The Economics of Nature

The Economics of Nature
Managing Biological Assets

G. Cornelis van Kooten
University of British Columbia, Vancouver, Canada

Erwin H. Bulte
Tilburg University, Tilburg, The Netherlands

First published 2000

2 4 6 8 10 9 7 5 3 1

Blackwell Publishers Inc.
350 Main Street
Malden, Massachusetts 02148
USA

Blackwell Publishers Ltd
108 Cowley Road
Oxford OX4 1JF
UK

Library of Congress Cataloging-in-Publication Data

Van Kooten, G. C. (Gerrit Cornelis)
   The economics of nature : managing biological assets / G. Cornelis van Kooten ; Erwin H. Bulte.
      p. cm.
   Includes bibliographical references (p.).
   ISBN 0-631-21894-7 (hardbound : alk. paper) – ISBN 0-631-21895-5 (pbk. : alk. paper)
   1. Nature conservation – Economic aspects. 2. Sustainable development – Environmental aspects. I. Title. II. Bulte, E. H. (Erwin Hendricus), 1968-

QH75.V374 1999
333.95 21 – dc21
                                                                99-43556
                                                                CIP

British Library Cataloguing in Publication Data

A CIP catalogue record for this book is available from the British Library.

Typeset in Times New Roman, 10pt by the authors
Printed in Great Britain by T J International, Padstow, Cornwall

This book is printed on acid-free paper.

CONTENTS

Tables

Figures

Preface

The idea for this book began in 1995 when the senior author spent a sabbatical leave at Wageningen Agricultural University (later renamed Wageningen University). As a result of this visit, we began a fruitful research collaboration that culminated in the current text. The collaboration has been interesting because our views of the world have often clashed, which has made this text all the more remarkable. We benefited from a great deal of discussion, and give and take, in the writing of many sections of the book. Lest this be taken as another example of disagreement among economists, however, it is well to point out that for the greatest part we have been in agreement.

We wrote this book with three purposes in mind. First, we wrote it as a text for students studying natural resource economics, resource management and forest management. In this regard, it is aimed at senior-level undergraduate and graduate students. In our experience teaching this material, undergraduates cannot be expected to understand much of the mathematics, but they can understand the underlying story. Further, many chapters do not employ much mathematics and can be included in an undergraduate course with few problems. The main exceptions are Chapters 7 (dynamic optimisation) and 10 (endangered species), which require an ability to grasp the essentials of optimal control theory. Students unfamiliar with traditional, constrained static optimisation solutions may also have trouble with Chapters 2 (consumer welfare theory) and 3 (producer welfare theory), and parts of Chapter 5 (nonmarket valuation). Nonetheless, they should have no trouble with Chapters 4 (rent and rent capture), much of Chapter 5, and Chapters 6 (project evaluation), 8 (sustainable development), 9 (biological diversity), 11 (forest management) and 12 (tropical deforestation).

Our second purpose was to provide a reference book that could prove valuable to economists, ecologists, foresters, biologists and other researchers interested in biological assets.

Finally, we wrote this book in order to bring an economics perspective on the conservation of biological assets and sustainable development more generally. It is our view that proper application of economic principles can lead to greater global well being, while, at the same time, protecting ecosystems from degradation. By failing to understand the economic consequences of many well-intentioned policies, decision makers have frequently brought about environmental deterioration, the very thing they sought to avoid. It is our hope that the principles we present and the many examples we provide will eventually lead to better policy design and implementation. We hope that, at the very least, policy analysts and those responsible for implementing policy will take our arguments seriously. By so doing, we might do a better job managing the earth's ecosystems.

Many people have made contributions, directly or indirectly, to this work. During the past five years, the material contained in this book has been used in undergraduate and graduate classes at the University of British Columbia, Tilburg University and Wageningen University. As a result, many students have contributed to the text in subtle ways. A number of Ph.D. students at UBC have read large portions of the manuscript and/or provided background material. They include Sen Wang, Patrick Kinyua, Bryan Bogdansky, Brad Stennes, Takuya Takahashi, and Harry Nelson. We want to thank Mette Asmild for her painstaking reading of an earlier draft, and Emina Krcmar-Nozic, Bill Wilson, Daan van Soest, Quentin Grafton, Maria Leon, Louis Slangen and Ruud van Gorkom for their contributions. Comments by Jack Knetsch, Cees Withagen, Henk Folmer and Louise Arthur on various chapters are greatly appreciated. None of these people should be held responsible for any errors that remain.

Retha Gerstmar, Kathy Synkary, Connie Ho, Loreen Stevenson, Cynthia Suh, Wilbert Houweling and Dineke Wemmenhove have contributed with many background services. Moral support from Ilan Vertinsky, Wim Hijman, Roel Jongeneel, Paul Berentsen and Alison Burrell is also appreciated.

Particular thanks are due to Arie Oskam who greatly encouraged the senior author by providing a place and atmosphere where *wetenschap* could be pursued unhindered, and to Moura Quayle for providing him the opportunity to profit from this environment. He also wishes to thank the Mansholt Institute, the Sustainable Forest Management National Centre of Excellence at the University of Alberta, and the Social Sciences and Humanities Research Council for research support. Without it, we could not have worked together the way we have. Finally, we wish to thank those near and dear to us for putting up with many hours of neglect.

1 Managing the Earth's Biological Assets

The United Nations' Conference on Environment and Development (UNCED) at Rio de Janeiro in 1992, also known as the "Earth Summit", is widely considered to be the source of the most recent wave of discussions about sustainable development and sustainable forestry. It marked the culmination of the environmental movement's efforts to bring to the attention of the world the idea that the globe is on a non-sustainable path of development. Three important agreements were signed as a result of UNCED: accords on climate change, biological diversity and forestry.

The United Nations' Framework Convention on Climate Change committed signatories to stabilise atmospheric greenhouse gas (GHG) concentrations, with developed countries to reduce their GHG emissions to the 1990 level by 2000 (article 4). This commitment was renewed and enhanced at a December 1997 Conference of the Parties to the Convention on Climate Change in Kyoto, Japan. Since climate change is considered one of the most pressing environmental problems facing global society (Clinton and Gore 1993), it is discussed in greater detail in Chapter 11, but then in relation to forestry (a manageable biological asset).

A Convention on Biological Diversity was also signed at UNCED. Biological diversity, or biodiversity, is:

> the variability among living organisms from all sources, including *inter alia*, terrestrial, marine and other aquatic ecosystems, and the ecological complexes of which they are a part: this includes diversity within species, between species and of ecosystems' [article 2] ... [T]he Convention not only provides important international recognition of and impetus to the need to conserve global biological diversity at all levels, but poses a challenge to ecologists, economists and scholars from other disciplines to provide further insights into the fundamental economic and ecological role of biological diversity. (Barbier et al. 1994, p. 10)

The Rio Summit's main document, "Agenda 21", also contained a Statement of Principles on Forests that set forth non-binding principles on forest use, management and protection, which applies to temperate as well as tropical countries. UNCED spawned the UN Commission on Sustainable Development (UNCSD) and its working group, the Intergovernmental Panel on Forests (IPF). Further, UNCED set the stage for international efforts, such as the Intergovernmental Working Group on Forests, the Helsinki Process, the Montreal Process, and the International Tropical Timber Organisation, among others. The binding Helsinki intergovernmental ministerial agreements and the non-binding Montreal agreement represent a key development, because they outline for the first time a common understanding of measures to monitor biological and social conditions at the national level associated with most of the world's temperate forests. Since they are directed specifically at temperate and boreal forests, the Helsinki and Montreal Processes have influenced moves to protect old-growth, temperate rain forests in the US Pacific Northwest and British Columbia, Canada.

Prior to Rio, there had already been a United Nations Conference on the Human Environment in Stockholm in 1972. It was this conference that first popularised the term sustainable development, although this is often credited to the report of the World Commission on Environment and Development (WCED 1987) chaired by then prime minister of Norway, Gro Brundtland (see Chapter 8). There were also two World Conservation Strategies (1980 and 1991) that linked biodiversity and sustainable development, and justified this on economic as well as scientific and moral grounds (Barbier et al. 1994, p. 10). Further, a number of global conventions and multilateral treaties pertaining to the protection of biological assets have been signed, including conventions on the protection of plants (1951), wetlands (1971) and trade in endangered species (see Chapter 10).

The Global Environmental Facility (GEF) was established already in 1991 as part of a collective agreement to transfer funds and rights over development for the purpose of conserving the earth's resources and environment – to protect the global environment and promote sustainable economic growth. GEF is managed by the United Nations' Development Programme (UNDP), the United Nations' Environmental Program (UNEP) and the World Bank. GEF covers incremental costs of activities that benefit the global environment in four focal areas: climate change, biological diversity, international waters, and stratospheric ozone. As they relate to the four focal areas, activities that degrade land, primarily desertification and deforestation, are also eligible for funding. Investments would be considered on a project-by-project basis, using the principle of marginal costs. If a project met all of the appropriate criteria, GEF would pay only the difference between costs and any benefits that the project provides the host country. Projects are funded that provide global as opposed to just local benefits.

Some US$1.5 billion was made available to GEF in its first five years. While GEF was meant to be a temporary measure for the purpose of learning how to transfer funds on a global basis, it was restructured and replenished with over US$2 billion in 1994. Currently 156 countries participate in GEF, but a country must be a party to the Climate Change Convention or the Convention of Biological Diversity to receive funds from the GEF in the relevant focal area. GEF projects must be country driven, incorporate consultation with local communities and, where appropriate, involve non-governmental organisations in project implementation.

While management of nature and conservation of biological assets are clearly priority issues for public policy makers, they do involve real economic tradeoffs. Having extensively analysed the conservation and exploitation of natural resources over the past 50 years, economists have useful insights to offer policy makers. One of these is that, while market failure resulting from ill-defined property rights or public goods' externality, say, causes environmental degradation and over-exploitation of biological assets, government intervention may not always be a panacea in correcting the market failure. It is now well known that government intervention to correct market failure may produce a more insidious failure, namely policy failure. Indeed, public policies in arenas outside the environment, such as employment, agriculture and taxation, may unwittingly contribute to unsustainable development of biological assets.

Nonetheless, there remains an important role for government. One role is to define and enforce property rights to biological assets. This often leads private agents to promote the conservation of nature. Yet, it is simply not possible to privatise many biological assets and environmental amenities. Certain biological assets are not traded on markets and never will be, so the specification of property rights to those assets is nigh impossible. Sometimes constitutions, historical practice, laws and institutions prevent countries from granting property rights over certain resources to private agents. In these cases, government intervention is unavoidable if the resource (species, environmental amenity) is at all to be conserved. In that case, implementing appropriate government policy for protecting (perhaps saving) biological assets, and for managing nature more generally, becomes important. In this book, we grapple with the question of determining appropriate policies for managing nature and conserving biological assets. The focus is on policy analysis using economic tools. We attempt to include all of the relevant economic costs and benefits, including nonmarket ones. We employ economic efficiency models that take into account the biological dynamics, and present case studies to illustrate how various models are used to analyse policies related to nature management.

One purpose of this book, therefore, is to provide the tools required for economic analysis of issues related to the social desirability of conserving natural resources, and of issues related to the three accords considered at Rio de Janeiro. We provide tools useful for managing biological assets. Among the tools are well-known ones, such as dynamic optimisation and cost-benefit analysis, but also less conventional methodologies that rely on controversial techniques such as fuzzy logic. The focus of the book, however, is broader than merely introducing the economic tool-kit. We also apply the tools to a number of case studies, including preservation of endangered species, tropical deforestation, temperate forest management and loss of biodiversity. And we aim to draw some general conclusions based on our findings. We argue that the economic case for large-scale conservation of nature appears to be weak. While market and policy failure have undoubtedly contributed to the demise of the natural environment, strict economic reasoning suggests that in many instances conversion of "nature" may simply be rational.

Throughout this book, we consider natural resources as "biological assets". In essence, society chooses a portfolio of assets that it wishes to retain. Biological assets can be included in the portfolio (as a component of aggregate wealth), or they can be excluded, but the choice is made through the political and other institutions that constitute civil society. If biological assets are not considered a form of wealth (something worth retaining in the "investment" portfolio), then they are converted into reproducible (or human-made) capital. This conversion implies disinvesting in natural capital, and is one particular interpretation of "development" used in this book. Disinvestment in biological assets implies their inevitable decline; for example, it can take the form of a reduction in biodiversity, clearcutting of old-growth and tropical forests, harvest to extinction of large mammals (whales, elephants), build-up of atmospheric greenhouse gases that cause climate to change, and so on.

Disinvestment can be "irrational" from society's point of view, but can be caused by market or policy failure. But it can also be economically rational, in the sense that the social rate of return to biological assets lags behind the rate of return to other assets. Species with an intrinsic rate of growth below that of the market rate of interest may need to have increasing economic value to society in order to be worthwhile preserving, or special pleading may be needed to ensure their survival. The reason is that efficient portfolio management often suggests disinvestment in less productive assets.

Obviously, to analyse the potential role of biological assets in the human portfolio, we need to consider their value. The first part of the book ("basic tools") provides the technical and conceptual tools that are relevant for assessing the value of biological assets. In the second part of the book ("applications"), we apply these concepts to specific case studies, such as conservation of biodiversity (Chapter 9) or endangered species (Chapter 10). We find that, typically, biological assets are less competitive at the margin than perhaps hoped for by the international conservationist community. We find that, quite often, the opportunity cost of conserving biological assets is significant, and that conversion of natural capital into reproducible capital in the future may well be consistent with economic efficiency considerations. Some caveats are discussed in the final chapter, however.

The first part of this book examines cost-benefit analysis (CBA) from both a theoretical and practical perspective. Included in this discussion are problems of measuring consumer and producer welfares (Chapters 2 and 3, respectively), the measurement and capture of resource rents (Chapter 4), valuation of commodities not traded in markets, of which nature and biological assets are likely the most important (Chapter 5), and examples of how to apply CBA (Chapter 6).

The problem with cost-benefit analysis as generally practised is that, while it considers future costs and benefit, it is essentially static. CBA does not take into account the effect of biological growth and harvest on extinction, and does not seek to determine optimal population sizes of wildlife populations, for example. The necessary background for economic dynamics is provided in Chapter 7. Exploitation of the commercial fishery is used as a motivating example, although other examples are also presented.

Chapter 8 deals with the concept of sustainable development, addressing definitional and other issues. For example, how do we know that a system is sustainable? What are indicators of sustainability? We also discuss the potentially conflicting relation between economic efficiency, as paramount in the natural asset approach to conservation, and "sustainability", which is ultimately rooted in equity and ethical considerations.

Economic and other issues related to biological diversity are the focus of Chapter 9. Topics examined in that chapter include measurement of numbers of species and biodiversity, extinction, and the economics and politics of endangered species legislation. Threatened and endangered species are considered in greater detail in Chapter 10, where the plight of some large mammals is examined, particularly the African elephant. The Convention on International Trade in Endangered Species of Wild Fauna and Flora, which was signed in Washington in 1973, opened the way for a trade ban on ivory in 1989. In Chapter 10, the extent to which elephant populations have declined in Africa (particularly rates of decline) and the impact of the trade ban are examined. It turns out that a main problem with elephant conservation is poaching, and its corollary, government anti-poaching enforcement. Also considered in Chapter 10 is the possibility of game cropping as a means of conserving wildlife ungulates, and the issue of whether whaling should be resumed (even to a limited extent).

The topic of Chapters 11 and 12 is forestry. In Chapter 11, the economics of forest management are considered (including the question of optimal forest rotation ages), as is the role of forestry in mitigating climate change. The focus in Chapter 11 is primarily temperate forests, while Chapter 12 deals with tropical deforestation. Since tropical deforestation is associated with species loss, this chapter is linked to Chapter 9. However, the focus in Chapter 12 is not species loss and biodiversity but, rather, economic models of deforestation and the factors that are thought to contribute to deforestation.

In the final chapter (Chapter 13), we discuss some caveats related to the use of economic efficiency analysis in studying biological assets, putting into perspective the economic approach to nature management. One caveat is the following. Throughout the book, we set out to estimate the economic value of natural assets, and where possible to incorporate all relevant components of "total economic value" associated with investing in nature. Unfortunately, there are limits to what is currently quantifiable. For example, some services of nature, such as those associated with resilience and stability, are extremely difficult (or impossible?) to quantify (let alone approximate in monetary terms). We discuss such benefits, but are unable to include them in the numerical analyses. Evidently, this biases our findings. While we may underestimate the true economic value of nature by doing so, this is something that the reader will have to decide when confronted with our results. In addition, it should be stressed that economic thinking is but one approach (albeit an important one) for allocating scarce resources, and that different allocations (portfolio selections) may be preferred due to, for example, equity or ethical considerations.

So why is an economics of nature needed? As we show in the chapters that follow, economists can bring to bear a broad array of tools for studying policy related to the stewardly use and protection of biological assets. These tools show the folly of some, often well-meaning, policies. Such policies might lead to the impoverishment of society, resulting in the degradation of some biological assets because they are not valued as highly as previously or cannot be protected as before. On the other hand, economic analysis might suggest policies that, while perhaps not bringing about the results desired by some, go a long way to protecting nature in the real world of politics and economics.

2 Consumer Welfare Measurement

The objective of this chapter is to provide a theoretical background to cost-benefit analysis that includes commodities not normally traded in markets. Our concern is with natural resource commodities that are traded in markets (such as logs), environmental goods that affect the production or consumption of goods that are traded in markets (e.g., energy, housing), and environmental goods that are desired for their own sake (e.g., biodiversity). We begin with a review of consumer demand theory, followed by measures of changes in the well being of consumers when prices of one or more goods change as a result of a public policy. Quantity restrictions are examined and, finally, the effects on welfare of changes in the availability of an environmental good are considered.

2.1 Consumer Demand Theory

Empirical demand estimation is necessary for public policy analysis in two important and related ways. First, estimates of price and income elasticities are useful for determining the direction and magnitude of changes in the quantities and prices of one or more commodities that might occur when a particular government policy affects any of the determinants of the demand for (or supply of) those commodities. Second, estimates of the demand parameters are needed to obtain measures of the gain or loss in consumer welfare as a result of some public policy. Although a simple statistical or empirical demand relationship might be useful for evaluating the direction and magnitude of price and quantity changes, such relationships are not be appropriate for measuring consumer welfare. Consumer demand theory is based on the existence of a utility function (Georgescu-Roegen 1968, p. 262). Only then is it possible to use the demand for wood products, say, to measure the change in consumer welfare (utility) when a restriction on timber harvests results in an increase in their price. Since economists are often preoccupied with the need to make welfare judgements, or quantitative assessments of the gains and losses of public policies, demand functions derived from utility maximisation are a necessary prerequisite. But a theory of preferences and utility maximisation is also needed in the case of amenities (such as biodiversity) that are not traded in markets. How is it possible to measure whether people are better or worse off (and by how much) when the availability of wildlife habitat, or hiking trails, is increased unless such a change can be traced back to their preferences for such commodities? In this section, we present the background theory for measuring changes in well being that arise from changes in government policies, particularly as these relate to the natural resource commodities discussed later in this book. The theory also serves as background for measuring costs and benefits in project evaluation.

The primal problem

It is postulated that the consumer maximises utility subject to a budget constraint. Formally, the consumer's problem is to

(2.1)

$$\text{maximise}_{\{q_i\}} \quad U = \varphi(q_1, ..., q_n)$$

$$\text{subject to} \quad m = p_1 q_1 + \cdots + p_n q_n,$$

where φ is the utility function, q_i is the quantity of the ith good or service consumed by the individual, p_i is its price, m is the total amount of income (or budget) available to the individual, and n is the total number of goods and services in the economy. The utility function must satisfy a number of properties, including that it be quasi-concave and twice differentiable – $\partial\varphi/\partial q_1 \geq 0$, $\partial^2\varphi/\partial q_i^2 \leq 0$ (Deaton and Muellbauer 1980, pp. 26–30). The Lagrangian function associated with problem (2.1) is:

(2.1′) $\quad L = \varphi(q_1, ... , q_n) + \lambda (m - p_1 q_1 - \cdots - p_n q_n),$

where λ is the shadow price of income – the amount by which φ will increase with a unit increase in m – or Lagrange multiplier (McKenzie 1983, pp. 22–3). Solving problem (2.1′), and assuming that the second-order conditions are satisfied, gives the Marshallian or ordinary demand functions:

(2.2) $\quad q_i = q_i(p_1, ..., p_n, m) , i = 1, ..., n.$

A monotonic transformation of the utility function φ, say $U = u[\varphi(q)]$, such that $du/d\varphi > 0$, does not affect the resulting demand functions. However, a monotonic transformation of the utility function may change the sign of the derivative of the marginal utility of income with respect to expenditure, i.e., $d\lambda/dm$.

The ordinary demand functions (2.2) can be substituted into the objective function – the utility function in (2.1) – to obtain the indirect utility function:

(2.3) $\quad U = \varphi[q_1(p_1, ..., m), ..., q_n(p_1, ..., m)] = v(p_1, ..., p_n, m).$

The indirect utility function assumes that the optimising problem has been solved. It has the important property that the ordinary demand functions can be recovered from it using Roy's identity (Varian 1992, pp. 106–7):

(2.4) $q_i = - \dfrac{\partial v / \partial p_i}{\partial v / \partial m}$.

Thus, it is possible to derive the Marshallian demand functions by starting from the direct utility function or from the indirect utility function.

The dual problem

Problem (2.1) is known as the primal problem; the associated dual problem is:

(2.5)

$$\text{minimise}_{\{q_i\}} \quad \sum_{i=1}^{n} p_i \, q_i,$$

$$\text{subject to} \quad U_0 = \varphi(q_1, \, ..., \, q_n),$$

where U_0 is a given level of utility. Solving problem (2.5) provides the Hicksian or compensated demand functions:

(2.6) $q_i^c = q_i^c(p_1, \, ..., \, p_n, \, U) \, , \, i = 1, \, ..., \, n.$

In the dual problem, rather than allowing utility to change (as in the derivation of the ordinary demand function), we allow income to change as needed to maintain the original level of utility. Thus, since there is no income effect (see below), the slope of the compensated demand function is generally steeper than that of the ordinary demand function. It is also why we use the term "compensated" – individuals are compensated to keep utility at a given (target) level – even though "compensation" could imply taking income away. The fact that individuals are "compensated" to remain at some reference level of utility says something about property rights – it assumes that the individual has a right to this reference level of well being. This is further discussed later in this chapter.

Now substituting the compensated demand functions (2.6) into the objective function gives the cost-of-utility or expenditure function:

(2.7) $m = p_1 \, q_1^c \, (p_1, \, ..., \, p_n, \, U) + \cdots + p_n \, q_n^c \, (p_1, \, ..., \, p_n, \, U) = e(p_1, \, ..., \, p_n, \, U).$

The expenditure function is the amount of income or budget required to attain the given level of utility, and satisfies certain properties discussed by Deaton and Muellbauer (1980, pp. 38–41). The compensated demands can be recovered from the expenditure function using Shephard's lemma (Varian 1992, p. 74):

(2.8) $q_i^c(p_1, \, ..., \, p_n, \, U) = \dfrac{\partial e}{\partial p_i}$.

In addition, solving (2.7) for U gives the indirect utility function; the ordinary demands can then be obtained from the indirect utility function using Roy's identity (2.4).[1]

Restrictions on demand systems

Functional forms for demand systems are often chosen on the basis of empirical expediency rather than as a result of optimisation. The demand systems are then made to conform to utility maximisation by applying certain restrictions that follow from the theory. Three restrictions on the set of consumer demand equations can be identified. If an estimated demand system satisfies these conditions, we can be assured it is the result of utility maximisation, with the results usable for welfare, or cost-benefit, analysis.

(1) *Adding up* Differentiating the budget constraint with respect to total expenditure m, while keeping prices constant, gives:

$$(2.9) \qquad p_1(\frac{\partial q_1}{\partial m}) + \cdots + p_n(\frac{\partial q_n}{\partial m}) = 1.$$

This implies that the sum of the marginal propensities to consume the n commodities must equal 1.0. Upon multiplying each term by $(q_i m)/(q_i m)$, (2.9) can be written in elasticity form as:

$$(2.10) \qquad w_1 \xi_1 + \cdots + w_n \xi_n = 1,$$

where w_i is the ith budget share and ξ_i is the income elasticity of good i. Equation (2.10) is referred to as the Engel aggregation condition.

Differentiating the budget constraint with respect to any price, say p_j, while keeping income and all other prices constant, gives:

---

[1] It is possible to recover the expenditure function from the indirect utility function simply by solving (2.3) for m. Shephard's lemma (2.8) can then be used to obtain the compensated demands. Further, it is possible to derive the inverse of the Marshallian or uncompensated demand function using the Hotelling-Wold identity:

$$p_i = p_i(q, m) = \frac{\frac{\partial U}{\partial q_i} m}{\sum_{j=1}^{n} q_j \frac{\partial U}{\partial q_j}}, \forall j = 1, ..., n, \text{ where } q = (q_1, ..., q_n) \text{ is a vector of quantities.}$$

It is also possible to obtain the inverse compensated demand function using the Shephard-Hanoch lemma (Weymark 1980).

(2.11) $p_1 \dfrac{\partial q_1}{\partial p_j} + p_2 \dfrac{\partial q_2}{\partial p_j} + \cdots + p_n \dfrac{\partial q_n}{\partial p_j} = -q_j.$

This can be written in elasticity form as:

(2.12) $w_1 \xi_{1j} + w_2 \xi_{2j} + \cdots + w_n \xi_{nj} = -w_j,$

where ξ_{ij} is the cross price elasticity of demand for good i with respect to the price of good j and ξ_{ii} is the own price elasticity of demand. Equation (2.12) is referred to as the Cournot aggregation condition. Engel aggregation and Cournot aggregation are variants of the adding-up condition.

(2) **Homogeneity** The ordinary demand functions are homogeneous of degree zero in prices and income.[2] Therefore, doubling all prices and income will not affect the demand for a commodity. Applying Euler's theorem to the demand function (2.2) gives:

(2.13) $t\, q_i = \dfrac{\partial q_i}{\partial p_1} p_1 + \cdots + \dfrac{\partial q_i}{\partial p_n} p_n + \dfrac{\partial q_i}{\partial m} m,$

where t is the degree of homogeneity. Dividing both sides by q_i and since $t = 0$, the homogeneity condition can be written in elasticity form as:

(2.14) $\xi_{i1} + \cdots + \xi_{in} + \xi_i = 0.$

(3) **Symmetry** The Slutsky equation can be derived from the relationships obtained above (Boadway and Bruce 1984, p. 38). At the consumer's equilibrium, the ordinary and compensated demands are equal; that is, $q_i^c(P, U) = q_i(P, m)$, where P is the price vector $(p_1, \ldots, p_n)$. Substituting for m gives $q_i^c(P, U) = q_i[P, e(P, U)]$. Finally, differentiating with respect to p_j gives $\partial q_i^c/\partial p_j = \partial q_i/\partial p_j + (\partial q_i/\partial m)(\partial m/\partial p_j)$, which, upon rearranging and using Shephard's lemma (2.8), results in the Slutsky equation:

(2.15) $\dfrac{\partial q_i}{\partial p_j} = s_{ij} - q_j \dfrac{\partial q_i}{\partial m},$

where $s_{ij} = \partial q_i^c/\partial p_j$ is the compensated Slutsky substitution term. Symmetry requires that $s_{ij} = s_{ji}$ and that the matrix of substitution effects, $S = [s_{ij}]$, is symmetric and negative semi-definite, which implies that $s_{ii} \leq 0$ for all $i = 1,\ldots,n$ (Deaton and Muellbauer 1980, pp. 43–4).

---

[2] A function $f(x_1, \ldots, x_n)$ is homogeneous of degree t if $f(kx_1, \ldots, kx_n) = k^t f(x_1, \ldots, x_n)$, where $k > 0$.

These demand system restrictions are generally satisfied in one of two ways. First, one can postulate a proper functional form for the direct or indirect utility function, and derive the demand equations as indicated above. Since one begins with a utility function specification, the derived Marshallian demand functions automatically satisfy the above properties. However, several approaches have been developed to avoid directly specifying the utility function *a priori*. One is to employ duality theory and specify a functional form for either the indirect utility function or the expenditure function. As McKenzie and Thomas (1984) show, duality theory permits the investigator directly to specify a large number of different functional forms for the demand system without *a priori* knowledge of either the direct or indirect utility function, although the functions must satisfy certain homogeneity requirements.

A second approach is to specify directly a functional form for the system of demand equations to be estimated (without the homogeneity requirements of McKenzie and Thomas) and, during estimation, impose the restrictions of demand theory (adding up, homogeneity, symmetry and negative semi-definiteness of the matrix of substitution effects). The Rotterdam model of Barten (1964; 1968) is an example. This approach allows explicit testing of the demand theory restrictions, but the general conclusion of such tests has been that the empirical evidence contradicts demand theory (Deaton and Muellbauer 1980, p. 70). Finally, a third approach has been to use flexible forms (e.g., translog, Fourier) to approximate the true, but unknown, direct or indirect utility function or expenditure function. Examples are found in Christensen et al. (1975), Simmons and Weiserbs (1979), and Gallant (1981). Once again, the results of these studies provide evidence for rejecting consumer demand theory.

Utility maximisation: Some issues

Difficulty in specifying and estimating demand functions is only one of the problems that resource economists face. Another problem is related to non-market values. What is the social cost of a reduction in biodiversity? Does the benefit from increased water quality exceed the cost of measures that improve water quality? How valuable is backcountry skiing compared with timber harvest? How does one make trade-offs between timber harvest and backcountry skiing? That is, how many trees should be left to prevent erosion of benefits associated with skiing? Similar questions can be asked with respect of scenic amenities, camping, hiking and other outdoor recreational activities. As discussed in Chapter 5, the task of measuring the benefits of such things as improved access to recreation, better air or water quality, and preservation of biodiversity is an onerous one that may only make sense if it is grounded in consumer theory.

Although forming the theoretical foundation for consumer welfare measurement (see next section) and cost-benefit analysis (Chapter 6), not all economists are satisfied with utility maximisation. We briefly identify four issues.

1. As already noted, the empirical evidence from demand system estimation suggests that people do not behave as utility maximisers. The theoretical

restrictions of demand theory do not generally hold in practice. This has usually been attributed to lack of quality data for estimating demand equations.

2. Evidence from experimental markets, where economists and psychologists directly test whether utility functions have the assumed properties of consumer demand theory, overwhelmingly suggest that people do not behave as if they maximise their utility subject to constraints. People behave in a way that is contrary to notions in economics. Knetsch (1989, 1995, 2000), for example, argues that utility functions are not smooth as postulated, but that property rights determine rates of marginal substitution between commodities. Indifference curves are kinked at the endowment, or reference state, with losses valued more highly than gains (Kahneman and Tversky 1979). People are willing to pay less to purchase an endowment (say a mug) than what they would require to part with it. (We return to this issue later in this chapter and in Chapter 5, with regards to our discussion of non-market and public goods that are not traded in markets.) Experimental markets have shown that preference reversals are more common than thought, so that utility functions are not always transitive. Ostrom (1998) summarises work demonstrating that people do not behave as rational economic agents (as utility maximisers) in situations where individual and social choices may conflict. However, she argues that, in the absence of a new generation of models that recognise human limitations and fickleness, the use of models that assume rationality (such as those based on constrained utility maximisation) can profitably be continued.

3. Ethical and philosophical arguments have also been levied at utility maximisation. Winrich (1984) argues that the preference relation can never be both complete and consistent (transitive) because it denies the inclusion of preferences themselves in the choice set. Ignoring preferences as an object of choice results in self-reference, so the assumed preference (utility) function of demand theory cannot exist. Sagoff (1988b, 1994) raises ethical concerns about the use of utility functions, particularly in the context of willingness to pay measures, which are used in environmental economics. This issue is considered again in Chapter 5 in the context of contingent valuation.

4. In the context of nature conservation and forestry, it is useful to consider one additional point that has been neglected in literature for the most part. The concept of utility as used in modern consumer demand theory is not the same notion as that used by the marginal economists at the turn of the century. Early economists distinguished between utility and *ophelimity*; utility is directly comparable across individuals (in a cardinal sense), but *ophelimity* refers to (ordinal) preferences and can not be compared among individuals. Thus, the material welfare school

> made a distinction among the types of satisfactions that could be derived from goods. Indeed, goods, the motives for acquiring them and the satisfactions yielded by their consumption were arranged in a hierarchy that proceeded from the "purely economic" or "material" at one end to the purely noneconomic or nonmaterial at the other. It was stressed that there was no hard-and-fast line separating the economic part of the scale from the noneconomic, although the extremes were clearly distinguishable. (Cooter and Rappoport 1984, p. 513)

Those goods that fall clearly into the category of material well being, such as food, clothing, housing, heating and rest, constitute the components of utility. But people also have preferences (desires) over goods and services that are not necessary to physical living (and admittedly there will be debate about where the line should be drawn). These non-necessary goods constitute components of *ophelimity*.

Georgescu-Roegen (1966) clearly rejected the idea that all human wants could be reduced to a common basis (*ophelimity*), opting instead for retention of the "Principle of the Irreducibility of Wants". He also accepted the "Principle of the Subordination of Wants" (1966, p. 195), which implies Gossen's law of satiable wants, or a bliss point (1968, p. 262). Knight (1944) also accepts the notion of satiety, whereas consumer demand theory, which is based on ordinal preferences (*ophelimity*) assumes nonsatiation. As Georgescu-Roegen argues: "It has long been observed that human needs and wants are hierarchized. In fact, as the reader may convince himself by looking at random in the literature, this hierarchy is the essence of any argument explaining the principle of decreasing marginal utility" (1966, p. 194).

To what extent, then, is nature conservation necessary – providing utility (in the classical sense) rather than *ophelimity*? This is a difficult question to answer. Some components of (and flows provided by) nature are needed for human survival, but likely not all. Further, it may be possible to manage landscapes and ecosystems in ways that enhance nature's contribution to utility – in ways that make nature more useful (and subservient) to human needs. The distinction between utility and *ophelimity* does raise doubts about many of the welfare measures that economists use in cost-benefit analysis (and discussed in the next section). Nonetheless, these are the only measures of well being that are available and they do enable economists to make useful insights about forest and other ecosystem management. Therefore, we echo Ostrom (1998), arguing that in the absence of an alternative theory, we continue to rely on insights from models that assume utility maximisation.

2.2 Measuring Changes in the Well Being of Consumers

In this section, the theory of welfare measurement is examined from the viewpoint of developing usable measures of changes in consumer welfare resulting from government policies or other factors that affect prices of goods traded in markets or that affect the availability of environmental amenities. There exist a number of theoretical measures of consumer welfare. The most important of these are Marshallian consumer surplus (S), compensating variation (CV), equivalent variation (EV), compensating surplus (CS) and equivalent surplus (ES). The latter two measures are used principally in non-market measurement. Each of these measures is discussed in the following sections, and problems concerning their use are highlighted.

Consumer surplus

The French engineer Dupuit first introduced the concept of consumer surplus in 1833. Consumer surplus, S, is used to measure the welfare that consumers get when they purchase goods and services. The general concept is well-known to economists and is simply the difference between an individual's marginal willingness-to-pay and the market price. The marginal willingness-to-pay curve is the individual's *ordinary* demand curve (denoted D in Figure 2.1). If the price of a commodity is given by p_0 in Figure 2.1, then consumer surplus is given by the area denoted by a. The consumer surplus is determined as follows. The consumer will purchase q_0 units of the commodity at a price p_0. The value that the consumer attaches to an amount q_0 of the commodity is given by area $(a + b + c)$ – the area under the demand curve. (The demand function can, therefore, be thought of as a marginal benefit function.) Since she must sacrifice an amount equal to area $(b + c)$ to purchase the commodity, the consumer gains area a – the consumer surplus.

In applied welfare economics, we are generally not interested in total consumer surplus but, rather, in the change in S that an action (e.g., a program to protect biodiversity by reducing timber harvests) may bring about. Suppose, for example, that a policy reduces price from p_0 to p_1 (Figure 2.1). Initially, the consumer purchased q_0 units but, given price p_1, q_1 units of the commodity are purchased. Prior to the reduction in price, the consumer surplus was given by area a. After price is reduced, the consumers can purchase the same quantity (q_0) as previously, but they pay less for it. Therefore, they gain area b that is the difference between the amount they paid for quantity q_0 when price was p_0 and the amount they pay for the same quantity at the lower price p_1. However, by increasing purchases of the commodity from q_0 to q_1, the consumer only pays an amount given by area e, but she places a greater *value* on the additional purchases, a value given by area $d + e$. Therefore, by increasing purchases from q_0 to q_1, the consumer gains a surplus given by area d. Thus, the *change* in S due to a reduction in the price of the commodity is given by area $b + d$. Total S from purchasing q_1 units of the commodity at a price of p_1 is given by area $a + b + d$.

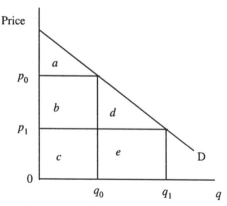

Figure 2.1 The Notion of Consumer Surplus

Now consider what happens when a government policy results in a change in the income received by a consumer. A fall in income causes the demand function to shift inwards, but the fall in income should not be measured by the loss in consumer surplus (i.e., as the area above price and between the original and income-changed demand functions). Rather, it is measured by the change in income itself. Since the purpose of the consumer surplus measure is to provide a monetary measure of the change in consumers' well being, it is the change in income and not S that is the best measure of welfare change. Indeed, S need not equal the change in income.

Now consider what happens to consumer welfare when both income and price change simultaneously. Suppose income increases from m_0 to m_1, while price rises from p_0 to p_1. The situation is illustrated in Figure 2.2 where consumers initially purchase q_0 at price p_0. We consider two cases:

1. **Price increases, then income increases** The loss in consumer surplus due to a price increase is given by the area under $D(m_0)$; that is, the loss in S is given by ΔS = area c. Since the increase in income is given by $m_1 - m_0$, the net welfare change for consumers is given by $m_1 - m_0$ minus area c.
2. **Income increases, then price rises** Once again the change in income is given by $m_1 - m_0$. However, now S is measured under $D(m_1)$ rather than $D(m_0)$. The loss in consumer surplus due to the price increase is, therefore, given by ΔS = area $(c + d + e)$, and the net welfare gain to consumers is $m_1 - m_0$ minus area $(c + d + e)$.

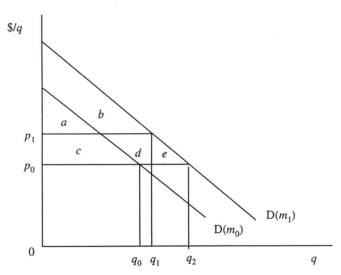

Figure 2.2 Change in Consumer Surplus due to Change in Income and Prices

The difference between the two measures given by paths (1) and (2) is area $d + e$. It is important to note that the measurement of consumer surplus is dependent on whether income changes before or after price changes. That is, *consumer surplus measures are path dependent and, hence, are not unique.*

Another type of path dependency occurs when more than one price changes at any given time, keeping income constant. Suppose the prices of two goods, q_1 and q_2, fall from p_1^0 to p_1' and p_2^0 to p_2', respectively. We need to consider whether the goods are complements or substitutes, and whether, for measurement purposes, the price of q_1 is considered to change before or after the price of q_2 changes, although in practice they change at the same time. If these are the only goods in the economy they must be substitutes.

Complements. Consider Figure 2.3 where panel (a) represents the q_1 (wood doors) market and panel (b) represents the q_2 (door frames) market. A reduction in the price of one commodity will shift the demand curve of the other commodity to the right when the goods are complements. Consider two cases:

1. ***First p_1 falls, then p_2 falls*** The initial fall in p_1 increases consumer surplus by area b and shifts the demand for q_2 to $D_2(p_1')$. When p_2 falls, the gain in S is area $\beta + \delta$ and the total change in S is given by $\Delta S =$ area $b + \beta + \delta$.
2. ***First p_2 falls, then p_1 falls*** In this case, the change in consumer surplus is given by $\Delta S =$ area $\beta + b + d$.

The difference between the measures derived from paths (1) and (2) is given by the difference between areas d and δ in this case where the goods are complements.

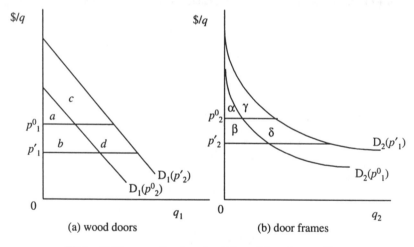

Figure 2.3 Consumer Surplus when Prices of Complements Change

Substitutes. The appropriate measures for calculating the change in S when q_1 and q_2 are substitutes (say, wood doors versus metal ones) can be derived via Figure 2.4. Reductions (increases) in the price of wood doors shift the demand for metal doors to the left (right). Once again, it is necessary to consider two possible paths.

1. **First p_1 falls, then p_2 falls** The change in consumer surplus is ΔS = area ($s + t + w$).
2. **First p_2 falls, then p_1 falls** In this case, the appropriate measure is given by ΔS = area ($w + x + s$).

The difference between the measures derived from paths (1) and (2) is given by the difference between areas t and x in the case where the goods are substitutes. Recall that, for complements, the difference was given by the difference between areas d and δ. In each case, the two areas need not be "close" or approximately equal to each other in magnitude. The problem of path dependency is discussed further in the Appendix to this chapter.

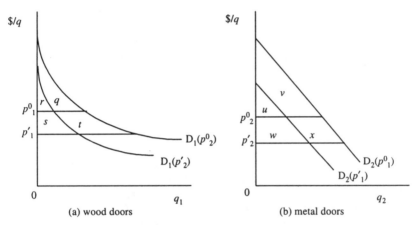

Figure 2.4 Consumer Surplus when Prices of Two Substitute Goods Change

Derivation of consumer surplus

Suppose a consumer faces an infinitely small change in prices and income that may have been brought about by a particular government policy. The impact on the consumer's utility of such a small change can be determined by total differentiating the indirect utility function (2.3):

$$(2.16) \quad dv = \frac{\partial v}{\partial p_1} dp_1 + \cdots + \frac{\partial v}{\partial p_n} dp_n + \frac{\partial v}{\partial m} dm.$$

Applying Roy's theorem and recalling, from the first-order conditions to problem (2.1), that $\lambda = \partial v / \partial m$ is the marginal utility of income, the change in utility can be written as $dv = - \lambda \, \Sigma_i \, q_i(P, m) \, dp_i + \lambda \, dm$. Since $\lambda > 0$ and is approximately constant for an infinitesimally small change in prices and income, it is possible to divide both sides by λ and still obtain a perfectly adequate measure of welfare change; namely, $dW = dv/\lambda = dm - \Sigma_i \, q_i(P, m) \, dp_i$.

However, as McKenzie argues, "a considerable jump in reasoning is required if we are to say that this differential equation is also acceptable when expressed in terms of discrete changes" (1983, p. 24); that is, when expressed as $\Delta W = \Delta m - \Sigma_i \, q_i(P, m)$ Δp_i. In particular, the assumption that λ is constant is valid only under restrictive conditions.

Consider a move from an initial situation 0 to some final situation 1 caused by a change in prices and income resulting from some public policy. The discrete welfare change is given by:

$$(2.17) \quad \Delta U = \int_L (dm - \Sigma_i \, q_i(P, m) \, dp_i),$$

where $\int_L$ is the line integral which gives the measure of welfare change along the path L. Dividing both sides of (2.17) by λ gives:

$$(2.18) \quad S = \frac{\Delta U}{\lambda} = -\Sigma_i \int_0^1 q_i(P, m) \, dp_i + \Delta m.$$

This money measure of the change in welfare is the Marshallian consumer surplus. The first term on the right-hand-side (RHS) of equation (2.18) is a line integral that depends upon the path of integration; that is, the value of the integral depends upon the order in which the prices are varied (see Appendix to this chapter). If only one price varies then (2.18) may be a good approximation of the change in consumer welfare. However, if more than one price changes, S may be neither a unique nor a consistent measure of welfare change.

The argument is sometimes made that, in practice, errors of measurement will occur; therefore, the difference in the measured values of welfare change obtained from (2.18) by following different paths are likely to be insignificant. However, Chipman and Moore (1976) argue that this attitude is inappropriate because it takes the position that "the existence of error [is] a reason for compounding it with more error" (p. 81).

The problem with the consumer surplus measure concerns λ. One can only divide both sides of (2.17) by λ to obtain (2.18) if λ is constant, which can only occur under one of two rather restrictive assumptions (Chipman and Moore 1976; Just et al. 1982, pp. 361–3). First, S provides a consistent measure of welfare change if preferences are homothetic. Preferences are homothetic if the ratio of the consumption of any two commodities is independent of the income level, or $(\partial(q_i/q_j))/\partial m = 0$. This implies that the uncompensated demand curves have unitary income elasticity (the Engel curves are straight lines emanating from the origin) and exhibit the property that $\partial q_i/\partial p_j = \partial q_j/\partial p_i$ (Silberberg 1978, p. 25). In addition, it implies that λ is a function of income only, and not prices.

Second, the marginal utility of income (budget) will be a constant if preferences are "vertically parallel" (see Appendix to this chapter). Then the marginal utility of income is independent of income and of the prices of all the commodities except the numeraire commodity, say q_n. The income expansion paths are straight lines parallel to the q_n axis. Thus, any increase in income is spent entirely on good n. When preferences are vertically parallel, the utility function can be written as $U(q_1, q_2,..., q_n)$ $= q_n + g(q_1, ..., q_{n-1})$.

Constancy of the marginal utility of income implies that there is no income effect when the price of a commodity changes; that is, the commodity is assumed to be such a small component in one's budget that changes in its price do not affect income. This is hardly a realistic assumption when demand functions for broad categories of consumption are generally estimated. Further, "the assumption that marginal utility of income is independent of numeraire prices and income is an assumption about preferences, and nothing can be inferred concerning preferences from the fact that a particular commodity under consideration absorbs a negligible proportion of the consumer's income, other than that fact itself" (Chipman and Moore 1976, p. 91).[3] Constancy of λ is discussed further in the Appendix to this chapter.

Compensating and equivalent variations

Marshallian consumer surplus is not a true measure of welfare change. It can be shown that S may, in some situations, be an ambiguous measure of changes in consumer well being; but it is also not a true measure of welfare by its very construct. Neither the compensating variation nor the equivalent variation measure of consumer welfare suffers from the path dependency problem.

Compensating Variation (CV)

The CV of a move from situation 0 to situation 1 is the amount of compensation to be provided, or the amount of income to be taken away, to leave the individual as well off in the new situation as she is in the old one. Suppose that there are two commodities q_n and q_1, where q_n is a composite good consisting of all other goods in the bundle or simply the numeraire. In Figure 2.5, the consumer is initially at point 0 on the indifference curve U_0; in the figure, parallel lines have the same style. A reduction in the price of q_1 from p_1^0 to p_1^1, or P^0 to P', and an increase in income from m_0 to m_1 due to some public policy enables the consumer to move to point 1 on the higher indifference curve U_1. The CV of the public policy is given by $m_1 - e_K$, where e_K represents the minimum expenditure required to attain the utility level U_0 at the new set of prices (point K in Figure 2.5).

More generally, the CV of a change in prices and incomes is given by:

---

[3] Also see Knight (1944) for further elaboration. As for S, Knight argues that *"the area under a demand curve has no economic meaning whatever"* (p. 315, emphasis in original).

(2.19) $CV = m_1 - e(P^1, U_0) = m_0 - e(P^1, U_0) + \Delta m = e(P^0, U_0) - e(P^1, U_0) + \Delta m,$

where $\Delta m = m_1 - m_0$, P^0 is the vector of initial prices $(p_1^0, ..., p_n^0)$, and P^1 is the vector of final prices $(p_1^1, ..., p_n^1)$. (Initial income m_0 is the income needed to attain utility level U_0 given initial prices; final income m_1 is the income needed to achieve U_1 given final prices.) Since the expenditure function is continuous in prices, $CV =$

$$\int_{P^1}^{P^0} \sum_{i=1}^{n} \frac{\partial e(P, U_0)}{\partial P_i} \, dp_i + \Delta m,$$ or, using Shephard's lemma (2.8) and reversing the order of integration,

(2.20) $$CV = - \int_{P^0}^{P^1} \sum_{i=1}^{n} q_i^c (P, U_0) \, dp_i + \Delta m.$$

Path dependency is not a problem since, for the compensated demand functions, $s_{ij} = s_{ji}$, so that the symmetry condition holds automatically.

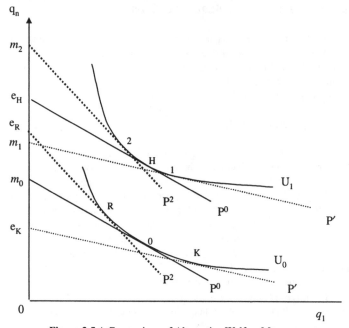

Figure 2.5 A Comparison of Alternative Welfare Measures

CV cannot be given a "clean bill of health" as an unambiguous measure of changes in consumer welfare, however, since CV is also an inconsistent measure, just as S. This can be seen from Figure 2.5. The CV of a move from 0 to 1 is $m_1 - e_K$.

Suppose instead that prices rise to P^2, but that income is also raised to enable the consumer to still move to U_1. The CV in this case is measured by the move from 0 to 2, and is $m_2 - e_R$, which is not the same as $m_1 - e_K$. While the two CV measures should be identical, this is not the case. Boadway and Bruce (1984, pp. 201–2) argue that the correct relative ranking between situations 1 and 2 can be obtained by comparing them with each other, rather than comparing both with situation 0; in that case, situations 1 and 2 will turn out to be identical. That is, the CV measure of welfare is consistent for the case of binary welfare comparisons. However, it is unlikely that binary comparisons are the only ones to occur in practice. Situations 1 and 2 are usually to be compared via situation 0 since it is the status quo situation. The CV welfare measure will also be a consistent money metric if preferences are homothetic (McKenzie 1983, pp. 34–5). As Chipman and Moore (1980) have shown, CV is a valid measure of welfare change only under the same conditions for which consumer surplus (S) is a valid measure – when preferences are either homothetic or indifference curves are vertically parallel (λ is constant).

Equivalent Variation (EV)

The EV of a move from situation 0 to situation 1 is the minimum amount of compensation an individual is willing to receive, or the maximum amount she is willing to pay, to forgo a move from the initial to the final situation. In this case, the reference level of utility is that which would occur in situation 1, the final situation. In Figure 2.5, $e_H - m_0$ is a measure of EV in terms of q_n, and e_H represents the minimum expenditure required to achieve U_1 *at the old set of prices* (point H in Figure 2.5). Thus,

$$(2.21) \quad EV = e(P^0, U_1) - m_0 = e(P^0, U_1) - m_1 + \Delta m = e(P^0, U_1) - e(P^1, U_1) + \Delta m.$$

Since the expenditure function is continuous in prices, and using Shephard's lemma (2.8) while reversing the order of integration, (2.21) can be written as:

$$(2.22) \quad EV = - \int_{P^0}^{P^1} \sum_{i=1}^{n} q_i^c(P, U_1) \, dp_i + \Delta m.$$

Once again, since the EV measure is in terms of the compensated demand functions, the welfare measure (2.22) is path independent; the order in which the price changes are taken does not affect the value of EV.

It appears that both CV and EV are unambiguously defined. They differ only with respect to the reference set of prices as can be seen by comparing expressions (2.19) and (2.21). EV relies on base prices while CV relies on the prices which exist in the new situation, although any set of prices could, in principle, be used to construct a measure of welfare change.

Comparing Welfare Measures

McKenzie (1983) argues that only EV constitutes a true measure of welfare change since CV is an inconsistent measure. EV relies on the original prices that are empirically observable, while final prices may not be known or known only with difficulty. The EV of a change from situation 0 to situation 1 is given by $e_H - m_0$; similarly, the EV of a change from situation 0 to situation 2 (with a different set of prices and income than situation 1) is also given by $e_H - m_0$ (Figure 2.5).

Three additional points need to be raised. First, we can reverse the situation in Figure 2.5 so that point 1 with m_1 and P^1 constitutes our starting point, and we consider an increase in price to P^0 and a reduction in income to m_0, or a move to point 0. This reverses all of our results: what we previously identified as compensating variation is now equivalent variation and vice versa, except that one is the negative of the other. Thus, the compensating variation of a move from 1 to 0 is equal to the negative of the equivalent variation of a move from 0 to 1. Likewise, the EV(1→0) = − CV(0→1).

Second, if the indifference curves are asymptotic to the vertical axis, then the EV of a price reduction could be unbounded, while the CV is limited by the amount of income available to the individual. In the case of an adverse effect (e.g., a price increase), the CV may be unbounded (i.e., the amount of compensation required may be infinite), while the EV is bounded by the amount of income available.

Finally, consider Figure 2.6. Recall from our discussion on duality in consumer theory that the compensating demands are a function of prices and utility – q_i^c $(p_1,...,p_n,U)$, $\forall\ i = 1,...,n$. Therefore, the CV of a price reduction from p_1^0 to p_1^1 is given by the area under $q_i^c(P,U_o)$ and between the price lines (i.e., area a). The EV of the price change, on the other hand, is given by the area under $q_i^c(P,U_1)$ bounded by the price lines, area $(a + b + c)$.

Consumer surplus is measured as the area under the Marshallian demand curve, $q_i(p_1, ..., p_n, m)$, $\forall\ i = 1,...,n$, and bounded by the price lines, so that in Figure 2.6 the change in consumer surplus of a reduction in the price of q_1 is given by area $(a + b)$. Ignoring the signs on the welfare measures (i.e., considering only absolute values), EV serves as an upper bound on the measure of consumer surplus, while CV serves as a lower bound in the case of a reduction in price: $CV \leq S \leq EV$. The inequality signs are reversed for a price increase from p_1^1 to p_1^0: $CV \geq S \geq EV$. Willig (1976) has shown mathematically that one can expect areas b and c to be small compared to area a, or that $EV \approx S \approx CV$. This conclusion has been challenged, however, by mounting empirical evidence to the contrary (see below).

Measuring EV and CV from Market Data

Compensated demand curves are a function of utility and thus not observed. Nonetheless, compensating and/or equivalent variation can be measured using market data, although all such measures are necessarily approximations of the true measure. We illustrate a simple method, described by Boadway and Bruce (1984), that employs Taylor series expansion and the Slutsky relation. Other methods are discussed by McKenzie (1983) and Vartia (1983).

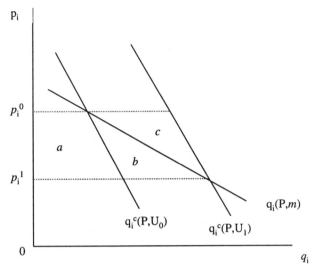

Figure 2.6 Relationship between S, CV and EV for a Single Price Change

Approximations of both compensating and equivalent variation can be found by taking a Taylor series expansion of the expenditure function about either the initial set of prices or the final set of prices. Taking a Taylor series expansion of the expenditure function $e(P^1, U_0)$ about the initial prices, while keeping utility at the original level, gives:

(2.23)

$$e(P^1, U_0) = e(P^0, U_0) + \Sigma_i \left(\frac{\partial e(P^0, U_0)}{\partial p_i} \right) \Delta p_i$$

$$+ \tfrac{1}{2} \Sigma_i \Sigma_j \left[\frac{\partial^2 e(P^0, U_0)}{\partial p_i \partial p_j} \right] \Delta p_i \, \Delta p_j + R,$$

where R represents the higher-order terms which are assumed to be negligible. Substitute this result in (2.19). Then, using result (2.8) and that $s_{ij} = \partial q_i^c / \partial p_j$ ($i, j = 1,...,n$), and upon rearranging, an approximation for CV is

(2.24) $CV \approx - \Sigma_i q_i^c(P^0, U_0) \Delta p_i - \tfrac{1}{2} \Sigma_i \Sigma_j s_{ij}(P^0, U_0) \Delta p_i \, \Delta p_j + \Delta m.$

The RHS terms in expression (2.24) are evaluated at the original prices and utility. The estimated (observed) Marshallian demand functions can be used to determine the approximation to CV, but only under restrictive conditions. At the original equilibrium (situation 0), the compensated and ordinary demand functions intersect. Hence, it is possible to use the estimated demand function, evaluated at the original equilibrium, in place of the (unknown) compensated demand function to evaluate the first term on the RHS of expression (2.24). Similarly, since the Slutsky equation can be written as $s_{ij} = \partial q_i/\partial p_j + q_j \, \partial q_i/\partial m$, the empirically estimated demand functions can be used to evaluate the second term on the RHS (Boadway and Bruce 1984, pp. 219–20). The s_{ij} are evaluated at the initial point using empirical estimates of the consumer demand functions. However, higher-order terms in the Taylor series approximation of CV cannot be evaluated from market data, which is why only a second-order Taylor series expansion is used.

An approximation of equivalent variation can also be found from equation (2.21). A second-order Taylor series expansion of the expenditure function $e(P^0, U_1)$ about the final prices, with the final level of utility held constant, gives the following:

$$e(P^0, U_1) = e(P^1, U_1) + \Sigma_i \left[\frac{\partial e(P^1, U_1)}{\partial p_i} \right] \Delta p_i$$

(2.25)

$$+ \tfrac{1}{2} \Sigma_i \Sigma_j \left[\frac{\partial^2 e(P^1, U_1)}{\partial p_i \partial p_j} \right] \Delta p_i \, \Delta p_j + R,$$

where R is the remainder which is approximately zero. Substituting into (2.21), and making the same substitutions as above, gives the following approximation of EV:

(2.26) $EV \approx \Sigma_i q_i^c(P^1, U_1) \Delta p_i + \tfrac{1}{2} \Sigma_i \Sigma_j s_{ij}(P^1, U_1) \Delta p_i \, \Delta p_j + \Delta m.$

It is possible to evaluate the first two terms on the RHS of (2.26) in the same way as for CV, but at final prices rather than original prices.

When the expenditure function is used to determine either CV or EV, and the expenditure function cannot be explicitly written, then a second-order Taylor series approximation can be used to approximate CV or EV. However, as McKenzie notes (1983, pp. 114–6), the subsequent measures rely on the ability of a second-order Taylor series expansion to measure EV and CV with sufficient accuracy. Calculations by Mckenzie (1983, pp. 171–3) indicate that such an approximation may not be sufficiently accurate, and he advocates an alternative approach (see van Kooten 1988).

We need to ask whether or not this distinction between EV, CV and S is worth all the fuss we have accorded it. First, why are there two different but equally valid or true measures of welfare change, CV and EV (S is not a theoretically valid measure), which may or may not be of the same magnitude? The reason is that the two measures depend upon the assignment of property rights. Second, why do we worry about differences between these measures if, as Willig (1976) has demonstrated, the three measures are nearly the same? These questions are addressed further below.

2.3 Public Goods and Welfare Change

Public goods have the characteristic that, once they are provided, no one can be excluded from "consuming" them. Examples include clean air, biodiversity and other environmental amenities. In addition to CV and EV, Hicks introduced the concepts of compensating and equivalent surplus. The compensating surplus (CS) is defined as the "compensating payment or offsetting income change [that] will make the individual indifferent between the original situation and the opportunity to purchase the new quantity of the good whose price has changed" (Freeman 1979a, p. 37). Equivalent surplus (ES) is the income change required to keep the person consuming the old quantity of the good whose price has changed, so that the consumer is indifferent to the new situation. Instead of permitting individuals to move along their indifference curves, adjusting to new prices, CS and ES require that an individual consume the new bundle or the old bundle, respectively. Thus, CS and ES are relevant in the case of quantity restrictions or public goods, whose quantity is fixed from the perspective of the individual. The welfare measure is then given by the vertical distance between the indifference curves at the reference consumption bundle.

These concepts can be considered with the aid of Figure 2.7. Let Q be a composite commodity such that $Q = \sum_i p_i q_i = m$. The budget line is horizontal since consumers do not pay for the public good (G) directly – there is no price associated with G and the consumer cannot vary the amount she consumes. We measure the welfare change due to a change in the quantity of the public good from G_0 to G_1 in terms of good Q. Since m is fixed, we do not change the level of expenditures on Q. In the diagram, E_0 represents the original consumption level and E_1 the final (or proposed) level of public good. Then, the compensating surplus for a price reduction is given by the vertical distance BE_1, while the equivalent surplus is given by the distance E_0A. If the indifference curves are vertically parallel, then the ES is equal to EV and the CS is equal to CV.

Mathematically, we write the utility function augmented by the public good as $U = \varphi(q_1, ..., q_n, G)$. When the budget constraint, $m = \sum_i p_i q_i$, is minimised subject to an arbitrary utility level, the resulting expenditure function is $e(p_1 ..., p_n, G, U)$. Previously we saw that the compensated demand curves could be obtained as $q_i = \partial e/\partial p_i = q_i^c(p_1, ..., p_n, G, U)$. Since the public good G is not traded in markets and, hence, no price is attached to it, its shadow price (w) is found by differentiating the expenditure function with respect to G. This gives the Hicksian (compensated) *inverse* demand function or marginal willingness to pay for changes in G:

$$(2.27) \quad w = \frac{-\partial e}{\partial G} = q_G^{-1}(p_1, p_2, ..., p_n, G, U),$$

where the minus sign is needed to permit portrayal of the function in the usual positive or northeast quadrant. The benefit to the individual of a non-marginal increase in the supply of G is:

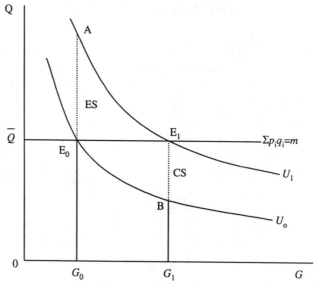

Figure 2.7 A Comparison of Compensating and Equivalent Surplus

$$(2.28) \quad \text{benefit} = \int_{G_0}^{G_1} q_G^{-1} (p_1, ..., p_n, G, U) \, dG.$$

This is either the CS or ES measure of the welfare change depending on the level of utility at which it is evaluated.

As an example consider $U = q_1 q_2 G$ and $m = p_1 q_1 + p_2 q_2$. Minimise the cost subject to U, obtain the demands, substitute into U and solve for the expenditure function. The expenditure function is $e = (4p_1 p_2 U)^{½} \div G$. Then, $w = -\partial e/\partial G = (p_1 p_2 U)^{½} \div G^3$. The benefit to the individual of an increase in the supply of G is given by the area under the inverse compensated demand function as indicated by the shaded area in Figure 2.8. This welfare measure is the compensating surplus of the quantity change and, hence, is equal to the CS measure indicated in Figure 2.7 (i.e., vertical distance $E_1 B$).

If the level of the public good were to be reduced from G_1 to G_0, the CS measure now asks how much would be required as compensation for the individual to put up with less of the public good (i.e., CS = − ES); the CS measure is now vertical distance AE_0. The ES measure indicates how much to take away in order for the individual to be as well off with the original quantity of the public good as with the new (lesser) quantity. This is vertical distance $E_1 B$ and, thus, the ES in this case would equal the negative CS from moving in the opposite direction.

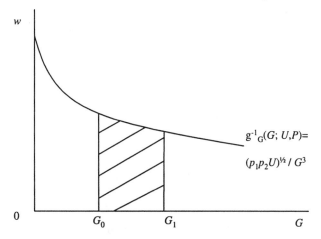

Figure 2.8 Compensating Surplus Benefit Measure of Change in a Public Good

Compensating and equivalent surplus are important concepts when it comes to measuring the value to consumers of certain goods and services that are *not* traded in markets. In the case of market goods, equivalent variation and compensating variation can be derived from estimated market transactions. But markets do not exist for such goods as recreational experiences, scenic amenities, old-growth forests, certain wildlife species, and so on. In such instances, it is necessary to employ either the CS or ES concept if one is to obtain any measure of value whatsoever. The measure that is employed depends on the property rights. If, in Figure 2.7, individuals have a right only to the original level of the public good – G_0 on the indifference curve U_0 – then CS is the appropriate measure. As shown in Chapter 5, determining CS requires one to know what individuals would be willing to pay (WTP) for the higher level of the amenity (G_1). Alternatively, if individuals have the right to G_1, the nature preserve, say, and thus utility level U_1, ES is the appropriate welfare measure. To determine ES in the case of non-market amenities, it is necessary to ask what individuals would be willing to accept (WTA) as compensation (also referred to as compensation demanded) to forgo the higher level of the public good – to forgo the nature preserve. Based on Willig's (1976) results, economists expected WTA and WTP to be relatively close (Just et al. 1982), but empirical evidence indicates that there is substantial difference between these welfare measures.

Two reasons have been postulated for large differences between WTA and WTP. Evidence from contingent valuation surveys (Chapter 5) and experimental markets (see Knetsch 2000 for a review) indicates that individuals become attached to a particular endowment, requiring a higher level of compensation to part with something than they would be willing to pay to obtain it. For example, in one experiment, Kahneman et al. (1990) find that individuals with a mug must be paid on average \$7 to give it up, while those without one are only willing to pay an average of \$2 to purchase the same mug. Almost all studies that ask people to value changes in the availability of a public good (e.g., environmental quality, nature preserves) find that WTA exceeds WTP by a substantial amount (Knetch 1989, 1995). As noted above, gains from a reference state are valued less than losses, implying that the utility function is not continuous at the endowment (Kahneman and Tversky 1979). This has sometimes been referred to as the endowment effect – the empirical evidence indicates that indifference curves are "kinked" at the endowment bundle of goods and services (Knetsch 1995).

The alternative explanation is due to Randall and Stoll (1980), Hanemann (1991) and Shogren et al. (1994). Randall and Stoll (1980) initially argued that WTP and WTA (ES and CS) are identical if there is perfect substitutability between two goods, so they can be treated as equivalent to money. This is the same as arguing that the two indifference curves in Figure 2.7 are straight (parallel) lines that angle downwards from left to right, in which case $AE_0 = E_1B$. However, their case applied to goods traded in competitive markets with no transaction costs. Hanemann (1991) argues that goods, such as health, species diversity and nature preserves, are lumpy or indivisible and markets for them are incomplete. Then the indifference lines are curved (as in Figure 2.7), resulting in a divergence between WTA and WTP. Indeed, an increase in income elasticity or a decrease in the degree of substitutability between the good in question and all other goods increases the divergence between WTA and WTP (as is clear from the Slutsky equation). Since there are few substitutes for many environmental amenities and biological assets, one would expect a divergence between WTA and WTP. Thus, the divergence falls within traditional theory. But this is not an explanation for the observed difference between WTP and WTA for goods where there are adequate substitutes, such as mugs and candy bars. Using experimental data, Shogren et al. (1994) demonstrate that for goods for which substitutes are plentiful (such as candy bars and mugs), WTP and WTA converge with repeated market participation, but for goods with few substitutes (such as food purchases where health risks are involved) they did not converge with repeated participation. This evidence supports Hanemann's (1991) contention. However, the study by Shogren et al. (1994) is the only one to demonstrate a convergence between WTP and WTA. Further, Knetsch et al. (1998) found these results could be attributed to the failure of the Vickery auction, which failed to reveal people's valuations accurately.

2.4 General Equilibrium Considerations

In the foregoing sections, we were concerned with measurement in a single market or, when more than one price changed, the sum of consumer welfare measurements in several markets. What has been ignored in this discussion is production possibilities – it may simply not be possible to increase output. When the production frontier is encountered, one would expect resource rents to rise as well as wages and the rent on capital. In these circumstances, a general equilibrium framework is needed for measuring welfare changes as the compensated demand functions are no longer appropriate for calculating CV and EV. We illustrate how welfare measures change in these circumstances by constructing a general equilibrium demand curve for a single consumer economy. Finally, we consider general equilibrium welfare measurement.

We first consider how the effect on welfare measures of general equilibrium considerations and then how might measure welfare impacts across markets in practice.

General equilibrium demand curve

The general equilibrium or Bailey's demand curve is a theoretical construct that takes into account constraints on production. A single person economy is assumed so that indifference curves and production possibilities can be shown on a single diagram. In Figure 2.9(a), the production possibility frontier is denoted by zz'. The individual is assumed to be in equilibrium at point E. A policy that increases the price of good q_1 is indicated by the steeper price, with the tangency on the indifference curve shifting from E to K'. However, the latter point is beyond the transformation frontier. Hence, rather than moving to K' on the original indifference curve, the consumer would move to point K on a lower indifference curve, but still on zz'. A new demand curve can be traced out that takes into account the production constraint – the general equilibrium or Bailey demand function. It is shown in Figure 2.9(b) and denoted bb'. Also shown in Figure 2.9(b) are the compensated and ordinary demand functions, denoted cc' and dd', respectively.

Under conditions of general equilibrium, the true measure of consumer welfare loss due to an increase in the price of q_1 from p_1^0 to p_1' is not area $(\alpha + \beta + \gamma)$ in Figure 2.9(b), but rather area $(\alpha + \beta)$. This is because the general equilibrium demand curve takes into account impacts in other markets and, thereby, the overall constraints in the economy. Finally, notice that the consumer surplus measure of welfare change is less than the true measure of welfare change (and less than compensating variation) for price increases, but that it is greater than the true welfare change (and greater than CV) for price reductions.

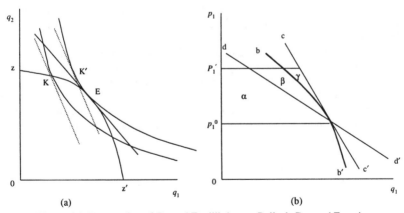

Figure 2.9 Construction of General Equilibrium or Bailey's Demand Function

Measuring welfare in one market with distortions in other markets

For much practical policy analysis, impacts in other markets can be taken into account by measuring indirect benefits (Harberger 1971). However, there is often confusion about when indirect benefits (or costs) actually occur and, hence, when they may be included in cost-benefit calculations. Indirect benefits are measured in markets that are affected by changes in the market impacted by the government policy. For example, government policies in one market may increase price and reduce output in that market. Impacts are also felt in related markets through the cross price elasticities of demand because consumers shift expenditures toward other goods. What is often neglected in this case is that welfare impacts are to be measured only when there are distortions in the indirectly affected markets.

> The task of measuring indirect benefits can thus be reduced, first, to ascertaining those industries or activities in the economy for which marginal social benefit (MSB) is likely to differ from marginal social cost (MSC); second, estimating the magnitude of the difference, for each industry, per unit change in its output and, third, estimating the likely change (ΔQ) in the output of such industries as a consequence of the project being evaluated. Having done this, the estimation of indirect benefits can be calculated by the formula $\Sigma_i(\text{MSB}_i - \text{MSC}_i) \Delta Q_i$, where the subscript i varies over all industries for which $\text{MSB}_i \neq \text{MSC}_i$. (Harberger 1972, p. 48)

In their survey of cost-benefit analysis, Prest and Turvey (1974) come to the same conclusion: "we need worry about secondary benefits (or, for that matter, costs) only to the extent that market prices fail to reflect marginal social costs and benefits. The real problem concerning secondary benefits (and costs) is thus a matter of second-best allocation problems" (p. 690).

Indirect benefits are to be included in cost-benefit analysis only when there is a distortion in at least one market indirectly impacted by the project or government policy. As Just et al. (1982) note, "effects in nondistorted markets are completely captured by equilibrium measurements only in distorted markets" (p. 459). Examples of distortions include government-sanctioned price supports, taxes and monopoly. The theoretical framework for including indirect benefits (or costs) to consumers is illustrated in Figure 2.10, where three markets for building materials are assumed.

Suppose that government policy (e.g., US quota on imports of Canadian lumber) causes a shift of the supply curve for lumber from S_1^0 to S_1^1, with the supply-restricted quantity set at q_1^R. The price of q_1 increases from p_1^C to p_1^R as a result of government intervention. While area $(p_1^C \alpha \beta\ p_1^R)$ is simply an income transfer from consumers to producers, the direct social cost of the government policy is given by area $(\alpha \gamma \tau)$ – a direct cost.

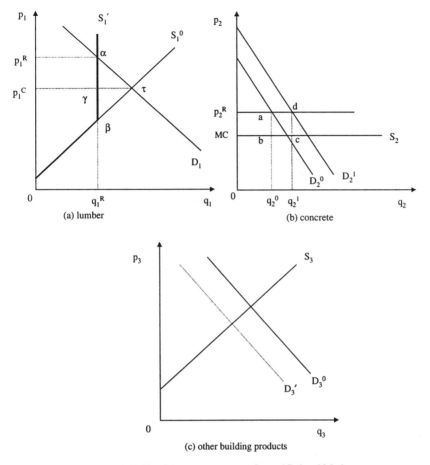

Figure 2.10 Welfare Measurement across Several Related Markets

In the market for concrete (q_2 in (b)), we assume that the marginal cost of production is below price due to the existence of a market distortion (e.g., monopoly) that causes price to be above marginal cost. For ease of exposition, we assume that the supply curve for q_2 is perfectly elastic (i.e., that there are constant returns to scale production).[4] For small changes in output, it is also possible to assume that the difference between output price and marginal production cost remains constant as output expands. Given that goods q_1 and q_2 are substitutes, the demand curve for q_2

---

[4] With upward sloping supply, welfare measurement is more difficult as a new marginal revenue curve would likely have to be identified whenever demand shifts; but the basic approach remains the same. For the case of a small country under free trade, a perfectly elastic supply means domestic producers can supply as much as they want at the world price.

shifts from D_2^0 to D_2^1 and consumers increase purchases from q_2^0 to q_2^1. If the price distortion in market (b) remains equal to the distance ab, then area ($abcd$) in market (b) is an indirect benefit of restricting supply in market (a). (If q_1 and q_2 are complements, then the measurable loss in welfare in market (b) is given by the height of the distortion times the reduction in quantity purchased.) The reason that it is a benefit is that society's marginal valuation of q_2 is greater than the marginal cost of providing these goods; whenever MSB > MSC, more of the good should be produced.

The increase in the price of q_1 will also shift the demand curve for all other building materials (market (c)), with the direction of any shift depending on whether q_1 and q_3 are complements or substitutes. No welfare loss or gain is to be measured in that market since marginal social cost remains equal to marginal social benefit (Harberger 1971; Just et al. 1982, p. 459).

In summary, the total cost of the lumber quota is equal to area ($\alpha\beta\tau$) in panel (a) minus the benefit (ignoring other externalities) in panel (b) given by area ($abcd$). It is important to note that area ($\alpha\beta\tau$) > area ($abcd$). The overall welfare of society must be reduced as a result of a supply restriction on lumber. Otherwise, it would imply that the distribution of consumer expenditures among markets was not efficient to begin with. Consumers could have been better off by re-allocating their total expenditures on food in a different fashion.

Appendix: Consumer Surplus and Path Dependency

Suppose all prices and income change from $(p_1^0, ..., p_n^0, m^0)$ to $(p_1^1, ..., p_n^1, m^1)$. Then

(A2.1) $\Delta U = v(p_1^0, ..., p_n^0, m^0) - v(p_1^1, ..., p_n^1, m^1) = \int_L dv,$

where $\int_L$ is a line integral which depends upon the particular path chosen. Total differentiating the budget constraint and the utility function yields, respectively,

(A2.2) $dm = \Sigma_i p_i \, dq_i + \Sigma_i q_i \, dp_i$ and

(A2.3) $dU = \Sigma_i U_i \, dq_i = dv.$

Substituting the first-order condition $U_i = \lambda p_i$ into equation (A2.3) gives:

(A2.4) $dv = \Sigma_i \lambda p_i \, dq_i.$

Substituting (A2.4) into (A2.1) and replacing $\Sigma_i p_i \, dq_i$ from (A2.2) gives:

(A2.5) $dU = \int_L \lambda \, (dm - \Sigma_i q_i \, dp_i).$

This line integral gives an exact measure of ΔU regardless of the path chosen (Just et al. 1982, pp. 360–5).

It turns out that the term after the integral sign in equation (A2.5) is an exact differential or exact integral (McKenzie 1983, p. 26). An exact differential is, "An expression M(x,y) dx + N(w,y) dy is called an *exact differential* if and only if a function w = f(w,y) exists such that df(x,y) = M(x,y)dx + N(x,y)dy" (Thomas 1968, p. 536). We then have the following:

> *Theorem*: Let M(x,y,z), N(x,y,z) and P(x,y,z) be continuous, together with their first-order partial derivates, for all real values of x,y, and z. Then a necessary and sufficient condition for the expression Mdx + Ndy + Pdz to be an exact differential is that the following equations be satisfied: $\partial M/\partial y = \partial N/\partial x$, $\partial M/\partial z = \partial P/\partial x$, $\partial N/\partial z = \partial P/\partial y$. (Thomas 1968, p. 591)

An exact differential implies path independency.

Now, we have: $dm - q_1\,dp_1 - q_2\,dp_2 - \cdots - q_n\,dp_n$. By the above theorem, this is an exact differential if and only if: (i) $\partial m/\partial p_i = \partial q_i/\partial m$, $\forall\ i = 1, ..., n$; and (ii) $\partial q_i/\partial p_j = \partial q_j/\partial p_i$, $\forall i \neq j$, conditions identical to those identified by Just et al. (1982, p. 364).

One problem remains. It is not possible to measure the change in utility because we do not observe λ, the marginal utility of income (budget). How can equation (A2.5) be converted into a money metric? One way is to assume that λ is constant over the path of integration. Then,

$$(A2.6) \quad S = \frac{\Delta U}{\lambda} = \int_L (dm - \Sigma_i\, q_i\, dp_i),$$

where S is a money measure of welfare; (A2.6) is identical to (2.18). Alternatively, one can assume that λ is not constant, but that it is also not a function of either m or p_i ($\forall\ i = 1, ..., n$). Then $S = \Delta U/\lambda$ is *not* proportional to ΔU but varies as λ varies. While (A2.6) still holds, one needs to investigate conditions under which S is unique.

Recall Roy's identity, $q_j = -(\partial v/\partial p_j)/(\partial v/\partial m)$. Rearranging gives $-\lambda q_j = \partial v/\partial p_j$, where $\lambda = \partial v/\partial m$. Differentiating with respect to expenditure m yields:

$$(A.2.7) \quad -\lambda\left(\frac{\partial q_j}{\partial m}\right) - q_j\left(\frac{\partial \lambda}{\partial m}\right) = \partial\left(\frac{\partial v}{\partial p_j}\right)/\partial m = \frac{\partial^2 v}{\partial p_j \partial m} = \frac{\partial^2 v}{\partial m \partial p_j} = \frac{\partial \lambda}{\partial p_j}.$$

Note that $\partial \lambda/\partial p_j = \partial \lambda/\partial m = 0$ implies that $\partial q_j/\partial m = 0$ ($\forall\ j = 1, ..., n$). But this cannot hold because $m = \Sigma_j\, p_j q_j$ implying that $\partial m/\partial m = 1 = \partial(\Sigma_j\, p_j\, q_j)/\partial m = \Sigma_j\, p_j\, (\partial q_j/\partial m)$. Therefore, one of the following must be true:

1. λ is constant with respect to all prices, but not with respect to income. This is the Marshallian definition of constancy of marginal utility of income.
2. The numeraire is defined as the *n*th good and, hence, λ constant implies constancy of the marginal utility of the *n* th good, that is, of money. Note that, from $U_i = \lambda p_i$ and $p_n = 1$, we get $\lambda = U_n$. *As a result, S cannot possibly be unique when all prices and income change.*

Three conditions that could lead to a unique measure of S (i.e., path independency) can now be identified.

1. $\partial \lambda / \partial p_i = 0$, $\forall i = 1, \ldots, n$ and $dm = 0$. All prices can change but income cannot. This condition will result in path independency if an only if consumer utility is homothetic, which holds if and only if all income elasticities are unity.
2. is constant and $\partial \lambda / \partial p_i = 0$, $\forall i = 1, \ldots, n - 1$, where q_n is the numeraire commodity or money.
3. Path independence does not imply constancy of λ, but "that λ change at the same rate for each of the price changes (when connected by relative expenditures on the goods)" (Just et al. 1982, p. 365). At most, λ can be constant with respect to all prices but not income, or with respect to income and the first $(n - 1)$ prices.

Now, Marshall's postulate states that, if there is an abundance of some good in the system, say q_1, the marginal utility (MU) of that good will be constant over some range: $MU_1 = constant \Rightarrow \partial MU_1 / \partial q_1 = 0$. The assumption of vertically-parallel (or if the reference good is on the ordinate, horizontally-parallel) indifference curves is somewhat different than Marshall's postulate, although Marshall's postulate is a special case. First, to ensure that indifference curves are convex to the origin, we must have $d^2 q_2 / d q^2_1 > 0$. The assumption of vertically-parallel indifference curves implies that

$$(A2.8) \quad \partial (\frac{-dq_2}{dq_1}) / \partial q_1 = \partial (\frac{MU_{q1}}{MU_{q2}}) / \partial q_1 = 0.$$

How is this related to Marshall's postulate? Assume $U = \varphi(q_1, q_2)$. Then $dU = \varphi_1 \, dq_1 + \varphi_2 \, dq_2 = 0$, which implies that $- dq_2 / dq_1 = \varphi_1 / \varphi_2$. Then, taking the derivative in (A2.8) and, upon rearranging,

$$(A2.9) \quad \partial^2 U / \partial q_1^2 = (\varphi_1 / \varphi_2) (\partial^2 U / \partial q_1 \partial q_2).$$

Since φ_1, $\varphi_2 > 0$, sign $[\partial^2 U / \partial q_1^2] = sign[\partial^2 U / \partial q_1 \partial q_2]$. Three cases arise:

1. $\partial^2 U / \partial q_1^2 = 0$, which is simply Marshall's postulate. This implies that $\partial^2 U / \partial q_2 \partial q_1 = 0$ and, therefore, q_1 and q_2 are *independent* in consumption.
2. $\partial^2 U / \partial q_1^2 < 0$ which implies $\partial^2 U / \partial q_2 \partial q_1 < 0$ and, therefore, q_1 and q_2 are *competitive* on consumption.
3. $\partial^2 U / \partial q_1^2 > 0$ which implies $\partial^2 U / \partial q_2 \partial q_1 > 0$ and, therefore, q_1 and q_2 are *complements* in consumption.

Therefore, Marshall's postulate is a special case of the assumption of vertically parallel indifference curves; it is a more restrictive case. Vertically parallel indifference curves imply that, as income rises or falls, *ceteris paribus*, the amount of q_1 purchased remains unchanged. Then there is no income effect.

3 Producer Welfare and Aggregation of Well Being

Consider first the case of the single competitive firm producing wood products, say. The firm is assumed to be maximising profit. Alternatively, we can assume that the firm is maximising expected utility $E(U)$, where $U = \varphi(\pi)$ is the utility function and π is profit, although such an assumption generally requires that the decision maker's risk attitude be taken into account, and that is beyond the scope of the current discussion. The firm's input supply curve is assumed to be perfectly elastic as is the demand function for its products. That is, the firm is a price taker in both input and output markets. We are concerned with the welfare impacts on producers whenever some policy causes changes in output (or input) prices.

In the short run, a firm's fixed costs are considered foregone. Thus, the firm will produce wood products as long as revenues exceed variable costs. In the short run, the firm earns profit given by the difference between total revenue (TR) and total costs (TC), where the latter is the sum of total variable cost (TVC) and total fixed cost (TFC), $\pi = \text{TR} - \text{TC} = \text{TR} - \text{TVC} - \text{TFC}$. Although the focus of the next chapter, we define *rent* to equal profit (rent = TR − TC = π) and quasi-rent as the excess of total revenue over total costs: Quasi-Rent = TR − TVC = π + TFC. We then ask to what extent are profit, rent and/or quasi-rent good measures of producer welfare? The answer depends on the notions of compensating and equivalent surplus developed in the previous chapter.

Now consider what is meant by compensating and equivalent variation in the case of producer welfare. Suppose, as in Figure 3.1, that the price of the firm's output increases from p_0 to p_1 as a result of some public policy. Then the

> *compensating variation* associated with the price increase is the sum of money that, when taken away from the producing firm, leaves it just as well off as if the price did not change, given that it is free to adjust production (to profit-maximizing quantities) in either case. ... The *equivalent variation* associated with the price increase is the sum of money which, when given to the firm, leaves it just as well off without the price change as if the change occurred, again assuming freedom of adjustment. (Just et al. 1982, pp. 52–3)

In Figure 3.1, profit is higher at p_1 than at p_0 by area p_1abe. This area is also equal to the area above the marginal cost (MC) curve between P_0 and P_1, or area p_0acp_1. Area p_1abe (= area p_0acp_1) is the compensating variation (CV) of the price increase. Similarly, profit is lower at p_0 than at p_1 by the same area p_0acp_1, which measures the equivalent variation (EV) of the price reduction. Therefore, the change in profit associated with a price change is an exact measure of both the CV and EV as long as price is not below the shut down price (p_S in Figure 3.1). Following Marshall, the area above the firm's short-run supply curve and below price measures producer surplus, as long as the firm is operating at or above its shutdown point. The change in producer surplus of either a price increase or a price decrease is given by area p_0acp_1. The producer surplus is identical to quasi-rent.

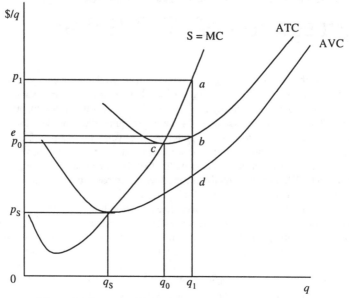

Figure 3.1 Concepts of Rent, Quasi-Rent and Producer Surplus

3.1 Measuring Producer Surplus via the Input Market

Suppose that output can be produced using one input, so $q = f(x)$. Let r denote the input price (cost of input to the firm) and $f'(x)$ the marginal physical product of input x in production of output q. In this case, it is quite easy to measure the change in producer surplus in the input market alone. In Figure 3.2, the demand curve for input x – the value of marginal product curve (VMP $= f'(x) \times p$, where p is output price) – will shift to the right when output price increases. Then area ψ in Figure 3.2 is a measure of producer welfare that is identical to area p_0acp_1 in Figure 3.1.

Changes in input prices

Suppose input price falls from r_0 to r_1. In this case, the *compensating variation* is the "sum of money the producer would be willing to pay to obtain the privilege of buying at the lower price (that is, which would leave the firm just as well off at the lower price)". The *equivalent variation*, on the other hand, is the "sum of money the producer would accept to forego the privilege of buying at the lower price (that is, which would leave the firm just as well off at the original price)" (Just et al. 1982, p. 58).

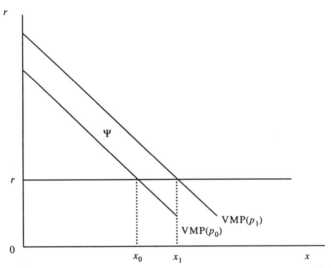

Figure 3.2 Producer Surplus Measured in the Input Market: Increase in Output Price

Now consider Figure 3.3 and suppose input price falls from r_0 to r_1. In the input market depicted in panel (a), this is represented by the downward shift of the price line (from r_0 to r_1). However, in the output market, panel (b), the supply curve shifts to the right, from $S(r_0)$ to $S(r_1)$. Given that the input price is r_0 and the associated quantity is x_0, then total cost is $r_0 x_0$ = area $b + c$, while total revenue is given by area $a + b + c$. The difference, area a, is producer surplus and is equivalent to area α in panel (b), ignoring the possibility of shutdown. Now, when the price of the input falls to r_1, the new total cost is area $c + e = r_1 x_1$, while the total revenue is area $a + b + c + d + e$. The difference, area $a + b + d$, is the producer surplus. Therefore, area $b + d$ measures the increase in producer welfare that results from the reduction in input price. This area is identical to area β in the output market (panel (b)).

Simultaneous Changes in Input and Output Prices

Suppose that input price rises from r_0 to r_1 while, at the same time, the output price rises from p_0 to p_1. How do we measure the welfare change? The net welfare change can be measured in either the input market or the output market as illustrated in panels (a) and (b), respectively, in Figure 3.4. Before any change occurs, producer surplus is area $b + c$, which is equal to area $\beta + \mu$. When the input price rises, producer welfare *decreases* by area c in the input market. This is equal to area μ in the output market. Now output price increases and producers gain area a = area α. Therefore, the net gain (or loss) in producer welfare is area $a - c$ = area $\alpha - \mu$. It is easy to verify that we obtain the same result if we begin with an output price increase followed by an increase in input price. That is, unlike consumer surplus, measures of producer surplus are path independent.

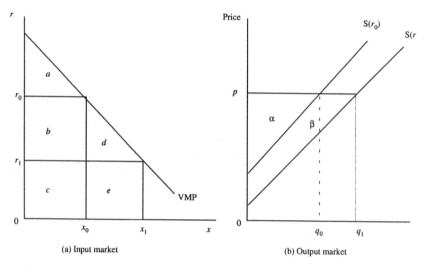

(a) Input market   (b) Output market

Figure 3.3 Welfare Measures in Input and Output Markets: Reduction in Input Price

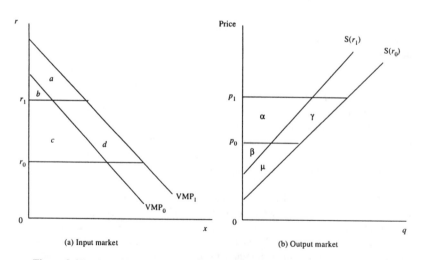

(a) Input market   (b) Output market

Figure 3.4 Producer Welfare Measures when Both Input and Output Prices Change

Multiple Inputs

When we have more than one input, the measure of producer welfare gain (or loss) due to price changes is more difficult to measure. The value of the marginal product curve does not represent the demand curve in input markets when $\partial MP_i/\partial x_j \neq 0$, where MP_i is the marginal physical product of input i. For example, labour (L) on a fishing vessel influences the marginal productivity of fuel (F). If the production function for fish is specified as $q = \gamma L^{\beta} F^{\alpha}$, then $\partial MP_F/\partial L = q\beta\alpha/LF \neq 0$. However, the derived input demands that result after all other inputs have been adjusted to their optimal levels can be used to measure producer welfare changes. Once again there is path independency and, hence, it is possible to measure welfare changes in sequential fashion.

Consider Figure 3.5 that illustrates the case of moving from the original situation (p^0, r_1^0, r_2^0) to (P^1, r_1^1, r_2^1). We assume that $p^1 > p^0$, $r_1^1 < r_1^0$ and $r_2^1 > r_2^0$.

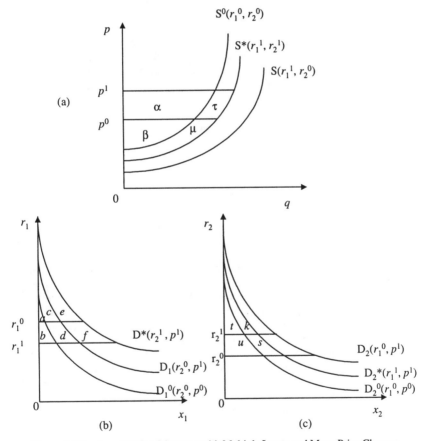

Figure 3.5 Producer Welfare Measures with Multiple Inputs and Many Price Changes

The output market, the market for input x_1 and the market for input x_2 are shown in panels (a), (b) and (c), respectively. Assume that x_1 and x_2 are substitutes in production; then a reduction in the price of x_2 will reduce the demand for x_1. The superscript * on the functions represents their final position. (There is no reason why S* lies to the right of S^0 in Figure 3.5(a). The analysis does not change if S* is positioned to the left of S^0.)

The change in producer welfare can be measured in each market or sequentially. In the output market, producer surplus initially equals area β. Thus, the increase in producer surplus equals area $\alpha + \tau + \mu$. In the market for x_1 (panel (b)), the initial producer surplus (or quasi-rent) is given by area a, while the final producer surplus is given by area $a + b + c + d + e + f$. Hence, the gain in quasi-rent is area $b + c + d + e + f$. In the market for x_2 (panel (c)), producer surplus is initially given by area $t + u$. Final quasi-rent is given by area $t + k$. The change in producer welfare is measured by area $k - u$ in panel (c). In summary, we have that the change in producer surplus is given by area $\alpha + \tau + \mu$ in panel (a), by area $b + c + d + e + f$ in panel (b), and by area $k - u$ in panel (c).

We can also derive a measure of producer surplus in sequential fashion. One case is considered although others are also possible. Assume that the output price rises first, followed by a reduction in the price of input x_1. Finally, the price of input x_2 is assumed to increase. Then we have the following sequence of welfare measurement: the gain in quasi-rent due to a rise in p equals area α; the gain in quasi-rent due to a fall in r_1 equals area $b + d$; and the loss in quasi-rent due to a rise in r_2 equals area $u + s$. The total change in producer surplus is equal to area $\alpha + b + d - u - s$. This area should be identical to those derived above. We could calculate similar areas for other cases although we will need to identify on the diagrams $S(r_1^0, r_2^1)$, $D_1(r_2^1, p^0)$, and so on.

Resource income and backward-bending supply

So far we have considered measures of consumer surplus and producer surplus, but we have not considered the impact of income changes on the demand for commodities when income change is the result of changes in input prices. That is, so far we have treated income as an exogenous variable although, in reality, income varies directly with changes in the prices of inputs. Individuals own factors of production from which they derive income. Changes in the prices of factors have a direct effect on income (e.g., via changes in wage rates or resource rents); income, in turn, impacts directly on the demand curves for final commodities. Hence, the area above a resource supply curve is fully analogous to the area below a consumer demand curve if consumers, as factor owners, earn income from that resource.

Similar to our notion of Hicksian (compensated) demand curves, we can construct Hicksian (compensated) supply curves. Compensated supply is determined for a given level of utility (holding other prices fixed). The compensated supply curve is conditioned on utility, whereas the ordinary supply curve is conditioned on the level of exogenous income. Using the Hicksian supply curves, it is possible to find the compensating and equivalent variations of a change in wage rates either from the indifference map (not shown here) or as an area above the compensated supply curve.

Consider the backward bending supply curve for labour (L) in Figure 3.6. The backward bending supply function is derived from utility maximisation, where utility consists of leisure and income, with the slope of the constraint determined by the wage rate (see Mishan 1981, p. 214). The Hicksian (compensated) supply curves for the utility levels $U_0 < U_1 < U_2$ are denoted $H(U_i)$ in Figure 3.6, and have positive slope even though the ordinary supply curves might have a negative slope as a result of the income effect associated with an increase in wages – workers purchase more leisure as wages increase. The area above the compensated labour supply curve $H(U_1)$ gives the compensating variation of a wage change from w_1 to w_2, namely, area $a + b + c$. The equivalent variation of the wage change is given by the area above $H(U_2)$, or area a.

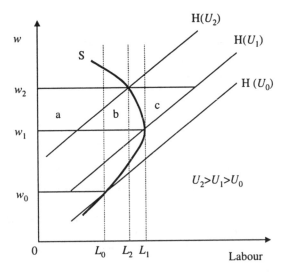

Figure 3.6 Welfare Measures and Compensating Supply of Input Curves

Now consider Figure 3.7 and assume that income consists of an exogenous and endogenous component. Endogenous income is earned income, obtained by selling a factor of production. Exogenous income is income from net wealth, government transfers and so on. The labour market is depicted in Figure 3.7(a). The wage rate is assumed to fall from w_0 to w_1, while the price of the consumer good (shown in Figure 3.7(b)) also falls from p_0 to p_1.

In this case, the welfare measures are path dependent unless the following path independency condition can be met: $\partial q/\partial w = \partial L/\partial p$. (Path dependency is discussed in the Appendix to Chapter 2.) Consider the following two paths.

1. ***First p falls, then w falls*** Given the original demand curve $D(w_0)$, the gain in consumer surplus is given by area $\alpha + \beta$. The reduction in the consumption

commodity's price shifts the labour supply curve inward from $S(p_0)$ to $S(p_1)$. The reduction in wage rates implies a loss in producer surplus equal to area *a*. In this case, the lost producer surplus (or quasi-rent) is a loss to the resource supplier in her role as consumer.

2. *First the wage rate falls, then p declines* Given the original supply curve, S_0, we measure the loss in producer surplus due to a reduction in wages by area $a + b$. The reduction in wages results in a reduction in income and, therefore, causes the demand curve for the consumption commodity to shift inward. When the price of this good falls from p_0 to p_1 the gain in consumer surplus is area α.

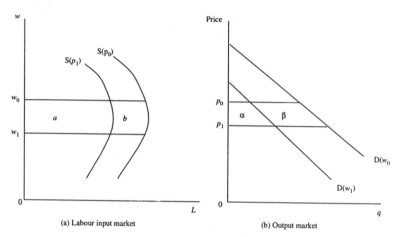

(a) Labour input market   (b) Output market

Figure 3.7 Welfare Measures when Resource Prices affect Income and Final Prices Fall

The net gains in welfare in the two situations are area $\alpha + \beta - a$ along the first path and area $\alpha - a - b$ along the second, with the difference equal to area $\beta + b$. Only if area β = area b are the two measures of welfare gain the same.

Missing Labour Markets and the Environment

When wages increase, individuals may respond by supplying more or less labour to the market, depending on the strength of the income effect. This may have an impact on resource management, especially in developing countries where markets for labour are typically less than perfect. Bulte and van Soest (1999) analyse the effect of rising prices of agricultural output on soil management by a rural household. In particular, what happens to the optimal nutrient stock in the soil when agricultural prices change? Barrett (1991) argues that rising prices have little or no impact on the nutrient stock that the household chooses to "hold" because higher prices affect both marginal benefits and costs (foregone future production) of soil mining, with the total effect being neutral on balance. This finding may not hold when the income effect is strong, which can be demonstrated as follows.

Typically households are assumed not to maximise profits or income but utility, which may encompass a broader set of objectives. Assume the following household objective function:

(3.1) $\int_0^\infty U(c^M, c^L)e^{-rt}\, dt,$

where U is an (additively separable) instantaneous utility function; c^M is consumption of manufactured goods (a traded commodity purchased by the household); c^L is consumption of leisure (defined as time not spent farming); and r is the household's discount rate. The household budget constraint is:

(3.2) $P^M c^M = P\, g(R, S, L^D) - \omega L^H.$

The LHS of (3.2) represents expenditures on consumption goods, where P^M is the price of manufactured goods. Household income (the RHS) consists of the (net) revenues of household production minus costs of hired labour. More specifically, P is the (exogenous) price that the household receives for its output and $g(\cdot)$ is the quantity produced. Production is a function of labour allocated to production (L^D), the stock of nutrients in the soil (S) and the use (extraction) of nutrients (R) by the household. Barrett (1991) discusses this production function in greater detail, noting that it is strictly concave in all its arguments. Finally, ω is the prevailing wage rate and L^H is the quantity of labour hired (or sold, when L^H takes negative values) by the household.

The nutrient stock changes over time as a result of decisions by the household. These include agronomic activities that reduce the nutrient stock and soil conserving activities (e.g., planting shelter belts, building ridges and/or terraces, green manuring, and applying mulch) that increase nutrients. The nutrient dynamics are described by the following differential equation:

(3.3) $\dfrac{dS}{dt} = \dot{S} = z(L^i) - R,$

where $z(L^i)$ is nutrients added to the stock as a result of investment, with $z'(L^i) > 0$. Soil quality (nutrient stocks) can increase or decrease over time depending on household choices.

Further, assume that the household can allocate time to three different activities – direct production (L^D), investments in conservation (L^i) and leisure (c^L). Given a fixed endowment of time available within the household ($\overline{L}$), equilibrium requires that demand for time equals supply:

(3.4) $L^D + L^i + c^L = \overline{L} + L^H.$

The household maximises (3.1) subject to constraints (3.2), (3.3) and (3.4). The tools for solving this problem are provided in Chapter 7; here we merely state the main results. It follows that $dS/dP > 0$ when the household can hire and sell labour L^H. Increasing the price of agricultural output P induces the household to invest in the soil as the value of the marginal product of the inputs (including the nutrient stock) increase. As a result more labour will be allocated to soil conservation.

If labour markets do not exist, so that (3.4) needs to be written as $L^D + L^I + c^L = \overline{L}$, dS/dP can be positive or negative. Specifically, $dS/dP = f(\eta)$, where $\eta = c^M U_{MM}/U_M$ (subscripts refer to partial derivatives); that is, η is the elasticity of marginal utility of consumption. Now, $dS/dP > 0$ if $\eta < 1$, while $dS/dP < 0$ if $\eta > 1$. If $\eta > 1$, a 1% increase in consumption of manufactures results in a more than proportional reduction in marginal utility, U_M. Higher prices make the household better off, and tend to increase demand for both manufactures and leisure. As it is not possible to compensate for extra leisure consumed by the household by hiring extra labour, labour allocated to soil conservation L^i may fall, thus reducing the optimal nutrient stock. Higher prices for agricultural output do not always translate into soil conservation, however, due to the income effect (see Bulte and van Soest 1999).

Backward-Bending Supply and Exploitation of Biological Assets

Backward bending supply curves also show up in natural resource systems, although interpretation of areas above such functions as welfare measures is troublesome. As we discuss in Chapter 7, growth of commercial fish species or wildlife herbivores is often characterised by a carrying capacity and maximum sustainable yield (MSY) population. The supply curve can be constructed intuitively as follows. When prices are zero (the species has no value) and there is no other disturbance to the system, the population will be at its carrying capacity. Suppose that the species' value increases. Then, at some price, it becomes worthwhile to begin harvesting the species; early on the population is sufficiently abundant that relatively little effort is required to harvest animals. As prices rise, more effort is attracted to the exploitation of the species, causing the supply of harvested animals to increase. As effort increases, harvest will exceed growth and population falls. Further increases in price result in greater effort and greater harvests (supply). However, once effort increases beyond that needed to achieve MSY, biologically excessive harvesting occurs and the species declines. As Clark (1990, pp. 131–44) shows, the supply curve then bends backwards as the price of the species increases further (see Figure 3.8). This is true not only for an open-access resource but also for one that is optimally controlled; it is true for both the case where the (single) resource owner faces an infinite demand elasticity or a downward sloping demand function. The exact shape of the supply curve will also depend on the discount rate that is used. In the case of a zero rate of discount, the supply curve is no longer backward bending, but approaches the MSY harvest asymptotically as price increases (Clark 1990, p. 137).

Is it possible to measure the rent associated with the exploitation of the fish stock, or species of wildlife herbivore (e.g., elephants), from the supply function? In the case of open-access, the rent is all dissipated, so there is no rent. In all other cases, it is the discounted supply curve that is drawn. Since the supply curve is not a marginal cost curve, rent cannot be determined directly (see Mishan 1959, 1981), but must be calculated in the ways indicated in Chapter 4.

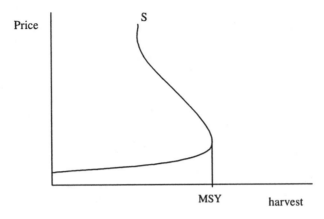

Figure 3.8 Backward-Bending Supply for Fish or Herbivores

Sequential measurement versus measurement in a single market

Earlier we showed that when a producer faces multiple price changes, welfare could be measured sequentially or in a single input or output market. In the case where factor markets determine (endogenously) the income constraint of the consumer, the same result holds. Consider the case of a (short-run) producer whose optimisation problem is:

(3.5)

maximise $\quad \pi = \sum_i p_i q_i - \sum_j r_j x_j; \qquad i = 1,...,n; \, j = 1,...,k$

subject to $\quad f(q_1, ..., q_n; x_1, ..., x_k) = 0,$

where f is the implicit production function. The consumer/resource supplier's problem can be stated in similar fashion:

(3.6)

minimise $\quad m = \sum_j r_j x_j - \sum_i p_i q_i$

subject to $\quad U(q_1, ..., q_n; x_1, ..., x_k) = U_0,$

where m is expenditure needed to attain U_0 and, to make the problem mathematically equivalent to the producer problem, we write $f(q_1, ..., q_n; x_1, .., x_k) = U(q_1, ..., q_n; x_1, ..., x_k) - U_0$. Mathematical equivalence implies that "areas behind firm supply and demand curves are related to the firm's quasi-rent exactly as areas behind a consumer's compensated supply and demand curves are related to (the negative of) expenditures necessary to attain a given utility level" (Just et al. 1982, pp. 143–4).

Consider, as an example, an increase in both consumer commodity prices (from

p_0 to p_1) and wage rates (from w_0 to w_1). The example is illustrated in Figure 3.9. Suppose $H(p_0)$ and $H(p_1)$ are compensated supply curves for the same utility level, and likewise that $D^c(w_0)$ and $D^c(w_1)$ are compensated demand functions for that same utility level. Further, assume that the consumption commodity is essential so that positive quantities are consumed at all times. Similarly, a positive amount of labour is always supplied. These assumptions are crucial to the analysis that follows.

Given w_0 fixed, a price increase results in a loss of welfare equal to area y. This welfare loss can be measured in the input market by area d. Similarly, an increase in the wage rate results in a gain of area $b + c$ for a given price level p_1. In the commodity market, this gain is measured by area $x + v$. Finally, the net welfare gain of a shift from (w_0, p_0) to (w_1, p_1) is measured by area $b - d$ = area $v - y$, if and only if labour is essential to the person's well-being (in which case area $b - d$ is an exact measure of welfare) and q is essential (in which case area $v - y$ is an exact measure of welfare). Finally, these are a measure of EV or CV depending on whether the reference utility function is the final or initial one, respectively.

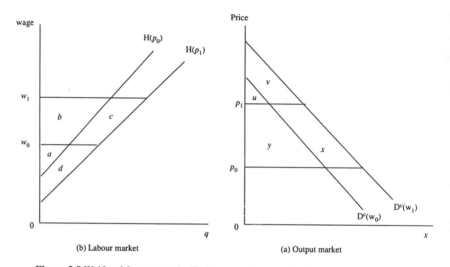

Figure 3.9 Welfare Measures under Endogenous Incomes: Equivalent Approaches

Quantity restrictions

Quantity restrictions are common in natural resource systems. In the fishery, quotas are used to restrict harvests, while, in forestry, lumber quotas have been used by the United States to keep out lumber from Canada, thereby maintaining high domestic prices and making available rents to US producers. These former is likely an example of output restrictions (fish is sold to final consumers), while the latter is an example of an input restriction (lumber is used to build homes).

Consider first the case of an input restriction. Suppose the following single-output profit maximisation problem: $\pi = p\,f(x_1, x_2, \ldots, x_k) - \sum_j r_j\,x_j$: $j = 1,\ldots,k$. The solution requires that $pf_i/r_i = pf_j/r_j = 1$ ($\forall i \neq j$, $i,j = 1,\ldots,k$), where f_i is the marginal physical product of input x_i in production of this output. That is, the value of the marginal product of input x_i divided by its input price must equal the VMP of input x_2 divided by its input price. This relationship describes the expansion path for production in input space. The further requirement, that $pf_i/r_i = 1$, $\forall i$, indicates which point on the expansion path is globally optimal.

With a quantity restriction on an input, $pf_i/r_i = pf_j/r_j$ still holds ($\forall i \neq j$, $i,j = 1,\ldots,k$), but the further requirement that $pf_i/r_i = 1$ ($\forall i$) cannot be maintained, even for some inputs. Thus, a restriction on the availability of input x_1, say, raises f_1 so that $pf_1/r_1 > 1$. To stay on the expansion path, the marginal physical product of all other inputs must be increased. This is done by lowering input use. The result is a decline in output – say, from q_0 to q_R in Figure 3.10. For example, if timber harvest is reduced by public fiat, one would expect a decline in wood product output and a fall in the number of forest sector workers. Assuming that output price is unaffected (see below for the case where demand elasticity is finite), the welfare impact of the restriction on input x_1 can be measured in the output market as the loss in producer surplus, area α in Figure 3.10. It can also be measured in the input market as a loss in consumer surplus, as shown above.

A quantity restriction on output is similar, and can also be analysed using Figure 3.10. Again assuming that demand elasticity is infinite, if quantity is restricted to q_R, where previously it was q_0, the loss in producer surplus is given by area α. Thus, a fish quota in one region will result in a loss of producer surplus. However, given that the analysis in Figure 3.10 is static, it is not clear that the quota will make producers worse off in the long run. A dynamic analysis is required (see Chapter 7).

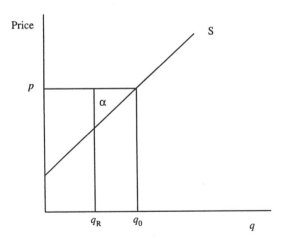

Figure 3.10 Welfare Loss due to an Input or Output Restriction

3.2 Aggregation of Economic Welfare

Previously, discussion of welfare measures concerned only the individual consumer or producer. Now we need to find some method for aggregating over all producers and consumers. In this section, we consider aggregation of both consumers and producers, and then look at how government policies at the aggregate level affect different groups (i.e., producers and consumers) in society. In the concluding section of this chapter, we consider aggregation of welfare more generally, and the issue of how one might compare projects using such things as social welfare functions and compensation tests.

Aggregation of producer welfare

Measures of producer surplus are generally not path dependent and therefore are unambiguous. As long as an input is essential to production, an exact measure of producer welfare is given by producer surplus (i.e., quasi-rent) or consumer surplus in the input market, with equivalent and compensating variation being equal. We can examine aggregation of gains when we have two producers. First, we examine the case of an increase in output price, then a reduction in input price.

Consider Figure 3.11. As a result of a price increase producer #1 gains area x, producer #2 gains area y and together they gain area x + y = area z. This is true since supply curve S is simply the horizontal summation of the individual producer supplies, S_1 and S_2. If the analysis is conducted in a single diagram then this would be clear. Note that these areas of welfare gain are measures of compensating and equivalent variation.

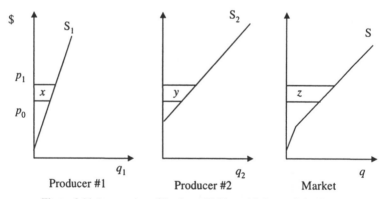

Figure 3.11 Aggregation of Producer Welfare with Output Price Increase

Now consider a reduction in input price from r_0 to r_1 as illustrated in Figure 3.12. In this case the gain to producer #1 is given by area α, the gain to producer #2 is area β and the gain to both is given by area τ = area $\alpha + \beta$. In this case, the derived, aggregated input demand D is equal to the horizontal sum of the individual input demands ($D_1 + D_2$), and the areas are exact measures of both the equivalent and the compensating variation.

It is important to note that, in the case of producers, the areas we have measured satisfy the Scitovsky compensation criterion (see section 3.3 below). That is, even in the case where producer surplus changes occur in a number of different markets and affect many producers, as long as the sum of producer surplus changes over the several markets is positive, the Scitovsky compensation criterion is satisfied. That is, it is possible for gainers to compensate losers so that both gainers and losers are at least as well off as they were previously.

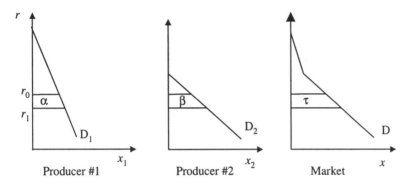

Figure 3.12 Aggregation of Producer Welfare in Input Markets

Aggregation of consumer welfare

Aggregation of consumer welfare is a much trickier problem because consumer surplus derived from the Marshallian demand curve is not an accurate measure of either compensating or equivalent variation in most cases. While we can aggregate in the same way as we did in the case of producer surpluses, we must keep this point in mind. An additional problem arises if we cannot weight consumers equally. It may be possible to construct weights for different groups, but whenever different weights are applied, a value judgement is made, beyond that of allocating the same weight to everyone (which is itself a value judgement). The issue of weighting different groups is beyond the scope of this discussion (see Dreze and Stern 1987).

Welfare effects impacting more than one market

In order to consider multiple-market analysis of welfare impacts, we first distinguish between vertical and horizontal market structures. Vertical market structures occur where a clearly defined marketing channel exists. Extraction to final market distributing of wood products is an example where firms at each stage in the channel purchase inputs only from preceding sawmilling, transportation, or logging firms. In contrast, a horizontal market structure occurs when firms sell to a variety of industries and purchase their inputs from a variety of sources.

Consider first the case of a vertically related market shown in Figure 3.13. Suppose q_k is the final output (panel (b)) and q_{k-1} is the input (panel (a)) used to produce q_k. What is the welfare effect of a price change in the final output market q_k? $S(p^0_{k-1})$ and $S(p'_{k-1})$ represent the short-run supply curves for output q_k in panel (b). In panel (a), S represents the input supply curve; and $D(p^0_k)$ and $D(p'_k)$ represent the derived input demand curves for different prices of q_k. We assume that $p_k^0 > p'_k$. When output price falls from p^0_k to p'_k, the derived input demand curve shifts from $D(p^0_k)$ to $D(p'_k)$ – an inward shift to the left. Input price falls from p^0_{k-1} to p'_{k-1}, thereby causing short-run final output supply to shift down from $S(p^0_{k-1})$ to $S(p'_{k-1})$. Hence, rather than output falling from q^0_k to q'_k when output price falls from p^0_k to p'_k (i.e., firm's sliding down $S(p'_{k-1})$), the firm reduces output to q''_k, that is, the firm slides down the all-other-markets-adjusted supply curve S*.

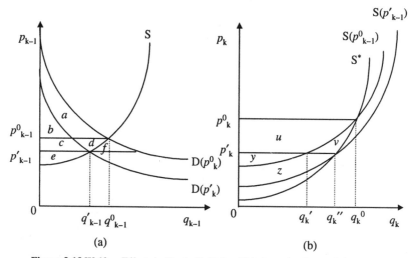

Figure 3.13 Welfare Effects in Vertically Related Markets: An Output Price Change

The welfare effects of the price change are as follows. Prior to the price change, producer surplus is area $u + y$; after the price change, producer surplus is $y + z$. The net change in producer surplus, compensating or equivalent variation, is given by area $u - z$ which represents a loss in welfare. This change in quasi-rent can also be represented by areas under derived demands in the input markets. In panel (a), the net change in quasi-rent (net loss) is area $a - c$. The loss given by area $a - c$ equals the loss measured as area $u - z$.

There is an additional welfare change to be considered, however. The change in input price has a welfare impact on the suppliers of q_{k-1}. Previously their producer surplus equalled area $c + d + e$. Now it is equal to area e only. Hence, they have lost an amount given by area $c + d$. The total reduction in welfare is thus equal to area $a + d$.

Now suppose the functions of the input supplying and final output firms were integrated into a single firm. Then S* would be the appropriate supply curve for the single firm and, assuming that there are no other inputs whose prices might change, area $u + v$ is the appropriate measure of welfare change. Further, area $u + v$ = area $a + d$ in this scenario. We can also show that area $c + d$ = area $v + z$.

S* is a particular type of supply curve and should not be confused with a long-run supply curve (Mishan 1981). It is simply the equilibrium supply curve that allows for equilibrium adjustments of input prices and their use as output price changes. The area above this curve and below the price line measures the change in producer surplus in all the input markets as well as in the output market. That is, the producer surplus area measures the change in welfare not only for the final output producers but also for the input suppliers at each stage of the process. If the industry supply curve in the first input market is perfectly elastic (i.e., flat), then

$$(3.7) \qquad \Delta R^*_k = \sum_{j=1}^{k} \Delta R_j = \Delta R^*_{k-1} + \Delta R_k \,,$$

where R refers to producer rents as areas above the associated supply curves but below price.

Unless we can determine the S* curve in a given output market, thereby obtaining ΔR^*_k as the measure of welfare change, it is necessary to investigate more than one market in order to find the total welfare change of a final change in output price.

Analogous results are obtained when input price changes in a vertically related industry structure. An equilibrium (derived) demand curve D* can be found for q_k by permitting the prices of q_{k+1} to change, and then tracing the effects on the derived demand for q_k back into the q_{k+1} market (through shifts in the supply of q_{k+1}, which is a function of p_k). Once again, assume a hypothetical merger of the two industries. The derived demand curve D* would then be the demand curve used by the firm since it appropriately measures the effect of changes in output price (due to input price changes) on derived demand. The change in consumer surplus can be measured as an area underneath this demand curve.

Finally, in general, we have a vertical market with q_N being the final consumer demand commodity and its demand is perfectly elastic. There is only one input into q_N, namely, q_{N-1}; there is one input into q_{N-1}, namely, q_{N-2}; and so on. Then the total change in consumer surplus for this group of industries as a result of a price change in input market q_k is

$$(3.8) \qquad \Delta C^*_k = \sum_{i=k+1}^{N} \Delta C_i = \Delta C^*_{k+1} + \Delta C_k \,,$$

where C represents the producer benefits measured as areas under the appropriate derived demand curves, but above price.

Now consider the welfare effects of a policy that alters both the supply and demand prices. Assume that the vertical structure (vertical chain) consists of q_0, q_1, ..., q_N and that a change in the price of q_k occurs. What is the welfare effect? It is simply the forward sum of consumer surpluses, as given by equation (3.8), and the backward sum of producer surpluses as given by equation (3.7). That is,

$$(3.9) \quad \Delta W^*_k = \Delta R^*_k + \Delta C^*_k = \sum_{j=1}^{k} \Delta R_j + \sum_{i=k+1}^{N} \Delta C_i .$$

Equation (3.9) can also be written as:

$$(3.10) \quad \Delta W^*_k = \Delta R_0 + \Delta C_N + \sum_{j=1}^{k} R_j + \sum_{i=k+1}^{N} \Delta R_i.$$

These equations hold true only if the input supply curve is perfectly elastic for q_0 and the demand curve is perfectly elastic for q_N. Surplus measures defined with respect to fully adjusted equilibrium curves have validity, at least in the purely vertical economic framework, and, therefore, can be used to determine the welfare impact in a single market, the kth one in the above example.

In the case of horizontally related markets similar results can be shown to hold.

Welfare impacts in one market: Empirical considerations

The implication of the foregoing discussion is that "net social welfare effects over the economy as a whole of intervention in any single market can be measured completely in that market using equilibrium supply and demand curves of sufficient generality" (Just et al. 1982, p. 192). Indeed, it can further be shown that, if distortions exist elsewhere in the economy, the analysis

> extends directly to take account of all *private* social welfare effects (not necessarily government effects) in the entire economy of intervention in a single market if (1) the supply and demand curves used for analysis in the market of interest are conditioned on all other distortions which exist in the economy, (2) all consumer and resource suppliers adjust along compensated demand and supply curves, (3) no existing distortions are in the form of price ceilings or floors, and (4) competitive behavior prevails throughout the economy. To the extent that consumers and resource owners do not react along compensated curves, the actual private welfare effects are approximated to the extent that compensated equilibrium prices and adjustments approximate noncompensated equilibrium prices and adjustments. (Just et al.1982, p. 199)

Hence, it is necessary only to estimate general supply and demand functions for a single market, the market immediately impacted by the policy. For welfare measurement, it is necessary only to consider areas above the other-markets-adjusted equilibrium supply curve and below the other-markets-adjusted equilibrium demand curve.

In general, we estimate a supply curve such as

(3.11) $q^s = a_0 + a_1 p + a_2 r$,

where q^s and p are the quantity and price, respectively, in the market under consideration, r is the input price (or index of input prices) used in producing q, and a_i are estimated coefficients. The supply curve in equation (3.11) is the ordinary supply curve. To find the equilibrium supply curve, we first estimate

(3.12) $r = b_0 + b_1 p$,

where b_0 and b_1 are estimated coefficients. Substituting (3.12) into (3.11) yields

(3.13) $q^s = (a_0 + a_2 b_0) + (a_1 + a_2 b_1)p = \alpha + \beta p$.

This is the equilibrium adjusted supply curve.

A similar result holds for demand. The ordinary demand curve for q_0, for example, is estimated from an appropriately specified equation as follows:

(3.14) $q^0 = f(p, p^A, m)$,

where p^A represents the price of other goods and m represents income. We can substitute for p^A by finding p^A as a function of p and m.

In general, however, we would like to estimate the equilibrium-adjusted supply and demand curves simultaneously. It is possible to estimate the following supply and demand equations:

(3.15a) $q^s = q^s(p^s, \tau_s)$

(3.15b) $q^d = q^d(p^d, \tau_d)$,

where p^s and p^d are the supply and demand price, respectively, and τ_s and τ_d are the parameters that affect supply and demand, respectively. It should be noted that Equations (3.15) depend on the assumption that p^s and τ_s, and p^d and τ_d, are separable in the respective p^s_d and p^d_d equations:

(3.16a) $p^s_d = p^s_d(p^s, \tau_s)$

(3.16b) $p^d_d = p^d_d(p^d, \tau_d)$

where p^s_d and p^d_d represent all prices and exogenous income in the economy that serve as determinants of ordinary supply and demand, respectively.

Finally, it is recommended that producer and consumer welfare impacts be measured in a single market using data from estimated fully adjusted demand and supply curves whenever possible. If these cannot be estimated simultaneously (because of statistical problems), they can be determined separately. If distortions exist in other markets, welfare measurements can be made as suggested in Chapter 2.

Aggregate welfare impacts: An illustration

The concepts of welfare defined in the previous sections can be used to evaluate the economic efficacy of government programs and policies. By assuming that all individuals are to be treated equally, whether they are producers or consumers or whether they are rich or poor, it is possible to determine the gains and losses of various public policies simply by summing all of the welfare measures. Gains and losses accruing at different points in time are weighted depending upon when they accrue. This is called discounting and is considered further in Chapter 6. Here we assume that all the welfare gains and losses occur in the same time period.

To illustrate the usefulness of the welfare measurement concept, consider the case where the government invests funds in research and development (R&D) aimed at improving tree growth. At the same time, government policy results in a restriction on timber harvest. This restriction may be due to endangered species legislation that affects private forestland owners (see Chapter 9) or it may be the result of a decision to reduce timber harvests on publicly owned lands. The situation can be analysed with the aid of Figure 3.14. The estimated demand and supply functions, S* and D*, respectively, represent full adjustment in other, related markets. Market equilibrium before any government intervention occurs at price p_c and quantity q_c.

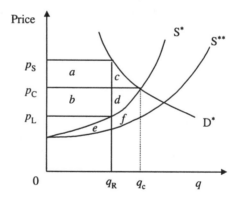

Figure 3.14 Aggregate Welfare Effects of Quota and R&D: Summing Producer and Consumer Surpluses

Suppose the harvest restriction implies that no more than q_R can be harvested in any given period. Based on the original supply S* and ignoring income transfers between consumers and producers, the welfare loss due to a restriction in harvests is given by the sum of the reduction in consumer surplus and loss of producer surplus (area $c + d$). Government-sponsored R&D investment shifts the timber supply from

S* to S**. In the absence of a harvest restriction, there is a gain in welfare equal to area $e + f$. The harvest restriction compounds the loss identified by the area $c + d$. The total dead-weight loss due to allocative inefficiency (i.e., resources are inappropriately employed) is given by area $c + d + f$ if the supply function S** is used at the basis for the analysis. However, the welfare loss from the two public policies – harvest restriction and increase in R&D expenditure – is given by area $c + d + f - e$ plus the added cost to the government of implementing the policy package. If the gain in welfare, area e, exceeds the loss, then the overall effect of this policy package will be to enhance social well-being.

Why is the government likely to impose restrictions on timber harvest? One reason is to achieve environmental objectives, such as preservation of wildlife habitat and protection of watershed or scenic amenity values. Such nonmarket benefits have been ignored in the foregoing analysis. Methods for estimating the benefits of protecting and preserving biological assets are examined in Chapter 5, while an example of their use in cost-benefit analysis is provided in Chapter 6.

3.3 Compensation Tests and Social Welfare Functions

Economic policy is about making comparisons of economic situations, which requires knowledge about the desirability of the change that an action seeks to bring about. In the real world, choices lead to gains by some and losses by others. To avoid making value judgements in this context, a number of compensation tests have been devised (during the 1940s and 1950s) in an effort to find a basis to compare states that is founded on efficiency. However, as we note below, attempts to devise a criterion based solely on efficiency criteria, and without resort to ethical judgements, are simply not available and economists' policy recommendations are often a matter of faith. An excellent discussion of compensation tests can be found in Nath (1969), and Chipman and Moore (1978).

Pareto Criterion

The Pareto criterion is the most unambiguous as it provides an unequivocal method of comparing two situations. According to this criterion, a public program is considered desirable only if at least one person gains by the program while no one loses.

Kaldor-Hicks Compensation Criterion

The Kaldor-Hicks compensation test (Kaldor 1939; Hicks 1939) states that there is an unambiguous increase in society's welfare in moving from one state to another if the gainers of a public program can hypothetically compensate the losers and still be better off than in the absence of the project. Hence, the Kaldor-Hicks principle is compatible with making the poor still poorer, as long as the rich gain enough. If compensation is actually paid, the principle is nothing more than the Pareto criterion.

Scitovsky Reversal Paradox

Scitovsky (1941) recognised that, just as some state of the economy Q_2 can be considered better than situation Q_1 on the basis of the Kaldor-Hicks compensation test, state Q_1 can be demonstrated to be better than state Q_2 on the basis of the same test. Just as, in moving from Q_1 to Q_2, the gainers could compensate the losers and still be better off, the gainers in a move from Q_2 to Q_1 could compensate the losers and be better off. (The reason is that the distribution of income differs between Q_1 and Q_2.) Hence, Q_1 is better than Q_2 at the same time that Q_2 is shown to be better than Q_1. As a result, Scitovsky proposed the reversal (double) criterion: A project which moves the economy from state Q_1 to state Q_2 is deemed to increase social welfare (i.e., is efficient) if the gainers from the project can compensate the losers, but the losers cannot bribe the gainers to oppose the project.

Unfortunately, Scitovsky's criterion breaks down if the choice is to be made from more than two possible situations. Thus, it is possible for Q_2 to be superior to Q_1, Q_3 to be superior to Q_2, and Q_4 to be superior to Q_3. However, in comparing Q_1 and Q_4, Q_1 is found to be superior to Q_4, implying that transitivity of choices does not hold (Nath 1969, pp. 100–01).

Little's Criterion

Little (1957) felt that the income distribution must be admitted as an explicit ethical variable so that "every reader of the economist's conclusions can decide this issue (equity) for himself" (p. 11 footnote). He proposed a three-fold criterion:

    (a) Is the Kaldor-Hicks criterion satisfied?
    (b) Is the Scitovsky criterion satisfied?
    (c) Is any redistribution good or bad? (1957, p. 101)

If either (a) or (b) and (c) are satisfied, then the policy is deemed desirable.

Nath (1969, pp. 107–9) demonstrates that there is a flaw in the Little criterion. In particular, an economic state X may be superior to an original state Q_1 on distributional grounds, but inferior to Q_1 on the basis of the Pareto criterion, to which Little claims to adhere. This paradox results because Little compares between X and Q_1 through some intermediary state Q_2, and, as a result, violation of the Pareto criterion (X is Pareto preferred to Q_1) is not obvious. One way to avoid this problem is to judge between states on distributional grounds only. In summary, Chipman and Moore (1978) consider the Little criterion as a

> wholesale retreat from the basic tenet of the New Welfare Economics, which was that the Compensation Principle can take the place of distributional value judgements in the formation of policy recommendations. Perhaps still more noteworthy is the fact that if one accepts Little's approach, one no longer has any basis for advocating measures that would remove existing discrepancies between marginal rates of transformation, i.e., one no longer has any basis for advocating efficiency and Pareto optimality as necessarily desirable goals. (p. 578)

One is forced to conclude that there is no satisfactory, scientific method for choosing between different states of the economy and, therefore, among a variety of public programs. As a result, public decisions are made in the political arena rather than by appeal to scientific authority. This implies a continued role for the economists, albeit one that is diminished in terms of technical sophistication.

Society is often willing to trade-off a reduction in overall welfare for a better distribution of income – equity versus efficiency. Economists argue that income transfers should be done as efficiently as possible and, further, that the cost of increased income equality (measured in terms of lost allocative efficiency) be made explicit (see also Chapter 6). Likewise, society might want to protect biological assets at the cost of reduced allocative efficiency. Again, economists argue that the trade-off should be made explicit; see, for example (Simon 1996, p. xxxiii).

Social Welfare Functions

More than just a Pareto principle is needed in order to rank projects. A complete and consistent ranking of social states ("projects") is called a social welfare ordering. If this ordering is continuous, it can be translated into a social welfare function (SWF), which is a function of the utility levels of all households such that a higher value of the function is preferred to a lower one. The SWF is defined as: $SWF = w[u_1(q_1), u_2(q_2), ..., u_n(q_n)]$, where u_k is the utility of person k as a function of the bundle of goods and services available to that person for consumption or trade, q_k. A priori there is little one can say about the specification of the SWF. Arrow (1951) has shown the impossibility of constructing a SWF that satisfies certain fundamental requirements that are associated with democratic, capitalist economic systems. Hence, the SWF is based on normative judgements. Utilitarianism requires that the SWF be maximised, but constrained by the production possibilities.

Using contract theory, Rawls (1971) proposed a lexicographical SWF (Figure 3.15). He argued that, under a veil of ignorance and in an initial position where one did not know one's lot in society (whether poor or rich, or of the current or some future or past generation), people would first agree upon a fundamental principle of liberty. Once it was satisfied, the contractarian approach would lead one to choose, as a social welfare rule, the Rawlsian objective of enhancing the well being of the worst off group in society. Rawls permits gains to those who are better off as long as these enhance the prospects of the worst off.

The SWF associated with cost-benefit analysis takes a more extreme position, namely that people are to be treated equally. In that case, a person with few goods (one in poverty) is treated the same as one who has more than enough (a rich person). Both are treated equally in deciding among projects – the distribution of income does not matter, only the sum of the utilities of the members of society, with a poor person's utility treated on par with that of a rich person. This is represented in Figure 3.15 by the downward sloping 45° line.

Finally, the more general utilitarian approach is to permit trade-offs among individuals, which was the objective behind the various compensation tests. The SWF in this case is represented by a curved line, with curvature a function of the marginal rates of substitution between the utility of one person and that of another. In other words, the shape of the utility function depends on the value judgements one makes about how the well being of one person is to be compared to that of another.

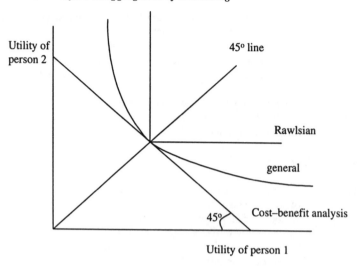

Figure 3.15 Three Specifications of the Social Welfare Function

Other social welfare functions are possible, including choices based on intuition. However, other rules for evaluating projects lack the rigour associated with the utilitarian approach, particularly as used in cost-benefit analysis, which is discussed further in Chapter 6. The contractarian and utilitarian approaches are considered again in Chapter 9 (section 9.2), but in the context of species preservation and their non-anthropogenic rights.

4 Resource Rents and Rent Capture

In the preceding two chapters, we examined theoretically correct measures of consumer and producer welfare, respectively. Producer welfare measures did not take into account natural resource inputs, but, because of their unique character compared to human-created capital resources, there is a welfare component associated with them that needs to be treated separately. This is the subject of the current chapter.

The concept of rent is closely associated with land and originally was not used in conjunction with any other resource. A review of the economics literature reveals that rent has a different meaning to different authors, with differences in meaning often being very subtle. The classical notion that rent accrues only to land is broadened to include all types of natural capital, which may be defined as the "nonproduced means of producing a flow of natural resources and services" (Daly and Cobb 1994, p. 72). The resource owner is potentially able to capture the economic rent, or surplus, without affecting the optimal behaviour of firms or economic agents. As we illustrate in this chapter, the instrument used to capture rents will in the end determine whether behaviour is affected or not.

A consistent definition of economic rents and quasi-rents is helpful in identifying available rents and the effect that various instruments for rent capture have on output decisions. Defining rents and quasi-rents at least clarifies what rents accrue, in theory, to what factors of production. The definitions of rents are applied in this chapter to forestry (both in temperate and tropical regions) and to the fishery, where the resource owner's objective is to collect as much of the economic rent as possible. In this chapter, we examine theoretical aspects of natural resource rents and mechanisms that resource owners, generally governments, can use to capture those rents. The issue of property rights is of paramount importance here, and will be addressed in the context of the fishery.

4.1 What is Rent?

David Ricardo (1817) along with Adam Smith (1776) deserve credit for the classical notion of rent, which is often referred to as *Ricardian rent*, and just as often *differential rent*. (For subtle differences between Ricardian and differential rent, see Alchian 1987). Ricardian rent is the infra-marginal return to a heterogeneous natural resource. In Ricardo's classic example, increasingly greater levels of rent accrue to land of successively greater productivity, with land at the extensive margin (discussed below) receiving no rent. The existence of the rent is explained by diminishing returns for the variable factors of production. Defining the concept in proportional rather than marginal terms, Ricardo noted that "rent invariably proceeds from the employment of an additional quantity of labour with a proportionately less return" (Ricardo 1817, p. 37). Given an identical price per unit of a variable input applied to a fixed factor to produce a homogeneous product, profit maximisation ensures that the value of the marginal product would be identical across the fixed factor of production irrespective of productivity. Thus, the value of the last additional unit of the variable input would be the same as for the more productive units of the fixed factor. At the extensive margin, however, no Ricardian rent is earned as the average product would be identical to the marginal product such that total revenue would equal total cost. For the fixed factor of higher productivity, each successive unit of the variable input reduces its marginal product until the value of the marginal product equals the price of the variable input. Until the last unit of the variable input is applied, each successive unit contributes more to revenue than it does to costs. The sum of these surpluses constitutes Ricardian rent.

The concept of Ricardian (land) rent is illustrated with the aid of Figure 4.1, where AC represents average cost and MC marginal cost of producing grain. Field *A* represents a more productive fixed factor (land) than does field *B*, and likewise *B* more productive land than *C*. The rent on all fields is determined by output price, *p*, which is determined by the intersection of demand and supply in the final goods market. Supply in turn is determined from the sum of the marginal costs of each of the fields producing the crop. Thus, fields *A* and *B* earn rents, but the marginal field *C* does not; field *C* is located at the extensive margin of cultivation. It is wrong to determine rent on field *A* as the difference in returns on that field and those on field *B*, since *B* also earns rent. The rent accruing to *A* and *B* is determined in comparison to *C*.

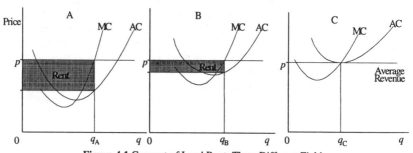

Figure 4.1 Concept of Land Rent: Three Different Fields

It was Ricardo's contention that, as the price of grain rises (e.g., due to increases in population), less and less fertile (i.e., increasingly marginal) land would be brought into production. As agricultural product prices rise, an economy will expand its agricultural production onto marginal land, land that could not be profitably cultivated at a lower price. With an increase in price, however, farming can earn enough to cover all expenses, including an adequate return on capital used in crop production. When marginal land is brought into production, this implies that the owner of better land (more fertile land, land experiencing better weather or land situated nearer markets) will earn a differential rent.

The Ricardian concept of rent was extended and clarified as a result of Johann von Thuenen's 1840 critique. Von Thuenen (1966) considers rent as a function solely of location, and not fertility or climate, since land quality in the "isolated state" is uniform, with rent differentials arising from transportation costs. Because it is focused on location, the von Thuenen model has been used to study spatially separated markets and to estimate outdoor recreation benefits of parks or nature areas, where visitors travel from different locations (see Chapter 5). It has also been used, for example, to explain urban development and location decisions by pulp and paper mills in the southern USA.

Consider Figure 4.2 where a single city-state is surrounded by land of uniform quality. Different land uses form concentric rings about the city (located at the origin) as suggested by the rings below the horizontal axis. Land nearest the city is used for growing vegetables, dairying and grains (use A). Next is a ring of forestland (B) followed, respectively, by pastureland (C) and hunting (D) areas that are the farthest from the centre. The reason for this pattern lies with rent differentials that are the result of transportation costs.

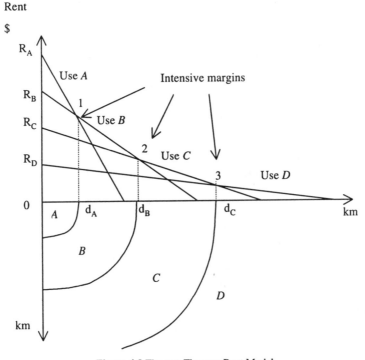

Figure 4.2 The von Thuenen Rent Model

If vegetables are grown next to the city, there is essentially no transportation cost associated with marketing them. Thus, the farmer located nearest the city can earn a rent given by $0R_A$ on the vertical axis. For farmers located at a greater distance from market, a transportation cost is incurred and this reduces the rent that they earn, but they continue to earn a normal profit in addition to any rent they may obtain. As the distance to market increases, the rent accruing to land use A declines as indicated by the rent-distance-to-market function for land use A. The same is true for the other land uses. For these land uses, the rent is lower if the activity were to take place at the market, or next to the city. Of course, that is why land uses A are undertaken nearest the city, and not other land uses.

The rent-distance functions differ among land uses because revenues and costs of production vary; they decline at different rates because transportation costs are not the same. At the point labelled 1, the rent-distance function for land use A intersects that of B from above. Thus, beyond distance d_A the return to land use B is greater than the return to land use A, if production and transfer costs are taken into account. Therefore, for distances from market up to $0d_A$, land use A will dominate; for distances from market between $0d_A$ and $0d_B$, land use B will dominate; and so forth for land uses C, D and any others. The changes in land use occur at the intensive margins – the margins of land-use transfer. The extensive margins occur where the rent-distance functions intersect the horizontal axis – all differential rent associated with the activity is dissipated. The result of landowners pursuing land uses that result in rent maximisation is concentric rings of similar land use about the city (assuming land of equal quality throughout the region).

Notice that farmers located near the city earn the highest rents and those living farther away earn lesser rents, even where land is employed in the same uses. In this case, it is location and not land quality that determines the rent; transportation cost is the key to rent differentials. Again, in principle, it would be possible for the authority to tax away the rent without changing the land use pattern, but it would depend on the rent capture mechanism employed. Rent has already been captured, however, if land is sold and the land price includes the capitalised value of the rent, as one would expect.

Marx distinguished two types of differential rent. First, as the price of agricultural output rises, production will expand onto marginal land and, thus, land of better quality will earn rent (or higher rent), as argued above. Second, when prices rise, farmers put more effort (labour, fertilizer) into producing crops on land that is not marginal. These efforts yield additional rent as the difference between total revenue and total variable cost increases, but this rent accrues to human investment and not to the land, thus constituting quasi-rent (see below). This second concept of differential rent is important because, in Marx's view, it is the better and not marginal soils that regulate the price of production, although marginal soil gains differential rent of the former type when price increases and poorer soil becomes marginal. Although differential rent of the first type does not affect the price of output, the same is not true of quasi-rent. Attempts to capture this rent will adversely affect investment decisions (as returns to fixed factors are reduced) and thus impact output and prices.

Transfer price or opportunity cost

An essential component in the definition of Ricardian rent and all rent is the notion of a transfer price or opportunity cost. This was first described by J. S. Mill in 1848 when he noted that the rent land could earn in an alternative activity constituted a cost that must be paid if it is used in some other activity. Earnings to the factor of production over and above the transfer price constitute rent. In the classical view, however, economic rent is the "payment to a factor of production over and above the minimum necessary to induce it to do its work" (Currie et al. 1971). The modern view of rent is that it is the payment to a fixed factor over and above the minimum amount necessary to keep it in its current use. The difference between the two concepts is whether the fixed factor is supplied at all in the economy and whether it is supplied in its present activity. Applying the notion of a transfer price to Ricardian rent, it is implicit that the heterogeneous natural resource has the same opportunity cost, irrespective of its productivity. In the case of natural resources, Ricardian rent would be the difference between total revenue and total cost for the natural resource less its transfer price. In the case where the transfer price is zero (e.g., for oceans as discussed in Chapter 7), the classical and modern definitions of Ricardian rent are identical.

In determining the economic rent for forestland, for example, all economic costs must be subtracted from the estimated revenues including, where applicable, an opportunity cost, depletion or user charges, a premium for risk, conservation costs, depreciation, and a normal rate of return for capital. The difficulty in measuring each of these cost components is what makes the determination of the rent and its capture difficult and controversial. For example, two forest sites that are identical in terms of productivity may differ in terms of distance to market and transportation costs. The site with the lower transport costs would, *ceteris paribus*, have a higher Ricardian rent. Alternatively, two sites may have equal access costs but differ in their productivity, so that, given the same inputs, one stand will yield more timber than the other at any instant in time, again generating a greater Ricardian rent. Sorting out these differences can be a difficult task in practice.

Resource and scarcity rents

Scarcity rent results from the natural scarcity of a natural resource.[1] Given perfect competition, it is equal on a per unit basis to the difference between the marginal revenue and the marginal cost of production (see Figure 4.3). As its name implies, a scarcity rent can only exist when there are (natural or legal) restrictions placed on the supply of a factor from natural capital and a corresponding limitation on the produce obtained. A scarcity rent, unlike a Ricardian or differential rent, can occur even if the

---

[1] The term scarcity rent has been used differently by other authors. It is defined in a similar fashion by Howe (1979) in reference to nonrenewable resources as "the user costs of the marginal unit being extracted at any point in time and, under appropriate market conditions, the market value of these marginal *in situ* resources" (p. 78).

units of the factor of production from the natural capital stock are identical (i.e., having all the fields in Figure 4.1 of identical quality, with the same average and marginal cost curves). For example, irrespective of demand, a given area of forestland exploited on a sustained yield basis can only provide a certain level of wood volume. The resource rent arises from the natural scarcity of the resource that restricts the supply of the output and is a function of the "marginal conditions of the economic calculus" (Conrad and Gillis 1985, p. 35). For resources where the marginal cost of exploitation equals the output price, the scarcity rent will be zero.

Even where the scarcity rent is zero, there may still exist a Ricardian or differential rent. This is illustrated in Figure 4.3, where the flow of services from land (Q) is restricted to an amount Q^o by physical limits to the availability of land, or by government decree. Here MC represents the marginal costs of extracting the services from land, such as logging and transportation costs in the case of forestry. The differential rent is not quasi-rent since all returns accruing to the human investment are already taken into account; the differential rent properly accrues to the remaining factor, the land itself. The resource rent is equal to the differential rent plus the scarcity rent, if any, as indicated in Figure 4.3. It is the area below price and above the marginal cost curve.

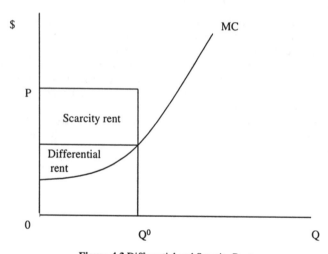

Figure 4.3 Differential and Scarcity Rents

Quasi-rents

The term quasi-rent refers to any payment made to a (human-created) capital asset that is fixed in supply for the time being; any return to the "sunk" component of capital represents quasi-rent (Ruzicka 1979, p. 47). It is commonly defined as the difference between total revenue and total variable cost, but this is not quite correct if there exist scarcity and Ricardian rents, as argued above. The usual definition of quasi-rent – those earnings over and above that required to keep a firm in business in the short run – only considers the pecuniary returns to (human-created) factors of production and assumes this determines their allocation. But Mishan (1959) has shown that to be inadequate. A quasi-rent need not only accrue to a fixed asset but also to labour services and other factors of production where their employment is fixed over the short run. These quasi-rents are returns that accrue to firms from past investments and innovative practices and are not attributable to the natural capital stock. In contrast to resource rent, the capture of quasi-rents can change the efficient behaviour of firms, often causing them to reduce investment and thereby the socially optimal level of output of the good or service in question.

Quasi-rents differ from differential rents associated with resource rent because they are returns required to keep human factors of production employed in resource extraction. In forestry, for example, several types of quasi-rents exist. Investments in processing facilities or capital improvements required as a condition of receiving a forest license may generate quasi-rents, as may investments in the trees themselves (silvicultural investments). Improvements can take the form of direct investments in the growing stock, such as replanting, fertilization or thinning. This has been termed preserving the conservable flow, or the inherent productivity of a site (see below). The return from direct investments in the stock itself should accrue to the persons responsible for the expenditures. They should accrue to the owner of the site or trees only insofar as the owner has invested in the improvements. No such problem arises with restrictions in harvesting that increase costs so long as such costs are fully deductible. Finally, some quasi-rents may accrue to the firms from entrepreneurial innovation. To the extent rents vary across firms due to innovations and are not attributable to variations in the resource itself, such rents should accrue to the firm. These rents provide the necessary incentives for firms to engage in entrepreneurial activity. A summary of the foregoing types of rents is provided in Table 4.1.

Table 4.1: Definitions of Various Types of Rent and Implications for Taxation

Type of rent	Definition	Implication for taxation
Resource	sum of scarcity and Ricardian rents	Taxation of rents does not affect behaviour of
- Scarcity	- difference between marginal revenue and marginal production cost that can only come about as a result of the natural or policy-induced scarcity of a resource.	firms or resource suppliers if the correct rent capture mechanism is chosen
- Ricardian or differential	- the excess of the market value of supramarginal (non marginal) units of *in situ* resources over current scarcity rents.	
Quasi-rent	returns that accrue to resources supplied out of human and human-created capital, and which are not attributable to natural capital. In that sense, they are the difference between total revenue and total (variable) cost.	Taxation of rents affects long-run efficient behaviour of firms and resource suppliers

Other types of rent

It is informative to discuss stock rents and land productivity rents, two terms that have appeared in the forestry literature (Luckert and Haley 1993; Luckert and Bernard 1993). They do not represent new types of rent but special sets of circumstances that generate one of the previously discussed types of rent. Stock rent has been used to describe the rent accruing to the harvest of old-growth timber, which far exceeds the present value of future returns in continuous rotations. These "stock" rents represent no previous investments so that all of the rent is a resource rent, with scarcity rent likely associated with high-grade lumber products that can come only from old-growth, temperate rain forests.

Land productivity rents are a combination of resource rents and quasi-rents, if silvicultural improvements have taken place. For land dedicated to timber management, timber rotations are chosen to maximise the present value of all future harvests. Where returns from harvesting exceed costs, this creates a stream of rents over time. The capitalised value of these rents is usually vested in the owner of the trees, who is usually the owner of the land as well. Consequently, land productivity rents for a site reflect those future rents. In a competitive market, the price of timberland would be a measure of the land productivity rent.

4.2 Agricultural Land and Rent Capture

Public-sector capture of economic rents has long been an important policy issue among economists. Rents can be an important source of government revenue and their appropriation, in theory, can take place without destroying economic incentives. For example, if one assumes absolute fixity of some resource, say agricultural land, then rents on land could be expected to rise over time as agricultural output prices increase. This led Walras also to argue for the nationalisation of land and, in its absence, for a tax on rents (Larmour 1979). Likewise, in 1879, Henry George (1929) put forward three arguments.

1.   Private ownership of land is inherently monopolistic.
2.   Rent is economic surplus not generated by entrepreneurship.
3.   Therefore, land should be owned by the public or, if privately held, the surplus should be taxed away.

George advocated a single tax of land rent, believing that rising prices for agricultural outputs would drive up rents so that, by capturing those rents, all future government programs could be funded from this tax.[2]

Here we examine a particular aspect of that problem, namely, rent and taxation in the context of soil depletion. It is possible to define land rent net of soil depletion. Depletion constitutes the sale of the substance of the resource, and the corresponding payment is not income but a transfer, comparable to the sale of title to land itself.

---

[2] This "single tax" fit George's overall political philosophy. For him, land had a peculiar place in society, so he focused on land tenure and equity and efficiency issues inherent in the private capture of land rents. Henri Gossens also argued for a single tax but his book appeared one year after that of George (1880 versus 1879), but it is unlikely that these economists were aware of each other's writings (Larmour 1979).

Therefore, to properly analyse land rent – that income which can be taxed away without affecting output decisions – one must examine four economic aspects or characteristics of land or soil (Gaffney 1965).

Perdurable component (pure flow) The perdurable component of soil rent is determined by location, climate, subsoil, drainage, inexhaustible nutrients, macro-relief, and so on. It is a pure flow resource with no critical zone. Under ordinary circumstances, the pure flow is enduring, permanent or non-perishable; but it can be affected by human actions such as strip mining, flooding due to construction of reservoirs, paving, and so on. It is indestructible due to neglect or abuse incident to farm operations. The question is, What contribution does this matrix make to land rent? What is the implication for taxation?

To understand this characteristic and its relationship to rent, consider two examples pertaining to location and fertility, respectively. (These examples can easily be related to Figure 4.1.) Two farmers have identical costs, yields, crops, macro-relief, and so on, but are located at different distances from the grain elevator. Jones trucks grain 5 miles to the elevator, while Smith trucks it 50 miles. Suppose each gets $4 per bushel (bu) at the elevator. Subtracting transportation costs, the farm gate prices for Jones and Smith are $3.97/bu and $3.78/bu, respectively. Smith receives $0.19/bu less than Jones. Since Smith stays in business (i.e., earns a normal profit), Jones must earn an economic rent of $0.19/bu. The $0.19/bu. can be taxed away without affecting Jones' decision regarding what to produce and how to produce it – the tax does not affect resource allocation. This ignores the fact that Smith might also be earning rent (in terms of Figure 4.1, Jones might represent field *A* and Smith *B*). Hence, this estimate of rent is possibly incomplete.

Next, consider the case where Smith and Jones have identical farms next to each other, but Smith's soil is more saline than that of Jones. Hence, Jones' yield is greater by 5 bu/ac. Since Smith stays in business, the economic rent per acre which can be taken from Jones by taxation is 5 multiplied by the farm gate price; if that price is $3.90/bu, the annual rent accruing to Jones is $19.50/ac. If land markets function perfectly and all of the rent is not taxed away, then Jones' land is also worth more than that of Smith by $19.50÷*i* per acre, where *i* is the real interest rate.

Subject to the *ceteris paribus* assumption, other factors such as macro-relief have a similar impact. This notion of rent, then, is differential rent. The implication for taxation is that all differential rent can be taxed away without changing the farmer's input-output decisions. This conclusion only holds if the rent has not already been capitalised in land values that the current landowner has paid. An attempt to tax it away would result in substantial loss to the current owner, who might have to sell the land at a loss as a result. Nonetheless, the land remains in agricultural production. This illustrates the income redistributional nature of rents and their collection.

Conservable flow (flow with critical zone) The conservable flow element of virgin soil fertility is that which takes some pain to keep in the original state, but is worth those pains because they are less than the cost of replacement and less than the present value of future income. Examples of conservable flow elements of the soil are humus and thin topsoil. Conservation in this case is effort devoted to reducing the loss of the virgin flow resources that may but need not be deteriorated by use. Liquidation of a conservable flow component of the soil is considered to be inefficient because soil can never be rebuilt so cheaply as the cost of conserving the virgin soil.

Now consider the rent attributable to this characteristic of the soil. The net rent is equal to the net income (including as a cost the normal rate of return) due to conservable flow elements of the soil minus conservation costs. This is the value that can be taxed away without affecting production decisions.

Revolving fund (stock resource) That element of virgin soil fertility that is not economical to conserve but is economical to replace or renew with materials imported from offsite is referred to as the revolving fund. It is a stock resource much like inventory. Examples of the revolving fund component are nutrients such as nitrogen and phosphorous that can be replaced by fertilizer, and, in some cases, moisture that can be replaced by irrigation water. Revolving fund components leave the soil and become embodied in crops and livestock.

The income imputed to the revolving fund is not a part of rent. Rather, it is a return to an improvement to the site, analogous to the return on capital tied up in storing grain – it is quasi-rent as defined in the previous section. After initial depletion of the virgin material, each decision to reinvest is an independent one that requires its own incentives. It represents a sacrifice of human alternatives – an opportunity cost.

Expendable surplus (finite fund) The expendable surplus is similar to the perdurable matrix except that the former is infinite, while the expendable surplus is a finite stock. The expendable surplus is often very large and, hence, its emplaced (nonuse) value is very low at the margin. Elements of the expendable surplus are not economical to replace when they are expended. In the case of the perdurable matrix, the resource fund is infinite and all income accruing to it is rent. However, when the fund is finite, a depletion charge is to be subtracted from the imputed income. Rent is equal to the imputed income minus the depletion charge.

Consider, as an example, excess topsoil of 250 centimeters (cm) and its exploitation by sod farming. Assume the technology of sod farming is such that the growing and sale of grass sod removes 5 cm of topsoil every year. Then it is not until after 50 years that all of the excess topsoil becomes depleted. It is at that time that the topsoil must be considered to be like conservable flow, and steps must be taken to ensure that further soil loss either does not occur or occurs at a rate that does not affect the future availability of the resource. This might mean that soil is depleted (eroded) at the same rate as it is replaced or that soil is rebuilt by intermixing of the layers below the humus and green manuring (adding humus).

When sod farming begins, the amount of surplus used this year has no effect on the amount available next year. Removing sod this year strips 5 cm of the excess (surplus) topsoil from the 250 cm excess base, but it is still possible to strip away 5 cm next year. After 50 years, the land can no longer be used for sod farming but, under our assumptions, is still available for crop production. The appropriate depletion charge today is the contribution of 5 cm of topsoil to the liquidation value discounted to the present. Suppose the liquidation value of 5 cm of topsoil is $1,000 (the return in a given year over normal cropping, or its opportunity cost).[3] Then the current year depletion charge is equal to $1000 \div (1 + i)^{50}$, where i is the interest rate. The depletion charge next year is $1000 \div (1 + i)^{49}$, and so on for following years. The depletion charge is very small early on but increases each year as the expendable surplus becomes fully depleted.

The depletion charge is equal to the user cost (Howe 1979, p. 75). User cost is defined as the opportunity cost associated with mining or harvesting a unit of resource today. This opportunity cost is what the marginal unit of the resource would be worth, in present value terms, had it been left *in situ* and mined or harvested at its most opportune time in the future. The amount of income that can be taxed away is equal to the income from the expendable surplus minus the depletion charge.

A summary of the foregoing discussion is provided in Table 4.2. In the analysis, we attributed land values to soil characteristics. However, the characteristics found in the perdurable matrix include elements that have nothing to do with the soil *per se*. They include location, climate, macro-relief and so on. The one thing that prevents us from valuing land according to physical attributes or things such as agricultural productivity is the other uses of land and externalities (e.g., blowing dust). Land values cannot be related to soil characteristics except in very rare circumstances.

Table 4.2: Resource Rent from Various Components of Soil

Perdurable Matrix	Net income from this source is *all* rent
Conservable Flow	Rent = Net Income – Conservation Costs
Revolving Fund	Income is a return similar to any return on capital investment. This is quasi-rent, so no rent is available to be collected
Expendable Surplus	$\text{Rent}_t = \text{Income}_t - \text{Depletion Charge}_t$

4.3 Taxation, Charges and Rent Capture in Forestry

Timber producing jurisdictions usually have a number of goals with respect to forest management, including maintaining employment, meeting environmental objectives, maximising tax revenue and so on (van Kooten 1995a). Here we only consider the goal of rent capture, which should occur with as little distortion as possible to economic efficiency. The objective is to transfer resource rents from private logging companies (or concessionaires) to the public land or resource owner. In this section, we review some methods of rent capture in forestry and describe the possible distortions they may impose on rotation, harvesting and management decisions. The resource owner is interested in capturing resource rents, but not quasi-rents that are attributable to factors of production other than the land itself. We also describe how

---

[3] The landowner cannot remove (or mine) topsoil at a faster rate. The standard Hotelling rule for optimal depletion of a mine (Dasgupta and Heal 1979) does not hold as inter-temporal reallocation is restricted. See also Chapter 7 for inter-temporal resource use.

rents may be dissipated and the implications for rent capture. As examples, we examine rent capture in British Columbia, Canada, and Indonesia.

Rent capture and efficiency

One way to determine whether a method of rent capture distorts decision making is to assess its effect on the extensive and intensive margins. The extensive margin for forestry is explained with reference to heterogeneity *across* sites or stands of timber and is illustrated in Figure 4.4(a). Suppose that there are N forest stands that can be harvested, arranged from left to right on the horizontal axis in terms of decreasing financial profitability. Financial profitability is determined by harvest costs (which are higher in steep terrain), transportation cost to mills (distance increases costs), and so on. The line ab represents the rent function, with the vertical distance between the rent function and the horizontal line at zero representing the resource rent, or simply the price of logs (p) minus marginal cost of harvesting the logs (c). Firms will harvest stands up to K, leaving KN stands unharvested because harvesting those would cost more than they yield in benefits at the margin ($c > p$). Forest stands OK constitute the working forest. Imposition of a uniform stumpage fee (to collect rents) will shift ab to the left, reducing the number of stands that firms can profitably harvest. If stumpage fees are already in place (i.e., assume ab includes existing stumpage fees), a reduction in fees will shift ab to the right, increasing the number of stands that yield rent, encouraging firms to harvest a greater number of sites. An increase in log prices will also shift ab to the right. Tenure arrangements and administratively set harvest levels can prevent expansion of the working forest into marginal areas, however. In that case, the greatest impact of changes in output prices and stumpage fees occurs at the intensive margin.

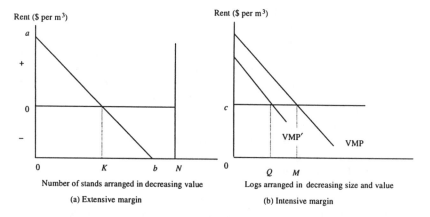

Figure 4.4 Extensive and Intensive Margins for Timber Harvesting

Figure 4.4(b) is similar to Figure 4.4(a), but illustrates the intensive margin. It refers to what happens at the stand rather than the forest level. Here, rather than arranging stands in decreasing order of financial profitability along the horizontal axis, trees (logs) are arranged in order of financial profitability, according to species and diameter. Large logs of the most valuable species are the most profitable, and generate the most rent. For illustration, marginal cost (c) is assumed not to vary by log size and quality in Figure 4.4(b) (but see below). Yet, there comes a point where the marginal cost of harvesting an additional tree or log is less than the revenue it provides once all costs of bringing it to the mill gate or export point are taken into account. Marginal revenue is the marginal value product (VMP) of a log, which is equal to the price (p) of logs times the marginal physical product of the log. Marginal physical product falls with declining log diameter. The difference between VMP and marginal cost equals the resource rent at the stand level; the intensive margin is found where VMP and c intersect. The effect of (an increase in) stumpage fees on the intensive margin can be shown either by shifting VMP inwards or marginal cost upwards.

Suppose that the government increases stumpage fees. This is represented by an inward shift of VMP to VMP′, and a leftward shift of the intensive margin from M to Q. Loggers want to harvest trees of a larger size, leaving logs of sizes in the range MQ and smaller on the ground, or standing as trees, a practice known as "high grading". To prevent high grading, governments often implement utilisation standards. For example, forest companies may be required to harvest trees with a diameter greater than 10 cm, even though they lose money on any trees that they harvest and haul to the mill that are less than 15 cm in diameter.[4] In British Columbia, if companies are found to be leaving logs that meet the utilisation standard for a site, the Forest Ministry will harvest the stand, charging the company both harvesting costs and associated stumpage fees. Whether this occurs in other jurisdictions frequently depends on the ability of governments to enforce regulations, with corruption at the local level reported as one obstacle leading to the high grading of sites.

A common supply restriction in timber management is the sustained yield requirement or, alternatively, a requisite that harvests be nondeclining or greater than some minimal level over a specified time period. In British Columbia, where some 95% of all of the forestland is publicly held, the Ministry of Forests determines a sustained yield harvest level, or Allowable Annual Cut (AAC). The Province sets the AAC based on the Ministry's calculation of the amount of forestland that can economically and biologically support harvesting. By definition, the limit to timber production is determined by those timber stands whose returns will just cover the cost of harvesting. Those stands constitute the extensive margin and by definition would earn no rent. If the Province errs in determining the extent of the land base, two possibilities arise. The first is that the AAC has been set too low – more timber could be harvested profitably. In this case, the resource rent is scarcity rent and is the margin between the revenues and costs for that stand at the artificially created margin.

---

[4] One BC forest company reported to the senior author that utilisation standards reduce the average value of logs by some \$17 per m³ in the BC interior.

The other possibility is that the AAC has been set too high, and firms incur a loss by harvesting at the margin. Because of the uncertain nature of administrative calculations, the Ministry does allow limited flexibility for firms to shift their cutting patterns within a five-year period. To the extent that the Province's AAC is a binding constraint on total production, a scarcity rent may be created reflecting the difference between marginal revenue and marginal cost of timber production.

A simple diagram can be used to illustrate concepts related to rent capture on public forestland. In Figure 4.5, individual trees (logs) on a concession are arranged in terms of quality from highest to lowest, where quality is determined by a tree's standing or stumpage value. This is reflected by the downward sloping derived demand curve, which is now equal to marginal revenue (MR) rather than VMP since log prices are not fixed. In practice, MR is likely a stepwise function (Ruzicka 1979; Vincent 1990). MC_{SR} refers to the short-run, private marginal cost of logging trees and transporting them to the mill. Marginal costs rise for the usual reasons, but also because costs per m^3 are smaller for large logs of high quality than for logs of lower quality and size. These costs are short term because, in most cases (e.g., both in BC and Indonesia), forest companies only have short-term rights to forestland – 25 years in BC and 20 years in Indonesia. Forest companies (or logging concessionaires) with short-term tenures ignore the costs of protecting expected future returns, say, by safekeeping during logging operations smaller (or larger) trees that are then left to regenerate.

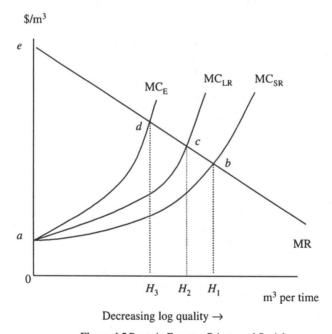

Figure 4.5 Rents in Forestry, Private and Social

The curve MC_{LR} represents the marginal costs of extraction when long-run impacts are taken into account (the sum of short-run marginal costs and the marginal costs of protecting future expected returns, or user cost). Finally, MC_E represents the (short- plus long-run) private marginal costs of logging operations, plus the environmental or externality costs of logging (see Chapter 6). When tenure rights or concessions are short term, volume H_1 will be harvested and rent equals area *abe*. If loggers have rights to future harvests, so they take into account the user cost, they will reduce harvests to H_2 by leaving more trees standing on a site and harvesting fewer sites at the extensive margin. The associated level of current rent from logging (and transportation to the mill) is area *ace*. (There will be future rents as well, but we ignore these in this discussion.) Finally, if the externality effects of logging are taken into account, only the volume H_3 should be harvested in the current period. The social rent given by area *ade* is, therefore, less than the market rent.

The government should permit the logging firm or concessionaire to harvest only the amount H_3, discourage high grading and capture as much of the rent as possible (as it is the resource owner). Economic efficiency deals with the optimal harvest quantity (where MC = MR), while rent capture deals with the distribution of the surplus (total area between MC and MR). Efficiency and rent capture are separate (but related) issues.

Vincent (1993) argues that, based on empirical evidence from tropical countries, the differences between MC_{SR} and MC_{LR} are insignificant. This is due to the fact that investments in natural forestry (e.g., by leaving some small trees standing) do not pay off due to the long rotation ages and, in tropical countries, high rates of discount. This is the case for boreal forests as well (see Chapter 11). In practice, we need only determine MC_{SR}, for which information may be available, and not worry about having to estimate user costs. Vincent (1993) also suggests that logging could result in environmental or external benefits, as well as costs. It is not clear, therefore, whether MC_E lies to the left of MC_{SR} (as drawn in Figure 4.5) or to the right.

Methods of rent capture

Several methods of rent capture may be employed to collect economic rents (Hyde and Sedjo 1992; Vincent 1993). We illustrate four such methods using Figure 4.6. The concessionaire is assumed to harvest H_1 and the available rent to be captured is given by area *abe* minus the fixed cost, otherwise quasi-rent would be captured. We ignore quasi-rent and assume that economic efficiency occurs at H_1 (although H_3 in Figure 4.5 may actually be socially optimal).

First, a fully differentiated royalty or tax would enable the authority to capture the entire area *abe*. Royalties would vary by tree species, size of tree, land quality, harvest costs by site, delivery costs and so on. Such royalty discrimination is impractical, however, particularly in tropical countries where there are many tree species and the monitoring ability of Forest Ministries is limited, but also in developed countries. Informational requirements are simply too great.

A second method of rent capture is a uniform fixed royalty (r_U), which is also referred to as the uniform specific royalty (Vincent 1993). This is shown in Figure 4.6 by an increase in MC to MC + r_U, where the vertical distance between the two curves is held constant at the fixed rate ($r_U = ad = cf$). The concessionaire reduces harvest levels from H_1 to H'. The rent collected by the government amounts to area *afcd*, while the concessionaires receive a windfall of *dce*. Area *cbf* is the rent lost to high grading because concessionaires leave felled and/or standing trees on the site to avoid excessive timber charges. Therefore, it is recommended that the uniform and fixed stumpage fee be levied on standing timber as opposed to logs when they have been removed from the site, say at a government check point or weigh scale (Vincent 1990).

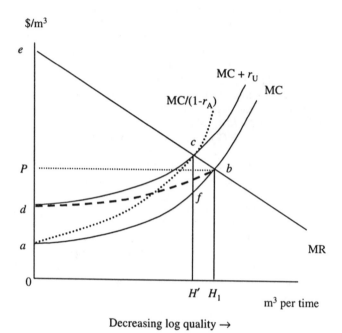

Decreasing log quality →

Figure 4.6 Methods of Rent Capture in Forestry

That the uniform fixed royalty distorts harvest levels and leads to high grading is easily demonstrated. In the absence of fees and future considerations, the concessionaire will maximise the following profit function:

(4.1) $\pi = p(H) H - C(H)$,

where $p(H)$ is price as a function of the harvest and $C(H)$ is the total cost of harvesting and delivering logs to the mill gate or export point. The first-order condition requires that $p'(H)H + p(H) = C'(H)$, or MR = MC. Solving gives H_1 in Figure 4.6. With the uniform royalty, the profit function (4.1) becomes

(4.2) $\pi = p(H) H - C(H) - r_U H$.

The first-order condition now requires that MR = MC + r_U. Solving for H give $H' <$ H_1 for some value of r_U. If r_U is set high enough, harvest volume could potentially be reduced to below H_3 (the point identified in Figure 4.5), which could imply that not enough trees are harvested even from society's point of view.

As noted by Hyde and Sedjo (1992), the incentive to "trespass, high-grade, and ignore off-site environmental values" (p. 346) is greatest for the best sites and best trees. This is clear from Figure 4.6. Better quality sites and trees are found near the origin where the difference between the tax and marginal cost is greatest.

A third method of rent capture is an *ad valorem* royalty ($0 \le r_A < 1$) set as a proportion of the selling price or revenue. The profit function (4.1) can now be written as:

(4.3) $\pi = (1 - r_A)\, p(H)\, H - C(H)$.

The necessary condition for a solution is now MR = MC/$(1 - r_A)$. The royalty on revenue, shifts the MC curve upwards by MC/$(1 - r_A)$ as indicated in Figure 4.6. For convenience, we show a royalty that shifts MC so it intersects MR at c (so that $H' <$ H_1 maximises the concessionaire's profit).

The effect of the royalty on harvest level (efficiency) is the same as for the fixed rate royalty (efficiency declines as high grading occurs), but the distribution of the rent is different. The government gets *acf*, while the logging company gets *ace*. Again *cbf* is the rent lost due to high grading. For the same harvest level (degree of high grading), the government collects less rent under the *ad valorem* royalty on revenue (or price) than under the uniform fixed royalty. Further, the fixed royalty is easier to administer, thereby reducing administrative costs relative to the royalty on revenue.

Finally, from a theoretical perspective, it does not matter whether one assumes that prices vary according log quality (MR is downward sloping) or price is horizontal (demand is infinite) as in Vincent (1990) and Hyde and Sedjo (1992). The essential difference between these cases is the size of the royalty required to get to H', being higher in the case of the flat price (P in Figure 4.6).

A fourth method is to levy an *ad valorem* royalty ($0 \le r_P < 1$) on the difference between price and marginal cost for each log. In essence, this is a profit tax. The effect of this levy is illustrated mathematically and with the aid of Figure 4.6. In this case, the profit function is

(4.4) $\pi = (1 - r_P)\, [p(H)\, H - C(H)]$.

The optimality condition in this case requires that MR = MC, as in the case where there are no fees. The royalty-adjusted MC curve in Figure 4.6 shifts up, however, but intersects MR at the original level of harvest H_1. For example, if the royalty-adjusted MC is given by segment *db*, the government collects an amount *abd* of the rent, leaving *dbe* to the concessionaire. The important point is that such a tax on rent does not distort economic efficiency. The only problem is that the Ministry must know not only selling prices but also something about marginal costs of harvesting and delivering timber to a mill or exporter. In that case, a fully differentiated royalty can also be used, but then to capture the entire rent. Unlike with a fully differentiated royalty, however, an *ad valorem* tax on net revenue only might work in practice if one does not attempt to calculate the net revenue on each and every log, but only on the company's net return from the site in each year.

Hyde and Sedjo (1992) recommend a fifth method for collecting rents, namely, to charge a competitively bid lump sum fee for the right to harvest a particular site. In theory, this will capture the entire area *abe* in Figures 4.5 and 4.6. This method is used in the USA, where the federal government auctions off the harvest rights to tracts of public forestland. This approach is also employed in BC under the Small Business Enterprise Program through competitive bidding for Minor Timber Sale Licenses. In theory, competitive bidding for harvesting rights should extract the *expected* economic rents from forest companies. It does not, however, ensure that the resource owner collects all the economic rents as it is an *ex ante* rather than an *ex post* method of rent capture. Thus, if firms' expectations are incorrect due to unexpected changes in demand or technological advances (or because they use a different discount rate than the government), the appropriate amount of rent will not be collected. An example of this was the disequilibrium in timber prices caused by speculative bidding in the US Pacific Northwest (Mattey 1990; Perez-Garcia and Lippke 1991). Operators were willing to pay more for the wood than it was worth as they anticipated higher lumber values that never materialised.[5]

Another problem with competitive bidding may arise when the timber rights represent a small proportion of the total requirements of the successful bidder. In this case, competitive bidding may reflect variable costs, not fixed costs. Attempts to use these bids as a measure of the rent available for the entire resource will then result in the collection of quasi-rents (Schwindt 1992). Furthermore, in times of excess capacity, firms may be willing to bid prices in excess of the actual timber value since they attach a premium to remaining in business (and expect to recoup their losses at a later date).

A third problem may arise where there are a limited number of bidders. In his classic work, Mead (1967) showed that the gap between the appraised upset price and the actual bid received for federal timber in the US Pacific Northwest varied directly with the number of bidders. Further studies have suggested that concentration on either the buyer or seller side may not lead to competitive outcomes. For example, Brannlund et al. (1985) looked at buyer concentration in Scandinavian pulpwood markets, arguing that pulp companies exercised their market power in terms of how prices are set by distance and through systematic importation of foreign wood. Binkley (1991) has made similar assertions about market power in pulpwood markets in the American South.

---

[5] Mattey (1990) described the US Pacific Northwest stumpage market of the early 1980s, while Perez-Garcia and Lippke (1991) focused on the late 1980s. Mattey describes how bids exceeded prices based on current values, and the resulting problems when the anticipated increased lumber prices never materialised. Perez-Garcia and Lippke predicted a potential problem, based on another run-up in bid prices similar to the previous period, although record lumber prices shortly thereafter may have obviated their conclusions. Firms might also have different discount rates (which likely differ from that of government), and this affects bidding.

The principal advantage of competitive bidding is that it should not change the optimal behaviour of firms or the extensive or intensive margins. This is because the firm has every incentive to maximise the net return from the forestland. However, in the case where there are other distortions, such as insecure tenure, firms may not have the incentive to preserve the conservable flow from the site in the absence of regulations, and economic efficiency may not be assured.

Other methods of rent capture that may be employed include land rentals and land productivity taxes. Land rentals are an arbitrary annual payment that does not distort resource use provided the charge does not exceed the forestland's economic rent. Land productivity taxes are based on an estimate of forestland productivity or the annual growth rate of the trees at a site multiplied by an expected price for the timber. The charge, therefore, is based on a site's "best use" value and not on the value of the actual inventory or harvesting costs. Provided that the charge is set so that an amount equal to or less than the economic rent is collected, the behaviour of firms is unaffected. The optimal area based charges suggested by Nautiyal and Love (1971) are an example. The problem with the land rental and productivity taxes is setting the appropriate rate of rent capture.

Finally, the efficiency distorting effects of the most common rent collection methods, uniform fixed royalties and *ad valorem* royalties on revenue or price, can be mitigated to some extent by regulations that prevent high grading. The regulations themselves can be a source of inefficiency, however, and can lead to higher social costs.

Rent capture in British Columbia

Two forest tenures are found on public forestland in BC. The first are Tree Farm Licenses (also known as Forest Management units in other parts of Canada) that guarantee forest companies access to timber in the area of the license for a period of 25 years, with the possibility of renewal. In exchange, firms must provide secondary manufacturing facilities (sawmills, pulp mills) and draw up management plans that are subsequently approved by the Ministry of Forests. The government sets five-year harvest targets, with firms having the flexibility to shift harvest levels within that time frame. While forest companies had previously not been responsible for reforestation (it was a public responsibility), recent policy changes shifted responsibility to the companies, first enabling the companies to charge such expenses against stumpage fees but later imposing all of the cost on the companies (as a cost of harvesting). Since rotation ages exceed 50 years, the length of tenure is inadequate to get firms to take into account the effects of current decisions on future timber availability. Further, vagaries in government policies concerning the Tree Farm Licenses led the private forest companies to view the tenures as ephemeral.

The second form of tenure is a harvest permit that only grants the logging company the right to a certain volume of timber. The permits require the concessionaires to submit harvest plans, but forest management responsibility resides solely with the government. Tenures are granted via competitive bids, although the process takes into account local employment impacts, the use to which logs are put and other such factors in addition to the bid amount. The Ministry of Forests is responsible for reforestation, but may employ special silvicultural contracting firms to plant trees (Wang et al. 1998; Wang and van Kooten 1999).

The method of rent capture, or stumpage system, previously employed in BC for most public land was based upon the Rothery formula. A simplified formulation of the method is: $S = P - C - R$, where S is stumpage or the assessed potential charge paid by the harvester of a site to the resource owner, P is the timber price, C is operating costs, and R is an allowance for risk and a normal rate of profit, all measured on a per cubic meter basis. Rent is determined by simply deducting total costs from total revenues. This approach is also used to calculate reserve prices, or the upset price, for timber sales on Federal lands in the United States. Luckert and Bernard (1993) refer to these as Residual Conversion Return (RCR) methods of appraisal.

The original stumpage system applied in BC used appraised values for P, C and R and not actual values, mainly because competitive markets are generally unavailable as a result of widespread public ownership and associated tenure arrangements. A distinction is made between Coast and Interior; trees on the Coast tend to be larger and used primarily for high-quality grades of lumber, with residual wood "sold" as wood chips for pulp, while those in the Interior are used for lower grade lumber, studs and wood chips. On the Coast, P was given as the price of logs in the Vancouver log market, which is a residual market. In the Interior, the value of logs is based upon random length lumber, stud and chip prices and estimated conversion factors. The appraised operating costs are estimated from surveys for an operator of "average efficiency". There was a minimum stumpage charge of 3% of the Average Product Value (APV) in the Interior, and 6% of the APV on the Coast, even if the above formula indicated a negative stumpage value, and charges were levied on the timber removed using uniform but species specific rates.

This system caused a number of distortions predicted by economic theory (see above) and discussed in the BC context by Pearse (1976) and Percy (1986). It resulted in high grading as firms had an incentive only to harvest those trees that provide a net return equal to or in excess of average stumpage, with remaining trees generally left on the ground. Thus, the stumpage system shifted the intensive margin to the left and distorted firm behaviour. This incentive for firms to harvest fewer trees from a stand with a per unit stumpage charge explains why the Province specified minimum utilisation rates for timber stands. In addition, the USA argued that the system did not collect enough rent within the Province, and, by failing to do so, the Provincial Government was subsidising the forest industry. In response, the BC Government adopted a new stumpage system in 1987 (modified in 1994) called Comparative Value Pricing (CVP). The new system was meant to meet the government's requirements for increased revenues and to eliminate the need for an export tax as required by the Memorandum of Understanding between the respective national governments (Grafton et al. 1998).

The CVP system changed many of the features of the stumpage system. In 1987, minimum stumpage rates were set at 25 cents per cubic metre, with all species in the same stand averaged together to determine the stumpage rate. Most importantly the stumpage system changed from a Rothery or residual value approach to an *ad valorem* approach, with stumpage charges ultimately determined as a percentage of the selling price of timber products. Specifically, the government now establishes target rates and uses relative values to allocate stumpage fees across the Province. This leads to a "waterbed effect", since a decrease in one operator's stumpage in one area means a concomitant increase in that of another operator. The actual formula is: $VI = P - OC$, where VI is the value index for the cutting authority, P is the selling price of logs on the Coast and lumber and chips in the Interior, and OC is operating costs. The resulting VIs are then aggregated to calculate an average VI or Mean Value Index (MVI), with negative rates reset at the minimum stumpage. The MVI is then used to determine what will be the average stumpage or base rate, given that the physical harvest changes from quarter to quarter. The base rate is then compared to the required revenue target, with the MVI adjusted upwards or downwards in an iterative process until the expected stumpage billed equals the base rate. The resulting base rate is then used to determine the individual stumpage for each cutting authority as a Base Rate + (VI – MVI).

At the same time, the deductibility of costs changed dramatically, as major licensees assumed responsibility for management costs, road-building and reforestation – the latter two previously treated as dollar for dollar credits against stumpage (Wang et al. 1998). Under the new system, silvicultural and development costs are incorporated in determining stumpage values, but are no longer fully deductible. Since recent changes in the BC Forest Practices Code (see Chapter 6) have increased operating costs and contributed to a 65% increase in average logging costs per cubic metre from 1992 to 1995, this potentially has an adverse impact on the viability of the industry.[6] Obviously, transferring funds in excess of the rent implies that firms earn less than normal profits, which may give rise to disinvestment.

It should be noted that, although stumpage payments make up the bulk of direct forest revenues, the government also collects several other (indirect) taxes. These include the sales tax, the corporate capital tax, logging taxes and property taxes. In addition, there are general methods of taxation that allow the Province to collect a share of the rents. To the extent that uncollected economic rents increase the profits of forest companies, any applicable corporate profit taxes should appropriate a share of the rent. It is the direct payments that are specifically designed to capture the rent in the forest industry.

The proportion of available rent that was captured by the BC government over the period 1970 to 1994 is provided in Figure 4.7. Rent capture varied between a high of 174% (in 1981) and a low of 22% (1977). Rent capture averaged 71% over the 25-year period. As the following discussion of Indonesia illustrates, the BC government has on occasion performed no better than developing countries in capturing forestry rents, although rent capture has generally been higher overall.

---

[6] Not including operating costs in calculations of stumpage has supposedly contributed to two high-profile bankruptcies (Grafton et al. 1998). In Spring 1998, the government reduced stumpage fees by some $8 per m^3 to help forest companies stem losses due to a US countervail duty on lumber and weak Asian markets, followed by further reductions in early 1999.

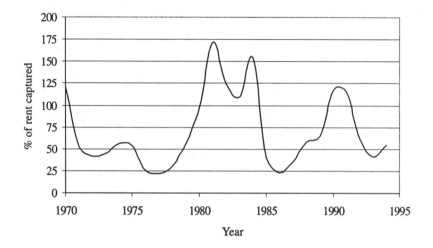

Figure 4.7 Rent Capture in BC, Percentage of Available Rent Captured

Rent capture in Indonesia

Indonesia accounts for about 10% of the earth's remaining tropical rainforests, ranking third behind Brazil and Zaire. In 1996, some 450 logging companies operated on about 55 million ha of forestland; there were over 500 forest concessions. Wood and wood products accounted for US$5,500 million in export revenues in 1994, or some 15% of total exports. In Indonesia, forestland is primarily in the public domain and, hence, sustainable exploitation should be a source of public revenues. In this subsection, we briefly discuss some aspects of rent capture in Indonesia. In contrast to BC, where rent capture has been relatively high at times and may even have resulted in hardships for forest companies on occasion, the situation in many developing countries is just the opposite – countries have generally been unsuccessful at capturing forest rents. Failure to capture economic rents contributes to excessive short-run exploitation, and inevitable waste of valuable resources.

The tenure arrangements in Indonesia have some things in common with those in British Columbia. Since the 1960s, forest companies have been given 20-year tenures (compared to 25 years in BC), but they are inadequate given that the next crop of trees becomes available some 35 years later. The Forest Ministry determines the annual harvest quota for each company.

Indonesia has a long history of log export trade restrictions. In 1985, an outright ban was introduced, but it was replaced by restrictively high taxes on exports in 1992 in order to comply with GATT rules (Barbier et al. 1995). The purpose of trade restrictions was to industrialise the forest sector, creating employment in secondary manufacturing. These policies reduced the domestic price of fibre, thereby encouraging waste, as cheap fibre was substituted for technologies that would use less fibre to produce the same amount of output. By reducing the value of standing timber, trade restrictions made forestland more valuable in alternative uses, meaning primarily agriculture. Thus, two forces have operated against each other – lower fibre prices have reduced supply of fibre as it reduced incentives to cut trees (but wood wastage has offset this effect to some extent), while the opportunity cost of converting land to agriculture has increased the incentive to cut trees (see Chapter 12). Finally, Indonesia also imposed substantial taxes on sawnwood exports in 1989 in order to shift activities toward plywood, although the tax was also meant to improve overall competitiveness and efficiency in sawmills (Barbier et al. 1995).

As forests are located on public lands, forest revenue systems should convert stumpage value into government revenues. Companies are charged a one-time license fee in order to obtain a concession to cut trees, but the fee is small. Annual Land and Improvement Taxes are also levied, but are generally small (because forest concession land is the lowest valued class of land in calculating these taxes) and is calculated only on one-twentieth of the total area of the concession. A volume-based scaling and grading fee is also assessed when harvest occurs. Each harvested log is graded and scaled under the supervision of a Forest Ministry official in order to assess royalties due to the government. The Ministry officials are completely reliant on the logging concessionaires for transportation, room and board, which creates conflict of interest (Teter 1997).

Two royalties account for 95% of the government's forest revenues. The first is a reforestation fee that, between 1980 and 1988, amounted to no more than a performance bond – the fee was returned to the companies based on compliance with forest management guidelines. In 1989, this was converted to the current reforestation fee, becoming the single largest of the government's forest levies, accounting for nearly 65% of annual forestry receipts. The flat charge was raised from $4 to $7 per m^3 in 1989, raised to $10 per m^3 in 1990, and increased again in 1993, but not thereafter. However, in 1993, the reforestation fee was made to vary according to two species groups and three geographic areas. Revenues from this program are earmarked for the establishment of industrial plantations, but the program has been considered a failure. A possible reason is that disbursement of funds requires the approval of the President of Indonesia, who also has the discretion to use the money for non-forestry purposes (Teter 1997).

The second form of royalty is the Forest Products' Royalty, which is an *ad valorem* tax that automatically adjusts for changes in market prices (e.g., inflation). The royalty amounts to 6% of the market value of logs (to have been raised to 10% in late 1996), with charges on teak and mahogany much higher than charges for the most common categories, meranti and mixed hardwoods. As with the reforestation fee, special low rates apply to wood chips and waste wood to encourage efficient use of fibre, and to logs from industrial timber plantations to encourage investments in plantation forests. With the fall in market prices brought about by Indonesia's ban on log exports in the early 1980s, plywood and sawn timber producers experienced a windfall at the expense of the royalty. Further, illegal harvests continue to depress domestic prices, thereby reducing royalties. (Although official records put log production at some 26 million m^3, estimates based on the output of wood products suggests that actual log production is closer to 40 million m^3.) As a result of better monitoring and enforcement of logging rules by the Forest Ministry and rising domestic log prices, revenue collection began to increase in the mid-1990s. Disbursement of revenues from the Forest Products' Royalty is more transparent than in the case of the reforestation fee, with 35% designated for forestry programs and the remainder going to regional and local governments.

The evidence suggests that the Indonesian government has not succeeded in capturing a great deal of the forest rent, although it has done better more recently. Estimates of rent capture differ depending on whether potential or actual rent is used as the benchmark. Potential rent is based on logging companies operating in open markets, so prices of freely traded logs from Sabah and Sarawak in Malaysia are used to calculate the resource rent. Actual rent focuses on private profitability under existing trade regulations; it is the basis for the calculations used in the case of BC, for example. To estimate actual rents, it is necessary at least to determine domestic log prices, but this may be difficult if log prices reflect transfer prices rather than competitive market prices. Obtaining information about transfer prices or logging costs from forest companies in Indonesia is also difficult. Further, government levies vary by species and location, as do production costs. In BC, such data are more readily available as a result of government regulations, standard accounting practices, and regular data collection by Statistics Canada. Thus, in the case of Indonesia, one would expect less agreement among researchers on the extent of rent capture.

Repetto and Gillis (1988) use potential rents as the basis for calculating the extent of rent capture in Indonesia. They estimate that log exports from Sumatra and Kalimantan between 1979 and 1982 (prior to the log export ban) generated potential rents of approximately $62 per cubic meter. However, total identifiable government revenues (timber royalties, land taxes, reforestation fees and other charges) averaged no more than $28 per m^3, implying that, over this period, the government captured only 45% of the rents available from log exports. Timber that was domestically processed received even more favourable treatment: tax rates were lowered and investment incentives were provided to stimulate processing. An inefficient domestic industry was erected that, at least initially, generated economic losses and required more than average input of wood per unit of output. Repetto and Gillis (1988) have estimated that

> between 1979 and 1982 the potential economic rents generated by log production, whether for further processing or direct export, exceeded US$4.95 billion. Of this, the government's share, collected through official taxes and fees, was $1.64 billion. Five hundred million dollars of potential profits were lost because relatively high cost domestic processing generated negative economic returns. The remainder, $2.8 billion, was left to private parties. (p. 21)

Marchak (1995) estimates that the share of potential rent captured has fallen to 10–20% (Table 4.3). The World Bank (1993) estimates that actual rent amounted to $40–$45 per m^3, and that the government collected 19–33% of this rent. Whiteman (1996) estimates that actual rent equaled $44 per m^3, with the government collecting 61% of the rent. Other studies suggest that the government captured somewhere between 25% and 57% of the available (actual) rents (Teter 1997).

Table 4.3: Economic Timber Rents in Indonesia: Potential and Collected Revenue (US$ millions)

	1989	1990
Economic rent per cubic meter log	99.24	94.66
Rent captured by license fee	5.00	6.00
Property tax, royalty reforestation fee	7.00	10.00
Total rent captured per m³ log	12.00	16.00
Log production (1000 m³)	31,215	26,000
Total economic rent	3,098[a]	2,461
Total collected revenue	253[b]	416
Percentage of rent captured	8%	17%

Source: Marchak (1995)

[a] Total amount if US$16 per m³ is realised

[b] Converted from RP447 billion revenue

Finally, because domestic log prices amount to a subsidy and are therefore a poor indicator of the true rents, it is necessary to examine rents in secondary manufacturing. Plywood is sold in international markets, and accounts for 70% of Indonesia's wood product exports by both value and volume. Estimates reported by Teter (1997) indicate that capture of these rents has increased from just over 10% in 1987 to nearly 40% in 1995.

The failure to capture rents has resulted in greater than normal profits for timber contractors. According to Repetto and Gillis (1988), excess profits resulted in a rush on concession contracts by private contractors (the so-called timber boom) and stimulated logging activity. Sub-optimally large areas of forestland were selectively logged and, as a consequence of roads constructed to transport the logs, opened up for shifting cultivators and settlers. (See Chapter 12 for a discussion of the relations between commercial logging and enhanced agricultural conversion.) Excess profits also stimulate short-run deforestation because concessionaires are not sure whether the favourable terms of the concession contracts will persist. Concession rights are typically not acquired by competitive bidding, but by negotiation. This process clearly opens the door for "side payments" and favouritism, which may provide the concessionaire with little formal rights. To forestall risk of renegotiating or revision of contract terms, a rational concessionaire should enter the property immediately, harvesting the trees as quickly as possible. The opening up of closed forests is also promoted by a timber revenue system that promotes high grading. This suggests that rent capture and economic efficiency may be linked; it appears to depend on the institutional framework.

Rent dissipation in forestry

The discussion on rents has so far assumed that a forest site will naturally yield (maximum) economic rent. In reality, there are a number of ways that economic rent and even quasi-rents can be dissipated, transferred or simply not realised. The most damaging type of rent dissipation from an economic point of view arises from market and policy failures that prevent the most efficient use of resources and benefit no one (see Chapter 12). These market distortions dissipate rent through the misallocation of resources, such as capital and labour, and through inappropriate rotations and harvest practices. Such distortions can arise from inappropriate forestry regulations, or policy failure. For example, uncertainty over tenure of forestland and harvesting rights may reduce investments and reduce the quasi-rents from the site that would otherwise have occurred under more appropriate tenure arrangements (see next section). In both the cases of BC and Indonesia, forest companies have tenure rights that are shorter in duration than the time required for the next round of harvest on a site.

In the standard theory of forestry, the owner of the resource balances the costs of silviculture today against future benefits, appropriately discounted (see Chapter 11). Luckert and Haley (1993) and Pearse (1985) have pointed out that most stumpage systems deduct current silvicultural costs from current harvests. Both companies and the government treat silviculture as a mandatory expenditure associated with timber harvest. In this case, the government is transferring rent from one period to the next, although, if such investments are not profitable (Benson 1988), the rent may be partially or totally dissipated. Rules requiring the planting of trees on sites where natural reforestation is more profitable, or employing more intensive silviculture where returns do not warrant doing so, result in the dissipation of rent.

In some cases, rent may be dissipated to achieve other social objectives, such as maximising employment in economically depressed regions. For example, a pulp mill on BC's northern Coast was provided hundreds of millions of dollars in subsidy payments (beginning in 1998) to continue production and prevent loss of employment. Yet, the mill is unlikely to survive in the longer run because fibre needs to be obtained from areas that are too distant from the mill to make logging profitable, a situation exacerbated by environmental regulations. Pursuing regional development or employment objectives is likely to be inefficient. Rarely is an attempt made to measure directly the costs and benefits of such actions, and rent is likely to be dissipated through forgone opportunities.

Transfer of the economic rent from the owner of forestland to other economic agents is a related consideration. Copithorne (1979) suggests that this type of rent dissipation has occurred in BC because of an unexplained wage differential between BC and Ontario forestry workers. Percy (1986) observed the same wage differential but concluded that much of the difference is explained by a higher productivity of workers in BC rather than rent dissipation. Yet another way economic rents can be lost to the public landowner is through capture and retention by forest companies. It has been suggested that economic rents left uncollected may be transferred outside of the forestry sector through transfer pricing by vertically integrated companies. This may take the form of overpricing inputs or under-pricing outputs. Such appropriation of economic rents should be evidenced by companies with higher than normal profits taking into account risk premiums, but Pearse (1980) observed that BC forest companies compare unfavourably with manufacturing industries in Canada based upon measures of financial performance.

The imposition of utilisation rates at harvest sites may also dissipate rents, as does the method of allocating harvesting rights. In BC, firms holding long-term cutting rights (Tree Farm Licenses or Forest Licenses) are required to build and operate processing facilities. Logs harvested under a company's permit may be more valuable to another company, or as an export, rather than being used in the local mill. Where logs are not utilised in their highest value use, the economic rent is reduced or dissipated. As noted above, this has been the case in Indonesia. In addition, the very means that governments employ to collect the rents may also impose distortions on efficiency and reduce the total rent available (see above; also Gillis 1988, pp. 98–105).

Governments restrict log exports for industry development, employment and well-being reasons. It is argued that, by preventing log exports, processing is encouraged, thereby leading to greater employment and economic development. Economic development is confused with economic well being in this case. Indeed, Margolick and Uhler (1986) show that social well being might even be enhanced if log export bans are relaxed, while Pearse (1993a) argues further that log exports could lead to higher and not lower employment. From economic theory, log export restrictions reduce the value of standing timber and lead to inefficiencies in the use of fibre. Thus, log export bans dissipate the available rent.

There is a further danger that, once firms commit capital or other investments, governments can take opportunistic advantage of these sunk costs. To the extent firms realise this, they will minimise their investments, thereby decreasing timber harvests and available rents.

An increasingly contentious area of indirect rent capture pertains to the interaction between the forestry sector and other parts of the environment and economy. The general problem in economic terms is that of externality, or interactions between various agents that lie outside market transactions. One example of this is the amenity value of forestland, where timberland provides benefits to recreationists. In the economic literature, this problem is solved through setting different tax levels, which cause the private timber owner's decision of the harvest level and/or rotation period to coincide with the socially optimal choice (Englin and Klan 1990). Although theoretically it is straight forward to resolve this problem (see Chapter 11), the uncertainty in determining many of these non-timber values makes such an exercise difficult in practice (Nautiyal and Resenyck 1985). Many governments resolve this divergence between the private and social optima by directly regulating where and how much timber can be cut, so those measurements of values are presumably already incorporated into the decision to permit harvesting.

Another example is changes in environmental standards that require significant pollution control expenditures by forest-resource companies. These include the well-known regulations that require pulp mills to reduce drastically certain effluents and eliminate others (but raise welfare elsewhere in society). Less well-known restrictions are ones like those that were placed on sawmills in BC for a short period; these prevented sawmills from burning their wastes to generate electricity that could then be sold into the provincial power grid (to prevent electricity prices from falling). The question here is whether the government should permit the increased costs of disposing wastes to be included in their estimation of operating costs (at least for the sawmills). If these costs are not included, this is a rent transfer in the short run from sawmills to the beneficiaries of such a policy. In the long run, if quasi-rent is being captured (appropriating some profits that need to cover the costs of properly disposing of this waste) then capital would exit the sawmill industry. The outcome is not so obvious for pulp mills, since the price they pay for their input is largely determined by negotiations with the sawmills. Offsetting some of the impact on pulp mills is that the Federal tax code is fairly generous in allowing water and air pollution control expenditures to be written off quickly.

Finally, the same issues arise with codes of forest practice that many countries have adopted. To the extent costs are imposed and cannot be recovered fully either through the stumpage or income tax system, rent will be transferred from the forestry sector to others in society.

4.4 Property Rights and Rent Dissipation in Fisheries

Much of the foregoing discussion on rent capture and rent dissipation is also relevant for fisheries. For example, the "intensive margin" in agriculture and forestry now returns as the "discard margin". But one important characteristic of marine fisheries (and many other resources, for that matter) has not yet been addressed. Property rights, or their absence, play a central role in natural resource economics and the management of biological assets. Fish are migratory and cross national boundaries, making it difficult to assign property rights to private individuals or even nations. As a consequence, fish stocks have often been harvested under conditions where no one has a right to the fish, resulting in over exploitation.

In this section, we present different property regimes and implications for rent dissipation. Although the discussion focuses on the fishery, the results apply equally to many other resources and biological assets. Ill-defined and enforced property rights have played an important role in the demise of African elephant populations (Chapter 10), while, in forestry, lack of well-defined property rights is an especial problem in developing countries. Tropical deforestation is primarily caused by advancing slash-and-burn agriculture and, locally, by excessive collection of fuelwood (Chapter 12). We also consider some policy instruments that can be used to enhance "rational" use in cases where some form of public or non-governmental organisation (NGO) ownership exists.

Property rights and rent dissipation

Property rights can be understood as characteristics that define the rights and duties associated with the use of a particular asset or resource. According to Bromley (1999), natural resources are exploited under one of four property regimes.

1. *State property* Individuals may be allowed to use (exploit) the resource but only according to the rules imposed by the state or its managing agency.
2. *Private property* In this case, the private owner has the right to utilise and benefit from the exploitation, conservation or sale of the resource, as long as no (socially unacceptable) externalities are imposed on others. Private ownership does not imply absence of state regulation (control), as private property cannot exist without state sanction and protection.

3. *Common property* In this case, a group of owners manages the resource, excluding those who are not members of the group. Members of the group have specified rights and duties, as do non-members as they must abide by exclusion.

4. *No property rights* (*res nullius*) When there is no assigned property right, open or free access is the result. Under open-access, each potential user of the resource has complete autonomy to utilise the resource since none has the legal right to keep another potential user out.

In practice, resources are often held in overlapping combinations of these regimes (Feeney et al. 1996), and it is possible to shift from one (dominant) regime to another when conditions change. Failure to enforce or manage properly a state or common property resource (which is frequent) leads to open-access (e.g., Newfoundland cod fishery, many endangered large-game species). The switch from common and state regimes to open-access as a result of population growth is well-documented (Murty 1994; Bromley 1999). Sethi and Somanathan (1996) provide additional reasons why social norms might break down (e.g., rising prices, and diminution of damages that sanctions such as cultural isolation entail due to migration), although this need not necessarily happen.

The absence of property rights (open-access) has resulted in excessive depletion of resources and biological assets for the following reason. The cost of exploiting a resource consists of two distinct components: the private extraction costs and the unobserved opportunity cost, or the value of the resource *in situ* – the user cost. The intuition behind user cost in the context of a renewable resource is as follows: harvesting a unit of the resource today means that that this unit and the growth (offspring) it causes are not available for future consumption. The (future) value of uncaught fish and unharvested trees depends on many different factors, including the discount rate, future markets for the resource, technological developments, reproductive features and so on. A sole private owner aiming to maximise profits will maximise the discounted value of this rent, and treat the resource as an asset. Hence, the value of uncaught fish prevents a rational fisherman from over-fishing the stock, but only as long as she expects to be the one to benefit from this "investment". Private property may result in a conservative harvesting policy. In the absence of externalities and given similar discount rates, the same applies for state ownership (Fisher 1981).

An open-access resource exists if there is no possibility to exclude firms attracted by excess profits, although their entry will compete away those profits. If there is unrestricted access to the resource, no person can be sure of who will benefit from the value of uncaught fish. In an open-access situation, no individual fisher has an economic incentive to conserve the resource, and none can conserve efficiently the resource by delaying harvest. Doing so will only enhance the harvest opportunities of competitors, which is the tragedy of open-access. One might say that the individual does not care about escaped fish, and discounts future harvests at an infinite rate (Neher 1990). New fishers will be attracted to the fishery, or existing ones will expand their efforts so long as fishers earn more than the opportunity cost of their effort, cE, where c is the cost of effort E. In *bionomic equilibrium*, all rent is dissipated, and total cost equals total revenue, rather than marginal cost being equal to marginal benefit.[7] The situation where marginal cost exceeds marginal benefit is usually referred to as *economic overexploitation.*

It is only since the late 1970s that exclusive economic zones (EEZ) have been established, within which governments or intergovernmental organisations have obtained the ability to implement fisheries policies. This implies that, at least within the EEZs, open-access has been transformed into a state property or common property regime, although this has not guaranteed survival of many fisheries. There are few, if any, commercially valuable open-access fisheries in the world today. Conrad (1995) notes that, what might appear to be a managed fishery, may in practice be one where open-access conditions are approximated; *de facto* open-access can arise if management regulations are ineffective.

Gordon (1954) was the first to explain why established fisheries were often characterised by a lot of old vessels making little or no profits. He developed a simple static model of rent dissipation based on zero discounting, constant prices and the conventional yield-effort function $y = qEx$, where y is yield, q is a catchability constant, E is effort (a choice or control variable) and x is *in situ* stock level. His model is illustrated in Figure 4.8. TR_1 represents total revenues for the base case, and is a concave function because of the concavity of the underlying growth function for the biological asset. (See Chapter 7 for more information on growth functions). TC_1 describes total cost; $TC = cE$, where c is assumed constant. (Ignore TC_2 and TR_2 for now.) Rent dissipation occurs at an effort level of E_1. Then, $\pi(x,E) = (pqx - c)E = 0$, where π is profit; hence, for an interior solution, $x_1 = c/pq$. Clearly, this is excessive compared to the two well-known benchmarks: (1) x_{MSY} (or E_{MSY}) corresponding with maximum sustained yield, and (2) efficient harvesting where marginal benefit equals marginal cost (E^*) and rent (= π) is maximised. That E^* is to the left of E_{MSY} depends on the implicit assumption of zero discounting. As the discount rate (r) increases, E^* moves to the right and eventually approaches E_1 as r goes to infinity.

When effort is socially excessive, the stock is smaller than is socially optimal; for the current model specification and assuming steady-state harvesting, effort E is readily translated into stock size x (see also Neher 1990). Effort beyond E_{MSY} is referred to as *biological overexploitation.* Depending on the growth function and the specification of the production function, the stock may be driven to extinction under open-access. Extinction will occur for positive stock levels as long as x_1 is smaller than minimum viable population levels (see Chapter 7). For the production function $y = qEx$, the catch per unit of effort, y/E, goes to zero as x approaches zero. With constant prices, rent dissipation will occur before the stock is totally depleted. However, depletion may occur during the approach to equilibrium (see Chapter 7).

---

[7] Fixed costs are ignored in this line of reasoning as they affect both entry and exit into the fishery. A consequence of considering fixed (sunk) costs is a "gap" between entry and exit, as fishers only enter when both variable and fixed costs can be covered, but will not leave the fishery until revenues fall short of variable costs.

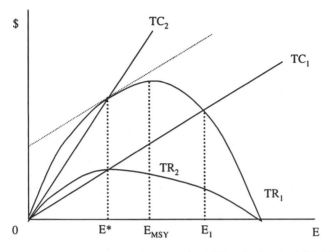

Figure 4.8 Rent Dissipation (E_1) and Optimal Effort (E^*) in a Static Model

Common Property

We might well ask whether public resources should be privatised, because private owners take the value of *in situ* resources into account, which should avoid the adverse effects of open-access. Although this issue is taken up again in Chapter 6, here we provide some observations about the transition from one form of property regime to another, and especially the role of common property. If property rights are completely defined and costlessly enforced, privatisation of natural resources enhances efficiency; but, in the real world, problems arise (Baland and Platteau 1996). While generally promoting economic efficiency, the actual process of privatisation may raise equity concerns. The newly established owner of the resource collects the rents (if any) that had previously been shared among those who exploited the resource under open-access; see also Weitzman 1974 on this distributional issue.

In addition to the distributional consequences, transaction costs are likely to increase when the property regime is altered. When privatisation "hurts" former resource users and the legitimacy of the new property rights regime is questioned, enforcement costs may be considerable. This has been the case in BC's salmon fishery, for example. Costs of enforcing catch limits have risen dramatically as existing fishers have rejected the federal government's reallocation of rights over the fishery to natives. Unless former rights' holders are compensated (which is rare due to budget constraints), any gains in efficiency could be lost due to increased transaction costs.

In addition to transaction costs, privatisation may not enhance efficiency if privatisation leads to imperfect competition (so that harvests are below the social optimum) or externalities are prevalent. Further, some biological resources are mobile (e.g., fish, migratory waterfowl), so owners will have an incentive to take the animals on their territory before they migrate elsewhere, a characteristic associated with open-access. In some cases, denying former users access to a resource (because of privatisation) increases pressure on resources in other areas. Privatisation might also increase uncertainty about conflicting resource claims, leading to a breakdown of traditional codes or norms of behaviour and aggravating rather than improving management outcomes (Baland and Platteau 1996).

These and other considerations (see Chapter 6) suggest that privatisation is not a panacea, but that governments will likely have some role to play in resource management. Some analysts favour management by a group of individuals (common property) over both state and private ownership. For example, in the preface to Baland and Platteau (1996), Mancur Olson argues that "in view of the absolutely appalling record of most of the national governments of the poorest countries, the potential of the smaller rural communities in these societies cannot be ignored" (p. x). However, while common property can be efficiently managed (so-called regulated common property), it could also exhibit features of open-access (unregulated common property), as discussed below.

Management of unregulated common property can be modeled as a game in which everyone's welfare can be improved by practising constraint, but it is in no one's interest to do so. Ostrom (1998) refers to this as the social dilemma. The social dilemma paints a pessimistic picture about the potential of (small) groups to manage jointly a resource as individuals fail to do what is in their overall best interests. The result is that common resource stocks are overexploited and public goods are under provided. Baland and Platteau (1996) discuss why some commons are regulated, while others are unregulated and "wasted". To illustrate, consider the decisions by two fishers to allocate effort (number of boats) to a fishery and three circumstances that are viewed as games – a traditional prisoners' dilemma, the so-called chicken game and the assurance game. The payoffs under each of the games and strategies (effort decisions) are provided in Table 4.4.

Table 4.4: Pay-off Structures for Common Property Management

		Number of boats chosen by B under:					
		Prisoners' Dilemma		Chicken Game		Assurance Game	
		1	2	1	2	1	2
Number of	1	(5,5)	(3,6)	(5,5)	(3,6)	(5,5)	(1,4)
boats by A	2	(6,3)	(4,4)	(6,3)	(1,1)	(4,1)	(3,3)

In the prisoners' dilemma game, both fishers gain 5 units if they only send out one boat, for an overall gain of 10. If one fisher sends out two boats while the other sends out only one, the former will gain 6 units and the latter 3. If both fishers send out two boats, each will gain 4 units for an overall gain of 8 units. Irrespective of the other fisher's behaviour, it is always optimal for a fisher to send out two boats. Consider fisher A in Table 4.4. Compared to sending out one boat, she gains 1 unit by sending out two boats if B sends out one boat (6 minus 5) or two boats (4 minus 3). Thus, an effort of two boats on the part of each fisher is the dominant strategy. The game predicts overexploitation and a sub optimal outcome (8 < 10) for society.

The chicken game is similar but payoffs under overexploitation (each fisher employs two boats) is now (1,1) rather than (4,4). Now there is no dominant strategy;

because the optimal number of boats for a fisher to send out depends on the expectation regarding the other fisher's effort. There are two Nash equilibria with payoffs of (3,6) and (6,3), where no fisher unilaterally wants to deviate from his strategy. Note that, in contrast to the prisoner's dilemma above, one fisher exercises constraint in this equilibrium. The Pareto efficient payoff (5,5) is not an equilibrium outcome in a one-shot game such as this because, if any fisher decides to exercise restraint, the other will find it in her interest to send out two boats.

Finally, consider the assurance game where the payoff matrix is different than for the other cases, except that the payoff when each fisher sends out one boat remains the same as before (Table 4.4). Now, if fisher A decides to use only one boat, the payoff to B will be highest by also employing only one boat (as the gain is 5 as opposed to 4). However, when a fisher fears that the other might put out two boats, he will respond by also sending out two boats (and gain 3 instead of 1). While cooperation is the Pareto efficient outcome, it may not materialise if insufficient trust exists. In fact, three equilibria are possible (two strategies where one fisher puts out one boat and the other two, and a strategy where both send two boats). Depending on the expectations held by the fishers, the Pareto efficient equilibrium may or may not materialise, although one would expect it to have a better chance in this case than in the previous ones. The final outcome depends on the characteristics of the resource and the groups involved. As Baland and Platteau (1996) note "the focus of the analysis is no more on the irresistible tendency of individuals to overexploit the commons. It is being shifted to human encounters involving problems of trust, leadership, co-ordination, group identity and homogeneity or heterogeneity of group members" (p. 114).

Repetition of a "game" may get individuals to cooperate and exercise constraint if future cooperation is conditional on present "good behaviour". Cooperation is in fact the more common outcome, although not as common as might be hoped or efficient (Ostrom 1998). Cooperative behaviour is expected if the "game" is indefinitely or infinitely long. Otherwise our knowledge from dynamic economic models that are solved using backward induction (see Chapter 7) suggests that defection is likely. If the series of interactive decisions that the players take is finite and known for a prisoners' dilemma game, it is always optimal to defect in the final period (in the same way that it is optimal to defect in the one-period prisoners' dilemma game). Given that this is the case in the final period regardless of behaviour prior to that event, it is also optimal to defect in the next to last period. Reasoning backwards, defection would be the outcome in every period. Fortunately, most "games" dealing with common property resources are indefinitely repetitive and, further, evidence suggests that people do not calculate in the rational manner required for backward induction (Ostrom 1998).

Indeed, empirical evidence indicates that the prisoners' dilemma framework is unduly pessimistic, even for one-shot games. There is a tendency for participants to cooperate even in one-shot games, although rigorous explanations of such behaviour are lacking (Ostrom 1998). Decisions are clearly based on notions of fairness, cultural norms and other factors that are not usually taken into account in game theoretic models.

Ballad and Plateau (1996) argue that cooperation is more likely when the number of common property "owners" (participants in a game) is small as opposed to large. Small communities tend to be close knit, generally sharing the same ethos and beliefs, and interacting frequently; people know each other, discussing matters and making decisions face-to-face (Ostrom 1998). This results in more efficient management in the sense that user costs of resource are taken into account. Further, there is less possibility and incentive to free ride when the number of members in the commons (N) is lower. Monitoring and enforcement costs are generally lower and benefits from investments in resource improvements received by one person (1/N) are higher, while the ability and desire to shirk is lower. Clearly, if the right conditions are met, common property management can be considered a viable alternative to private or state ownership.

In developing countries, common property ownership plays a larger role than in industrialised countries. In the latter, communities tend to be larger and more mobile, causing a breakdown in some of the important factors needed to make common property ownership work, importantly close-knit, largely immobile communities with a common ethos and shared beliefs. The needed characteristics are likely to be met in (parts of some) developing countries, where common property also has an important role in distributing income and preventing marginalisation of people. Markets for factors such as labour in developing countries are often imperfect. Common property resources may play the role of *employer of last resort*, providing some security to the poor and deprived. Many households can survive because they can gather products such as wood, herbs, fuel and spices from local common forests. Other markets are imperfect as well, thus allowing common property resources to play a useful role. Common property resources sometimes enable households to pool risks (e.g., livestock producers that move their animals over an extensive area to use forage more efficiently in response to local variations in yield). Common property resources may perform the role of a communal bank, thereby mitigating existing credit market imperfections. This happens if individuals are allowed extraordinary access to the resource in times of particular need, such as a wedding or a funeral.

This discussion indicates that the case for common property is likely strongest in small communities in developing countries. In developed countries, private ownership or state ownership with usufruct rights (e.g., forest tenures) may be better options for allocating natural resources in an efficient manner. In choosing between these two types of ownership, it is likely that each case would have to be decided on its own merits. We return to some of these topics in the examples we present in later chapters.

Management instruments

In this section, we focus on state property and the problem of managing the fishery. For the case of commercial fishing, the issue of property rights allocation has been partially resolved by extended jurisdiction. For many years, coastal nations only controlled fisheries within a small zone ranging from 3 to 12 miles from shore. Widespread depletion of near-shore and pelagic fish stocks resulted in a provision of the UN Convention on the Law of the Sea in 1982 that extended a nation's territorial waters to 200 nautical miles (360 km), thereby enabling better management of the fishery by reducing the problem of open-access.[8] The bulk of commercial fish harvesting takes place in territorial waters. For example, in the late 1980s, 80% of commercial fishing by the EU member states takes place in territorial waters (Salz 1991). While extended jurisdiction is an important first step, it will be meaningless unless proper management is instituted; open-access could remain a problem, but with fishers of the same country competing for the stock as opposed to fishers from many nations (Anderson 1977; Harris 1998).

What are some management instruments that can be applied to combat excessive harvesting and rent dissipation – encourage fishers to apply E^* rather than E_1? Necessary prerequisites for successful resource management, irrespective of whether the issue is management of elephants or fish stocks, are that a governing body has:

1. (formal) property rights,
2. the authority and political will to issue regulations, and
3. the ability to enforce regulations at reasonable cost.

We return to this below. Here we only mention that conventional economics has traditionally devoted little effort to issues concerning political will and enforcement, although Graves *et al.* (1994), Salvanes and Squires (1995), and Sutinen and Anderson (1985) are exceptions. Disregarding these issues, however, may have severe consequences.

According to Hartwick and Olewiler (1998), economic policies to regulate fisheries need to:

1. ration effort in the fishery,
2. regulate the harvest to maintain efficient stocks of fish, and
3. recognise that any policy may affect the distribution of income through effort reduction and changes in rents.

They add that many existing regulations are designed to sustain the fishery and increase the incomes of fishers, not to reach an economic or social optimum.[9] Horan et al. (1999) analysed the implications of a managing agency that maximises a social welfare or political preference function, with the welfare of consumers, fishermen and labourers in the sector as arguments in the objective function (with possibly different weights attached to the welfare of these groups). They found that "optimal stocks for policy makers" are likely completely different than the ones specified in conventional models. The economics literature is concerned mainly with the conditions required to

---

[8] Fishing jurisdiction for many valuable stocks was not easily assigned among adjacent fishing nations. Rettig (1995) describes the problems associated with transboundary stocks – stocks partly outside the exclusion zone and subject to open-access exploitation, stocks straddling the fishing zones of adjacent countries and highly migratory shared stocks – and the management tools that could be implemented to deal with them.

[9] Anderson (1989) argues that, for most commercially interesting fisheries, economic and biological data for determining optimal harvests are not available. Pearse (1980) suggests using regulation to allow a safe catch to be obtained as efficiently as possible.

reach optimal harvest and effort levels, and the identification of an optimal steady-state stock. As Rettig (1995) notes, fishing is constrained by informal social conventions and codes of behaviour, but social aspects are often ignored in economic analysis. Common assumptions are that the growth function of the fish stock is known, and that the behaviour of fishers can be predicted and controlled. Both assumptions are often violated in practice. If policies tend to overlook the economic forces behind over-exploitation, this leads to regulatory measures that may temporarily reduce the level of over-fishing, but which still include the market signals that cause over-exploitation. The usual outcome of declining fish stocks can be attributed to policy failure (Ludwig et al. 1993).

Most of the public regulation alternatives can be classified as follows (Tahvonen and Kuuluvainen 1995; Hartwick and Olewiler 1998; Conrad 1995):

1. *Closed seasons* limit harvesting during crucial periods when the fish population is reproducing.
2. *Gear restrictions* limit the use of catching devices that are "too effective" or try to preserve the habitat of the harvested population.
3. *Limited entry* is used by the authorities to restrict the number of fishing vessels, by first licensing vessels and then restricting their number (sometimes through the purchase of licenses if all existing vessels are grandfathered a license).
4. *Aggregate catch quotas* shorten the fishing period, with monitoring used to bring about cessation of fishing when the cumulative harvest equals the aggregate quota.
5. *Taxes* can be imposed on the catch or on one or more specific inputs.
6. *Individual transferable quotas* (ITQ) limit the level of harvest for each individual fisher per fishing period, with owners of quota able to sell them to other fishers (with government sometimes purchasing quota to reduce overall harvests).
7. *Establishing ownership* by forming cooperatives brings moral suasion to bear on individual behaviour.

The aim of closed seasons and gear restrictions is to reduce the effectiveness of harvests or increase the real cost of fishing. (A similar issue was discussed in the context of rent dissipation in forestry, but the purpose of regulation in that sector is different.) Conrad and Clark (1987) refer to these policies as the economic perversity of purely biological conservation. The effects are easily demonstrated with the aid of Figure 4.8. If TR_1 indicates the total revenue curve for the fishery, then, under conditions of open-access, the bionomic equilibrium is at E_1. If the regulator wants to control effort, and bring it back to, say, E^*, one possible way to do this is to rotate the total cost curve TC_1 upwards to TC_2. Imposing inefficient harvesting techniques and closing the fishery for long times (idling vessels) will increase the costs of fishing.[10] While these policies may meet the goal of stock conservation ($x = x^*$ in the new

---

[10] Until the 1950s, gill netters in Bristol Bay, Alaska, were barred from using engines, resulting in Alaskan fishers competing against Japanese and Soviet fishers in the Bering Sea using sailboats (Tietenberg 1996, p.286).

equilibrium), they will still cause economic inefficiency (e.g., excessive working hours for fishers and large expenditures on capital and equipment to achieve the desired level of harvest). Economic efficiency requires that the level of annual harvest reflects the true value of the fish stock and that harvest takes place at the lowest possible cost. By increasing the cost of harvesting, the regulations reduce the income level of fishermen as rents are dissipated through inefficiency as opposed to over fishing. Regulations may also have an ecological basis, for, as Conrad (1995) notes, gear restrictions (e.g., minimum mesh size) may be designed to permit young fish to escape, thereby enhancing recruitment in later periods.

Closed seasons have an additional effect, similar to one that occurs when the number of vessels in a particular fishing area is limited: closed seasons lead to a phenomenon called "capital stuffing". With short seasons, the harvesting capacity of existing vessels in the long run is increased by investments in more powerful engines, larger nets or better electronic detection devices (radar) to find fish. As a result, the danger of over-fishing remains if there are no binding constraints on total catch. Harvest capacity may increase with more fish caught in a given period. Anderson (1995) refers to input restrictions as "rubber yardsticks", and uses a game theoretic approach to model the manager-fishers' struggle, with the latter always having the last move. Furthermore, scarce resources are wasted as capacity becomes excessive or operational decisions of fishers are distorted. The reason why excessive investments in harvesting capacity are likely to be undertaken is that fishers still have strong incentives to start harvest at full capacity, because being too slow at the beginning of the season could result in a lower future share of the total annual quota.

The fundamental problem of open-access is that fishers have no incentive to take into account the (shadow) value of fish left in the sea. Conrad and Clark (1987) demonstrate that a management agency can force fishers to recognise this cost by imposing the shadow price as a tax on harvests. This tax reduces the revenue to the fishery for each unit of effort employed. This is illustrated in Figure 4.8 by the new revenue parabola TR_2 (= $(P - t)y$, where P is output price and t is the per unit tax). Fishers now set $TR_2 = TC_1$, yielding the desired amount of effort E^*.

While the resulting outcome is theoretically efficient and does not involve tedious monitoring of effort, some problems remain. First and foremost is that this regulatory measure may be politically infeasible (Munro and Scott 1985). The tax transfers all of the economic rent from the fishing industry to the government, and fishers will use their political power to prevent such a policy from being implemented (Harris 1998). Second, the authority may have difficulty in computing the varying shadow prices, which depend on factors such as demand for fish and biological processes. Third, enforcement of a harvest tax and its collection may be difficult (Hartwick and Olewiler 1998). Finally, taxes can be inflexible, which is hard to reconcile with fluctuating fish stocks (Rettig 1995).

An alternative to a tax on harvests would be a tax on effort. Effort is often measured as the number of vessel days devoted to fishing during a particular year (Conrad and Clark 1987). The effect of such a policy would be similar to that of increasing harvest costs by imposing inefficient regulations. The difference is that resources are not wasted through inefficient harvest processes, but are collected by the government instead. At least two different tax schemes are possible. First, a head tax can be levied on every fisher in the sector. An example is a simple license fee f that shifts the total cost curve up ($TC_2 = cE + f$), unless the tax is not paid every period, in which case it is considered a fixed or sunk cost by fishers. Second, a unit tax t on effort can be imposed so $TC_2 = (c + t)E$, which rotates the total cost curve upwards. In principle, both taxes could lead to optimal harvest levels. Apart from the difficulties associated with taxing (noted above), in reality it is difficult to define and measure "effort", because fishers have the incentive simply to substitute types of effort that are not taxed for types that are taxed. Empirical studies of substitution possibilities between restricted and unrestricted inputs in fisheries indicate that harvest technology is typically not of fixed-proportions (Squires 1987; Campbell 1991; Dupont 1991), contrary to what is usually assumed in the literature.

Another means of regulating a fishery is via quotas, which can be interpreted as allocating property rights to part of the stock to individual fishers or groups of fishers. The authority simply limits the quantity of fish that can be harvested in a given period. The moratorium on harvests of North Sea herring in the late 1970s and early 1980s is an extreme example of such a quota. The Common Fisheries Policy (CFP) of the EU is based on a quota system. Typically, one first determines the total allowable catch (TAC), which is based on biological, economic and often political considerations. The TAC is then distributed among member states, which use it as a basis for their national policies. National quotas may be distributed amongst the fishers (as in the Netherlands), or the fishery can simply be opened up, and remain open until the national quota is reached.

While a quota system may result in optimal harvesting levels (provided that the authority has access to all the relevant data, and that monitoring and enforcement occur), a quota system will not always result in efficient allocation of effort. If the fishery is opened up until the country's TAC is reached, it is possible to end up in a situation where fewer fish are caught with more effort as firms rush to capture quota before others get there first. Again this results in "capital stuffing", with fishers investing in more powerful engines and search-and-catch capacity for an ever-shorter fishing season. Further, investments in extra capacity are necessary in the processing and retailing sectors to handle the large irregular quantities of fish that are dumped on the market for an ever shorter time interval.[11] Rents are likely to dissipate; the situation is similar to an open-access fishery, except that fish stocks are supposedly protected from over-exploitation by the quota.

Open-access problems can be overcome if property rights are allocated at the firm or fisher level. If a fisher has the right to harvest a certain quantity in a specified time interval, she will decide to use her effort so that harvest costs are minimised if discounted prices are constant, for example, or that her supply is concentrated in periods of high demand and high prices. Economic efficiency occurs at the firm level, but from society's point of view it is still possible to improve the allocation of effort by allocating harvest to least-cost fishers. Quota can be allocated to low cost firms by

---

[11] Tahvonen and Kuuluvainen (1995) examine the wasteful harvesting of salmon in Sweden. Salmon is available for a short time at low prices, but at Christmas when prices are high, it is imported. Harris (1998) discusses the case of Newfoundland fishers competing to deliver cod in Europe, thereby driving down prices as opposed to spreading out deliveries over time.

cumbersome administrative procedures, by auctioning them off, or by allowing trade in quota.

Quota constitutes a property right, and thus has value. The price of the quota is the value of the *in situ* resource, which is simply the market price minus the marginal harvesting cost, or the scarcity rent. Of course, enforcement of quota rights is a necessary condition for quota prices to reflect scarcity rent. For example, ITQs for flatfish species were introduced in The Netherlands in the early 1980s, but quota prices did not rise until, in the late 1980s, the government made it clear that enforcement would be taken more seriously. Quota value increased from 17 guilders per tonne in 1986 to 70 guilders in 1987. Without monitoring and enforcement, *de jure* property rights are of little value. This may be a particular problem in developing countries (Andersson and Hgazi 1991).

Firms with low costs will bid more for quota; likewise, if quota is tradable, low cost firms will buy quota from high cost firms, thereby making everyone better off. In equilibrium, the price of transferable quota is equal to the resource rent (Clark 1985; Anderson 1995), although, if vessels are not easily abandoned as the industry disinvests, then quota prices may be higher as fishers seek to cover variable costs only. The impact of quota and an optimal tax are identical in the sense that a socially efficient allocation of effort results, but only if information about biological and economic conditions is available and enforcement is adequate. There is fear that rights will eventually end up in the hands of a few large firms, although a recent analysis of the effect of transferable catch quota on the structure of the Dutch fleet did not provide much support for this hypothesis (Davidse 1995).

Other problems with quota (tradable or not) pertain to high grading and multiple-species' fisheries (Copes 1986). If some specimens of a species are more profitable than others, say, because of size, discarding may occur (Harris 1998). With high mortality rates associated with discarding, the outcome of an ITQ system will be less than desired by the authority. This is similar to the forestry problem where logs are left on the ground because it does not pay to remove them from the site (the intensive margin). A discard margin exists not only for fish of the same species, but also for the case of by-catch. In this case, fishers throw away fish for which they do not have a quota. Discarding by-catch may be mitigated to some extent by short-term lease or spot markets for species caught as by-catch. The by-catch problem is particularly acute for tropical marine ecosystems that have a greater variety of species (Eggert 1998).

Distribution of quota is similar to distribution of income, and this adds to the political complexity of implementing quota schemes that is similar to the problem of allocating tradable pollution permits. Both auctioning off quota and taxes generate public revenue, and income is transformed from the fishery to the government, which may be resisted by fishers (as noted above). If, instead, quota are distributed among fishers on historical grounds (known as grandfathering), extant fishers receive a gift at the expense of society as a whole. Since fishers are a small, readily identifiable and easy to organise group, and because their individual losses or gains are greater than those of individual taxpayers, they have the incentive to lobby government for policies that favour them, while governments have an incentive to meet their demands. This is in contrast to the more general population of taxpayers. This might explain why, in Canada, the federal government purchases quota at market prices that reflect not only scarcity rents but access to unemployment insurance benefits that are not available to other groups in society.[12] That is, the government is paying the capitalised value of scarcity rents that really belong to the public sector to begin with, plus the capitalised value of sector-specific government subsidies. In addition, government activity to buy quota has increased their price. This is certainly an example of effective rent-seeking on the part of fishers.

Finally, we consider some empirical evidence of the effect of management on rent dissipation in marine fisheries. Bulte et al. (1998) analysed the development of rent in European fisheries by looking at a time series of prices for the major commercial species. (Data on prices are often readily available, while cost data are harder to obtain.) It was hypothesised that, after implementation of the Common Fisheries Policy, some return of previously "dissipated" rents would occur as restricted harvesting should translate into higher prices. The results indicated that prices of fish were significantly higher than could be expected from existing trends. Thus the CFP was interpreted as somewhat successful.

Some qualifications are important. As elaborated upon earlier, (scarcity) rent is defined as price minus marginal harvesting costs. Since fishery policies can result in increased harvesting costs, analyses of rent should be based on combinations of price and cost information. The importance of ineffective and inefficient regulation is demonstrated by Dupont (1990), for example, who showed that potential rents in Canada's west Coast fishery had dissipated to a great extent due to capital stuffing, fleet redundancy and sub-optimal fleet composition. More recently, they have been dissipated due to a fishing dispute between Canada and the USA over Pacific salmon (Munro et al. 1998). The results above are based solely on prices, and therefore present only part of the story. However, by analysing secondary sources, Bulte et al. (1998) argued that increases in cost over time did not keep pace with price increments, so that at least some rent was captured after implementation of the CFP.

None of this implies that current policies are optimal. It only suggests that the situation would have been worse in the absence of CFP. There is considerable evidence that current fish stocks are sub-optimally low, with potential rents dissipated through an inefficient fishery fleet. According to a report by the Commission to the Council and the European Parliament on the CFP, the income foregone through sub-optimal fishery management in the EU is around $2.5 billion annually (Schmidt 1993).

Wilson (1982) is critical about the implications of conventional fishery economics for policy makers. He points to the lack of attention for transaction and informational costs, and the simplified and unrealistic assumptions with respect to fishers' behaviour and fish biology. Wilson concludes that the social costs of unregulated fishing are typically less than might be expected on the basis of accepted theory (e.g., fishers switch from one species to another when the population gets depleted and harvesting costs increase) and that attempts to regulate will usually

---

[12] The federal government is buying quota in order to transfer it to Aboriginal people as part of its Aboriginal strategy.

imply higher than anticipated costs. These two effects limit the range of economically feasible management options.

Wilson *et al.* (1994, p. 291) argue that failing fishery policies in the past are not so much caused by "political and economic interests that manage to overturn basically good scientific advice", but rather that "the scientific concepts are fundamentally flawed and lead to ineffective policies". The latter would be due to, among other things, the use of simple single species models, and disregard for the complexity of fisheries' systems that preclude predictability of the sort required to exercise management (Ludwig et al. 1993). We expand on this concern in Chapter 7.

5 Valuing Nonmarket Benefits

Given the inevitability of ongoing environmental and social change, humans need to evaluate decisions regarding environmental development and interactions with natural ecosystems. Several difficult questions are raised. How do we quantify environmental change? How do we assess what proportion of the changes in the environment are caused by human activities as opposed to being the result of inherent natural variability (e.g., as in the case of climate change)? How do we value environmental changes, or changes in the availability of a public good (e.g., changes in species diversity)? How can we value ecosystem resilience, say, when we have an imperfect understanding of how ecosystems function and where thresholds exist? In response to these and many similar questions, the US National Research Council (1996) identified the development of improved social science and risk assessment tools as the top priority in environmental research and development. Specifically, research programs to improve analytical tools for nonmarket valuation and cost-benefit analysis (CBA) were identified as needing immediate attention.

Inclusion of the costs and benefits of changes in the availability of commodities not normally traded in the market place, such as recreational services and clean water, is an important component of CBA. It is also important in land use planning where multiple uses of land exist and tradeoffs need to be made. Such tradeoffs can only be properly evaluated if the value of land in each of its uses is considered, and that includes taking into account the values of goods and services not traded in the market place. Nonmarket values are explicitly recognised in social CBA, which is the topic of Chapter 6. In this chapter, methods for estimating nonmarket costs and benefits are examined. The discussion is cursory due to the nature of the topic – there are many methods available and research in this area is prolific.

It is possible to distinguish indirect and direct approaches to obtaining information about nonmarket goods and services, or public goods. The *indirect approach* uses information on goods and services traded in markets to value the public good in question. In some cases it may be possible to derive an *expenditure function* (as in Chapter 2) between market-traded goods and the public good, and from it draw inferences about the demand for the public good or environmental amenity. The indirect approach relies on information derived from market observations to say something about the value of an amenity that is not traded in the market. Alternatively, *choice-based models* employ information about a related activity (as opposed to the environmental good itself) to provide estimates about the values of public goods. Examples of this method include the *travel cost method* for valuing recreational sites and voter behaviour (the activity), especially where citizens vote on government budgets that deal directly with expenditures on public goods (referred to as *voter referendum*). This information can be used to say something about the value of the public good in question.

The *direct approach* uses questionnaires or surveys to elicit directly an individual's *willingness-to-pay* (WTP) for more of a public good or her *willingness-to-accept* (WTA) compensation, or compensation demanded, to forgo or have less of the public good. Therefore, it is also referred to as the *income compensation approach*. WTP is often used to measure compensating surplus, while WTA is often used to measure equivalent surplus. Since this approach requires individuals to respond to hypothetical questions in a survey setting, it is also referred to as the *contingent valuation method* (CVM) if actual values are requested, or the contingent behaviour method if a behavioural response is desired. Alternative approaches in this genre include contingent ranking, choice experiments (or *stated preferences*), which require respondents to state their preference between situations (much like in marketing surveys), conjoint analysis and other techniques that are briefly discussed in this chapter; see also Smith 1997. Our purpose is to introduce the reader to various approaches to measuring nonmarket or extra-market benefits.

5.1 Expenditure Function Approach

There are two ways to observe data about unpriced or nonmarket values – through physical linkages or through behavioural linkages. Estimates of the values of nonmarket commodities can be obtained by determining a physical relationship between the nonmarket commodity and something that can be measured in the market place. One means is to estimate a *damage function*, which provides a physical relation between damage from, say, pollution and emission levels, and relates damages to monetary values. Alternatively, and depending on the situation, one can determine replacement costs for the resources that are lost (Pearce and Warford 1993, pp. 125–6). Behavioural linkages, on the other hand, are traced through individual utility functions. These then appear as demands for market goods. By considering the effect upon the demands for related private goods, it may be possible to say something about the value of public goods.

Market valuation of public goods via physical linkages

A public good, G, can be an input into production. An example is ozone, with an increase in tropospheric ozone resulting in lower crop yields. An estimate of the benefits of cleaner air is then given by the loss in net returns to farmland, or the loss in value due to reduced crop yields. In the case where a public good is a factor input, the production function becomes $q = f(x_1, ..., x_n, G)$, where $x_1, ..., x_n$ refer to the n factor inputs (e.g., capital, labour and fertiliser) purchased in markets and G is the public good, perhaps clean air or water (Freeman 1979a, pp. 63–8).

What effect will a change in G have on the production of the good in question? This will depend, in part, on the effect that a change in G has on the output price of q. Suppose that there are constant returns to scale and G does not affect returns to scale.

(Constant returns to scale implies a horizontal supply function.) Also assume for the moment that the changes in the output of q are sufficiently large to affect output price, i.e., that the demand for q is downward sloping. An increase in the availability of G only decreases the cost of producing every level of output. A good example is irrigation; an increase in G might represent a reduction in water salinity. Although the costs of producing crops are unaffected, yields will increase because water is less saline. The supply or marginal cost function is a horizontal line as shown in Figure 5.1. An increase in G reduces marginal cost causing a shift in supply, say from S to S', and reduction in price from p_0 to p_1. All of the gain from the reduction in the price of q accrues to consumers in the form of consumer surplus, given by area A in Figure 5.1. Thus, the demand for the market commodity q provides information about the benefit of an increase in the availability of G.

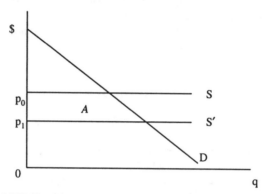

Figure 5.1 Welfare Measure with Constant Returns to Scale in Private Market

A second situation is one where an increase in G does *not* affect the price of the final output q and we no longer have constant returns to scale production. For example, a reduction in the salinity of irrigation water in a local region is unlikely to have an impact on crop prices since these are determined in a much larger market. Thus, the demand function for q is a horizontal line as shown in Figure 5.2.

A reduction in the marginal costs of producing q (from MC to MC') resulting from an increase in G will provide no benefits to consumers. All the benefits, given by area B in Figure 5.2, accrue to producers or, rather, to the owners of the fixed factors of production. Then how does one measure area B?

If producers are price takers in output markets, they are likely price takers in input markets; then the benefits of an increase in G accrue to owners of the fixed factor, land, since the owner of the fixed factor is the residual income claimant. The benefits of an increase in G are simply equal to the change in profits or fixed factor income – the increase in rent (see Chapter 4). Since increases in rent are capitalised in land values, changes in the land values of those farmers now using less saline water can be used to measure the benefits of improved water quality. If the production unit is small relative to both input and output markets, then changes in land values are a good indicator of the change in producer benefits. Otherwise, farm budget studies are needed to reveal the required data.

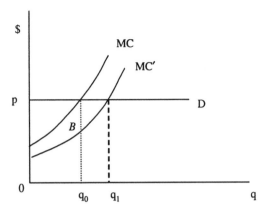

Figure 5.2 Welfare Measure with Infinite Elasticity of Output Demand

Finally, consider the case where an increase in the availability of G significantly increases the availability of q (local fresh vegetables), thereby shifting supply from S to S' and causing the price of q to fall (in the local market). Then there is both a change in consumer surplus and producer surplus due to the change in G (purer irrigation water). How does one estimate this area in practice? To obtain an estimate of the change in consumer surplus, it is necessary to estimate the ordinary demand function and calculate the appropriate area under it. The producer surplus is determined in the fashion discussed in the preceding paragraph. It is measured by the change in the net income of factor inputs.

If government agricultural policies support crop prices, then actual or market prices overstate social benefits. In this case, farm budget studies are required to determine the extent of producer benefits. Assuming that other crop prices are competitively determined (likely a heroic assumption), consumer benefits can be calculated in the same manner as above, but it will be necessary to include in the calculations the government support payments themselves as a cost to taxpayers. In all cases, it is worthwhile recalling the concept of *opportunity cost* and using it as a guide in calculating the benefits and costs of changes in the availability of a public good.

The above approaches are difficult to apply in practice. One means of doing so is through the damage function. Several studies have estimated damage functions for soil erosion for the Palouse region of eastern Washington and western Idaho, and for Saskatchewan (Walker and Young 1986; van Kooten, Weisensel and de Jong 1989). The physical component of the damage function provides information about the estimated yield loss when topsoil is removed, with topsoil loss related to particular agronomic practices. Given a physical relationship, it is possible to assess the value of topsoil, a commodity not traded in the market place, using information about crop yields, production costs and crop prices. It turns out that estimated damage functions for Saskatchewan and the Palouse region have steep slopes (high marginal damages) when topsoil depth is low, but slopes near zero (low to zero marginal damage) at topsoil depths that characterise most farms in the two regions. Damage from soil erosion in these regions is correspondingly small.

In Mali, a similar approach to that used in the Canadian and US studies was used to estimate a relationship between yield and soil loss. In contrast to the North American studies, costs of soil erosion in Mali were estimated to be significant, as high as 1.5% of GDP (Pearce and Warford 1993, pp. 23–4).

Damages from deforestation have also been valued in indirect fashion. Deforestation reduces the availability of wood for burning in some regions, with animal dung being used instead. The animal dung, in turn, is no longer available as a fertiliser in crop production, thereby reducing agricultural output. Since dung is bought and sold on markets, it can readily be valued. Using dung values, the costs of deforestation in Ethiopia are estimated to be some US$300 million annually (Pearce and Warford 1993, p. 25).

Market valuation of public goods via behavioural linkages

Behavioural linkages are more common than physical linkages, but they require a behavioural response to changes in the nonmarket commodity, and this response must somehow be measured. If there is no response to marginal changes in water quality, for example, then it is not possible to determine its value, even if it has value on average. Market valuation of public goods via behavioural linkages assumes that an individual's utility function includes the public good (G) as an argument: $U = U(q_1, q_2, ..., q_n, G)$, where q_i ($i = 1, ..., n$) represents goods that are traded in the market place.[1] As indicated in Chapter 2, the inverse Hicksian or compensated demand function can be determined, with the total benefit to an individual of an increase in the supply of the public good G given by the appropriate area under the inverse compensated demand function (equation (2.28)). This benefit is either the compensating or equivalent surplus of the change in the supply of the public good depending on whether the person has the right to the original or final level of the public good, respectively.

The tasks we are engaged in amount to detective work – we are attempting to measure the value of a change in the availability of a public good that is not traded in the marketplace using market data for related or affected goods and services. Of course, there are problems associated with investigations of this kind. The problems that are encountered in this particular piece of detective work concern the method by which the public good G enters the utility function. Several cases are discussed.

---

[1] The problem of aggregating over individuals is potentially serious, but usually ignored. This problem might be overcome by assuming a representative individual and multiplying the result by all persons in society.

Separability It is possible to partition goods in the utility function according to their "closeness". Suppose that there are six goods in the utility function and they are partitioned as $U(q_1, q_2, q_3, q_4, q_5, q_6) = \phi[u^1(q_1, q_2), u^2(q_3, q_4), u^3(q_5, q_6)]$, where ϕ is a monotonic transformation. A good q_1 is weakly separable in the utility function if changes in its availability affect only purchases of q_2, but not of q_3 and q_4. That is, a utility function is weakly separable if the marginal rate of substitution (MRS) between any pair of goods in the same group is independent of the availability of goods outside of that group (Freeman 1993, p. 101). The demand for q_1 (or q_2) is a function only of p_1 and p_2, and the expenditure share of that subset of goods. (The assumption of separability clearly simplifies econometric estimation of ordinary demand functions.) However, the MRS across two subsets of goods, say MRS(q_2,q_3), is not necessarily independent of the availability of goods in the third subset, say q_5. More generally, a utility function that is weakly separable in the public good G can be written as $U(q_i, q_j, G) = \phi[u^1(q_i, q_j), u^2(G)]$, $\forall i \neq j$, $i, j = 1,...,n$, where q_i and q_j refer to market goods (of which there are n). Weak separability implies that residual traces of changes in G might be found in the demands for the market goods.

Alternatively, for the case of six goods considered above, the utility function is strongly separable if it is written as $\phi[u^1(q_1, q_2) + u^2(q_3, q_4) + u^3(q_5, q_6)]$. In this case, the MRS across two subsets of goods, say MRS(q_2,q_3), is independent of the availability of goods in the third subset, say q_5. If G is strongly separable in the individual's utility function, so that utility is written as $\phi[u(q_i, q_j,) + v(G)]$, $\forall i \neq j$, $i,j = 1,...,n$, then purchases of other goods are unaffected by changes in the availability of G. Thus, while changes in the provision of the public good affect the level of utility, it is impossible to find a record of this impact in the market place.

Complements Perfect complementarity between a market good and an environmental good implies that they must be consumed in fixed proportions, say $q_1/G = k$, with consumption of q_1 equal to $\min(q_1/k, G)$. Then the amount of the market good consumed will be determined solely by the availability of the public good, but only as long as p_1 is below some critical value, say p_1^*. As G increases, purchases of q_1 will also increase because the individual will thereby increase her utility, and marginal WTP for G is positive. However, if the price of the market good is above p_1^*, the individual purchases less G than required to fully utilise the available amount of the public good and the marginal WTP for it is zero. This happens, for example, when area available for recreation exceeds the ability of recreation users to utilise the area – there is always recreation area that is under-utilised. There is no simple way to determine marginal WTP for G, however, and examples of perfect complementarity between an environmental amenity and a market good are difficult to envision (Freeman 1993, pp. 103–4).

Suppose, instead, that there is weak complementarity between the market commodity q_i and the public good G, so that the utility from consuming q_i increases with increases in the availability of G, *ceteris paribus*. For example, there is complementarity between water quality and demand for drinking water. If the demand for q_i (drinking water) is zero, the marginal utility of G (water quality) is zero (assuming that water for drinking is the only private good that depends on water quality and water quality does not give utility by itself). For welfare measurement, an increase in the availability of the public good must cause an outward shift in the demand function of the complementary good q_i. Then, under some restrictive conditions, the area above market price and between the new and old demand curves for q_i serves as an estimate of the benefit of increasing G. Without weak complementarity, there would be nothing to measure.

Consider Figure 5.3, where p^0 is the price of the market good (q) that is a weak complement of the environmental amenity G. Also assume that there is associated with some threshold level of the public good, G^*, a choke price for q, p^*, above which there will be no demand for the market activity. In other words, the compensating demand for q has a vertical intercept at some price: $h(p^*, G, U) = 0$. It is assumed, therefore, that there is some level of expenditure on other goods and services that sustains utility at the level indicated when $q = 0$. An additional requirement is that the derivative of the expenditure function be zero at the choke price: $\partial e(p^*, G, U)/\partial G = 0$.

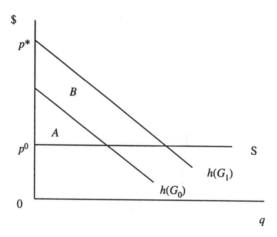

Figure 5.3 Welfare Measurement in Private Market under Weak Complementarity

Suppose that there is an increase in the availability of the environmental amenity from G_0 to G_1. This shifts the Hicksian demand functions for q from $h(G_0)$ to $h(G_1)$. Calculation of the benefit associated with this measure is divided into three stages (Freeman 1993, pp. 106-8). First, the price of q increases from p^0 to p^*, and the individual is compensated for the loss of area A. Second, the improvement in environmental quality causes an outward shift in demand for q, as indicated, but there is no gain in utility because q is priced at the choke price p^*. Finally, the reduction in price from p^* to p^0 results in a gain given by area $A + B$. The net gain is given by area B, since the consumer was compensated A in the first step. This is the compensating or equivalent variation measure of welfare depending on the reference level of utility for the compensated demand functions.

There remains a problem relating the compensated demand curves back to something that can be estimated. If the ordinary demand curves are used to determine the welfare estimate, Freeman (1993, pp. 110–11) shows that the error of measurement can be positive, negative or zero – the errors are of unknown sign and magnitude. However, exact welfare measurements can be used that permit one to recover the compensating demands from market demands (see Chapter 2).

Substitutes In the case of substitutes, welfare measurement often relies on knowledge of the underlying utility function. This is because the marginal WTP for the environmental amenity (w_G) can be expressed in terms of the price of a relevant market good multiplied by the MRS between it and the environmental amenity (Freeman 1993, p. 113): $w_G = p_i \, MRS(G, q_i)$. It is only in the case of perfect substitutes that it is possible to reduce w_G to something useable. Expenditures on private goods that substitute for the environmental amenity (e.g., in-house water filtration systems, bottled water) are examples of *defense expenditures* or *averting expenditures*. The degree to which such expenditures are truly representative of the benefits of improving water quality depends, of course, on the degree of substitutability between, say, purchased goods and municipal water quality (see also Chapter 6).

Averting measures related to drinking water, for example, are easily defined by consumers' purchases of bottled water or home water filtration systems (Chapter 6). In effect the consumer is combining market purchases (in-house water filtration) with the available level of the environmental amenity (water quality) to produce the preferred degree of water quality. Essentially, they produce a good $z = f(G, q)$, where $f(\cdot)$ can be considered a household production function (see below). Determination of the household expenditure function usually comprises two steps: first to see whether action is being taken to avoid contaminants in the water (e.g., bottled water, water filters, boiling), and second to measure the amount of money spent on averting action. The problem is an econometric one. First a binary logit or probit regression is used to determine factors that lead individuals to take averting action. The actual defense expenditures can then be adjusted using these results and employed as a measure of the potential benefits of public policies that change the availability or quality of the environmental amenity.

A marginal change in spending on the household good z is an appropriate measure of welfare change associated with marginal changes in G. This is not the case, however, if improvements in the environmental amenity are non-marginal. As environmental quality improves, people will reduce spending on q to produce z. If the change is large enough, there will be an income effect associated with reduced spending on q so that people will wish more z, thereby increasing purchases of q accordingly. For example, in the case of bottled water, people may purchase bottled water because they acquire a preference for the convenience and fresher taste of bottled water, and not because they seek to avoid a real or perceived externality.

Finally, even if it is not possible to derive appropriate welfare measures based on averting behaviour (especially in the case where substitutability is not perfect), defense expenditures do provide some guidance. If an individual's defense expenditures exceed their stated value for improvements in environmental quality, say, then the stated value is not reliable. We discuss elicitation of stated values below. First we consider an example to demonstrate how tracing behavioural linkages can be useful for valuing changes in the availability or quality of environmental amenities. We use coral bleaching and its effect on utility from diving as a motivating example for the methodology discussed above.

The Cost of Coral Bleaching

In the summer of 1998, experts noted large-scale bleaching of coral in the Indian Ocean that is, among other factors, allegedly caused by El Nino. When water temperatures increase beyond a certain threshold, coral animals expel the algae with which they live in symbiosis. Without the algae, coral appears white (hence the term "bleaching"), but, if the temperature does not return to its "normal" range within a period of some months, the coral dies. It has been estimated that about 80% of the coral near the Maldives has died as a result of coral bleaching, although it is not known if this is an irreversible event, and some coral species seem to be more sensitive to temperature changes than others. Coral bleaching will likely affect the Maldives economy, which is heavily dependent on diving tourism. In addition, divers visiting the Maldives will experience a loss in well-being, *ceteris paribus*. We are interested in how one might measure this loss in utility.

Divers visiting the Maldives can still enjoy good coral diving if they change their behaviour slightly. Specifically, they can choose to (i) dive deeper where water temperatures are likely constant, or (ii) dive further from the harbour, visiting the few undisturbed patches (recall that 20% is unaffected). Diving further implies spending more time on the boat and using more fuel to arrive at the destination. Assume that the behavioural response to coral bleaching is costly, and that the cost increment is somehow measurable. Divers can "produce" a diving experience D. First, assume that the diving experience is a function of the quality of coral (c) and diving gear plus effort to get to the diving location, G. The diving production function is:

$$(5.1) \quad D = D(G; c),$$

The diver faces the following budget constraint:

$$(5.2) \quad I = PG + B + x$$

where P is the price of diving gear; B is the bid amount (see below); and x is other goods purchased by the diver, with the price of x set to 1. Divers have the following utility function:

$$(5.3) \quad U = U(x, D) = U[x, D(G; c)].$$

We can now define the Lagrangian function $L = U(\cdot) + \lambda(I - PG - B - x)$, and solve for the first derivatives with respect to the choice variables x and G. The first-order conditions give:

$$(5.4) \quad U_x P = U_D D_G,$$

where subscripts refer to partial derivatives of the function. Total differentiating utility and income:

(5.5) $dU = U_x dx + U_D D_G dG + U_D D_c dc = 0$

(5.6) $dI = dx + PdG + dB = 0.$

Equation (5.5) can be rewritten as:

(5.5′) $dx = -\dfrac{1}{U_x}(U_D D_G dG + U_D D_c dc).$

Similarly, rewrite (5.6) as

(5.6′) $dx = -PdG - dB.$

Combining (5.5′) and (5.6′) yields:

(5.7) $PdG + dB = \dfrac{1}{U_x}(U_D D_G dG + U_D D_c dc),$

which can be rewritten as

(5.7′) $(PU_x - U_D D_G)\,dG + dB = \dfrac{1}{U_x} U_D D_c dc.$

Finally, substituting the optimality condition (5.4) in equation (5.7′), and solving, gives:

(5.8) $\dfrac{dB}{dc} = \dfrac{P}{D_G} D_c.$

The compensating variation, or change in bid amount that keeps the diver at his original utility level (thus compensating for the loss in coral quality), is a function only of the price of diving gear and the diving production function. The diver is indifferent between the old situation (income plus pre-coral bleaching diving) and post-coral bleaching diving if an income transfer of amount dB/dc is provided.

To estimate the welfare loss for divers as a result of coral bleaching, one approach is to construct a diving production function $D(\cdot)$, and proceed as outlined above. The welfare loss is modest if (i) coral is not an important input in diving experiences (D_c is small), or (ii) the incremental cost associated with the behavioural response (going deeper or further) is small (either because P is low, or because D_G is great).

Property values, benefit estimation and hedonic pricing

A particular example of nonmarket measurement using market transactions for other goods is the hedonic pricing method that studies property values. Hedonic pricing assumes that environmental characteristics and public goods affect the productivity of land in production or its desirability in consumption. The structure of land prices and rents reflects these environmentally determined productivity/desirability differences. The best example of individuals choosing the amount of public goods they want occurs with respect to the choices they make concerning house purchases. People choose to live in areas that have cleaner air or less crime, they choose to live near airports or along highways, and they choose to live on quiet or on busy streets. The choice is determined by what they are willing and able to pay for housing. Hedonic pricing exploits these choices by estimating implicit prices for house characteristics that differentiate closely related housing classes. In this way, it is possible to estimate demand curves for such characteristics or public goods as air quality and noise. Thus, the hedonic pricing technique requires that the following three questions be answered in the affirmative:

1. Do environmental variables systematically affect land prices?
2. Is knowledge of this relationship sufficient to predict changes in land prices from changes in air pollution levels, say?
3. Do changes in land prices accurately measure the underlying welfare changes?

If any of these is not answered in the affirmative, the methodology can not be applied.

Hedonic pricing is a two-stage procedure (Freeman 1979a, 1995). Begin by letting Q be a composite consumption good (with price equal 1), C a vector of housing characteristics, N a vector of neighbourhood characteristics, and G a vector of environmental amenities. For example, C includes such things as size of lot, number of rooms, age of house, number of bathrooms and liveable floor space; N measures proximity to a fire station, nearness to shopping, distance to the city centre, zoning characteristics of the neighbourhood, and so on; and G constitutes such things as the crime rate, air quality and noise. The public goods must differ among neighbourhoods (or houses) and must somehow be measurable; for example, air quality and the neighbourhood crime rate can be measured, as can distance to the nearest fire hall and/or fire hydrant. It is assumed that the urban area as a whole can be treated as a single market for housing services and that people choose to purchase a housing bundle that best satisfies their utility over these characteristics, subject to their budget, m. Hence, they are assumed to have information on all the alternatives and are able to buy anywhere in the urban area (subject to their budget). The supply of housing and its characteristics is not modeled, so housing prices are assumed to be in equilibrium.

The price of the ith house, P_i, is a function of its various characteristics and amenities:

(5.9) $P_i = P(C_i, N_i, G_i)$.

Relation (5.9) is often referred to as the *hedonic or implicit price function* and is obtained by regression. The implicit price of a private characteristic of housing in the region of concern is found by partial differentiating the hedonic price function with respect to that characteristic. If c_1 is the number of rooms in a house, then $\partial P/\partial c_1$ is the implicit price of a room. This is the amount that an additional room will add to the value of a house, *ceteris paribus*. It is the additional amount that must be paid if an individual chooses a house with a higher level of c_1.

The utility of the household living in house i is given by $u(Q, G_i, C_i, N_i)$. It is assumed that preferences are weakly separable in housing and its characteristics so that the demands for housing characteristics are independent of the prices of other goods. The budget constraint for a household that occupies the ith house is $m - P_i - Q = 0$. The Lagrangian function is:

(5.10) $L = u(Q, G_i, C_i, N_i) + \lambda(m - P_i - Q)$.

The related first-order conditions are (with the i subscript denoting the household in house i):

(5.11) $\dfrac{\partial u}{\partial g_j} - \lambda \dfrac{\partial P_i}{\partial g_j} = 0$

and

(5.12) $\dfrac{\partial u}{\partial Q} - \lambda = 0$,

where $g_j \in G$. Solving (5.11) and (5.12) gives:

(5.13) $\dfrac{\partial u / \partial g_j}{\partial u / \partial Q} = \dfrac{\partial P_i}{\partial g_j}$,

which is the first-order condition for environmental amenity g_j. Condition (5.13) says that a house buyer will purchase additional amounts of each amenity as long as the WTP for those amenities is greater than the cost of purchasing them. In equilibrium, the marginal WTP for an additional unit of the environmental amenity just equals the marginal implicit price of that amenity.

The above analysis results in a measure of the marginal WTP for (shadow price of) the environmental amenity g_j, but it does not directly reveal the marginal willingness to pay function. To find the marginal WTP or bid function, a second step is required.

In the second stage, it is assumed that the individual purchases only *one* housing bundle (or, if more, that they are equivalent). The individual stays at some level of utility with the utility function being weakly separable in housing so that prices of other goods can he omitted in the specification of the marginal willingness to pay or bid function. The bid function for environmental amenity g_j by the individual who chooses the *i*th house is:

$$(5.14) \quad b_j = \frac{\partial P_i}{\partial g_j} = b_j\,(g_j, G^*, C, N, u^*),$$

where the *i* subscript is dropped for convenience, G^* is a vector of environmental amenities excluding g_j, and u^* is the reference level of utility. Equation (5.14) is also obtained by regression. Note that, if P_i in (5.9) is linear in g_j, then, from (5.13), the implicit price of an increase in the environmental amenity would be the same regardless of its current availability – the marginal value of air quality, say, does not change according to the level of air quality. When estimating the second stage of the hedonic technique, it is necessary (for estimation purposes) that the value on the LHS of (5.14) is variable, which is only true if (5.9) is nonlinear in g_j. Presumably , the value of an additional unit of clean air is worth more when air quality is poor than when it is good.

When there is a change in amenity g_j from g_j^0 to g_j^1, *ceteris paribus*, the change in the welfare of the individual who chooses the *i*th house is determined as:

$$(5.15) \quad W_{g_j^0 \to g_j^1} = \int_{g_j^0}^{g_j^1} b_j(g_{ji}, G_i^*, C_i, N_i, u^*)dg_j ,$$

This is the welfare for a single individual only. The aggregate welfare change W_g for a change in g_j is given by:

$$(5.16) \quad W_g = \sum_{i=1}^{n} \int_{g_j^0}^{g_j^1} b_j(g_{ji}, G_i^*, C_i, N_i, u^*)dg_j ,$$

where *i* indexes both houses and individuals, and the population is *n*.

A problem is that a change in one characteristic can change the quantities of the other characteristics a person desires and can even change the hedonic price function itself. This is similar to the standard identification problem of econometrics. First, b_j is not directly observable. It is calculated from $\partial P_i/\partial g_j$. Then b_j is regressed on the same variables used to estimate P_i. Since no additional data is utilised beyond that already contained in the hedonic price function, the coefficients on the regressors of

g_j are identical to those of P_i. Second, the amount of a characteristic and its marginal implicit price are both endogenous in the model, unlike most consumer purchases where price is exogenous. This makes it difficult to separate the effects of demand shifters from the price-quantity relationship itself. One approach to solving the identification problem is to find some truly exogenous variables that act as instrumental variables. But, even if the identification problem is resolved, it is the uncompensated bid function that is estimated, which raises questions about the validity of the welfare measures (as noted in Chapter 2).

Empirical studies that have used the hedonic pricing method to determine the effect of aircraft and traffic noise on housing prices find that there is a measurable effect. For aircraft noise, a one-unit change in the measure of noise (as related to human hearing and discomfort) resulted in housing prices that were 0.5–2.0% lower, while traffic noise reduced house prices by 0.1–0.7% per decibel (Lesser et al. 1997, p. 281).

5.2 Recreation Demand and the Travel Cost Method

To assess benefits from recreation, the travel cost method emerged as perhaps the first technique for valuing nonmarket benefits (Clawson 1959; Thrice and Wood 1958). The travel cost method is a type of revealed preference model where

1. individuals are observed to incur costs so as to consume commodities related to the environmental amenity of interest, and
2. the commodities consumed are not purchased in a market where prices are determined by supply and demand.

A number of different approaches are available for estimating welfare gains/losses in what is generally termed the "travel cost" framework, and some are examined in this section. The original travel cost method was no more than an empirical means of deriving a demand schedule, without the theoretical background necessary for welfare measurement.

A theoretically appropriate version of the travel cost model can be illustrated with the aid of Figure 5.4 (due to Edwards et al. 1976). Assume that there is a single recreational site and that consumers have the option of staying home or travelling to the site and participating in recreational activities. The amount spent on all other goods and services (indicated by $) is plotted on the vertical axis and the number of days spent at the site (d) is plotted on the horizontal axis. Since recreation is not a necessity, in the sense that individuals can live without it, the indifference curves do not intersect the horizontal axis; however, they do intersect the vertical axis since some amount of one's budget must be spent on "all-goods-other-than-recreation" to survive.

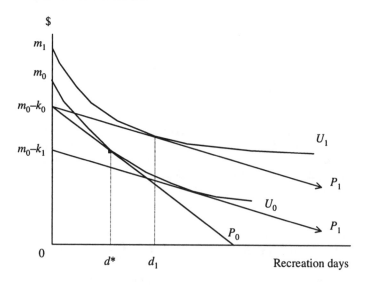

Figure 5.4 Constructing a Theoretical Recreation Demand Model

Now assume that the individual starts with some initial income m_0 (equal to an equivalent amount of goods whose price is 1). Further, suppose that the cost of getting to the site (the travel cost) is k_0, and the entry fee or price of q is initially P_0. If recreation is to take place, the budget line begins at the point labelled $m_0 - k_0$ because this is the amount of budget available for recreation at the site once one takes into account the cost of getting to the site. Given that the indifference curve through m_0 (U_0) is tangent to the budget line with slope determined by P_0, the person is indifferent between staying home and going to the site and staying for d^* days. If the entrance fee to the park were greater than P_0, then the person would stop visiting the site altogether. That is, for prices less than P_0, the individual will participate in recreation, but not for prices above this critical value. Thus, d^*, k_0 and P_0 are critical values for the given budget, travel cost and entry fee – the individual will either participate in recreation for d^* or more days, or not at all.

Now, if the entry price were reduced to P_1 ($< P_0$), the individual would take d_1 days of recreation at the site, enabling her to get on an indifference curve (U_1) that is higher than that going through m_0. The equivalent amount of income to this level of utility is given by m_1. From equation (2.19) in Chapter 2 and Figure 5.4, the compensating variation of an increase in the entry price (from P_0 to P_1) is given by $k_1 - k_0$.

Finally, the travel cost itself influences decisions. At a price of P_0, an increase in the travel cost to k_1 will prevent the person from going to the site for recreation. If the entry fee were subsequently reduced to P_1, then the individual can still attain U_0, but she remains indifferent to staying home or visiting the site.

It is clear that the graphical analysis in Figure 5.4 can be used to derive a demand curve such as $R = d(P, k, m)$, which differs from the demand curve $R = t(P', m)$, where P' refers to travel costs plus entry fee. In this case, not only does income shift the demand function, but so does the travel cost. The point is that the approach discussed with reference to Figure 5.4 can be used to formulate a demand function that can be empirically estimated: demand is a function of entrance fees, consumer income, travel cost and the prices of complements and substitutes. In principle, data can be collected on each of these variables. Furthermore, the model provides theoretically sound estimates of well being.

Household production function approach

The household production function approach begins with Becker's (1965) household production model. Households combine market purchased goods, $q = (q_1, ..., q_n)$, with time t_z to produce the commodities $z = (z_1, ..., z_m)$ from which they obtain utility. The production function is $z = f(q, t_z)$, with elements of z and q being identical in some cases. What distinguishes recreation from other household products is that time and q are combined to produce recreational experiences rather than other household products. Thus, the problem facing a household with respect to recreation decisions can be represented by (Bockstael 1995):

(5.17)

$$\text{Maximise} \quad U(z)$$

$$\text{subject to} \quad (m_0 + w(t_w))\,(1 - \tau) - c(z, t_z, p) = 0 \text{ and } T - t_w - t_z\,z = 0$$

In problem (5.17), the household seeks to maximise utility as a function of all goods (where q is collapsed into z), although the focus is on recreation. The first constraint in (5.17) is a budget constraint, where m_0 is annual non-wage income and $w(t_w)$ is annual wage income as a function of the time spent working, with total income corrected for taxes where τ is the marginal tax rate on any income received. The final expression in the budget constraint, $c(z, t_z, p)$, is a joint marginal cost function for purchases of all z (similar to the above production function); in this case, p is the marginal money cost associated with purchases of goods and services. The second constraint is a total time (T) constraint, with time allocated to working and producing z, with t_z being a vector of per unit time costs for producing z.

By substituting the second constraint into the first, assuming work time t_w is a choice variable, a constant wage rate w^* and that p_z is a vector of constant marginal money costs for each commodity, the model can be written as (Bockstael 1995):

(5.18)

$$\text{Maximise} \quad U(z)$$

$$\text{s.t.} \quad (m_0 + w^*\,(T - t_z\,z))\,(1 - \tau) - p_z\,z = 0$$

Solving gives the demand functions for z:

(5.19) $z = z[p_z + (1 - \tau) w \, t_z, (1 - \tau)(m_o + w \, T)]$.

In (5.19), the demand for recreation is a function of (1) prices that are equal to z's marginal money cost plus its time cost, and (2) full, after tax income if all available time is used for work.

There are a number of problems with the household function approach to travel cost. Time spent accessing the recreation site is "some fraction" of the individual's wage rate, while the model assumes that individuals can freely substitute work and leisure. Since data for the travel cost model are often obtained by surveying recreationists, it should also be possible to ask recreationists about the extent to which they can substitute work for leisure (but this is not done). The household production model fails to distinguish between on-site time and access time, with the former not valued in most models. Finally, if there are multiple destinations during a trip, there is no clear way of allocating fixed trip costs over sites (which is also a problem in the previous model).

The accepted welfare measure in the household production function model is the change in the expenditure function brought about by the change in the parameter of interest (price of entry, travel cost, site amenities, etc.). The expenditure function is calculated in the usual way (as discussed in Chapter 2).

Limited dependent variable models

In cases where it is not possible for the economic researcher to conduct her own travel cost survey, it may be possible to employ available information from parks, government agencies and so on. Such information may consist simply of number of visitors to a site (or to a number of different sites), along with a variety of variables that might include the origin, income level and other characteristics of visitors, and site specific data. If information on distance travelled is available, a travel cost approach might be used. If this information is not available, it may be possible to employ a count model that uses Poisson regression.

In the case where it is known only whether an individual visited a particular site or not, the following statistical model can be employed:

$q = f(x) + \varepsilon$ when $f(x) + \varepsilon \geq 0$ (person visits site)

$q = 0$ when $f(x) + \varepsilon < 0$ (person does not visit site)

where q is visits, x is a vector of available characteristics for visitors and non-visitors (e.g., distance from their residence to the site), and ε is a random error term. The model is generally estimated as a probit or logit function, but any distribution function can be used. The nature of the models employed is discussed further with respect to the random utility recreation demand model and the binary choice, contingent valuation method. Suffice to say, the problem is that we do not obtain information on persons who do not visit the site. For these situations, economists employ a variety of approaches that include sample selectivity tests and use of truncated observations.

Travel cost model with site attributes

The traditional travel cost model explains demand for number of trips over a specified time horizon (a season or year) for either one or several recreation sites or activities. The number of trips is decided within a planning horizon where diminishing marginal utility is associated with increasing frequency of trips. Traditional travel cost models have been estimated for single sites; demand systems have been estimated for multiple sites; and single equation models have been estimated for multiple sites, incorporating characteristics that vary over sites. When valuation of a price change at a single site (or its complete elimination) is required, a single-site demand curve can be used. However, behavioural models need to capture substitution among recreational sites if environmental quality changes are to be valued; variation in quality can often be found only by looking across sites with varying quality dimensions. Originally, recreation demand models were used to value sites and to predict how changes in travel costs and entry fees would affect demand. Now, however, they are used to assess the welfare effects (benefits or costs) of changes in environmental amenities or the quality characteristics of the recreational experience. Therefore, we wish to look at models that explicitly incorporate site attributes.

Hedonic Travel Cost

The hedonic pricing method can also be applied to recreation demand estimation, but the problems involved are complex. Simply, total household expenditures on recreation at a particular site take on the role of property value in the hedonic or implicit price function. Expenditures by a large number of households engaged in recreation at more than one site are regressed on a variety of private and public characteristics of the various sites. Again, by partial differentiating the hedonic price function with respect to any of the public attributes, an implicit price for that attribute is obtained. In the second stage, the implicit prices for the attribute are regressed on household characteristics, particularly income, and the amount of the attribute available, howsoever measured. The resulting equation is the demand function for the attribute. The area under the demand function can then be used to measure the benefit of a change in the amount of the public good. In practice, it is not easy to implement hedonic pricing.

The hedonic travel cost method seeks to identify the demand for the various amenities associated with the physical attributes of recreational sites, and thereby the benefits of changes in site attributes. In this respect it is similar to the hedonic price method described in conjunction with the value of housing. However, the hedonic travel cost method is more closely aligned with the travel cost approach described above. Indeed, it is possible to derive the benefits of a change in attributes using the travel cost approach, but this requires that one estimate the demand for a site before and after the change in attributes occurs (Wilman 1988). Welfare measurement is illustrated with the aid of Figure 5.5.

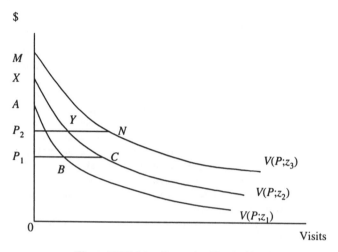

Figure 5.5 Valuing Recreation Site Attributes

In Figure 5.5, the curves labelled $V(P; z)$ represent the demand for recreation visits as a function of travel costs P (where P includes travel cost, time and entry fees) and site attributes z (e.g., number of wildlife species observed). Attributes shift the demand function; thus, the demand for visits when site attributes are z_2 lies outside the demand when attributes are z_1, and likewise for z_3. Suppose there are two sites that the recreationist might wish to visit. Site 1 has a travel cost of P_1, while site 2 has travel costs of P_2. The demand functions for the two sites differ according to the level of physical attributes available at each site; suppose the demand functions are $V(P; z_1)$ and $V(P; z_2)$ at sites 1 and 2, respectively. Then the net benefits of recreation at site 1 are given by area ABP_1, while the net benefits of choosing site 2 are given by area XYP_2. If site 1 is chosen over site 2, then area ABP_1 must be greater than area XYP_2.

Now suppose that the attributes at site 1 change (e.g., some bird species is now observed at the site) so that the demand curve associated with site 1 is no longer $V(P; z_1)$ but $V(P; z_2)$, which is identical to that for site 2. Since site 1 was chosen previously, it will be chosen again. The net benefit of the improvement in attributes at site 1 is given by area $(XCP_1 - ABP_1) =$ area $AXCB$. If, on the other hand, attributes at site 2 were to change from z_2 to z_3, so that the new demand function is $V(P; z_3)$, then the benefit of such a change will depend upon whether the recreationist shifts away from site 1 or not. If site 1 continues to be the preferred site, the benefits of the improvements at site 2 are essentially zero. If site 2 is now chosen over site 1, the measure of benefits is given by area MNP_2 minus area ABP_1.

While the travel cost method is based on a marginal utility condition describing the choice of the number of visits to a site, the hedonic travel cost technique is based on a marginal utility condition describing the choice of site quality and, implicitly, the actual site itself. The travel cost method requires observations on a wide range of recreationists who have come various travel distances in order to be able to identify the demand curve for trips. With regard to the demand for attributes, the travel cost method works best if site choice remains fixed as the visit level changes.

The hedonic travel cost procedure works best when the visit level remains fixed as the site choice changes. The hedonic method seeks to measure the demand for site characteristics or attributes directly. It requires only that the sample of users be spread around at various sites within a recreational area (e.g., national park or forest area) so that they face various costs of using a particular site. These costs vary due not only to travel distances, but also due to the physical attributes of the sites. In this way, a demand function for site attributes can be identified.

While the theoretical model upon which the travel cost method is based does not really permit visits to more than one site, it can easily be modified in practice to allow for the use of several sites. The same is not true of the hedonic price approach. It requires that individuals select only one site out of the ones that are available.

Random Utility Recreation Models (RURM)

The extra time and money an individual is willing to spend to access a site with more desirable amenities provides useful information for valuation of those amenities. The RURM relies on discrete choice among a finite set of alternative sites on any given trip occasion rather than the continuous choice of how many recreational trips to take in an arbitrary period of time. Compared to traditional models (that work best when substitution is not an issue), RURMs work best if substitution among sites is an important element of the decision problem. This then yields information about the importance of site amenities in the decision.

The random utility recreation model focuses on "where to go" on a given choice occasion; that is, the choice is that of deciding where to go on one of the trips taken within the arbitrary period, conditioned on the taking of recreational trips during that period. The individual or household gets utility $v_j(g_j, m - p_j - wt_j)$ from visiting site j on a given choice occasion, conditional on the probability of taking a trip. Vector g_j consists of quality characteristics at site j, m is the budget for recreation (so separability of the utility function is assumed), and $p_j + wt_j$ is cost of accessing site j. Then,

$$(5.20) \quad v_j(g_j, m - p_j - wt_j) = \max[v_s(g_s, m - p_s - wt_s) \; \forall \; s \in S],$$

where S is the set of all available recreational sites (Bockstael 1995). Assume v_j are linear so that

$$(5.21) \quad v_j(g_j, m - p_j - wt_j) = \alpha_0 g_j + \alpha_1(m - p_j - wt_j) + \varepsilon_j,$$

where the distribution of ε_j determines the choice of regression model. The probability that the individual chooses site j is:

$$(5.22) \quad Pr(j) = \frac{e^{\alpha x_j}}{\underset{s \in S}{\bigcup} e^{\alpha x_s}},$$

which is found by regression analysis. In (5.22), x_i refers to the set of explanatory variables that determine why one site is preferred to another (e.g., household income, size, ages of members, etc.). Depending on whether one assumes a cumulative logistics or cumulative normal probability distribution, the model is estimated as a multinomial logit or probit, respectively. The problem with the multinomial logit is that it imposes independence of irrelevant alternatives (Herriges and Kling 1997; Maddala 1983).

In many applied situations, however, it is necessary to assume that the "odds" of choosing one alternative over another are independent of one or more of the alternatives available in S – it may not be possible for a recreationist to identify all the sites in S. Then, the "odds" of choosing one site over another are (Bockstael 1995):

$$(5.23) \quad \frac{Pr(i)}{Pr(k)} = \exp[\alpha_0 (g_i - g_k) + \alpha_1(p_i + wt_i - p_k - wt_k)].$$

Income (m) does not change over the alternatives in the pairwise case and so does not enter the equation to be estimated. Another problem is linking the choice of number of trips over a season with the choice of site on a particular trip because the error terms are clearly linked.

Finally, it can be shown that an appropriate measure of welfare associated with the RURM is (Bockstael 1995):

$$(5.24) \quad W \approx \frac{1}{\alpha_{price}}\left(\ln \sum_e v_i g_i^1 - \ln \sum_e v_i g_i^0 \right),$$

where α_{price} is the estimated coefficient on the price term, which needs to be assumed equal to the marginal utility of income. This is a measure of the compensating surplus associated with changes in site attributes.

5.3 The Contingent Valuation Method

Nonmarket values associated with forests, for example, are classified into use and nonuse (or passive use) values. Use values refer to the values individuals place on activities such as outdoor recreation and the unpriced benefits that accrue to society as a result of particular forest ecosystem functions, such as water storage and cleansing, and waste assimilation. Compared to nonuse values, use values can be said to derive from direct physical contact with the resource (consumption of services), although distinction is made between consumptive use (e.g., fishing, hunting) and non-consumptive use (e.g., wildlife viewing). Although it is generally thought that the methods for measuring use benefits, such as the travel cost method and hedonic pricing, provide reasonable estimates of true values because they rely on market data, there remain technical and other difficulties with these methods (see, e.g., Sagoff 1994; Randall 1994). These are likely less onerous and certainly less controversial than those associated with the measurement of passive use benefits. However, the aforementioned methods have very little applicability to the real problems we now face (Knetsch 2000). Rather, there is great demand for passive use values.

In this section, we focus on the methods and difficulties of valuing nonuse benefits – the benefits derived from individuals' demands to preserve forestlands and biodiversity, say – using the contingent valuation method (CVM). Nonuse values are thought to include existence values independent of any behaviour related to current use, as well as bequest, option, altruism and other inherent values.[2] While nonuse values are generally estimated using the traditional contingent valuation method, other methods have been proposed (e.g., conjoint analysis, choice experiments, fuzzy contingent valuation). Some of these are discussed in section 5.4.

CVM attempts explicitly (via surveys) to elicit information concerning the minimum level of compensation required by an individual to forgo a public good (compensation demanded) or the maximum amount the individual would be willing to pay to obtain the nonmarket amenity. Because a survey is used, this approach is often referred to as the direct approach in contrast to the indirect approach of determining the value of nonmarket commodities from information about market transactions for other, related goods and services.

> Contingent valuation devices involve asking individuals, in survey or experimental settings, to reveal their personal valuations of increments (or decrements) in unpriced goods by using contingent markets. These markets define the good or amenity of interest, the status quo level of provision and the offered increment or decrement therein, the institutional structure under which the good is to be provided, the method of payment, and (implicitly or explicitly) the decision rule which determines whether to implement the offered program. Contingent markets are highly structured to confront respondents with a well-defined situation and to elicit a circumstantial choice upon the occurrence of the posited situation. Contingent markets elicit contingent choices. (Cummings et al. 1986, p. 3)

The contingent valuation method is needed when amenities to be valued are assumed to leave no behavioural trail for economists to employ.[3] This assumption has been questioned by Larson (1993), who argues that purchases of nature books, watching nature films, memberships in nature organisations and so on constitute a behavioural trail that can be used for valuation. However, his interpretation requires

---

[2] Existence value is the value of simply knowing that an environmental asset exists, while bequest value is WTP to endow the future generation with the asset. Option value, which is a measure of people's risk aversion to factors that might affect future access to or use of environmental or biological assets, is not a component of nonuse value (Carson et al. 1997). Option value is discussed further in Chapter 9.

[3] CVM can also be used to value goods traded in markets, which is useful for testing how well hypothetical responses to purchasing decisions correspond to actual ones (Harrison 1989; Kahneman and Knetsch 1992a; Knetsch 1995; 2000).

untestable assumptions that restrict individual preferences (Bockstael and McConnell 1993).

An important use of contingent valuation surveys is to determine preservation values for such things as tropical rain forests (Kramer and Mercer 1997). Preservation value is somewhat different from passive use value in that it includes option value in addition to existence and bequest values. Preservation values can be substantial. For example, Kramer and Mercer found that US residents were willing to make a one-time payment of $1.9–2.8 billion (assuming 91 million households) to protect an additional 5% of tropical forests. Preservation benefits for wildlife were estimated by Canadian economists to be in the neighbourhood of $68 million per year for Alberta residents (Phillips et al. 1989), while preservation of old-growth forests is valued at perhaps $150 per household per year (van Kooten 1995b). A summary of some studies on the preservation of wildlife species and nature is provided in Chapter 9. This evidence suggests that ignoring preservation values in the management of natural resources could lead to substantial misallocation of these resources.

CVM has been approved by the US Department of the Interior for implementing regulations under the Comprehensive Environmental Response, Compensation, and Liability Act (CERCLA) of 1980 and its amendments of 1986. In 1990, the US Oil Pollution Act extended liability to oil spills (as oil was not considered a hazardous waste). A 1989 decision by the District of Columbia Court of Appeals involving CERCLA in the case of *Ohio v. Department of Interior* affirmed the use of CVM and permitted inclusion of nonuse values in the assessment of total compensable damages (Castle et al. 1994). Thus, in the USA, CVM is used both for determining compensation when firms or individuals damage the environment and in cost-benefit analysis. Similar requirements for use of CVM in Canada and other countries do not exist, at least officially. Presumably this explains why economists in the USA have devoted more attention to CVM than economists in Europe and Canada.

As noted, the contingent valuation method uses questionnaires or surveys to elicit directly how much individuals are willing to pay for an increase in the availability of a public good or how much they would demand in compensation to forgo the increase. As discussed below, the valuation question can be elicited using either an open-ended or dichotomous choice (sometimes awkwardly referred to as "closed-ended") format. The individual responses to the survey are then used to obtain a median or mean household value for the unpriced or nonmarket commodity. The contingent valuation method has been criticised because it requires an individual to respond to hypothetical situations. As a result, various types of bias may occur and these biases can only be removed through proper design of the contingent device and proper training of those responsible for gathering the required data. In the following paragraphs, we briefly discuss these issues (Bishop et al. 1995; Mitchell and Carson 1989; Cummings et al. 1986).

In the remainder of this section, we first consider the underlying theoretical and empirical foundations of the contingent valuation method. Then problems associated with contingent valuation surveys are presented. Since some argue that the contingent valuation method is fundamentally flawed, we consider some of the fundamental objections to the CVM approach. Alternative approaches for obtaining benefit estimates using a survey device are discussed in section 5.4.

Welfare measurement using CVM: Theory

The contingent valuation method uses surveys to elicit either WTP for a hypothetical change in the availability of an environmental amenity, such as improved water quality, or willingness-to-accept compensation (WTA), or compensation demanded, to forgo the change. The maximum amount a consumer is WTP for improved water quality is a measure of compensating surplus (CS), while minimum WTA is a measure of equivalent surplus (ES) (see Chapter 2). Whether CS or ES is elicited depends on whether, in the contingency, the respondent has the right to the change (ES), or not (CS) and must pay for it. The two most widely used methods for eliciting WTP or WTA are the open-ended and dichotomous choice (DC) approaches. Kealy and Turner (1993) recognised that, if contingent values are sensitive to question format, the validity of either one or both of the methods is questionable. The two approaches assume different things about the respondent's knowledge of her utility function.

Open-ended Model

Until the paper by Bishop and Heberlein (1979), the standard approach to eliciting information about nonuse values in a CVM framework was to employ an open-ended format. Because no values are suggested to responds (all values are possible), this is also called the continuous value approach. After providing the necessary information about the contingency to be valued (Mitchell and Carson 1989, 1995), the researcher would simply ask questions of the following types: "What is the maximum amount that you would be willing to pay in an increased water bill to improve water quality from 12mg. nitrates per litre to 6mg. nitrates per litre?" "What is the maximum amount you are willing to pay in increased income taxes for a program [described in detail in the survey] that will increase by 500 the number of grizzly bears in Alaska?" The target nitrate level or number of bears to be preserved can be varied across respondents, but often is not. The first question could be modified so that it asks about minimum compensation demanded to forgo an improvement in water quality. The second question could be modified in similar fashion. The answers to the open-ended question are then summed and divided by the number of respondents to obtain an average value of WTP or WTA for a household.[4] Assuming that the characteristics of households in the sample are similar to those in the population (which can be tested), an estimate of total WTP (value of the contingency) is obtained by multiplying average sample WTP by the total number of households in the target population.

Alternatively, one can estimate a bid curve,

(5.25) $W = f(g, m, s)$,

---

[4] In CVM surveys, there is often no significant difference between the answers respondents provide as individuals and those they provide when asked to behave as a representative of a household (Hausman 1993).

where W is the stated WTP or compensation demanded, g is the target nitrate level in water (for the first question above) or number of bears (second question), m is income, and s is a vector of respondent characteristics that might affect WTP (e.g., age, education, attitudes, household size). Differentiating (5.25) with respect to g results in an inverse Hicksian demand curve. There is no *a priori* assumption about the functional form of (5.17), except that it must satisfy the requirements of an expenditure function; Sellar et al. (1986) recommend the use of a function that is quadratic in g. A linear tobit can also be used as it is considered sound from a theoretical standpoint (Halstead et al. 1991).

The open-ended format may lead to strategic behaviour by respondents who know full well that it is unlikely they will have to pay the amount declared, although the survey instrument should identify clearly how the stated amount is to be paid (Mitchell and Carson 1995). Some researchers have found that open-ended formats lead to lower average WTP than do dichotomous choice formats, but this too might be evidence of strategic behaviour by respondents (Boyle et al. 1996). However, with improvements in survey design (including better pre-testing procedures), more confidence has been placed in the open-ended format.

A variant of the open-ended approach is for the researcher to hone in on an individual's WTA compensation, or maximum WTP, using a bidding procedure. The interviewer suggests a particular value and then increments this value up or down (depending upon the respondent's answer) until the actual WTP or WTA is found for the contingency in question.

According to Hanemann and Kriström (1995), it is only if the respondent is thought to have a complete preference ordering, without any uncertainty, that it is appropriate to elicit WTP or WTA directly. If this is not the case, they argue, a dichotomous choice approach may be preferred.

Dichotomous Choice Model

A number of arguments have been raised in favour of dichotomous choice over the open-ended approach (Hanemann and Kriström 1995). First, the DC format best mimics an actual market choice. In actual markets, consumers are confronted with the choice of purchasing or not purchasing a commodity at a given price. A DC contingent question does the same thing. For example, in DC format the previous open-ended question about water quality would be: "Would you be willing to pay $A to improve water quality from 12 mg. nitrates per litre to 6 mg. nitrates per litre: yes or no?" "Would you be willing to pay $A to increase by 500 the number of grizzly bears in Alaska?"[5] Answering yes or no simply makes more sense. Second, DC is less stressful for the respondent. Third, the DC approach is thought to provide greater incentive for respondents to answer truthfully, avoiding strategic behaviour. This is only true, however, if respondents can be convinced that their valuation is tied to a real payment. Fourth, the DC format provides the same set of guidelines for all

---

[5] In practice, $A varies from one survey to the next, but it may take as few as 4 to 6, or many more, different values of A, with the highest value of A determined by pre-testing the survey.

respondents to use in determining their responses (Weisberg et al. 1989). Finally, the DC format addresses uncertainty.

Of these arguments, the first and last are probably the most powerful, although there may be some problems associated with the uncertainty argument. The major objection to DC is that it may result in higher values than the open-ended, or continuous, approach as a result of "yea-saying" – respondents are inclined to "vote" in favour of the bid amount by the nature of the question format (Ready et al. 1996; Boyle et al. 1996).

There are three sources of uncertainty. First, there is measurement uncertainty, which is the form of uncertainty addressed by the random utility maximisation model discussed below. Second, preferences are uncertain. It may be possible to address this form of uncertainty by asking respondents how certain they are about their answer, and then use appropriate econometric methods (Li and Mattson 1995; Li 1996). However, it is difficult to conceive of respondents identifying the extent of their uncertainty to a DC question, as preference uncertainty concerns the inability of the respondent to make a proper tradeoff between the environmental good in question and income. The issue is not one of uncertainty about an assigned value, but lack of cognitive ability (see below). The third source of uncertainty originates with the commodity or contingency that is to be valued. Respondents may be uncertain about what it is that they are valuing, having no experience with it and perhaps never having seen it. For example, most people have never seen spotted owl and may not even know what preservation of its habitat might entail; yet they are asked to value existence of the owl. Most people's notions about wilderness, wildlife species and biodiversity in general are simply wrong; they do not know what these things mean, what management or non-management entails, and so on (Budiansky 1995).

Some uncertainty can be resolved by providing more information to the respondent, but there remain sources of uncertainty that can not be addressed with more information. This is likely true for both the amenity that is to be valued (how can respondents know what biologists do not know?) and, given that the amenity is perfectly known, the tradeoff between it and income in the preference function. Only in some cases can uncertainty be (partly) resolved by providing survey respondents with more information about what is to be valued. Respondents to contingent valuation surveys lack knowledge, or have only vague knowledge, about the amenity to be valued, and the appropriate approach may well be to use a linguistic approach to value what is essentially a concept or notion (Zadeh 1965; McNeill and Freiberger 1993). Preference uncertainty of this kind has not been addressed in CVM.

Measurement Uncertainty: Random Utility Maximisation

Welfare measurement in the dichotomous choice model is based on the random utility maximisation (RUM) model (Hanemann 1984). Let $u(j, m; s)$ be an individual's utility function, where j is an indicator variable (taking on 1 if the respondent accepts the opportunity to pay for the contingency and 0 if she rejects the opportunity), m is income, and s is a vector of respondent characteristics. The RUM model begins by assuming that the respondent knows her utility function, $u(j, m; s)$, with certainty, although some components are unobservable to the researcher and are treated as stochastic. Then, from the perspective of the investigator, the respondent's utility function is a random parametric function:

(5.26) $u(j, m; s) = v(j, m; s) + \varepsilon_j, \quad j = 0, 1,$

where ε_0 and ε_1 are independent, identically distributed (iid) random variables.

The problem confronting the researcher is demonstrated with the aid of Figure 5.6. The individual originally has an amount g_0 of the amenity available to her, and is located at point K where the horizontal budget line m intersects the indifference curve, $u(X)$ or $u(Y)$. The question is whether a respondent to a survey would be willing to pay the (bid) amount $A for the opportunity to have g_1 ($> g_0$) of the amenity.

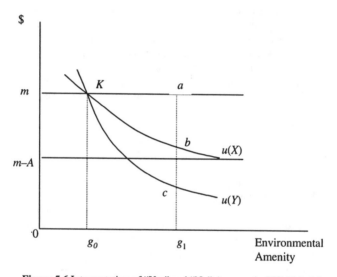

Figure 5.6 Interpretation of "Yes" and "No" Answers in RUM Model

An individual Y with utility map represented by the indifference curve $u(Y)$ will choose to pay the amount indicated because the compensating surplus for this person ($CS_Y = a - c$) exceeds the payment A. Thus, with budget constraint $m - A$, she is still able to move to a higher level of utility. Individual X, on the other hand, will choose not to accept the opportunity to pay $A for the environmental improvement because compensating surplus ($CS_X = a - b$) is less than $A. Thus, before an individual i will accept bid $A, $CS_i > (a - b)$. Since the observer does not know which indifference map applies, utility is a random variable.

The individual, however, knows for sure which choice maximises her utility. Then the probability that she will accept the opportunity to pay $A for the amenity is given by:

(5.27) $P_1 = \text{Pr}\{\text{respondent will pay } \$A\} = \text{Pr}\{v(1, m - A; s) + \varepsilon_1 > v(0, m; s) + \varepsilon_0\}$,

and the probability that the respondent is unwilling to pay the stated amount is $P_0 = 1 - P_1$. If ε_0 and ε_1 are independent, identically distributed (iid) random variables, $(\varepsilon_0 - \varepsilon_1)$ and $(\varepsilon_1 - \varepsilon_0)$ will have the same distribution (Hanemann 1984). The probability in (5.27) can then be re-written as:

(5.28) $P_1 = \text{Pr}\{\text{WTP} > \$A\} = F_{wtp}(\Delta v)$,

where $\Delta v = v(1, m - A; s) - v(0, m; s)$, and F_{wtp} is a cumulative distribution function, generally chosen to be the cumulative standard normal distribution or the cumulative logistics distribution,

(5.29) $P_1 = F_{wtp}(\Delta v) = \dfrac{1}{1 + e^{-\Delta v}}$.

Other distributions, such as the Weibull, exponential (a special case of the Weibull), log-normal and log-logistic, are also used in empirical work. The error term in the regression, $\varepsilon = (\varepsilon_1 - \varepsilon_0)$, is iid, as noted above.

Assume that the utility function is linear: $v(j, m; s) = \alpha_j + \beta m$, with $\beta > 0$ and $j = 0, 1$. Then,

(5.30) $\Delta v = \alpha_1 + \beta(m - A) - \alpha_0 - \beta m = \alpha_1 - \alpha_0 - \beta A$.

For the utility function $v(j, m; s) = \alpha_j + \beta \ln m$, $\beta > 0, j = 0, 1$,

(5.31) $\Delta v = \alpha_1 + \beta \ln(m - A) - \alpha_0 - \beta \ln m$

$$= \alpha_1 - \alpha_0 + \beta \ln(1 - A/m) \approx \alpha_1 - \alpha_0 - \beta(A/m).$$

Denoting $\phi = P_1$ in the cumulative logistics function (5.29), we can solve for the bid amount in each of the linear and semi-log functional forms of the utility function:

(5.32)   linear: $A = \dfrac{1}{\beta} \left[(\alpha_1 - \alpha_0) + \ln \left(\dfrac{1}{\phi} - 1 \right) \right]$

(5.33)   semi-log: $A = \dfrac{m}{\beta} \left[(\alpha_1 - \alpha_0) + \ln \left(\dfrac{1}{\phi} - 1 \right) \right]$.

The binary response probabilities in (5.27) or (5.28) can also be written as:

(5.34) $P_1 = \text{Pr}\{M > A\} = 1 - F_M(A)$,

where M is the respondent's maximum WTP for the environmental amenity, whether an improvement in water quality or protection of more spotted owl habitat, and $F_M(\cdot)$ is the cumulative density function of M (again taking on one of the functional forms discussed above). The compensating welfare measure can be either the median (M^*) or mean (M_μ) of this distribution. As Hanemann (1984) points out, either is a valid measure to use, although they can give quite different welfare estimates. The median is simply that value of M where the estimated probability that a respondent answers yes to the contingent question is 0.5. If the goal of the analyst is to determine whether the policy to change the level or availability of an environmental amenity will pass a referendum vote, then the median is the appropriate measure to employ. If the payment vehicle used in the CVM survey is a tax increase, then any tax increase less than the median WTP estimate would presumably pass (Johansson 1993). Of course, a referendum would be preferred, except that in some jurisdictions such votes are not usual. The mean WTP, on the other hand, is the appropriate measure to employ for cost-benefit analysis and is given by:

$$(5.35) \quad M_\mu = \int_0^\infty \left(1 - F_M(A)\right) \, dA.$$

Both the mean and median are indicated in Figure 5.7, with the mean simply the area under the distribution. The mean can be infinite due to nonconvergence of the tail of the cumulative distribution, which is a particular problem in the case of WTA – as demonstrated by Hanemann (1984) in his recalculation of Bishop and Heberlein's (1979) original welfare values (see Table 5.1 below). One approach has been to truncate the distribution at the largest value of $A used in the CVM survey. The above integral would stop at the highest elicited value, thereby ignoring the tail of the distribution. However, the median measure would be unaffected.

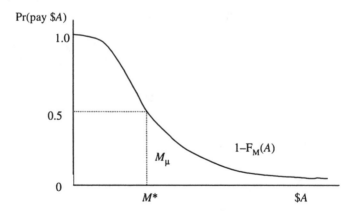

Figure 5.7 Welfare Measures in DC Models: Median (M^*) and Mean (M_μ)

The median and mean measures can, on occasion, provide substantially different passive use values for a resource. In the case of the March 24, 1989 *Exxon Valdez* oil spill in Alaska, estimates of WTP to prevent damages varied widely. For the Weibull, exponential, log-normal and log-logistic cumulative functional forms, median WTPs were found to be US$31, $46, $27 and $29, respectively, compared to respective estimates of mean WTPs of $94, $67, $220 and infinity (Harrison and Kriström 1995, p. 37). Given an estimated 90 million US households, choice of functional form and whether the mean or median welfare measure is employed can lead to differences in damage estimates of 1,000% or more. The median appears to be a lower bound estimate, but there is no reason to prefer it over the mean in assessing damages or benefits simply because it yields lower estimates.

Other measurement issues are discussed by Adamowicz et al. (1989). Further, Hanemann (1984) derives all of the aforementioned properties for the case of compensation demanded.

Extending the Basic Dichotomous Choice Model

The dichotomous choice model has been extended in several directions. There has been an attempt to hone in on, or fine tune, the elicited WTP or compensation demanded. This is done by using a follow-up question to the original DC one; hence, the method is known as the double-bounded approach, where the use of a single question is referred to as the single-bounded approach (Kanninen 1993). Suppose the initial question asked a respondent to provide a yes-no answer to a willingness to pay "bid" of A_0. A probability distribution is assumed about A_0, such that the true bid lies to the left of A_0 if the respondent answers "no" and to the right of A_0 if the respondent answers "yes". The nature of the follow-up question is such that a value higher than A_0, say A_U, is asked in a second DC question if the response to A_0 was "yes", and a value below A_0, say A_L, if it was "no". This partitions the probability distribution about A_0 into four zones – moving from left to right there is a (no, no) zone for a "no" response to A_L; a (no, yes) zone for a "yes" response to A_L and "no" to A_0; a (yes, no) zone for a "yes" response to A_0 but "no" response to A_U; and a (yes, yes) zone for "yes" responses to both A_0 and A_U. This procedure improves the quality of the estimated welfare measures (Kanninen 1993; Harrison and Kriström 1995; Hanemann and Kriström 1995).[6]

A second extension of the model has been to address preference uncertainty. Li and Mattsson (1995) were the first to ask respondents how certain they were about their responses to the DC question. If someone responded "yes" to a bid of A, but subsequently indicated that they were less than 50% certain about their answer, they were interpreted to have responded "no" with a certainty equal to 100% minus the stated level of certainty (so that the certainty of the "no" response exceeded 50%). This is rather arbitrary (van Kooten et al. 1999).

---

[6] A problem with the two-question, extended DC method is that a respondent's answer to the second question is not unrelated to the amount proposed in the first question – there is an anchoring problem.

Preference uncertainty can be illustrated via Figure 5.8. In this figure, three indifference curves are used – a linear indifference curve that exhibits perfect substitutability (u_0u_0), one that exhibits perfect complementarity or lexicographical preferences (u_1u_1), and an in-between case (u_2u_2) (Hanemann and Kriström 1995). The compensating surplus of an increase in the environmental amenity from g_0 to g_1 ranges from zero to total income m depending on the individual's preference map, which is unknown to the researcher. For perfect complements (u_1u_1), CS = 0; for perfect substitutes, CS = $a - c = m$; and for the in-between case, CS = $a - b$.

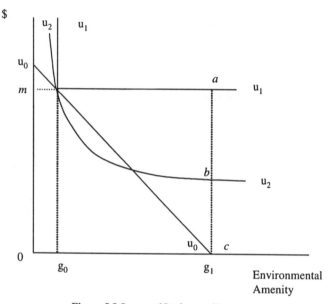

Figure 5.8 Source of Preference Uncertainty

Hanemann and Kriström (1995) (and Li and Mattsson 1995) talk about preference uncertainty related to the respondent, but they fail to make a clear distinction among the different types of uncertainty identified above. The RUM model addresses uncertainty in measurement and Li and Mattsson combine this with the uncertainty that respondents have about their yes-no response to the DC question. Perhaps, true preference uncertainty pertains less to uncertainty about whether the respondent's compensating surplus is greater or less than the bid amount (and the trustworthiness of the response), than to cognitive uncertainty about what is valued or about how they in fact make tradeoffs between the environmental good and income. It seems to us that true preference uncertainty cannot be addressed in the DC framework.

Finally, conventional methods that employ the log-logistics, log-normal, Weibull and other distributions implicitly rule out the possibility that respondents have non-zero probability for a zero WTP (in Figure 5.7 this is indicated by a 1.0

value for WTP = 0). To take into account a large number of zero respondents, Kriström (1997) suggests the use of a spike model, with the spike occurring at zero WTP. He argues that there are three ways to view negative responses to the bid price. First, WTP is below the bid price. Second, there are some goods or amenity services over which the consumer has no preference; they do not enter into the utility function. Finally, the good or amenity does not contribute positively to utility, with the respondent not even willing to purchase it at zero price. That is, the respondents have negative WTP.

Castle et al. (1994), and others, have also noted that, while environmental and other programs are assumed to result in gains to citizens, there are likely to be losers as well. Consider a program to protect grizzly bears, or increase their numbers. While many would favour such a program, there are others who would prefer to see a reduction in bear numbers (*viz.*, hikers who are afraid of being attacked). The latter would attach negative value to such a program. Likewise, the literature has focused on positive WTP for protection of old-growth forests. However, some would prefer to see some development of such forests, as opposed to keeping them solely as wilderness. For example, Portney (1994, p. 13) suggests that some will derive satisfaction from knowing that development (e.g., of wilderness) provides well-paying jobs, a benefit of development that could, in principle, be estimated using CVM. A case can also be made for assigning nonuse value to development – logging roads that provide access, clearcuts that are planted to grass or other species of trees, and thinning of old-growth stands may provide nonuse benefits to some. Nonuse benefits can be attached to the development (loss) of wilderness as well as to its protection. Empirical support for the possibility that development has nonuse value comes from Sweden, where Drake (1992) found that people attached positive nonuse value to retaining landscapes in agriculture as opposed to letting them revert back to their natural state as forests. In that case, equation (5.35) needs to be modified as follows:

$$(5.36) \quad M_\mu = \int_0^\infty \left(1 - F_M(A)\right) dA - \int_{-\infty}^0 F_M(A) \, dA,$$

where the last term on the RHS of (5.36) takes into account those with negative WTP.

Many respondents to CVM questions state that their WTP for the contingency is zero. The spike model takes this into account. Kriström (1997) employs a spike model to examine two Swedish studies – a proposal to re-route the Sweden to Finland ferry to prevent shoreline erosion in the Stockholm archipelago, and another to close Bromma airport in Stockholm (Arlanda airport 40 km outside Stockholm is the main airport). In the case of the ferry, 446 out of 575 respondents (or 77%) declined to pay anything to re-route the ferry. A traditional logit distribution function, which permits negative values (recall that log-normal, Weibull and other distributional functions do not permit negative values) resulted in estimated mean and median WTPs of –US$ 340. From the spike model, on the other hand, the estimated mean WTP was +US$200, while estimated median WTP was zero.

For the Bromma airport study, respondents were first asked their preferences regarding the future of the airport, with a slight majority favouring an expansion of air traffic as opposed to a reduction. Those who preferred a reduction in air traffic from Bromma over an increase were subsequently asked what they would be willing to pay for reducing activity at the airport. Only 7% of the sample provided a positive WTP to reduce activity at the airport. Some 18% of the sample indicated a negative WTP (i.e., preferred an increase in activity at Bromma airport), while 75% indicated indifference or zero WTP. Thus, the spike is estimated to be 0.75. The median WTP is clearly zero, while mean WTP is also estimated to be zero if a symmetrical distribution is assumed. The traditional approach finds a positive mean WTP.

It is clear that it is necessary to address questions of a zero response to CVM questions using either a spike model or some other methodology.

Contingent valuation survey techniques: Some issues

Contingent valuation surveys enable economists to measure the value of commodities and services that do not leave a footprint in the market place, either because they are separable from privately traded goods and services in individuals' utility functions or they are separable in the production function. Surveys using questionnaires enable one to obtain information about such amenities in a direct fashion. A good contingent valuation survey (1) communicates the attributes to be valued, (2) communicates the terms of the bargain (see below), and (3) is consistent with economic theory. If the mechanism for obtaining responses is not consistent with economic theory, it is not clear what the resulting responses mean. Some problems with the survey approach (at least as identified by its practitioners) are as follows.

1. The survey approach places individuals in hypothetical situations with which they may be unfamiliar. They are unable to respond in a meaningful manner to the questions that are subsequently posed about these situations. To prevent this, the interviewer can use explanation, pictures or other props to identify clearly the hypothetical situation to which the respondent is required to respond.
2. The relationship between the respondent and the interviewer may influence the values provided; the problem is that the observer is in the picture influencing outcomes. Questions pertaining to willingness-to-pay to have access to a resource or to have more of some public good, and questions pertaining to the compensation demanded for being denied access or having less of the public good, are subjective and the respondent may provide answers that she thinks the interviewer wants to hear. Thus, the respondent is not a *neutral* participant. This problem is likely the easiest to overcome by proper training of interviewers.
3. The respondent is not neutral to the hypothetical situations that are laid out. She may either *bias* the results up or down depending upon whether she thinks that the responses will, for example, prevent others from accessing a recreational site by making it either too expensive or less attractive. Responses may also be given in such a way that the value of the contingency is overstated because the respondent knows that she will not bear the cost of providing the public good

(free-rider problem), or the respondent may purposely understate her WTP in order to escape charges. This form of bias or strategic behaviour can be prevented by inclusion of a realistic payment device whereby the respondent recognises that she will indeed be required to pay for the proposed change.

4. *Starting point bias* is a problem in some instances. This refers to the value that is initially suggested by the researcher to the respondent. If the value is lower than that which the respondent had in mind, the respondent may revise values downward; likewise, they may be revised upwards. Pre-testing can be used to overcome the problem of realistic starting values. Further, one can avoid starting point bias by using open questions (i.e., not suggesting starting values).

Different types of surveys are also available to researchers.

1. *Mail surveys* are the lowest cost and perhaps the easiest to administer. Sample selectivity may be a problem, but can be addressed to some extent by using econometric tools that test and correct for sample selectivity bias. Other problems occur because those who are sent surveys may not be able to comprehend the material in the survey, due to high overall illiteracy rates.[7] This can account for low response rates in some instances. It is also possible that those completing the surveys are those who have strong feelings one way or another about the issue, so mail-outs are likely beset by response bias. Further, it is difficult to get accurate lists of names for survey purposes and one does not have control over the survey itself. Follow-up is very important. It is often recommended that non-respondents be contacted at least two times following the initial mail-out. Reminder cards can be used, followed, if necessary, by a telephone call and second mail-out if the telephone contact leads to a positive response. To increase response rates, respondents can be offered token compensation for time completing the questionnaire, say $5 or $10, although this raises the costs of mail surveys.

2. *Telephone surveys* are perhaps twice as expensive as mail surveys. Nonetheless, the advantages of telephone interviews are that they are reasonably low cost, result in a high response rate, and enable the interviewer to answer respondents' questions when necessary. Although the surveyor can respond to questions regarding clarification, interviewer bias does enter in. One problem concerns choice of respondent: rather than choosing the person who answers the phone, the interviewer can ask for the person in the household who is over age 18, say, and whose birthday is next. Call back based on a household listing obtained at first contact is a more expensive method. Another problem with telephone surveys is information overload. Questions must be kept simple so individuals can easily keep track of items over the telephone. Yet, telephone interviews are

---

[7] Illiteracy is defined in the broad sense; while individuals who are considered illiterate may be able to read, comprehension is low and there is a general inability to do arithmetic calculations.

often preferred to mail-out surveys (Portney 1994), although the preponderance of telemarketing has "poisoned the well" for telephone surveys to some extent.

3. ***In-person surveys*** are the most expensive means to elicit information, but they have the highest response and "success" rate. The major problem with this method is bias that arises due to personal contact, but again this source of bias can be overcome by training surveyors and through pre-testing.

It is important to pre-test any contingent valuation survey extensively. Using focus groups in one's pre-test helps the researcher to understand how and what people are valuing. Further, samples should be split so that the dimension of a particular item in the questionnaire can be asked in different ways. It is then possible to test if the phrasing of the question affects the answer or value provided, but this adds to the number of completed surveys needed for statistical significance. The current state of the art favours mail-out surveys, but only if all the conditions of proper survey design are satisfied.

The purpose of contingent valuation surveys is to get individuals to reveal values that correspond to the actual values that people put on commodities in real markets. Doing so is referred to as validity. If respondents do not answer honestly or meaningfully, validity is threatened. There are three kinds of validity tests.

1. ***Content validity*** focuses on the wording of questions in the actual survey. Questions need to identify clearly the items to be valued and the "terms of the bargain". The latter refers to the mechanism by which actual payment occurs, to whom the payment is made (from whom funds are received), in what form monies are paid or received, and how any funds raised are to be used in implementing the contingency.

2. ***Construct validity*** results when a survey's questions are consistent with economic theory; the responses can then be related to meaningful theoretical concepts. One measure of validity in these cases is to compare values from the contingent valuation survey with values obtained from market methods such hedonic pricing.

3. ***Criterion validity*** relies upon comparisons with laboratory experiments. For example, one might wish to compare hypothetical responses to WTP and WTA for hunting permits with those obtained from a simulated market for permits. Some comparisons of simulated market values and contingent values are provided in Table 5.1. It appears that contingent markets are able to provide estimates of value that correspond well with those provided by simulated markets. The greatest difference in values (in Table 5.1) is between WTP and compensation demanded (see Chapter 2 and below).

Is the contingent valuation method a panacea?

There remains controversy over the use of CVM for valuing biodiversity and wilderness preservation. Some environmental economists (perhaps the majority) vigorously defend CVM as a valid theoretical and empirical means for estimating the benefits (costs) of changes in the availability of environmental goods; see, for example, Hanemann (1994) and Smith (1992). Their view is supported in CERCLA and other legislation. The CERCLA decision grants equal standing to expressed and revealed preference, accepts nonuse values as a legitimate component of resource value, and favours restoration of a damaged natural environment over compensation (Gregory et al. 1993).

Table 5.1: Contingent Values and Simulated Market Values

Commodity	Valuation Method	Dollar Values	
		Contingent	Simulated Market
For compensation demanded			
Goose Permits	Dichotomous choice	$101 ($83.16)[a]	$63 ($31.02)[a]
Deer Permits	Sealed-bid auction	$833	$1,184
Deer Permits	Dichotomous choice	$420	$153
For willingness-to-pay			
Goose Permits	Dichotomous choice	$21 ($5.30)[a]	--
Deer Permits	Sealed-bid auction	$32	$24
	Sealed-bid auction and bidding	$43	$19
Deer Permits	Dichotomous choice	$35	$31

Source: Bishop and Heberlein (1990, pp. 97–8).
[a] Hanemann's (1984, p. 340) corrections to values originally calculated by Bishop and Heberlein (1979) are provided in parentheses. Bishop and Heberlein calculate areas under the curve (means), but arbitrarily truncate the calculation of mean to avoid infinite numbers. Hanemann's median values are provided in parentheses. Mean values for WTA for goose permits are $∞ and $114.22 for contingent and simulated markets, respectively, and $15.54 for WTP.

Defenders of contingent valuation methods have focused almost exclusively on its ability to provide monetary values in situations where none would otherwise exist (even as a starting point for negotiating damages), arguing that its shortcomings are best overcome by rigorous survey design and practice (Hanemann 1994; Arrow et al. 1993). However, CVM has also been criticised by economists, philosophers, psychologists and lawyers, resulting in questions about its use in litigation and in cost-benefit analysis (Knetsch 1995; Diamond and Hausman 1994; Hausman 1993; Kahneman and Knetsch 1992a, 1992b; Irwin et al. 1993; Kahneman et al. 1990; Sagoff 1988b, 1994; Niewijk 1992, 1994). The reasons for dissatisfaction or outright rejection of the method vary.

Ethical Norms and Valuation of Environmental Amenities

Rational values involve standards for truth; moral values involve standards of conduct; aesthetic values involve standards for appreciation; spiritual values involve standards of meaning of life; and economic values involve standards for choosing among goods and services. Consider a social hierarchy, where personal consumption goods are lowest in the hierarchy, protection of global ecosystems and concern for the well being of the least fortunate are ranked higher, and questions about who we are and how we relate to the world are highest. As a person deals with complex questions that are relatively high in the social hierarchy, many issues deal with intangibles or ill-defined "things". As More et al. (1996) argue, tangible goods have value because they allow us to fulfil certain functions, with market prices facilitating these choices.

However, a person's willingness to pay, say, to preserve minke whales in the Atlantic Ocean – a much less tangible amenity – may relate more to helping provide a person with an identity (what kind of person am I?), rather than reflecting any intrinsic value of wildlife. While this view may justify the use of economic analyses for valuing nonmarket goods, because all nonuse values are tied to the fulfilment of human goals and are really off-site values, it is important to be clear about what is really valued. Is it the resource, knowledge of the resource, the satisfaction people derive from the resource, or the satisfaction they derive from doing something to preserve nature, rather than preserving whales *per se*, that is being valued?

Do individuals make decisions based on market values or on a set of wider values based on social norms (or commonly accepted values)? The debate in the literature is intense about this point (Sagoff 1988a 1988b; Kahneman and Ritov 1994; Blamey et al. 1995; Common et al. 1997; Crowards 1997; Gowdy 1997). One view is that contingent valuation "actually captures a hodgepodge of market values and broader values and forces them into the indifference framework of market exchange" (Gowdy 1997, p. 27). The other view is that values are derived from economic theory. "It is utility – whatever its source – that matters for total value. Motives are essentially irrelevant and acceptance of consumer sovereignty is one of the most enshrined principles of economics" (Carson et al. 1996).

Sagoff (1988b) proposes that people make choices according to "citizen values" or "consumer values", depending on the context in which the choice is placed. There are values other than economic ones that are important to individuals when they make choices as a citizen as opposed to consumer; then ethical values matter (Sagoff 1994; More et al. 1996). Sen (1977) had previously pointed out that concepts of economic rationality are both too weak and too strong because humans have a capacity for maintaining multiple preference scales. Humans are cognisant of social duties that might conflict with personal welfare and may hold a land or environmental ethic that leads them to make decisions in a decidedly nonmarket fashion. Hence, individuals might reject offers to value an environmental resource or may provide answers that have no relationship to their true WTP.

Empirical research provides some support for the notion that individuals value environmental goods for reasons other than private benefits (Kahneman and Knetsch 1992a). One problem concerns "imbedding" of values within a questionnaire. Thus, an individual may respond that she is willing to pay $25 per year towards preserving grizzly bear when asked only about this wildlife species. Summing over individuals leads to a large value for grizzly bear. If the same individual were asked about her WTP to preserve all wildlife species, the answer may also be $25. Out of that amount, the person may only be willing to pay $15 towards the preservation of big game species; out of the $15, the individual may only be willing to contribute $5 per year for preservation of grizzly bears. Likewise, studies have found that individuals are willing to pay the same amount to preserve one lake full of fish as they would to save all fish in the region (Knetsch 2000). One conclusion is that, while people are interested in the environment and protecting biodiversity (saving species), they are irrational in how they make decisions about environment and biological assets. Alternatively, people may simply purchase the moral satisfaction of having made their contribution toward society by paying to save the environment or protect species (or contribute to cancer research, etc.). If it is moral satisfaction that individuals are actually purchasing, and not the contingent commodity, this raises questions about the validity of contingent valuation surveys.

Individuals might assign value to environmental goods out of an altruistic motive beyond that related to future generations (bequest value). People might value public goods, such as wildlife species, because these confer benefits upon others. It is useful to distinguish two types of altruism – non-paternalistic, in which an altruist gains utility from increasing the well being of others, and paternalistic, in which an altruist values the use of a particular resource by others. Paternalistic altruists believe that the availability of some environmental goods (wildlife species in tropical rain forests) is of benefit to others (forest dwellers) even if they gain no direct utility from their existence; the altruist derives utility only from knowing that the forest dweller has access to the wildlife species (regardless of whether the forest dweller desires them). Diamond and Hausman (1994) allege that altruistic externalities might result in double counting of benefits, but McConnell (1997) shows that altruism has no impact on benefit estimates if it is non-paternalistic and that benefits for paternalistic altruists can legitimately be used in valuation without problems associated with double counting.

Property Rights and Endowments

As noted in Chapter 2, empirical studies find a large disparity between WTP and WTA for both environmental amenities and goods normally traded in markets, even though one would expect these to vary only by a small amount. Yet, recommended best practice is to elicit WTP in CVM surveys (see, e.g., Arrow et al. 1993). This assumes, in essence, that the respondent has to pay for the right to the environmental amenity, even where the amenity has deteriorated through carelessness or some other reason – the property right or endowment is assumed not to reside with the respondent. As a result, many survey respondents provide answers that can only be interpreted as protest against the contingent property right.

There are several reasons why WTP is considered best practice. Almost all CVM studies employ WTP with the values generated considered "reasonable" for whatever reason, although Arrow et al. (1993) consider such values to be on the high side. WTP makes people more cognisant of their budget constraints; WTP is bounded, while WTA could be unbounded. Yet, in many cases the appropriate measure is compensation demanded (Knetsch 1993). Finally, in the determination of punitive damages (damages over and above compensation for injuries to the plaintiff) in lawsuits, both sides have come to accept WTP as the appropriate measure of nonuse value. The wrongdoer accepts WTP because it results in lower values than WTA, while the plaintiff accepts WTP because it addresses the punishment aspect ("the sense of community outrage") (Knetsch 2000).

In practice, the size of punitive damage awards is erratic and unpredictable. However, when those setting damage awards are able to use awards from other cases as a guide, unpredictability and variability are nearly eliminated. Therefore, as a practical matter, it may only be necessary to determine the perceived severity of environmental damage to decide the associated punitive damages (i.e., value the damage). That is, with input from stakeholders, governments can establish *ex ante* awards for different types of environmental damages. The courts would then use these values as a guide for situations not covered. Limits on damage payments would be used to ensure that businesses are not forced into bankruptcy (with significant job loss) due to litigation arising from accidental environmental damage, not caused by negligence on the part of the firm. This approach constitutes a way to get around the discrepancy between WTP and WTA, as both are considered valid welfare measures (Knetsch 2000).

Cognitive Ability of Survey Respondents

One criticism of CVM is that it seeks to elicit values for natural resources from respondents who may lack the cognitive ability to make such assessments. Respondents to surveys often provide zero answers because of their inability to attribute value to something that they have a difficult time valuing, if they can ever ascribe a value to it (Sagoff 1994; Gregory et al. 1993; Stevens et al. 1991). Psychologists consider four possibilities:

1. Preferences exist and are stable, well-defined and easily measured.
2. Preferences exist and are stable, but are not easily measured because some of the resulting measures are biased.
3. Preferences exist and are stable, but all measurements are biased.
4. Preferences may not exist in many situations or, if they do exist, they are not stable or well-formed.

The main criticism is that CVM itself creates preferences and bias because context or familiarity matters.

It is possible to rank or value items with which one is familiar, but this ability declines as the degree of familiarity falls. For example, consider the following items listed from highest to lowest degree of familiarity (familiarity declines as one goes from category 1 to 7):

1. Groceries
2. Appliances
3. Automobiles
4. Homes
5. Recreational activities
6. Air and water quality
7. Nature (environment and species preservation)

Valuing changes in the hypothetical availability of commodities in each of these categories becomes increasingly difficult as one moves from categories 1 through 7. Psychologists argue that it is likely impossible to place dollar values on hypothetical changes in the availability of commodities in categories 6 and 7.

This has led some to argue that, rather than employing CVM, it is necessary to help decision makers to "construct" their preferences for public goods. This approach would bring together all the stakeholders involved in a choice about some public good, help them construct their preferences about the good, and thereby lead to a policy choice. While discussed in more detail in the next section, we note that the major objection to this approach is that the stakeholder group may not be representative of the larger society.

Payment Instrument

There are other issues of concern that are not addressed, including protest responses related to the payment instrument. Although much research has gone into improving the payment device, many respondents indicate that they are against an increase in taxes because, while they may have a positive WTP for the contingency, they are against the current allocation of budgets. In this context, Sagoff (1994), for example, cites the large number of non-responses in most contingent valuation surveys.

How Valid are CVM Measures of Benefits?

The controversy surrounding CVM was sufficient that the US National Oceanic and Atmospheric Administration (NOAA) commissioned a panel led by two Nobel prize-winning economists (Kenneth Arrow and Robert Solow) to review the state of the art and make recommendations concerning the implementation of CVM (Arrow et al. 1993). The findings by the NOAA panel are summarised in the following points.

1. The CVM "technique is likely to overstate 'real' willingness to pay" (p. 4604).
2. External validation of the CVM results is needed before one can reliably use the answers provided by survey respondents.
3. Relatively few CVM surveys "have reminded respondents convincingly of the very real economic constraints within which spending decisions must be made" (p. 4605).
4. CVM frequently provides sketchy details about the project(s) to be valued and this calls into question the estimates of value that one thus derives from this information. However, if respondents were to be provided detailed information, it is unlikely that they would have the cognitive ability to proceed from the information given to answer the survey questions, often answering different questions from that elicited (p. 4605). While some of this information overload might be identified and addressed in pre-testing, there is no way to eliminate the problem.
5. Related to 4, in asking individuals to place value on an environmental commodity (such as a biological species), surveys often fail to apprise respondents of the current level of availability and/or existence of the commodity elsewhere (say in another country). Thus, average and not marginal values are elicited. As we discuss further in Chapters 9 and 10, relying on average as opposed to marginal nonmarket values leads to the wrong conclusions about species preservation – it is marginal and not average values that count in designing appropriate natural resource policies.
6. Open-ended questions are unlikely to be reliable and, therefore, survey respondents should be asked to respond to a dichotomous choice (yes-no) question where WTP is provided.

7. Questions concerning potential sources of bias need to be included in questionnaires. In addition, dichotomous choice questions should be followed by an open-ended question asking why the respondent "voted" the way she did.
8. Outcomes should be compared with those provided by expert panels and, wherever possible, *an actual referendum should be used.*
9. Careful pre-testing of surveys is required and in-person surveys are preferred to mail-out surveys.

The NOAA panel provided support for the use of CVM, arguing that CVM "studies can produce estimates reliable enough to be *the starting point of a judicial process of damage assessment,* including lost passive-use values" (p. 4610, emphasis added). Whether this constitutes an endorsement of CVM is not at all clear. Some of the NOAA recommendations have been adopted, including follow up questions that seek to determine the reasons why respondents provide particular answers to some of the survey questions (e.g., reasons for zero WTP). Others have not been followed, including rejection of in-person surveys in favour of mail outs. Despite the NOAA panel, controversy continues.

There have also been refinements to the methodology, mainly in terms of econometric approaches and development of alternative means of eliciting value information. At this stage, however, one can only state that contingent valuation methods are evolving and that, in the absence of a market-based approach to valuation of nonmarket (environmental) amenities, CVM or some other direct elicitation procedure will likely be around for some time to come. A major reason (noted above) is that CVM has come to be accepted in litigation.

5.4 Other Direct Valuation Methods

In this section, we consider some alternatives to the contingent valuation method. In some cases, the methods refine CVM, but in others they deviate substantially from the underlying notions of CVM.

Choice experiments

Adamowicz and his colleagues have proposed a promising alternative to CVM; see, for example, Adamowicz (1995), Adamowicz et al. (1998), and Hanley et al. (1998). Rooted in the marketing literature, this approach has been referred to as choice experiments (CE) or stated preferences. While the methodology has been used primarily to value recreational sites, Adamowicz et al. (1998) apply CE to the estimation of nonuse values.

Unlike CVM, CE does not require survey respondents to place a direct monetary value on a contingency. Rather, individuals are asked to make pairwise comparisons among environmental alternatives, with the environmental commodity (alternatives) characterised by a variety of attributes. For example, a survey respondent is asked to make pairwise choices between alternative recreational sites or activities, with each distinguished by attributes such as the probability of catching a fish, the type of fish, the amenities for fishermen (e.g., availability of boat rentals), distance to the site, and so on. It is the attributes that are important, and it is these that are eventually assigned monetary value. In order to do so, one of the attributes must constitute a monetary touchstone (or proxy for price). Distance to a recreational site might constitute the proxy for price, but, more generally, one of the attributes will be an entry fee or an associated tax, et cetera. Once the values of all attributes are known (from the value of the one and the pairwise rankings), the overall value of the amenity is determined by assuming additivity of the attributes' values. Of course, it is possible that the total value of the amenity is greater than the sum of its components (or vice versa).

Design of the choice experiment is crucial. Suppose that there are five attributes that constitute the choice model design i (Hanley et al. 1998):

$$(5.37) \quad Z_i = f(A_i, B_i, C_i, D_i, E_i),$$

where A, B, C, D and E refer to attributes, and Z is the environmental amenity that these attributes produce. If A, B and C take on four possible levels, and D and E take on three possible levels, then the total number of combinations is $(4^3 \times 3^2)$. In CE, it is typical to offer respondents two alternative designs of the environmental good and the option to choose neither. Each triple is known as a choice occasion and implies a possible combination of $[(4^3 \times 3^2) \times (4^3 \times 3^2)]$ pairwise comparisons. Using design theory, it is possible to determine the subset of all possible pairwise comparisons needed to estimate the parameters in the model.

Hanley et al. (1998) point out a number of advantages of the CE approach.

1. It enables one to value the attributes that comprise an environmental commodity, which is important as many policy decisions involve changing attributes rather than the total gain or loss of an environmental commodity. For example, when a wilderness area is developed as a result of timber harvest, not all of its attributes are lost. Attribute valuation is also important because of its use in prediction.
2. Choice experiments avoid the "yea-saying" problem of dichotomous choice surveys as respondents are not faced with the same "all-or-nothing" choice.
3. It may offer advantages over CVM when it comes to the transfer of benefits (e.g., transfer of estimated benefits for water quality improvements in one jurisdiction to those in another).
4. Repeated sampling in CE enables consistency testing that is not possible in CVM.
5. CE may be a means of getting around the embedding problem mentioned above. Finally, in the case of nonuse benefits estimation, by allowing some attributes to take on levels both above and below the status quo level, it is possible to estimate both WTP and WTA compensation (Adamowicz et al. 1998).

The theory underlying CE is similar to that presented above with respect to the random utility maximisation model in the case of recreation. Indeed, one obtains a hybrid travel cost model. Assume an indirect utility function:

(5.38) $u_i = v_i + \varepsilon_i$,

where ε_i are iid as before. Then the probability that site k is chosen over j is given by

(5.39) $P_{kj} = Pr(v_k + \varepsilon_k > v_j + \varepsilon_j)$.

Equation (5.22) applies here as well, and the model is estimated as a multinomial logit, implying that choices are consistent with independence of irrelevant alternatives. Consumer surplus estimates for changes in attribute levels can be derived in a fashion similar to those of equations (5.23) and (5.24) by interpreting the coefficient on the price attribute as equal to the marginal utility of income.

CE differs from conjoint analysis because, with the latter, respondents are asked to rank all of the alternatives from highest (best) to lowest (worst). Such a ranking can then be used to infer the importance of the attributes that characterise each alternative within one's preference function. Conjoint measurement is a marketing technique that uses revealed choice among goods with different characteristics (as in hedonic pricing) with a survey that asks people to choose among or rank hypothetical alternatives (contingent ranking) to impute the values of the characteristics. It is used primarily to predict the potential for new products, but efforts to apply this technique to the valuation of nonmarket commodities in ways different from CE are underway (Smith 1997).

Constructed preferences

Gregory et al. (1993) propose a multiattribute-utility-theory, contingent valuation, or MAUT-CV, approach to address the inability of respondents in a contingent valuation exercise to make holistic assessments about environmental resources. Individuals do not know the value of the resources they are asked to value, but "are constructing them, with whatever help or cues the circumstances provide" (p. 181). Thus, rather than attempting to uncover environmental values, Gregory et al. (1993) argue that the analyst's task is to help individuals discover those values by helping them work towards "a defensible expression of value" (p. 179). In essence, their approach is to work with stakeholder groups of less than 100 people, having them develop comprehensive, hierarchical attribute trees and then having them rank attributes on a 0–to–100 scale.

> Once all the pieces [of the tree and assigned utility values] are in place, [a] combination rule specifies how to calculate the total utility for any particular plan, program, or scenario. This total utility will be expressed using a single arbitrary *utile* unit of measurement. For contingent valuation, these units must be converted to dollars. In theory, this conversion need only be made at one place in the model. (Gregory et al. 1993, p. 189)

The MAUT-CV method also has the advantage that it is able to address uncertainty as components with probabilities can be built into the model, so that the final calculation is an expected value. It is unlikely that it can address disparity between WTP and

WTA (between the value placed on gains versus that on losses) as the results could be varied by using differing "paths" to help people discover their "values".

Fuzzy logic and its potential for nonmarket valuation

Respondents to CVM surveys are often unfamiliar with the environmental amenity that they are asked to value. This may be because they are simply unfamiliar with the commodity, having little experience with it, or because the commodity is not readily describable in "crisp" language. How does one place a value on an "ecosystem", or on an "old-growth forest" when ecologists and foresters are unable to provide unambiguous definitions of these systems? Clearly, if we ask people in a CVM survey to place value on "old growth" or on an "ecosystem", or on caribou or minke whales, different people will have different images of each of these "commodities". Unlike market goods, environmental amenities cannot always be defined; they are best described as being a vague commodity. In that case, fuzzy logic may offer insights that might lead to improved methods of valuation. In this section, we provide a brief introduction to fuzzy logic and describe two possible methods for valuing nonmarket commodities using fuzzy set theory.

Brief Introduction to Fuzzy Logic

Multivalued or "fuzzy" logic was first introduced in the 1920s and 1930s to address indeterminacy in quantum theory. The Polish mathematician Jan Lukasiewicz introduced three-valued logic and then extended the range of truth values from {0, ½, 1} to all rational numbers in [0, 1] and finally to all numbers in [0, 1]. In the late 1930s, quantum philosopher Max Black used the term "vagueness" to refer to Lukasiewicz' uncertainty and introduced the concept of a membership function (Kosko 1992, pp. 5–6). Subsequently, in 1965, Lofti Zadeh introduced the term "fuzzy set" and the fuzzy logic it supports.

Zadeh's (1965) concern was with the ambiguity and vagueness of natural language, and the attendant inability to convey crisp information linguistically. The word "hot", for example, may be used to communicate many things; the information it imparts is context dependent and, thus, the term itself may be considered ambiguous. "Hot" may refer to temperature, spiciness or trendiness. Once the frame of reference is identified to be temperature, the information conveyed is still not clear, as the subjective perception of heat by one person is not necessarily congruent with the perception of heat by a second person. There is no absolute temperature at which a thing may be said to have attained membership in the set of things that are "hot" and at which it may be said to have ceased to be merely "warm". Subjective interpretations of the term will allow for an overlap of temperature ranges. Thus, an object may be said to be "warm" by some while it is judged "hot" by others. In essence, it is accorded partial membership in both of the sets – it displays some of the requirements for being a "hot" thing while retaining some of the requirements for being a "warm" thing. It is this concept of partial membership that is central to the theory of fuzzy sets.

Now consider the idea of partial membership more formally. An element x of the universal set X is assigned to an ordinary (crisp) set A via the characteristic function μ_A, such that:

$$\mu_A(x) = 1 \qquad \text{if } x \in A.$$
(5.40)
$$\mu_A(x) = 0 \qquad \text{otherwise.}$$

The element has either full membership ($\mu_A(x) = 1$) or no membership ($\mu_A(x) = 0$) in the set A. The valuation set for the function is the pair of points $\{0,1\}$.

A fuzzy set $\tilde{A}$ is also described by a characteristic function, the difference being that the function now maps over the closed interval $[0, 1]$. Thus, an element may be assigned a value that lies between 0 and 1 and is representative of the degree of membership that x has in the fuzzy set $\tilde{A}$.[8] If $\mu_A(x) \in (0, 1)$, then element x has only some but not all of the attributes required for full membership in a set. A membership function describes the grade or degree of membership, with the membership function viewed as a representation of a fuzzy number (Klir and Folger 1988, p. 17). It is in this form that fuzzy set theory is used to deal with vague preferences. Then, $\mu_A(x) = 1$ means that the decision maker is very satisfied, while $\mu_A(x) = 0$ indicates that the decision maker is completely unsatisfied, with intermediate values indicating degrees of partial satisfaction. Membership functions are crucial to fuzzy set calculus. Set-theoretic operations for fuzzy sets were originally proposed by Zadeh (1965), including the intersection of two fuzzy sets $\tilde{A}$ and $\tilde{B}$ as:

$$(5.41) \quad \mu_{\tilde{A} \cap \tilde{B}}(x) = \min\{\mu_A(x), \mu_B(x)\} \ \forall \ x \in X,$$

and union as:

$$(5.42) \quad \mu_{\tilde{A} \cup \tilde{B}}(x) = \max\{\mu_A(x), \mu_B(x)\} \ \forall \ x \in X.$$

Hence, the intersection $\tilde{A} \cap \tilde{B}$ is the largest fuzzy set that is contained in both $\tilde{A}$ and $\tilde{B}$, and the union $\tilde{A} \cup \tilde{B}$ is the smallest fuzzy set containing both $\tilde{A}$ and $\tilde{B}$. Both union and intersection of fuzzy sets are commutative, associate and distributive as is the case for ordinary or crisp sets. Further, the complement $\tilde{A}^c$ of fuzzy set $\tilde{A}$ is defined as:

$$(5.43) \quad \mu_{\tilde{A}^c}(x) = 1 - \mu_{\tilde{A}}(x).$$

---

[8] Generally membership functions are normalised so that there exists at least one $x \in X$ such that $\mu_A(x) = 1$, and $0 \le \mu_A(x) \le 1 \ \forall \ x \in X$.

Fuzzy logic deviates from crisp or bivalent logic because, if we do not know $\tilde{A}$ with certainty, its complement $\tilde{A}^c$ is also not known with certainty. Thus, $\tilde{A}^c \cap \tilde{A}$ does not produce the null set as for crisp sets (where $A^c \cap A = \phi$), so fuzzy logic violates the "law of noncontradiction". It also violates the "law of the excluded middle" because the union of a fuzzy set and its complement does not equal the universe of discourse – the universal set. $\tilde{A}$ is properly fuzzy if and only if $\tilde{A}^c \cap \tilde{A} \neq \phi$ and $\tilde{A}^c \cup \tilde{A} \neq X$, where X is the universal set (Kosko 1992, pp. 269–72).

Fuzzy numbers are used to describe fuzziness and subsume membership functions. We distinguish two types of fuzzy numbers that are important for evaluating environmental resources. First is the notion of fuzzy class or quantity (Cox 1994) that is most frequently associated with fuzzy sets and membership functions. Linguistic descriptors are often used but, no matter how well one is able to describe a particular resource aspect, it will always remain vague. As an example, consider the set of "ponds". A "pond" ceases to be one when it becomes so large that it is conceived of as a "lake", or when it becomes so small that it is better thought of as a "puddle". But all three concepts – puddle, pond and lake – are fuzzy and dependent on the surface area of the water body to be classified, although other factors might enter into the classification, such as the water body's permanency or suitability for certain activities. If surface area is the distinguishing feature, then the fuzzy sets might look like those in Figure 5.9.

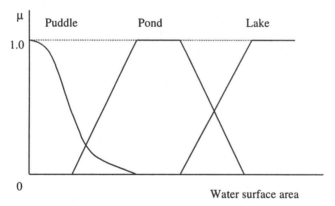

Figure 5.9 Comparison of Several Fuzzy Sets

Fuzzy sets can take a variety of functional forms – they can be linear, piece-wise linear, one-sided (as in the case of "puddles"), two-sided (as for "ponds"), bell-shaped, triangular, symmetric, asymmetric, and so on. Fuzzy sets can also overlap. Hence, a body of water can be classed as both a "puddle" and a "pond" at the same time, although (usually) with differing degrees of membership. It is the researcher's task to construct the relevant parameters that characterise the fuzzy sets "puddles", "ponds" and "lakes", although surveys of experts, say, can be used to specify the forms of the fuzzy sets.

The second type of fuzzy number is associated with fuzzy variables. In this case, the problem is not that of fuzzy set – the extent to which an element is a member of a vague set; rather, it is imprecision in value. For example, "pond" is a fuzzy class or quantity – a problem of fuzzy set – because it is not clear what surface area (or degree of permanency) is required to be sure that a "pond" is not a "lake" or "puddle". In contrast, if a waterfowl biologist estimates the size of a body of water from a satellite photograph to be 2 ha, it could be just as well be 1.5 ha or even 3 ha. This is an example of a fuzzy variable. In this case, fuzzy numbers represent approximations of a central value and can be described by distributions about that value. Such distributions can be symmetric or asymmetric. They are constructed as membership functions, which should not be confused with probability distributions as has been demonstrated by Kosko (1992, pp. 263–94; see also Fedrizzi 1987). In this case, the fuzzy approach provides an alternative to RUM.

In summary, fuzzy numbers are used either to express the idea of fuzziness about what something is (how it should be classified) or imprecision about the value of a particular variable (Cox 1994, pp. 351–3). The only difference is that a fuzzy quantity implies vagueness in classification, while a fuzzy variable indicates uncertainty about its value. When the amenity to be valued is not well defined or known to respondents (or to anyone else for that matter), we have vagueness in classification. What exactly is the amenity to be valued? While linguistic terms and fuzzy classification are one means for dealing with some of the confusion about what exactly is to be valued in CV surveys (Li 1989), fuzzy numbers can also be used to deal with imprecision in the values that are elicited.

A concept required for working with fuzzy numbers is that of the α-*level set*. The α-level set A_α is simply that subset of $\tilde{A}$ for which the degree of membership exceeds the level α, and is itself a crisp set (an element either meets the required level of α or it does not).

(5.44) $A_\alpha = \{x \mid \mu_A(x) \geq \alpha\}$, $\alpha \in [0, 1]\}$.

A_α is an upper level set of $\tilde{A}$. The use of α-level sets provides a means of transferring information from a fuzzy set into a crisp form. Defining an α-level set is referred to as taking an α-cut, cutting off that portion of the fuzzy set whose members do not have the required membership or possibility value. It can be argued that the level of the α-cut is a measure of the reliability of the imprecise coefficient. The more trustworthy the central value of the fuzzy set, the higher is the α-cut.

For additional information on fuzzy logic, a general background to the theory and its applications is provided by McNeill and Freiberger (1993), while technical discussions are found in Bandemer and Gottwald (1996) and Zimmermann (1996).

Fuzzy Contingent Valuation: Forest Preservation in Sweden

To illustrate how fuzzy membership might be used to estimate nonmarket values, we construct a fuzzy WTP membership function using the results of a contingent valuation survey of Swedish residents undertaken during the summer of 1992 (Li and

Mattsson 1995). The survey asked respondents whether they would be willing to pay a given amount "to continue to visit, use, and experience the forest environment as [they] usually do". Bid amounts took one the following values: 50, 100, 200, 400, 700, 1000, 2000, 4000, 8000 and 16 000 SEK. Since the authors were interested in preference uncertainty, they used a post-decisional confidence measure based on a follow-up question that asked respondents how certain they were about their yes-no answer. A graphical scale with 5% intervals was used. The researchers also collected data on household income, the respondent's age, gender, education level, and average annual number of forest visits. The analysis below is based on 389 usable surveys.

We first assume that the individual's response to the question of how certain she is about her answer to the choice problem is a measure of the "fuzziness" of the WTP response and not the utility function itself nor of the amenity to be valued. We construct a fuzzy set of acceptable bids with various degrees of membership. Although choice of form of the membership function affects the results, this is no different than choice of the cumulative distribution function in the RUM model (section 5.3 above). If a respondent answers "yes" to the dichotomous choice question, it is assumed she would then be willing to pay any lesser amount, so that we can construct a one-sided fuzzy set. It is therefore also a measure of the fuzziness of the WTP estimate.[9] The bid amounts are first converted to a proportion of respondent's income. We assume that all respondents are willing to pay zero percent of their income to preserve the forest; we assign the maximum value of 1 to a bid of zero, interpreted as full acceptability in the fuzzy set of "acceptable bid values as a proportion of income". For respondents who accept a bid, their response to the certainty question, $x \in [0, 1]$, denotes the degree of membership of the associated bid in "acceptable bid values as a proportion of income". For the person who rejects a bid, the complementary fuzzy number is used, via (5.43), to indicate the degree of acceptability. Since no respondent was willing to pay 10% or more of household income towards forest protection, fuzzy numbers were truncated at the "tithe amount". Measuring bid as a proportion of income along the abscissa and x along the ordinate, we can construct a fuzzy number for WTP for each respondent.

The approach is explained with the aid of Figure 5.10. Person #1 accepts with 90% certainty a bid that is 2% of household income. The fuzzy number takes on a value of 1 if there is no cost for forest protection. The degree of certainty in his/her WTP declines linearly at a rate of 0.05 for each percent of income that must be contributed, until at 10% it falls to zero. Person #2 rejects with 95% certainty a bid that constitutes 4% of income, which is interpreted as having a degree of membership of 0.05 in the set of acceptable bids. Again, assuming linearity, the person would be totally certain (membership in the fuzzy set is zero) that they would not contribute if asked to contribute anything above 4.21% of income.

---

[9] The questionnaire used for this illustration was not designed to deal with fuzzy categories. Respondents simply do not know with certainty what might constitute an acceptable bid. This interpretation is similar to that provided by Li and Mattsson (1995).

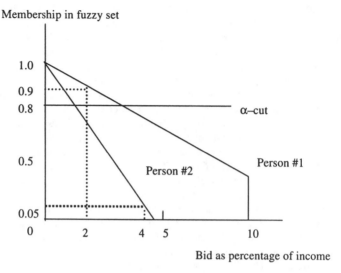

Figure 5.10 Membership Functions for Bids as a Proportion of Income

Also indicated in Figure 5.10 is an α-cut of 0.8. For that value of certainty, person #1 would contribute 4% of income to protect the forest, while person #2 would only contribute 0.842% of income. Alternatively, suppose that #1 had an income of $40,000, while #2 had an income of $50,000. Then, person #1 accepts a WTP offer of $800 with 0.90 certainty, and based on the fuzzy number that was constructed in Figure 5.10, a request to pay $1600 for forest protection with membership of degree 0.8. Person #2, on the other hand, rejects paying $2000 (4% of income) to protect forests with 0.95 certainty (implying acceptance with 0.05 degree of certainty). Based on the derived fuzzy function for person #2 drawn in Figure 5.10, this person would accept paying 0.842% of their income, or $421, with degree of membership of 0.8. The total amount the two would pay together would be $2,021 or an average of $1,010.50 per household with 0.8 degree certainty. For each respondent, we can plot the actual dollar amount on the abscissa and α on the ordinate. For each level of α, then, we determine an average WTP.

The results of this approach are summarised in Figure 5.11. They are not directly comparable to those reported by Li and Mattsson (1995), where a binary yes or no response is interpreted to be its binary opposite if the subsequent level of certainty associated with the response is below 50%. For fuzzy WTP, a "yes" response is also a "no" response, except with different degrees of membership as determined by fuzzy complementarity. Li and Mattsson estimate four different (but crisp) mean WTPs for their uncertainty-adjusted model, depending on the version of the model used and whether or not responses are truncated at 16,000 SEK or not. These range from a low of 7352 SEK to a high of 12,817 SEK.

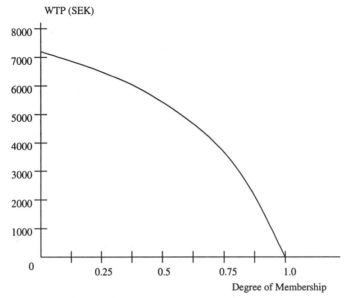

Figure 5.11 Fuzzy WTP for Continued Use of Forest Environment

Our calculations provide a fuzzy WTP number that ranges from 0 to 7300 SEK, below the average values obtained by Li and Mattsson. The crisp value used to represent WTP depends on the degree of membership or α-cut chosen. The results indicate that respondents would certainly be willing to pay nothing to guarantee that the forest environment will be preserved. From Figure 5.11, they would be willing to pay on average about 1800 SEK, with membership value 0.9, for forest protection, but 5000 SEK with membership value 0.5. Thus, the higher the α-cut or membership value for the fuzzy WTP number, the greater is our confidence that respondents consider it to be an acceptable amount to pay for forest protection.

In Figure 5.10 the membership function was assumed to take on only positive WTP values. This was done for convenience only because we had one observation on which to base the membership function. The function could just as well be chosen to be single-peaked (in the same way as for the spike model), taking on negative and positive values. Indeed, a true fuzzy design would focus attention of the construction of the membership function, eliciting the necessary information from survey respondents. In the end, however, choice of a membership function is not different than choice of functional form for the distribution of WTP. Choice of the membership function in Figure 5.10 is no different than choice of a Weibull or log-logistic distribution function in standard CVM. Clearly, more research is required into fuzzy contingent valuation methods.

Fuzzy Pairwise Comparisons

A second approach that uses pairwise comparisons and a market touchstone, much like the choice experiments, is that of fuzzy pairwise comparisons. Fuzzy pairwise comparisons were first used by van Kooten, Schoney and Hayward (1986) to study farmers' goal hierarchies for use in multiple-objective decision making. The fuzzy pairwise method results in a ratio scale that can then be used to value nonmarket goods and services if one of the items in the set has a known market value. Fuzzy pairwise comparisons require that, if there are k items, all are compared in pairwise fashion; thus, there are $k(k-1)/2$ pairwise comparisons that need to be made. Items can then be ordered. Respondents are asked not only to choose between two items, but to indicate an intensity of preference between the items.

A measure of the intensity of preference between two items, A and B, is made by marking on a line, with endpoints denoted A and B, the degree of preference for one over the other; a mark placed at the centre of the line indicates indifference. A measure of the intensity of the preference of item A over item B is determined by measuring the normalised distance from the left-hand-side endpoint (where A is assumed to be located) to the respondents mark, where the line is of unit length after normalisation. Denote this distance by r_{AB}. If $r_{AB} < 0.5$, then A is preferred to B; if $r_{AB} > 0.5$, B is preferred to A; if $r_{AB} = 0.5$, A is equally preferred to B; and $r_{AB} = 1 - r_{BA}$.

Van Kooten et al. (1986), and van Kooten (1998), develop a measure indicating the intensity of preference among items. This concept can be understood as the degree of membership of a fuzzy number. Once all of the pairwise measures r_{ij} are obtained, the measure of intensity for item j, m_j, is determined as:

$$(5.45) \quad m_j = 1 - \sqrt{\frac{\sum_{i=1}^{k} r_{ij}^2}{k-1}},$$

where the numerator in the second term on the RHS is the Euclidean norm, the denominator, $(k-1)^{1/2}$, is its maximum value, and k is the number of items that are ranked by the fuzzy pairwise comparisons. Assume that, as a result of fuzzy pairwise measures, we obtain the following matrix of normalised distances:

Item	1	2	3	4
1	0	0.2121	0.9697	0.1212
2	0.7879	0	0.5606	0.4242
3	0.0303	0.4394	0	0.3485
4	0.8788	0.5758	0.6515	0

The matrix indicates that $1 \succ 2$, $1 \succ 4$, $2 \succ 4$, $3 \succ 1$, $3 \succ 2$ and $3 \succ 4$, where $\succ$ denotes "preferred to". Using the above formula, the preference intensity scores are as follows: $m_1 = 0.4227$, $m_2 = 0.3904$, $m_3 = 0.6757$ and $m_4 = 0.2863$. Further suppose that item 3 is valued at \$100. Then, by independence of irrelevant alternatives (one's preference between oranges and apples does not depend on whether or not a grapefruit exists in the choice set), item 4 is valued at $42.37 (= $100 × 0.2863/0.6757).

Values obtained using fuzzy pairwise comparisons are compared in Chapter 6 to those obtained using both an open-ended and dichotomous choice CVM instrument. The results indicate that the fuzzy methodology could be a viable alternative to standard CVM.

5.5 Discussion

In this chapter, we have provided a brief review of the state of the art in the valuation of goods and services that are not traded in markets. It is our impression, however, that the field of nonmarket valuation is at a threshold. While damage functions are increasingly used to value loss in environmental goods such as soil and trees, their use in practice is limited. Likewise, the travel cost method and hedonic price technique are too limited in their applicability to current environmental concerns. This leaves the contingent valuation method as the most popular means for measuring nonmarket values. However, insights and critiques from the emerging field of behavioural economics (or economic psychology), and evidence from CVM itself, indicates that the values obtained from surveys may not reflect people's true worth. While the debate over CVM and the search for new techniques (some of which were identified here) continues, we feel that a significant challenge remains.

In the remaining chapters, we assume that the values obtained for biological assets and other environmental amenities using methods discussed in this chapter are a good indicator of their true value. Yet, as we demonstrate, this is not very helpful from a policy perspective. What is needed is information about how nonuse values change as the availability of the amenity varies. Decisions are made at the margin and it is marginal and not total values that are important. We begin in the next chapter by considering cost-benefit analysis, providing examples of the use of nonmarket values in cost-benefit studies. In later chapters on biodiversity (Chapters 9 and 10), we employ nonmarket values to evaluate species preservation in a dynamic context. Clearly, there is a demand for nonuse values, but the supply or provision of such values is limited.

6 Evaluating Natural Resource Policy

Since planners and decision makers are frequently required to choose among two or more alternative programs, or policies, project evaluation plays a key role in public investment planning. Project evaluation is a term used to describe any consistent set of criteria – financial, economic or social – that can be used to judge whether potential public investment projects are likely to achieve stated policy objectives. Objectives might be to increase employment, diversify the economy of a particular region, increase the number of individuals living in a certain location (e.g., the far North of Canada), attain the largest net social economic benefit for the public expenditure, or protect the American burying beetle (*Nicrophorous americanus*). Only the restricted objective of economic or allocative efficiency – to achieve the greatest net *economic* benefit for society – is addressed by social cost-benefit analysis (CBA).

Unless the CBA practitioner is fully cognisant of the methodology and underlying theoretical foundation of cost-benefit analysis, there may be confusion about what needs to be measured and how. For example, one may have trouble distinguishing between the economic *benefits* of a project and the economic *impacts* of a project. The former refers is a welfare measure, while the latter is a measure of economic activity, but it has no meaning for welfare as defined in earlier chapters. That is, objectives other than economic efficiency cannot properly be considered in the cost-benefit framework as these are generally considered to be income transfers in applied welfare economics.

Further, there is a difference between a financial accounting of costs and benefits (one taken by the private sector, say) and economic or social CBA, which takes into account externalities, such as nonmarket values, as well as private costs and benefits. The accounting stance, or viewpoint, one takes regarding what to include in the analysis affects what the decision maker or analyst includes as costs and benefits. As a result, CBA is as much art as it is science.

In this chapter, we describe the methodology of social cost-benefit analysis and consider its role in the evaluation of several natural resource policies. The examples we use are from actual cost-benefit studies. While the methodology described in the examples is applicable to *social* evaluation of land and resource projects in general, CBA is not the only evaluation technique (Smith 1986). The methods and issues discussed in this chapter and those that follow will, hopefully, clarify problems that might be encountered in the analysis of projects.

In this chapter, we begin by examining the role of government in the economy and the associated need for project evaluation. The history of cost-benefit analysis leading to multiple accounts analysis is examined in section 6.2, while sections 6.3 and 6.4 discuss choice of discount rate and the mechanics of CBA, respectively. Three case studies are provided in section 6.5. Our conclusions ensue in section 6.6.

6.1 Policy Evaluation and the Role of Government

Government intervention in the economy through direct investment has long been taken for granted. More recently, economists have applied insights from the New Institutional Economics (Furubotn and Richter 1997) to question whether public or private provision of goods and services is preferred. While the goods and services in question relate to health care, education and prisons, it can equally apply to provision of many environmental amenities (e.g., recreation, watershed protection, and wildlife habitat). Shleifer (1998) and Hart et al. (1997) make the case for private provision of health care, schools and other services that are usually associated with government provision. The reasons for private provision are that it leads to incentives for innovation and cost minimisation, but possibly at the expense of quality. Where cost of provision is important and quality is less important, the case for private provision is strongest. However, even where quality is important, the ability of government to use contracts to get what it wants could mitigate the need for public provision. While private firms providing a service have an incentive to innovate so as to reduce costs, contracts can be written in ways that prevent deterioration of quality as a result of cost-minimising efforts or encourage innovation to improve quality (e.g., via performance incentives). Public ownership or provision may be preferred when the adverse effect of cost reduction on quality is large, quality improvements are unimportant, or government employees have weaker incentives in quality improvement than private owners (Hart et al. 1997).

In addition to the quality-cost of provision tradeoff, corruption and patronage are important in deciding whether public or private provision is preferred. Corruption and patronage are opposite sides of the same coin. Corruption occurs when private firms are effectively able to lobby or "bribe" government officials to extend them favours (e.g., providing contracts for provision of services with weak or vague performance clauses). Patronage occurs when government (elected) officials favour particular constituents in return for their support (e.g., public service union workers are provided large pay raises, environmental groups are given freedom to protest even if they break the law). Where corruption is a severe problem, the case for in-house provision is enhanced; where patronage is a problem, the case favours privatisation.

In the mainstream literature, accepted reasons for government intervention in the economy are linked to market failure, particularly externality. There are three forms of externality:

1. Ownership or technological externality (e.g., pollution, open-access).

2. Public goods externality – the market will not provide nature reserves, or protection of biodiversity, as incentives are lacking.
3. Technical externality – falling long-run average costs leading to natural monopoly)

Governments can use public ownership, regulation, taxes or public expenditure on the provision of goods and services to achieve the socially optimum level of provision, or correct the market failure. Governments might also intervene in the economy on the basis of actual or perceived inter-temporal inefficiency, and on income inequality or equity grounds.

It is now recognised in mainstream economics that government itself can be a source of failure in the economy. This source of failure is labelled policy failure (see, e.g., Panayotou 1993a). As noted, the new institutional economists point to possibilities of corruption and patronage as a source of policy failure. Even well meaning policies, some of which are meant to correct market failure, can lead to a worsening environment or reduction rather than improvement in the overall well being of society. An example is provided in section 6.5, where government regulations of forest practices are designed to protect environmental amenities (correct a market failure), but the result in a diminution of social welfare. Likewise, government agricultural policies in developed countries have led to environmental deterioration, although the original aim of such policies was to protect family farms. Government policies are also a contributing factor to tropical deforestation, as shown in Chapter 12. Policy failure may be a greater source of failure within the economy than market failure.

What can cost-benefit analysis contribute? CBA offers primarily a consist criterion for evaluating the costs and benefits of government intervention through direct investment, regulations or other policies, leaving the final decision to the political process. Consider water resource development projects, which are often not provided without government intervention. Although water development projects enhance navigation, flood control and water supply, the major benefits are often electrical power generation, water for irrigation and water for recreation. Electric power generation and irrigation projects have elements of technical externality since they require enormous investments, so marginal costs inevitably lie below price once the project is built, and benefits are disbursed to many individuals in society. Hence, such projects may not be provided privately or, if they are, they are smaller in capacity than desired from a social point of view. Provision of recreation, on the other hand, is a proper function of government because of its public good characteristics; in particular, it is unlikely to be provided privately since those who bear the direct costs of facilitating the recreational activity frequently can appropriate only some of the benefits. Finally, public investment in water projects may serve as a catalyst for economic development. For these reasons, a strong case can be made for public investment in the development of water resources.

Although public investment in the economy is justified in many situations, this does not imply that the government should pursue all investments that might be deemed worthwhile, however the term "worthwhile" is defined. Indeed, the government's ability to pursue certain investments is limited by the availability of funds. Therefore, given the limited amount of public funds, some method of determining which investments are worth pursuing and which are not must be agreed upon – and the mechanism for doing this is known as *project evaluation*. Smith (1986) discusses several approaches to project evaluation, but CBA is probably the most comprehensive. However, because cost-benefit analysis is a more restrictive concept than project evaluation *per se*, it often constitutes an input into the broader politics of policy evaluation.

Whenever project evaluation is undertaken, it is important for the practitioner to recognise, and to identify clearly, the viewpoint that is taken. If economic efficiency is important to the decision then cost-benefit analysis is an appropriate tool to employ, but its limitations must be recognised. CBA has been criticised precisely because it focuses on economic efficiency only, while the objective of most public programs is not simply, or even principally, economic efficiency. CBA also embodies an ethic that is not acceptable to everyone, namely, utilitarianism. For example, some cannot accept measuring everything in monetary terms or they argue that CBA may be largely irrelevant or relevant to only a small part of the problem of evaluating public projects and programs (e.g., Layard 1972, pp. 61–2; Self 1972). Clearly, it needs to be understood that political feasibility and acceptability are important aspects of project evaluation

There have been attempts to modify the cost-benefit methodology to address some of the criticisms. Dreze and Stern (1987), and Squire and van der Tak (1975), for example, recommend including value judgements about income distribution directly in the social CBA calculations by using distributional weights for specific regions, income classes, and so on. To obtain knowledge about the weights amounts to discovering society's tradeoff between economic efficiency and income distribution. This task is identical to discovering society's welfare function, which may be impossible (Arrow 1951). Thus, most economists do not consider it proper to include income distributional considerations within the CBA framework. It is our view, by including subjective value judgements social CBA's contribution is watered down, because it is then possible to derive several (contradictory) conclusions about economic efficiency from the same information.

Despite these objections, cost-benefit calculations are important, not only because they are one of the criteria used to evaluate projects, but because they provide data concerning the costs of pursuing objectives other than economic efficiency. Cost-benefit analysis enables one to determine tradeoffs among objectives.

There are two important points that should be made. First, economists trained in welfare economics frequently refuse to consider alternatives to economic efficiency as having any validity in policy analysis since these approaches have to do with social and political matters that are beyond the scope of economic science. In fact, some economists stress that CBA cannot embrace the wider considerations that the political system must deal with, but whether these criticisms relate to the economist's inability to quantify certain items is not clear. Yet, there is nothing wrong with a practice of quantifying the quantifiables and leaving the qualitative factors (sometimes referred to as "intangibles") as additional considerations. This argument leads to the concept of *multiple accounts*, which is discussed in the next section. Second, and related to this, it is not possible to mix measurement tools since this results in confusion about, and possible misrepresentation of, the project analysis. Thus, for example, it is not possible to construct a benefit-cost (B-C) ratio by including the regional development impacts resulting from the implementation of a water resource project as secondary benefits. A portion of such impacts may constitute benefits from the project, but only under special circumstances. This is discussed further below.

6.2 A Brief Background to Cost-Benefit Analysis

As the government's role in the economy expanded, it was necessary for decision-makers to develop guidelines to determine whether public funds spent on various government activities were achieving their aims. One guideline developed by US legislators in the Flood Control Act of 1936 required that the benefits of water development projects, "to whomsoever they may accrue", should exceed all the social costs related to the development of the project.[1] This requirement was subsequently expanded upon in the economics literature, culminating in what is now known as cost-benefit analysis.

As a result of the 1936 Flood Control Act, an Inter-Agency River Basin Committee, with representatives from the Department of Agriculture, the Army Corps of Engineers, the Bureau of Reclamation and the Federal Power Commission, was set up to develop procedures for testing whether benefits exceeded costs. The Sub-Committee on Costs and Budgets published criteria for the appraisal of water resource projects in the so-called "Green Book" of 1950. The US Inter-Agency Committee on Water Resources published a revised edition of the "Green Book" in 1958. In that same year, McKean (1958) and Eckstein (1958) published procedures for evaluating the economic efficiency of projects. Since then, Mishan (1971), Harberger (1972), the Treasury Board Secretariat of Canada (1976), Sassone and Schaffer (1978), and many others have outlined procedures for conducting cost-benefit analyses.[2]

In 1961, the US Secretaries of the Interior, Agriculture, Army, and Health, Education and Welfare were requested to review evaluation standards for water and related land resources development projects. Their recommendation (US Inter-Agency Committee on Water Resources 1962) was that development, environmental preservation and individuals' well-being should be considered equal objectives. The suggested approach was to formulate plans on the basis of economic benefits and costs, but constrained by environmental preservation and well-being objectives. The result was that preservation and well-being were not actually given equal status with

---

[1] The first application of BCA occurred in 1902 "when the US River and Harbor Act directed the Corps of Engineers to asses the costs and benefits of all river and harbor projects" (Bentkover 1986).
[2] The literature on project appraisal is profuse and it would be inappropriate to document all of it here. It should be noted that much of the early literature originated with the World Bank and other development agencies (e.g., Gittinger 1982; Squire and van der Tak 1975; Little and Mirrlees 1974; Dasgupta et al. 1972).

development or economic efficiency, as the former were simply a constraint on the latter. Subsequently, further effort was expended on the development of guidelines for conducting project evaluation.

The methodology for performing project evaluations, particularly social cost-benefit analyses, began to take concrete form with the US Water Resources Council's "Principles and Standards" (P&S) for water project evaluation, which appeared in the *US Federal Register* in 1973 and 1979 (US Water Resources Council 1973, 1979). In 1973, the US Water Resources Council (hereafter WRC) identified four objectives for project evaluation.

1. All the benefits and costs of a project had to be considered in the evaluation, regardless of who bore the costs and who received the benefits. This is the objective of national economic development.
2. Impacts on the environment had to be calculated and included in the cost-benefit analysis. This implied that the nonmarket benefits of recreation, environmental degradation, etc., had to be taken into account.
3. The regional benefits of resource development projects were to be included explicitly in the analysis, making it possible to justify a project on the basis of its regional development benefits.
4. Finally, the impact of a project on social well-being had to be taken into account. For example, the analyst or planner was to take into account the impact of the project on certain groups in society (e.g., on blacks or on those with lower incomes). This objective, then, required explicit consideration of social issues in evaluating resource development projects.

The 1973 P&S for evaluating projects focused only on the first objective. The 1979 P&S attempted to extend the evaluation methodology to the second objective. It is clear that, for water projects, the measured benefits from recreation were to be included, while, for environmental programs, the benefits of improving air and water quality were also to be determined. (Unlike 1973, the 1979 P&S included detailed instructions for evaluating projects.) The last two objectives were not addressed in the 1979 P&S, perhaps because the WRC did not feel these could be handled within the P&S framework then proposed.

In 1982, the 1979 P&S were repealed, only to be reinstated the following year (WRC 1983). Given the requirements of various pieces of US legislation relating to water (and other) resource developments, a method for including items 2, 3 and 4 into the evaluation process had to be found. Such a method was developed in the 1983 "Principles and Guidelines" (P&G); by recognising non-commensurability among the various objectives, which was not explicitly done in the earlier P&S, the WRC adopted a *multiple accounts* approach to project evaluation. The 1983 P&G are currently in use in the USA, but have not been wholeheartedly adopted by other countries (although they do serve as a guideline).

The four accounts that are now identified in the P&G (WRC 1983) are similar to the four categories indicated above. The difference between the approaches is the recognition that the various accounts deal with different issues and are not commensurable. Thus, the 1983 P&G include a description of methods for displaying the different accounts. The four accounts can be summarised as follows:

1.   National Economic Development (NED) Account
2.   Environmental Quality (EQ) Account
3.   Regional Economic Development (RED) Account
4.   Other Social Effects (OSE) Account

Cost-benefit analysis is used only to evaluate those items that can be measured in dollar terms, namely, those found in the NED account and quantifiable components of the EQ and RED accounts. The items that cannot be monetized are to be presented in each of the EQ, RED and OSE accounts and are briefly described in the following paragraphs.

The main tool used to analyse the RED account has historically been input-output analysis. As noted above, the main fallacy that has been made in the past (and continues to be made by many involved in project evaluation) is to include values obtained from input-output analysis in the cost-benefit values (Stabler et al. 1988; Hamilton et al. 1991). The RED account recognises that these items are not directly comparable – that benefits to a region may be costs to the nation as a whole, indicating that the RED account focuses on income transfers (e.g., income transfers to Canada's maritime provinces to help them cope with loss of the fishery). By separating the NED and RED accounts (and the other accounts as well), the incompatibility between economic efficiency and income distribution (or equity) is explicitly recognised.

According to the P&G, environmental items that are to be displayed in the EQ account are ecological attributes, cultural attributes and aesthetic attributes. Ecological attributes include functional aspects of the environment (e.g., assimilative capacity, erosion, nutrient cycling, succession) and structural aspects such as plant and animal species, chemical and physical properties of air, water and soil (e.g., pH of rainfall), and so on. Cultural attributes are evidence of past and present habitation that can help in understanding and propagating human life. Aesthetic attributes include sights, scents, sounds, tastes, impressions, etc., of the environment. It is clear that these attributes would be difficult to measure in monetary terms (see Chapter 5), although they can be measured in other ways. These include both quantity indicators that employ numeric and non-numeric scales and quality indicators such as "good" and "bad". It is obvious, however, that the EQ attributes need to be presented in a clear and concise fashion if they are to be of use in the decision making framework.

Several principles govern the planning process with respect to the environmental quality account. Both an interdisciplinary approach and public involvement are required in the planning process, although the means for involving the public is left to the discretion of the planning agency. The EQ account is designed to assist agencies in meeting the requirements of the US National Environmental Policy Act (NEPA) of 1969 and the NEPA guidelines established by the US Council on Environmental Quality. As such, the procedures established by the WRC are meant to facilitate water resource planning to satisfy the aforementioned requirements, plus environmental requirements under the Endangered Species Act (1973), the National Historic Preservation Act (1966), the Fish and Wildlife Coordination Act (1972), and the

Coastal Zone Management Act (1972), and their subsequent amendments. Finally, as discussed below with respect to costs and benefits (NED account), the EQ attributes need to be displayed in a way that highlights the comparison between the "with project" and "without project" scenarios.

The OSE account includes any items that are not included in the other three accounts but are important for planning. While the US WRC's Principles and Guidelines provide no procedures for evaluating other social effects, it does indicate that such effects include "urban and community impacts; life, health, and safety factors; displacement; long-term productivity; and energy requirements and energy conservation". They also include effects on income distribution, employment, population distribution, fiscal effects on State and local governments, quality of community life, and so on. While some of these effects can be measured in monetary terms and, thus, included in the NED account, others need to be displayed using guidelines similar to those of the EQ account. It appears that public agencies have substantial freedom within the planning process to include whatever items they wish in the OSE account and how they are to be displayed.

Since the publication of the P&S, and P&G, the basic techniques of evaluation have been extended to the appraisal of all US government projects and programs, particularly environmental regulatory programs.

In Canada, guidelines for project appraisal were established in 1976 by the Federal Treasury Board Secretariat, but these are vague and, in most instances, not very useful to the practitioner. One reason is that they appeared before the 1979 P&S were released in the USA; alternatively, it is likely that the political system in Canada, that relies on income transfers via specified projects from the central government to the provinces mitigates the development and use of strict evaluation criteria. Project evaluation guidelines have also been developed by most provinces, but many of these are internal documents and unavailable to the general practitioner.

One of the most comprehensive cost-benefit studies ever undertaken concerned a third airport for London, England. The Roskill Commission, which reported in 1971, had been asked to recommend where a third London airport should be located, and when it should be built (Layard 1972, p. 61). The first step that the Commission took was to provide a draft cost-benefit analysis. An overview of the study's CBA is provided by Flowerdew (1972), with criticism by Mishan (1972).

In practice, the cost-benefit methodology is often not strictly adhered to in making decisions about public investment projects. For example, there is no evidence that the US Bureau of Reclamation used cost-benefit guidelines in determining whether to construct many of the dams that were placed on rivers in the western USA during the decades of the 1940s, 1950s and 1960s (Reisner 1986). Perhaps this is because social CBA methodology was in its infancy, but it could also be the result of political factors or project evaluation criteria other than social cost-benefit analysis.

A problem occurs with the multiple accounts approach to cost-benefit analysis when all of the accounts are given equal status – when no account is given precedence over any other account. In that case, proponents of any one account are not required to seek compromise, conceding to trade off one benefit for another, but they tend to become entrenched their position. We return to this in Chapter 9 where we consider preservation of species. If species are to be preserved at all cost, then there are insufficient funds to preserve all species. While compromise might lead to some middle ground for species preservation, say, the decision in the multiple accounts framework often boils down to choosing between one of two extreme policies. For example, the middle ground might be a policy that leads to a 50-50 chance that a particular species survives for the next 100 years. However, the decision amounts to a choice between the policy that gives the species a 95% chance of survival (the impossibly expensive option) and the one that gives the species less than a 10% chance of survival (the "do nothing" option). In British Columbia, where the multiple accounts philosophy treats all accounts as equal, protection of wilderness areas may even be threatened by the failure to compromise (van Kooten 1995a).

6.3 Choice of Social Discount Rate

Benefits and costs accrue at different points in time. Since $1 today is worth more to an individual (or society) than that same dollar received at some future date (say, next year), it is necessary to discount future benefits and costs. The calculation of net present value (NPV) and the B-C ratio is sensitive to the rate of discount (interest rate) that is employed in CBA. What, then, is the appropriate rate of discount to use in weighting future costs and benefits? For many years there have been disagreements among economists on the right conceptual basis for social discount rates – the rate at which society should be willing to substitute present consumption for future consumption at the margin (Johansson 1987, pp. 161–2). In addition, there is disagreement on whether or not an adjustment for risk is appropriate for government projects, and on the nature and size of the adjustment assuming one is required.

Broadly speaking, there is a school of thought that advocates use of the opportunity cost of capital rate (OCC), which is based on the productivity of capital; a second school advocates using the marginal rate of time preference (MRTP). Proponents of the OCC rate argue that government investments divert funds that would otherwise go into private investment, and referred to as the "crowding out effect". Crowding out may result in a decrease in wealth for society as profitable investment opportunities are foregone. The MRTP is the rate at which one is willing to trade present consumption for future consumption. The MRTP typically is the sum of two components – the pure rate of time preference (a measure of impatience) and a term that is the product of the elasticity of marginal utility of consumption and the rate of change of consumption. The latter constitutes a judgement that future generations are probably better off (richer), such that the marginal benefit of additional revenues is lower. Hence, even if we have zero pure time preference, future costs and benefits are still discounted if consumption is growing and the utility function is concave in consumption.

The marginal rates of time preference of individuals in society may differ. This enables them profitably to trade current and future incomes (individuals who value the present more highly will borrow from those who value the future more) until their rates are equal. In a first-best world without taxes, transaction costs, uncertainty and external effects, the equilibrium rate of time preference associated with many individuals is called the social rate of time preference (SRTP). By definition, this represents the rate at which society is willing to trade off present for future consumption. Efficiency requires that in such a first-best world the SRTP is equal to the social opportunity cost rate (Clark 1990; Pearce and Turner 1990). Trading among consumers and producers will result in a situation where both the SRTP and the social opportunity cost of capital rate are equal to the market interest rate.

Determination of society's discount rate (or the SRTP) is difficult for a number of reasons. First of all, individuals themselves are not consistent with respect to the rates of time preference they use, with an individual choosing different rates depending on the circumstances. Evidence from behavioural economics indicates that people commonly discount future losses at a lower rate than future gains, and that they use higher rates to discount outcomes in the near future than those in the distant future (Knetsch 2000). Further, individuals may have different preferences with respect to the environment, for example, in their role as citizens than in their role as consumers (Sagoff 1988a). Such preferences are usually expressed politically.

Society may also choose to save more collectively than the sum of all individual savings decisions (Marglin 1963). The government is considered a trustee for unborn generations, whose wealth will (at least in part) depend on the state of the environment that they inherit, so real consumption (and rates of return on invest-ments) may not grow, and may even decline, when we degrade the environment. Further, because of risk and uncertainty (giving rise to "risk premiums"), society's rate of time preference will be lower than that of individuals as society as a whole is better able to pool risks; certain individual risks are mere transfers at the level of society. While individuals face real chances of death, society does not really face such a risk. All in all, these more or less ethical arguments suggest that society's rate of discount is lower than that of individuals making up the society. The social discount rate is likely lower than the opportunity cost of capital rate or the marginal rate of time preference, but it is not immediately clear how much lower.

The argument becomes more complex when we realise that the simplifying assumption of a first-best world without taxes, risk or uncertainty in which MRTP and OCC rate coincide does not exist. For example, introducing a tax on corporate profits and/or on individual incomes will affect equality of OCC and MRTP. With taxes, the required rate of return for private parties should be higher than the marginal rate of time preference, implying that too few investments are undertaken and that a bias exists against longer-term investments. Hence, in the real world, the OCC rate is likely to exceed the MRTP. It is not clear which rate should prevail as the basis of the social discount rate, given that a case can be made for both the MRTP and the OCC?

Some authors, notably Harberger (1972), have argued that the correct discount rate r should be a weighted average of the return to private investment (OCC) and foregone consumption (MRTP): $r = \alpha OCC + (1 - \alpha)MRTP$, where α is the fraction of a dollar of public spending that displaces private investment and $(1 - \alpha)$ displacing consumption. As pointed out by Zerbe and Dively (1994), however, the Harberger rate is theoretically incorrect because it ignores what happens to the proceeds of public investment (e.g., these could be reinvested).

The theoretically correct approach is as follows: the consumption value of investment should be discounted at the SRTP (or the MRTP corrected for ethical considerations and external effects), but displacement of private investment should also be taken into account (Zerbe and Dively 1994, p. 283; also Bradford 1975; Musgrave 1969).[3] The effect of the OCR is thus taken into account in discovering the change in consumption produced by a private investment. In contrast to the above approach, the analysis is extended to both the costs and the benefits of the investment. The latter is taken into account by distinguishing the fraction β of the proceeds from public investment that is returned to private capital. Depending on the magnitude of α and β, simply discounting with the corrected SRTP while ignoring the impact for the private sector may be overstating ($\alpha > \beta$) or understating ($\alpha < \beta$) a project's NPV.

In a number of cases, simply using the SRTP without further adjustments – simply discounting ordinary costs and benefits – is warranted. This is the case when analysis indicates that benefits and costs affect private capital in the same proportion. Also, the effect of crowding out may be non-existent, as in an open economy where there is a high degree of capital mobility (see Zerbe and Dively 1994). The trend of increasing global capital mobility implies that errors of applying the SRTP will in most cases be small (Lind 1990), although it should be recognised that there are still many developing countries where capital markets are rudimentary or controlled by governments.

Next consider the matter of empirically estimating the SRTP, or the discount rate to apply in CBA. In general, the SRTP has been identified with the after tax real return on safe investments (where ideally we would like to use expected real rates of return). Since such returns are a function of the state of the economy (growth, inflation), they will typically not be constant over time. According to Zerbe and Dively (1994, pp. 287–8), real rates between 4% and 5% before taxes seem appropriate for the 1980s and early 1990s for the USA, which corresponds with an after tax return varying from 2.70 to 4.25%. Note that this number is quite a bit lower than the rate of return on private investments, which typically ranges from 15 to 25%.

The discount rate and biological assets

The discount rate has profound effects on the portfolio of assets that society wishes to maintain. It is usually assumed that high discount rates are detrimental for the environment and nature conservation. One interpretation is as follows. As will be explained in Chapter 7, efficient management of biological assets implies, among other things, that the current benefits of extraction are equal to the user cost, or potential future benefits foregone. Increasing the discount rate implies, *ceteris paribus*, that the user cost declines, which favours current extraction, conversion of land from nature to cultivation, and consumption. Another interpretation, based on

---

[3] The shadow price of private capital, or the net present value of consumption from $1 of private investment, is a concept that can be used to convert those public investments that displace private funds to consumption equivalents. This implies that one simply convert all benefits and costs to consumption equivalents using the shadow price of capital, and then discount these by the SRTP.

substitution possibilities between different forms of capital (see Chapter 8), is that higher discount rates are consistent with a higher opportunity cost of capital, or marginal productivity of human-made capital. Simple portfolio management then suggests that the stock of biological assets should be depleted until the rate of return on investments in natural capital has increased until it is equal to the rate on competing goods (i.e., investment in human-made capital). This is discussed further in the following chapters.

Some caveats apply to the suggested inverse relation between discount rates and environmental quality. First, since many resource extraction industries are capital intensive, higher discount rates lead to lower NPV (as costs occur early on while benefits stretch into the future). This may slow down conversion in early phases (Toman and Walls 1995). Second, if capital is an input into the extraction process, marginal extraction costs may rise for higher discount rates, thereby slowing down extraction (Sweeney 1993). Finally, Pearce and Turner (1990) mention that a higher discount rate may reduce the overall level of economic growth, thereby restraining demand for natural resources. This is formally demonstrated by Rowthorn and Brown (1995), who study biodiversity loss due to habitat conversion, and conclude that higher discount rates tend to make production more labour intensive:

> Failure to discount future utilities might eventually result in an unacceptable rate of habitat destruction. By making the discount rate positive we can move output growth onto a lower trajectory and reduce the demand for land for use in production. Thus, one rationale for discounting could be to preserve the environment. (Rowthorn and Brown 1995, p. 33)

6.4 Mechanics of Cost-Benefit Analysis

In the remainder of this chapter, we focus only on social CBA as a tool for evaluating projects.[4] We provide a discussion of the methodology of cost-benefit analysis and, in the following section, examples of how to apply CBA in practice.

There are several important assumptions that should be pointed out, however, as many are ethical in nature and may not be acceptable to all in society. By stating these assumptions up front and given that cost-benefit analysis is based on a strong theoretical foundation, it contributes to rational analysis of public investments.

1. Only marginal changes in the economy are to be evaluated. That is, the impact of projects to be evaluated is small compared to national output.
2. There are no significant distortions in other markets. Those that exist must be taken into account either by using shadow prices or by measuring indirect net benefits or costs in other markets (see Chapter 2).

---

[4] The theoretical foundations of CBA have been well documented by Harberger (1972), Boadway (1974), Just et al. (1982), and Boadway and Bruce (1984), among others. They are also provided in Chapters 2 and 3.

3.   The status quo or some other distribution of income is taken as given. Usually CBA is based on the existing income distribution.
4.   The tastes, income and wealth of the current generation are the starting point for the desires and ability to pay of future generations.
5.   All individuals are treated equally so that a marginal dollar accruing to a rich person is valued the same as a dollar going to a poor person.
6.   Either uncertainty is absent or the public's attitude toward risk can be represented by changes in the discount rate.

It is clear that these assumptions impose limits on the interpretation of the results of project evaluation using CBA. However, if these presuppositions are recognised, cost-benefit analysis becomes a useful tool for analysing public policies.

Economic efficiency is simply defined. First, it is necessary to calculate the present value of all the social costs (PVC) of a proposed project as:

$$(6.1) \quad PVC = \sum_{t=0}^{T} \frac{C_t}{(1+r)^t},$$

where C_t refers to *all* of the project-related costs incurred by society in year t, the life of the project is T years, and r is the rate of discount. The costs are calculated for each year; these are costs over and above those that would be encountered in the absence of the project. The *"with-without"* principle of CBA is important since it illustrates the economic concept of opportunity cost. The term C_0 is sometimes referred to as the capital or construction cost.

Likewise, it is necessary to calculate the present or discounted value of all the social benefits of the project (PVB):

$$(6.2) \quad PVB = \sum_{t=0}^{T} \frac{B_t}{(1+r)^t},$$

where B_t refers to *all* of the benefits that result from the project in year t, regardless of who in society receives them. Again benefits are defined as the difference between benefits that accrue with the project in place as opposed to without it.

The next step in determining economic efficiency is to calculate the difference between PVC and PVB; the present value of net social benefits or simply net present value (NPV) is defined as NPV = PVB – PVC. If NPV > 0, then the project adds to the welfare of society and is deemed to be economically efficient. If NPV < 0, the present value of costs is greater than the present value of benefits and the project should not be pursued because society will be made worse off overall. Such a project should only be undertaken if the attainment of some other objective such as income redistribution warrants the overall loss to society.

The formula for making cost-benefit calculations is straightforward. Problems occur in the choice of discount rate and in measuring the actual costs and benefits. In particular, there is controversy about what is to be included in the measurements. The concept of economic surplus is important in this regard.

For a given project, one could identify three types of benefits or costs:

1. Benefits and costs for which market prices exist and for which these prices correctly reflect social values (see Chapters 2 and 3).
2. Benefits and costs for which market prices exist, but these prices do not reflect social values (e.g., labour input that would otherwise be unemployed) (Sassone and Schaffer 1978, pp. 63–95).
3. Benefits and costs for which no market prices exist because the commodities (e.g., recreation, water quality, historic sites) are not generally traded in the market place.

The first two types of benefits and costs are most easily included in a CBA, while the last category of benefits (or costs) is frequently presented as additional considerations because these values are difficult to obtain.

All projects with a positive NPV should, in principle, be undertaken because they add to the welfare of society, but budget constraints prevent this from happening. Therefore, a project with a positive NPV may not proceed because an alternative project has a higher NPV. When there are a large number of projects and programs available to decision makers with a limited budget, it is necessary to rank projects. This can be done by comparing the social benefits on a per \$1 basis of social costs; a B-C ratio can be constructed for this purpose, namely, $B/C = PVB \div PVC$. As long as $B/C > 1.0$, the project is worthwhile undertaking since, for every \$1 society spends, it gains more than \$1. While all projects yielding a B-C ratio greater than 1.0 should be developed, if there are a number of different projects competing for limited funds, the B-C ratios can be used to rank the projects. Projects are then chosen from the highest to the lowest B/C, until either all of the available funds are expended or there are no more projects with a $B/C > 1.0$. What is confusing is that other B-C ratios may be constructed to examine particular aspects of a project.

1. It may be useful to determine the benefits accruing to each \$1 spent by the government. In this case, one subtracts from benefits the private costs and divides the result by public costs only; i.e., $(PVB - PVC_{private}) \div PVC_{public}$, where PVB is defined in (6.1), $PVC_{private}$ and PVC_{public} refer to the present values of private and public costs, respectively. Thus, a distinction is made between costs incurred by the private sector and those incurred by the government.
2. If it is necessary to distinguish between capital costs and the costs associated with the operation, maintenance and routine replacement (OM&R) of a facility, the B-C ratio might be written as $(PVB - PVC_{OM\&R}) \div C_0$, where $PVC_{OM\&R}$ is the present value of the OM&R costs, and C_0 represents the capital or construction costs of the project. (If construction of the facility requires a period in excess of one year, then C_0 can be thought of as the present value of capital costs.) For example, the authority might purchase a biological preserve but hand it over to a non-governmental organisation for operation.

3.   Finally, one might wish to determine the impact of each $1 of project costs only. The present value of associated costs (AC) is then subtracted from social benefits and divided by project costs. An example of associated costs are the increased on-farm costs that result when a water resources project is built for irrigation purposes. Then the B-C ratio can be written as (PVB − AC) ÷ PVC$_{Project}$. This concept of the benefit-cost ratio can also be interpreted as the "direct costs" B-C ratio.

None of these representations of the B-C ratio should replace NPV and the social B-C ratio; they can be presented as additional considerations. This has occurred in cases where the government has constructed irrigation works but ignored the associated costs of agricultural improvements; see, for example, the discussion in PFRA & Saskatchewan Water Corporation (1985).

One alternative to providing a project's NPV or its B-C ratio is to present annualised net returns. This is done by calculating NPV and then dividing it by the discount rate using the bond formula: $V = Y ÷ r$, where V is the value of the bond (NPV), Y is the annual yield of the bond and r is the discount rate. Annualising NPV is equivalent to finding Y. Of course, the bond formula can also be used to provide annualised benefits or costs (see Chapter 11 for examples).

It is unimportant for economic efficiency whether the project is funded locally or by taxpayers outside the project region. However, in the latter case there will be additional benefits that need to be evaluated, but only if the outside funds are tied to that particular project and would not be available under any other circumstances. Even in this situation, the benefits are difficult to measure, constitute a transfer from individuals outside the region, and may not even accrue to current residents in the region. Therefore, applied welfare economists correctly ignore them.

The one thing that should not be ignored in the evaluation of public projects is government inefficiency. Not only can the marginal excess burden of tax collection be onerous, but the costs of making funds available for projects often add further costs that are overlooked in determining the actual costs of a public project.

Finally, the internal rate of return (IRR) criterion is an alternative to NPV and the B-C ratio in selecting the most efficient projects, but it is not widely used by natural resource economists although it is used in private industry. In principle, IRR yields the same ranking of projects as NPV and the B-C ratio, as long as care is taken in specifying reinvestment alternatives. The IRR is found by setting NPV equal to zero and solving for the discount rate or IRR:

$$(6.3) \qquad \sum_{t=0}^{T} \frac{B_t - C_t}{(1 + IRR)^t} = 0,$$

where T is the length of the time horizon. To find IRR requires solving a higher-order function, which implies multiple solutions. Although solving for IRR is simple to accomplish numerically on a computer, this requirement and the possibility of multiple solutions (i.e., determining which is appropriate) are some of the reasons for the unpopularity of this criterion. The basis for project selection is to compare the internal rate of return with an appropriate discount rate; if IRR is greater than the selected discount rate, the project is a desirable one. This criterion can also be used to rank projects.

6.5 Applications of Cost-Benefit Analysis

In this section, we provide examples of how CBA can be used in evaluating public investment projects or policies relating to the environment. We examine policies to reduce ground-level ozone, water quality improvements and environmental regulations relating to forest practices. The examples are based on real world problems, with the latter two illustrating the difficulty of using nonmarket benefits.

Ozone damage and opportunity cost

Damage to crops in the lower Fraser River Valley of British Columbia occurs as a result of ozone (O_3) concentrations that exceed certain critical levels at various times during the growing season. Ozone is the result primarily of automobile emissions and is found to diminish very little in concentration with distance, even 100 km from the pollution source. The crops that are most sensitive to damage in the Fraser Valley are green beans, while potatoes and forages are not affected very much by ozone pollution. The most common method of measuring damage is to multiply the reduction in crop yields by the output price. However, this is not correct and could lead to overestimates of actual ozone damage. The following discussion illustrates some of the pitfalls that need to be avoided.

Government often subsidises agricultural production, although the actual degree of subsidy depends upon the particular crop. Some crops receive no direct subsidy while others are highly subsidised, with the farmer receiving as much as double the market price. Market price may be what the commodity trades for locally, in which case the government effectively subsidises consumers, or it may be the world price (adjusted for transportation costs). The correct price for valuing crop damage is the market or world price – the price that consumers could obtain the commodity for if there were no restrictions (e.g., import quotas or tariffs) on their purchases of the commodity.

Further, the government frequently subsidises purchases of inputs by farmers. This is done either through the tax system or through actual subsidy payments to agricultural producers or input suppliers. If ozone damage occurs, the inputs, and *the change in input use*, need to be valued at their opportunity cost, not the prices that the farmer pays. In this case, the original net revenue received by the farmer needs to be reduced, and the damage from ozone pollution is less than otherwise indicated. Subsidies are a problem in other resource industries besides agriculture.

Finally, the concept of opportunity cost requires that adjustment be made for alternative land use. Suppose that land in the Fraser Valley can be used to grow either beans or potatoes. The annual net revenue from beans is $600 per ha, but it is only $550 ha^{-1} if potatoes are grown. As a result of ozone damage, assume that net revenue from beans declines to $450 ha^{-1}. If one continues to grow beans, then one would say that the cost of ozone pollution is $150 ha^{-1} per year. However, suppose that, for the same ozone concentrations, the net revenue from potatoes falls to only $500 ha^{-1}, because they are less sensitive to ozone. If this is the case, then the real damage from ozone pollution is not $150 ha^{-1}, but, rather, $100 ha^{-1} because farmers can grow potatoes instead of beans when they know that ozone damage is likely to occur.

Water quality improvements and composting livestock wastes

As another example of cost-benefit analysis, we consider the benefits of improving water quality by composting livestock wastes. Livestock wastes are a major source of groundwater pollution in Europe, North America and elsewhere. Water problems include bacteria, salinity, sediment, pathogenic organisms, toxic material, and nutrient (nitrate) pollution. A national survey on pesticides in drinking water wells in the USA discovered that about 52% of community wells have detectable amounts of nitrate, 10% of wells contain at least one pesticide, and 7% may contain both nitrates and pesticides (Abdalla et al. 1992). Similar problems have been found in the Abbotsford aquifer region of south-western British Columbia, Canada.

The Abbotsford aquifer covers approximately 100 square kilometres (km) in SW BC and an additional 100 square km in NW Washington State in the USA. It is the largest of the approximately 200 aquifers in the lower Fraser River valley, and is an important source of residential, industrial and agricultural water. In 1981, groundwater supplied 44% of the water for the area between Surrey and Chilliwack on the south side of the Fraser River, and from Maple Ridge to the district of Kent on the north side. Groundwater provides almost all of the water requirements for the residents of Abbotsford, as well as a large portion of water for other uses.

The aquifer has failed to meet Canadian water quality standards for nitrate-nitrogen concentrations on a number of occasions. Nitrate-nitrogen concentrations have often exceeded the 10mg/l – 10 parts per million by volume (ppmv) in drinking water – concentration limit set out by the Canadian government in its *Guidelines for Canadian Drinking Water Quality*. The nitrate-nitrogen concentration limit is meant to prevent *methaemo-globineamia*, also known as "blue baby syndrome". Children who develop the disease have bacteria in their intestinal microflora that break down nitrate into toxic nitrite. In adults nitrate can be broken down to nitrite, which can synthesise with other chemical substances (*amines*) to create ones that can cause cancer. The long-term effect of nitrate consumption in children, older infants and adults is unknown, but it is thought ruminant animals such as cattle and sheep can also develop the disease.

Wastes from livestock-intensive agriculture and their application to berry and other crops during periods of heavy rainfall are blamed for the nitrate pollution problem. Therefore, the BC Ministry of Agriculture, Fisheries and Food (MAFF) determined that composting of manure was the most appropriate means of mitigating the problem. Agricultural scientists and policy makers appear to favour composting as this results in an environmentally benign product that provides organic matter to soil. Composting of manure (as well as a number of other methods of dealing with manure not considered here) is not thought to be financially feasible. The government has also ruled out penalties as these would mean that producers in the region would be disadvantaged relative to those located off the aquifer. As a result, because composting is not privately profitable, subsidies are likely needed. To justify such intervention, it is necessary to determine that individuals value improved water quality more than the required subsidy – that is, that the discounted social benefits of improving water quality exceed the discounted social costs. Since the benefits are nonmarket in nature, it needs to be shown that these are significant.

Net Costs of Composting Manure

The total amount of animal waste produced each year on the aquifer is about 890,000 tonnes, and it costs some C$36-$70/tonne to compost manure (Hauser et al. 1994). Then, the annual cost of reducing these wastes to compost is between $32.0 and $62.5 million. Assuming that revenues are $8-$15/tonne, or $7.1-$13.4 million per year, the shortfall is $18.6-$55.4 million. This must be covered by the willingness of households affected by poor drinking water quality to pay for improvements to water quality.

Social Benefits of Improving Water Quality

Three studies have been conducted to determine the social benefits of improving water quality in the Abbotsford region. Each study employs a different means for estimating benefits, although each relies on a contingent device.

Van Kooten (1998) employed fuzzy pairwise comparisons, with a mail survey instrument, to determine the benefits of water quality improvements. From the predicted preference intensities for two ranked items (water quality and a 33-inch colour television – the market touchstone), respondents' intensity of preference for water quality relative to the colour television was determined using relation (5.37). Intensity of preference depended on whether the respondent owned land in the agricultural land reserve (ALR) and on whether they owned or rented their residence. Those owning both land and their residence valued improvements in water quality by a factor of 1.836 over the television, or about $248 per year (if the television is valued at $1,350). Those who owned their place of residence but did not own land in the ALR valued improvements in water quality at $193/year, while those who owned no property whatsoever valued it at $242/year. If individuals perceive the price of the television to be lower than $1,350, say only $900, then improvements in water quality are valued at $165, $128 and $161, respectively. In general, improvements in water quality are valued higher by those with ALR land.

Hauser et al. (1994) used an open-ended contingent valuation question imbedded in a mail-out survey of households in the Abbotsford area. They obtained estimates of WTP of $55.35-$114.71 (depending on the regression model used for the bid functions) for those with ALR land, and $80.00-$114.71 for those with no land in the ALR.

Finally, van Kooten, Athwal and Arthur (1998) conducted a telephone survey in which they elicited WTP for water quality improvements in the Abbotsford region using a dichotomous choice format. Three levels of improvement were presented to respondents – eliminating the problem entirely, reducing the pollution so that the Canadian drinking water standard was always met (from an assumed 12 mg/l to 10 mg/l), and a reduction of water pollution by half (from an assumed 12 mg/l to 6 mg/l). Mean WTP (truncated at $300) was estimated from the logit models to be $160.54–$209.54, depending on the proposed reduction in water quality and the regression model employed. Median values ranged from $8.18 to $161.51.

A comparison of the three studies suggests that the method of fuzzy pairwise comparisons provides results that are "in line" with those obtained by more traditional methods. A comparison of the open-ended and dichotomous choice approaches lends some support to the hypothesis that DC formats lead to higher values of WTP because of "yea-saying". However, given that the approaches used in the two studies differ substantially, it is difficult to draw a definitive conclusion from these results. Further, the fuzzy approach supports the values from the dichotomous choice instrument.

Cost-benefit Results

The population of the District of Abbotsford is about 25,000. Almost all residents in the District depend on groundwater. Assuming 2.5 individuals per household, we find that about 10,000 households use groundwater. Using the largest of the above estimates of the annual WTP for improvements in water quality ($248 per household), the total social benefit of composting livestock wastes equals C$2.48 million per year. This amount is insufficient to cover the estimated annual costs of $18.6–$55.4 million. Of course, this analysis is based on an all-or-nothing decision – either compost all wastes or none. In the next example, we show that a non-marginal cost-benefit analysis may be inadequate. While cleaning up all wastes will be to the detriment of society's well being, it is likely that, at the margin, composting some wastes could lead to an improvement over the current situation. The information for making such an assessment is not currently available.

Evaluation of British Columbia's Forest Practices Code

In response to growing pressure from the general public, the BC Government has taken steps to protect forestlands, of which it owns more than 95% of the Province's total. Among these steps is the 1994 Forest Practices Code, which regulates harvesting to protect environmental amenities by, for example, reducing the size of clearcuts, implementing riparian corridors and leaving seed trees. In this subsection, which summarises more-detailed analysis in van Kooten (1999a), we provide an economic evaluation of BC's Forest Practices Code to illustrate the difficulty of CBA in the context of evaluating policy related to nature preservation. CBA is meant to provide decision makers with measures indicating whether overall social well being is increased or decreased as a result of a particular public program or policy.

On the benefit side, what is important are nonmarket values – outdoor recreation, protection of biodiversity, scenic amenities provided by forest landscapes, wildlife habitat, watershed protection and so on. Also important, but not calculated here, are the possibility that more timber might be available in the future, and the quasi-option value associated with preservation of old growth (logging old growth is a type of irreversibility) (see Chapter 10; Arrow and Fisher 1974).

Measuring nonmarket benefits can be a problem (Chapter 5). On the cost side, foregone benefits from timber harvest are most important. In principle, these are relatively easy to measure, but that is not always the case, as shown below. If the discounted benefits to society from the Forest Practices Code exceed the discounted costs, then the well being of BC's citizens is improved by the policy. If not, then the Code results in the overall impoverishment of the Province's citizens, even though some individuals or groups might be made better off. In essence, it is necessary to demonstrate that the value citizens place on the environmental amenities that are protected by the Code exceed the costs of the Code.

Costs of the Forest Practices Code

The major costs of the Forest Practices Code are measured by lost surplus in the markets for stumpage and wood products. Consider first the stumpage or forest-level market in Figure 6.1. The marginal costs (MC) of growing and harvesting timber for commercial purposes consist of silvicultural costs (if any), and road construction and logging costs. The value of stumpage is given by P_s, which exceeds MC because of resource scarcity.

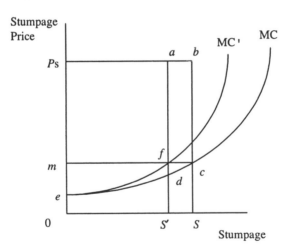

Figure 6.1 Lost Rents in Stumpage Market

Since the stumpage available for harvest in any given period is limited on average to S, which is equal to the allowable annual cut (AAC) that is determined by government fiat, the scarcity rent is given by area P_sbcm, while the differential rent is given by area mce. As indicated in Chapter 4, scarcity rents are simply the result of existing stands of natural and mature trees that came into being without human intervention. Differential rents, on the other hand, relate to differences among stands, with some stands being more valuable than others because they are closer to the mill or the terrain is not as steep. The differential rent is related to logging and transportation investment. Together these constitute the producer surplus or total economic rent accruing to the trees.

The Code does two things at the forest level. First, the amount that can be harvested is reduced from S to S' – there is a reduction in the AAC; the available economic rent is reduced by area *abcd*. Second, the marginal cost of forest operations increases from MC to MC'. This results in a reduction in producer surplus equal to area *def*. The cost associated with the Code, as measured in the timber market, is then given by area *abcef*.

The wood products market is also affected by a reduction in the availability of fibre. The economic surplus is measured in this market and not in the stumpage market because, given government regulation, it is not possible to determine a derived demand for stumpage. The welfare in the wood products market is illustrated in Figure 6.2. In the figure, it is assumed that BC producers face a horizontal demand for their products, whether that be pulp, lumber or other wood products. Reductions in the supply of BC wood products could raise world prices because of BC's market power. However, this response is likely to be short lived as higher prices stimulate wood product supply from other producing regions, technical advances in the use of wood products and greater use of non-wood substitutes. In the longer term, therefore, BC firms likely face a horizontal demand for their products.

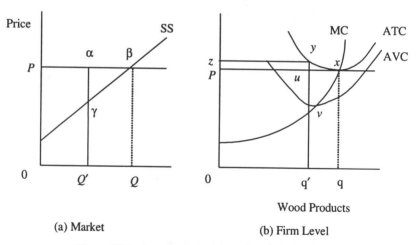

(a) Market   (b) Firm Level

Figure 6.2 Producer Surplus Loss in Wood Products Market

A reduction in fibre availability has the effect of restricting the output of wood products, as illustrated in Figure 6.2(a) by a shift in output from Q to Q'. Given the supply curve SS, and output price P, the loss in producer surplus is given by area αβγ, which is a quasi-rent. The case of an individual mill or firm is indicated in panel (b). The reduction in fibre availability means a reduction in mill output from q to q', with the sum of the individual reductions in output totalling the output reduction by the industry as a whole. For the individual mill, the reduction in output results in excess capacity as production slides up the average total cost (ATC) curve from point x to y in Figure 6.2(b). However, only marginal costs and average variable costs (AVC) are relevant to the calculation of the true economic loss, which is given by the producer surplus or the area above MC and below price. This is area uvx in panel (b), which is also equal to the difference between total revenue and total variable cost. The sum of these firm-level areas over all producers or mills is equal to the area in panel (a). To obtain the total economic loss, we add over the stumpage and wood product markets.

Given that there is little or no information about the curves in Figures 6.1 and 6.2, measuring the costs indicated above is difficult. Nonetheless, it is possible to gain some insight into the magnitude of these costs. In addition, there are costs that have not been considered above, but are discussed below. The costs associated with the Forest Practices Code can be summarised as follows.

Foregone Scarcity Rent The reduction in AAC is one important cost of the Code. Current provincial AAC is 72.1 million m^3-22.3 million m^3 on the Coast and 49.8 million m^3 in the Interior (Saunders 1993, p. 13). The Code is projected to reduce the AAC by 6% for the first ten years after implementation (BC Ministry of Forests 1996), although reductions of 10% might be expected in the coastal (temperate rain) forest (Saunders 1993). The foregone economic rent (area *abcd* in Figure 6.1) includes returns to fixed capital, surplus captured by unions (if any), and government stumpage fees, rents, taxes and royalties. Based on estimates of BC forest sector rents by Percy (1986), and by Grafton et al. (1998) (see Chapter 4), the surplus is roughly $25 per m^3, although it varies from one year to the next. This rent is not available in perpetuity, however, because, as firms harvest more and more second growth timber, the available scarcity rent falls since second-growth logs are worth less. It is assumed that only half of the $25 per m^3 of rent is available after 30 years. Using a 4% discount rate, the $12.50 per m^3 available for 30 years can be converted into a perpetuity equivalent of $8.65 per m^3. In that case, the net adjusted surplus is $21.15 per m^3. Multiplying this surplus by the reduction in AAC determines the economic value of the lost timber. Assuming the reduction is 10% on the Coast (2.23 million m^3) and 6% in the Interior (2.99 million m^3), the cost amounts to C$110.4 million per year.

Increased Delivered Wood Costs: Lost Differential Rent As a result of increased costs of road building (more roads need to be built as size of clearcuts is reduced by more than 50%), road maintenance, changed logging practices and so on, harvest costs will increase. An in-depth study of changes in delivered wood costs as a result of the Code was conducted by McIntosh et al. (1997). Delivered wood costs increased as a result of added costs of planning and administration, and forest practices. In the former category, the greatest cost increases were in the form of additional plans, amendments to approved plans, greater inventory requirements, administrative delays, and various costs associated with increased need for permits. Increased costs of forest practices are associated with reductions in cut-block size, road and landing requirements, greater soil conservation, protection of riparian areas and green-up requirements. These Code-related costs have increased delivered wood costs by $19.68 per m^3 on the Coast and $8.41 per m^3 in the Interior. (The higher costs on the Coast are due to steeper terrain, greater biodiversity and lack of a winter "deep freeze", when logging takes place in the Interior.) The total increase in this component of costs then amounts to some $69.0 million per year, which is an estimate of area *def* in Figure 6.1.

Loss of Producer Surplus in the Wood Products Market: Quasi-Rent There is no readily available information to estimate the loss in producer surplus in the wood products market from a reduction in AAC. A reduction in AAC will mean that mills will either have to obtain logs or fibre elsewhere (e.g., from Alaska, Alberta, Saskatchewan), causing the AVC and MC curves in Figure 6.2(b) to rise. It could also lead to reduced output, which results in excess capacity and higher per unit costs as fixed costs are spread over a reduced output. For sawmills these are estimated by Saunders (1993, p. 41) to cost $113.7–$229.0 per annum for the first five years after the Code's implementation. Saunders converts this to an annual cost of $20.2–$40.8 million in perpetuity using a 4% rate of discount. COFI (1994, pp. 2-5) estimates the increased costs of excess capacity in pulp mills to be $77–$156 million per annum for the first ten years of the Code, or annual cost of $25.0–$50.6 in perpetuity at 4%. Both Saunders and COFI use reductions in AAC of 10% and 20%, thus giving them a range of values. In terms of Figure 6.2, the excess capacity estimates by Saunders and by COFI are equal to area *Puyz*, but then summed over all mills.

Increases in excess capacity are the result of inappropriate plant investment, but such investment is a fixed cost and such costs are unrelated to estimates of economic costs in a welfare sense – they are "water under the bridge". Nonetheless, given that estimates of the costs associated with excess capacity are all that is available, these are used to develop crude approximations of the loss in producer surplus.

Assume that ATC and MC are linear over the range *q'q* in Figure 6.2(b), and that the slopes of ATC and MC are identical in absolute terms over the ranges *yx* and *vx*, respectively. For sawmills, the cost of excess capacity (area *Puyz*) is $113.7 million when AAC is reduced from 72.10 million m^3 to 64.89 million m^3; the height of the rectangle (distance *uy*) is thus 1.752. Similarly, for pulp mills, distance *uy* is 1.187 (= $77.0 million ÷ 64.89 million m^3).[5] It is possible to calculate the loss in producer surplus for sawmills and pulp mills on the Coast and in the Interior. The results are presented in Table 6.1. Total foregone producer surplus as a result of the Forest Practices Code is estimated to be $7.671 million, or some $307,000 annually.

---

[5] Although not actually needed for calculating producer surplus (area *uxv* in Figure 6.2(b)), it is possible to calculate the slope of MC. For sawmills, *ux* is 7.21 million m^3 (assumed 10% reduction in AAC), the slope of segment *yx* is -243.0×10^{-9} (=*uy* + *ux*), and then the slope of MC over the relative range *vx* is 243.0×10^{-9} (by assumption). Similarly, for pulp mills, the slope of MC is 164.6×10^{-9}.

Table 6.1: Code-Related Producer Surplus Reductions in Sawmill and Pulp Mill Sectors

	Coast	*Interior*	*TOTAL*
Sawmills	$1.953 million	$ 2.619 million	$4.572 million
Pulp mills	$1.324 million	$1.775 million	$3.099 million
TOTAL	$3.277 million	$4.394 million	$7.671 million

Increase in Government Administration Costs Saunders (1993, pp. 16–9) estimates the increase in costs to government because of the Code to be $49.0–$71.0 million annually. These cost estimates may be low if overhead costs by the Forest Renewal BC (FRBC) are any indication. FRBC is a publicly-owned corporation created in 1994 and charged with investing forest resource rents of some $500 million per year back in the forest sector. Overhead amounts to some 40% of expenditures (Hamilton 1997). We assume that overhead expenses amount to 20% of expenditure, or $100 million annually.

Social Adjustment Costs While job losses and consequent reductions in forest sector wages are important considerations in formulating policy, these do not comprise an economic cost in the true sense. Many displaced forest sector workers will find jobs at lower pay, but this constitutes an income transfer, not an economic cost. However, there are economic costs brought about by the displacement in forest sector workers. These are the costs of job search, retraining and moving, plus the psychological costs on workers and their families, and costs associated with, for example, increased alcohol abuse, crime and so on. Similar costs are incurred by merchants and communities, while the federal and provincial governments incur added costs in administering unemployment insurance and welfare schemes. (The actual payments made under these programs are a form of income transfer and not an economic cost.) The social adjustment costs are difficult to measure. Assuming 1.57 direct jobs per 1,000 m^3, some 8,200 forest sector jobs will be lost as a result of the Code. Since forest sector workers have low education levels and experience difficulty finding alternative employment (even at lower wages), an adjustment cost of $40,000 per forest sector worker is assumed. The social adjustment cost amounts to about $325.0 million. Additional jobs will be lost elsewhere in the economy, but such workers are likely to experience lower adjustment costs. Assuming an employment multiplier of 2.5 and an adjustment cost for those workers of $10,000, the social adjustment cost outside the forest sector is $123 million. Thus, the total adjustment cost is $448 million, or using a 4% discount rate, some $17.9 million on an annualised basis.

Lost Nonmarket Amenities While the benefits of the Forest Practices Code will be primarily nonmarket in nature, there will be lost amenity values because there will be "negative public reaction to coarse woody debris" (Saunders 1993, p. 10) that is to be left on cut over sites according to the Code's regulations. These and other such costs are not quantified here – they are assumed to be negligible.

Other Costs As noted above, reductions in the supply of BC wood fibre will raise world prices, at least in the short term. This increases the welfare of producers (including government) because rents will be higher for the AAC that remains available, but consumers are worse off. However, higher prices stimulate supply from elsewhere and substitute products that will reduce prices in the longer run. Some of the increase in supply may come from regions that are ecologically more sensitive than BC and, to the extent that such areas are valued by BC residents, this constitutes a cost. Substitute products may be less friendly for the environment than wood products, with the environmental damage that they cause also attributable to the Code. These costs (and benefits) are difficult to trace and value, and are assumed to be negligible or to cancel one another.

A summary of all the aforementioned costs of the Forest Practices Code is provided in Table 6.2. The economic costs of the Code, as estimated here, are $297.6 million per annum. Of course, there is substantial uncertainty associated with such a point estimate, perhaps as large as 50% of the value reported here. For comparison, the BC government collected an average $953.0 million in rent per year over the period 1990-1994, compared to available annual rents of $1609.6 million (Grafton et al. 1998). Thus, the Code's costs (irrespective of the large estimated variance) are large compared to rent collection. Compared to estimates of the Code's costs, however, estimates of the benefits of the Code are likely to be even more uncertain.

Table 6.2: Estimated Annual Costs of BC's Forest Practices Code ($ mil)

Cost of foregone economic rents	110.4
Increased harvest costs	69.0
Lost producer surplus in wood products	0.3
Increased government administration costs	100.0
Social adjustment costs	17.9
TOTAL	**297.6**

Benefits of the Forest Practices Code

If the Forest Practices Code is to benefit the citizens of the province of British Columbia, and increase their well being as defined above, it is necessary that the benefits exceed these costs. The benefits of the Code need to be determined from non-timber uses and this requires the estimation on nonmarket values. Expenditures by tourists cannot be used as a measure of benefits, since expenditures are not the same as benefits (Chapter 2; van Kooten 1995b, c). The benefits of the Forest Practices Code are primarily nonmarket in nature. They consist of use and non-use benefits. Recreation is the major use to be affected by the Code. Non-use benefits derive from forest attributes, such as biodiversity, because individuals derive utility from simply knowing that these amenities exist even if they are unlikely to ever visit the area where they are found (existence value) or from passing on such amenities to the next generation (bequest value). In the analysis that follows, it is assumed that the amenities that the Code seeks to protect are similar to those that the Province's Protected Areas Strategy seeks to preserve.

Recreation Benefits The BC Ministry of Forests (1991) has estimated forest recreation use benefits, *plus* the value that recreationists attach to the future option of continuing to pursue these activities. These are provided by forest region in columns (4) and (5) of Table 6.3. Forest recreation use and wildlife viewing are valued at about $40 million per year, while preservation for purposes of future recreation and wildlife viewing (option demand) is valued at slightly more than $147 million per year. Thus, forest recreation is valued at $187.0 million annually. Forest recreation benefits on an annual per hectare basis and by forest region are provided in column (4) of Table 6.4. Each hectare of forest is valued at about $11.80 in forest recreation, with the highest value ($34.00 ha^{-1}) occurring in the Vancouver forest region and the lowest value ($1.49 ha^{-1}) in the Prince Rupert forest region. Such an allocation assumes that all recreation value is attributed to mature forest area, which is clearly not the case. Thus, the values reported in Table 6.4 are high and any other means of allocating benefits over hectares would result in much lower per ha values for recreation.

Table 6.3: Population of BC and Forest Recreation Use and Preservation Values by Region, $1992

Region	(1) Total population	(2) Adult population	(3) Regional % of adult population	(4) Recreation use value ($mil/y)	(5) Recreation preservation value[a] ($mil/y)	(6) Nonuse Benefits[b] ($mil/y)
Vancouver	2,102,460	1,583,017	74.5%	4.54	111.13	339.22
Prince Rupert	83,048	53,602	2.5	4.97	4.49	11.49
Kamloops	328,398	239,572	11.3	10.03	11.23	51.34
Prince George	161,769	105,411	5.0	6.83	8.22	22.59
Nelson	148,195	104,840	4.9	8.15	9.40	22.47
Cariboo	59,495	39,376	1.8	5.11	2.87	8.44
TOTAL	**2,883,365**	**2,125,818**	**100.0**	**39.62**	**147.34**	**455.53**

Source: BC Ministry of Forests (1991, pp. 15, 48–9, 51)
[a] Recreation preservation value includes preservation for purposes of future recreation and future wildlife viewing.
[b] Estimated as follows: household WTP for non-use benefits is estimated at $300 per year. Divide adult population by 1.4 to get number of households and multiply by $300 (see text).

Table 6.4: Mature Forest Area, Recreation Expenditures by Area, by Forest Region, $1992

Region	(1) Mature Timber ('000s ha)[a]	(2) Recreation Use Value ($ ha^{-1} yr^{-1})[b]	(3) Recreation Preservation Option Value ($ ha^{-1} yr^{-1})[b,c]	(4) Total Recreation Benefits ($ ha^{-1} yr^{-1})[b]
Vancouver	3402	1.34	32.67	34.00
Prince Rupert	6367	0.78	0.71	1.49
Kamloops	2373	4.23	4.73	8.96
Prince George	9596	0.71	0.86	1.57
Nelson	1390	5.86	6.76	12.62
Cariboo	3565	1.44	0.81	2.25
Total (Average)	**26 693**	**(1.48)**	**(5.52)**	**(11.80)**
Interior (Average)	**23 291**	**(1.51)**	**(1.56)**	**(3.06)**

[a] Source: BC Ministry of Forests (1992b)
[b] Source: Calculation
[c] This is the value of retaining the option to pursue recreational activities at some future date.

There is very little information about the potential impact that the Forest Practices Code will have on recreational benefits. It could be argued that recreational values may, on balance, be unaffected by the Code if site characteristics are taken into account. The reason is that the Code will bring about better access because of an increase in road building. This will be a positive benefit. Further, there exists evidence that wilderness recreation is less highly valued than developed recreation (Edwards et al. 1976), suggesting that protection of wilderness attributes beyond some amount is unlikely to enhance benefits from recreation and may even reduce them. On the negative side, recreational values might be reduced because site attributes are adversely affected (e.g., coarse woody debris or too many roads) and there may be restrictions on access and/or the types of activities that can be pursued (e.g., hunting, motor homes, all-terrain vehicles and snowmobiles may be banned).

To determine the extent to which the Forest Practices Code increases recreational benefits, it is assumed that Code-induced reductions in AAC (10% on the Coast, 6% in the Interior) increase the area of mature forest that has wilderness-type attributes by a similar amount. This increase in wilderness attributes is then assumed to increase recreation benefits by similar percentages over what they are currently. Thus, recreation benefits increase by $11.6 million on the Coast (Vancouver forest region) and by $4.3 million in the Interior (all other forest regions), for a total increase of $15.9 million per year. It is important to recognise that this is an arbitrary assumption, as are some of the ones used to obtain estimates of non-use benefits. No information about the relationship between nonmarket benefits and land characteristics is available, nor do economists generally elicit it (but see Section 5.4 for some exceptions).

Non-use Benefits It is likely that the increase in non-use benefits is the most significant aspect of the Code. But it is not clear how the Code will affect such benefits. A significant future research effort will be needed to make the link between the forest attributes that the Code seeks to protect and their economic value. For example, we do not know (and do not attempt to measure) possible adverse effects of logging operations on fish habitat (see, e.g., Aylward 1992, p. 52). At this stage, the data are unavailable and some detective work is required to provide even cursory estimates of potential benefits from contingent valuation data that do exist. This is done below.

Given the paucity of information, a number of assumptions will need to be made. For BC, a government study (Vold et al. 1994) found that households were, on average, willing to pay $136 per year to double the amount of wilderness in the province from 5% of BC to 10% of BC; households were also willing to pay $168 per year to triple the amount of wilderness preserved from 5% of the province to 15%. A US study by Hagen et al. (1992) found the annual non-use or preservation value of spotted owl habitat, which they equated to old-growth ecosystems in their survey, to be as much as US$200/household (about C$300 per household) – the largest value found in any of CV studies on spotted owl or protected areas. In this study, therefore, some scenarios assume that households would be willing to pay as much as $300 annually for increasing wilderness protection from its current level to that under the Province's Protected Areas Strategy (BC Ministry of Forests 1992a); *this value is high compared to other studies*. If households consist of 1.4 adults on average, it is possible to calculate the total non-use benefits by forest region; total annual non-use benefits are $455.5 million (col. (6), Table 6.3).

Estimated non-use benefits of $455.5 million per annum cannot simply be added to annual estimated forest recreation benefits of $15.9 million to obtain the total benefits attributable to the Forest Practices Code. The reason is that the non-use benefits are a total value, while recreation benefits are the additional benefits associated solely with the Code. If the non-use values identified here are representative of true WTP, these values cannot all be attributed to changes in forest practices. Given that the Code protects wilderness attributes, much of the value needs to be attributed to the preservation of intact ecosystems, as occurs under the Protected Areas Strategy. Suppose that the value of $300 per household per year was determined at the time that 8% of the Province's land, or 7.582 million ha, was officially protected. In 1994, 8.9% of the Province's land base was protected, but area in Provincial Parks (constituting by far the largest area set aside) had increased by 42.3% since 1987, to 7.6 million ha (BC Ministry of Environment, Lands and Parks 1996). Then, the $455.5 million represents total WTP (total non-use benefits) from increasing wilderness protection beyond 7.6 million ha.

Decisions are necessarily made at the margin. Hence, it is necessary to determine the marginal WTP function for setting aside further wilderness. Without additional information, it is simply assumed that the marginal WTP function is linear as shown in Figure 6.3, where $u'(W)$ represents marginal utility (marginal WTP) as a function of wilderness (W) and W^0 is the current amount of wilderness.

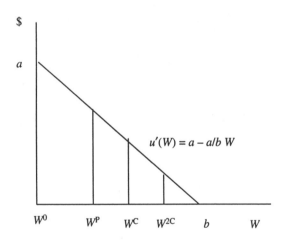

Figure 6.3 Marginal Willingness-to-Pay for Protection of Wilderness

Let W^P represent the area that is protected under the Province's Protected Area Strategy (11.4 million ha) and $W^C - W^P$ the area equivalent (AAC converted to area) protected by the Code, and which has similar wilderness attributes to other protected area. Thus, the non-use benefits of the Code are determined as the area under the marginal utility function, $u'(W)$, between W^P and W^C.

The area protected by the Code remains protected next year as well, and the year thereafter, and so forth. The area protected the second year is over and above $W^C - W^P$, and is equal to the area under the marginal utility function, $u'(W)$, between W^P and W^{2C} in Figure 6.3. The benefits of protecting this area are lower than those associated with $W^P - W^C$, but this benefit is also available in the second year and thereafter. To obtain the total non-use benefit, it is necessary to calculate the discounted value of this stream of increasing benefits, at least increasing to the point where the marginal benefit function cuts the abscissa. Negative benefits (or costs of too much protection) are ignored.

Neither a nor b is known; only the area under the curve is known and fixed (equal to $455.5 million). However, once a is known, b is also known because $b = 2A/a$, where A is the area under the curve. Parameter a is the amount households are willing to pay to protect the next hectare of wilderness, given that they already have W^0. As a starting point, we begin with a value of $120 per ha, which is obtained by dividing $455.5 by the difference $W^P - W^0$. Of course, the higher the value of a, the steeper the slope of the marginal preservation function.

To simplify the calculations and because the Province's target of protecting 12% of BC's land base applies equally to the Coast and Interior, the calculations are conducted for the Province as a whole (i.e., $W^0 = 7.6$ million ha). Assume standing inventories of approximately 400 m^3 per ha on the Coast and 200m^3 ha^{-1} in the Interior. This is low for mature stands, especially on the Coast, but serves our purpose since it increases the estimate of non-use benefits attributable to the Code. Using these values to convert AAC to area results in the protection of an additional 20,525 ha each year. Further, since non-forest lands constitute some 45% of the land area, the Code actually protects an additional 30,000 ha every year. Non-use benefits from the Code are provided in Table 6.5 for various values of a. Total discounted benefits are calculated using a discount rate of 4%, and are then annualised. A scenario with double total non-use benefits ($900 million rather than $455.5 million) is also presented; this scenario is meant to address potential unaccounted for ecosystem benefits (e.g., protection of salmon habitat, weather regulation, carbon sink). From Table 6.5, maximum annual non-use benefits of the Code are between about $40.5 million and $80.0 million.

Table 6.5: Estimated Annual Non-use Benefits of BC's Forest Practices Code, 1992 ($ mil.)

Assumed non-use value of marginal ha before PAS and Code (a)	Value to BC Household of Protecting more Wilderness Attributes	
	$300 (Max. stated WTP)	$600 (WTP plus non-measured benefits)
$ 40	25.9	29.1
$ 80	38.8	51.6
$100	40.4	60.4
$120	38.8	67.5
$160	25.9	77.0
$180	14.5	79.2
$200	--	79.8
$240	--	76.2

Summary

The costs of the Forest Practices Code are estimated to be approximately $297.6 million annually. Recreation benefits are estimated at $15.9 million per year, while non-use benefits are calculated to be $40.5–$80.0 million annually. Not included in the benefits of the Forest Practices Code are those primarily non-use benefits that accrue to people living outside BC. There are two issues. First, it is not clear that one should count benefits to those outside the Province unless they are prepared to compensate BC residents for their foregone timber rents and other costs associated with the provision of forest ecosystem amenities. Second, given that the calculations provided in the last column of Table 6.5 are based on an unrealistically high level of benefits over and above those provided by (then) existing parks and other protected areas, the higher non-use benefit values might take into account benefits to non-residents. Even with these caveats, it is clear that the costs of the Forest Practices Code exceed benefits by a significant amount, by almost $200 million annually.

One could well ask why the provincial government would want to impose such costly regulations on the forest sector. One reason is that there needed to be changes in BC forest practices, because existing practices simply were not sustainable; they consisted of large clearcuts in mountainous terrain, with significant soil erosion, wood fibre wastage and so on. Although fish and other critical wildlife habitat were threatened by these practices, as was the ability to grow trees on a sustainable basis, by the early 1990s these damages were already being addressed by other means before the Code was brought to bear (see, e.g., Chapter 11). Further, protection of many of the attributes associated with non-use benefits (including protection of critical habitat and preservation of biodiversity) were also being addressed by initiatives, such as the Protected Areas Strategy (which sought to protect 12% of each of the Province's biogeographical zones), timber supply reviews, and the Spotted Owl Recovery Team (which identified northern spotted owl nests and declared areas around them off limits to loggers).

Political factors were also present. The Forest Practices Code may have enabled the government to claim the moral high ground while appeasing their environmental constituency. At the same time, the regulatory legislation was designed to counter charges and boycotts of BC forest products by the international environmental movement (as were some of the other forestry initiatives). These factors are difficult to quantify as benefits, if indeed they can be considered as such.

The economist can only compare costs and benefits, and it is difficult to argue that the political benefits are large. Although they may well be large, it is necessary to make this case. Otherwise, one can only conclude from the analysis presented above that, even under the most optimistic estimates of non-use benefits, the Forest Practices Code will result in a significant reduction in the well being of BC citizens.

6.6 Conclusions

Cost-benefit analysis is a powerful tool for evaluating public and private projects, and even government programs (e.g., forest harvest regulations). It constitutes the practical aspect of economic efficiency, and confronts the policy maker with a stark choice. This is not to suggest that the decision maker needs to choose the project or program that yields the highest social benefit as calculated by economists. Rather, CBA forces the decision maker explicitly to take into account the inevitable tradeoffs that choice entails. This we see as the primary purpose of CBA – to aid in the selection of projects and in courses of action. In this book, those courses of action involve biological assets and nature. The only remaining consideration is the link between economic efficiency and the dynamics of the biological or natural system that we evaluate. This element is discussed in the next chapter.

7 Economic Dynamics and Renewable Resource Management

In this chapter, basic concepts of the economics of renewable resource management are introduced. Unlike exhaustible resources, renewable resources have regenerative capacity and there exists the possibility of steady-state harvest of the resource, whether timber from forests or fish from the ocean. The analysis of exhaustible resources represents a "degenerate case" of zero resource growth that is not treated explicitly in this book (Dasgupta and Heal 1979). Nonetheless, it is possible to deplete a renewable resource or drive it to extinction, either as a result of natural causes or by mismanagement, including the failure to address open-access. As shown in this Chapter, deliberate extinction may in some cases even be economically efficient. In the case of renewable resources, growth functions constitute some of the constraints (or equations of motion) associated with inter-temporal optimisation. An example of an objective function might be the maximisation of net present value or the discounted stream of net returns from exploitation of the resource. This stream of net benefits should include nonmarket values in addition to market values. The growth and production functions are generally quite different for various resources, but the general insights of the basic theory spill over into management of fisheries, wildlife and forests, although differences remain for reasons usually associated with institutions.

Fisheries and wildlife economics are different from the economics of forestry, for instance, because of the prominent role of property rights (which play a role in deforestation, as indicated in Chapter 12) and search costs (fishers have to go out and find fish). Since search costs are possibly influenced by the size of the wild stock, there may be an incentive to maintain fish and wildlife populations at relatively high levels. Alternatively, typical forestry problems concern the optimal rotation of an even-aged stand and multiple use values (as illustrated in Chapter 6 and discussed in Chapter 11). Further, fishery and wildlife models typically attempt to determine steady-state stocks where harvests equal incremental increase, whereas harvesting in traditional forestry models involves both incremental growth and standing stock, as discussed in Chapter 11.

7.1 Background

A basic understanding of the biology of (single) renewable resource stocks is necessary to analyse management of these resources, although it might also be argued that the biology of ecosystems and food webs needs to be better understood (a topic addressed below). Two simplified models that describe fertility, mortality and growth characteristics of a population are the logistic growth function and the Gompertz function.[1] The logistics growth function is given as:

$$(7.1) \qquad G(x) = \gamma x (1 - \frac{x}{K}),$$

while the Gompertz function is:

$$(7.2) \qquad G(x) = \gamma x \ln \frac{K}{x},$$

where x is the population (or stock), γ is the intrinsic growth rate of the resource and K is the carrying capacity of the ecosystem for the population.

The logistics growth curve in (7.1) has the shape of a bell or parabola, as illustrated by curve I in Figure 7.1. When the stock is small, growth will be modest, even under the most favourable conditions. In terms of the fishery, the reason is that there are few female fish to produce offspring. Growth of the stock will also be small when the population is close to its maximum size – when it has filled its niche in the ecosystem. When the stock has expanded to K, it has reached its carrying capacity and the ecosystem is not able to support further growth. Possible reasons are food scarcity or spreading of diseases because of high population densities.

A more complete illustration of the growth function includes the concept *minimum viable population* (MVP). This corresponds with the population level below which, without intervention, the population would decrease and eventually approach zero. It is the smallest population that gives a species a good (say 95%) chance of survival for a long period of time (say, the next 100 years). To determine whether a species has a good chance of survival, it is necessary to conduct *population viability*

---

[1] These biological models fit the so-called Schaefer approach in the fishery. In contrast, the Beverton-Holt approach follows separate cohorts (age classes) through time; harvest of separate cohorts requires a (unavailable) knife-edge selectivity of harvest method. Since modelling the economics of multi-cohort fishing is complicated, the Beverton-Holt model has not been a successful foundation for economic models (Munro and Scott 1985), although Flaaten and Kolsvik (1996) and van Kooten et al. provide examples for the fishery and wildlife ungulates, respectively. Discrete time analogues of nonlinear equations (difference equations) may produce chaos, depending on the value of the parameters used (Gleick 1987; Grafton and Silva-Echenique 1997). Duarte (1994) examines the complex interaction between policy measures and harvesting, on one hand, and stock behaviour, on the other, in unstable dynamic systems.

analysis. This consists of studying the chances of a population surviving under various assumptions about its habitat (e.g., size of habitat that is protected), harvest and reproduction levels, predation, genetic deterioration, and so on. A modified logistics growth function that accounts for a minimum viable population is:

$$(7.3) \qquad G(x) = \gamma x \left(\frac{x}{\text{MVP}} - 1 \right)\left(1 - \frac{x}{K} \right).$$

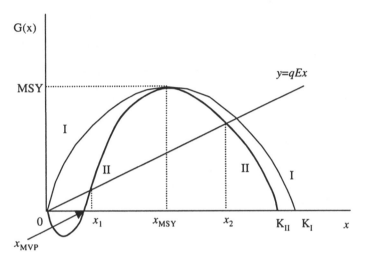

Figure 7.1 Logistics Growth Functions

This modified logistics growth function (7.3) is depicted by curve II in Figure 7.1. It has a non-concave interval with negative values for $G(x)$ at low stock sizes, so that the growth function intersects the horizontal axis at x_{MVP} (see Clark 1990). The growth function is *purely compensatory* if $x_{\text{MVP}} = 0$ and $G(x)$ is strictly concave, as curve I in Figure 7.1. It is *depensatory* if $G(x)$ is initially convex and later concave (but not shown in Figure 7.1). Finally, the function is said to exhibit *critical depensation* if $x_{\text{MVP}} > 0$, and $G(x)$ initially convex and later concave, as curve II. K_{II} is a stable equilibrium whereas x_{MVP} would be unstable. When the actual population deviates from the equilibrium population x_{MVP}, the equilibrium population cannot be restored without intervention, as (natural) population growth is negative when $x < x_{\text{MVP}}$ and positive when $x > x_{\text{MVP}}$.

Besides the growth function, a yield or production function $y(t)$ is needed to describe the management model. A common and general production function (especially in fishery and wildlife modeling) incorporates a biological stock term x (which is usually absent in forestry models). Fisheries are commonly divided into "schooling" and "searching" fisheries, with the distinguishing feature being whether the species in question has the propensity to school in large numbers. Neher (1990) mentions as possible reasons for schooling migration courses and defense against predators; well-known examples of schooling species are herring, anchovies and tuna. It has been found that the size of schools does not decrease much as the overall biomass of the stock decreases, although this implies that there are less schools as overall numbers fall. Since large schools of fish are relatively easy to find, searching (and catching) costs are likely not much influenced by the size of the stock. This implies that, for schooling fish, the rationale for increasing populations to reduce harvest costs is less than for the case of a search fishery. This, in turn, means that their optimal stock size will typically be lower (see below). Moreover, if property rights are not well established or enforced, the risk of extinction is higher, as low harvest costs imply that it pays fishers to keep fishing and reduce the stock, even if the stock is near the x_{MVP} level. The difference between schooling and searching fisheries is formally as follows. For searching fisheries, harvesting $y(t)$ is a function of effort (E) and the size of the stock (x); hence, $y(E,x)$, with $\partial y/\partial E > 0$ and $\partial y/\partial x > 0$. For the schooling fishery, the latter term is of less importance, and often ignored in mathematical analyses, so harvest is given by $y(E)$. The production (yield) function can be written as:

(7.4) $y(t) = qE(t)^{\alpha}x(t)^{\beta}$,

where q is a (possibly species-dependent) catchability constant and effort E measures the inputs devoted to harvest.[2] The equation of motion (state equation) for the renewable resource problem is:

(7.5) $\dfrac{dx}{dt} = \dot{x} = G(x(t)) - y(t)$.

Sustained yield harvesting is defined to occur when x, y and E are all constant over time, so that the LHS of (7.5) should equal zero, or $y = G(x)$. In the Schaefer (1957) model, the parameters α and β of the production function (7.3) are set to one, and the growth of the stock is described by the logistic growth function (7.1). Then in equilibrium:

(7.6) $y = qEx = \gamma x(1 - \dfrac{x}{K})$.

Solving for x gives:

(7.7) $x = K(1 - \dfrac{qE}{\gamma})$,

---

[2] Alternative forms sometimes applied in fisheries economics is the exponential, or Spence production process: $y(t)=x(t)(1 - e^{-qE(t)})$ (Amundsen et al. 1995).

which implies

(7.8) $y = qEx = qEK(1 - \dfrac{qE}{\gamma})$.

This sustained yield (harvest) function is parabolic. If harvests exceed growth ($qE > \gamma$), the resource stock is asymptotically depleted and eventually y and x approach 0 (Conrad and Clark 1987). This is the case because, for sufficiently high values of E, the harvest function $y = qxE$ is steep and does not cross the growth function at a positive growth level (Swanson 1994b). Alternatively, if the growth function displays critical depensation (i.e., a convex curve with negative growth for $0 < x < x_{MVP}$, and a well-behaved concave segment for $x_{MVP} < x < K$), two possible equilibria exist for a certain input of E. In Figure 7.1, a stable equilibrium occurs at x_2 and an unstable one at x_1. This is readily verified as harvest is linearly increasing in x for a given level of effort ($y = qEx$) and crosses the growth function twice. Increasing the value of E rotates the yield curve $y = qEx$ upward, and when effort exceeds a certain level, the population may be driven below MVP levels and hence to extinction.

As indicated in Figure 7.1, rapid growth of the stock is possible with moderate stock sizes. Growth is at its maximum when $G'(x) = 0$ (and $G''(x) < 0$). The associated harvest is maximum sustained yield (MSY), and the corresponding stock size is x_{MSY} in Figure 7.1. For the logistic growth function, $G'(x) = 0$ at $x_{MSY} = \frac{1}{2} K$ (such that $G(x) = \gamma K/4$), and for the Gompertz function $x_{MSY} = K/e$, with $G(x) = rx/e$ (where e = 2.71828...). Harvesting $G(x_{MSY})$ at stock levels of x_{MSY} has been promoted for many years by fishery and forestry ecologists alike. It was considered good policy to search for the largest harvest that can be sustained forever. For a long time, economists argued that x_{MSY} is a seriously flawed management concept. Neher (1990) puts forward three different arguments tailored for the case of a fishery but applicable to forestry as well. First, and perhaps least important in this respect, the steady-state analysis does not give any insight into the dynamics of approaching the optimal stock size. A tradeoff arises between adjustment costs and bridging time that is overlooked in the ecological model.

Second, prices and costs are disregarded in the MSY concept. As mentioned, harvest costs are likely to be influenced by stock size for searching species because it is easier to find fish or wildlife when there are more of them in a given area. Since excessive harvest costs are a waste of the economy's productive resources, it may be worthwhile to increase stock size (and density) by settling for smaller harvests, and arrive at a steady-state stock size to the right of x_{MSY}.[3]

---

[3] Multiplying $G(x)$ of Figure 7.1 by the price of fish transforms it into a revenue curve. Marginal harvesting costs can be represented by a declining function of stock size in the same Figure. Then the optimal stock size will be the one where the slope of the revenue curve is equal to the slope of the cost curve (i.e., marginal harvest costs are equal to marginal benefits). This point of tangency is to the right of x_{MSY} (Pearce and Turner 1990; Tietenberg 1996).

Third, discounting is ignored in the MSY concept. Harvesting transforms *in situ* renewable resources into monetary assets ("money in the bank"). Since both money in the bank and fish in the sea are productive assets, with the first growing at the interest rate r and the latter producing offspring at an average rate of $G(x)/x$ and a marginal rate of $G'(x)$, the assets can be compared. Disregarding harvest costs for the time being, the problem can be represented as:

(7.9)   Maximise $V = \int\limits_{0}^{\infty} P(t)\, y(t)\, e^{-rt}\, dt$

subject to (suppressing time notation)

(7.10) $\dot{x} = G(x) - y$,

where V refers to the discounted present value and P to output price. Along with (7.10), the necessary conditions for an optimum are (see Appendix I):

(7.11) $P - \lambda = 0$

and

(7.12) $\dot{\lambda} = [r - G'(x)]\, \lambda$.

From (7.11), the shadow price of the stock (i.e., the increase in the objective function from increasing the *in situ* stock by one unit) is equal to the market price of the resource (with zero marginal harvest costs). Condition (7.12) indicates that, for an optimum steady-state ($\dot{\lambda} = 0$), arbitrage gains are ruled out as the growth rate of the shadow price should equal the "net rate of interest", $r - G'(x)$. Combining (7.11) and (7.12) yields:

(7.13) $\dfrac{\dot{P}}{P} + G'(x) = r$.

Thus, rising prices ($\dot{P} > 0$), say because of changing preferences, encourage conservation as it motivates the resource owner to build up future stocks.

The intuition is as follows. Along an optimal path, (7.13) must hold. Given a certain (exogenous) value for r, the higher $\dot{P}/P$, the lower the required value for $G'(X)$ to balance the LHS and the RHS of (7.13). Since $G(x)$ is concave over the interval of stock sizes relevant for resource managers, namely, $x_{MVP} < x < K$, lower values of $G'(x)$ correspond with greater stock sizes. For the logistics growth function, $G'(x) = \gamma - (2\gamma x)/K$ and $G''(x) = -(2\gamma)/K < 0$. Hence, $G'(x)$ is a monotonically declining function in x, that crosses the horizontal axis at $x = x_{MSY} = \frac{1}{2}K$. Similarly, with constant prices, $r = G'(x)$, so that high discount rates correspond with high values for $G'(x)$, which in turn translates into small stocks. The relative strength of the countervailing effects of discounting on the one hand and (harvesting costs) and rising prices on the other determines whether optimal economic stock size is bigger or smaller than maximum sustained yield.[4]

Other reasons why MSY is not to be trusted as a management objective are:

1. harvesting $G(x_{MSY})$ will not necessarily be sustainable over the long run due to natural fluctuations of the stock (although similar criticism applies to other rigid policy prescriptions, see Grafton and Silva-Echenique 1997);
2. relations between interdependent species are ignored; and
3. preservation values are not included. The latter is a serious omission in the case of large marine mammals.

7.2 Optimal Population Size and Economic Dynamics

If society wants to maximise its welfare from exploiting and preserving a renewable resource stock, or if firms with well-defined property rights want to maximise profits, x_{MSY} is generally not the optimal stock size. In this section, optimal stock size is determined by finding a steady-state solution for the optimal control problem that represents society's effort to maximise its well being. Represent the management problem as:

$$(7.14) \quad \text{Maximise } V = \int_0^\infty U(y, x)\, e^{-rt}\, dt$$

$$(7.15) \quad \text{subject to } \dot{x} = G(x) - y,$$

where U indicates utility derived from either exploiting the stock or preserving it (i.e., both harvest levels and *in situ* stock are arguments in U).

Assume a downward sloping inverse demand function $P = D(y)$, and assume that utility is separable in harvesting and conservation, $W(x)$, so that $U(y,x) = \int D(y)dy + W(x)$. Then, if the resource in question is exploited with a simple multiplicative yield function ($y = qEx$), this management problem can be rewritten as:

---

[4] For the North Sea herring fishery, Bjorndal (1988) shows that the economically optimum population is lower than x_{MSY}, which equals about 2 million tonnes (Mt). For discount rates ranging from 0% to 20%, Bjorndal estimates that the optimum economic stock size ranges from almost 1.6 Mt down to 1 Mt. Both the biological and economic stocks are greater than the 1996 stock of about 500,000 tonnes. This is because herring are a schooling species where stock size has little impact on harvest costs.

$$(7.16) \quad \text{Max } V = \int_0^\infty \left[\int_0^{y(t)} D(s)ds + W(x) - cE \right] e^{-rt} dt = \int_0^\infty \left[\int_0^{y(t)} D(s)ds + W(x) - \frac{cy}{qx} \right] e^{-rt} dt,$$

where c is the per unit cost of effort. Assuming an interior solution, the necessary conditions for an optimum are (see Appendix I):

$$(7.17) \quad D(y) - \frac{c}{qx} - \lambda = 0$$

and

$$(7.18) \quad \dot{e}(t) = [r - G'(x)] \lambda(t) - W'(x) - \frac{c}{qx^2}.$$

Equation (7.17) defines the shadow price or rent (λ) accruing to the resource on a per unit basis, namely, price minus marginal harvesting costs. This is the rental rate or value that a resource owner can charge for each unit of harvest. Condition (7.18) indicates under what condition society is indifferent to holding a marginal unit of the stock *in situ*, when the alternative is to harvest and invest the revenues elsewhere in the economy (at rate r). This condition is a non-arbitrage condition, similar to the Hotelling rule for non-renewable resources (Neher 1990; Clark 1990). The increment in the shadow price should be equal to the "net rate of interest", $r - G'(x)$, multiplied by the shadow price, but augmented by two terms. The two additional terms on the RHS represent the benefits to society of holding one extra unit of the stock *in situ*: it is a direct source of future utility for conservationists and, with the current specification of the harvest function, it reduces future harvesting costs.

Differentiating (7.17) with respect to time gives:

$$(7.19) \quad \dot{e}(t) = D'(y) \dot{y}(t) + \frac{c}{qx^2} \dot{x}(t).$$

Setting (7.19) equal to (7.18) and solving for $\dot{y}$ gives:

$$(7.20) \quad \dot{y}(t) = \frac{1}{D'(y)} \{ [r - G'(x)] [D(y) - \frac{c}{qx}] - W'(x) - \frac{c}{qx^2} G(x) \}.$$

The optimal stock size is found by setting all time derivatives equal to zero. When $\dot{x} = 0$ harvest should be equal to the regenerated fraction of the stock: $y = G(x)$, which follows directly from (7.15). The optimal size of the stock is found from (7.20). Setting $\dot{y} = 0$ and rearranging terms gives:

(7.21)　$r = G'(x) + \dfrac{W'(x)qx^2 + cG(x)}{x(qxD - c)}$.

In equilibrium, the social rate of time preference must be equal to the marginal product of the stock in production, $G'(x)$, plus a complicated stock term. With fish, trees or wildlife, society is compensated for delaying harvest because the stock increases. Hence, the rate of return on holding the marginal unit of stock can be decomposed in two parts: (i) the return from increased stock growth $G'(x)$, and (ii) the return from increased preservation value and reduced costs. The numerator of the stock term reflects the combination of future marginal cost savings from leaving a unit of the resource *in situ* because less effort will be needed when the stock is denser (population density is greater), and future marginal utility from this denser stock. These savings and gains are "discounted" by the current marginal rent due to harvesting (the denominator). Since $W'(x)$ and $cG(x)$ are both positive, the stock term is positive. The larger this term, the higher the optimal steady-state stock. Given a certain value of r, a higher realisation of the stock term corresponds with lower required values for $G'(x)$ to balance the LHS and RHS of (7.21). Again, since $G''(x) < 0$ this implies that stock size should increase.

If the Hamiltonian is nonlinear in the control variable (as in the current situation), the optimal approach path to the equilibrium solution is found with aid of equations (7.15) and (7.20). The differential equations $\dot{x} = 0$ and $\dot{y} = 0$ can be depicted in a phase-plane diagram with x plotted against y. The combination of these equations is often called an autonomous system of differential equations, as the right-hand-sides of these equations are not explicit functions of time t. The equilibrium is the intersection of the two *isoclines* (i.e., the curves where $\dot{x} = 0$ and $\dot{y} = 0$). From (7.15), we know that the x-isocline is the curve $y = G(x)$. To determine the y-isocline, we need to specify the demand curve and determine the utility provided by preservation. An example is provided in Chapter 10 for the management of the African elephant, with the basic results repeated in Figure 7.2. In the absence of stock dependent harvest costs and preservation values, the $\dot{y} = 0$ equation would reduce to the vertical line $x = x^*$, where $G'(x^*) = r$.

The two isoclines divide the graph into four quadrants (or *iso-sectors*), labelled I through IV in Figure 7.2. Each quadrant has a *directional* (indicated by two arrows) that indicates the movement of a point (x, y) over time. In the figure, a point would move to the right if $\dot{x} > 0$ (and to the left if $\dot{x} < 0$) and upwards if $\dot{y} > 0$ (downwards if $\dot{y} < 0$). The signs of $\dot{x}$ and $\dot{y}$ come from the differential equations. For example, for $y > G(x)$ or points above the $\dot{x} = 0$ isocline, catch exceeds regeneration and the stock declines over time (hence a point moves to the right as indicated by the directionals in quadrants I and II of Figure 7.2). A unique trajectory passes through each given point in the phase-plane. From quadrants II and III in Figure 7.2, a point moves in the direction of the equilibrium, with one trajectory in each of quadrants II and III actually converging to (x^*, y^*). In quadrants I and IV, there is a trajectory that passes through the equilibrium point, but any shock from equilibrium in the directions of quadrants I and IV sends the system away from equilibrium. These trajectories are indicated by dark lines in Figure 7.2 and are referred to as a separatrices. The separatrix through quadrants II and III is a stable branch, while the other is unstable. Points lying off the separatrices move in the directions indicated. (See Simon and Blume 1994, pp. 689–708 for a description of how to construct such phase-plane diagrams).

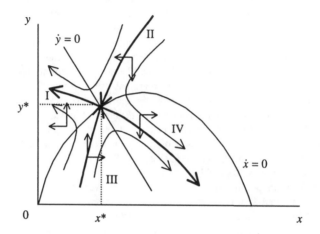

Figure 7.2 Phase-Plane Diagram: Saddle Point Equilibrium

The equilibrium described in Figure 7.2 is a saddle point. One separatrix is a stable branch, while the other is unstable. Further, any trajectory other than the stable branch would be unsustainable (a trajectory is shown for each of the four quadrants). Initially the trajectories that start in quadrants II and III (shown in the figure) approach the (unstable) equilibrium (x^*, y^*), but later veer off and diverge from it, so that, eventually, either $y(t) = 0$ or $x(t) = 0$ as t→∞. Trajectories starting in quadrants I and IV would move immediately towards $y(t) = 0$ or $x(t) = 0$ as t→∞. Because of the one stable separatrix and one unstable one, the point (x^*, y^*) describes a saddle point, which is typical of nonlinear models.

For models involving more than one state variable, numerical methods must be used to determine the approach dynamics. For the one state, one control system, the separatrices can be computed by linearising the dynamical system and finding the eigenvalues and associated eigenvectors near the equilbrium point (see Appendix I). The eigenvectors determine the directions along which the separatrices approach the equilibrium point; for example, Conrad and Clark (1987, pp. 52–6) numerically solve for the optimum approach path, or the separatrices themselves, using the Runge-Kutta algorithm. Typically, separatrices are obtained by iterative numerical integration, and dozens of numerical integration algorithms exist. It is of interest to note that the separatrices converge to the steady-state equilibrium (x^*, y^*), but the approach velocity slows as one gets nearer to the equilibrium. The steady-state is reached when *t* reaches infinity; this is in contrast to most rapid approach path (MRAP) models where the equilibrium will be reached in finite time (see below).

The above analysis is based on the convenient but unrealistic assumption that exploitation costs are directly related to harvesting effort, or $C = cE$. Clark et al. (1979) explicitly recognise that non-malleable capital is pervasive in renewable resource management. Relaxing the assumption that human-made capital (H) can be regarded as a flow variable has a profound influence on (short-run) optimal resource management. More specifically, under the assumption that capital investments in vessels and gear are completely irreversible (i.e., there is no market for excess capacity), but subject to depreciation, they find that the *x-H* phase-plane is divided into three separate regions where it is optimal to:

1. not harvest or invest,
2. harvest at full force and not invest, and
3. invest at full force by increasing H to a value determined by a switching function (see also Clark 1985).

Although the optimal policy converges to the same steady-state stock as determined by the variable cost model, Clark et al. (1979) demonstrate that it may be optimal to have an excessively high capital stock and a severely depleted fish stock in transitory phases. Boyce (1995) turns their linear model into a nonlinear one, and also finds that temporary phases with excess capacity and small stocks may be optimal in the short run. This may, for example, shed new light on the often heard claim that fish stocks are "over fished" over the entire world: (temporarily) reducing (fish) stocks below their optimum stock size may be economically efficient when investments are irreversible. On the other hand, with irreversibilities in exploitation, such as could occur with harvesting near MVP and with tropical deforestation, temporary over-harvesting may no longer be an optimal management strategy.

The Hamiltonian in the simple model above is not linear in the control variable (see Appendix I); hence, the optimal approach dynamics are gradual and the equilibrium is not reached in finite time. Nonlinearity may be caused by a downward sloping demand curve for the harvested product, or by the manner in which harvesting costs $C(y)$ are specified.[5] Instead, if the current value Hamiltonian would have been linear in $y(t)$ – for example, when $H_c = Py - cy/qx + \lambda(G(x) - y)$ – then the optimal approach path to the steady-state solution would have been a MRAP or a bang-bang solution. A linearity condition is both necessary and sufficient for the optimality of MRAP solutions (Conrad and Clark 1987).

The switching function for this case is defined as follows: $s(t) = \partial H_c / \partial y = P - c/qx - \lambda$. Depending on whether the net revenue per unit harvest ($P - c/qx$) exceeds the shadow value λ of an additional unit of the stock or not, harvesting is conducted either at its maximum feasible level or not at all. This corresponds to the following rule for harvesting when the stock is out of equilibrium:

---

[5] It is a matter of preference whether E (effort) or y (harvest) is the control variable. Neher (1990) refers to the former model specification as the *primal*, and the latter as the *dual*.

(7.22) $y(t) = 0$ whenever $x(t) \leq x^*$ and $y(t) = y_{MAX}$ whenever $x(t) > x^*$.

In finite time, the stock will settle back to its optimal size. When $s(t) = 0$, $y = y^* = G(x^*)$. This bang-bang solution is simple and elegant, but not realistic in most cases.

Managing population quality: Micro-evolution of species

In addition to population size (a quantity measure), attributes of population *quality* (e.g., in terms of genetic diversity) may be relevant for policy makers. Munro (1997) studied the impact of human activities (such as harvesting or pesticide applications) on biological micro-evolution. Human actions are assumed to affect the relative fitness (and thus reproductive success) of some species and individuals of species over others, and this will, in turn, affect the genetic composition of future generations. Examples include the positive effects of using pesticides on the relative fitness of resistant insects (Munro's case) and the favourable effect of lower limits on fishnet mesh size on smaller adult fish. The effect of human actions on genetic composition of future populations is sometimes anticipated and purposeful (as in the case of selective breeding) and sometimes overlooked, possibly with detrimental consequences.

To include micro-evolution in bioeconomic modeling, Munro (1997) adds a differential equation to describe how selection pressures determine the proportions of the population with a particular trait over time, and then links this changing proportion to population growth. We briefly describe his model of the spread of insect resistance causing damage to agricultural crops.

Consider a diploid organism, with alleles A and a at a single locus, implying that three genotypes can be distinguished: AA, Aa, and aa. Assume a is the allele conferring resistance to pesticides, and that A is dominant. Absolute fitness of the susceptible phenotype (consistent with genotypes Aa and AA) in the absence of the pesticide is W, while W_a ($< W$) is absolute fitness of the resistant strain (the strain with genotype aa). Denote p as the proportion of alleles that are of type A and $(1 - p)$ the share that are of type a. Average fitness is described by:

(7.23) $\overline{W} = p(2 - p)W + (1 - p)^2 W_a$.

Recall that, when both parents are of the Aa genotype, offspring will have genotype AA (with probability ¼), Aa (½) and aa (¼). The evolution of p over time is described by:

(7.24) $\dot{p} = (\dfrac{W}{\overline{W}} - 1)p$

Now, in the absence of pesticides, p will tend to 1 as time goes by and as $W > \overline{W}$. The next step is to translate these findings into population growth of the insect species under consideration. (We do not do this here, but focus, rather, on the main idea.)

Munro (1997) assumes that management (applying pesticides that reduces fitness of non-resistant strains) reduces the fitness of genotypes *AA* and *Aa* by φ, where φ is a choice variable, with associated cost $c(\varphi)$. Applying pesticides affects average fitness, population growth and the development of the proportion of susceptible individuals, but leaves resistant individuals unaffected. If the modified fitness W' of the susceptible phenotype is smaller than W_a, p will fall to zero.

Munro examines pesticide application for a myopic planner, who incorrectly assumes that $\dot{p} = 0$ (or who ignores the effect of φ on evolution of the insect species), and a fully rational planner.[6] The myopic planner's time plan for φ(t) will not be time consistent and will require constant updating as p changes. Perhaps not surprisingly, Munro demonstrates that the value of p is higher under perfect foresight and the equilibrium insect stock is lower, compared to the myopic case. This illustrates that both quantity and quality attributes of populations may have economic consequences, and that human behaviour can affect both.

7.3 Extinction

Extinction or loss of viability of a species can be a deliberate or an inadvertent event.

> Commercially important species are often overharvested to economic depletion (many fisheries and forest dwelling species), to near extinction (the blue whale, right whale, northern elephant seal, American bison, black rhino, white rhino, for example) or to extinction (Stellar's sea cow, great auk, Carribean monk seal). Overexploitation, usually combined with habitat destruction and/or introduced species threatens about one-third of the endangered mammals and birds of the world. (Lande et al. 1994, p. 88)

Deliberate extinction is dealt with in the realm of economics, and a short discussion is provided below. The model introduced here is extended and applied in Chapters 9 (biodiversity) and 10 (endangered species). In addition to predictable and controllable systematic pressures, such as hunting and habitat destruction, extinction of species may be caused by stochastic perturbations that elude prediction, because they are or appear random and involve uncertainty. While maintaining a (small) population of a species may be an economically attractive option, due to the vagaries of nature, survival of such populations is not guaranteed. This issue, with which ecologists are more familiar than economists, is treated briefly in a separate subsection below.

Bioeconomic models and extinction

Human caused extinction of plant and animal species in general (and the threat of extinction of certain high-profile animal species in particular) is a problem that biologists have brought to the attention of policy makers. Swanson (1994a, b) argues

---

[6] Pest control is a public good as it affects damage on own and neighbouring crops; thus individual farmers will likely under supply this good.

that the economics of biodiversity loss, or the narrowing of the gene pool through the loss of many (unknown) species, and extinction of species are essentially the same general problem.

> Human societies must select a portfolio of assets from which they derive a flow of benefits, and one important part of this portfolio is the range of biological assets upon which we depend. ... Given capital constraints it will sometimes be optimal to disinvest in one asset and invest the receipts in another asset; that is, it will be socially optimal to engage in conversions between assets to equilibrate returns. ... The fundamental force driving species decline is always the relative rate of investment by the human species. It is the human choice of another asset over a biological asset that results in the inevitable decline of that species. (Swanson 1994b, p. 805)

Recall again equation (7.21), which essentially states that, in a steady-state, the resource is to be maintained at a level that equates the return from that asset with the return from other assets; r (on the LHS) measures the opportunity cost of capital, or the competitive return. In (7.21), the return from investing in the biological asset depends on three factors:

1.   The marginal growth rate of the asset $G'(x)$
2.   Nonuse values of the stock $W'(x)$
3.   Stock dependent harvest costs, such as search costs

If it is not possible to balance the RHS and LHS of (7.21) for positive stock sizes (or, for critical depensation, for $x > x_{MVP}$), the species in question is not a competitive investment. In Swanson's words: "slow growth relative to other assets in the economy is in and of itself a route to species extinction. Resources, even biological resources, must be competitive as productive assets if there is to be a force for their retention in a world of scarce resources" (p. 807). Sometimes, the threshold value for r compatible with viable populations is called the "critical rate". Hence, when biological assets are considered inferior assets, they are removed from the human portfolio. Swanson (1994b) describes three different routes to bring about species decline.

Stock disinvestment entails removal of the stock and subsequent sale, with the receipts allocated to the acquisition of other, more competitive assets. This is the conventional "optimal extinction" scenario developed by Clark (1973a,b, 1990)-the LHS and RHS of equation (7.21) cannot be equated for positive stock x. A necessary condition is that it is profitable to harvest the very last individual (or breeding pair) of the population, or at least harvest the population down to MVP: $P > c(y,x)$ for $x = 0$ or $x = x_{MVP}$.

If the cost of transforming the "inferior" resource stock into another asset is prohibitively high, an equilibrium stock exists and, depending on the size of this equilibrium population relative to MVP, extinction may or may not be the result. Hence, extinction is at least partially determined by the development of costs and prices as the stock is drawn down. Among other things, this implies that extinction is less likely when harvest costs are stock dependent, such that harvest costs increase when the stock is reduced. Similarly, Farrow (1995) argues that large stocks are safer from extinction than small stocks, as drawing them down may imply that prices decrease, so that the profitability of continued exploitation is eroded.

There are other concerns. First, the *opportunity cost* of harvest effort plays an important role. If opportunity costs are low (e.g., because alternative employment opportunities for fishers and/or poachers are scarce), exit from the unprofitable resource sector will be slow (as long as revenues cover *variable costs*, harvesting may continue), and the probability of extinction is greater. Second, for some renewable resource industries, such as the fishery, the "braking impact" of harvest costs on effort may be obscured when multiple species are exploited. One possible reason for near extinction in the case of blue whales (Spence 1973) is that whalers were not very selective in the choice of whales harvested – most of the products obtained from blue whales can also be obtained from most other whales, albeit in smaller quantities. This implies that it is the cost of harvesting *any* type of whale that determines whether whaling will continue, not the cost of locating and killing a blue whale. Similarly, elephants and rhinos are typically poached jointly (see Chapter 10).

In the absence of price effects, Cropper (1988) shows that extinction of a small renewable resource stock may be optimal for a profit-maximising agency, even if the marginal growth rate at MVP exceeds the discount rate, $G'(x_{MVP}) > r$, and the asset thus seems a worthy investment. Necessary conditions for this to happen are that (1) the growth function exhibits critical depensation (curve II in Figure 7.1) – i.e., a positive minimum viable population for the species exists – and (2) that it is profitable to harvest (some) members of the species below MVP. The reason is that the net discounted benefits of refraining from harvest for a time sufficient to build up the small stock to sizeable proportions are smaller than the discounted benefits from current depletion.

Swanson (1994b) notes that it is not often the case that "stock disinvestment" is the prime cause for species decline, as there is no "demand" for most of the species threatened today. As discussed in Chapter 9, biodiversity loss is not confined to marketable species. Indeed, projected extinction rates are mainly based on unknown species, so another force is at work.

Base resource allocation refers to the situation where "base resources", such as land, are not allocated to the asset, because those resources are better used elsewhere (allocated to more competitive assets). The above discussion basically ignored opportunity costs of species conservation. This is logical. Most literature on the economics of extinction is based on work done by Colin Clark, who was especially interested in the fishery. While marine resources may have low opportunity costs (there are few competing uses for the sea), land-based resources often do compete with alternative uses such as agriculture (e.g., habitat suitable for elephants). For the survival of "on-shore" biological assets, it is necessary that these assets are allocated so-called base resources R by decision makers, as habitat available to species is an endogenous decision variable. Swanson (1994b) proposes to make the carrying capacity (K) of the species concerned a function of the base resources allocated to the survival of the species.

The growth function of a biological asset thus shifts inwards as less base resources are allocated to it, and outward if the reverse holds. This implies that the base model should be described as follows:

(7.25)   Maximise$_{y,R}$ $$V = \int_0^\infty \left[\int_0^{y(t)} D(s)ds + W(x) - \frac{cy}{qx} - rp_R R \right] e^{-rt} dt,$$

(7.26)   subject to $\dot{x}(t) = G(x, R) - y(t),$

where ρ_R is the "price" of the base resource (usually land) and is based on the flow of benefits that this resource could generate in its next best alternative. This implies that policy makers no longer maximise the difference between revenues and costs of exploitation, but rather the difference between revenues and the sum of harvest costs and opportunity costs. This new model contains the extra control variable R and, upon solving, yields an additional condition for the "optimal allocation of base resources" that the species will obtain. Not surprisingly, "a species will receive allocations of base resources only to the extent that the species is able to generate a competitive rate of return from this use" (Swanson 1994b, p. 813). This means that a rapid rate of growth may not be sufficient to rule out extinction as an optimal strategy; the returns from alternative land use options are also relevant. Extinctions may thus be the result of "undercutting", which seems to be consistent with species loss due to tropical deforestation, caused mainly by converting forests into agricultural lands (see Chapters 9 and 12).

Reallocation of management services refers to the refusal to allocate management services to the asset, giving preference to the use of scarce management resources in other, more competitive assets. Under open-access, no one can be excluded from entering the industry (as shown in Chapter 4) and effort is attracted to the sector as long as harvesting is profitable – as long as rent is not totally dissipated. Eventually, the system reaches a sub-optimally low stock equilibrium. If prices are sufficiently high or exploitation costs are sufficiently low, the stock may be totally depleted (i.e., it is privately profitable to harvest the last individual in the stock) or driven below MVP levels. Harvesting biological assets under conditions of open-access is often considered a factor contributing to the demise of potentially valuable biological assets. Under open-access management, the selfish behaviour of individuals results in inadvertent extinction. If the resource in question had been managed under another regime (see next section), extinction or the loss of worthwhile resources would not have occurred. While this insight may be true for some cases, Swanson (1994b) has questioned this line of reasoning, arguing that "it is important to know why productive assets potentially worthy of investment would be subjected to [an open-access] regime. ... It is more likely that open-access regimes are caused by decisions not to invest in diverse resources" (p. 814). Bromley (1999) provides other compelling reasons based on institutional arguments.

Management services are just another form of an ancillary resource required for the survival of many biological assets, and allocation of these services is subject to similar considerations as the base resources. Hence, a resource stock will only receive attention and management services if it is able to generate a competitive rate of return. If maintaining *in situ* biological assets is considered an unworthy investment, no management services are provided, and harvesting takes place under wasteful conditions of open-access. Formally, this can be modeled by modifying the objective function as follows:

$$(7.27) \quad \text{Max}_{y,R,M} \; V = \int_0^\infty \left[S(y;R,M) + W(x) - \frac{cy}{qx} - r\rho_R R - r\rho_M M \right] e^{-rt} \, dt,$$

where ρ_M is the price of a unit of management services; M is the level of management services provided; and $S(y;R,M)$ describes social benefits of harvesting generated by the levels of investment in base resources R and management services M.

Open-access regimes are not a state of nature but an endogenous policy choice. While this is an interesting insight and presumably true for resources that are harvested under open-access conditions for extended periods, it leaves undisputed that in some cases temporary conditions of open-access may be caused by other factors, such as lack of information. For example, there may have been a period when decision makers considered the "bounties of the oceans" as endless, so that management was not deemed necessary. In other cases, defining property rights may have been difficult due to complex institutional constraints (especially involving multiple nations) that may have temporarily impeded appropriate management. Open-access may also arise as traditional common property management regimes come under pressure from, for example, migration, population growth or rising prices. This is discussed in section 7.4.

Ecological considerations and extinction

As argued above, biological assets have to compete for a position in the human portfolio, and only assets representing "worthy investments" (where "worthy" may be defined in terms of both market and nonmarket values) are selected. Due to an assumed concave growth function, the relative rate of return to (many) biological assets can be manipulated: reducing the stock x (for a given level of base resources) typically implies increasing $G'(x)$. Hence, to increase the rate of return of *in situ* stocks of biological assets, they are kept at "low" levels. In a deterministic world, this does not pose any particular problem. However, the concept of population viability may well be more complex than usually modeled by economists (Grafton and Silva-Echenique 1997). If economists consider the concept "minimum viable population", it is treated as a known and constant number, or an additional parameter in the growth function (see section 7.1).

This simple, deterministic view of the world is not consistent with the way ecologists view extinction (Soulé 1987; Quammen 1996). In addition to "controllable pressure", such as hunting and habitat conversion, population viability is affected by stochastic perturbations. To be more specific, maintaining low populations of biological assets relative to competitive assets may be risky for the following reasons:

1. *demographic stochasticity*, or accidental variations in birth rates, death rates and the sex ratio (Pindyck 1984);
2. *environmental stochasticity*, or fluctuations in species abundance due to variations in weather, food supply, predators, parasites and/or competitors (e.g., Olsen and Shortle 1996);
3. *catastrophes*, or extreme (non-continuous) cases of environmental stochasticity (such as drought or floods) where population size is significantly adjusted downwards; and
4. *genetic stochasticity*, or the vagaries by which certain harmful alleles become more common or rare in a population.

In small populations, two harmful genetic processes are at work. First, helpful alleles may become rare and eventually disappear due to the random process of genetic drift, which strips a population of its genetic variety, thus reducing its capacity to respond to changing circumstances (Quammen 1996). Second, harmful recessive alleles may manifest themselves due to inbreeding. The total sum of harmful recessive alleles within a population is known as the genetic load. Since a species with a small population is often forced to inbreed, recessive alleles may manifest themselves (i.e., occurring in a homozygous rather than heterozygotous situation). The result is called *inbreeding depression*.

Demographic and environmental stochasticity are unlikely to wipe out large populations of an animal species, while small populations are sensitive to small "shocks" (e.g., if by chance all four Mauritius kestrels remaining in the 1970s would have been males, the species would have gone extinct).7 Also, for obvious reasons, large populations are safer from genetic drift and inbreeding depression than small populations. Hence, rather than binary, as assumed by economists, the degree of safety of a population is (monotonically) increasing in stock size x. We develop a formal model of population viability later in this chapter.

The discussion of genetic stochasticity suggests that the lowest historical population may be relevant for population viability, rather than the current stock. This lowest level then acts as a bottleneck through which the population has moved in terms of genetic variation, restricting the ability to respond to future changes in the natural environment. To make matters worse, due to ongoing genetic drift and inbreeding of small populations (or populations that have once been reduced to low levels), the entire concept of steady-state may be open to dispute.

---

7 The probability that N individuals are of the same sex (be it male or female) is given by $(\frac{1}{2})^N$. For the case of the 4 remaining Mauritius kestrels, this implies that the probability of extinction due to an unfavourable sex ratio was equal to 1/8. For the case of the Northern subspecies of the white rhino (20 individuals) this number has fallen to 0.000002. Similarly, with 500 individuals, this chance has dropped to essentially zero!

Introducing stochasticity has far-reaching impacts on extinction probabilities. This is demonstrated by Lande et al. (1994), who analyse extinction risk in fluctuating populations. In a numerical model, they allow for variation in population growth due to demographic and environmental stochasticity and find that incorporating stochasticity into optimal harvesting strategies results in faster extinction of the target population (see also May 1994). Due to environmental and demographic stochasticity, eventual extinction will be the fate of any population. Viewed from this angle, conservation of species merely implies forestalling their eventual and inevitable demise. However, the average time to extinction is sensitive to the harvesting regime, and postponing extinction can be considered the aim of conservationists. The main results of Lande et al. (1994) are as follows. First, even for discount rates below the deterministic critical rate (see equation (7.20)), the biological asset is in trouble as the average time to extinction is greatly reduced for low but positive discount rates. May (1994) concludes that "estimates of critical discount rates based on deterministic models may often be optimistically high" (p. 43). Second, for species with growth displaying critical depensation, the critical rate itself is lower in stochastic models than in deterministic models. Third, if the aim is to maximise the average time to extinction, the appropriate policy for zero discount rates is to refrain from harvesting when the stock is below the carrying capacity K, and harvest at full force when the stock is (temporarily) greater than K. Economic discounting reduces the optimal harvesting threshold below the carrying capacity, but, not surprisingly, harvesting should be more careful than in deterministic models; see also Ludwig et al. (1993); and Hilborn et al. (1995).

7.4 Property Rights and Dynamics

In Chapter 4, we examined alternative property rights regimes. The value of *in situ* resources prevents a rational owner from over-exploiting this stock, and may thus contribute to a conservative harvesting policy. Similarly, if sufficient trust and social pressure exist, common property regimes may be successful in managing resources; cultural norms, ideology and value systems are important determinants of the actual extent of selfish behaviour and "free riding" (Bromley 1999). Hence, the absence of private property rights does not necessarily imply that management will fail.

Sethi and Somanathan (1996) consider additional situations and evidence from experimental economics (controlled experiments in a laboratory environment), providing a theoretical underpinning for this observation. They develop an evolutionary game-theoretic model to explain why common property management "guided by social norms of restraint and punishment may be stable ... against invasion by narrowly self-interested behaviour" (p. 766). It is assumed that the proportion of individuals choosing a particular behaviour increases when the payoff to that behaviour exceeds the average payoff in the population, and vice versa. Failure to meet social norms may result in a variety of sanctions, ranging from cultural isolation to the sabotage of equipment. It is assumed that those sanctions are both costly to inflict and incur.

Consider the model employed by these authors. There are three groups in a society of n persons: *Defectors D* (devoting high effort E_H to the harvesting process and ignoring the negative externality imposed on others); *Cooperators C* ; and *Enforcers F*. The latter two groups adopt low effort levels E_L, with enforcers sanctioning defectors while cooperators do not. The respective payoffs for these groups are as follows:

$$(7.28) \quad \begin{aligned} \pi_D &= E_H(A) - s_F \, \gamma n \\ \pi_C &= E_L(A) \\ \pi_F &= E_L(A) - s_D \, \delta n. \end{aligned}$$

where the price of the resource is 1; A is the average product of effort (a function of aggregate effort E); s_i ($i = D, C, F$) is the proportion of players belonging to a certain group; γ is the cost incurred by a defector when punished by an enforcer; and δ is the loss in welfare associated with sanctioning. It is assumed that enforcers sanction all defectors. Higher exploitation effort for defectors implies that this group earns a higher payoff than the other groups, unless the damage suffered as a result of sanctioning is sufficiently high to offset this advantage. Cooperators do better than enforcers (who bear the cost of punishing defectors), unless there are no defectors.

Next, assume the following equation describes the dynamics of group size:

$$(7.29) \quad \dot{s}_i \, \dot{s}_i = s_i(\pi_i - \bar{\pi}).$$

where $\bar{\pi}$ is the average payoff in the population. A steady-state is defined as a state in which the proportions of players in the three different groups are constant over time. From (7.29), it is clear that this is only possible when all groups earn equal payoffs: $\pi_i = \bar{\pi}$. A state consisting solely of defectors is such a steady-state. Other possibilities are any state without defectors. (With three groups of players a state can never be a steady-state as enforcers always do worse than cooperators. Similarly, a steady-state with cooperators and defectors is not possible as the latter will always "out-compete" the former.) Hence, "if the damages from sanctions are sufficiently high relative to the benefits derived from self-interested resource exploitation, there exists a set S of steady-states which consists of a mix of cooperators and enforcers" (Sethi and Somanathan 1996, p. 774). If the initial population is sufficiently close to this state, the population will be driven to it. The size of the set of steady-states and its basin of attraction is a function of the parameters. The "norm of restraint" breaks down as:

1. the intensity of local sanctions declines (e.g., because of the cultural isolation of the community declines over time, incursions by outsiders who are immune to local sanctions, or population growth), or
2. the net returns from resource exploitation increases (e.g., because of new technologies or higher prices).

Such a breakdown of social norms will imply lower resource stocks (or even extinction of the resource in question) and, in most but not all cases, higher levels of extraction effort.

A situation much like open-access results if common property breaks down. The static case of open-access was discussed in Chapter 4. The *dynamics* of open-access can be demonstrated using a simple model. Under the assumption that entry and exit in the fishery occur with a time lag, a simple entry-exit function can be formulated as:

$$(7.30) \quad \dot{E} = \frac{Py - cE - \alpha}{E} \, v.$$

In (7.30), v is a response parameter that describes the speed with which effort responds to profitability in the fishery, and α is a cut-off rate of return for the industry equal to the opportunity cost of capital multiplied by the number of vessels (or rE) (Hartwick and Olewiler 1998; Conrad 1995). If the stock has a quadratic growth function with parameters a and b, and we use the production function of the Schaefer model, then, in the steady-state, the following must hold:

$$(7.31) \quad \dot{x} = ax - bx^2 - qEx = 0,$$

which implies that (i) the stock has been depleted ($x = 0$), (ii) no harvesting takes place ($E = 0$, $x = a/b$), or (iii) an interior solution exists, with $x = (a - qE)/b$. Equation (7.30) can be rewritten as:

$$(7.32) \quad \dot{E} = v \, (pqx - c - r)$$

In equilibrium, exit and entry must balance; hence, $\dot{E} = 0$ so (7.32) can be solved for x:

$$(7.33) \quad x^{\infty} = \frac{c + r}{pq}.$$

Combining the two isoclines in a phase-plane diagram yields the steady-state equilibrium for the open-access fishery, which is not the same as that for the optimally managed fishery (of Figure 7.2). Depending on the various parameter values and starting conditions, $E(0)$ and $x(0)$, the isoclines may intersect in the interior of the phase-plane. In Figure 7.3, the case of pure compensation is illustrated, with the approach path *I* leading to the stable equilibrium x^{∞}. Approach path *II*, on the other hand, leads to extinction. Thus, it is possible that, even if an interior solution exists, excessive entry and delayed exit will deplete the resource before equilibrium is reached. This is particularly the case if the open-access situation is characterised by depensation (Clark 1990, pp. 189–92).

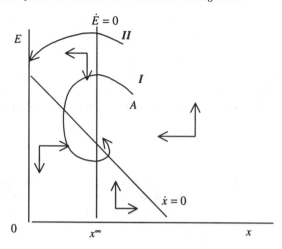

Figure 7.3 Open-Access Dynamics

An important assumption underlying Figure 7.3 is that the various parameters (e.g., r, K, c and v) are constant over time, which is unlikely in practice. In this case no open-access equilibrium may exist (Conrad 1995). The dynamics of open-access resources have been analysed by various researchers, especially the case where different countries exploit the same stock. Applying the model is easier when the discrete time analogue is used, as data on stocks and output are often recorded in discrete (say, yearly) intervals. For the case of the north pacific fur seal in the late 1800s, exploited by a number of countries during the migratory phase in their reproductive cycle, Wilen (1976) calculates values that predict a positive steady-state, with stock extinction *unlikely* (i.e., observations on effort and stock levels were consistent with path I in Figure 7.3). Amundsen et al. (1995) reach a similar conclusion for minke whale exploitation in the North Atlantic. In contrast, Bjorndal and Conrad (1987) found that the North Sea herring was probably saved from extinction when, after decades of *de facto* open-access management, the authorities decided to stop harvests for a number of years. Their model predicted that, without the ban, extinction might have occurred in 1983. Under the moratorium, which lasted in some sectors until 1981 and in others until 1984, the stock (temporarily) recovered.

7.5 Uncertainty in Resource Exploitation

So far, we have considered management of biological assets under conditions of certainty. This is clearly a simplification as many management choices take place under uncertainty. The benefits of exploiting and conserving assets often involve random components. When utility is a function of the first two moments (mean and variance) of the probability distribution of income (or wealth), the Capital Asset Pricing Model (CAPM) can be used to study asset management. CAPM states that the expected return on any asset is equal to the risk-free rate plus a risk premium, where the premium is a function of the covariance between the asset's return and some efficient portfolio of assets (Varian 1992). For the level of assets that society chooses to maintain, it makes a difference whether the uncertainty of investing in biological assets is independent, positively or negatively related to rates of return elsewhere in the economy. For given levels of biological and human assets, the uncertainty that society faces is higher (lower) when the return to those assets is positively (negatively) correlated. This is an incentive to reduce (increase) the *in situ* stock of biological assets.

Little evidence exists on this issue. It is usually assumed that stochasticity in "returns" from biological assets is independent of the marginal productivity of capital. That is, analyses typically focus on uncertainty in, for example, growth of renewable resources, stocks of *in situ* resources, future technology, etc., in isolation from other markets or capital stocks in the economy. Typically, the rate of return on investments in biological assets is equated to the exogenous and constant discount rate. Along these lines, much effort has been made to incorporate aspects of uncertainty in resource management.

Before turning to an example, we briefly review some insights derived from exhaustible resource models that can also be applied to biological assets or renewable resources. Uncertainty can relate to, for example, future demand or technology, property rights, or the size of the stock. Some sources of uncertainty (e.g., with respect to future tenure rights) imply that a rational resource owner (risk averse or not) accelerates depletion. Uncertainty in this case can be modeled as a Poisson process, and the mean arrival rate of the uncertain event in question (say, the probability of expropriation in any period Δt) can be added as a risk premium to the discount rate.

This is not a general result, however. Uncertain demand in the form of a shifting demand curve may have no impact on risk-neutral resource owners. For risk-averse owners depletion may be accelerated or postponed, depending on the characteristics of uncertainty. If uncertainty is positively related to time (such as with prices following a random walk), the resource owner is less certain about prices farther in the future, and thus risk-averse owners tilt exploitation towards the present. If uncertainty is related to the amount supplied (revenues are defined as price times quantity, so that revenues will be more uncertain when supply is large), the risk-averse owner will typically try to spread supply more evenly over time – from early periods, when supply is relatively large according to Hotelling's model, to future periods where supply and variations in returns are relatively small.

Pindyck (1980) demonstrated that risk-neutral and risk-averse resource owners alike should increase exploitation when exploration is modeled as a stochastic process. With (nonlinear) stock effects on extraction costs, equally big upward and downward deviations from the mean value in a stochastic model do not outweigh each other, which is a consequence of Jensen's inequality.[8] In Pindyck's model,

---

[8] Jensen's inequality states that, if x is a random variable and $f(x)$ is a convex function of x, then $\varepsilon[f(x)] > f(\varepsilon[x])$. Thus, if the expected value of x remains the same but the variance of x increases, $\varepsilon[f(x)]$ will increase. (Dixit and Pindyck 1994, p.49)

future marginal extraction costs are higher, resulting in faster depletion than along the certainty equivalent path.

In addition to uncertainty associated with future demand and technology, property rights (which may not be very secure even for land-based resources such as timber) and stock size, management of renewable resources often involves uncertainty in reproduction of the stock. Pindyck (1984) argues that the natural rate of growth of the stock is stochastic for virtually all resources. In a model with well-defined property rights and endogenous prices, he demonstrates the role of uncertain asset growth. The standard equation of motion (7.5) is replaced by:

$$(7.34) \quad dx = [G(x(t)) - y(t)] \, dt + \sigma(x(t)) \, dw,$$

where $G(x)$ is a growth function, $y(t)$ is harvest at time t, and $dw = \varepsilon(t)\sqrt{dt}$. Here $\varepsilon(t)$ is a serially uncorrelated and normally distributed error term with unit variance, implying that $w(t)$ is a Wiener (stochastic) process (see Appendix II to this chapter). The current stock x in this model is known, but the instantaneous change is the stock is partly random. Pindyck's (1984) objective function is (suppressing time notation):

$$(7.35) \quad \text{Maximise}_{\{y\}} \int_{0}^{\infty} [p - c(x)] \, y \, e^{-rt} dt,$$

where p is price per unit and $c(x)$ is the stock-dependent harvest cost function.

Solving (7.35) subject to the deterministic equation of motion (7.4) gives the following expression for the optimum stock:

$$(7.36) \quad G'(x) - \frac{c'(x)y}{p-c} = r.$$

Pindyck solves the model with the random equation of motion (7.34) using the recursive method of stochastic dynamic programming (see Appendix II), obtaining the following solution:

$$(7.37) \quad \frac{E\left(\dfrac{d(p-c)}{dt}\right) - c'(x)y}{p-c} + G'(x) = r + \sigma'(x)\,\sigma(x)\,A(x),$$

where E is the expectations operator and $A(x)$ can be thought of as an index of absolute risk aversion. The interpretation of (7.37) is that the market interest rate is augmented by a risk premium equal to the increase in stock growth variance attributable to the marginal *in situ* unit times the index of risk aversion (Pindyck 1984). Fluctuations reduce the value of the stock and, because their variance is an increasing function of the stock level, there is an incentive to reduce the stock. From (7.37), it is evident that the expected capital gain required to hold a unit of the resource *in situ* is higher, and *ceteris paribus*, the rate of extraction is higher so less of the stock will be held *in situ*.

Pindyck demonstrates that rent and the extraction rate are affected by random growth in two other ways. First, since $G(x)$ is a concave function, stochastic fluctuations in the stock level reduce the expected rate of growth, which is an implication of Jensen's inequality. This results in increased scarcity and reduced extraction. Second, since the cost function $c(x)$ is typically convex, fluctuations in the stock level increase expected extraction cost over time, which again is an implication of Jensen's inequality. This effect reduces rent and increases the rate of extraction. Pindyck concludes that, given a particular stock level x, the net effect of uncertainty on the current rate of extraction is ambiguous. More ambiguity arises if, in addition to stochastic growth of the resource, a stochastic stock of pollutants is modeled (Olsen and Shortle 1996)

Extinction revisited: Minimum viable populations and uncertainty

We now expand the discussion in section 7.3 by considering a simple model that captures catastrophes and demographic and environmental stochasticity. For this purpose, we expand on the forgoing stochastic models. Assume that, *ex ante*, society is risk neutral. The objective function can be specified as:

$$(7.38) \quad \text{Maximise}_h \int_0^\infty [B(h, x) - c(h, x)]e^{-rt}dt$$

where $B(h, x)$ are benefits from harvesting h units of the species ($\partial B/\partial h > 0$) and nonuse values associated with population abundance x ($\partial B/\partial x > 0$); $c(h,x)$ are harvest costs (with $\partial c/\partial h > 0$, $\partial c/\partial x < 0$); and r is the (social) discount rate. Maximisation takes place subject to the following stochastic processes:

$$(7.39) \quad dx = [G(x, f) - h]dt + \sigma_1(x)dw_1 - j(x)dq$$

$$(7.40) \quad df = \sigma_2(f)dw_2.$$

In (7.39), it is assumed that expected growth G of the resource is a function of current stock size x and stochastic food (or prey) availability f.[9] Since f is treated as a random variable, environmental stochasticity is included in the model through the impact of food availability on (net) regeneration.

---

[9] Alternatively, we could have modeled additional interactions with the environment by including, for example, predators or pests P, such that $\partial G/\partial P < 0$. We do not pursue this further here in order to keep the discussion simple.

The term $j(x)dq$ describes the disruptive effect of catastrophes on population size. In the absence of catastrophes, the expected change in species abundance over the period dt is $G(x, f) - h$. The term $\sigma_1(x)dw_1$ on the RHS of (7.39) represents random disturbances in the stock due to demographic variation. As above, the term dw_1 is an increment of the stochastic, Wiener process w_1 (with Brownian motion), such that $dw_1 = \varepsilon_1(t)\sqrt{dt}$, where $\varepsilon_1(t)$ is a serially uncorrelated and normally distributed random variable with zero mean and unit variance. Assume $\partial\sigma_1/\partial x \geq 0$ and $\sigma_1(0) = 0$. Catastrophes cause infrequent but discrete changes (or jumps) in species abundance. Assume that catastrophes can be modeled as a Poisson process. Let α be the mean arrival rate of a catastrophe, such that the probability of occurrence of such an event over the time period dt is given by αdt; the probability of no catastrophe is simply $(1 - \alpha dt)$. Now, $dq = 0$ with probability $(1 - \alpha dt)$, and $dq = u$ with probability αdt, such that $uj(x)$ is the jump (downward adjustment) in species abundance after a catastrophe has occurred (Dixit and Pindyck 1994).

The stochastic process in (7.40) describes food availability over time, which is simply assumed a function of a random component, due to, for example, weather fluctuations. Again, we assume that w_2 is a Wiener process.

Assume $E(dw_1 dq) = E(dw_2 dq) = 0$, and that $j(x) = x$ so that, if a catastrophe occurs, q falls by some fixed percentage ξ $(0 \leq \xi \leq 1)$ so that $(1 - \xi)$ times the initial population size remains after an event. This implies that $dx = [G(x,f) - h]dt + \sigma_1\sqrt{dt}$, with probability $\frac{1}{2}(1 - \alpha dt)$; $dx = [G(x,f) - h]dt - \sigma_1\sqrt{dt}$ with probability $\frac{1}{2}(1 - \alpha dt)$; and $dx = -\xi x$ with probability αdt. Hence, the expected change in x over time, $(1/dt)E(dx)$, is defined as $[G(x,f) - h](1 - \alpha dt) - \alpha \xi x$. Define ρ as the correlation coefficient between dw_1 and dw_2. Note that ρ is also the covariance per dt for dw_1 and dw_2 since the standard deviation per unit of time for these processes is equal to 1.

By Ito's lemma, dynamic programming can be used to maximise this model (see Appendix II). As $E(dw_1 dw_2) = \rho dt$, Bellman's fundamental equation of optimality can be written as:

$$(7.41) \quad rV(x, f) = \max_h \{B(h, x) - c(h, x) + [G(x, f) - h]V_x + \tfrac{1}{2}\sigma_1^2 V_{xx}$$

$$+ \tfrac{1}{2}\sigma_2^2 V_{ff} + \sigma_1\sigma_2\rho V_{xf} - \alpha[V(x, f) - V((1 - \xi)x, f)]\},$$

where $V(x, f)$ is the optimal value function (see Appendix II). An optimal solution requires that $\partial B/\partial h - \partial c/\partial h - V_x = 0$. This merely implies that, for an optimal solution, the shadow price of the renewable resource (V_x) should be equal to the marginal benefit of harvesting the species. Substituting the optimal harvest level h^* in (7.41) and differentiating with respect to x gives:

$$(7.42) \quad rV_x = (\frac{\partial B}{\partial h} - \frac{\partial c}{\partial h} - V_x)\frac{\partial h}{\partial x} - \frac{\partial c}{\partial x} + \frac{\partial B}{\partial x} + \frac{\partial G}{\partial x}V_x + (G - h)V_{xx}$$

$$+ \tfrac{1}{2}\sigma_1^2 V_{xxx} + \frac{\partial\sigma_1}{\partial x}V_{xx}\sigma_1 + \frac{\partial\sigma_1}{\partial x}V_{xf}\sigma_2\rho + \sigma_1\sigma_2\rho V_{xxf} + \tfrac{1}{2}\sigma_2^2 V_{xff} - \alpha\xi V_x,$$

which is evaluated at h^*. Next, take a second-order Taylor series expansion of $V(x,f)$ and again differentiating with respect to x gives:

(7.43) $dV_x = V_{xx}dx + V_{xf}df + \frac{1}{2} V_{xxx}dx^2 + \frac{1}{2} V_{xff}df^2 + V_{xxf} dx\, df,$

which is readily rewritten as:

(7.44) $dV_x = V_{xx}[(G(x,f) - h)dt + \sigma_1 dw_1 - xdq] + V_{xf}\,\sigma_2 dw_2 + \frac{1}{2} \sigma_2{}^2 V_{xff}dt$

$$+ \frac{1}{2} V_{xxx}(\sigma_1{}^2 dt + \alpha\xi^2 x^2 dt) + V_{xxf}\sigma_1\sigma_2\rho dt.$$

In deriving (7.44), we substituted (7.38) and (7.39) for dx and df, respectively, and have used the knowledge that $(dw_i)^2 = dt$, $dw_1 dw_2 = \rho$, $(dt)^2 = (dt)^{3/2} = dw_i dq = 0$. Taking the expectation of (7.44), noting that $E(dw_i) = 0$, and dividing by dt provides the expected rate of change in the marginal value of the renewable resource $(1/dt)E(dV_x)$. Now, substitute this result in (7.42) and note that, for an optimum solution, $\partial B/\partial h - \partial c/\partial h - V_x = 0$ holds. The optimal *in situ* stock of the renewable resource is then implicit in the following condition:

(7.45) $(r + \alpha\xi) - \dfrac{1}{V_x} \{[\dfrac{\partial\sigma_1}{\partial x}\sigma_1 + \alpha\xi x]V_{xx} - \frac{1}{2} V_{xxx}\alpha\xi^2 x^2 + \dfrac{\partial\sigma_1}{\partial x}\sigma_2\rho V_{xf} \}$

$$= \dfrac{\partial G}{\partial x} + \dfrac{1}{V_x}\{\dfrac{1}{dt} E(dV_x) + \dfrac{\partial B}{\partial x} - \dfrac{\partial c}{\partial x}\}.$$

This condition is an extended version of Pindyck's stochastic golden rule (7.37) discussed above. It states that, at the margin, the resource owner (society) is indifferent between harvesting the resource and investing the proceeds elsewhere in the economy (LHS) and holding the resource *in situ* (RHS).[10] The marginal benefit from conserving a unit, or the expected rate of return, consists of

1. the effect on resource growth,
2. the expected capital gain,
3. marginal nonuse values, and
4. the depressing effect of stock size on harvest cost.

Since $c(h,x)$, $B(x)$ and $G(x,f)$ are likely nonlinear in x they are affected by stochastic fluctuations in x, even though the expected values of these disturbances equal zero. Again, this is due to Jensen's inequality. Stochastic fluctuations reduce the expected growth rate, thus increasing scarcity and reducing optimal harvest levels, and increase expected catch costs, creating an incentive to increase harvesting to

---

[10] This becomes clearer after $(B_h - c_h)$ is substituted for V_x, and $(1/dt)E[d(B_h - c_h)]$ for $(1/dt)E[dV_x]$.

reduce future cost increments (Pindyck 1984). This indicates that the effect of (random) changes on optimal harvest policies is analytically ambiguous.

The LHS of (7.45) describes the social opportunity cost of conservation, which is more complex. The first term is the social opportunity cost of capital, augmented by a term that comes from the Poisson disturbance. It is well known that, if a benefit stream is interrupted as a result of a Poisson event (with arrival rate α), the expected present value of the stream of benefits can be calculated as if it had never ceased, but α must be added to the discount rate (Dixit and Pindyck 1994, p. 87). In this specific case, however, the species is not extinguished entirely after a random "event", but merely reduced in abundance. This explains why we adjust the arrival rate downwards (i.e., multiply with $\xi \leq 1$). Nevertheless, the profitability of investing in conservation of the *in situ* stock is reduced, and this term provides an incentive to reduce the optimal stock. The second term on the LHS is Pindyck's "risk premium" (Pindyck 1984, p. 294), adjusted for the possibility of jumps (the adjustment is $\alpha \xi x V_{xx}/V_x$). Pindyck's original risk premium is the increase in stock growth variance attributable to the marginal *in situ* unit multiplied by an implicit index of absolute risk aversion ($-V_{xx}/V_x$). However, the possibility of a stock-dependent catastrophe further unambiguously increases the (expected) rate of return that is demanded by a resource owner to conserve the marginal *in situ* unit.

The third term is a correction for non-marginal changes in stock size due to "catastrophes". Since the curvature of $V(x, f)$ is not necessarily constant over the range of values that x can take, such non-marginal changes will affect the level of absolute risk aversion (unless $V_{xxx} = 0$). Depending upon the shape of $V(x, f)$ (i.e., depending on whether $-V_{xx}/V_x$ increases or decreases as x falls), this implies an incentive to decrease or increase *in situ* stock levels, respectively.

The fourth term on the LHS is an adjustment to the expected rate of return required to hold the marginal unit *in situ*. The sign on this term depends on V_{xf} and ρ, and is analytically ambiguous; when $\rho V_{xf} >(<) 0$, the adjustment term is negative (positive); hence, the required rate of return decreases (increases), so the adjustment represents an incentive to increase (decrease) the optimal stock; see also Olsen and Shortle(1996).

Even though nonuse values are included as an argument in the model, species survival (population viability in the long run) is by no means assured. When, for example, the opportunity cost of capital or the probability of catastrophe is high, the economically optimal stock size may well be so low that, in the short or medium term, the stock is driven to extinction because of chance effects. Indeed, it may even be economically optimal to harvest the very last individual of the species, although rising harvest costs and marginal nonuse values probably prevent this from happening.

The above model is based on the assumption that a manager maximises net (social) benefits. Using this model, it is possible to consider population viability of the species at the preferred stock size. The concept MVP is usually considered a more restrictive concept, and used in a different context. More specifically, the use of MVPs has been advocated in the context of sustainable management. Assume that, say for ethical reasons, minimum viability requirements are imposed as constraints on harvest decisions. This might imply abandoning the optimising framework spelled out above. Assume that we are interested in managing a fish stock such that the probability of extinction in the next T years is below a certain acceptable level (say, this probability should be no more than 5%). Then, it is possible to compute sufficiently prudent management regimes that accommodate this concern. Of course there is a clear trade off, because the net present value of exploitation and conservation in the "sustainable scenario" will be lower than in the efficient management scenario solved above. This is true unless the sustainability constraint is redundant; implying that efficient management does not result in unduly risks for the species at hand.

Meta-populations: Stochastic and spatial aspects

In addition to questions pertaining to intertemporal issues, management of biological assets often involves spatial aspects. This has largely been ignored in the economics literature (Sterner and van den Bergh 1998). In this section, we apply some basic spatial elements that originate in ecological theory to our resource model. A boost for spatial analysis in ecological science came from the theory of island biogeography (MacArthur and Wilson 1967). This theory concerned the colonisation of an island from a mainland source, but it has increasingly been applied in a more general context as mainland habitats become increasingly fragmented due to human development (Quammen 1996; also Chapter 9). Further, the term meta-population is used to describe a set of local populations of a single species that interact as members migrate between locations (Hanski and Gilpin 1991).

With meta-populations, survival of a local population, or survival of the species itself, is determined by the ability of migrants to re-colonise areas (known as "patches") where a local population has gone extinct. One example is the re-colonisation of Yellowstone National Park with wolves from (meta-)populations elsewhere when those in the Park went extinct (Budiansky 1995, p. 179). Another is the plight of the Concho water snake (*Nerodia harteri paucimaculata*), which is threatened by water development projects in Texas. It survives only because of migration and re-colonisation of habitats where the snake went extinct as a result of the vagaries of population dynamics and external events (Quammen 1996, pp. 592–602). Analysis of meta-populations has both a spatial and a stochastic element.

Levins (1969, 1970) introduced the meta-population concept in ecological science. For simplicity, he ignored local (or conventional) dynamics and assumed that any local population is either at zero or at its carrying capacity (K). Denote by $s(t)$ the fraction of habitat patches occupied by a species at time t, and assume that the spatial arrangement of patches is of no importance. Then, the rate of change in the fraction of occupied patches (ds/dt) is equal to the difference between the colonisation rate and the extinction rate. (This is analogous to conventional population models where changes are described by the difference between the birth and death rates.) For a set of assumptions concerning colonisation and extinction, a steady-state for the fraction of occupied patches is readily computed.

To analyse the consequences of meta-population dynamics for harvesting regimes, we consider the simplest meta-population conceivable; that is, a meta-population consisting of just two local populations, between which migration is possible (Bulte and van Kooten 1999a). Denote these populations as X and Z, and the numbers of individuals in each by x and z, respectively. Assume that influx of individuals in any population is a function of the vacant niche, defined as the difference between carrying capacity and actual abundance, and species abundance in the other population.

More specifically, assume that migration from population Z to population X is denoted as $\alpha(K_X - x)z$, and that the process of individuals moving from X to Z is represented by $\beta(K_Z - z)x$. In these expressions, K_X and K_Z denote the carrying capacities of X and Z, respectively, and α and β are population specific parameters. This specification subsumes most common biological interconnections between subpopulations as described in the ecological literature, such as the sink-source (or one-way migration), fully integrated and limited-distance cases. The sink-source case is consistent with either α or β equal to zero. The fully integrated case is consistent with α and β greater than zero, and possibly of equal value.[11]

The objective function of the resource manager can be written as:

$$(7.46) \quad \text{Maximise } E \int_0^\infty B(h_X, h_Z, x, z)e^{-rt}dt,$$

where E is the expectations operator; B are net benefits of exploitation (and possibly conservation) of populations X and Z; h_i is harvesting of the respective populations; and r is the (constant) discount rate. Maximisation takes place subject to the following stochastic processes (see Appendix II):

$$(7.47) \quad dx = [G(x) - h_X + \alpha(K_X - x)z - \beta(K_Z - z)x]dt + \sigma_X(x)dw_X, \text{ and}$$

$$(7.48) \quad dz = [F(z) - h_Z + \beta(K_Z - z)x - \alpha(K_X - x)z]dt + \sigma_Z(z)dw_Z.$$

$G(x)$ and $F(z)$ describe net regeneration of the respective subpopulations. Since ecological circumstances for the two local populations are potentially different, we allow for different regeneration functions. The terms $\sigma_i(\cdot)dw_i$ represent random disturbances in population abundance due to demographic or environmental stochasticity. The term dw_i is an increment of the stochastic Wiener process w_i.

Ito's lemma and dynamic programming are used to solve the problem. The optimal population level is implicit in the following equation:

$$(7.49) \quad r + [\alpha z^* + \beta(K_Z - z^*)][1 - \frac{V_z}{V_x}] - \frac{V_{xx}}{V_x}[\sigma_x \frac{\partial \sigma_x}{\partial x^*}]$$

$$= G'(x^*) + \frac{1}{V_x}[\frac{\partial B}{\partial x^*} + \frac{1}{dt}E(dV_x) + \sigma_z \frac{\partial \sigma_x}{\partial x^*} \rho V_{xz}].$$

---

[11] The parameters α and β are potentially different. For example, for certain fish species, downstream migration may occur more "easily" than migration upstream.

Next, consider steady-state abundance for population Z:

$$(7.50) \quad r + [\alpha(K_X - x^*) + \beta x^*][1 - \frac{V_x}{V_z}] - \frac{V_{zz}}{V_x} [\sigma_z \frac{\partial \sigma_z}{\partial z^*}]$$

$$= F'(z^*) + \frac{1}{V_z} [\frac{\partial B}{\partial z^*} + \frac{1}{dt} E(dV_z) + \sigma_X \frac{\partial \sigma_z}{\partial z^*} \rho V_{zx}].$$

To solve for the steady-states, equations (7.49) and (7.50) and the corresponding equations of motion should be solved simultaneously. Hence, typically x^* can not be considered separately from, for example, $F(z)$ and K_Z. This finding is consistent with Brown and Roughgarden (1997), who also conclude that the biology of one population affects harvesting of another. Equations (7.49) and (7.50) state that, at the margin, the resource owner should be indifferent between current harvesting of an individual (unit) of the species (the LHS) and conserving that unit for future use (the RHS).

Consider the LHS of (7.49). The opportunity costs of conservation, or the benefits of harvesting, consist of

1. the opportunity cost of capital r,
2. the "migration effect", and
3. Pindyck's (1984) risk premium.

The latter is the compensation required for the increase in the local sub-population variance attributable to the marginal conserved unit multiplied by an implicit index of absolute risk aversion, $-V_{xx}/V_x$ (see above).

Consider the migration effect. Harvesting individuals from population X implies that migration to this local subpopulation will increase as the vacant niche is enlarged. Similarly, migration from X to Z will decrease as there are fewer individuals that can migrate. The marginal value of individuals in the two subpopulations, V_x and V_z, may differ due to stock effects in exploitation, accessibility, "image" and so on. Hence, the sign of V_z/V_x in the second term on the LHS of (7.49) is ambiguous, and so is the entire term. This implies that the migration effect may contribute to both investment and disinvestment in population X. For example, if, in the steady-state and at the margin, individuals in local population Z are more valuable than individuals in population X, the term capturing the migration effect is negative, and hence contributes to investment in stock X. This may seem counterintuitive, but building up population X implies enhancing net migration flows towards population Z, because of both an increased outflow of individuals and a reduced influx.

The RHS of (7.49) describes marginal benefits of conserving an individual of population x. Such benefits consist of

1. the marginal regeneration rate $G'(x)$ (which can be positive or negative, assuming a concave regeneration function);

2. perhaps marginal nonuse values, or possibly the marginal stock effect on exploitation costs $(\partial B/\partial x)$;

3. the expected rate of change in the marginal value of the species (or the expected "capital gain"); and

4. an additional adjustment factor or risk premium.

Analogous to Pindyck's risk premium, the fourth term on the RHS introduces an adjustment to the required rate of return on conservation due to stochasticity. The term $\sigma_Z(\partial\sigma_X/\partial x)\rho(V_{xz}/V_x)$ captures the fact that stochastic fluctuations in distinct local populations may not be independent ($\rho \neq 0$). Populations can be affected similarly (e.g., fluctuations due to El Niño affecting populations over vast areas) or in opposite fashion (e.g., abundance of migratory predator and prey species). Hence, the sign of this term is unknown. If $\rho V_{xz} > 0$, the term has a positive sign and hence tends to increase optimal abundance levels. The reverse holds when $\rho V_{xz} < 0$.[12]

The meta-population concept, or the effect of migratory individuals, thus has two distinct effects on steady-state harvesting. First, resource managers can partly manipulate migratory flows by determining the magnitude of the vacant niches. Increasing (decreasing) harvest effort depresses (increases) subpopulation levels and provokes a net influx (outflux) of migrants. When the marginal value of both local populations is different, so that $V_z/V_x \neq 1$, managers are able to "favour" the preferred population by depressing its abundance. The population that is valued less at the margin is allowed to be relatively abundant to provide a sort of sanctuary or overflow area. In contrast to Brown and Roughgarden (1997), who treat the biologically *more* productive population as a sanctuary, in this model, the economically *less* valuable population should take that role. When potential migratory flows are symmetrical (i.e., $\alpha = \beta$), the migration effect reduces to $\beta K_Z (V_z/V_x - 1)$, providing a simple benchmark. When inflows are more (less) likely than outflows, the term becomes more (less) important.

Second, migration is relevant when the stochastic processes that determine abundance over time are dependent. When upward fluctuations in one local population are matched by downward fluctuations in the other ($\rho < 0$), resource owners' overall exposure to shocks decreases. The risk term due to the meta-population concept thus mitigates Pindyck's risk premium (assuming $V_{xz} > 0$). As Pindyck's risk term is interpreted as an incentive to reduce stock size (local population abundance), this new risk term implies that the required premium declines, which is consistent with larger local populations, *ceteris paribus*. The reverse holds when subpopulations are affected in a similar fashion over time. In this case, investing in multiple local populations by refraining from harvesting can be considered extra risky, thus worthy of a higher premium. Due to concavity of the regeneration function, a higher risk premium typically implies reducing abundance.

---

[12] Stochastic fluctuations imply additional effects on optimal management because $B(\cdot)$, $G(x)$ and $F(z)$ are nonlinear, such that equally large upward and downward fluctuations in numbers of a subpopulation do not cancel out (Jensen's inequality). This adds to the ambiguity of the results discussed in the text. .

Incorporating the meta-population concept, or recognising migration of individuals between different local populations, is redundant only when the marginal value of local populations is equal *and* when stochastic processes are independent. If one of these conditions is violated, considering local populations in isolation will produce suboptimal management regimes. This implies that enlarging the scope of conventional bioeconomic models implies richer but more complex results.

7.6 Beyond Bioeconomic Models? Species Interaction

Clark (1990) argues that, with increasing demand on renewable resources, single species models are inadequate. He divides interactions between exploited populations in two broad classes: biological and economic. An example of the latter is the case of harvesting cost of blue whales in a multi-species fishery, where the stock size of one species affects the marginal harvesting cost of another species. Anderson (1977) refers to this as an example of a *technical interdependency*. Biological dependencies concern the competitive, communal and predator-prey relations that species have with other species (Begon et al. 1996). Interactions among species in economic models imply working with multiple-state variables. Analytical results tend to get fewer because of the associated mathematical complexities involved, and often we need to rely on numerical solutions for approach dynamics.

Most multi-species models that have been developed in recent years are partial models, in the sense that many important relationships and interactions are ignored. This may be due to incomplete knowledge of (marine) ecosystems. Clark (1990), for example, writes that no marine ecosystem has probably been studied in sufficient depth to warrant the use of sophisticated multi-species models.

An important feature of (partial) multi-species models is whether selective harvesting is possible or not. When multiple species are captured with the same gear, differentiation may not be possible. In those cases, however, in which ecologically interacting species can be harvested selectively, the standard theory developed in this chapter seems adequate, although it should be slightly modified to allow for these interactions. For example, consider the classical predator-prey model proposed by Lotka (1925) and Volterra (1931). Assume that the dynamics of predator (y) and prey (x) species interaction is described by the following dynamical system:

(7.51) $\dot{x} = rx - \alpha xy$

(7.52) $\dot{y} = -sy + \beta xy,$

where r, s, α, and β are parameters. According to this specification the predator species is needed to keep the prey population within bounds (for $y = 0$, x grows exponentially), with the predator going extinct without the prey (for $x = 0$, y declines at an exponential rate). In the absence of harvesting either species, an interior steady-state is possible and is described by $x = s/\beta$ and $y = r/\alpha$. By computing the eigenvalues of the linearised system (obtained by a first-order Taylor expansion about the steady-state) the stability of this equilibrium can be analysed (see Appendix I). Clark (1990, p. 183) demonstrates that the Lotka-Volterra system is unstable, as the system has imaginary eigenvalues: $d = \pm i\sqrt{rs}$ (where $i = \sqrt{-1}$) and that the trajectories are closed orbits with motion counter clockwise (the x-axis and y-axis are also trajectories). Small changes in the system destroy this property, however, resulting in diverging oscillations. Since observed patterns of predator and prey abundance are more stable than behaviour predicted by the basic model above, ecologists have attempted to add modifications to the model which enhance stability. One obvious approach to enhance stability is to assume density dependent growth of the species (i.e., add intraspecific competition by incorporating a concave growth function for the predator and prey species). This approach and others are discussed by Begon et al. (1996).

As a next step, harvesting can be added to the multiple species model. For example, Hartwick and Olewiler (1998) analyse the case of a simple predator-prey model with sharks and tuna, where the latter is a commercially valuable species. Not surprisingly, they conclude that it is socially desirable to subsidise shark harvesting such that the steady-state population of tuna rises and more tuna is available for human consumption. Similarly, Flaaten and Kolsvik (1996) examine a predator-prey relation where both predator and prey are commercially interesting species (here the predator is cod). In the context of a multiple cohort model with the opportunity cost of predation in the objective functional, they conclude that the optimal age at which to start harvesting is significantly reduced. Harvesting cod yields not only a commercially valuable product, it is also a kind of investment in the prey species – in this case, shrimp, herring, capelin and small cod. Unlike the conclusion reached by Hartwick and Olewiler, there is no need for subsidies to induce extra cod harvesting. In fact, they conclude that the optimal age in the Northeast Arctic is still high compared with the actual age of harvesting.

Flaaten and Stollery (1996) have examined the economic cost of predation of minke whales on economically valuable species such as herring and capelin. Because modeling the interactions among prey species (i.e., modeling a more complete multi-species model for the ecological system) proved to be very difficult, their model neglects these effects. It is shown that the cost of predation depends on the management regime for prey species (e.g., constant effort as opposed to constant catch policies), which is to be expected. In an empirical section it is shown that the economic cost of whale conservation, in terms of fishery benefits foregone, may be considerable (see also Chapter 9).

The case where selective harvesting is not feasible proves to be more difficult. Consider the case of combined harvesting of two ecologically independent populations x and z with differential productivity. If E represents effort devoted to joint harvesting, then $\dot{x} = rx(1 - x/K) - q_1 Ex$ and $\dot{z} = gz(1 - z/M) - q_2 Ez$, where r and g denote intrinsic growth rates and q_i, $i = 1,2$, is the (possibly) different catchability coefficient for the two species. Clark (1990) demonstrates that when such species are harvested jointly, the less productive population may be driven to extinction, whereas the other species continues to support the fishery. The ratios r/q_1 and g/q_2 are referred to as biotechnical productivity. As a general rule, populations with a relatively low biotechnical productivity (i.e., species with low growth rates and/or high catchability coefficients) are subject to extinction under joint harvesting conditions, provided that the cost-price ratio of the other species is sufficiently low to ensure sustained profitability of effort devoted to harvest. Extinction may occur under conditions of open-access, but it may also be optimal (even with zero discounting) for a profit maximising regulatory agency.

Anderson (1995) mentions another aspect of catching several types of fish simultaneously. Under a quota system this may cause problems as it may result in discarding fish for which no quota rights are held. Anderson describes a number of ways to address this issue, such as retroactive trading (i.e., buying and selling quotas after the harvesting has occurred) and allowing fishers to exceed current quotas with any overages today deduced from next period's allowable catch. See Clark (1985) for a more detailed analysis of multiple species and discarding.

Undeniably, the multi-species models discussed above enrich economic thinking, but they are still a first step in incorporating (modern) ecological science in economics. A key assumption underlying traditional theories of renewable resources is that long-term abundance of exploited species is directly and inversely linked with exploitation effort (e.g., Neher 1990; Conrad and Clark 1987). By controlling current effort and harvest levels, certain preferred future stock levels can be attained. When the optimal stock is reached, according to the theory, harvest can be made truly sustainable at a constant level (harvest is equated to net growth). This deterministic view of the natural world is the basis of most bioeconomic modelling, but it is increasingly being questioned.

In most bioeconomic models, for example, "density dependent" growth is assumed, while ecologists recognise that births, deaths and migration may also be caused by "density independent" factors. The latter effects then cause "noise" in population dynamics, some of which can be modeled as Brownian motion. However, bioeconomic analyses quickly become very complex indeed. In real life, populations (stocks) of renewable resources may not be stable and predictable. In fact, there is a "great variety of dynamical behaviours exhibited by different populations. Some populations remain roughly constant from year to year, other exhibit regular cycles of abundance and scarcity, and still others vary wildly, with outbreaks and crashes that are in some cases plainly correlated with the weather, and in other cases not" (May and Seger 1986). In addition to the well-known causes of disturbance, which obviously have severe consequences for the usefulness of conventional bioeconomic models, there is at least one more aspect that deserves attention.

There exists a growing sense among resource scientists that scientific effort should be directed at multiple species, community and ecosystem approaches (Budiansky 1995; Leakey and Lewin 1995; Wilson et al. 1994). The existence of predictable and stable equilibrium states has been called into question (Pahl-Wostl 1995), and is replaced by a view of ecosystems as self-organising systems, subject to change according to internal dynamics. The function and behaviour of the system as a whole is dictated by the relationships between members of the community and their environment. An ecosystem (or community), then, is defined as a network of compartments (species or functionally related groups of organisms) linked by interactions. When these interactions between different species in an ecosystem are explicitly modeled, the result may be complex, even chaotic, behaviour. It is well known that even simple nonlinear deterministic difference equations (and differential equations with a "time lag" in the regulatory mechanisms) of single species models may produce bizarre or chaotic dynamics (Gleick 1987).

Wilson et al. (1994) point out that "even relatively simple fish communities may be characterised by interactions that lead to chaotic population patterns, ... patterns of abundance in which the stock level of an individual species has no equilibrium tendency, but varies unpredictably within limits" (p. 294). Even in the absence of harvest pressure, populations of economically valuable species fluctuate over time. The mechanistic view of stability and predictability of species' populations, or even of ecosystems, moving inevitably towards a climax is giving way to a new paradigm based on the concepts resilience, cycles and natural fluctuations (Budiansky 1995).

Grafton and Silva-Echenique (1997), for example, focus on the chaotic properties of the system described by equations (7.51) and (7.52). Chaos occurs when the continuous time model is made discrete and the system parameters are in the chaotic range (see Gleick 1987). While the deterministic model suggests management strategies such as controlling total removals, controlling predators and prey enhancement are effective, the chaotic model suggests that management strategies that affect the system parameters (e.g., injecting contraceptives in predators; feeding prey to enhance reproduction) are most effective. Total removals will leave the system as chaotic as before (as this is equivalent to changing the initial conditions), while prey enhancement could cause a non-chaotic system to become chaotic. Mixed management strategies may also be effective in terms of learning about the system, but pursuit of a single strategy, as suggested by a deterministic model, could lead to extinction of one of the species.

The finding that real-life ecosystems may be very complex (Ludwig et al. 1993; Hilborn et al. 1995) or chaotic (Wilson et al. 1994) obviously has significant implications for the usefulness of bioeconomic modelling and the prescriptions derived from it. Such concepts as optimal stock, sustainable harvest and safe harvest standard lose their validity. Similarly, monitoring management programs by the state of *indicator species* (i.e., species whose state is thought to be highly correlated with the state of the system as a whole) is called into question. Again, such management relies on the existence of orderly and predictable relationships between the population of the indicator species and the integrity of its environment.

Clearly, much needs to be learned about the ways in which humans interact with nature. The purpose in the remainder of this book is to apply models presented in this chapter and the theory of previous chapters to various problems that humans encounter in their quest to manage nature. Management must be stewardly. It must occur in a way that contributes to economic well being (broadly defined to include nonmarket as well as market benefits), but without damaging those same natural systems. This is the challenge of what follows.

Appendix I: Deterministic Optimal Control Methods

The most useful technique for dealing with economic choices in dynamic settings is optimal control theory (Leonard and Van Long 1992; Simon and Blume 1994). Other well-known techniques to study dynamic problems are the calculus of variations

(Miller 1979; Chiang 1992; Kamien and Schwartz 1994) and dynamic programming, which is especially useful for empirical work (Kennedy 1986; Leonard and Van Long 1992). Since modern textbooks on environmental and resource economics often include a treatment of dynamic optimisation (e.g., Hanley et al. 1997), the treatment here is brief. We demonstrate the maximum principle with equality constraints in continuous and discrete time.

The maximum principle yields an open-loop solution, or "once-and-for-all" plan to which the resource owner should stick. The solution is a function of time only. The recursive method of dynamic programming tends to lead to closed-loop solutions, ones where the optimal decision is a function of the state variable at the beginning of each time period (Kennedy 1986). Closed-loop models are suitable, for example, when actors interact strategically or there are (stochastically) fluctuating populations. However, closed-loop solutions are not readily obtained for more complicated problems and their usefulness in analytical economics is rather limited (Leonard and Van Long 1992, p. 181). An exposition of stochastic dynamic optimisation is provided in Appendix II.

The standard optimal control problem can be represented mathematically as:

$$(A7.1) \quad \text{Maximise} \int_0^T R(x,u,t)\,dt$$

subject to

$$(A7.2) \quad \dot{x} = f(x(t), u(t), t),$$

$$(A7.3) \quad x(0) = x_0 \text{ and } x(T) = x_T, \text{ and } u(t), x(t) \geq 0.$$

where R is the objective functional; $x(t)$ is the state variable; $\dot{x} = dx/dt$; $u(t)$ is the control variable that is used to "steer" the state variable through time; T is the length of the planning horizon, which could be infinite; and $f(x,u,t)$ describes how the system changes over time as a function of the state and control variables and time. Starting and end-point conditions (if any) and non-negativity constraints are given by (A7.3) (Chiang 1992).

In renewable resource economics, for example, we might have

$$(A7.4) \quad f(x, u, t) = g(x, t) - h(x, u, t),$$

where $g(\cdot)$ is a growth function for some wildlife population, say as described by (7.1), and h is harvest as a function of the existing stock x and effort u. The objective function might then be:

$$(A7.5) \quad R(x, u, t) = Ph(x, u, t) - c(u, t),$$

where P is the price of a unit of harvest and $c(\cdot)$ is the cost of harvesting as a function of effort.

Assuming an interior solution (implying that the values taken by the controls and state variables in the optimal solution belong to the set of admissible controls and states), the problem can be solved using the (present value) Hamiltonian function (Clark 1990, pp. 91–5; Hanley et al. 1997, pp. 182–9):

(A7.6) $H(x, u, \lambda, t) = R(x, u, t) + \lambda f(x, u, t)$,

where λ is the dynamic equivalent of the Lagrange multiplier known here as the costate variable (there is one costate variable for each state variable, measuring the shadow price of an additional unit of that state variable). The Hamiltonian equals the value of the net returns plus the change in the stock valued by its shadow price. From the *maximum principle*, the first-order conditions for a maximum are (suppressing time notation):

(A7.7) $\dfrac{\partial H}{\partial u} = 0$ (optimality condition)

(A7.8) $\dot{\lambda} = -\dfrac{\partial H}{\partial x}$ (costate equation)

(A7.9) $\dot{x} = \dfrac{\partial H}{\partial \lambda}$ (state equation or equation of motion)

In addition, for an optimum solution the initial and endpoint conditions should be satisfied; hence, $x(0) = x_0$ and $x(T) = x_T$. Using the definition of the Hamiltonian, the system (A7.7)-(A7.9) can be rewritten as:

(A7.7′) $\dfrac{\partial R}{\partial u} + \lambda \dfrac{\partial f}{\partial u} = 0$

(A7.8′) $\dot{\lambda} = -\dfrac{\partial R}{\partial x} - \lambda \dfrac{\partial f}{\partial x}$

(A7.9′) $\dot{x} = f(x, u)$.

The optimal triplet $(x(t), u(t), \lambda(t))$ is a solution to equations (A7.7′)-(A7.9′), consisting of two differential equations and a first-order condition (A7.7′) for selecting the control variable. The conventional procedure for solving this problem is to eliminate the costate variable, and define a steady-state solution. The solution usually involves differentiating (A7.7′) with respect to time t, and solving for $\dot{\lambda} =$

$d\lambda/dt$. Next, the two expressions for $\dot{\lambda}$ are equated, and through subsequent substitution, which eliminates λ using (A7.7′), the problem is solved. The approach dynamics are of the bang-bang type (i.e., $u = u_{MAX}$ when the switching function $s(t) = \partial H/\partial u > 0$, and $u = 0$ when $s(t) < 0$) if the Hamiltonian is linear in the control variable u, and the approach is gradual (where the separatrices are computed numerically) if the Hamiltonian is not linear in u.

Often the endpoint $x(T)$ is not specified, but a transversality condition often needs to be invoked in order to solve the model explicitly. Leonard and van Long (1992, p. 254) provide an overview of common transversality conditions. Here, we only mention the most relevant conditions for resource economics. First, when terminal time T is fixed and there is no constraint on the stock $x(T)$, then, for an optimal solution, the following transversality condition should hold: $\lambda(T) = 0$. If the costate variable (shadow price) is positive, this implies that profits could be earned by further exploitation.[13] Second, when a terminal value exists, $S(x(T))$, the value of the costate variable equals the marginal terminal value of the stock: $\lambda(T) = \partial S/\partial x(T)$. Third, many non-renewable resource problems involve solving for the optimal "depletion time" of a fixed stock. Hence, T is not fixed but should be solved endogenously. The transversality condition in this case is simply $H(T) = 0$.

Discounting

Thus far, we have not considered discounting. Suppose that equation (A7.1) is written as:

$$\text{(A7.10) Maximise} \int_{0}^{T} R(x,u,t)e^{-rt}\,dt\,,$$

where r is the discount rate. The same approach can be used as above, in which case (A7.6) would be the present value Hamiltonian. However, it is often easier to work with the current value Hamiltonian, which is defined as:

$$\text{(A7.11)} \quad H_c \equiv H\,e^{rt}.$$

That is, the current value Hamiltonian H_c equals the compounded present value Hamiltonian. Then, we can let $\varphi = \lambda e^{rt}$, where λ is the discounted shadow price and φ is the current shadow price. The costate equation (A7.8) then becomes:

$$\text{(A7.12)} \quad \dot{\varphi} = r\varphi - \frac{\partial H_c}{\partial x}\,.$$

---

[13] Of course, given T finite, one might require that $x(T) \geq x_T$, in which case we would require that the Kuhn-Tucker conditions be satisfied, namely, that $\lambda(T) \geq 0$ and $[x(T) - x_T]\,\lambda(T) = 0$. This implies either that $x(T) = x_T$ or $\lambda(T) = 0$.

Consider the resource management problem above:

$$\text{maximise} \int_0^T \left(Ph(x,u) - c(u) \right) e^{-rt} dt$$

(A7.13)

subject to $\dot{x} = g(x) - h(x, u)$.

The current value Hamiltonian for this problem is $H_c(x, u, \varphi, t) = Ph(x, u) - c(u) + \varphi[g(x) - h(x, u)]$. Applying the maximum principle gives:

(A7.14) $\quad \dfrac{\partial H_c}{\partial u} = 0 \quad \Rightarrow \quad P\dfrac{\partial h}{\partial u} - \dfrac{\partial c}{\partial u} = \varphi \dfrac{\partial h}{\partial u}$

(A7.15) $\quad \dot{\varphi} = r\varphi - \dfrac{\partial H_c}{\partial x} \quad \Rightarrow \quad \dot{\varphi} = -P\dfrac{\partial h}{\partial x} + \varphi\left(r - \dfrac{dg}{dx} + \dfrac{\partial h}{\partial x} \right),$

plus the equation of motion in problem (A7.13). The first condition (A7.14) requires that the net marginal benefit of current harvest of the wildlife stock (as given by the LHS of the equation) is equal to the marginal benefit of leaving the resource *in situ* (marginal value of the stock). Equation (A7.15) gives the change in the costate variable over time – to prevent further arbitrage over time – ensuring that for an optimal solution the resource owner is indifferent between current and future exploitation. If this were not the case, gains could be achieved by intertemporally reallocating supply.

Equation (A7.14) can be solved for φ. Then $\dot{\varphi}$ is found by taking the derivative of φ with respect to time. Substituting φ and $\dot{\varphi}$ into (A7.15) and rearranging gives an expression for $\dot{u}$. The system of differential equations, the state equation and the expression for $\dot{u}$, can be analysed as illustrated in the discussion of Figures 7.2 and 7.3.

In order to determine whether the system diverges or returns to equilibrium after perturbation, it is common to analyse the local stability of the steady-state. Rewrite the differential equations as: $\dot{u} = w(x, u)$ and $\dot{x} = z(x, u)$. Obviously, in the steady-state, $w(x^*,u^*) = z(x^*,u^*) = 0$. If the differential equations are smooth, then the system can be approximated by a first-order Taylor series expansion:

$$\dot{u} = w(x^*, u^*) + \dfrac{\partial w}{\partial x}(x - x^*) + \dfrac{\partial w}{\partial u}(u - u^*) = \dfrac{\partial w}{\partial x}(x - x^*) + \dfrac{\partial w}{\partial u}(u - u^*)$$

(A7.16)

$$\dot{x} = z(x^*, u^*) + \dfrac{\partial z}{\partial x}(x - x^*) + \dfrac{\partial z}{\partial u}(u - u^*) = \dfrac{\partial z}{\partial x}(x - x^*) + \dfrac{\partial z}{\partial u}(u - u^*)$$

where the partial derivatives are evaluated at the steady-state. Stability is indicated by the eigenvalues of the matrix of partial derivatives ($a_{11} = \partial w/\partial x$, $a_{12} = \partial w/\partial u$, $a_{21} = \partial z/\partial x$ ($x - x^*$), $a_{22} = \partial z/\partial u$) at the steady-state: $A = \begin{bmatrix} a_{11} & a_{12} \\ a_{21} & a_{22} \end{bmatrix}$. These eigenvalues

can be obtained by solving: $\det [A - dI] = \begin{vmatrix} a_{11} - d & a_{12} \\ a_{21} & a_{22} - d \end{vmatrix} = d^2 - (a_{11} + a_{22})d +$

$(a_{11}a_{22} - a_{21}a_{12})$.

Let d_1 and d_2 be the solutions to this equation. Then the steady-state (x^*, u^*) is (1) an unstable node if d_1, $d_2 > 0$, (2) a stable node if d_1, $d_2 < 0$, (3) a saddle point if $d_1 < 0 < d_2$ or if $d_2 < 0 < d_1$, (4) an unstable spiral if d_1, d_2 are complex with positive real part, and (5) a stable spiral if d_1, d_2 are complex with negative real part (Simon and Blume 1994; Conrad and Clark 1987, p. 46).

Return to the issue of transversality conditions. When T is fixed at infinity (a common assumption in renewable resource models) then the transversality condition can be eliminated as $\lambda(\infty) = e^{-r\infty}\varphi = 0$, which will be assured for finite φ and positive discount rates. This implies that the model can be allowed to reach a steady-state, which is obtained by solving (A7.7')–(A7.9') for $\dot{\lambda} = \dot{x} = 0$ in the case of the Hamiltonian and solving (A7.14)–(A7.16) for $\dot{\varphi} = \dot{x} = 0$ in the case of the current value Hamiltonian.

Finally, to check whether the maximum principle conditions are both necessary and sufficient for a maximum solution, the Arrow sufficiency theorem can be applied (see Chiang 1992 for discussion; Kamien and Schwartz 1994 for proof). This comes down to checking whether the maximised Hamiltonian – substitute the optimal values of the control variable u into the (current value) Hamiltonian, $H^*(x,\varphi,t)$ – is concave in x for any given φ (i.e., the second derivative of the maximised Hamiltonian with respect to x should be non-negative). When the objective function $R(\cdot)$ and the RHS of the equation of motion $f(\cdot)$ are both concave in (x, u) and $\varphi > 0$, then the current value Hamiltonian $R + \varphi f$ is also concave in (x, u), and the conditions of the maximum principle are sufficient for a global maximum. However, the (current value) Hamiltonian can be concave in x even if R and f are not concave in (x, u). For details and additional information, see Kamien and Schwartz (1994) and Leonard and van Long (1992).

Discrete maximum principle and Bellman equation

The discrete-time problem can be stated as:

$$\text{Maximise} \quad \sum_{t=0}^{T-1} \beta^t R_t(x_t, u_t) + \beta^T S(x_T)$$

(A7.17)

$$\text{subject to} \quad x_{t+1} - x_t = f(x_t, u_t) \text{ with } x_0 = \bar{x}_0 \text{ (given)},$$

where x refers to the state variable, u to the control (decision) variable, T is the length of the time horizon, $S(x_T)$ is the terminal or salvage value, and $\beta = 1/(1 + r)$, where r is the discount rate. Define the discrete-time, current-value Hamiltonian as:

(A7.18) $H(x_t, u_t, \lambda_{t+1}, t) = R_t(x_t, u_t) + \lambda_{t+1} f(x_t, u_t)$.

The first-order conditions for an optimal are as follows:

$$\frac{\partial H}{\partial u_t} = 0 \qquad \Rightarrow \qquad \frac{\partial R_t}{\partial u_t} = -\lambda_{t+1} \frac{\partial f}{\partial u_t}$$

(A7.19) $\quad \beta \lambda_{t+1} - \lambda_t = -\dfrac{\partial H}{\partial x_t} \qquad \Rightarrow \qquad \beta \lambda_{t+1} - \lambda_t = -\dfrac{\partial R_t}{\partial x_t} - \lambda_{t+1} \dfrac{\partial f}{\partial x_t}$

$$\lambda_T = S'(x_T) \qquad \text{and} \qquad x_0 = \bar{x}_0.$$

These conditions are derived by writing the Lagrangian to problem (A7.17) in terms of (A7.18), as demonstrated by Kennedy (1986) and Conrad and Clark (1987). Simultaneously solving equations (A7.19) along with the constraint (equation of motion) in (A7.17) provides the solution to the discrete-time problem.

Problem (A7.17) can also be written as a dynamic programming (DP) problem. The Bellman equation is then:

(A7.20) $V_t(x_t, u_t, \lambda_{t+1}, t) = \max_{ut} [R_t(x_t, u_t) + \beta V_{t+1}(x_{t+1})]$,

where x_{t+1} is an explicit function of x_t and u_t. First-order conditions (A7.19) can be found from the Bellman equation by first setting $\partial V_t/\partial u_t = 0$, then differentiating both sides of (A7.20) by x_t (recalling that x_{t+1} is a function of x_t), and, finally, letting $\partial V_t/\partial x_t = \lambda_t$. As is clear from (A7.20), DP requires a backward solution algorithm to find the optimal decision set. This is described in greater detail below.

Appendix II: Stochastic Dynamic Optimisation

In this Appendix, we briefly discuss some basic principles of stochastic dynamic optimisation. A more complete review is found in Kennedy (1986), Taylor (1993), Dixit and Pindyck (1994), Kamien and Schwartz (1994), and other places.

Introduction to Ito calculus

A fundamental building block of most stochastic DP problems is the so-called Wiener process, or Brownian motion. Wiener processes have the following important properties:

1. They are Markov processes (i.e., the probability distribution for state values at time $t + 1$ depends only on their value at time t, and not $t - 1, t - 2, ...$).
2. They have independent increments (i.e., the probability distribution for changes over any finite interval is independent of other time intervals).
3. Changes in the process over any finite interval are normally distributed with a variance that increases linearly with the time interval (Dixit and Pindyck 1994, p. 63).

The Wiener process can be thought of as a continuous time version of a random walk.

Consider the Wiener process $z(t)$. Define $\varepsilon(t)$ as normally distributed with an expected value of zero and variance of 1, with the covariance between $\varepsilon(t)$ and $\varepsilon(t + j)$ being zero for all $j \in \Re$. The stochastic process $z(t)$ is related to $\varepsilon(t)$ and t as follows:

(A7.21) $\Delta z = \varepsilon(t) \sqrt{\Delta t}$.

Hence, over any finite interval z changes as follows:

(A7.22) $z(s + T) - z(s) = \displaystyle\sum_{i=1}^{n} \varepsilon_i \sqrt{\Delta t}$.

Since the ε_i are independent, the change $z(s + T) - z(s)$ is normally distributed with mean zero and variance $n\Delta t = T$. The latter point (see property 3 above) follows from the fact that Δz depends on $\sqrt{\Delta t}$ and not on Δt. By letting $\Delta t \to 0$, the continuous time version of (A7.21) is

(A7.23) $dz = \varepsilon \sqrt{dt}$

Note that $E(dz) = 0$ and $var(dz) = dt$. A fundamental property of the Wiener process is that $dz^2 = dt$ with certainty. This follows from these simple steps:

(A7.24) $var[z(t)] = \displaystyle\int_{0}^{t} ds = t$.

(A7.25) $dz^2 = (\varepsilon \sqrt{dt})^2 = \varepsilon^2 dt$.

The expected value of dz^2 is:

(A7.26) $E(dz^2) = E(\varepsilon^2 dt) = E(\varepsilon^2)dt = dt$.

By definition, $\mathrm{var}(\varepsilon) = 1$. This implies that the variance of dz^2 is:

(A7.27) $\mathrm{var}(dz^2) = E[(dz^2 - E(dz^2))^2] = E[(\varepsilon^2 dt - dt)^2] = dt^2 E(\varepsilon^4 - 2\varepsilon^2 + 1) = 0$

Thus, $\mathrm{var}(dz^2) = 0$ because $dt^2 = 0$. This implies that $dz^2 = dt$. The basic Wiener process can be generalised into more complex stochastic processes. For example, consider the following continuous-time stochastic process known as the Ito process:

(A7.28) $dx = a(x, t)dt + b(x, t)dz$,

where dz is the increment of a Wiener process, and $a(x,t)$ and $b(x,t)$ are known functions, representing drift and variance coefficients (Dixit and Pindyck 1994, p. 71). Since $E(dz) = 0$, $E(dx) = a(x,t)$. Commonly, $a(x,t)$ is referred to as the drift rate. Also, $\mathrm{var}(dx) = E(dx^2) - E(dx)^2$, which contains terms in dt, in $(dt)^2$ and $(dt)(dz)$, which is of order $(dt)^{3/2}$. For dt approaching zero, terms in $(dt)^2$ and $(dt)^{3/2}$ can safely be ignored, implying that the variance of dx is equal to $b^2(x,t)$.

In this chapter, some models with Ito processes for multiple variables were presented (i.e., the minimum viable population and the meta-population models). These represent simple extensions of the process discussed above, namely,

(A7.29) $dx = a_1(x, y, t)dt + \sigma_1(x, y, t)dz_1$ and

(A7.30) $dy = a_2(x, y, t)dt + \sigma_2(x, y, t)dz_2$.

The variables ε_1 and ε_2 may be correlated so that $\mathrm{cov}(\varepsilon_1,\varepsilon_2)$ can be different from zero. As the variance and standard deviation of ε_1 and ε_2 all equal 1, the correlation coefficient between x and y equals $\mathrm{cov}(\varepsilon_1,\varepsilon_2) = \rho$.

Ito processes are continuous in time but not differentiable. To differentiate functions of Ito processes, we make use of Ito's Lemma, which is a sort of Taylor series expansion. Ito's Lemma is also known as the fundamental theorem of stochastic calculus. Assume that $x(t)$ follows process (A7.28), and consider the function $F(x, t)$ that is at least twice differentiable in x and once in t (Dixit and Pindyck 1994, p. 79). Using normal calculus, the total differential of this function, dF, would be given by:

(A7.31) $dF = \dfrac{\partial F}{\partial x}dx + \dfrac{\partial F}{\partial t}dt$.

The total differential is usually defined in terms of first-order changes, as higher-order terms vanish in the limit. However, this is not the case when x follows an Ito process. Consider an extension that also includes higher-order terms:

(A7.32) $dF = \dfrac{\partial F}{\partial x}dx + \dfrac{\partial F}{\partial t}dt + \dfrac{1}{2}\dfrac{\partial^2 F}{\partial x^2}(dx)^2 + \dfrac{1}{6}\dfrac{\partial^3 F}{\partial x^3}(dx)^3 + \cdots$

Now from (A7.28) we find:

(A7.33) $(dx)^2 = a^2(x, t) (dt)^2 + 2a(x, t) b(x, t) (dt)^{3/2} + b^2(x, t) dt.$

Again, terms in $(dt)^2$ and $(dt)^{3/2}$ can be ignored as they approach zero for $dt \to 0$, so that $(dx)^2 = b^2(x, t)dt$. Using a similar approach, it is easy to show that $(dx)^3$ is zero. The correct total differential should, however, contain the one term from $(dx)^2$ that does not vanish:

(A7.34) $dF = \dfrac{\partial F}{\partial x} dx + \dfrac{\partial F}{\partial t} dt + \dfrac{1}{2} \dfrac{\partial^2 F}{\partial x^2} (dx)^2.$

Hence, compared to ordinary calculus, the total differential has one extra term. Substituting (A7.28) for dx yields:

(A7.35) $dF = [\dfrac{\partial F}{\partial x} a(x,t) + \dfrac{\partial F}{\partial t} + \dfrac{1}{2} b^2(x,t) \dfrac{\partial^2 F}{\partial x^2}]dt + b(x,t) \dfrac{\partial F}{\partial x} dz.$

Dynamic programming is a useful tool for dynamic optimisation under uncertainty. The key procedure for solving DP problems is backward recursion (even for a decision sequence that is infinitely long). The value function consists of just two components: the immediate payoff and a function that captures the (discounted) value all future decisions (Dixit and Pindyck 1994, p. 93ff.). For a problem with a finite time horizon, the ultimate "optimal decision" is readily derived with static optimisation techniques, as there is no future to consider. This solution is the value function for the penultimate decision. This, in turn, is the "value function" for the decision two periods from the end, and so on. The underlying principle is formally stated in Bellman's principle: "An optimal policy has the property that, whatever the initial action, the remaining choices constitute an optimal policy with respect to the subproblem starting at the state that results from the initial actions". (Dixit and Pindyck 1994, p. 100)

Denote the choice variable for the decision maker at time t by u_t, and the state variable by x_t. The value of the control variable at time t is contingent on the information available at time t, contained in x_{t-1}, which is the Markov requirement. Define $F_t(x_t)$ as the outcome, or the expected net present value of optimal future decisions. The decision maker will choose u_t to maximise the sum of the immediate payoff plus the discounted value of all future returns if the optimal path is followed in the future. The Bellman equation, or the fundamental equation of optimality, expresses this as follows:

(A7.36) $F_t(x_t, u_t) = \max_{u_t} \{R_t(x_t, u_t) + \beta E_t[F_{t+1}(x_{t+1})]\},$

where E_t is the expectation at time t. Note that (A7.35) is similar to (A7.19).

Consider a problem with a finite time horizon of T periods. Again let $S_T(x_T)$ be the end-period payoff, or salvage value. The problem for the decision maker in the next to last period is to find u_{T-1}:

(A7.37) $F_{T-1}(x_{T-1}, u_{T-1}) = \max_{u(T-1)} \{R_{T-1}(x_{T-1}, u_{T-1}) + \beta E_T[S_T(x_T)]\}.$

In words, the optimal decision at time $T-1$ is the one that yields the highest sum of the returns in period $T-1$ plus the discounted salvage in period T, where the salvage value depends on the period $T-1$ decision via the equation of motion (dynamic constraint). Once the period $T-1$ decision is made, the decision maker then solves for u_{T-2}, thereby finding $F_{T-2}(x_{T-2})$, and so on, until the optimal decision for the initial period is found. By re-tracing one's steps, the optimal path is followed.

When there is no finite time period, as in the models presented in this chapter, there is no salvage value function (or terminal payoff) $S_T(x_T)$. Instead, the problem retains its recursive structure, as in (A7.36), but it becomes independent of time t as such. Apart from a different starting state, the problem one period ahead is identical to the current one. In other words, the value function is common to all periods, so we can write $F(x_t)$ without a time label on the function symbol (Dixit and Pindyck 1994). We can rewrite (A7.36), or (7.37), as follows:

(A7.38) $F(x, u) = \max_u \{R(x, u) + \beta E[F(x'|x, u)]\},$

where x and x' are any two subsequent states (with x' preceding x in time). Deriving the optimal control is guaranteed by convergence when the discount rate is positive.

Now consider continuous-time dynamic programming. Assume each time period is of length Δt. Assume $R(x, u, t)$ is the benefit at time t (the rate of the benefit flow), with actual benefits over a period are given by $R(x, u, t)\Delta t$. Define r as the discount rate per unit of time, so that total discounting over an interval of length Δt is simply $1/(1 + r\Delta t)$. The Bellman equation becomes:

(A7.39) $F(x, t) = \max_u \{R(x, u, t)\Delta t + 1/(1 + r\,\Delta t)\, E[F(x', t + \Delta t | x, u)]\},$

Multiply by $(1 + r\,\Delta t)$ and rearranging gives (Dixit and Pindyck 1994, p. 105):

(A7.40) $r\,\Delta t\, F(x, t) = \max_u \{R(x, u, t)\Delta t(1 + r\,\Delta t) + E[\Delta F]\}.$

Then, dividing by Δt and letting $\Delta t \to 0$ yields:

(A7.41) $r\, F(x, t) = \max_u \{R(x, u, t) + \dfrac{1}{dt} E[dF]\}.$

In (A7.41), $(1/dt)E(dF)$ is the limit of $E(\Delta F)/\Delta t$. Equation (A7.41) is essentially a zero-arbitrage condition, consistent with the solution to optimal control models discussed above. It is convenient to think of the entitlement to a flow of benefits as an asset. The value of this asset is $F(x, t)$. A normal rate of return for this asset would be

$rF(x,t)$, which is the LHS of (A7.41). The expected total return of holding this asset is on the RHS. This total return is composed of two components: the immediate benefit and the expected rate of capital gain.

Now return to the Ito processes discussed above. Assume that the state variable is subject to a stochastic process:

(A7.42) $dx = a(x, t)dt + b(x, t)dz,$

where, again, dz is the increment of a standard Wiener process. Applying Ito's Lemma to the value function F gives:

(A7.43) $E[F(x + \Delta x, t + \Delta t | x, u)]$

$$= R(x,u,t) + \{F_t(x,t) + a(x,u,t)\frac{\partial F(x,t)}{\partial x} + \tfrac{1}{2} b^2(x,u,t) \frac{\partial^2 F(x,t)}{\partial x^2} \}\Delta t.$$

plus higher-order terms that go to zero faster than Δt. Bellman's equation can thus be written as:

(A7.44) $rF(x,t) = \max_u \{R(x,u,t) + F_t(x,t) + a(x,u,t)\frac{\partial F(x,t)}{\partial x} + \tfrac{1}{2} b^2(x,u,t)\frac{\partial^2 F(x,t)}{\partial x^2} \}.$

Stochastic dynamic programming

The case for using discrete stochastic dynamic programming (DP) to solve real-world problems has been made by Kennedy (1986) and Taylor (1993). The interpretation of closed- and open-loop control in stochastic DP is similar to that above. As an example, consider the decision to crop or fallow. By leaving land barren for one growing season, moisture is conserved, so two years of precipitation are used to grow the crop. This is clearly a discrete-time problem. The state variable is available soil moisture at spring planting time, which is influenced in stochastic fashion by the previous year's crop-fallow decision (van Kooten, Chinthammit and Wiesensel 1990; Weisensel and van Kooten 1990; van Kooten, Young and Krautkraemer 1997). The process is markovian.

The current decision to crop or fallow also affects the soil moisture level in the next period through the equation of motion,

(A7.45) $x_{t+1} = f(x_t, u_t, e_t),$

that governs the change in soil moisture level from one cropping season to the next. Soil moisture in the following year (x_{t+1}) is a random variable conditional on current year soil moisture (x_t), the decision taken (u_t) (crop or fallow), and a random variable

(e_t) representing *annual* rainfall and other random factors (e.g., evapo-transpiration, weeds). Now, assume that farmers maximise the present value of the *expected* income stream, subject to the biophysical constraints in the system. The return to farming in a given year, denoted R_t, is a random variable whose probability distribution depends upon soil moisture at planting time, x_t, as well as precipitation during the growing season and other factors (e.g., precipitation in the winter). The problem, therefore, is to maximise

$$(A7.46) \quad \sum_{t=1}^{T} \beta^{t-1} E(R_t \mid x_t),$$

subject to constraint (A7.45), where R_t is net income at time t, β is the discount factor (as before), and there are T periods in the time horizon.

Let $V_t[x_t(i, u_t)]$ denote the maximum expected value at time t given soil moisture $x(i)$ at time t. The backward recursive solution equation of stochastic DP for this problem becomes:

$$(A7.47) \quad V_t[x_t(i, u_t)] = \max_{u_t} \left\{ E[R_t(x_t(i)] + \beta \sum_{j=1}^{N} p(i, j, u_t) V_{t+1}[x_{t+1}(j)] \right\},$$

where $p(i, j, u)$ gives the probability that soil moisture will be at level j in the next period given that soil moisture in the current period is at level i ($i,j = 1, \ldots, N$), and that decision u_t is taken. There are N discrete soil moisture levels, each described by its two end points and a mid point. The probability transition matrices (one for each decision) can be obtained by estimating (A7.45) as a linear or log linear function for each decision (e.g., one regression of next period's soil moisture on this period's soil moisture when the decision was crop, another when the decision was fallow). The probability of attaining a particular soil moisture interval in the next period for a given level this period is found as follows. Substitute the current-period soil moisture mid point into the estimated equation to obtain a point estimate of next period's soil moisture. This estimate is the mean for a probability density function that has a standard deviation given by the standard error of the regression. The normal or log-normal density function is partitioned according to the moisture intervals, with the probability in each partition providing the probability of attaining that interval. This gives one row in the probability transition matrix for the particular decision. The remainder of the rows for that decision are found in like fashion, while the other regression result is used to calculate the transition matrix for the other decision.

For the crop-fallow, soil moisture problem, the equations of motion are given by a probability transition matrix for each of the crop and fallow decisions, summarised by the term $p(i, j, u)$. Based on the crop-fallow decision, any state (soil moisture level) is reachable from any other soil moisture level. In that case, it is possible for the choice of control (crop or fallow) to be dependent on spring soil moisture alone, and not time. By solving (A7.48) in recursive fashion, a repetitive solution is usually found after four to six iterations, and the solution method is known as *policy iteration*.

When soil depth (soil erosion) is taken into account, soil moisture is not a function of stochastic rainfall alone, but also of soil depth; the probability of moving from one soil moisture state to another is no longer dependent on stochastic rainfall alone, but on soil depth, which changes in irreversible fashion. The state variable is a combination of soil moisture and soil depth, and it is no longer possible to "reach" some of the states. That is, if soil depth is taken into account, some states are no longer "reachable" – higher soil depth states can no longer be attained in the system because soil erosion prevents it. The problem is solved in recursive fashion as before (using A7.48), but there is no convergence for the solution algorithm. The solution depends on the state of the system and time. This is known as *value iteration*.

In the case of policy iteration, one can determine the long-run probability that the system is in a particular state if the optimal policy is followed. Denote this long-run probability vector by π. Multiplying π by the vector of returns for the states gives the long-run expected net return.

To determine π, it is necessary to determine the probability transition matrix associated with the optimal decision strategy, denoted **P**. This matrix is constructed by taking, for every state, the row from the probability transition matrix associated with the optimal decision for that state. Then, π is found by solving $\pi = \pi\mathbf{P}$. Burt and Johnson (1967), Hardaker et al. (1997, pp. 221–6), and others recommend finding vector π as any one of the identical row vectors of Π, where Π is found as $\Pi = \lim_{n \to \infty} \mathbf{P}^n$. The problem is that, since all elements of **P** are less than one (but greater than zero), making n arbitrarily large causes $\mathbf{P}^n$ to collapse to a null matrix if quite a few elements of **P** are very small. Instead, Π can be found by solving $\Pi = \mathbf{D}(\mathbf{I} + \mathbf{D} - \mathbf{P})^{-1}$ (see Hastings 1973, pp. 114–5). In this expression, **I** is an identity matrix, **D** is a matrix of zeros except that the last column consists of a vector of ones, and **P** is the probability transition matrix with each row of **P** corresponding to the transition probabilities for the optimal decision associated with that state. The dimensions of **I** and **D** are identical to **P**.

8 Sustainable Development and Conservation

Sustainable development became a popular term in the (late) 1980s and 1990s for expressing the idea that economic growth must occur in harmony with the environment, and not at the expense of future generations. The term was coined by the World Commission on Environment and Development (or Brundtland Commission) as development that "meets the needs of the present without compromising the ability of future generations to meet their own needs" (1987, p. 8). This definition is not very helpful because it provides no guidance as to what it is that is to be sustained and how sustainable development is to be measured (e.g., what constitutes "needs"?) or put into practice. But it does highlight the political nature of the conflict (real or perceived) between economic growth and the environment: the definition is purposely vague so that it would receive unanimous political support, while many interpretations can be assigned to it (Daly and Cobb 1994, pp. 75–6).

It is important to recognise that sustainability and economic efficiency (as defined in previous chapters) are two different and possibly conflicting concepts. While economic efficiency is a relatively unambiguous concept ("maximise the net present value of society's well-being"), and cost-benefit analysis can be used to identify efficiency in the public realm, it can result in unequal distributions of welfare over time. Maximising net present value (NPV) may be to the detriment of distant generations (mainly because of discounting), but it is not inconsistent with compensation tests used in CBA (see Chapter 6). Thus, sustainability may be worth pursuing for moral reasons (justice and fairness), even though it does not necessarily maximise aggregate welfare – economic efficiency may be pushed aside because of concern about intergenerational equity. In addition to concerns about future generations, the sustainability concept is sometimes used to acknowledge environmental integrity and rights in nature (van den Bergh and Hofkes 1998).

There are more than 60 definitions of sustainable development (Pezzy 1989). While there is consensus that sustainable development concerns intergenerational transfer of natural resources, if not wealth, there are differing views about what this really implies. Yet, most definitions appear to have one or more of the following essential ingredients:

1. Concern with the long-term health of the environment.
2. Apprehension about the welfare of future generations.
3. Condemnation of rapid population growth.

4. Worry over whether it is possible to maintain economic growth in the face of resource scarcity.

Some components of the resource base are ultimately fixed – there are limits to the reserves of fossil fuels and to the ability of the atmosphere to absorb anthropogenic emissions of greenhouse gases – but others, such as solar and wind sources of energy, are limitless.

Judging by most literature, it appears that sustainable development is a relatively new concept, one that the scientific community has recently, and perhaps fortunately, stumbled across. Economists have been concerned with many of these issues, particularly resource scarcity, since at least the time of Robert Malthus, whose argument was alluded to above, namely, that food scarcity (due to a fixed land quantity, continued population growth and diminishing returns) would keep the majority of people in poverty. This same theme shows up in more recent times under various guises, including the Club of Rome's "Limits to Growth" research (Meadows et al. 1972), and now, in some forms, as sustainable development. It is in this respect that the debate is seen as one of neo-Malthusians versus the optimists.

Our goal in this chapter is to investigate some of the topics surrounding sustainable development, with a particular focus on economics. Unfortunately, many topics are addressed only in cursory fashion, mainly because of their complexity and because our focus is on nature conservation and management. We address the issue of subsitutability between reproducible and natural capital (section 8.2) and indicators and evidence of sustainability (section 8.4). We also address related concepts found in the economics literature, some long before the term sustainable development was coined (section 8.3). Before doing so, however, we examine what it is that needs to be sustained (the object of sustainability), viewpoints, and what is meant by sustainable consumption.

8.1 Background

Before considering what is meant by sustainable development, we address the question: what are we to sustain? We also consider the role of peoples' views on sustainability and what sustainable consumption (utility) implies.

What is to be sustained?

One answer to this question is that we want to sustain current per capita income. But whose per capita income is to be sustained – the incomes of those living in rich countries or of those living in poor countries, or do we wish to sustain global per capita income (output)? If global output is to be sustained, then, unless global per capita output can be raised (by reducing population or increasing output, or both), it may be necessary to redistribute incomes from rich to poor (say, for ethical reasons). However, redistributing income could result in adverse incentives, that actually reduce output. Clearly, without economic growth it is not possible to keep global per capita income at its current level unless we somehow deny opportunities for raising standards of living to those in developing countries. It is for this reason that the World Commission on Environment and Development (WCED) adds the word "development". It would seem that sustainability must include opportunities for raising the living standards of the poor, while maintaining those of the rich at current (or higher) levels. While this is a value judgement, it is realistic because the richest countries (Western Europe, North America, Japan) and those in the process of raising their living standards to the levels of the richest countries (Eastern Europe, Russia, Korea, Singapore) are unlikely to make significant sacrifice to their incomes. This is seen, for example, by the failure of the developed countries at Kyoto, Japan (in December 1997), to agree to meaningful trade sanctions on those nations that subsequently fail to meet CO_2-reduction targets. Moral suasion alone is likely inadequate to prevent climate change from occurring or to convince rich countries to accept declining living standards to help poor countries.

Rather than per capita income, perhaps it is the stock of total capital, or human plus natural capital, that is to be sustained. As discussed below, this object of sustainability creates its own set of problems. Perhaps, the object is to sustain growth, but then the same questions as those in the preceding paragraph arise: Whose growth is to be sustained? What rate of growth is to be sustained?

Some argue that it is the earth's ecosystems or life-support functions, varyingly referred to as the "environment", the "web of life" or the "stock of natural capital", that are to be sustained. For example, Common (1995) notes that "ecological sustainability is, then, not a well-defined state to be attained by simple rules. We can say it is the requirement that the resilience of the system is maintained through time" (p. 54). To some extent this implies a departure from the focus on human preferences and desires. A crucial issue is whether the structure and characteristics of the ecological system, as well as its dynamics, are maintained. Two concepts, resilience and stability, are of paramount importance (Holling 1973; Holling et al. 1995). Stability refers to the ability of populations to return to "equilibrium" after some disturbance, while resilience is a broader concept, measuring the propensity of ecosystems to retain their main features after some disturbance. It has been argued that system resilience is related to system diversity, complexity or interconnectedness (Common and Perrings 1992), suggesting that human impacts that reduce these properties should be avoided (see Chapters 9 and 10 for discussions concerning loss of biodiversity and species extinction). However, recent ecological insights indicate that links between complexity and stability, for example, may be extremely complex. Thus, adding species in stochastic multiple-species models does not necessarily reduce fluctuations in population size of the component species, and makes management more difficult (as noted in the previous chapter). Further, the links between stability of separate populations and system resilience may not be straightforward, and distinguishing crucial keystone species may be difficult (see Budiansky 1995).

In general, proponents of the "ecosystem stability" view tend to favour curtailing of economic activity, so that interactions between the economy and the environment do not negatively impact system resilience. But there is disagreement about the resilience of ecosystems, about how human activities affect the earth's ecosystems, and about the degree to which human intervention (management?) interferes with life-support functions. These are important questions as the opportunity costs of maintaining natural capital are almost certainly considerable. Those concerned about possible ecosystem collapse often argue that we must maintain natural capital at its current level, and, in some cases (as with greenhouse gases in the atmosphere), that steps should be taken to restore ecosystems to an earlier (better?) state, regardless of the costs involved. Yet, even among those who dissent with this view, there are few, if any, who would agree to economic development that would threaten the very continuance of human life. The debate, therefore, is reminiscent of, and has its parallels in, the aforementioned Malthusian debate about whether geometric population growth will be limited by arithmetic growth in agricultural output, thereby dooming everyone to live at a subsistence level (see, e.g., Zebrowski 1997, pp. 96–109).

When all is said and done, there is no consensus as to what is to be sustained. In order to investigate sustainability in a scientific fashion, bringing to bear scientific facts that are analysed in one or more theoretical frameworks, it is important that a definition of sustainability be rigorous. But definitions of sustainability typically lack rigor, as exemplified by the definition provided by the WCED. One can only conclude that attempts to define sustainable development need to be purposely vague if they are to be politically acceptable (as noted above), but this is not helpful for scientists seeking to measure and debate sustainability.

Viewpoints and sustainability

The role of investment is clearly important, and especially the form that such investment takes. Investment is to take place not only in natural capital (e.g., protecting biodiversity, planting trees), but also in reproducible capital (human made and knowledge). Much of the controversy about sustainability concerns

1. the allocation of resources for investment between natural and reproducible capital, and
2. consumption versus investment, since investment implies a need to sacrifice consumption.

Perhaps current generations place too much emphasis on current consumption, and not enough on investment. Of an earlier generation, John Maynard Keynes wrote that the West experienced progress because "owners [of capital] were free to consume profits but refrained from so doing, and workers to issue excessive demands but again did not do so" (Hall 1985, p. 160). It would appear that previous generations reduced consumption in order to provide more for future generations, but that this ethic has abated. The earlier generation focused on investment in reproducible capital, which required inputs of natural capital to produce. Would the earlier generation also have been willing to protect (invest in) natural capital?

In an interesting twist, White (1967) turned the ethical position of the earlier generation on its head. He argued that, by refraining from consumption and investing in reproducible capital, previous generations created the high levels of prosperity that brought about levels of consumption that led to an environmental crisis. Leaving aside arguments about the relationship between high levels of prosperity and environmental quality (see section 8.5), it is not clear whether it is prosperity *per se* or a change in society's ethics that is responsible for White's conclusion that the environment has deteriorated to the point of crisis.

The concept of sustainable development clearly involves an ethical dimension. Implicitly (if not explicitly), it requires judgements about the right relationship between people and the environment. Further, definitions of sustainable development, and much of the discussion surrounding it, suggest purpose, and purpose can be judged only on ethical grounds.

But differences exist for other reasons as well. The notion of sustainability "embodies deep conceptual ambiguities [that] ... cannot be easily resolved because they rest ... on serious theoretical disagreements that transcend disciplinary boundaries. In particular, economists and ecologists employ different conceptualizations for explaining the interactions of humans with their environment" (Norton and Toman 1997, p. 553). The underlying philosophical viewpoints of disciplines vary, which becomes a source of disagreement that is not easily resolved. As discussed later in this chapter, many biologists and ecologists take a neo-Malthusian view of resources and resource scarcity, while mainline economists are more optimistic about the ability of humans to manage their way out of environmental crises. Many ecologists have adopted a position that state intervention is required to protect natural systems, while economists, for the most part, emphasise the individual and property rights. While the former advocate state involvement, the latter perceive sustainability and environmentalism to be associated with (and caused by) increasing public intervention in matters dealing with private property; see, for example, Chant et al. (1990), Pearse (1993b) and Panayotou (1993a). Whatever position one takes, politics and special interests may well determine how sustainable development policies are implemented. Our view (admittedly rooted in economics) is that this could potentially be a problem since, in the absence of a clear definition of sustainability, well-intentioned policies may be enacted that could endanger the economic health of resource-based industries to the detriment of society and potentially the resources themselves. In Chapter 12, for example, we show how important property rights and incentives are with respect to tropical forest conservation.

Sustainable consumption (utility)

Consider as a social objective that of maximising net present value of utility over time, as represented by the following objective:

$$(8.1) \quad PV = \int_0^\infty e^{-rt} U(C_t)\, dt,$$

where r is the real rate of social time preference and C_t is consumption in period t. Since utility is a function of consumption, we can also state the objective function in terms of the discounted utility of consumption.

Define C_t^m as the maximum consumption level that can be held forever constant from time t onward, and $\bar{C}$ as the subsistence level of consumption. Alternatively, define U_t^m as the maximum utility level that can be held forever constant from time t onward, and $\bar{U}$ as the subsistence level of utility.[1] As alternative definitions of sustainability, Pezzey (1997) distinguishes three constraints on maximisation of net present value – three constraints on (8.1):

SD_1: Sustainable development	$C_t \leq C_t^m$, $\forall t$	$U_t \leq U_t^m$, $\forall t$
SD_2: Development is sustainable	$C_{t+1} \geq C_t$, $\forall t$	$U_{t+1} \geq U_t$, $\forall t$
SD_3: Development is survivable	$C_t \geq \bar{C}$, $\forall t$	$U_t \geq \bar{U}$, $\forall t$

SD_2 (non-declining consumption) seems to be too strong a requirement for sustainability, while SD_3 would seem to be too weak because it would permit a reduction in living standards to the subsistence level at some future date. Historically, SD_2 has been the most popular definition of sustainability, but it implies sustained development, not sustainable development (SD_1). Pezzey prefers SD_1 as a constraint on economic activities because it prevents consumption from growing without limit, and thereby reducing future consumption possibilities.

In practice, conflicts about sustainability "cannot be resolved without forming an ethical view of what intertemporal goal society should have" (Pezzey 1997, p. 453). Sustainability is not about choosing the "correct" discount rate to ensure that future generations are sufficiently well off, but about choosing how much the current generation will pass onto the future one. The discount rate that allocates between generations is endogenous to the ethical choice of how much to pass along to the next generation (see Howarth and Norgaard 1995 for a review). The decision is ethical because the current generation must decide whether to ensure that the future has the opportunity (is able) to be, or actually is, as well off as the current generation (Pezzey 1997, p. 451). Farmer and Randall (1998) go further, arguing that the current generation must even decide how many individuals there will be in the future (see below).

Inevitably, a sustainability constraint on economic activity must be politically acceptable. Pezzey (1997) argues that political developments in the late 1980s seemed to express support for sustainable development as an overriding constraint. But the realities (as opposed to the rhetoric) of developments since the WCED (1987) and the Earth Summit in Rio de Janeiro in 1992 indicate that people only have a preference for sustained development, and that it is not an overriding constraint – it does not take pre-eminent status.

---

[1] See seminal contributions by Dasgupta and Heal (1979) and Solow (1974), and an overview by Toman et al. (1995), for details on conditions that allow for constant consumption over time, specifically related to technological change and the elasticity of substitution between human and human-made capital and natural capital.

8.2 Sustainability Paradigms: Maintaining Capital Stocks

What form of capital should the current generation pass onto the next? Coal, petroleum, natural gas and minerals are examples of resources that are, by their nature, subject to exhaustion. If consumption continues at current rates, there will come a point in time when these resources are no longer available, although technical advances and new discoveries may delay their exhaustion. Obviously, sustainable development cannot imply that non-renewable resources are prevented from being depleted, or even kept at the current or some other level. It will be necessary eventually to replace the flow of services from non-renewable resources with services obtained from renewable ones. At the same time, it will be necessary to reduce input of natural resources and the environment per unit of standard of living, or output. This implies greater reliance on human capital (knowledge) and human-made capital, which are collectively referred to as *reproducible capital*. Reproducible capital is important, even though it is resource using, because it can substitute for natural capital to some extent; reproducible capital can reduce society's reliance on natural resources by increasing the usefulness of each unit of service provided by the non-renewable and renewable resource stocks.

The degree of substitutability between natural capital (whether renewable or non-renewable) and reproducible capital is the subject of considerable debate. Victor (1991) distinguishes two viewpoints regarding sustainability, which can be referred to as the ecological and the neoclassical paradigms – or strong and weak sustainability, respectively. Before examining each of these in turn, we must define weak and strong sustainability.

Daly and Cobb (1994) define weak and strong sustainability in terms of whether reproducible and natural capital are to be kept intact together (weak sustainability) or separately (strong sustainability). Weak sustainability requires a high degree of substitutability between reproducible and natural capital, while strong sustainability "assumes that they are complements rather than substitutes in most production functions" (p. 72). Barbier, Burgess and Folke (1994) also define weak and strong sustainability in terms of the substitutability between reproducible and natural capital. "As long as the natural capital that is being depleted is replaced with even more valuable human-made capital, then the value of the aggregate stock – comprising both human-made and the remaining natural capital – is increasing over time" (p. 54). This is weak sustainability. Strong sustainability, on the other hand, stresses that there are limits to substitutability between natural and reproducible capital; it "suggests that it is difficult to ensure that future economic opportunities are maintained without imposing some conditions on the depletion of natural capital" (pp. 55–6).

Strong sustainability: The ecological paradigm

Among others, Herman Daly and John Cobb (1994) favour strong sustainability for several reasons. First, some natural resources are essential for production, and their loss would constitute a catastrophic event. Second, even for production processes where natural capital is not yet an essential ingredient, substitutability declines as resource stocks are depleted. Finally, they argue that there are no substitutes whatsoever for many natural resources, especially wilderness – that the elasticity of substitution between natural and reproducible capital is zero, because of the unique character of some forms of natural capital. The implication is that certain stocks of so-called critical natural capital should be conserved, regardless of the opportunity cost of so doing.

The ecological position downplays the role of prices and technological change (Victor 1991). Prices are considered to be imperfect signals of resource scarcity because of market imperfections brought about by "a preponderance of large companies or powerful resource-owning governments, or because the environmental effects of resource extraction are not reflected in resource prices" (p. 201). Prices do not capture the interests of future generations, and, because they reflect conditions at the margin, cannot be used to value entire stocks of the resource. Prices cannot be relied upon to signal scarcity because resource owners likely have too optimistic a view of technological change; they will continue to supply scarce natural resources even as scarcity increases for fear of technical changes that will lower prices in the future. Further, private resource owners' time horizons are too short to bring about sustainable resource use. The short time horizon causes too many natural resources to be supplied, consequently depressing prices. The ecological view is pessimistic about the future contribution of technological change, which is considered too uncertain to rely on for solving environmental problems.

An implication for management is that it is not aggregate capital that should be maintained, but rather natural and reproducible capital separately. Even within the strong sustainability tradition, there are different views about whether natural capital is too broad of a category. Some advocate maintaining each separate element of the natural capital stock, or even all components and the structural relationships among them (Wackernagel and Rees 1997). Another position is that only specific, critical elements of the natural stock should be protected, while permitting substitution among others (see, e.g., Barbier and Markandya 1990; Pearce and Atkinson 1995). When substitution between different sub-classes of natural capital is allowed, however, one encounters an aggregation problem. Is it possible to compensate for SO_2 emissions in excess of critical loads by having a moratorium on herring harvesting? Is it meaningful to aggregate fish stocks, biodiversity and *in situ* exhaustible resources in physical units? Should monetary units be used instead? In section 8.4 we discuss an alternative approach – the ecological footprint – but it too employs a subjective aggregation measure (hectares). Depending on one's view with respect to substitution possibilities, management rules for biological assets can be formulated to correspond more or less to economic efficiency criteria as spelled out in Chapter 7.

The ecological view is clearly influenced by developments in biology and ecology. Concern about the demise of natural (biological, meteorological) systems is a common theme in the biology-ecology literature, and is at the heart of the strong sustainability perspective. The ecological view often supports some form of population control, regulations and/or incentives to prevent loss of species (see Chapter 9), agreements to limit trade in threatened and endangered species (see Chapter 10), international agreements to reduce CO_2 emissions (Chapter 11), subsidies or sanctions to prevent further tropical deforestation (Chapter 12), constraints on free trade (as these might lead firms to locate in countries with less concern about the environment), and other similar interventionist policies.

Weak sustainability: The neoclassical paradigm

The neoclassical paradigm is associated with Julian Simon (1996), Robert Solow (1974, 1986, 1993) and John Hartwick (1977), among others. It is the antithesis of the ecological (dubbed neo-Malthusian) view that natural capital imposes severe constraints on growth – that economic collapse might be brought about by ecosystem collapse. The neoclassical view is that, as resources become scarce, their relative prices will rise, which leads to conservation and substitution toward alternative resources and the development and use of new technologies (Scott and Pearse 1992). Rising relative prices cause substitution away from those resources that are becoming scarce. Neoclassicals point to empirical evidence indicating that this is exactly what has happened in the past and continues today. For example, the technology to produce electric automobiles that are capable of travelling distances of 150 to 300 kilometres on a single charge is already available, but the adoption of such technology is prevented by the relatively low price of gasoline.

The neoclassical view is that the elasticity of substitution between natural capital and reproducible capital is high, with some even going so far as to suggest that it is infinite (Simon 1996). Neoclassicals point out that there are two possibilities for sustaining growth. First, there is likely sufficient substitutability between reproducible capital and the non-renewable resource so that economic growth can be sustained while generating a continuous decline in the non-renewable resource stock. In the case of petroleum resources, this will be true if economies become more reliant on public transportation and/or people purchase only the most fuel-efficient vehicles (e.g., abandoning the current penchant for gas-guzzling sport utility vehicles). Second, technological change will inevitably enable society to shift from reliance on one non-renewable resource to another (e.g., trains converted from coal to oil), and finally to a renewable resource (e.g., solar energy). Although not denying that it is difficult to assess exactly how past technical change has affected the elasticity of substitution between natural and reproducible capital, economists point to the undeniable impact that technological advance has made (Lipsey 1996). As a result, they are optimistic about the potential for technological change in the future.

Indeed, it is the link between past evidence and future projections that is likely most contentious between the two positions, although interpretation of past evidence may well be a source of controversy in some cases. For example, based on current and historic trends, Simon (1996) does not consider population growth to be a problem, while Ehrlich and Ehrlich (1972, 1990, 1991), relying on the same data, maintain that population growth is *the* major threat to the environment and sustainable development. Biologists project that continued habitat destruction (*viz.* tropical deforestation) and over-indulgent lifestyles (e.g., demand for ivory and tiger bones) will result in the loss of a million or more species in the next ten years (Leakey and Lewin 1995). Yet, economists (and others) point to the fact that there have been few documented extinctions (see Chapter 9). Different viewpoints also exist with respect to natural resource scarcity (see below). Although interpreting the historical data differently in some cases, ecologists argue that the past is no guide to the future. However, Simon (1996, p. 27) maintains that, in the absence of other information, the past is a reliable guide to the future. Different views with respect to the future are apparent, for example, in the environmental Kuznets curve (EKC) debate. The EKC describes the relation between income and environmental degradation, and has inspired some researchers to speculate that it may be possible to "grow out" of environmental problems (see section 8.5).

The neoclassical economics' view on sustainability of resource capital pertains to the flow of income from capital. The objective is to maximise the annual income that can be derived from the natural resource over all remaining time – forever. We illustrate this concept with the example of a mine. The concept of *user cost* is important here. The user cost of removing ore from a mine today is the benefit one obtains from removing that same ore at some future date, appropriately discounted. Since the mine will eventually be depleted, it is useful to consider the sustainability of the resource revenue from that mine. El Serafy (1989) argues that the net revenue R from a non-renewable resource should be allocated into an income component (R_I) and a capital component (R_C). The capital component is to be set aside and invested at the real rate of discount, r. The amount of revenue allocated to the capital as opposed to income component is determined as follows: once the mine is depleted, the capital component will need to generate an annual income in perpetuity that is equal to the income made available during the period the mine is in operation. The implicit assumption is that natural and reproducible forms of capital are infinitely substitutable, so that the economy does not collapse when the mine is exhausted.

Consider a mine that generates a net revenue of $1,000 per year (= R_t) for a period of 10 years, which is the useful life of the mine. The general formula for determining the sustainable income from the mine, R_I, is as follows:

$$(8.2) \qquad R_{It} = r\,R_C = r \sum_{t=1}^{T} R_{Ct} (1+r)^t = r \left(\sum_{t=1}^{T} (R_t - R_{It})(1+r)^t \right),$$

where T is the time required to deplete the mine (10 years, in this case), R_{It} is the sustainable annual income, and the term in brackets on the right-hand side of the equation is the capital fund (e.g., plantation forest) available at the time the mine is closed. Numerically solving this equation for the mine using a discount rate of 4% gives R_{It} = $333.09 and R_{Ct} = $666.91. That is, the mine is able to provide a sustainable annual income of $333.09. The problem of determining the sustainable income (the equation to be solved) is complicated when R_t varies from one year to the next and when there is uncertainty, but these complications can be addressed and do not change the essential notion of sustainable income. Given certain assumptions with respect to the depletion path and substitutability between natural and reproducible capital, reinvesting resource rents implies that consumption can infinitely be maintained, even if the (exhaustible) resource stock is depleted.

Equation (8.2) is an example of the Hartwick rule for sustainability. Assume an economy exploits a non-renewable resource stock x, that is only used as an input in production. Define y as extraction, such that $dx/dt = -y$. Aggregate output Q is a function of labour, capital and the extracted resource, such that $Q = Q(L, K, y)$, where $dK/dt = I$. Consumption equals output minus investment: $C = Q - I$. The current value Hamiltonian associated with the problem of maximising consumption subject to the exploitation and investment dynamic constraints can then be written as:

(8.3) $H = Q(L, K, y) - I - \lambda y + \mu I$,

where λ and μ are the shadow prices (costate variables) of the *in situ* resource and capital, respectively. Solving yields the following necessary conditions for an optimum solution: (1) $Q_y = \lambda$, (2) $d\lambda/dt = r\lambda$ (the Hotelling rule), and (3) $\mu = 1$ (see Chapter 7).

Differentiating $C + I = Q$ with respect to time yields:

(8.4) $dC/dt + dI/dt = Q_L \, dL/dt + Q_K dK/dt + Q_y dy/dt$.

Assuming that Q_K equals r (the discount rate) in a competitive economy and that the labour force (population) is constant ($dL/dt = 0$), (8.4) reduces to:

(8.5) $dC/dt + dI/dt = rdK/dt + \lambda dy/dt$.

Hartwick postulates that resource rents should be invested, so that $I = \lambda y$ (Hartwick's Rule). Differentiating with respect to time yields:

(8.6) $dI/dt = yd\lambda/dt + \lambda dy/dt$.

Substituting (8.6) in (8.5) gives:

(8.7) $dC/dt = - yd\lambda/dt + rdK/dt$.

Since the last term on the RHS of (8.7) can be rewritten as $r\lambda y$, and since the Hotelling rule applies ($d\lambda/dt = r\lambda$), expression (8.7) can be rewritten as:

(8.8) $dC/dt = - yd\lambda/dt + yd\lambda/dt = 0$.

Following the Hartwick rule will maintain the value of total national wealth (natural and reproducible) constant when appropriate shadow prices are used for valuation. Correct shadow prices are crucial to the argument, as emphasised by Toman et al. (1995). They argue that optimal (efficient) depletion may be too fast for sustainability (because the Hotelling rule is defined in differences, rather than absolute levels), causing the current resource price and rent to be low relative to what is sustainable. In this case, even full investment of the resource rent will not ensure enough capital formation for sustainability. Instead, resource rents should be measured using shadow prices reflecting the sustainability constraint. Estimating these prices is hard, and subject to great uncertainty. The Hartwick rule is a necessary but not sufficient condition for maintaining constant consumption.

The paradigms in contrast

A summary of the main positions of the neoclassicals and ecologists is provided in Table 8.1. It is the different viewpoints that lead one to be optimistic about the actual and potential for substitutability between natural and reproducible capital, and the other to be pessimistic. Reconciling these positions poses a tremendous challenge for the development and implementation of natural resource policy, and economic policy more generally. It cannot be done as long as long as "the current strategy of asserting, defending, and applying opposed, monistic systems of value in exclusive disciplinary contexts is continued" (Norton and Toman 1997, p. 565).

Table 8.1: Differences Between the Neoclassical and Ecological Views of Sustainability

Neoclassical (Economists)	*Ecological*
1. Focus is on what happens at the margin, because it is at the margin that decisions are made. The scale of the economy relative to the resource base is irrelevant.	1. Focus is on large-scale ecosystems and possibilities for irreversibility. There are scale effects – certain "triggers" could set in motion large-scale ecosystem processes that result in irreversible loss in ecosystem functioning.
2. Economists employ steady-state models that assume equilibrium.	2. Models in ecology focus on resilience and non-equilibrium dynamics.
3. The value system employed is utilitarian.	3. A value system must come from outside ecology as ecology does not have its own.
4. Monetary values are used to measure and "value" changes in environmental quality.	4. Monetary valuation is generally opposed, especially as it is applied to decisions affecting threatened, large-scale ecosystem productivity.
5. Prices play an important role signalling scarcity and, as a result, encouraging substitution and technological innovation. While unpredictable and difficult to measure, technological change has been shown to be a powerful factor in the past and will continue in that role in the future.	5. The role of prices and technological change is downplayed. Prices do not reflect reality because of the existence of externalities. Technological change is unpredictable and unreliable for solving future problems.
6. Discounting and present values are used.	6. Discounting is generally opposed, and the emphasis is on future generations.
7. The current generation owes the future opportunities equal to its own, which means maintaining a non-declining aggregate capital stock. Adequate investment needs to be maintained to compensate the future for the use (or degradation) of certain resources.	7. Safeguarding the functioning of large-scale ecosystems figures prominently in satisfying concerns about intergenerational fairness. Preservation of variety of ecosystem functions (with aesthetic services featuring prominently) is what matters for the future.
8. Attempts are made to measure the well being of various generations and then compare them (referred to as teleology, implying the making of decisions for the future generation).[a]	8. The rights of future generations trump the mere enjoyments of current generations, enjoyments that come at the expense of future well being. This is a rights-based theory, or deontology.[a]
9. The Safe Minimum Standard of Conservation allows trade-offs.[b]	9. The Precautionary Principle permits less scope for balancing costs and benefits.
10. Property rights of individuals feature prominently, with government's role specified as that of setting and enforcing the "rules of law", and, where justifiable, relying on the State to correct externalities.	10. Individualism is seen as a source of environmental degradation. State intervention is needed to protect ecosystems.

[a] See Norton and Toman (1997).
[b] SMS is discussed in section 8.3.

While an interdisciplinary approach might resolve some of the issues, it may not be able to resolve those related to world or ethical viewpoints as opposed to theoretical approaches. Ecological economics is a recent field of study that attempts to bridge the gap between the two views, but the success of this endeavour is uncertain at this time.

It is important to stress that substitution possibilities between different forms of capital are an *empirical* matter (and not an ideological issue, although this sometimes seems the case), and that nobody really knows what will be feasible in the future. Until recently, economic models generally treated technical change as a residual, embodied in the time trend of regression models, although more recent theoretical work attempts to endogenise growth (see, for example, Romer 1994). To what extent is it possible to substitute reproducible capital and knowledge (management) for (some) natural resources? The empirical evidence of substitution possibilities is still fragmented, but some support exists for the claim that they are indeed limited. For example, using a macroeconomic model, Manne (1979) estimates that the elasticity of substitution between energy and other inputs is 0.25. Dasgupta (1993), on the other hand, is fairly optimistic, at least about the possibility to replace natural resources in production processes. He describes a series of innovative mechanisms, of which substitution of capital for vanishing resources is but one example. Other mechanisms include the development of new materials, and new technologies that increase efficiency in the use of resources, or that enable substitution of low-grade reserves for high-grade deposits. While depletion of (high-grade) deposits may force prices up, new technologies will drive them down. With the exception of hydrocarbons, Dasgupta does not foresee any problems for extended periods in the future. And even for fossil fuels, Dasupta is optimistic that hydrocarbons will not constitute a binding constraint, as alternatives become available as prices rise.

Natural capital is not just used in production, however, as natural ecosystems are also essential as a waste receptor and may be essential for mental health. Perman et al. (1996) note that "differences in (estimates of substitution possibilities) probably reflect, in large part, differences in the breadth of functions of the environmental resources being considered" (p. 120). Wilderness is often used to make the case that no substitutes exist for some natural capital, but Budiansky (1995) argues that wilderness is a matter of degree. There are no areas that have been untouched by humans and, even in the distant past, humans managed "wilderness" to suit their needs, usually by fire. There is some evidence that recreation in "managed" areas (e.g., certain types of production forest) is preferred over recreation in wild areas, implying that some form of (forest) management may be desirable. Similarly, many of the life-support services of nature are not only provided by unmanaged ecosystems, but are provided by ecosystems that have been dramatically altered. Hence, substitution possibilities *within* the set of natural capital are also important.

It appears that there is ample confusion about substitution possibilities. Yet, some minimum standard likely exists below which (aggregate) natural capital should not be reduced. While certain managed forests may serve as a substitute for "nature", both for recreation and as a waste receptor, it is unlikely that a combination of "virtual reality devices" and mechanical air cleansing can ever be a true substitute for forests. Concerning production possibilities, the case favoring the neoclassical view is relatively strong, but this does not mean it is the right one. Ethical issues come into play as well, and these may include sentiments concerning other life forms that likely make large-scale depletion of natural capital intolerable.

8.3 Sustainable Development: Related Concepts

In this section, we briefly address concepts related to the sustainability debate. Sustainable development includes ideas that economists have been considering for quite some time, particularly the notions of conservation and the safe minimum standard of conservation. In addition, we examine what is meant by coevolutionary development, a term that Norgaard (1984) adapted from biology. We consider coevolutionary development primarily for its insights. Finally, we turn to two central concepts of the neo-Malthusian tradition: population growth and resource scarcity.

Economics of conservation

An early definition of conservation defines it as a redistribution of use rates into the future. Depletion is then a redistribution of use rates toward the present. This definition of conservation is due to Ciriacy-Wantrup (1968), who some regard as the father of resource conservation. It requires that there be some benchmark distribution of use rates to begin with. Consider a hypothetical coal mine. There are four planning periods as indicated in Table 8.2 and four alternative plans for removing coal. Alternative #1 is the benchmark, perhaps the current rate of extraction. Relative to the benchmark rate of extraction, the second alternative is resource conserving since it redistributes use rates into the future – more of the resource is available in the future. The third plan is resource depleting, however, as use rates are redistributed toward the present – less coal is available in the future. The third plan has greater current consumption than either the benchmark plan or the second alternative.

Table 8.2: Extraction or Use Rates for a Coal Mine

| Alternative Plan | Planning Period | | | | Weighted Change in Use Rates (at 10%) |
| | 1 | 2 | 3 | 4 | |
		(tonnes/year)			
#1 (Benchmark)	4	3	3	2	--
#2 (Conservation)	3	3	3	3	
Change in use rate	-1	0	0	+1	0.331
#3 (Depletion)	5	4	2	1	
Change in use rate	+1	+1	-1	-1	-0.401
#4 (Unclear)	5	1	3	3	
Change in use rate	+1	-2	0	+1	0.131

A problem arises in attempting to categorise plan #4. It is not clear whether plan #4 is conserving or depleting since the net change in use rates is zero and there is no clear indication that all changes are either into the future or toward the present. Whenever there are a large number of pluses and minuses in the row indicating how the plan's use rates have changed from those of the benchmark plan, it is necessary to employ a weighting scheme. The weighting scheme should be one that accounts for the need to discount the future. Thus, weights should increase as the distance from the present time period increases. If the weighted change in use rates is positive, then there is resource conservation; if it is negative, depletion of the resource occurs.

Consider a system of weights that begins with 1.0 for the current period and increases 10% for each subsequent period. Then, the weighted change in use rates for alternative #4 is given by $+1 + (1.1)(-2) + (1.1)^2(0) + (1.1)^3(+1) = 0.131$. The weighted changes in use rates are provided for the alternative plans in the last column of the table; they show that alternatives #2 and #4 are resource conserving. Only the classification of plan #4 as conserving depends crucially upon the weights that are chosen, as it is clear that plan #3 is depleting.

Some argue that stewardship requires that resource availability in the future be weighted exactly the same as that in the present. In that case, the weighted change in the use rates for alternative #4 is simply zero, but this is not very helpful. Likewise, a zero discount rate cannot be used by a society to abrogate its responsibility in determining ethical issues pertaining to how much natural and reproducible capital to leave future generations (see below); treating current and future dollars equally is simply unrealistic, it does not work.[2] One problem with discounting is that people are unlikely to ever agree upon an appropriate weighting scheme. Nonetheless, the point remains that conservation is a comparative concept and one cannot judge whether something is conserving or depleting without reference to some benchmark, and that may require employing a weighting scheme that values the future more than the present.

Scott (1973) expands on Ciriacy-Wantrup's definition of conservation by taking explicit account of political and other factors.

> Conservation is a public policy which seeks to increase the potential future rates of use of one or more natural resources above what they would be in the absence of such policy, by current investment of the social income. The word investment ... covers not only such policies as investing the social income in restoration, education, and research, but also policies of reservation and hoarding of stocks. (Scott 1973, p. 30)

Scott's definition includes a method for achieving the objective of conservation, namely, by investing part of the social income. It is also based on six conditions (Scott 1973) including that, as a practical point, focus should generally be on a single resource within a defined geographical region, and that conservation should be measured in physical as opposed to monetary units. Further, Scott's definition is confined not to natural resources alone, as it recognises the necessity of trade-offs between investments in natural capital (e.g., preservation of ecosystems) and investments in human-made capital and knowledge. Importantly, this definition recognises that conservation is a political as well as a biophysical and economic concept.

---

[2] The discounting issue is revisited in Chapter 11 where we consider whether physical carbon should be discounted in calculating costs of carbon uptake. It turns out that, by not discounting carbon, methodological problems arise.

In Table 8.2, the resource is to be completely exhausted at the end of the planning horizon. Does this fact of exhaustion violate the concept of sustainable development? It may well be that the activity of exhausting a non-renewable resource does violate the concept of sustainable development, but only if the ability of future generations to meet their needs is compromised.

The safe minimum standard (SMS)

Ciriacy-Wantrup (1968) first used the term "safe minimum standard" and urged its adoption to allow for uncertainty in resource development and to increase "flexibility in the continuing development of society". As demonstrated by Bishop (1978), the safe minimum standard can be thought of in terms of game theory – it expands upon the *minimax* principle of game theory, as illustrated in Table 8.3. Two states of nature or outcomes, denoted by #1 and #2, are possible, but their occurrence is uncertain. Society has two strategies to cope with environmental uncertainty: extinction could possibly occur if the resource is exploited (E), while strategy S (for safety) leaves the resource in its current state. If the state of nature turns out to be #1, then there is no damage to the environment from "development". If the strategy had been to avoid development (strategy S), the benefits of development, given by x, are foregone. If exploitation (development) takes place, there is no loss. On the other hand, if the state of nature turns out to be #2, then development (strategy E) results in irreversible damage (i.e., extinction of one or more species) worth y. However, if strategy S is now adopted, there is no environmental loss, but society does lose x – the cost of implementing S.[3] The decision is determined in this "game" by choosing the strategy that minimises the maximum possible loss, i.e., choosing E if $x > y$ and choosing S if $x < y$, with equality of x and y indicating indifference.

Table 8.3: Matrix of Losses

Strategies	States		Maximum Losses[a]
	#1	#2	
E	0	y	y
S	x	x	x

[a] Assumes $x, y > 0$
Source: Modified from Bishop (1978)

There are problems with the game-theoretic approach. (1) The minimax solution is conservative, with E chosen if the costs of preventing extinction (x) are only slightly higher than the losses (y) to society under the worst conceivable future outcome. (2) Payoffs (and costs) are assumed to be known with certainty, while the distribution of income is ignored – it does not matter who gains or loses. (3) The approach is static because the probabilities of each state of nature are unknown, and have no effect upon the decision to be taken. There is no learning effect as time

---

[3] Bishop (1978) erroneously suggests that the loss would be x-y, but y is not a gain if strategy S is adopted.

passes. (4) More importantly, it fails to recognise that a decision not to develop a resource (e.g., construct a dam that floods a valley, harvest old-growth timber) constitutes a deferral – exploitation can still take place in a future period.

The safe minimum standard (SMS) of conservation modifies the minimax principle. The modified decision rule is: adopt S unless the social costs of doing so are unacceptably large. It is clear that this rule places development of natural resources beyond routine trade-offs, although the SMS does not permit deferral or non-development at a cost that is intolerably high. Failure to recognise that there are intolerably high costs to not developing a resource in some cases inevitably leads to dangerous conflicts within society (e.g., between loggers and environmentalists). Decisions regarding what level of costs is considered "intolerably high" and what trade-offs are acceptable are political ones. Randall and Farmer (1995) argue that intolerable costs could be defined as extreme deprivation for society, at least based on moral principles. Berrens et al. (1998) employ a much lower standard for intolerable cost. Their recommended threshold for exclusion is a one percent deviation of economic activity from the baseline.

The Precautionary Principle is similar to SMS, but it permits less scope for balancing costs and benefits, often blocking trade-offs. The Safe Minimum Standard, on the other hand, is all about trade-offs, with the purpose being to identify explicitly the trade-offs that are made (Norton and Toman 1997). As noted by Berrens et al. (1998) "the SMS will be unpalatable to some strong sustainability advocates, ... [but it] will be equally unpalatable to unfettered CBA advocates. As such the SMS approach may be identified as falling between weak and strong sustainability perspectives" (p. 158). It is unpalatable to advocates of cost-benefit analysis because it is unclear why irreversibility mandates a change in the decision rule: one decision criteria (CBA) is jettisoned for another (SMS), but only as long as the costs of avoiding irreversibility are tolerable. As Farmer and Randall (1998) point out, "an efficiency program cannot generate an SMS departure from the efficiency rule, just as strong sustainability clearly rejects the efficiency appeals to permit substitution in production and in consumption" (p. 291). In this regard, the Precautionary Principle is at least a consistent decision rule.

Farmer and Randall (1998) make the case for SMS despite the seemingly unjustified switch in decision criteria when faced by irreversibility on the grounds that most stakeholders involved in the decision consensus "do not possess well-defined, fully articulated ethical positions for sustainability" (p. 292). They argue that a "theory of sustainability must start with the question, What defines a moral agent to whom we have moral obligations?" (p. 2.93). To answer this question, and to address the issue of intergenerational equity, it is necessary to determine the specific numbers of future agents current agents are to "create" and how well off to make them (see also Howarth and Norgaard 1993, 1995). Farmer and Randall defend SMS on the grounds that, until there is a consistent moral theory delineating duties of present agents to each other and to future agents, avoiding irreversibilities has value that is not adequately captured in cost-benefit analysis. This, then constitutes a defence of the authors earlier position that, when it comes to resource management and possible irreversibility, cost-benefit analysis needs to be *constrained by the safe minimum standard* (Randall and Farmer 1995).

To illustrate the concept of a SMS, consider the northern cod fishery. In the late 1980s, it became apparent that stocks of cod were disappearing off the coasts of Newfoundland and Norway. Inshore fisheries in both regions experienced declines in catch and, more importantly, the cod tended to be smaller. The cod on the Grand Banks and the Barents Sea appeared to be in trouble, although the science permitted leeway for different interpretations (Harris 1998). The responses by Canada and Norway to the threat of a possible collapse in the cod fishery differed dramatically. While Norway imposed an immediate moratorium, which led to the recovery of stocks, Canada continued to permit fishing, even setting the total allowable catch on one occasion above what fishers were actually capable of catching with all their sophisticated gear. The northern cod stocks of Newfoundland collapsed and the fishery has yet to recover. It would appear that Norway implemented a SMS, while Canada did not.

One question remains. Suppose that a proper cost-benefit analysis, with the dynamics of the fishery included in the calculations, were conducted for both fisheries. Would the cost-benefit results have favoured a moratorium for both fisheries? Quite likely it would have. That is, an appropriate economic efficiency analysis would have led to a policy similar to one that follows the SMS. It would appear, therefore, that the role of the SMS is to permit the inclusion of intuitive values as a means for addressing uncertainty in cases where CBA is incomplete or key elements are uncertain.

Coevolutionary development

Economists often employ dynamic optimisation models that result in a steady-state solution and definitive approach paths (Chapter 7); ecologists, on the other hand, model large-scale systems where equilibrium is but a temporary state (see Table 8.1, points 1 & 2). For ecologists, it is the resilience of an ecosystem that matters; for economists, it is the policy insights. Is it possible to marry the two notions? Norgaard (1984) makes an attempt via the idea of coevolutionary development, which preceded and anticipated the debate about sustainable development.

Coevolutionary development is a concept derived from the biological notion of coevolution (Norgaard 1984). Coevolution refers to evolution based on reciprocal responses of two or more closely interacting species; it refers to the interaction of two or more plant and/or animal species over time. Impacts or changes in one species have an effect on other species that, in turn, impact on the former. Coevolutionary development extends the notion of coevolution among plant and animal species to include social as well as ecological systems. That is, coevolutionary development integrates the cultural or social realm, and all its human-made institutions, with the biological sphere. The concept is illustrated in Figure 8.1.

Human activities impact upon nature and nature, in turn, impacts on human systems, thereby affecting the development of cultural and economic institutions. The feedback effects continue in what becomes an infinite loop between the cultural and natural realms.

Coevolutionary development relies on a different concept of time than what is employed in more mechanistic (Newtonian) models. In classical mechanical models, time is not really present since all processes, even dynamic ones, are reversible in the sense that one can move backwards or forwards in time. Consider Figure 7.3. If the system is initially at point A, it will move towards the equilibrium (where $\dot{x} = 0$ and $\dot{E} = 0$ intersect). The approach dynamics is independent of time in the real sense – the system approaches equilibrium from A (along path I) regardless of *when* it is at point A to begin with. Ecologists would argue that the approach dynamics from point A to the equilibrium point (Figure 7.3) might change over time. Starting at A, the system might approach equilibrium today, but may follow a totally different dynamic path if it starts at A tomorrow. Indeed, the same starting point can lead to equilibrium one time, but to irreversibility (or extinction of x) another. This is how irreversibility and system scale-effects are to be understood, according to ecologists.

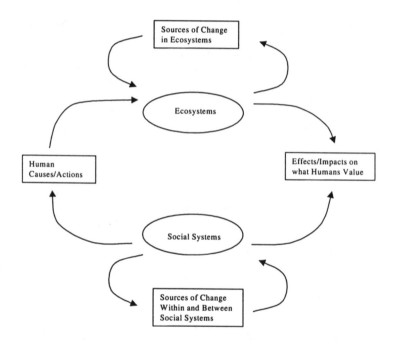

Figure 8.1 Coevolutionary Development: Interactions among Systems

For the economist, policies are meant to move the system along the Newtonian path, usually along an optimal path and towards equilibrium. The ecologist, on the other hand, is cognisant of the biophysical limits to the system and the laws of thermodynamics. In thermodynamics, time is continually running down since entropy – the amount of energy unavailable for work – increases over time. Nonetheless, time is still parametric since the system's location depends upon the starting point, and it is possible to select alternative starting points. In this sense, time is still reversible.

It is irreversibility that is important in environmental systems. As Norgaard explains:

> The basic assumptions of the neoclassical model [of economics] do not fit the natural world. The model assumes that resources are divisible and can be owned. It acknowledges neither relationships between resources in their natural environments nor environmental systems overall. It assumes that both the economic and environmental system can operate along a continuum of equilibrium positions and move freely back and forth between these positions. Markets fail to allocate environmental services efficiently because environmental systems are not divisible, because environmental systems almost never reach equilibrium positions, and because changes are frequently irreversible. (1985, pp. 382–3)

Solutions to the kinds of environmental problems that are usually proposed by economists, such as Pigou taxes/subsidies and regulation (Pearce and Turner 1990), presume a mechanistic, equilibrating world. But irreversibilities and disequilibria are a fact of life in ecological systems, so the notion that there exist once-and-for-all taxes or regulations that can be implemented by the authority to solve particular environmental (or other) problems is a myth.[4] Natural systems evolve and change over time, much as social systems do. The idea that there exists an economic or any other equilibrium may simply be unrealistic.

When it comes to environmental pollution, multiple pollutants may prevent equilibrium from occurring (see also Colborn et al. 1996). For example, methyl compounds and mercaptans are fairly safe and are individually benign, but they combine to form methylmercaptans that are deadly, even at low concentrations, and these are malign. Thus, if effluents containing methyl compounds and mercaptans enter a river, irreversible changes in the river's ecosystem are likely. The mix of species of aquatic life that exist in the river will differ from those originally in the river ecosystem. Further, recreation and municipal water users might be affected. Given that the entire ecosystem has been affected, it may be impossible to turn back the clock, even by eliminating the pollutants that first entered the river. The ecology may be permanently altered. Yet, simple economic models of market failure assume that an equilibrium can be found by realigning or properly specifying property rights (Coase 1960) – that the original situation can be "recovered". But reality is much more complicated.

Consider several examples of coevolutionary development. Through agronomic activities humans impact the ecosystem, intervening in nutrient cycles and disturbing the equilibrating mechanisms present in the natural system. The cultural or human system compensates for nutrient losses through management (e.g., application of fertilizers and pesticides, use of crop rotations that include legumes) and public policies (e.g., income support). These interventions could trigger further human and ecosystem responses, some of which are a surprise (Holling et al. 1995). For example, agricultural policies in North America and Europe during the 1980s were meant to support the family farm, but they encouraged environmental destruction that eventually undermined the sustainability of farming in some regions. In North

---

[4] This is not to be misconstrued as an argument against taxes, subsidies or regulation, but only a statement about their limitations.

America, for example, marginal land was cultivated and soil erosion increased, requiring offsetting set-aside programs. In Europe, the Common Agricultural Policy encouraged location of intensive livestock operations in coastal states (especially the Netherlands and Denmark), with the result that manure disposal became a major problem that needed to be dealt with. Entire ecosystems were affected as a result. Further, increasing land costs that made it increasingly difficult for families to purchase farms. While more recent policies attempt to increase reliance on markets while reducing or eliminating agricultural support programs, it may take decades to reverse this state of affairs (van Kooten and Scott 1995).

A second example is provided by tropical deforestation in the Amazon, which is considered in more depth in Chapter 12. By the early 1990s, the Amazon region of Brazil had become a focal point of criticism for the world's environmentalists. Historically, shifting or "slash-and-burn" agriculture constituted the institutional response to a tropical ecosystem that could not support large-scale permanent agriculture. Shifting agriculture gave the ecosystem a chance to respond to human intervention, and, with a small population to support, turned out to be sustainable. Then the Brazilian government provided public infrastructure (e.g., towns, schools, public buildings and roads) and incentives to cattle ranchers to develop parts of the region to produce large numbers of cattle for export. (Exports were needed by Brazil to pay back international loans that were made without due regard to project risks in an effort by banks to circulate "petro" dollars.) This resulted in rapid denuding of the tropical forests, with a consequent loss in wildlife habitat and species, and added atmospheric carbon dioxide (a cause of global warming) due to burning of the forest. As Norgaard (1984, 1985) argued, the agricultural development promoted by the new interventions in Amazonia resulted in interactions between the cultural system and the ecosystem that would be mutually destructive. If the region is to support the larger population, new institutions need to evolve, ones that are more efficient in their use of natural resources per unit of economic activity. By the 1990s such institutions were beginning to evolve, with subsequent reductions in rates of deforestation.

What does coevolutionary development tell us about policy and policy analysis? The interaction between nature and humans – the feedback mechanisms between the two – are important, but unpredictable, as are human responses to various policies. Further, a crucial element is that policy makers should realise that policies that worked well in the past may have adverse consequences in the future (or vice versa), and that constant adaptation to changing circumstances may be preferred over simple adherence to steady-state approaches. Moreover, some changes in the underlying relations between the social and biological system may be anticipated, such that more effective decision making is possible, but for the most part prediction is difficult because of inherent uncertainty (e.g., noise, luck, structural changes, mutations). Van den Bergh and Hofkes (1998) argue that the main lesson from the coevolutionary perspective is that policy makers should aim for preservation of biological diversity as this leaves open more evolutionary paths and reactions to future unanticipated environmental problems. Coevolutionary development provides a framework for thinking about sustainable development and the types of models that economists use.

In light of this, should economists abandon dynamic optimisation models and other mechanistic models that provide equilibrium solutions? It would be naïve to think that economists are not cognisant of the limitations of the models that they employ, but it would also be overly narrow to think that such models were anything but tools for thinking about management of biological assets. As noted by Ostrom (1998) in another context, until more realistic models are available, existing ones continue to offer insights that are useful to management. However, economists are busy developing new models and theories. In the last chapter, we examined insights from a chaotic model of the fishery. We also introduced the concept of fuzzy set theory as a means for addressing uncertainty in nonmarket valuation (Chapter 5), but it has also been applied to the management of biological assets (Ells et al. 1997; Krcmar-Nozic et al. 1999). On the theory side, the New Institutional Economics (discussed briefly in Chapter 6) offers promising insights into the management of natural resources that are only now beginning to be explored (e.g., Wang and van Kooten 1999). These developments are a response to criticisms of economic modelling, but they have not changed most economists' stand with respect to sustainability.

Population pressure

There are two components to the neo-Malthusian argument – population growth and resource depletion (which subsumes degradation of the environment). Consider first population growth. Environmentalists often view population growth as the main cause of poverty and the greatest threat to "spaceship earth;" they consider humans to be a curse upon the planet (Ehrlich and Ehrlich 1972, 1991; Smith et al. 1995). The following statement is typical of this view:

> Everything has been visited, everything known, everything exploited. Now pleasant estates obliterate the famous wilderness areas of the past. Plowed fields have replaced forests, domesticated animals have dispersed wild life. Beaches are plowed, mountains smoothed and swamps drained. There are as many cities as, in former years, there were dwellings. Islands do not frighten, nor cliffs deter. Everywhere there are buildings, everywhere people, everywhere communities, everywhere life. ... Proof [of this crowding] is the density of human beings. We weigh upon the world; its resources hardly suffice to support us. As our needs grow larger, so do our protests, that already nature does not sustain us. In truth, plague, famine, wars and earthquakes must be regarded as a blessing to civilization, since they prune away the luxuriant growth of the human race. (Bratton 1992, p. 76 as quoted by Beisner 1997, p. 97)

What is interesting is that Tertullian wrote this in Carthage around 200 AD when the total population of the earth was probably less than 500 million.

People are consumers, but they are also a resource capable of producing wealth under the "right" circumstances (which include certain liberties and freedoms as discussed by Hall 1985). People are the ultimate resource (Simon 1996). It is not surprising, therefore, to find ambiguous empirical evidence related to population density and income (see Table 8.4). There is no compelling evidence that links population growth to either poverty or environmental degradation (Simon 1996; Olson 1996; Eberstadt 1995).

Population growth often goes hand-in-hand with poverty and (local) environmental degradation, but the causality is defined in accordance with one's politics. Dasgupta (1995) argues that the causal links between population growth and size, and poverty and the environment, are complex. Simply showing that per capita income is positively correlated with population density, as suggested in Table 8.4 and statistically demonstrated by Olson (1996), says nothing about causality. Indeed, Olson (1996) demonstrates that it is differences in institutions that cause some countries to be rich and others poor, and that population is not that important. Further, while sheer population size multiplies per capita impacts on environmental degradation, population size and growth need not have exclusively negative implications for the environment. Rich countries generally have a cleaner environment than poor ones, regardless of population levels.

Table 8.4: Relationship between Population and Wealth

Country	Population (millions)	Area (mil km²)	GPD (US$bil)	Population per km²	GDP per person ($US)
Bangladesh	120.4	0.130		924.9	220
Brazil	155.8	8.512	372.7	18.3	2,392
Chile	14.2	0.757	17.3	18.8	1,214
China	1,198.5	9.751	541.0	125.2	451
Czech Republic	10.5	0.079	17.6	131.0	1,700
France	57.9	0.544	1,372.1	106.4	23,696
Germany	81.3	0.357	2,084.5	227.9	25,628
Japan	125.2	0.378	4,756.6	331.4	37,992
India	920.0	3.287	231.2	279.9	251
Malaysia	20.1	0.330	69.4	61.0	3,453
Netherlands	15.4	0.034	358.3	453.0	23,288
United States	260.3	9.809	6,050.4	26.5	23,240
Poland	37.9	0.313	22.5	123.4	594

Source:*The Europa World Year Book* 1996. *Volumes 1&2.*(London: Europa Publications,1996).

Population growth is endogenous and the determinants of fertility are generally known. The theory of demographic transition indicates that the death rate initially falls, but birth rates decline only after a lag. Population growth is high during this transitional stage (Perman et al. 1996, p. 288). According to the economic theory of fertility, households choose number of children by setting the perceived marginal costs of bearing and raising them to the perceived marginal benefits. Preoccupation with households as optimising units and the historical evidence that richer countries are associated with lower fertility rates has led some analysts to opine that high population growth rates in developing countries are a temporary and relatively harmless phenomenon (Kelly 1988). It is often thought that economic growth can be relied upon to reduce population growth (e.g., Simon 1996), but there is some evidence that the drop in mortality rates in many developing countries is a result of knowledge (technology) transfer and not income growth. As a result, the drop in mortality rates is not soon matched by a decline in birth rates, which might lead to rising populations that create the potential for a vicious circle of poverty and environmental degradation, at least in some countries (Perman et al. 1996).

While fertility behaviour may be rational from the perspective of the household, there may be collective failure due to external effects in reproduction. Dasgupta

(1995) describes two main motives for procreation and indicates how reproductive externalities may arise.

1. Children can be considered as ends in themselves, as they are generally wanted and valued. If every household's desired family size is an increasing function of the average family size in the community (e.g., for reasons associated with status), the community as a whole may end up in a sub-optimal equilibrium. Imitative behaviour encourages sub-optimally high fertility rates.
2. In some circumstances, children can be considered productive assets. Children can be both a source of security for old age, when public support for the elderly is absent or weak, and an income-earning asset when they are young. In developing countries where common property resources are frequent, children (extra hands) can contribute towards exploiting the commons for private gains, even though such behaviour is socially sub-optimal. This provides households with an incentive to raise extra children. A potentially adverse feedback relation may now be triggered: as the resource base gets depleted, households need to invest more labour effort to collect the desired inputs, which is an incentive to enlarge and produce yet more children.

Children are not only "hands" contributing towards common property exploitation, but the same hands can also be used to invest in sustainable resource management under different institutional arrangements (Dasgupta 1995). Children are also minds that help solve problems, providing new solutions; in that sense, they are the ultimate resource. The neo-Malthusian notion should be contrasted with the equally powerful ideas of Boserup (1965), who has described how changing population pressure may translate into different institutions and production techniques. The net effect of such changes on the environment should be determined on a case-by-case basis. For Kenya, for example, Tiffen and Mortimore (1994) have determined that increased population is consistent with more trees and less erosion. They argue that "increased population density has helped to make markets and information more accessible, thereby stimulating wise investments in new technologies, which have enabled output and incomes to rise faster than population growth, and which have restored and improved the resource base" (p. 1007).

We conclude that the impact of population growth on the environment is ambiguous, depending on, among other things, the institutional setting (i.e., presence or absence of relevant markets, tenure arrangements, *etc.*), and government incentives. Also, the outcome will depend on the environmental issue concerned; while it is easy to think of a growing population as having a favourable impact on soil conservation, a similar impact on protection of biodiversity is harder to conceive. In some cases, the combination of poverty and population pressure will have detrimental effects on the environment, thus perhaps justifying intervention (see also Pearce and Warford 1993). Dasgupta's (1995) review of efforts to reduce population growth suggests that issues related to power and gender within the household are crucial: "high fertility, high rates of female illiteracy, low share of paid employment and a high percentage working at home for no pay – they all hang together" (p. 1886). Education and employment of women may be especially important in efforts to reduce fertility.

Education and employment of women raise the marginal costs of child bearing and raising, thereby reducing the total number of children a household desires. Further, increasing state-sponsored (or private) social security for the elderly reduces the need to rely on children, thereby lowering the marginal benefits of children and, hence, numbers borne.

Resource scarcity

An important issue related to sustainability is scarcity of resources and environmental amenities. Economists have been concerned with resource scarcity since at least the time of Robert Malthus. Rather than monitoring physical quantities or measures (such as the reserve-to-consumption ratio, which is an unreliable indicator of scarcity), economists typically study resource scarcity by examining commodity prices (Hall and Hall 1984). (Prices are generally not a useful measure of scarcity for environmental services, such as waste receptor services, as these are not privately "owned".) When firms adopt efficient depletion paths, a much better but more difficult measure, because it is not observable, is the course of resource rents over time.[5] If the real (inflation-adjusted) price of a resource increases, this is a sign of increasing scarcity. If real commodity prices fall, this is evidence that either the demand for the resource has fallen (e.g., because less of the resource is required to achieve the same or a greater level of final product than previously) or that there is more abundant supply (possibly from a substitute). For example, more efficient means of harvesting timber and processing logs into lumber, and greater use of a tree's mass (less waste), increase the supply of wood products available from the same forestland. Planting faster growing species also increases timber supply. New discoveries, secondary or enhanced recovery, more efficient ways of extracting oil from tar sands, and the ability to pump oil from deep sea wells increase the supply of oil and gas. Fuel efficiency and alternative fuels (e.g., electricity, solar and wind) have reduced the demand for oil and gas. In addition, there often exists a sustainable backstop technology that is based on sustainable resource use (e.g., solar or wind power). A relatively plentiful non-sustainable resource (say, oil) may be used in the beginning of the growth process, but, as it becomes increasingly scarce and more expensive, the sustainable resource (say, solar power) is used as the substitute technology.

For whatever reasons (whether the result of economies of scale in production, technical change, substitution, imports, government policies or new discoveries), the real prices of many non-renewable resources have not increased over time. Empirical tests of the Hotelling rule (see the earlier discussion of the Hartwick rule) can be used

---

[5] Other scarcity indicators are (real) marginal extraction costs (see Barnett and Morse 1963, who worked with average costs for lack of marginal estimates), and marginal exploration and discovery costs, for which data are often also hard to find (see Peseran 1990). An important drawback of working with costs is that the measure is "backward looking", and fails to take into account expectations about future supply and demand (as do prices). For discussions, see Fisher (1981), Farzin (1995), Common (1995), and Hanley et al. (1997).

to analyse resource scarcity. We present two approaches to testing Hotelling's rule (Berck 1995; Withagen 1998). First, the price path of the resource can be analysed, as was done by Barnett and Morse (1963) in a seminal study of mineral prices over the period 1870–1957. They found that prices were non-increasing over that interval and rejected the hypothesis of increasing scarcity. In contrast, Slade (1982) found that the prices of many resources over the period 1870–1979 followed a U-shaped path, which is consistent with increasing resource scarcity over time. Recall that prices are the sum of marginal extraction costs and user costs or rents. Due to increased scarcity and technological progress, marginal costs and rent move in opposite directions. In early periods prices fall, because the decline in marginal extraction costs as a result of technological progress outweigh increases in user costs. In later periods, the reverse holds and prices rise. More recent work does not confirm her empirical results, however. For example, Slade (1991) shows that resource prices have been volatile after the sample period used in the earlier study, which is at odds with steadily increasing scarcity. Berck (1995) argues that the parameters of Slade's U-shaped path are not constant for different sub-periods, and that the price series may be more aptly modeled as a stationary series around a stochastic (rather than a deterministic) trend. This would invalidate the parameter estimates of the regression analysis (also see Ahrens and Sharma 1997). According to Berck and Roberts (1996), there is no evidence of rising prices over time.

Second, and theoretically more correct, some analysts have attempted to measure changes in resource *rents* (rather than prices) over time. As rents are not observed on markets, they have to be computed. For this purpose, an extraction cost curve can be postulated and estimated. Tests using this line of reasoning provide inconclusive support for the theory that extraction of non-renewable resources occurs along an optimal (economically efficient) path, with some refuting the theory (Halvorsen and Smith 1991) and others providing evidence consistent with theory (Stollery 1983).

Some caveats should be mentioned. Rents (and under some conditions prices) are good indicators of scarcity if certain conditions are satisfied. For example, resource owners should have perfect foresight. If resource owners have only access to imperfect information about future prices (which is likely the case as futures markets for resources are generally absent and "thin"), price paths may measure ignorance of decision makers rather than changing scarcity conditions (Norgaard 1990). Further, environmental costs associated with resource exploration and exploitation may curtail extraction before exhaustion occurs. In principle, environmental costs should be included as a component of (marginal) extraction costs, but we are not aware of any (net) price series that takes this cost component into account. A related point is that the resource base is actually infinite, but that extraction costs eventually become prohibitively high (Farzin 1992). Even though the resource will not be exhausted, resource rents are positive as extracting a unit of the resource today drives up future extraction costs. (The value of the *in situ* resource equals the discounted increment in future costs avoided.) Farzin demonstrates that the resource rent path is governed by the specification of the cost function, and rent can rise, fall or remain unchanged over time. This sheds new light on the theory of efficient extraction of exhaustible resources.

Interestingly and somewhat paradoxically, there is considerably more concern in the economics literature about depletion of stocks of renewable than of non-renewable resources. This is due to the questions associated with proper management of renewable resources, particularly with reference to institutional arrangements and the possibility of catastrophe. Resource management has not been properly implemented in many parts of the world, and commercial exhaustion of certain renewable resources (especially fish) and pollution remain serious problems (World Resources Institute 1995).

Overall, however, the majority of the dismal predictions of the "limits to growth" tradition have simply been proven wrong and there is little or no evidence to expect an impending resource shortage (Beckerman 1992; Scott and Pearse 1992). Nonetheless, widespread poverty in the third world, signs of environmental stress in large parts of the world, and overexploitation of some open-access and even common property resources are taken by some as a sign of impending scarcity. Clearly, as discussed above, the view one takes depends on one's view of sustainability.

As far as we are aware, only one person has been willing to wager that their view is the correct one. The late Julian Simon (1996, pp. 8–9) offered to bet anyone who cared to take him on that the future for ecosystems, environment and natural resources is not as bleak as suggested by "doomsayers", or even those in the ecological economics camp. We refer to this as Simon's bet. Simon argued that "supplies of natural resources are not finite in any economic sense", the long-run future of energy supplies is bright, food scarcity is not imminent, and population growth is not going to overwhelm the earth's ecosystems (pp. 5–7). He was optimistic concerning biodiversity and ecosystem health. Simon based his wager on historical evidence that indicates scarcity has not been a problem in the past, that humans have not been responsible for ecosystem collapse, that standards of living are rising, and that people's health (an indicator of ecosystem health) is better now than ever before. Biologists would dispute much of this (as noted in section 8.2), but, with the exception of Paul Ehrlich who lost some $1,000, none had taken Simon up on his wager.[6] None of this is a guarantee, however, that there will be no future resource scarcity or ecosystem collapse, but then we live in a world of uncertainty.

Consider the role of the government in more detail. It is interesting to note that, in 1891, the US Geological Survey predicted that there was little or no chance of finding oil in Texas. In 1926, the US Federal Oil Conservation Board predicted that the USA had only a seven-year supply of oil left, leading some to argue that the price of a gallon of gasoline would soon rise to $1. Similar predictions were made in 1939 and 1949, but none ever materialised (Maurice and Smithson 1984). The so-called energy crisis of the 1970s occurred primarily because price controls on oil in the USA (implemented by the Nixon Administration) meant that there was no incentive to encourage conservation (reduce demand), exploration for new sources of oil (increase supply), or investment in alternatives to fossil fuels (reduce demand). The energy crisis abated rapidly once price controls began to come off in 1979. Deregulation of

---

[6] Simon bet Ehrlich that the price of commodities thought to be scarce would actually decline over a 10-year period. The comparison involved prices at the beginning and end of the period, with Ehrlich actually choosing the commodities.

prices was complete in early 1981. As a result, energy consumption declined by 20% during that year and drilling activity increased by 50%. The resulting fall in energy prices led to the eventual collapse of the OPEC oil cartel. In 1995, the Paris-based International Energy Agency argued that energy supplies are not running out, but that deregulation, freer flow of products among countries and new technologies are making it possible to increase the supply of fossil fuels; indeed, it predicts that, by 2010, 90% of the world's energy consumption, which is forecast to rise by 34 to 45%, will be accounted for by fossil fuels (Moore 1995).

In Canada, the National Oil Policy of 1961 guaranteed western oil producers (mainly the Province of Alberta) a market for oil by preventing consumers west of the Ottawa River Valley from purchasing oil from sources other than western Canada. This resulted in Ontario prices for western crude that were 25 to 35 cents per barrel higher than what they would otherwise be. When world oil prices increased dramatically in 1973 as a result of OPEC, the federal government responded by freezing the price of all oil at $3.80/barrel. Taxes on exports and oil company profits were used to subsidise oil imports east of the Ottawa River Valley. Although the oil producing provinces (primarily Alberta) increased their royalty rates to capture a large portion of the resource rents, the low Ontario price and the export tax kept these rents well below their potential. In an attempt to offset the power of the western producing provinces and increase the available supply of oil, the federal government encouraged and subsidised exploration outside the producing provinces in northern and coastal areas.

Throughout Canada the low-price oil policy weakened concurrent policies to conserve energy, adopt energy efficient technologies and alternative fuels, and reduce polluting activities in general. Later, when domestic and world prices converged, these policies inadvertently were to give Canada's industry a competitive disadvantage relative to its trading partners who had already adopted energy-saving technologies. Although the federal government was forced to back away from its price freeze when Alberta decided to reduce oil production in 1980, the National Energy Program that was introduced in 1980 did not go the full step. It slowly increased domestic prices to the world level via phased-in price increases. The producing provinces and the primarily foreign oil companies continued to object to this policy because the resource rents available to them remained lower than under a free market. This redistribution of resource rents was objected to as a matter of discriminatingly unfair income redistribution, but it was the rent dissipation among Canadian consumers in the form of lower than world prices that likely led to inefficiency and resource misallocation (van Kooten and Scott 1995).

In retrospect, it appears that attempts to control prices of resource commodities led to increasing prices. An examination of oil, wood products, aluminum, copper, zinc, nickel and other resource commodities indicates that, while consumption has increased, real prices have either remained relatively constant or even declined. This indicates that there has been both an increase in the availability of the resource *in situ* and greater efficiency in mining and production. One is forced to conclude that, with few exceptions, there does not appear to be an impending shortage of natural resources. To reach the same conclusion about ecosystem resources that are not priced in the market place is not as straightforward. What the foregoing discussion does indicate is, that by somehow pricing ecosystem services, the chances of maintaining these resources may well be greatly enhanced.

8.4 Sustainability Indicators and Evidence

Ecologists and economists employ different indicators of sustainability. Depending on beliefs with respect to the degree of substitutability between natural and reproducible capital, analysts may prefer some "sustainability indicators" over others. Advocates of strong sustainability will probably prefer ecological indicators or direct biophysical measures (e.g., carrying capacity relative to exploitation, ecological footprints and measures of resilience), while advocates of weak sustainability will employ economic indicators, such as those associated with "green" national income accounting and "genuine savings" (Pearce et al. 1998). In terms of empirical progress, the indicators preferred by neoclassicals seem further advanced and less speculative. In this section, we briefly consider two opposing approaches. We present some empirical work related to weak and strong sustainability as defined above, and we discuss the so-called ecological footprint, a measure preferred by some ecologists.

Weak and strong sustainability: Evidence

A "weak sustainability index" developed by Pearce and Atkinson (1995) is complementary to environmentally adjusted national accounts, and addresses whether countries are on a sustainable path or not. As noted earlier, countries should seek to keep aggregate capital K (defined here as the sum of human-made K_M, human K_H and natural capital K_N) constant in order to satisfy the criterion of weak sustainability. The weak sustainability rule then boils down to the following condition:

$$(8.9) \quad S(t) - \delta_M K_M - \delta_H K_H - \delta_N K_N \geq 0,$$

where $S(t)$ represents aggregate gross savings at time t and δ_i ($i = K,H,N$) is the depreciation rate for the relevant capital stock. If δ_H is assumed to equal zero, there is no depreciation of knowledge and skills, which seems a reasonable assumption. An economy is assumed sustainable if it saves more than the depreciation on its reproducible and natural capital. Depreciation of natural capital takes the form of depletion (e.g., extraction of a non-renewable resource) and degradation (e.g., air and water pollution). Dividing by income m yields the basic condition for weak sustainability:

$$(8.10) \quad Z = \frac{S}{m} - \frac{\delta_M K_M}{m} - \frac{\delta_N K_N}{m} \geq 0,$$

where Z is the weak sustainability index.

Similarly, a strong sustainability criterion requires that $\delta_N K_N/m \leq 0$. Monetary valuation is used for this specific strong sustainability indicator (but see below for an alternative approach). Where sufficient information with respect to natural capital is available, it would be possible to produce additional, more segregated sustainability indexes. Pearce and Atkinson advocate a combination of weak and strong sustainability rules to address the complex issue of sustainability. Evidence for both weak and strong sustainability is presented for selected years and countries in Table 8.5.

The results indicate that many countries fail to pass the weak sustainability test. Pearce and Atkinson (1995) suggest that eight countries out of the 22 they investigate (not all of which are given in Table 8.5) have negative values for Z, with six of these found in Africa. Relatively high savings ratios contribute to, but are no guarantee for weak sustainability, as can be observed from Indonesia and Mexico. The fourth column indicates that not a single country meets the strong sustainability standard, because all values for $\delta_N K_N/m$ are positive. However, it should be added that data on both depreciation and accumulation of natural capital are incomplete, so that the results are biased in an unknown direction. Again, we emphasise that Table 8.5 provides a static picture for addressing an inherently dynamic issue; the potentially offsetting, but highly relevant factors of population growth and technological change are ignored, so these empirical results should be interpreted with care.

Table 8.5: Testing Sustainable Development for Selected Countries: An Indicator[a]

Countries	S/m	$\delta_M K_M/m$	$\delta_N K_N/m$	Z
Sustainable economies				
Japan	33	14	2	+17
Poland	30	11	3	+14
Costa Rica	26	3	8	+15
Zimbabwe	24	10	5	+9
US	18	12	3	+3
Brazil	20	7	10	+3
Marginally sustainable economies				
Mexico	24	12	12	0
Philippines	15	11	4	0
UK	18	12	6	0
Unsustainable economies				
Indonesia	20	5	17	-2
Nigeria	15	3	17	-5
Madagascar	8	1	16	-9
Mali	-4	4	6	-14

[a] Assumes $\delta_H = 0$.
Source: Selected from Pearce and Atkinson (1995)

Finally, as pointed out by Asheim (1986) and Pearce and Atkinson (1995), the Hartwick rule for investing resource rents should be adapted for open economies, implying that the results presented above should be corrected for international trade. Japan, for example, performs best according to Table 8.5, but this is partly due to the fact that Japan is a major importer of natural resources (e.g., wood and oil). Hence, while domestic natural capital is not subject to much depreciation, Japan may be drawing down natural capital stocks in its trading partners. Hartwick and Olewiler (1998) intuitively discuss why, in this case, the net investment figure Z should be adjusted downwards (i.e., why the importing country should save more than the sum of domestic depreciation of reproducible and natural capital to meet the criterion of weak sustainability). One interpretation is that the importing country will face rising prices in the future as stocks are depleted, and should save more today to counter this negative "terms of trade effect" tomorrow to keep consumption constant. Conversely, exporting countries such as Indonesia may be excused for not having positive Z-values; as resource prices rise in the future, it may be possible to maintain current consumption patterns without keeping aggregate capital constant. However, sustainability is an issue for the (very) long run, and whether "under-investing" is truly sustainable for extended periods is an open question.

Hueting's (1989) concept of sustainable income can be considered an intermediate approach between the focus on maintaining capital and biophysical measures (see below). While it is theoretically possible to value ecological damages and costs associated with deterioration of natural capital (see Chapter 5), this is often difficult in practice. Hueting (1989, 1992) therefore proposes a different sustainability indicator where it is not necessary to value (the loss of) environmental functions. Assume an extant societal consensus on threshold levels for environmental amenities and biological assets. Implicitly, it is assumed that the marginal benefits of environmental functions are equal to (or in excess of) the marginal costs of attaining those levels (Rennings and Wiggering 1997). Next, avoidance costs are estimated for achieving those standards; that is, an assessment is made to determine how much money has to be invested to ensure that the environment does not degrade to levels below what society considers acceptable. This yields the correct amount that can be used to compute sustainable income. As this income concept is based on explicit threshold values for (key) environmental functions, it is one step towards strong sustainability indicators.

The ecological footprint

Strong sustainability indicators often focus on scale aspects of production and consumption, on whether or not society exceeds the carrying capacity of the environment as a source and sink. It is assumed that a "sustainable scale" exists, and this scale is measured in absolute physical limits. There are several indicators that employ biophysical measures (see, for example, Rennings and Wiggering 1997 for a discussion), but we focus on the ecological footprint (EF).

Wackernagel and Rees (1996, 1997) take a strong sustainability stance, arguing that each generation should inherit a stock of essential biophysical assets that is no less than the stock of such assets inherited by the previous generation. What is the best approach to measure constancy of natural capital? How can the various essential components of natural capital be aggregated in a meaningful way? Wackernagel and Rees reject monetary valuation as this is "blind to ... biophysical realities" (1996, p.6), and instead propose the ecological footprint. The EF represents the natural capital requirements of an economy. It is variously defined as "the 'load' imposed by a given population on nature" (p.5) or "an accounting tool that enables us to estimate the resource consumption and waste assimilation requirements of a defined human population or economy in terms of a corresponding productive land area" (p.9). It is measured by "the aggregate area of land and water in various ecological categories that is claimed by participants in that economy to produce all the resources they consume, and to absorb all the wastes they generate on a continuous basis, using prevailing technology" (p.7). The EF is the area of land required to sustain economic activities – the common denominator is hectares of ecologically productive land, rather than dollars.

The footprint measure can be illustrated with the aid of Table 8.6, where the EF for Canada is calculated as 4.27 ha per person.

Table 8.6: Ecological Footprint for Canada (ha per person per year)

Item	Food	Housing	Transpor-tation	Consumer Goods	Services
Energy (land required to sequester carbon to offset fossil fuel emissions)	0.33	0.41	0.79	0.52	0.29
Degraded land (built up environment)	–	0.08	0.10	0.01	0.01
Garden (for vegetables & fruits)	0.02	0.002 (?)	–	–	–
Cropland	0.60	–	–	0.06	–
Pasture (for dairy, meat & wool production)	0.33	–	–	0.13	–
Forest (prime forest area assuming a MAI of 2.33 m^3)[a]	0.02	0.40	–	0.17	–
TOTAL	1.30	0.89	0.89	0.89	0.30

Source: Wackernagel and Rees (1996, pp.82–83)
[a] MAI refers to mean annual increment, or annual growth (see Chapter 11).

Annual energy consumed in the production of food requires 0.33 ha per person for sequestering the carbon released into the atmosphere from fossil fuel burning. For housing, 0.41 ha per person is required to offset the addition to atmospheric CO_2, while it is 0.79 ha annually for transportation. Food production also "consumes" 0.02 ha of land for growing fruits and vegetables, 0.60 ha of cropland and 0.33 ha of pasture per person. Housing construction requires 0.40 ha of forestland per person per year, while consumer goods needs 0.17 ha (presumably for paper and other wood products). Annually some 0.20 ha of "degraded land" are required per person for housing sites, transportation corridors, and production of goods and services. The EF for the USA is 5.1 ha, for eastern Europe it is 0.3 ha, while it is 0.4 ha per person for India; the world's EF is 1.8 ha per person.

What does the EF say about sustainability? Land area is finite by definition, and thus constitutes a clear upper limit for extraction. When the EF of a regional economy exceeds the region's size, the difference can be covered either by imports or by drawing down the stock of natural capital. Thus, Wackernagel and Rees (1997) argue that the ecological footprint is a useful yardstick for identifying and measuring sustainability. At the global level, the footprint must be smaller than the (essentially given) carrying capacity. The carrying capacity EF is calculated to be 1.5 ha per person, below the current EF of 1.8 ha; further, the average person in an industrialised economy currently has a significantly greater footprint (ranging from 2 ha per capita for Japan to 5 ha for the US) than the global carrying capacity. Therefore, a "sustainability gap" exists. When incomes in developing countries increase and approach Western standards, production and consumption patterns will inevitably mean that natural capital stocks need to be run down. Wackernagel and Rees argue that excessive depletion is already taking place: "our rough calculations suggest that the ecological footprint of all industrialized nations, representing less than 20% of the world population, is larger than the available ecologically productive land on earth" (1997, p.10). Hence, current economic activity is not sustainable, as determined by the EF.

How useful is the EF as a measure of sustainability? Unfortunately, the EF is less a scientific measure than one designed to raise public awareness and influence politics. From that perspective, however, it must be regarded a success. Proponents of the EF oppose the aggregation and substitutability inherent in a monetary metric, they are against discounting, and they reject marginal in favor of absolute (average) valuation. However, in the construction of the EF metric, the very same measurement issues (aggregation, substitutability, discounting, valuation) have not been dealt with in a meaningful way. Due to this imperfection, the EF is useless for policy analysis where trade-offs at each moment in time and over time are essential. Some of its shortcomings are highlighted in the next paragraphs.

First, about one-half of the footprint estimate for developing countries is associated with the need to assimilate carbon from fossil fuel burning – land as a carbon sink (see Chapter 11). This implies that the footprint is substantially overestimated if the greenhouse effect is not real after all, or less damaging than currently perceived if low-cost carbon abatement is somehow feasible in the future. As indicated in Chapter 11, the costs of sequestering terrestrial carbon rise substantially as more land is used for that purpose. Indeed, a mix of carbon abatement options is more cost effective than simply using land as a "carbon sink", even if such land use is currently cost effective *at the margin*. Further, terrestrial carbon uptake has a temporal dimension, but it is impossible not to discount physical carbon if the effectiveness of various land use options are to be compared (see Chapter 11). To calculate this component of the EF is fraught with a degree of difficulty not addressed in the EF metric.

Second, the EF is chosen because of its apparent "ease" at aggregating sustainable development data (especially compared to monetary measures); resource and waste flows are easy to measure, it is claimed, as is the conversion of such flows to "productive" land area. However, with some exceptions, little is known about what happens to wastes when they enter ecosystems (see, for example, how they are broken down, how long they reside in ecosystems, potential damages they cause), and even less is known about how to convert resource and waste flows into a productive land area – the aggregation problem.

Third, the EF depends on (implicit) assumptions about how one substitutes between various forms of nature and how they are aggregated. Thus, for example, land needed for carbon uptake is rated the same as productive cropland, or forestland, or "degraded" land (which supports activities that might well enhance productivity of other land categories). This clearly cannot be the case. The differences are addressed in part by assuming different yield factors for different land uses in different countries, presumably based on some measure of actual output. For Italy, pasture is given a yield factor of 6.5 while arable land has a yield factor of 1.49 (Wachernagel et al. 1999). These indicate that output in Italy is that much higher than the global average – Italian land (nature?) is that much "better". Although yield factors address differences in land quality among regions, economic factors are not taken into account. In less developed countries, economic incentives lead to low output levels, while subsidies in North America and Europe have resulted in higher agricultural output than would otherwise be the case. By using yield factors, the proponents of the EF are making judgements about the substitutability between various kinds of natural capital, and about the correctness of distorting economic incentives. As a result, solutions to environmental problems that depend on substitution cannot be studied using the EF tool.

Further, despite the strong sustainability stance of its proponents, the EF requires implicit judgements about the substitutability between natural capital and other forms of capital. The reason is that, in addition to the yield factors, various "weights" are used to convert human investment activities into land area. For example, in determining how much land is needed to cover a country's demand for wood products (say for construction), the footprint uses average annual growth rates of 2.0 m^3 ha^{-1} for Italy (Wackernagel et al. 1999) and 2.3 m^3 ha^{-1} for Canada (Table 8.6). The EF overestimates the land area required to provide human capital, in the form of housing say, because countries could use timber from forests in regions that yield 40 m^3 ha^{-1} per year or more. This requires an increase in trade, but it will reduce the globe's EF. The alternative is for countries to rely on timber harvests from primary and other less productive forests or on wood substitutes, such as cement and aluminum, which are much less environmentally friendly.

The point is that other ways of aggregating the same data, and other assumptions about substitution possibilities, can lead to opposite conclusions about local, regional and global sustainability. The EF is a metric that depends on how aggregation occurs.

Fourth, Van den Bergh and Verbruggen (1999) criticise the EF because, as it is currently measured, the footprint does not distinguish between sustainable and unsustainable land use, and thus abstracts from most real world policy issues (see, for example, intensification of agriculture).

Fifth, it assumes that land use is associated with single functions only, whereas it is well known that land often provides multiple products and services.

Finally, van den Bergh and Verbruggen point out that the EF is autarkic, against all but a minimum level of international and interregional trade. The reason is that trade enables unsustainable economic activities to continue by imposing costs on others in a fashion reminiscent of imperialism – environmental imperialism in this case. Van den Bergh and Verbruggen (1999) argue that "the ecological footprint hides the favourable impact of specialization, not merely in terms of efficiency, i.e. the standard trade story, ... but also in terms of environmental sustainability given the erratic clustering of people in space". Hence, while the EF may be an informative statistic at the global level, but certainly not the single dimensional yardstick for sustainability that many seek, it does not and cannot serve as a guide for policy making in the real world. It ignores the real world and the real trade-offs that need to be made. Regional footprints are even more confusing. As the critics note, the economies of urban areas and small densely populated countries like the Netherlands will never be sustainable, by definition. But what lesson are we to draw from that?

In summary, the EF is an attempt to replace extant measures of sustainability, both monetary (see Pearce and Atkinson 1995; Hueting 1989) and biophysical (Rennings and Wiggering 1997), with a single one. This is much like replacing measures of humidity, temperature and air pressure as indicators of weather with a single measure, altitude, since each of the former are (perhaps imperfectly) correlated with the latter. Clearly, this would lead to a much less useful indicator, just as the EF is a much less useful indicator of sustainability than the indicators its proponents wish to discard. Further, claims that the EF avoids problems of aggregation and substitutability (and even discounting) are empty ones that simply do not hold up under careful metrological scrutiny. Nonetheless, The EF can be used alongside other measures of sustainability to provide an indication of direction, but it should not be relied upon as a sole measure or even a reliable measure of how societies might "overshoot" their carrying capacities.

8.5 The Environmental Kuznets Curve

A relatively recent phenomenon in environmental economics is the so-called environmental Kuznets curve (EKC) hypothesis. According to this hypothesis, environmental damage first increases with income, but after a "turning point" declines. The hypothesis proposes an inverted U-shape relation between damage and per capita income.[7] It would be a comforting idea that environmental quality will, in the long run, improve as economies grow, with strong implications for policy makers. The implications for sustainable development run counter to the central hypothesis of the "limits to growth" research (Meadows et al. 1972). Obviously, the EKC concept is meaningless where there is a great potential for irreversibility of some environmental good (e.g., extinction of species or, perhaps, depletion of old-growth forests).

According to Grossman (1995), the effect of economic activity on the natural environment can be decomposed into three components. First is the "scale effect" that features prominently in the limits to growth tradition. This effect captures the simple intuition that more output, *ceteris paribus*, results in faster depletion of reserves and increases pollution. However, EKC adherents, who believe that the second and third mechanisms offset the scale effect, debate the *ceteris paribus* assumption. The second mechanism is the "composition effect", which refers to the possibility of a decline in environmental damage when the share of pollution intensive activities in GDP decreases over time. That is, the structure of the economy, or the goods and services produced, changes over time (International Bank for Reconstruction and Development, hereafter IBRD, 1992). The third mechanism is the "technique effect", which refers to potential changes in methods of production. The World Bank points out that enhanced efficiency, substitution and the introduction of clean technologies and management practices play an important role in determining the environmental impact per unit of economic activity (IBRD 1992).

The extent to which the composition and technique effects offset the scale effect is determined by incentives. As per capita income rises, the demand for environmental quality may increase, resulting in an "induced policy response"

---

[7] The original Kuznets curve, supported by empirical data, describes a similar relation between income inequality and per capita income (Kuznets 1955).

(Grossman and Krueger 1995; Selden and Song 1994). Hence, environmental regulations are expected to tighten as wealth (and education and awareness) increases. In addition to this effect, environmental quality may improve because fertility is assumed to be a declining function of income, or simply because there are more resources available for investment in clean production when income is higher (IBRD 1992; Beckerman 1992). Further, as pointed out by Perman et al. (1996), while many forms of regulation or control may benefit society, the initial resource cost could be prohibitively high for some economies.

The foregoing implies that economic growth is sometimes considered part of the solution rather than the source of environmental problems. Some researchers have been very optimistic about this finding. Beckerman (1992), for example, argues that "in the end, the best and probably the only way to attain a decent environment in most countries is to become rich". On the other hand, Stern et al. (1996), Arrow et al. (1995), and the World Bank (IBRD 1992) have been more careful and emphasised the role of proper policies. The empirical work indeed suggests that "becoming rich" will not be a panacea for environmental quality. Shafik and Bandyopadhyay (1992) argue that, while it is possible to "grow out" of some environmental problems, there is nothing automatic about doing so.

Some support for the EKC hypothesis comes from work by Shafik and Bandyopadhyay (1992), Panayotou (1993b), Selden and Song (1994), Cropper and Griffiths (1994) and Grossman and Krueger (1995). The results of Grossman and Krueger (1995) indicate that, at high-income levels, further increases in income may be detrimental to the environment. Hence, instead of an inverted U, environmental damage may describe an N shape – a re-linking of damage and economic growth after a period of de-linking. Most empirical work typically consists of fitting a single regression equation between degree of air pollution and income (Grossman and Krueger 1995; Selden and Song 1994; Panayotou 1993b), but the hypothesis has also been tested in the case of deforestation (see Chapter 12) and urban sanitation-clean water (Shafik and Bandyopadhyay 1992). The results do not point in a single direction, but indicate that environmental improvement is more likely to occur when it concerns a local environmental problem (*viz.* sanitation), where there is a clear link between cause and effect (Beckerman 1992). Other problems, notably those with global effects that occur in a relatively distant future (e.g., global warming) are more difficult to put into an EKC framework.

One approach to improving EKCs is searching for important omitted variables. Boyce (1994) and Torras and Boyce (1998), for example, argue that in addition to income levels, the distribution of income and measures of civil rights may be important in explaining environmental degradation. Access to information about environmental pressure and valuing of environmental degradation are likely affected by the degree of inequality in an economy. Considering the "induced policy response", one can expect that the demand for environmental amenities and the political will to respond to this demand are affected by income distribution. A more equitable distribution of income may lead more people to demand a cleaner environment, thereby giving a larger effective voice favouring higher environmental quality. It may also bring about a social harmony that is more conducive to the long-term perspective necessary to make investments in environmental quality (Sandler

1997). Scruggs (1998) is cynical about this line of reasoning, arguing that the effects of distribution are ambiguous; depending on the distribution of preferences across groups in society and the institutional rules, a more equitable income distribution may both enhance and mitigate environmental pressures.

Most studies that examine the EKC hypothesis are fraught with problems. Regression analyses tend to be biased and inconsistent due to simultaneity problems. Feedbacks exist between the state of the environment and economic growth (e.g., because a low-quality environment results in higher costs associated with illness and lower productivity of workers), and regression models fail to capture this source of bias. Another problem is related to international trade. While the data provide some evidence for a structural change in the economies of developed countries, this does not imply that a similar option exists for developing countries. Stern et al. (1996) cite evidence that the energy intensity of US imports has increased over time, with imports having, to a certain extent, taken the place of domestic production. As the structural change in the USA may have been "partly accomplished through specialisation towards activities with lower energy and resource intensities, it is not clear that the world as a whole can achieve a similar transformation" (p. 1156).

Estimated EKCs are sometimes used to project environmental damage in the medium term. Since the so-called turning points of many statistical EKCs lie in the vicinity of current mean income levels (turning point estimates range from several hundred US dollars to $12,000, with many outcomes close to $5,000), further economic growth seems to contribute to higher incomes and a cleaner environment. But an implicit assumption underlying this claim is that incomes are normally distributed. Stern et al. (1996) argue that the global distribution of income is highly skewed, with much larger numbers of people below world mean income per capita than above it. To evaluate the effect of economic growth on the environment, *median* rather than *mean* income may be relevant, and median income is not close to estimated turning points. Taking estimated EKCs as given and simulating the impact of economic growth on the environment, these authors demonstrate that matters could become worse before they get better. They conclude that EKCs are no justification for policy inaction. For sensible courses of action concerning the trade-offs that arise when sustainable development is pursued, however, policy makers will find little guidance in EKC relationships.

8.6 Conclusions

For economists, it is hard to draw clear conclusions from the discussions in this chapter, mainly because the principal issue of sustainability is rooted in fairness and ethics, rather than allocation and choice. Yet, economists have long ago addressed some of the key issues relevant to the current debate. Also, implementing sustainable development will require developing policies (economic institutions and instruments) to bring about sustainable development. The economist has a comparative advantage in measuring costs and benefits of proposed policies (see Chapters 2, 3, 5 and 6), and examining alternative institutions and market incentives for attaining sustainable development. This is not to dispute the need for more information from ecological sciences, especially with respect to issues related to stability, resilience, possible system collapse and human pressure on ecosystems.

One observation is that there are huge differences in extant interpretations of the sustainability concept. This is due to differences in ethical position and opinions about what to sustain. Further, the underlying assumptions (e.g., Cobb-Douglas production technology versus Leontief production) often determine model outcomes, thus driving management prescriptions. Ultimately, however, it is an empirical matter as to which assumptions are correct.

Many analysts have highlighted the difference between efficiency and sustainability by emphasising that internalising externalities and correcting market failures, while perhaps necessary for sustainability, are not sufficient for most interpretations of the concept. Toman et al. (1995) point out that "sustainability is perfectly consistent with intertemporal Pareto efficiency and intergenerational justice as expressed in other intertemporal social welfare criteria, but achieving sustainability would require different degrees and direction of collective intervention than the conventional prescriptions" (p. 158). Common and Perrings (1992), who describe a different type of model for "ecological sustainability" that highlights system resilience, also note that (their interpretation of) sustainability may conflict with consumer sovereignty, so that government intervention is necessary.

Unfortunately, governments often fail to take the appropriate measures, sometimes because the majority of individuals in society are against them, but more often because a small group conducts rent-seeking activities to avoid paying the cost of their responsibility for sustainable development. Too often the sustainable development process results in recommendations to make incremental changes to existing policies, along with suggestions to collect more information and improve existing management of resources. Unfortunately, the recommendations cover familiar territory, where the thinking and positions of various interest groups are well staked out, but there is often no real change in economic institutions and incentives that would truly lead to sustainable development. Another reason is that large, bureaucratic governments are themselves wasteful of resources and targets of rent seeking by political self-interests (see Chapter 6; Shleifer and Vishny 1998). By circumventing markets, governments misallocate resources and create an atmosphere that is not conducive to sustainable development. Governments should focus on the development of institutions that encourage investments in human and human-made capital that reduce reliance on natural resources and the environment, while redistribution of income towards the poor must be done in a manner that is fair and does not distort resource use.

9 Biological Diversity and Habitat

Approximately 1.4 to 1.8 million different organisms, ranging from mammals down to bacteria and viruses, have been described (Wilson 1988; Smith et al. 1995), but many more species remain undocumented. Slightly less than 1 million of the described species are insects, about 250,000 are higher plants and 4,500 are mammals. Biologists and ecologists, among others, are concerned with extinction of species and loss of biodiversity, often blaming this loss on economic development and population growth. For example, Leakey and Lewin (1995) argue that "the felling of tropical forests and the encroachment of wild places through economic development may soon be pushing as many as 100,000 species into extinction each year" (p. 6). Similarly, Ehrlich and Wilson (1991) note that, "if current rates of clearing are continued, one quarter or more of the species of organisms on earth could be eliminated within 50 years – and even that pessimistic estimate might be conservative" (p. 160). This compares with an observed loss of some one to two species each year, or about 600 documented animal extinctions since 1600 (see below). Such statements have little empirical basis, but, faced with low documented levels of extinction, reliance on predicted high rates of future extinction is a recurring theme (see, e.g., Sinclair 1999; Gowdy 1997, p. 35).

Biological diversity is difficult, perhaps even impossible, to quantify. Yet, one can make judgements about the likely potential of certain areas to have greater or lesser biodiversity than others. Tropical rain forests likely have more biodiversity than temperate rain forests, which, in turn, are likely to have greater biodiversity than boreal forest and prairie ecosystems. Areas with a great deal of biodiversity are termed "hotspots", while those with little biodiversity are sometimes referred to as biological "coldspots". When policies are being considered to preserve biodiversity, it is important to determine the level or scale at which biodiversity is to be preserved. If the goal is to maximise global biodiversity, the greatest effort, perhaps, should be directed at tropical hotspots, which are generally located in low-income countries where tropical deforestation constitutes a major threat to species loss. This strategy differs from one that seeks to preserve a representative of each possible ecosystem on earth, which has led to the adoption of nature preserves and land set asides around the globe (WCED 1987). Both these strategies differ from one that aims to preserve representative ecosystems in each country or locality. Preserving representative ecosystems in each political jurisdiction often results in inefficient allocation of global resources. For example, Sweden might spend monies protecting a particular habitat for a species that is locally endangered but found in relative abundance elsewhere, when those monies could have been better spent (achieving greater species protection) by preventing deforestation in Malaysia, say. It is often easier to implement a program of species protection locally than internationally, however, so it might be the case that, had the monies not been spent in Sweden, they would not have been spent at all.

It is useful to point out that individuals and/or organisations do not decide directly upon how much biodiversity to preserve. Rather, decisions are made about the way in which resources and habitat are used. Thus, the public owner of an old-growth forest has to make a choice as to the amount of the total forest to harvest. The farmer (private woodlot owner) makes decisions about draining sloughs (harvesting trees) based on both her preferences and attitudes concerning the activity and the economic incentives she faces. Economic incentives include such things as market prices, interest rates, the individual's (firm's) net worth, government regulations and incentives (e.g., corporate and personal tax rates, input rebates or tax write-offs, capital depreciation allowances), and the general economic and political milieu.

Issues about biodiversity involve the aggregate of all public and private decisions about land use. Policies designed to achieve an objective unrelated to biodiversity may inadvertently lead to reduced biodiversity. The destruction of tropical rain forests is an often-cited example (see Chapter 12), but subsidies to agriculture – another contemporary phenomenon – have also resulted in reduced biodiversity, as they have brought about the destruction of wildlife habitat by encouraging cultivation of marginal farm lands (van Kooten and Scott 1995). It is important to recognise that there are many private and public decisions that can have an adverse effect on biodiversity, not just those relating directly to wildlife habitat, forestry and agriculture.

In this chapter economic issues pertaining to the preservation of biological diversity are examined. We begin in the next section by examining rates and causes of species loss, and the meaning and measurement of biodiversity. In section 9.2, we explore ethical issues related to biodiversity. In many countries, preservation of biodiversity is addressed by setting aside or preserving areas that are representative of particular ecosystems. In section 9.3, we focus on economic thinking about biodiversity and, in particular, provide some indication of its value. This is followed in section 9.4 with evidence that countries are moving in the direction of preserving land for protection of biodiversity. The conclusions ensue.

9.1 Biological Diversity: Background

Erwin (1991) points out that "biodiversity can be equated with species richness, that is the number of species, plus the richness of activity each species undertakes during its existence through events in the life of its members, plus the nonphenotypic expression of its genome" (p. 751). Smith et al. (1995) argue that biodiversity can apply to the diversity of proteins within a cell, genes within a population, or species within an ecosystem. Commonly, however, biological diversity refers to the richness, variation or number of different species of living organisms. While concerns over loss of biodiversity (generally extinction or extirpation of species) have usually focused on tropical forests, biodiversity in other regions cannot be ignored.

What are species?

Preservation of biodiversity is often synonymous with preservation of species. But what is meant by the term species? Smith et al. (1995, p. 126) refer to this issue as "one of biology's grand old debates". Consider Figure 9.1, which indicates where the American burying beetle (*Nicrophorous americanus*) fits in the animal kingdom. The system of classifying species used in Figure 9.1 is attributable to Carolus Linnaeus (1707–1778), a Swedish botanist at the University of Uppsala. In his *Systema Naturae* (1st edition 1735; definitive edition for animal taxonomy 1758), Linnaeus gave

> each species a two-word (or binomial) name, the first (with a capital letter) representing its genus (and potentially shared with other closely related species), and the second (called the trivial name and beginning with a lower case letter) as the unique and distinctive marker of a species. (Gould 1995, p. 421)

(A subspecies is identified with an additional trivial name, also beginning with a lower case.) According to Linneaus, species were to have the characteristic that there would be no hybrids (offspring from two individuals of different species) or mutations (organisms that are genetically unlike their parents), but he discovered that both occurred. Thus, either evolution was occurring on a regular and observable basis much more often than was realised or species were too narrowly defined.

Kingdom: *Animalia* (animals)
Phylum: *Arthropoda* (invertebrate animals with jointed legs)
Class: *Insecta* (insects)
Order: *Silphidae* (carrion beetles)
Genus: *Nicrophorous* (burying beetles)
Species: *americanus*

Figure 9.1 Taxonomy of the American Burying Beetle

Charles Darwin himself subscribed to the former view because the (gradual) evolutionary process would result in a continuum of characteristics between species, making it difficult to define species with precision. He writes: "I attribute the passage of a variety, from a state in which it differs very slightly from its parent to one in which it differs more, to the action of natural selection in accumulating ... differences of structure in certain definite directions. Hence I believe a well-marked variety may be justly called an incipient species" (1979, p. 107).

While there are different species of burying beetles, there is only one species of *Homo sapiens*, even though one can readily see that a person from northern Europe is different from a person from Asia. How does *Nicrophorous americanus* differ from *Nicrophorous orbicollis*, a slightly smaller but similar-looking beetle? And how do these species of burying beetle differ from *Nicrophorous tomentosus* (which becomes active in mid-June and reproduces in September or later, while *N. orbicollis* becomes active in April and reproduces before early September) and from *Nicrophorous defodiens*, which is active just before sunset (while *N. tomentosus* and *N. orbicollis* are nocturnal)?

So what distinguishes species? Geneticists use differences in DNA, or the genetic code, as a measure of "distance" between species, enabling them, under the assumption of gradualism, to determine the time to nodes in the evolutionary "tree" (Gribbin 1985, pp. 326–30). Differences in DNA do not appear to be a means of defining species, however. The reason is that species have many genes in common with other species. For example, the DNA of humans, chimpanzees and gorillas are "identical along at least 98% of their length" (p. 342). Since individual organisms have genes that are not identical to other organisms within a species, where does one draw a dividing line between species, as any choice would be arbitrary? Do we divide species when 99 or 99.9% or less of genes is shared? When do individual organisms become separate species? Taxonomists, on the other hand, employ traditional tools of observational differences to distinguish species. Moran and Pearce (1997) note that "a species may be defined as whatever a competent taxonomist says it is ... [so] a worrying implication is that the number of existing species will immediately depend on how a species is defined" (p. 102). Clearly, defining a species is a fuzzy concept (McNeill and Freiberger 1993, p. 64).

One definition of a species is due to Ernst Mayr (1982): "A species is a reproductive community of populations, reproductively isolated from other populations, that occupies a specific niche in nature" (p. 273). This threefold definition – reproductive community of populations, reproductively isolated from other populations, and occupying a specific niche – is overly narrow. Again, and not surprisingly, Mayr notes several pages earlier that taxonomists are "trying to define the undefinable" (p. 267).

The definitional problem has implications for measurement and policy, because biodiversity measures and policies based on them require precise identification of species. For example, under the United States' Endangered Species Act (ESA), the US Fish and Wildlife Service spent more than $2.5 million (1/4 of the F&WS's 1990 budget of $10.6 million) to save Florida's dusky seaside sparrow (*Ammodramus maritima nigrescens*), but the last individual was lost in 1987. Subsequent DNA tests revealed that *A. m. nigrescens* was indistinguishable from other Atlantic coast subspecies of seaside sparrows (Mann and Plummer 1992). If true speciation and pseudo-speciation are considered on an equal footing, it is difficult to target scarce resources to save species that truly add to biodiversity. Further, it is difficult for the objective observer to take serious claims about species loss if, for example, one counts on an equal footing (not necessarily equal value) as separate species the African elephant (*Loxodonta africana*) (only close relative is the Asian elephant, *Elephas maximus*) and the American burying beetle (*N. americanus*), with related species *N. tomentosus*, *N. orbicollis*, *N. defodiens* and others.

At what rate are species disappearing?

There is a good deal of concern with extirpation of species. Harvard biologist Edward O. Wilson is considered a "relentless populariser of the theory that 'we are in the midst of one of the great extinction spasms of geological history', ... [arguing] that fifty thousand or more species a year are being driven to extinction" (Budiansky 1995, p. 164). Leakey and Lewin (1995), and Sinclair (1999), argue that some one million species will become extinct over the next 10 years, and that this is a conservative estimate. Hughes et al. (1997), Wilson (1988, p. 11), Myers (1979) and others make similar claims. Is there evidence to support such claims?

The basis of claims for high rates of extinction is the species-area curve (Wilson 1988, p. 11; Hughes et al. 1997). The species-area curve relates the number of species (S) to land area (A):

(9.1) $S = cA^z$,

where c and z are arbitrary constants to be determined empirically (MacArthur and Wilson 1967). This relation is not a law of nature, but an assumed (empirical) relationship. It is accepted by some scientists because it works – it gives "correct" answers – although statistical verification of the species-area curve and estimation of the parameter values are mainly based on sparse evidence from small islands. Major criticisms of the species-area function are that it ignores the patchy distribution of habitats and that it is an *ad hoc* and continuous relation between habitat area lost and species loss. For most reasonable parameter values of c and z that are applied in the literature, the species area curve precludes the possibility of catastrophic or discontinuous effects, which are often a concern of ecologists (see Budiansky 1995 for a popular but critical discussion).

The species-area curve is used to predict extinctions, but before that can be done, it is necessary to determine how many species exist in a particular region or island, or globally. Conducting a census of the world's store of biodiversity is impossible. Nonetheless, estimates of the number of species have been made. Estimates of discovered species range as high as 1.8 million and, if one adds in undiscovered species, total estimates range between 2 and 14 million or more, depending on the investigator. The methodologies employed involve extrapolation from known information. For example, one researcher used data from Britain to estimate that there are 6 million species of insects. He used the ratio total insect species to butterflies in Britain as a starting point. There are 67 species of butterflies in Britain and about 22,000 insect species in total. Because so many people are amateur butterfly enthusiasts (*lepidoterists*), some 17,500 butterfly species have been identified globally. By assuming that there are in reality 20,000 species of butterflies globally (as we have clearly been unable to find all species), multiplying the ratio of insects to butterflies for Britain (22,000 ÷ 67 = 328.36) by 20,000 results in an estimate of 6.5 million species (Mann and Plummer 1995, pp. 39–40).

In similar fashion, a researcher fumigated 19 Panamanian linden trees, collecting all of the dead beetles that fell out of the canopy. Each tree had some 1,200 species of beetles, which was the only insect counted by the researcher. Assuming that beetles account for 40% of all insect species, the canopy of each tree has some 3,000 insects. Further, assuming that the lower parts of the tree (including rooting zone) are only half as species rich as the canopy, and that the insects found in the lower half differed from those in the canopy, each linden tree contains some 4,500 species of insects. Supposing that 13.5% of the species found in the linden trees are not found in other tree species implies that 600 insects are uniquely associated with the linden tree. If this is the case for all species of tropical trees, of which there are some 50,000, then there must be some 30 million species of insects (Mann and Plummer 1995, p. 41). While each of the assumptions appears reasonable, their cumulative effect is staggering. To these totals must then be added 1.6 million species of fungi, a million nematodes, 10 million species of creatures living on the ocean floor, and so on, and the tally of species runs near 100 million.

To illustrate how estimates of species loss are obtained from estimates of total species, let S_0 and A_0 be the initial number of species and area of tropical forest, respectively, and S_1 and A_1 the species and area after one year. The species-area relationship can be rewritten to eliminate c as follows (Pimm et al. 1995):

$$(9.2) \qquad \frac{S_1}{S_0} = \left(\frac{A_1}{A_0} \right)^z.$$

The shape of the species-area curve is determined by z. According to Pimm et al. (1995), the value of z lies between 0.1 and 1.0, and is often taken to be 0.25. This implies that the rate of change in the number of species is 25% of the rate of change in habitat size. Lugo et al. (1993) claim that z does not exceed 0.7. They also point out that the value of z increases as the area under consideration becomes smaller: "Islands tend to have z factors of about 0.35, while comparable continental areas have z factors of about 0.20" (p. 106). Further, the z factor is different for trees than plants; for the Caribbean, with islands of about 1,500 km^2, the value of z is 0.12 for tree species and 0.23 for all plant species (p. 106). As a rule of thumb, it is often assumed that for every 90% loss in habitat, the number of species that can be supported is cut by 50%.

Given S_0 is some 9.4 million species (2/3 of 14 million) and assuming an annual rate of deforestation of 0.8% (Hughes et al. 1997; see Chapter 12), then $S_1 = S_0 (A_1/A_0)^z = 9.40$ million $(1 - 0.008)^{0.25} = 9.38$ million. The projected number of species lost annually is thus 20,000, which is approximately 80,000 times higher than the natural, or background rate of extinction (Leakey and Lewin 1995, p. 241). For $z = 0.2$, 15,000 species are projected to be lost annually, while, for $z = 1.0$, more than 75,000 species per year are projected to go extinct as a result of tropical deforestation. Ehrlich and Wilson (1991) write that "extinction due to tropical deforestation alone *must* be responsible for the loss of 4,000 species annually" (p. 759, emphasis added). The problem is that the

> species-area curve (in a mainland situation) is nothing more than a self-evident fact: that as one enlarges an area, it comes eventually to encompass the geographical ranges of more species. The danger comes when this is extrapolated backwards, and it is assumed that by reducing the size of a forest, it will lose species according to the same gradient. (Heywood and Stuart 1992, p. 102)

At the risk of "collaborating with the devil" (Mann 1991, p. 736), many have questioned the extent of species extinction (Simon and Wildavsky 1984; 1995; Simon 1996, pp. 439–58; Mann 1991). Critics have pointed to the weaknesses of three key assumptions. First, what is the exact rate of habitat loss? Is nibbling at the fringes of a forest comparable to cutting large tracts of forest on an island? What forest ecosystems are actually converted and does some secondary forest return after some years have passed? Some of these issues are addressed with regards to tropical deforestation in Chapter 12. Second, the shape of the species area curve itself is called into question, as noted in the above quote for example. Finally, as noted above, the number of species S remains unknown, and there exists a wide range of estimates. Yet, S is needed to determine rates of species loss. It seems prudent, therefore, to interpret estimates of rates of extinction with great care.

Using the species-area curve, for example, researchers predicted that 50% of the species in Brazil's State of Sao Paulo should have disappeared as a result of reducing the original natural forests by almost 90%. However, an exhaustive list of extinctions compiled by the Brazilian Society of Zoology indicates that only two birds and four butterflies had gone extinct over the period that deforestation was occurring. One of the birds has recently been seen again, while the song of the other was unknown (making it almost unidentifiable as the lost one should it "re-appear"). The four butterflies had not been observed for decades, but no special effort was made to look for them. While ignorance or lack of data could explain the difference between predicted and actual extinctions, it appears that recorded extinctions in the Amazon are inversely related to the effort to tally them (Mann and Plummer 1995, pp. 69–70; also Budiansky 1995, pp. 67–8). Further, even with the loss of 90% of total habitat area, it appears that enough representative samples of all types of microhabitat remain to ensure survival of the great majority of species and biodiversity (Budiansky 1995).

Nee and May (1997) go even further, suggesting that, even if 95% of all species disappear, more than 80% of the earth's genetic diversity would be retained, because many species are genetically not very different so that losing a significant share need not have grave consequences for overall genetic diversity. And Lugo et al. (1993) point out that the species-area relation appears to overestimate extinction rates (p. 106). They report studies that used z values as low as 0.15, but even for such low values actual extinctions remained below predicted levels. For example, these researchers report a case where, with 90% net deforestation (after loss of 99% of the primary forest), only 11.6% of bird species was lost.

So how prevalent is species extinction? Some evidence is found in Table 9.1 and Figure 9.2, which rely on data from the International Union for the Conservation of Nature and Natural Resources (IUCN) (Edwards 1995; World Conservation Monitoring Centre, hereafter WCMC, 1992).[1] The documented extinctions in modern times have been few, at least compared to (pre-) historical rates of extinctions (Leakey and Lewin 1995). For example, the fossil record suggests that an extinction event during the late Permian period resulted in the loss of 44% of the families of fish

---

[1] The IUCN was founded in France in 1948 as the International Union for the Protection of Nature, changing its name to the one on which the acronym is based in 1956. It became the World Conservation Union in 1993, but retains the acronym IUCN.

and 58% of those of tetrapods (WCMC 1992, p. 197).[2] Most modern extinctions have taken place on islands and are the result of hunting, with habitat destruction playing a significant but lesser role (p. 199). From Figure 9.2, it is clear that "around 75% of recorded extinctions ... have occurred on islands; almost all bird and mollusc extinctions have been recorded on islands. ... Very few extinctions have been recorded in continental tropical forest habitat, where mass extinction events have been predicted to be underway" (Edwards 1995, p. 218).

Table 9.1: Documented Extinctions of Animal Species by Region, 1600–1994

Region	Mammals	Birds	Reptiles	Amphibians	Fishes	Invertebrates	Total
Africa	7	34	12	1	1	50	105
Antarctica	1	0	0	0	0	0	1
Asia	8	12	0	1	2	25	48
Europe	3	5	0	0	0	24	32
N.and Cen. America	37	27	6	2	30	162	264
Oceania	25	36	2	0	2	104	169
S. America	2	0	0	0	1	3	6
Unknown	0	1	0	0	0	0	1
TOTAL	83	115	20	4	36	368	626

Source: Edwards (1995)

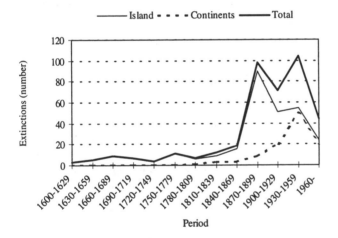

Figure 9.2 History of Extinctions by Type and Historical Period

---

[2] Leakey and Lewin (1995) suggest that some 30 billion species have appeared on earth, but only 30 million remain. The Big Five of mass extinctions "comprises biotic crises in which at least 65% of [marine animal] species became extinct in a brief geological instant. In one of them, which brought the Permian period and the Paleozoic era to a close, it is calculated that more than 95% of marine animal species vanished" (p.44). Almost as many terrestrial species also vanished (p.49).

One researcher has indicated that "60 birds and mammals are known to have become extinct between 1900 and 1950" (Whitmore and Sayer 1992, p. 55). In the eastern USA, forests were reduced over two centuries to less than 5% of their original extent. Forested area has increased dramatically over the last half century as forests have become more valuable for recreation, scenic amenities, and so on, while the land's value in agriculture has declined. During the period of destruction, however, "only three forest birds went extinct – the Carolina parakeet (*Conuropsis carolinensis*), the ivory-billed woodpecker (*Campephilus principalis principalis*), and the passenger pigeon (*Ectopistes migratorius*). Although deforestation certainly contributed to the decline of all three species, it was probably not critical for the pigeon or the parakeet" (Whitmore and Sayer 1992, p. 85; Farrow 1995). While little is known about the extinction of most species, good data generally exist for birds and mammals, and it suggests that about one species goes extinct per year (p. 94).

As stated above, about 600 extinctions of animal species have been documented since 1600, which is consistent with the "normal turnover rate" for species. The fossil record suggests that the average lifespan for a species is approximately 2 million years. Given that there are almost 2 million species known to science, it is expected that about one species per year becomes extinct. Hence, 600 animal extinctions in roughly 400 years is about normal. Smith et al. (1995) note a number of caveats, however. First, the majority of extinctions are vertebrates, constituting only a small fraction of all species, albeit a well documented share. This suggests that many more species may have gone extinct, but remain unnoticed. Second, the rate of extinctions in the twentieth Century has been higher than in previous centuries, although this may be attributable to greater capacity to document extinctions. Third, and finally, some 10 to 30% of well-studied groups (e.g., mammals, birds) are listed as being threatened or endangered by the IUCN. They conclude, therefore, that future rates of extinction could well be higher than recorded rates, although the future rates would not be of the magnitude of 100,000 per year.

Lack of data is clearly a big problem in assessing whether we are in the midst of an extinction spasm or not. It seems that some ecologists are overly worried about this problem (Mann 1991, p. 736), but that others prefer to err on the safe side ("precautionary principle;" see Chapter 8), purposefully claiming excessive rates of extinction. Some authors have tried to reconcile observations with theory by expanding scientific jargon with new phrases, such as "committed to extinction" (Heywood et al. 1994). Actual extinction rates have lagged behind theoretical predictions, but for some this can be explained by understanding that "extinction is a gradual process on an uncertain time scale" (Heywood et al. 1994, p. 105). The suggestion is that many populations of currently living species are no longer viable and will become extinct in the (near) future. It is of course also possible that predicted extinction rates are simply wrong. As Smith et al. (1995) note, extinction estimates "rely partly on untested assumptions and shaky extrapolations" (p. 127).

Suppose that there are indeed large numbers of undocumented (unmeasured) extinctions, but we do not know these are taking place. Do we assume they are occurring nonetheless? It seems imprudent to formulate public policy on undocumented and unknowable extinctions, as there are certainly very real (opportunity) costs involved with conservation. For the economist, it is not the number of extinctions that is important, but, rather, the foregone economic value of the species concerned. Thus, if 10,000 species are projected to go extinct out of a total 50 million species, this might be less important than 1,000 species going extinct out of 3 million. Many species could go extinct in a given year with no (actual or potential) loss of value, but it is also possible that the loss of one or two species is very costly. It all depends on the (marginal) value of the soon-to-be-extinct species (see below).

In addition, to uncertainty about both the total number of species and current extinction rates, there is a debate about the *underlying causes* of biodiversity decline. Swanson (1995) distinguishes four schools of thought.

1. *Portfolio choice* "Human society has a choice in regard to the amount of biodiversity that will be retained along its development path, and this choice has thus far been made in a haphazard fashion" (Swanson 1995, p. 2). (This portfolio selection argument is also discussed in Chapter 7.) A crucial element of this reasoning is that biodiversity decline is an outcome of society's own free will. Path dependency in development – that developing countries copy the route to development taken by industrialised countries, which consists of exploiting natural capital – may also play a role. Swanson (1995) argues that humans have accumulated knowledge that is specific to the management of certain plant and animal species. This knowledge is a non-rival good, creating a non-convexity in the human choice set. Human choice selects those species for the portfolio for which knowledge is freely available, and thus previous selections (and experiences) determine later choices.

2. *Market failure* It is believed that there are significant external effects and (global) public good features of biodiversity that are not accurately valued and included in current decision making. In other words, the relative ability to appropriate flows from natural capital compares poorly with the similar ability to appropriate flows from human and physical capital. Among other things, there may be an insurance value and an information value of biodiversity that is currently (partially) overlooked. For example, there is no institution that captures information from natural capital as an analogue to "intellectual property rights" for human capital. The result is socially excessive loss of biodiversity (most often through excessive habitat conversion).

3. *Policy failure* Not only is biodiversity conservation undervalued, but governments have often promoted inefficient conversion of natural capital into other assets through subsidies, tax cuts, and so on. Ignorance, and possibly corruption, lobbying or political favoritism, may result in the subsidising of biodiversity loss, and thus play an important role in patterns of biodiversity decline. This is particularly well-documented for tropical forests (see Chapter 12).

4. *Development* By expanding, human societies and economies necessarily leave less room for other species, and possibly ecosystems. Typically, economists tend to disregard this stream of thought as it neglects essential feedback reactions of changing relative scarcity on behaviour (but see Chapter 8).

The decline in biodiversity, at whatever rate, could possibly be caused by a combination of the above factors, but it might also be caused by other factors (including ethical attitudes).[3] Separating the relative factors indicated above, as well as many other factors, is an impossible task, partly due to the many interlinkages that exist. For example, population growth will have an impact on institutions governing resource use and trigger policy reactions, while institutions and government incentives will determine the development path chosen.

The *direct* causes of biodiversity decline are better understood than the underlying factors. Consider the animal species that have gone extinct since 1600 (extinction causes for plants are less well documented). According to WCMC (1992), who estimates that 486 animal species have gone extinct (there remains disparity in estimates of extinction), 114 have become extinct from deliberate or accidental introductions of exotic species, 98 from habitat destruction and 80 from overexploitation (e.g., hunting and trapping). This leaves 189 species for which the immediate cause is unknown. The major direct causes of biodiversity decline are habitat conversion, introduction of exotic species and overexploitation. These direct causes are often interlinked, as are the underlying causes. In the future, global climate change and ozone layer depletion (particularly sensitive for amphibians) may play an important role too. Establishing causal relations between underlying and direct causes of diversity decline is an important area for future research.

Measuring biodiversity

Operational definitions of biodiversity focus primarily on the larger or more visible wildlife species, although the importance of micro-organisms certainly cannot be ignored. But, from a practical standpoint, biodiversity frequently focuses on animal species (mega-fauna) that are found at the top of the food chain. In some cases, it is possible to focus only on *keystone* species because they are critical to maintaining the ecosystem in which they live. (Some mammals, birds, amphibians and reptiles are often considered keystone species, but vascular plants and fungi might also take this role.) However, ecologists now believe that keystone species are rare – there are few species that control or are vital to the larger ecosystem (Holling et al. 1995, pp. 73–4). In most cases, loss of one or several species does not affect the ability of other species in the ecosystem to survive; other species readily fill the vacated niche. Ecosystems are in continual flux. Resilience and not catastrophic collapse is the common result (Budiansky 1995, p. 183; Mann and Plummer 1995, p. 131).

Measurement of biodiversity involves three *aspects*:

1. The *scale* aspect focuses on spatial attributes. *Alpha diversity* refers to species richness (numbers) within a local ecosystem, while *beta diversity* reflects differences in alpha diversity as one moves from one ecosystem to another across

---

[3] Grizzle and Barrett (1998) reconcile some viewpoints regarding the role of ethics in environmental degradation. This is also addressed in the next section in regards to discussion of viewpoints aspect of biodiversity measurement.

a landscape. *Gamma diversity*, on the other hand, pertains to species richness at a region or geographic level, say within a biogeoclimatic zone. Gamma diversity is likely more important than alpha and beta diversity, because, even in the absence of human intervention, the latter two are affected by local catastrophic events such as wild fire. Gamma diversity is unaffected by local natural events, but can be affected by larger (perhaps global) events that affect large regions (e.g., climate change).

2. The *component* aspect of biodiversity concerns the identification of what constitutes a minimum viable population (MVP) for survival and propagation of a species. For example, genetically unique salmon stocks on Canada's West Coast are threatened and, in order to determine their survival potential, it is helpful to know the minimum viable population for various stocks. This knowledge is useful in targeting scarce resources for protecting stocks. It is likely better to target efforts at stocks where numbers exceed MVP as opposed to stocks where numbers are already below MVP (see Chapters 7 and 10; also Quammen 1996). However, Soulé (1987, p. 181) argues that, even when a species falls below its MVP, it might still be possible to save the species from going extinct: "there are not hopeless cases, only expensive cases and people without hope". Examples of apparently hopeless cases are the (northern) white rhinoceros (of which no more than 20 animals were alive in the 1920s) and the Mauritius kestrel (of which no more than two pairs were known to exist in the wild in the mid–1970s). With human intervention, both species have made a reasonably successful come back, although future viability is by no means assured and the expense of saving these species was large.

3. Finally, there is the *viewpoints aspect*, with viewpoints ranging from the practical to the moral and aesthetic. Not everyone takes the same view of nature, and religious motivations impact one's view. For example, the "Japanese public [is] far more inclined than the American to emphasize control over nature" (Kellert 1995, p. 110). Nelson (1997) attributes this to a Puritan influence in America that did not occur in Japan.[4] Puritan worship is characterised by holiness and separation from the world, which was a theme that proponents of nature preservation adopted, speaking of nature in the same religious tones as used by Puritans. Not surprisingly, those who wished to preserve wild spaces for purposes of reflection, mental well being, getting away from it all or getting in touch with nature also had an exclusionary view of nature conservation – nature is to be preserved only for them (Nelson 1997; Budiansky 1995, pp. 3–66).

While no index of biodiversity can capture all aspects, it remains important from a scientific and policy point of view to make the effort. How else can we know if a certain policy to protect biodiversity is effective? A measure of biodiversity can provide insights and information for policy making, but it is almost always incomplete.

---

[4] White (1967) makes a similar observation when he attributes the ecological crisis to economic growth resulting from a Calvinist work ethic.

Measures of biodiversity are illustrated with the aid of Table 9.2. *Richness* measures alpha species diversity or number of species, while *evenness* attempts to measure perceived diversity or the distribution of populations of various species represented in the ecosystem. In Table 9.2, ecosystems D and E have the greatest richness, but D is perceived to be more diverse because individuals are more evenly distributed across species (greater evenness). Richness and evenness need to be combined to produce an index of biodiversity. One such index of diversity is Shannon's index (*H*) (Pielou 1977):

$$(9.3) \qquad H = - \sum_{i=1}^{n} p_i \log_{10} p_i, \qquad 0 \le H \le 1,$$

where p_i is the proportion of all individual organisms accounted for by species *i*, $\log_{10}$ refers to base 10, and *n* is the total number of species in the ecosystem. *H* represents a measure of average rarity that varies between 0 and 1, with lower values indicating less biodiversity. According to the Shannon index, ecosystem D has the greatest biodiversity.

Table 9.2: Diversity Indexes for Hypothetical Ecosystems

Species	Ecosystem					
	A	B	C	D	E	F
1	43%	74%	62%	23%	92%	100%
2	32	13	13	17	2	
3	25	13	13	17	2	
4			12	16	2	
5				16	1	
6				11	1	
Measure of Biodiversity						
Richness	3	3	4	6	6	1
Evenness	0.977	0.685	0.781	0.984	0.225	0
Shannon	0.466	0.327	0.470	0.769	0.175	0

Source: Adapted from Bunnell et al. (1991)

Weitzman (1992, 1993) proposed a measure of biodiversity that enables one to prioritise and target species to be protected. It is based on a measure of genetic distance between species, and is found by solving the following dynamic programming equation:

$$(9.4) \qquad V(S) = \max_{k \in S} [V(S \mid k) + d(k, S \mid k)],$$

where $S \mid k$ refers to the set of species *S* without species *k*, and $d(k, S \mid k)$ is the genetic distance between *k* and $S \mid k$. Backward recursion to solve this equation (see Chapter 7) results in a "tree" (or cladogram) such as that found in Figure 9.3. Distance between any two species is given by the height of the "tree", measured from the bottom to the "tree" to the node that is common to the two species. In the limit, the measure of biodiversity derived from the dynamic programming algorithm is directly related to the Shannon index as follows:

(9.5) $V = \dfrac{H}{2}$.

In Figure 9.3, species 1 and 2 are closely related (in a genetic sense). If it is not possible to save all species, loss of either species 4 or 5, for example, might be tolerated (in terms of the effect on overall biodiversity) as long as the other species does not go extinct.

If both species were to go extinct, however, there would be a large reduction in biodiversity. Thus, if two species can be saved out of a set of species then the most distantly related species should be spared. The most valuable species is the one that is most distant from the others. When a species is removed from a set, then the most distant species changes, but the farthest species always remains the most valuable one. With a budget constraint, the strategy that minimises the loss of extinction is the one that permits one species of a closely related pair to go extinct, *ceteris paribus*.

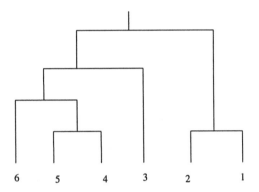

Figure 9.3 Dynamic Programming Tree for Constructing a Pure Measure of Biodiversity

In choosing those species to target with conservation programs, it is necessary to consider the probability that a collection of species will continue to exist at some future time. Since disparate policies lead to different collections of species over time, it is necessary to use discounting.[5] Assume that all species are equally valuable in their contribution to biodiversity – the concern of policy is with preservation of biodiversity and not individual species. Then consider three policies that provide the expected collections of bird species over the four periods found in Table 9.3.

In Table 9.3, policy C is preferred if the objective is to maximise the expected number of species available after 4 periods, while B is preferred if discounting is employed. Although the debate will likely be between those favouring B and C (those for and against discounting), policy A might be the compromise choice if it is

---

[5] Discounting of a physical entity is also required in the context of carbon sequestration, as discussed in Chapter 11.

revealed that each period represents 25 years. In addition to the "preservation effectiveness" of each program, final policy choice will also require that information be available on the conservation budget, the costs of all possible conservation programs, and the benefits of species over and above their contribution to biodiversity. The latter requirement violates the assumption that all species are equally valuable, and is discussed further below.

Table 9.3: Expected Collections of Bird Species over Four Periods under Three Policies

Policy/Period	1	2	3	4
A	200	198	125	100
B	200	199	125	99
C	200	190	125	101

Suppose that species 3 and 4 in Figure 9.3 are relatively abundant, but species 5 is endangered. Suppose further that the budget for protecting species requires a decision maker to choose between two equally costly conservation programs: one reduces the probably that species 3 goes extinct in the next 50 years from 0.010 to 0.005, while the other reduces the probability of species 5 going extinct in the next 50 years from 0.440 to 0.435. The program to be chosen depends on a number of factors, but, as demonstrated by Weitzman (1993) and by Solow et al. (1993) in the case of crane preservation, it is possible that resources are best spent enhancing the survival chances of the more abundant species 3 and ignoring the endangered species 5. The reasons are that 5 is close to 4, so its loss reduces biodiversity less than the loss of 3, and its chances of survival are much less than for species 3.

What happens if species are not equally valuable? It is important to distinguish between preservation of a particular species for its own sake and preservation because it is part of the "web of life" and contributes to biodiversity. For example, people may want to preserve the whooping crane (*Grus americana*) because it has value to them apart from its contribution to biodiversity. This is different than arguing for its preservation because its loss would mean a reduction in biodiversity. Indeed, as the above authors show, if a conservation program is to preserve biodiversity in the crane family (*Gruiformes: Gruidae*), then such a program is best directed at species other than the whooper.

The forgoing analysis suggests that efforts to save the whooping crane or the dusky seaside sparrow may be ill-advised – funds could better be spent elsewhere. However, if survival of a particular species has very high economic value to society, the benefit of a conservation program directed to a specific species might exceed its costs. This is likely true for the whooper but not the dusky. Weitzman (1998), and Metrick and Weitzman (1998), solve a model, aptly called "Noah's Ark Problem", that aims to maximise the degree of genetic diversity, plus direct utility from a species, subject to a budget constraint. They propose a priority ranking based on the criterion that $R_j = (D_j + U_j)(\Delta P_j / c_j)$, where D_j is distinctiveness of species j, U_j is the direct utility of j (likely high for the whooper), ΔP_j is the measure by which the survivability of species j is improved, and c_j is the cost of improving the survivability of j by ΔP_j. The cost of improving survivability represents the space a species occupies on the ark (nowadays measured in monetary units).

Using public spending as a proxy for Noah's ranking, they found public spending to be inconsistent with a ranking based on this criterion. Priority setting in the context of the US Endangered Species Act (see next section) is either perverse or, more likely, explained by "an overpowering role for omitted unobservable charisma-like factors" (p. 32). Thus, direct utility of species may be more important than survivability, distinctiveness, or costs of conserving the species. Spending decisions do not correlate well with scientific rankings. This finding is consist with Metrick and Weitzman (1996) – birds and mammals are ranked higher than fish, amphibians and reptiles.

Loomis and White (1996) report household willingness to pay to preserve species increases with opportunities to view the species. While they report relatively high WTP values for some species (see Table 9.5 below), again WTP appears to be correlated to species profile. This does not bode well for spiders, worms, burying beetles and the host of species that constitute biodiversity. However, as saving high profile species in the wild ultimately implies conserving (setting aside?) their habitat, less charismatic species may take a free ride.

9.2 Economics, Values and Endangered Species Legislation

In this section, we consider the viewpoints aspect of biological diversity, focusing in particular on the validity of attaching dollar values to biodiversity. The discussion provides support for the imposition of constraints on human behaviour to protect biodiversity, but such constraints must be carefully thought out because they should not conflict too much with other values in society. In this regard, we also examine the role of private property and *takings*.

If biodiversity is to be accorded either first-principle or pre-eminent value status (biocentrism), then anthropocentric valuation is not acceptable (Ehrenfeld 1988). Most economists reject the argument that biodiversity should be preserved *at all costs* because species have intrinsic value and that humans are duty bound to preserve all species. The duty-based approach does not survive critical scrutiny when one assumes that there are at least two moral goods – preserving biodiversity and enhancing the life prospects of the world's worst-off people. Which takes pre-eminent status? Randall (1991) makes the case that "the claims of humans trump those of non-humans". Further, if biocentrism is "carried to its logical conclusion, only a hunting and gathering society would be permitted" (Castle 1993, p. 286). It is clear that, while humans should make some sacrifices for biodiversity, these cannot be unlimited. And, as noted in Chapter 8 in the context of sustainable development, humans are unwilling to make preservation of all species an overriding constraint on their behaviour. "The question is not whether a reduction in biodiversity will occur, but whether it will be conducted out of complete ignorance and neglect or not" (Swanson 1992, p. 66). Economics can guide decision making in this regard.

Christian writers have also pointed out that species have value beyond an anthropocentric one. They argue that humans are in a position of stewardship and, therefore, have an obligation to prevent species from going extinct (Cobb 1988). Species do have intrinsic value to the Creator and humans do not have the right to destroy species wantonly. Rather, since humans are considered to be the pinnacle of creation (created in the image of God), they have a stewardship responsibility for creation. However, that obligation has been abrogated as a result of sin. While the Christian view points to sin as the root cause of irresponsible behaviour toward creation, this aspect of the Christian viewpoint is often forgotten (Beisner 1990, 1997). Importantly, the Christian view asserts that sin prevents realisation of effective policies for achieving a harmonious relationship between humans and the environment. Along with humanity's fall into sin, the creation also became "polluted" or imperfect (Schaeffer 1972; Grizzle and Barrett 1998). Thus, while Christianity states that humans have an obligation to preserve the creation, it also points to our inability to achieve what is desired. This, then, could provide a case for the imposition of constraints on human behaviour, constraints imposed by the authority.

Other religions also stress the importance of human responsibility to the environment, but they have had no greater or lesser success in applying this ethic in practice than Christianity. Further, secular and non-secular approaches need not necessarily be in opposition to each other.

Philosophical (secular) approaches to decision making concerning biodiversity are essentially limited to utilitarianism, libertarianism and contractarianism. Utilitarians consider maximisation of social utility to be the basic criterion of morality, with social utility defined either as the sum, or the arithmetic mean, of the utility levels of all individuals in the society. Utilitarianism underlies cost-benefit analysis. Although the "...environmental movement has witnessed an intensive search for an environmental ethic not based on utilitarianism", none has been found (Castle 1993, p. 285). Nonetheless, the utilitarian ethic has not gone unchallenged, especially by biologists (see, for example, Sinclair 1999).

The social welfare function of utilitarians can be specified as:

$$(9.6) \qquad W = W[U_1(m_1), U_2(m_2), ..., U_n(m_n)],$$

where W is total society welfare, U_i refers to the utility of the i th individual in society, m_i is the individual's income (representing the ability to purchase goods and services, including biological assets), and there are n individuals in society. As noted in Chapter 6, CBA assumes additive (strong) separability of the social welfare function, so that total social welfare is simply the (unweighted) sum of the welfares of the individuals in society. This assumes that all individuals count and they count equally. If the marginal utility of income is constant and equal across individuals, then welfare is simply the sum of everyone's income. The problem with utilitarianism is that it permits large losses for some (sacrifice of some) as long as others (the majority) gain more than what those individuals lose.

One variant of utilitarianism suggests that species be included in the summation of welfares. This implies expanding (9.6) to include the utility of (individual members of?) species. However, assignment of a species' utility, which is then included in the universal "sum", is a human task, so the utilitarian cannot avoid anthropocentric valuation.

Libertarianism originates with classical liberal philosophy; central to libertarian ethics is the concept of individual rights and private property, even to the point that "taxation of earnings from labour is on a par with forced labour" (Nozick 1974, p. 169). Support for this position is found in the takings clause of the US Constitution, which says that private property cannot be taken for public use, without compensation (Epstein 1985). Exceptions to compensation might occur where compensation is in-kind (e.g., an owner is prevented from erecting signs, compensated by the fact that other owners are also prevented from doing so) or the entire society is threatened. Debates over rights and privileges with regard to the use of natural resources (e.g., grazing or timber harvesting "rights") are ongoing. Most would reject libertarian philosophy because it places onerous limits on public control over private decisions, often requiring the public to provide compensation to landowners to protect species (see below with respect to takings). Libertarians are, nonetheless, quite likely to be receptive to cost-benefit analysis, but with restrictions on what can be done to reduce the welfare of some in order to enhance the total welfare of all. Libertarians would clearly give pre-eminent status to humans.

The contractarian approach to public decision making was originally formulated by Rawls (1971). (The Rawlsian social welfare function requires that the well-being of the worst off individual or group in society be maximised, with the worst off continually changing.) A contractarian case for preserving biodiversity relies upon thought experiments. In some experiments, the possibility that one is "born" non-human is accepted. Preservation of all species relies upon the notion that one has a chance of being "born" into a non-human species that might become extinct. Therefore, similar to the Rawlsian principle that gives priority to the least-off individuals in society (but subject to the principle of liberty), it is concluded that extinguishing any species is wrong. However, while equality between humans and non-humans might be acceptable to deep ecologists, it cannot be the foundation upon which to base a society (Castle 1993).

Another problem with this approach is that it is based on a presupposition (that differences between humans and non-humans are only biological) that has no more right to priority claim than an alternative presupposition, including one that results in an opposite conclusion. Modification of the contractarian argument to permit only satisfaction of human preferences leads to the possible inclusion of the SMS constraint as a component of a just constitution. The cost-benefit approach emerges as a second-best result: "a plausible contractarian solution is to maximise net benefits (to satisfy preferences) subject to a SMS constraint (because participants in the "veil of ignorance" process would insist on it)" (Randall 1991, p. 17); see also Bishop (1978); Randall (1988); Randall and Farmer (1995); and Farmer and Randall (1998).

Finally, Kant's "categorical imperative" ("I ought never to act except in such a way that I can also will that my maxim should become a universal law") is often cited as an important source of inspiration, but naturalistic writers have extended the "respect for persons" (Kant's original idea) to non-humans (Watson 1979). Needless to say, much of current economic thinking is probably not consisten with this "deep ecology ethic". While the utilitarian framework has been challenged, it has yet to be replaced.

Takings

The Fifth Amendment to the US Constitution (November 1791) states: "nor shall private property be taken for public use, without just compensation". This amendment is frequently called the "takings clause" and has recently been the subject of much debate. Takings occur, for example, when governments expropriate property to make way for a new road. Such takings are known as a *titular taking* – literally a taking of title to the property – and are accepted as long as the owner is provided with fair market value, or *direct compensation*. Taxes to pay for armed forces or police protection provide compensation in the form of security, while taxes used to build roads, sewers and so on provide similar indirect benefits. Taxing the better off to provide for the less fortunate also provides *in-kind compensation* in the form of social stability (and satisfying altruistic motives). Social stability might also be used to justify universal medical coverage.

While a social safety net provides in-kind compensation to those who pay the bill, no compensation is provided when social programs encourage abuse, constitute an income transfer from poor to rich (or even rich to rich), or impose one group's idea of what is best for society upon another. The latter may be particularly relevant in the context of biological asset management (see Simon 1996).

Suppose that you purchase a beachfront property with the hopes of building a house at some future date. Houses are built on the lots on either side of the property, but, after your purchase, the government passes a law preventing further development to protect a species of marine life. The new law constitutes a *regulatory taking*. Is such a taking fair? Under the US Constitution, such a taking might require compensation depending upon the circumstances, although courts have been slow in recognising these forms of compensable takings for two reasons. First, the bureaucracy's ability to fight lengthy legal cases is better than that of citizens, with litigants sometimes passing away before cases are concluded. Second, definitions of "property" and "compensation" are not always clear.

In an actual case, the state of South Carolina was ordered by the US Supreme Court in 1992 to buy Mr. David Lucas' beachfront lot at market price if it wanted to prevent anyone building on the property. After gaining title to the property, however, South Carolina sold the lot to a developer. There are few citizens who would argue against providing compensation in the aforementioned case because they can envisage it happening to them. It is personal.

In Canada, the concept of private property is similar to that in the United States, but private property is not explicitly protected in the Constitution (although constitutional proposals during 1992 included a clause pertaining to private property). *Expropriation* of private property (*condemnation* of property for public purpose) is permitted with or without compensation, and such laws vary from one province to another. Each province has its own legislation concerning compensation in the case of government *expropriation* of private property rights, but the general principle of compensation for takings is well known in Canada. However, rights with respect to regulatory takings are not as clear (see Schwindt and Globerman 1996 for examples). Further, the Peace, Order and Good Government provision of the current Constitution can be used by the federal government to *take* private property from individuals without compensation (van Kooten and Scott 1995; van Kooten and Arthur 1997). Although not explicitly referred to as takings, other democratic countries have some provision in constitutional law to prevent the government from taking property from citizens without compensation.

The true economic test of whether a policy to protect the environment is worthwhile or efficient is this: if those who benefit from the policy are able to compensate the losers and still be better off, the program is worth undertaking (see Chapter 3). Efficient outcomes do not, in principle, require that compensation be paid, but not requiring gainers to compensate losers will, in practice, give them an incentive to overstate the true value of their gains. Stroup (1997) points out, for example, that biologists have no economic incentive to limit their demands because they have no requirement to compensate landowners. Governments may be tempted to pursue environmental goals only because they are able to shift the burden of their implementation onto private individuals who have no power to prevent "wipeouts". If governments had to pay compensation in all circumstances, they would be more likely to avoid policies that bring about large wipeouts but few benefits. Therefore, such outcomes are likely to be more efficient, and efficient outcomes are desired because they utilise less of society's scarce resources, including environmental ones.

Takings and endangered species legislation

People place economic value on endangered species preservation, and many of the services provided by protection of such species are not captured in markets. Hence, government intervention may be justified. In the United States, Congress passed the Endangered Species Act (ESA) in 1973 and re-authorised it in 1988. (An earlier version of ESA existed, but it required little beyond monitoring of endangered species.) ESA was interpreted by the Courts to mean that species were to be saved *at all costs*, which was not what Congress had intended (Eisgruber 1993). ESA established a duty to preserve all species, but the duty itself was impracticable. Shortly after ESA was enacted, the Congress established the Endangered Species Committee, comprised of relevant agency heads and other representatives, to resolve conflicts between federal government projects and ESA – an attempt in other words to get around ESA. Environmentalists dubbed the Committee the "God Squad", but it has rarely met since it was established and even less often taken action to over-turn Court decisions.

Establishment of the Endangered Species Committee itself suggested that there was something wrong with ESA. First of all, the duty to preserve all species regardless of cost is an impossible one. The US Fish and Wildlife Service's budget for doing so amounted to a mere $10.6 million in 1990, although States and other non-government organisations added to that amount. Even so, not more than $100 million was available, although the amount required for the USA is likely to be billions of dollars. Brown and Shogren (1998) illustrate the budgetary problems by noting that, of the 1,104 species in the USA that are listed as threatened (228) or endangered (870) in July, 1997, slightly more than 40% have approved recovery plans. To make matters worse, there is evidence that there are nearly 200 species that should qualify as threatened or endangered (T&E), but the budgets for listing them are inadequate. Budgetary limits only allow listing of species at a rate of about 100 per year. Listing does not ensure survival, nor does the development of a recovery plan. Implementing a recovery plan may or may not ensure survival, but implementation could also be very costly.

The power of ESA rests with its provisions to restrict economic activities, even on private lands. This is particularly relevant as an estimated 75 to 90% of the species listed as T&E under ESA are found on private land, and many of these landowners complain that the costs of complying are too high (Shogren 1998). In the past, ESA did not require compensation for private property owners, although law and jurisprudence are slowly changing (Innis et al. 1998). ESA set up perverse incentives, causing landowners to destroy wildlife habitat, especially habitat for species that were under consideration for ESA listing. That this occurs has been documented (e.g., see Mann and Plummer 1992, 1995), with Brown and Shogren (1998, p. 7) referring to this as the "shoot-shovel-and-shutup" strategy. To prevent such behaviour, tradeoffs clearly have to be made, and failure to recognise this may have detrimental effects on conservation.

By casting social and environmental policy into the wishful mode, as ESA does, "the perfect society to which we aspire in theory may become a powerful enemy of the good society we can become in fact" (Sagoff 1988a, p. 200). The problem is one of fairness: the burden or cost of species protection is borne by a small number of private landowners, while the benefits accrue to the larger society. Alternatively, a small group (say developers and/or home buyers) could benefit from action to rid a property of a species about to be listed, while society loses due to the reduction in biodiversity. A middle ground usually exists, say a compromise where a developer agrees to build less housing units and makes some efforts to protect habitat of an important wildlife species so that its probability of survival increases over what it would be had development taken place without restriction. ESA does not encourage such compromises.

How successful has ESA been? Even though twenty-five years is too brief a period to evaluate policies related to extinction, the evidence indicates that ESA has been a mixed success at best. By August 1994, 920 domestic and 532 foreign species (or 1,452 species in total) were listed under ESA (Edwards 1995, p. 239). Of these, 134 had been listed prior to 1973. During the first 20 years of ESA, 721 species were added, but only 21 were removed. Of those removed, seven were declared extinct, but only one went extinct under the watch of the Fish and Wildlife Service. The others were lost prior to ESA. Further, nine species should not have been listed and five were taken from the list because they had recovered – three birds on Pacific islands affected by World War II recovered, one species recovered due to a ban on hunting, and one species recovered when DDT spraying was banned. Brown and Shogren (1998) report that 11 species have recovered and subsequently been removed from the list. Clearly, ESA has not been a complete failure, but it has also not been an overwhelming success. Possibly one species has been saved as a result of ESA. By prohibiting hunting of the American alligator, the species has recovered, but not to the point where it has been de-listed due to concern that it will be mistaken for crocodiles, which can be hunted legally.

It is clear that ESA is a pipe dream. It is simply too costly to save everything, and the majority of citizens are against efforts to do so, although they are not against protecting biodiversity in cases where it is "reasonable" to do so. The extent to which people are willing to pay to protect endangered species is still poorly understood. Brown and Shogren (1998), for example, have crudely summed benefits estimated by several surveys valuing specific endangered species, and obtained the implausible result that people would pay over 1% of the US GDP for less than 2% of all endangered species. This suggests that policy makers can probably not rely on the many isolated estimates of nonuse values that abound in the economic literature to formulate sensible policies (also see below). Mann and Plummer (1995) make several suggestions for improving ESA. They argue that a system for making choices about species preservation must have the following elements.

1. It must be ethical. It must encourage balancing the interests of different groups and social classes, and different values. Tradeoffs must be permitted, and it should not be possible for benefits to accrue to many with costs borne by a few, or costs borne by many for the benefit of a few. People must have a say in the decision-making process, and yet they must feel they have a responsibility for biodiversity.
2. It must be practical in the sense that goals can be attained and measures for attaining these goals must exist. Private landowners must not be provided perverse incentives. Rather, it will be necessary to use public funds to compensate owners and encourage them to make efforts to protect rather than destroy endangered species. Private owners cannot bear all the costs, but, rather, should be rewarded for good stewardship. Participation in efforts to save endangered species on one's property should be voluntary. Further, the notion of *take* should be modified so that those who actually destroy an individual of an endangered species are held responsible, but to exclude harm caused by habitat transformation (p. 233).
3. More knowledge is needed. Biologists often know too little about endangered species, with some species listed that turn out not to be endangered or threatened. More resources are required for information gathering.
4. It must be political so that biodiversity gets the same attention in budget considerations as defence, health care, regional development and education. It is not at all clear that conservation of biodiversity holds a moral trump card over other investments. Hence, including ESA in the realm of cost-benefit analysis also seems worthwhile. By so doing, it is likely that awareness of species preservation and funding to bring it about will increase. Since it is impossible to protect all species, trade-offs will need to be made, and this best occurs in the political arena.

A number of different approaches can be used to protect species and, specifically, their habitat. Rather than put the onus on private landowners, covenants between landowners and communities could be used to protect habitat. These covenants consist of legal agreements that restrict what a landowner can do with her property, with the landowner compensated for such a restriction. In essence, the community purchases certain development rights to the property. Innes et al. (1998) demonstrate that, without compensation, landowners have an incentive to develop too much of their land to avoid takings. When land owners are granted full compensation, however, excessive private investment is promoted because they have no incentive to take into account the probability that their land may turn out to be more valuable in a public use (e.g., as protected habitat). The researchers propose either lump-sum subsidies or more than full compensation for owners of undeveloped land. Obviously, compensation is costly for the government. A more efficient solution, therefore, might be to use a system of tradable development rights.

Shogren (1998) promotes such a market based approach to protect endangered species. He refers to this as "conservation banking".

> A bank is established when a parcel of land is protected. Public officials then assign credits to the land based on the value of its ecological services, and certify the long-term viability of these services. Developers then buy the credits and use them to offset environmental effects on their own land for which they would otherwise be liable. When all credits are purchased the banked land is protected in perpetuity, either by deed restrictions or transfers to a protector, often government. (Shogren 1998, p. 567)

This approach has the important advantage that it encourages landowners to search for the least-cost protection strategy, rather than imposing costly procedures on them, so that overall efficiency may be attained. As with tradable pollution permits, low cost developers sell credits whereas high cost developers must buy them. A similar approach is used by some non-governmental organisations (NGOs), such as Ducks Unlimited and The Nature Conservancy, in their dealings with private landowners to preserve waterfowl habitat, for example. Ecologists will be quick to point out that defining equivalent "ecosystem services" (thereby enabling fair trade) will be difficult and possibly demand more from our understanding of substitution possibilities than is (currently) available.[6]

What the US experience with ESA shows is that a "preserve at all costs" attitude results in large amounts of money being targeted at several high-profile species, while other species that could, perhaps, be saved at much lower cost get ignored. While several attempts have been made to amend or change the Endangered Species Act, environmentalists generally oppose these. This is surprising as the evidence increasingly suggests that ESA is not working and that a new approach is needed, one that relies to a greater extent on politics rather than science. Other countries are also considering legislation to protect endangered species (see, e.g., van Kooten and Arthur 1997), and it can only be hoped that the US experience will serve as a warning and a guide.

---

[6] Consistent with the concerns spelled out above, Shogren (1998) also indicates that conservation banking may be risky, as it ultimately depends on banks that are created by regulatory agencies "with differing missions, which can undermine the security of bank investments" (p.567).

9.3 Economic Values and Biodiversity

Richard Bishop (1978) identifies two broad economic methods for thinking about biodiversity, namely, Ciriacy-Wantrup's (1968) safe minimum standard (Chapter 8) and the Resources for the Future (RFF) approach associated with John Krutilla's (1967) famous article "Conservation Re-considered". Bishop shows that these approaches are similar and complementary. The RFF approach is not confined to Resources for the Future and involves two principal ideas – the notion of quasi-option value and nonmarket valuation (Chapter 5). Quasi-option value is related to the SMS and irreversibility, the main concern in discussions about biological diversity.

Resilience and quasi-option value

There is substantial literature in economics pertaining to preservation of endangered species, wildlands and biodiversity (Krutilla 1967; Ciriacy-Wantrup 1968; Arrow and Fisher 1974; Henry 1974; Bishop 1978; Fisher and Krutilla 1985; Fisher and Hanemann 1986, 1990; Fisher 1988). In the US Pacific Northwest, concern centres about endangered species and the preservation of old-growth forests. In the tropics, deforestation is blamed for the destruction of ecological systems and the subsequent loss of unknown numbers of plant and animal species. In the Great Plains region of North America, conversion of wetlands to agriculture forever alters both the landscape and the ecology. Preservation in each of these examples, as well as many others, is related to *uncertainty* and *irreversibility*.

Uncertainty is a problem because we do not know if a plant or animal species that becomes extinct contains information that may have enabled us to find an alternative source of liquid petroleum, a perennial variety of corn, or a cure for cancer. The potential benefits from any of these discoveries could be enormous. Consider, for example, the savings to society from the discovery of a perennial hybrid of corn. This would result in savings from not having to plough and seed the 28 million hectares that are currently planted to corn in the USA every year. It would also lead to increased carbon storage and a reduction in soil erosion because annual ploughing is no longer required and perennials are better able to bind the soil during periods of rain and/or wind. By delaying development of wildlands, it is quite possible that new information about the existence or value of a particular endangered species or an entire ecosystem becomes available. Similarly, as discussed below, uncertainty enters because the ecological role of many (harvestable?) species in ecosystems is not fully understood, so the potential implications of (local) extinction are unknown.

According to the World Conservation Monitoring Centre (1992, pp. 331, 361), most of the world's plants have been sampled for their value as a food source; while there are some 250,000 species of plants, only 3,000 are a source of food. About one-quarter of cancer drugs in use today were found by random testing of plants between 1955 and 1982. The US National Cancer Institute discontinued this work in 1982 due to its cost and, notably, its lack of success. A second program begun in September 1986 had collected some 116,000 samples by mid–1994, and screened 63,000 for their potential in the fight against cancer and AIDS using new techniques. Such programs are not very successful when compared with their cost, and other methods, such as combinatorial chemistry, are being used in their place. Yet, it might be useful for governments to take such long-shots, although the benefits appear to be small.

Irreversibility has both a biological and economic dimension. Ecologists are beginning to abandon the successional view of ecosystems, adopting instead an adaptive-cycle model of ecosystem change (Holling et al. 1995). The adaptive cycle consists of four phases: exploitation (by species), conservation, release (e.g., fire, pest, storm) and reorganisation. *Resilience, recovery* and *surprise* are the terms used to describe ecosystems. The concept *resilience* has drawn attention to basins of attraction around local equilibria, short-run responses to shocks and behaviour of systems towards equilibria, rather than properties of the long-run equilibria of the system itself (see Chapter 7). It has been observed, for example, that changes in ecological systems may involve sudden shocks, triggered by relatively small perturbations. It has also been observed that functionally different system states involve different equilibria, between which systems tend to "switch" (Perrings 1998). Resilience is a key concept that can apply to the time required for a disturbed system to return to some initial state (Pimm 1984), or to the magnitude of disturbance that can be absorbed before the system "flips" from one state to another (Holling 1973). Both interpretations can be considered measures of system stability. The first interpretation is especially relevant for behaviour near a stable equilibrium, whereas the latter assumes multiple locally stable equilibria among which switching is possible. Perrings et al. (1995) conclude that the link between stress and resilience loss is an alteration in the species mix of the system, or (local) extinction of species. There is "evidence that deletion of some species has minimal effect on at least the short term functioning of the system, whilst the deletion of others triggers a fundamental change from one ecosystem type to another" (Perrings 1998, p. 505).

The link between biodiversity and resilience of ecological systems is as yet ill understood. It has been argued that more complex or diverse systems are more "interconnected" or interdependent, and therefore less resilient. Losing one species may have repercussions for other species – one species may drag down another causing a cascade of extinctions. On the other hand, ecological resilience of systems is likely to depend on the number of species capable of performing critical functions, or the number supporting critical processes under different conditions. Biodiversity conservation then is expected to have significant local benefits, as it increases the perturbation that the system can withstand without losing self-organisation. It has been argued that today's redundant species (also called "passenger species") may well turn out to be quite useful tomorrow, when different ecological conditions prevail. This implies that conservation of an appropriate level of biodiversity is a necessary condition for sustainable management of any natural or managed ecosystem (Perrings 1998). This recommendation is obviously different from the conventional view that biodiversity conservation should focus on "hotspots".

It should be stressed that there remains uncertainty, and perhaps even controversy, about the "stabilising role" of biodiversity. In terms of the ecological benefits of diversity, beyond a certain level of biodiversity, ecosystem function does not improve when the number of species increases. Writing about experiments related to grassland ecosystems, Baskin (1994) points out that the "biggest gains in "stability", for example, come with the first 10 species in a system; beyond 10, additional species didn't seem to add much stability, perhaps because the essential functional niches had already been filled" (p. 203). Similarly, productivity of an ecosystem may be affected by diversity. Baskin (1994) also notes that "more diverse systems are more productive – at least up to a point. Most natural systems are well beyond that threshold, however, and they can often sustain some species loss without a drop in productivity" (p. 202). Random extinction of species may thus pose only limited problems, as long as there are substitutes available in the same functional group. In reality extinction of species is often not a random process.

The processes by which extinction occurs (whether human caused or not) are not well known and this makes it difficult for ecologists to determine exactly what actions might lead to extinction. How resilient are ecosystems? What are the implications for spotted owl of felling old-growth forests if this is done rapidly? What are the consequences if it is done very slowly? What is the likelihood of the spotted owl going extinct even if old-growth forests are protected (Montgomery et al. 1994)? What are the repercussions for the temperate rain forest ecosystem if the spotted owl goes extinct? The stochastic nature of ecological shocks suggests that population viability studies should include the probability of collapse and other stochastic processes affecting stock dynamics (see the discussion on MVPs in Chapter 7). It is in this stochastic framework, where exogenous shocks and management (or institutions) interact, that economists must seek answers to guide policy makers.

Economic irreversibility occurs when development has left an environment in a state that cannot be restored to the original, or restored to the original at a cost that exceeds the costs of preventing the degradation to begin with – the concept of conservable flow (see Chapter 4). Thus, if restoration to an original state is excessively costly, either in terms of the resources that must be allocated or the time required, economic irreversibility has occurred. It is only when the consequences of a decision can be readily altered at negligible cost to society that a decision can be said to be reversible.

It is clear that there is some value to delaying development in the current period if more becomes known about future benefits and costs in the next period. That is, the expansion of choice by delaying development of wildlands (and thus delaying loss of endangered species) represents a welfare gain to society. The value of this welfare gain is known as *quasi-option value*. By the same token, a reduction in the options available to society represents a welfare loss. Quasi-option value is a different concept than option value, which is also related to uncertainty.

First consider option value (OV). It is the additional amount a person would pay for some amenity, over and above its current value in consumption, to maintain the option of having that amenity available for the future, given that the future availability of the amenity (its supply) is uncertain (Graham-Tomasi 1995). Suppose that the maximum amount an uncertain individual is willing to pay to purchase an option to visit a nature park at some time in the future is that person's option price (OP). Then, following Ready (1995), we define option price as:

(9.7) $OP = E(CS) + OV,$

where CS or consumer surplus is the amount the individual is willing to pay to visit the park after she has made a decision to become a demander, with E(CS) being the expected consumer surplus obtained by multiplying CS by the probability of wanting to visit the park. Option value is then the difference between option price and expected consumer surplus: OV = OP − E(CS). Along with bequest value and existence value, OV is included as a component of preservation or nonuse value, and is obtained using contingent valuation or some other nonmarket approach (see Chapter 5).

CS and OP are always positive, and one would expect that OP ≥ E(CS) so that OV ≥ 0, but it turns out that OV can be negative (Ready 1995, pp. 575–78). This situation arises if CS = 0, *ex post*, in one of two states, say. If the marginal utility of income is the same in both states then OP ≥ E(CS) holds. However, if the marginal utility of income is not equal in the two states then it is possible for OV < 0. Suppose that income is much lower in state 1 than in state 2, so CS = 0 (*ex post*) in state 1, but the marginal utility of income in state 1 is also higher than in state 2, the higher income state. If the marginal utility of income in state 1 is sufficiently high, it could overcome the risk aversion effect so that OP < E(CS) and OV < 0.

Although OV assumes uncertainty in supply, it derives from risk aversion on the part of demanders. Quasi-option value (QOV), on the other hand, assumes uncertain benefits, but is derived under risk neutrality (Arrow and Fisher 1974). The basic idea is that, as the prospect of receiving better information in the future improves, the incentive to remain flexible and take advantage of this information also increases (Graham-Tomasi 1995, p. 595). It is not really the prospect of better information about the costs and benefits of delaying development that is important, however, but, rather, having access to better information results in greater revision of one's initial beliefs. Thus, it is "greater variability of beliefs" rather than "improvement of information" that leads one to choose greater flexibility over irreversible development.

To expand on this idea, consider the following example. If the current and future returns from the decision to harvest an old-growth forest are uncertain, then, in general, it is not correct to replace the uncertain returns by their expected values in calculating the present value of the decision to preserve the old growth. By waiting until the uncertainty is resolved, the actual value of the benefits of preserving the forest will be known, and this value will be different from the expected value. By using expected value in calculating the next period's benefit of preserving old growth, the value of preservation is likely underestimated. The difference between the value obtained using expected values and the true value once the uncertainty is resolved – the shortfall – is quasi-option value. This is the loss of options that an irreversible decision entails. Thus, if there is any chance that some uncertainty is resolved by delaying development, the decision to develop or preserve favours the preservation decision.

To summarise, as time passes, the decision maker gets more and better information about costs and benefits of maintaining the land in its present, reversible state. Thus, if the decision maker has to choose between developing and not developing land (whether or not to harvest a stand of primary timber), she can obtain additional information about present and future returns by delaying the decision. It is important to recognise that the problem's decision and information structure evolve through time; the decision is not a timeless one. The importance of quasi-option value for forest conservation is illustrated by Albers et al. (1996) for the case of forest conservation in Thailand. These authors illustrate that quasi-option value may be sufficient to shift the economic balance towards forest conservation when there is a choice between sustainable forest management and irreversible development.[7]

Graham-Tomasi (1995) provides a theoretical framework for analysing QOV. A decision maker wishes to maximise the discounted stream of future benefits from a parcel of agricultural land, say. The benefit function is given by:

(9.8) $\sum_t \beta^t u(x_t, q_t, s_t)$,

where benefits u are a function of the state of the system at a given time (x_t), the action that is taken at that time (q_t), and the resulting and unknown state of nature (s_t). The state of the system is described by variables that indicate the extent of agricultural/urban development of the land. The state of nature is described by such things as agricultural prices, price of land in residential or commercial development, international agreements, and so on, while the action taken could be one of delaying development (remaining flexible), partial development, or complete (irreversible) development. The discount factor is $\beta = 1/(1 + r)$ where r is the real rate of discount.

There are several constraints that need to be taken into account. The first involves the state equations:

(9.9) $x_{t+1} = g(x_t, q_t, s_t)$.

Equation (9.9) is a standard equation of motion that describes the state of development of the parcel of land, or its suitability for continued agricultural production. A second constraint describes how the decision maker's beliefs about the future change over time as more information becomes available. Suppose that the decision maker's beliefs about s at time t are summarised by the probability vector $\pi_t = \{\pi_{1t} \, \pi_{2t} \, ... \, \pi_{nt}\}$, where the number of unknown states of nature is n. Further, suppose that the decision maker receives *exogenous* information in each period of time described by the vector $y_t = \{y_{1t} \, y_{2t} \, ... \, y_{mt}\}$, where m is the number of possible bits of information that can be received in each period. Then, beliefs change from one period to the next according to

(9.10) $\pi_{t+1} = B(\pi_t, y_{jt})$, $j = 1, \, ..., \, m$,

where B might be Bayes' rule. Finally,

---

[7] These authors actually consider a problem with three different types of land use: preservation *P*, development *D* and an intermediate use *M* (say, agroforestry). In their model, it is possible to go from *P* to *P*, *D* or *M*, and from *M* to *M* or *D*. State *D* is a so-called "trapping state" in the transition matrix of a markov process (see Chapter 7).

$x_0 = x^0$ is the initial state of the parcel of land,

(9.11) π_0, y_0 are given,

$q_t \in Q(x_t)$,

where $Q(x_t)$ is the set of all possible actions. The problem is to choose q_t to maximise the discounted stream of future benefits (9.8) subject to (9.9), (9.10) and (9.11).

Because of its assumed markovian properties (equations (9.9) and (9.10)), the problem can be translated into dynamic programming, with the following Bellman equation:

(9.12) $V(x_t, q_t, s_t; y_t) = \max_q [E\ u(x_t, q_t, s_t) + \beta\ V(x_{t+1}, \pi_{t+1}, y_{t+1})]$.

where the expectations operator E is with respect to the decision maker's current information. Given sufficient information, this can be solved as a stochastic dynamic programming problem.

Quasi-option value is always non-negative for both renewable and non-renewable resource systems as long as there exists an "irreversibility effect" – "a relationship between better information and the flexibility of the initial positions" (Graham-Tomasi 1995, p. 603). One expects QOV to be positive, however, because the prospect of learning should always lead one to adopt the more flexible position – information has value. It is only when the amount learned increases with development, or that conservation provides less information than some amount of development, that QOV might be indeterminate.

The conclusion is that the discounted net benefits of development need to exceed the present value of the net benefits of preservation by a "substantial" amount before development should proceed. Thus, QOV does not imply that preservation or retaining flexibility will always be the preferred strategy. It is interesting to note that the safe minimum standard approach implies a similar bias favouring preservation, but here too the costs of preservation cannot be onerous (Chapter 8). Thus, the RFF approach and that of a SMS are similar (or at least consistent), as pointed out by Bishop (1978).

The greatest obstacle to employing QOV in applied cost-benefit analysis is the difficulty of measuring it. For example, in Chapter 11, we consider preservation of old-growth forests, but do not consider quasi-option value because we are unable to estimate its value. Option value can be measured using contingent valuation, but then as a component of preservation value. However, QOV measures a slightly different concept and, perhaps, the only way in which information can be found is by asking a panel of experts about the likelihood of obtaining more information by delaying development or, alternatively, permitting some small amount of development simply to obtain more information. For example, by cutting down some tropical trees, it may be possible to obtain information about the species and ecology of the region. However, neither of these approaches is satisfactory.

How valuable are species and their habitat?

Economists have sought to measure the value of individual species, collections of species and ecosystems (habitats). Total economic value (of ecosystems) constitutes three components.

1. Use values refer to such things as recreation, viewing, and pharmaceutical values of species. Use values are divided into consumptive use (e.g., hunting) and non-consumptive use (e.g., viewing). Both current and potential future values need to be considered.

2. Nonuse or passive-use value (also referrred to as preservation value) refers to the bequest, existence and option values that individuals attach to biodiversity. Perhaps the largest value of biodiversity is existence value – the sum of what individuals are willing to pay for knowing that certain species, or biodiversity more broadly, exists. Nonuse value also includes QOV, but not as a component of preservation value.

3. While use and nonuse values are measurable, in principle, ecosystems provide a third economic value that is perhaps not possible, or at least very difficult, to measure. This is referred to as the economic "glue" (or "infrastructure") value of ecosystems. It is the values provided by such things as watershed protection, waste assimilation, and the general "web of life" functions associated with ecosystems (Moran and Pearce 1997; Holling et al. 1995; Costanza et al. 1997). Since marginal benefits of the "web of life" functions may go to infinity (in other words, a minimum level of ecological infrastructure is necessary for human survival), total glue value is probably unbounded (Costanza et al. 1997, p. 8).

Consider one controversial and much-cited effort to estimate the global value of ecosystems. Costanza et al. (1997) summarise the valuation literature and estimate that the earth's ecosystems contribute some $33 trillion in benefits, significantly higher than global output (GDP) of $25 trillion (1994 is the base year). (Interestingly, nutrient recycling makes up more than half of the value of ecosystem services.) The authors group ecosystem services in 17 major valuation categories, ranging from climate regulation to nutrient recycling and through to recreational and cultural services. The results clearly indicate that ecosystems are important for human welfare. It is certainly possible to criticise the details of the various valuation studies that underlie the Costanza et al. study (see Chapter 5 for shortcomings of the various techniques). There may also be scope for criticism on the aggregation of services and techniques (e.g., replacement costs, WTP), which may have resulted in double counting. Despite this, we briefly focus on the bigger issue.

First, it is clear from Costanza et al. (1997) and the discussion surrounding it,[8] that valuing ecosystem services is a useful and worthwhile endeavour. This is because

---

[8] Additional discussion of the Costanza et al. (1997) study, and a reprint of the paper itself, are found in a special issue of *Ecological Economics* (Vol. 25, 1998).

society faces tradeoffs about nature every day and is forced to make choices. Better choices are made when more information is available.

Second, consider the issue of global value exceeding world GDP, which does not seem consistent with the observation that most valuation techniques are based on willingness-to-pay or some other method that relates to GDP (e.g., expenditures averting environmental damages). It seems as if a budget constraint is violated. The authors defend this by arguing that current GDP is not a proper measure of welfare, because it only includes marketed goods and services. Had ecosystem services been properly priced, the global price system and GDP would be very different (specifically, much higher). It is this hypothetical benchmark that is relevant.

Third, despite their claim, Costanza et al. (1997) do not estimate the marginal value of ecosystem services. Rather, they estimate total (global) value by multiplying social surplus (or price) per hectare by the number of hectares in the biosphere. This implies that their estimate of global value (US$33 trillion) may be considered a "serious underestimate of infinity" (Toman 1998, p. 58), as the global value should also include the "glue value" noted above. In any event, economists are interested in value at the margin rather than total value, and the global value provided by Costanza et al. is not helpful in this regard.

Ayres (1998) doubts that the product of price and quantity is a reasonable substitute for the sum of producer and consumer surpluses, as suggested by Costanza and his co-authors. He points out that, in an equilibrium, the shadow prices of most ecological services (that is, those services that are not a "binding" constraint) should be zero. As Daly (1998) points out, in the Garden of Eden there would be no scarcity of natural resources, so marginal utility would be zero even though wealth in the form of natural capital is at its maximum. For practical purposes, Ayres proposes to consider the cost of restoration, control and maintenance of ecological services as the best proxy for the value of the service flows. If this is accepted, the total value will be much more modest, and probably not exceed a few percent of GDP, although Tinbergen and Hueting (1991) produce estimates of up to 50% of global GDP. In what follows, we present some information supporting Ayres' proposition that, at the current margin, the shadow value of species and habitat may be low. We consider some aspects of total economic value related to species and habitat conservation in more detail.

The existence of undiscovered uses of wild species in industry, agriculture and medicine is often cited as the most important reason for preventing species from going extinct. Searching for these uses is referred to as "biodiversity prospecting" (Simpson and Sedjo, 1996a). Consider pharmaceutical uses. There are some 250,000 species of higher plants, and approximately 125,000 of these are found in tropical regions. To date about 47 major drugs have come from tropical plants. However, the value of genetic material in the development of drugs is small. More important is the human knowledge, R&D investment and marketing required to bring drugs to market. Further, combinatorial chemistry is an alternative approach to "looking for the needle in the haystack". The disadvantage of combinatorial chemistry is that many of its products often fail to pass laboratory tests for biological function.

Mendelsohn and Balick (1995) estimate that the net present value to a drug company of a successful drug developed by screening extracts from tropical plants (about 6 extracts per plant) is about $125 million before tax. Including taxes, this means that a company would only be willing to pay $0.90–$1.32 per ha of tropical forest. Since only some 38–56 screens are available to an individual firm, while there exist about 500 screens, the value of a successful drug to society is much larger, about $449 million per drug.[9] This translates into a total value of $147 billion or land value of $48 per hectare. While the authors conclude that the "potential value of undiscovered drugs is an additional incentive to conserve species-rich forests throughout the world" (p. 227), the values they provide are small and cannot, on their own, be used to justify protection of tropical species. Barbier and Aylward (1996) also note that "the potential economic returns from pharmaceutical prospecting of biodiversity are on their own insufficient justification for the establishment of porctected areas in developing countries"(p. 174).

The above values are average benefits provided by species (or total value), but preservation decisions are made at the margin and need to be justified on that basis. Focusing only on (potential) industrial, agricultural and pharmaceutical values, what is the sacrifice in value if an additional species is lost? Simpson et al. (1996), and Simpson and Sedjo (1996a, 1996b), argue that, even under the most optimistic assumptions, the value of marginal species is small, less than $10,000 at best. As the number of species increases, the value of a marginal species falls – from almost $3,000 when there are 250,000 species to a negligible amount when there are more than one million (Simpson and Sedjo 1996b).[10] If the value of marginal species is small, then, by extension, so is the value of a marginal hectare in biodiversity prospecting. This is seen in Table 9.4 where data are provided for selected tropical hotspots.

Biodiversity as a Competitive Asset

Now consider pharmaceutical value of biodiversity loss in more detail. We determine whether conservation of biodiversity is a competitive investment or not by considering various assumptions about the number of species S, and thus changes in S (ΔS). The approach is somewhat atypical as opportunity costs are not considered explicitly – the focus is exclusively on marginal benefits of conservation (or rather, the marginal cost of species extinction). The model is based on Simpson et al. (1996).

---

[9] New techniques enable scientists to stress plants and other organisms (e.g., by exposing them to light or heat) so that they produce additional genetic material not available at the time selection was made in the wild. Further, advances in automated screening enable a company to perform nearly 1 million screens a week compared to only 100 or so some 20 years ago, although this also benefits the combinatorial chemistry approach.

[10] Polasky and Solow (1995) criticise Simpson et al. (1996) for their assumption that, once a drug is found, finding the same drug by testing another species is redundant. The former suggest that, by allowing more "hits", it is possible to gain additional benefits from such things as quality improvements. Based on their analysis, however, the value of a marginal species does not increase dramatically.

Table 9.4: Maximum WTP to Preserve a Hectare for Biodiversity Prospecting, Selected Hotspots

Hotspot	Max. WTP	Hotspot	Max. WTP
Western Ecuador	$20.63	Cape Floristic province, S. Africa	$1.66
Southwestern Sri Lanka	$16.84	Peninsular Malaysia	$1.47
New Caledonia	$12.43	Southwestern Australia	$1.22
Madagascar	$6.86	Ivory Coast	$1.14
Western Ghats of India	$4.77	Northern Borneo	$0.99
Philippines	$4.66	Eastern Himalayas	$0.98
Atlantic Coast of Brazil	$4.42	Columbian Choco	$0.75
Uplands of western Amazon	$2.59	Central Chile	$0.74
Tanzania	$2.07	California Floristic province	$0.20

Source: Derived from data in Simpson et al. (1996)

Define the expected value of sampling biodiversity as $pR - c$, where p is the probability that any randomly sampled species yields a successful commercial product, R is the (net) revenue associated with such a successful "hit", and c is the cost of research and development. Sampling is treated as an independent Bernoulli trial with equal probability of success. Over time, society will demand new products, such as cures for new infectious diseases. This will increase the value of biodiversity prospecting. Define λ as the mean arrival rate of the "demand" for new products – the shocks to the demand function. The increase in total value of an additional species (i.e., marginal value) is given by:

$$(9.13) \quad V(S) = \frac{\lambda}{r} (pR - c)(1 - p)^S > 0,$$

where r is the discount rate. Due to redundancy in genetic information (once a successful product is found, further discoveries add little for that particular application), marginal value is a declining function of the number of species:

$$(9.14) \quad \frac{\partial V(S)}{\partial S} = \frac{\lambda}{r}(pR - c)(1 - p)^S [\ln(1 - p)] < 0.$$

Total economic cost as a result of losing ΔS species is measured as the relevant area under the marginal value curve, which is obtained by integrating (9.14):

$$(9.15) \quad \int_{S}^{S+\Delta S} V(S) \, dS = \frac{\lambda}{r} \frac{pR - c}{\ln(1 - p)} (1 - p)^S [(1 - p)^{\Delta S} - 1].$$

Assuming a constant rate of tropical deforestation, it is possible to compute the number of species that are projected to go extinct using the species-area curve, and then invoke (9.15) to compute the associated economic cost.

As an empirical example, in Figure 9.4, we plot the economic cost associated with decline in biodiversity (pharmaceutical benefit foregone) against various estimates of the number of extant species, using a deforestation rate of 1.0% (see Chapter 12). For the base scenario, we use the parameter values of Simpson et al. (1996): R = $450 million; c = $3,600; p = 0.000012; z = 0.3 (parameter in the species-area curve); $r = 10\%$; and $\lambda = 0.01$. The parameter values in each of the scenarios in Figure 9.4 are the same as for the base case, except in one case we double the assumed revenue of a successful hit ($R = \$900$ million) and in the other the probability of success is doubled ($p = 0.000024$).

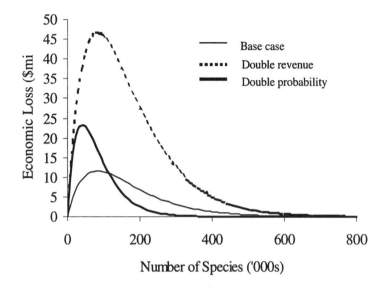

Figure 9.4 Loss of Pharmaceutical Value from 1% Habitat Reduction

The results indicate that, for the base case, economic costs are negligible for both low and high estimates of the number of species, and significant for somewhat average values. For low values of S (or few species), costs are low because the species-area curve predicts that very few species will go extinct as a result of deforestation. Costs are also low for high values of S because then the pharmaceutical value of the extinct species is negligible due to redundancy.

Essentially, marginal costs fall to zero when there exist some 600,000 species or more. The effects of doubling revenue per successful product R and doubling the probability that prospecting yields a successful commercial product p are also provided in Figure 9.4. The former increases the marginal costs of biodiversity decline, but does not qualitatively affect the main result. The latter increases the marginal value of species when there are few left, but decreases their value when biodiversity is higher. The marginal value falls relatively faster because increasing the probability of obtaining successful products from a given stock S will increase redundancy.

We conclude that uncertainty about the number of species (important to biologists) is nearly irrelevant from an economic perspective when total species exceed about 600,000. The economic cost of biodiversity decline for both modest estimates (say 4 million species) and high estimates (100 million species) are virtually zero. Further, conservation of biological assets may not represent a competitive investment. The marginal benefits of preserving species rapidly approach zero. The economic model is thus consistent with driving species to extinction for any positive opportunity cost (say, conversion of forestland to agriculture). Of course, it could be argued that benefits of biodiversity are understated when the focus is solely on pharmaceutical value.

Willingness-to-Pay for Species Preservation

Protection of species cannot be justified on the basis of their potential industrial, agricultural and pharmaceutical values. Rather, it needs to be justified by the benefits that individuals obtain from viewing (threatened or endangered) species or simply knowing that they exist. (This assumes that the species in question are not keystone species of special importance for ecosystem viability, and responsible for the ecosystem's "glue value".) Estimates of nonuse (or passive-use) values for selected wildlife species are provided in Table 9.5.

The estimates in Table 9.5 are derived from contingent valuation studies, employing either WTP to avoid loss of a species or WTP for a proposed gain in numbers. While such values are large when multiplied by the number of households, there are problems with such estimates.

Among these problems is that the link between the value assigned to a particular species and the area needed to protect its habitat is often left unspecified. If biologists are unable to make this link, one cannot always determine the opportunity cost (e.g., foregone timber production for the case of the northern spotted owl or marbled murrelet) of preserving the species, making it difficult to anchor WTP values in questionnaires. Opportunity cost is not a concern, however, if species are to be preserved at all cost. Further, the values reported in Table 9.5 cannot be added up because doing so could violate the respondent's budget constraint. Bishop and Welsch (1993) note that the adding-up problem may be mitigated if different species are considered substitutes.

> Adding up values of a number of species, ignoring that they may be substitutes ...
> could lead to theoretically invalid welfare measures. If species are substitutes, ...
> and consumers believe that several of them are about to become extinct, then
> simply adding up will overestimate their combined value. (p. 144)

Finally, economic theory suggests that the marginal utility of preservation declines as the size of the preserved stock increases – that the amount respondents are WTP to protect another individual of an animal or plant species declines as the stock of that species increases. Alternatively, people are willing to pay some amount to be sure that the species survives (i.e., that population is at least equal to the minimum viable population), plus a declining amount as the numbers of a species increases beyond MVP (Fisher 1996). Likewise, the amount people are willing to pay to preserve wilderness declines as more wilderness is available.

Table 9.5: Household WTP for Preservation of Species, 1993

Species	Gain, avoid loss or increase % chance of survival	Change in population elicited in survey (%)	Annual WTP ($US)	V if survey respondents view species; E if existence value only	Survey instrument:
Whooping crane	Avoid loss	100	31.81	E	dichotomous choice
	Avoid loss	100	49.92	V	dichotomous choice
Gray-blue whales	Avoid loss	100	33.33	E	payment card
Sea otter	avoid loss	100	28.88	E	payment card
Gray whales[a]	gain	50	17.15	E	open ended
	gain	100	19.23	E	open ended
	gain	50	26.50	V	open ended
	gain	100	31.51	V	open ended
Gray wolf	reintroduce		21.07[b]	E	dichotomous choice
	reintroduce		90.76[c]	V	dichotomous choice
Grizzly bear	hunt permit		36.58	V	open ended
Monk seal	avoid loss	100	119.70	E	dichotomous choice
Humpback whale	avoid loss	100	117.92	E	dichotomous choice
Bald eagle	avoid loss	100	15.40	E	dichotomous choice
	speed	Recovery	63.24	E	dichotomous choice
	avoid loss	100	32.94	E	dichotomous choice
	avoid loss	100	23.20	E	open ended
	gain	300	254.63	V	dichotomous choice
	gain	300	178.36	V	open ended
Striped shiner	avoid loss	100	6.04	E	dichotomous choice
Squawfish	avoid loss	100	8.42	E	open ended
Northern spotted owl	avoid loss	100	95.42	E	dichotomous choice
	chance[a]	30	28.09	E	open ended
	chance[a]	75	22.09	E	open ended
	chance[a]	100	44.25	E	open ended
Bighorn sheep	avoid loss	100	12.36	E	open ended
	hunt permit		29.86	V	open ended
Salmon and steelhead[a]	gain	100	31.29	E	open ended
	gain	100	88.40	V	open ended
Atlantic salmon	avoid loss	100	7.29	E	dichotomous choice
	avoid loss	100	8.10	E	open ended
Red-cockaded woodpecker[a]	chance[a]	99	10.64	E	open ended
	chance[a]	99	14.82	E	dichotomous choice
	chance[a]	99	9.52	E	payment card
Sea turtle	avoid loss	100	12.99	E	dichotomous choice

[a] Increase chance of survival by percentage indicated in the next column.
[b] Average of three studies.
[c] Average of four studies.
Source: Adapted from Loomis and Giraud (1997)

The vast majority of cost-benefit and contingent valuation studies have ignored these fundamental principles and focused on total WTP, with few studies having determined MVP size or measured marginal preservation benefits. Economists recognise that it is meaningless to know how much a species is worth, unless that species is at (or near) its minimum viable population.[11] Rather, one needs to think about marginal WTP to preserve species or ecosystems.

Some researchers have sought to elicit marginal WTP: Loomis and Larson (1994) for the case of gray whales; Brown et al. (1994) and Montgomery et al. (1994) for the northern spotted owl; Tanguay et al. (1993) for caribou; and Vold et al. (1994) and Rollins and Lyke (1997) for wilderness preservation in BC and Ontario, respectively. Others have used meta-analysis to estimate the relationship between WTP and changes in the availability of the public good; examples include Smith and Osborne (1996) for air pollution/visibility, Boyle et al. (1994) for groundwater quality, and Loomis and White (1996) for species preservation. However, in these and most other studies, estimated WTP is still for a rather substantial discrete change and generally not useful for policy purposes. The studies also ignore MVP, although some studies do elicit WTP to prevent total loss of the species.

To elaborate on this problem of measuring marginal WTP to preserve species or ecosystems, consider the nature of most contingent valuation studies. In general, a CVM questionnaire begins by providing survey respondents with information on some threatened or endangered species, and how past intervention (usually over-harvesting or destruction of habitat) has led to their decline. Then, the usual CV questions take one of the following forms (either in open-ended or dichotomous choice format, with only the former shown here):

1. What are you willing to pay to ban all future harvest of the species?
2. What are you willing to pay to prevent this species from going extinct?
3. What are you willing to pay for a management program that will increase the stock of the species by x animals ($x\%$) [where x is specified]?
4. What are you willing to pay to improve the chances of survival of the species by $x\%$ [where x is specified]?

Other variants have also appeared, but few enable the construction of a marginal WTP curve for preservation of the species. More often than not, total WTP to preserve the status quo level of stocks (avoid the loss of the species) is elicited (as with variants 1 and 2 above). Alternatively, if the survey elicits WTP for an increase in stocks (variant 3 and possibly 4), the respondent is not usually told how much it already costs them to maintain the current stock (a number that may not even be provided, and may not even be known), and whether she would agree to pay that amount. For example, in their review of eight groundwater quality studies, Boyle et al. (1994) point out that most studies "did not include information on the levels of these variables [contaminants] in the design of their contingent valuation survey instruments" (p. 1057). In general, albeit with some exceptions as noted above,

---

[11]Admittedly, the MVP concept is controversial (partly because of interdependence among species) and that is why we use the term "near". In some cases, harvest of animals is possible without having any bearing on the possibility of their extinction. People are likely willing to pay some amount to guarantee a species' survival (that population is at MVP or higher), but only declining additional amounts for numbers beyond MVP. CVM studies do not make this distinction, however (Fisher1996).

information about marginal WTP for preservation is not available; see, for example, Table 9.5. We illustrate the importance of minimum viable population and marginal considerations in the next chapters.

9.4 Nature Conservation and Protected Areas

Opinions are divided on how best to conserve biodiversity, with the debate often polarised between advocates of the so-called species approach and the ecosystem approach to conservation. The former emphasise the protection, both *in situ* and *ex situ*, of endangered, high-profile, vertebrate species, while the latter aim to set aside entire natural ecosystems that will capture as much species and diversity as possible. In Chapter 10, we focus on conservation of certain endangered species that require (networks of) protected areas for *in situ* conservation. Advocates of the systems approach argue that targeting of species implies that a few bird and mammal species receive almost all attention and dollars (which is consistent with actual ESA experience). On the other hand, advocates of the species approach may counter by arguing that charismatic mega fauna such as elephants and rhinos can play a key role in motivating conservation of certain areas, thereby enhancing survival probabilities of many less "appealing" species (a free rider effect). Selection of areas for this purpose would be easier and more effective if the following two propositions are true:

1. Habitats that are species rich for one taxon are also species rich for others.
2. Rare or endangered species occur in species-rich habitats.

Prendergast et al. (1993) have tested these propositions for Britain and found little support for either one: "species-rich areas ('hotspots') frequently do not coincide for different taxa, and many rare species do not occur in the most species-rich squares" (p. 335). Given limited areas available for *in situ* conservation, policy makers may face tradeoffs between conserving different groups of organisms, and also between conserving diversity *per se* and certain rare (high-profile?) species.

Soulé (1991) argues that the above dichotomy is false as it ignores the social context. He distinguishes eight different paths, or tactics, for biotic survival, varying by the degree to which it is artificial as represented by the level of human intrusion. He distinguishes:

1. *in situ* conservation (e.g., protected areas)
2. *inter situ* conservation (conservation outside protected areas, often times on relatively infertile lands)
3. extractive reserves (exploitation on a sustainable basis)
4. intensively managed ecological restoration projects
5. "zooparks" in secure locations for sensitive species
6. intensively managed production systems, such as agro-ecosystems and agroforestry projects
7. *ex situ* programs (e.g., botanical gardens and zoos)
8. completely artificial *ex situ* storage programs (e.g., germplasm and seed banks)

Successful nature conservation likely requires some combination of each of these forms of protection. According to Soulé, the level of population pressure and political stability will determine which approach is needed. For example, in areas of high population pressure, extractive reserves and agro-ecology systems may be more successful than wilderness parks in conserving biodiversity. Erwin (1991) notes that many protected areas exist only "on paper". This is consistent with Soulé's (1991) observation that, when either population pressure is high and/or political stability is low, protected areas may be poor vehicles to promote biodiversity conservation. Backup *ex situ* facilities may then be justified.

Protecting representative habitats will be a component of most conservation programs. In 1991, some 5% of the earth's land surface was protected (WCMC 1992, p. 451), although Erwin (1991) argues that no more than 3.2% of the planet's landmass was protected. Today, perhaps 7% of the globe's land surface is protected (see Table 9.8 below). The Brundtland Commission (WCED 1987) suggests that 20% of tropical forestlands be protected (p. 152), and that there be a three-fold increase in the amount of land set aside for species and ecosystem preservation (pp. 165–66). As a result, there appears to be international consensus that, as a rule of thumb, nations should commit 12% of their land base to protect biological resources. Therefore, many countries have either formulated or are in the course of designing plans to move towards this target. Is this an adequate level of protection?

Economic considerations

Although the initial purpose for maintaining scenic landscapes was for recreational use, the concept of protected areas has evolved, in recent years, to encompass habitats of endangered species and ecosystems rich in biodiversity (WCMC 1992). Protected areas constitute *in situ* protection of biodiversity and other environmental values. Along with *ex situ* facilities, they help sustain many species, including some in serious danger of extinction. But the establishment of protected areas was not originally oriented towards the conservation of biological diversity. In the past, it was often the case that protected areas were limited in size, while *ex situ* collections contained relatively little genetic material. Many parks were simply too small effectively to conserve intact ecosystems or provide for their inhabitants. For example, a considerable number of animals range outside park boundaries during certain seasons to find food (World Resources Institute 1992).

Creation of protected areas has not gone unopposed. Two reasons for this include lack of input from the grass-roots level and conflict with the local community's interest. In many developing countries, colonial administrators were the first to pass wildlife laws. The tendency has been to form "pristine areas" and evict local people, often without compensation. Hence, benefits from protected areas frequently extend beyond the sites to society at large (e.g., in the form of existence values, or hunting benefits for an international elite). Cost on the other hand are borne by local people, who have (forcibly) been moved or are bound by excessive restrictions in their use of these areas. By removing the incentives of local peoples in managing the areas for local benefits, non-sustainable activities, such as "illegal" land conversion and poaching, are difficult to avoid (see, e.g., Milner-Gulland and Leader-

Williams 1992a). Of course, there is also evidence that decentralising of property rights has had negative effects on the resource base. People may choose to exploit (common property) natural resources in an unsustainable fashion, or inefficiently, due to imperfect control by local communities. This may result in overexploitation and degradation of the resource (e.g., Lopez 1998; Baland and Platteau 1996).

Other problems have been ineffective management and insufficient funding to maintain protected areas. In many countries, the responsibility for managing protected areas is scattered among various agencies or ministries. Ironically, in many countries where parks are major sources of tourist revenue, very little is reinvested in conservation. A recent survey of protected areas suggested that development is seen to be the most common threat in North America, Europe and Oceania; Asia has suffered from inadequate management; protected areas in Africa are exposed to poaching; and regions in South America are particularly vulnerable to fire (World Resources Institute 1992).

Poaching is a particular problem in many developing countries because the values of products from some endangered and threatened species, such as rhinoceros, elephants, tigers and bears, are high compared to the incomes of people living in the regions where animals are found. This is illustrated in Table 9.6 for the case of tigers. Such high values suggest that it may be difficult to stop all illegal harvest activities, even within protected areas. This is discussed further in Chapter 10 where the economics of poaching are also examined.

Table 9.6: Average Prices Paid for Tiger Bones in Selected Countries (US$)

Country	per Kg	Value of whole animal	Average GDP per person
Cambodia	100	1,700	200
China	31–126	527–2,142	435
India	15–200	255–3,400	310
Laos	12–76	204–1,292	230
Nepal	100–130	1,700–2,200	180
Vietnam	100–375	1,700–6,375	220
Russia	20–300	340–5,100	2,100

Source: McNeely et al. (1995, p. 779)

The last decade has seen changes in strategies concerning protected areas. New conservation techniques that address the root causes of biodiversity loss are being implemented in several countries. One example is the CAMPFIRE project in Zimbabwe, where the local population has been granted user rights for wildlife and where some of the proceeds of safari hunting and tourism are returned to the community. CAMPFIRE gives locals a stake in conservation of scarce resources, and may reduce own "poaching" effort and tolerance for outside poachers (Hertzler and Gomera 1998).

One alternative is bio-regional management, a method that works for areas with high biodiversity value. This approach requires the establishment of a management regime to coordinate land-use planning of both public and private properties, and to define development options that will meet human needs without diminishing biodiversity. Bio-regional management attempts to manage whole regions with biodiversity in mind, while involving local people and integrating ecological, economic, cultural and managerial considerations at the regional scale. It represents a departure from the traditional practice characterised by arbitrary division of government responsibilities into isolated forestry, agriculture, parks and fishery sectors. With a view to integrating ecological, social and economic considerations, the bio-regional approach depends on eliciting cooperation among various interests for success, requiring cross-sectoral and, in some cases, transboundary cooperation and integration, as well as broad participation by all affected constituencies (World Resources Institute 1992).

Three priorities for selecting nature preserves that protect wildlife habitat have been suggested (Pressey et al. 1993).

1. Complementarity or efficiency recognises that there is a limit to the land and water area that can be devoted to conservation and, thus, seeks to protect a target representation of species with the smallest number of sites. The economist would be less concerned with the number of sites, focusing instead on reducing costs of providing sites to their lowest level.
2. Since the many indices of biodiversity are non-unique, there is a (large) degree of flexibility in the choice of sites to achieve the desired protection of species. This means that there is flexibility to choose sites in a manner that minimises the costs of their provision.
3. Finally, it is important to include sites that are irreplaceable – options for reservation are lost if the site is lost.

In applications of algorithms that attempt to meet these plus other criteria, it became evident that a rather small subset of the total sites available for reservation was needed (Csuti et al. 1997; Williams et al. 1996). In Oregon, it turns out that only 23 of 441 sites are needed to protect all 426 species of terrestrial vertebrates, while, surprisingly, sites of maximum species richness were found east of the Cascade Mountains as opposed to the temperate rain forests (Csuti et al. 1997). Although based on biological as opposed to economic concerns, the conclusion is that current policies likely attempt to protect too much area, with redundancy in terms of the species that do get protected while neglecting other species.

Using data on WTP for wilderness and species protection, van Kooten (1995b,c) found that British Columbia's policy to protect 12% of the land base was inefficient in economic terms – costs greatly exceeded benefits. It turns out that marginal benefits of wilderness (and wildlife habitat) protection decline to zero beyond about 14% (van Kooten 1995b). Marginal costs of protecting wilderness from all but the most benign activities are substantial; as a result, the economically optimal level of protection is probably closer to 6–8% (see also Chapter 11 where protection of temperate rain forest is considered). While a lower level of protection can easily be justified on biodiversity grounds, it is also important to target protection – reducing protection of redundant sites (e.g., large areas of temperate rain forest) while increasing protection of interior range lands.

In Chapter 12, we turn to tropical rain forest conservation, arguing that there is currently too much tropical forest because the opportunity costs of forest preservation (or the agricultural benefits foregone had the land been cleared) are often considerable. When balancing benefits and costs of habitat conservation, however, it is often assumed that development does not really constitute an irreversible process (or that similar habitat is available at some other location). Hence, quasi-option value is ignored. Ignoring quasi-option value implies underestimating the benefits of conservation.

Changes have taken place in recent years in the philosophy of protected areas management. Newly adopted programs have invariably expanded their focus. For example, the protection of freshwater and marine areas has grown in importance. In this regard, the Canadian government has expanded the National Parks system to include national marine parks, with some six national marine parks to be in place by the year 2000 (Government of Canada 1990, 1991). In this regard, Australia's Great Barrier Reef Marine Park, in which a large marine ecosystem and adjacent mainland areas are managed for sustainable development, is widely acclaimed as a success.

Defining protected areas

By definition, protected areas refer to sites that remain relatively undisturbed by humans and close to their natural state (Dixon and Sherman 1990). Several issues deserve clarification. First, the above definition does not necessarily refer only to areas that are extremely remote geographically or inaccessible because of topographical restrictions. We are primarily concerned with natural areas that are in danger of conversion, areas that are becoming increasingly scarce, or areas that are at risk. Second, the concept of a particular type of area becoming scarce or at risk embodies the recognition of agreed upon criteria that serve as a basis for making this determination. Criteria have been developed by the IUCN.

To be specific, the term "protected area" is an area of at least 1,000 hectares in IUCN management categories I–V (defined below), and managed by the highest competent authority, generally government or an internationally recognised NGO. Finally, the action required to establish a protected area needs to be specified and, once a protected area is created, the activities that are allowed should be clearly spelled out. In the current discussion, protected areas are designated natural areas such as ecological reserves, national or provincial parks, wilderness areas, and wetlands – any designation aimed at keeping natural areas relatively intact and restricting commercial development. The types of activities permitted include recreation, education and scientific research, and other uses sanctioned by IUCN agreements. IUCN categories of protected areas have been developed according to the perceived degree of human intervention.

The idea of protected areas was first championed by the IUCN in 1959 when it was awarded the task of maintaining a list of the world's national parks and equivalent reserves. Through its Commission on National Parks and Protected Areas (CNPPA), the IUCN has defined ten categories of conservation areas representing different levels of protection from strict nature reserves to multiple-use areas, all with varying degrees of local, regional and global importance. The categories are arranged in ascending order according to the degree of human use permitted.

I.   *Scientific reserve/strict nature reserve* The objective is to protect nature and
       maintain natural processes in an undisturbed state in order to have

312 Biological Diversity and Habitat

ecologically representative examples of the natural environment available for scientific study, environmental monitoring and education, and for the maintenance of genetic resources in a dynamic and evolutionary state.

II.   *National park* National parks are large natural and scenic areas of national or international significance for scientific, educational and recreational use. They are managed by the highest competent authority of a nation.

III.   *Natural monument/natural landmark* The objective is to protect and preserve nationally-significant natural features because of their special interest or unique characteristics.

IV.   *Managed nature reserve/wildlife sanctuary* These protected areas ensure the natural conditions necessary to protect nationally-significant species, groups of species, biotic communities or physical features of the environment requiring human intervention for their perpetuation.

V.   *Protected landscape* The objective of protected landscapes is to maintain nationally-significant natural areas characteristic of the harmonious interaction of people and land, while still providing opportunities for public enjoyment through recreation and tourism within the normal life-style and economic activity of these areas.

VI.   *Resource reserve* The objective of these protected areas is to maintain the natural resources of an area for future use, curbing development pending the establishment of objectives.

VII.   *Natural biotic area/anthropological reserve* This protected form enables existing societies living in harmony with the environment to continue their way of life undisturbed by modern technology.

VIII. *Multiple-use management area/managed resource area* These protected areas provide for the sustained production of timber, wildlife, forage and outdoor recreation, as well as waste assimilation; the conservation of nature is primarily oriented to the support of economic activities, although specific zones can also be designated within these areas to achieve specific conservation objectives.

IX.   *Biosphere reserves* Biosphere reserves are designed to preserve sites of exceptional richness with respect to the diversity and integrity of biotic communities of plants and animals within natural ecosystems for research, education and training purposes.

X.   *World heritage sites* The objective of a world heritage site is to protect unique natural and cultural sites of outstanding universal significance.

Of these categories, the last two are regarded international designations. Categories I, II and III are considered to be regions where protection is total, whereas IV and V are considered sites where protection is only partial. A summary of the most important features of each of the designations is provided in Table 9.7.

Table 9.7: IUCN Framework for Protected Areas Classification

	Designation	Main Uses
I	Scientific reserves and wilderness areas	Scientific research and education
II	National parks and equivalent reserves	Scientific research, education & managed recreation
III	Natural monuments	Scientific research, education & managed recreation
IV	Habitat and wildlife management areas	Scientific research, education & managed recreation
V	Protected landscapes and seascapes	Managed recreation

Source: World Conservation Monitoring Centre (1992)

Global distribution of protected areas: General trends

Areas that are in some sense "protected", in that access or forms of use are controlled, have existed for thousands of years. For instance, in India, protected areas in the form of forest reserves have existed since the fourth century BC, while hunting reserves have existed in Europe for several hundred years. Although these "protected areas" were exclusively used by the upper classes, they did serve the purpose of preserving biodiversity. Creating protected areas for the general public is a practice with a much recent history. In 1861, the first protected area in the world was created – Yosemite National Park in California (World Resources Institute 1992). A decade later, in 1872, Yellowstone was proclaimed a national park by the US government (Conservation Foundation 1987). Emulating the USA, many countries had either created national parks or developed plans for their creation by the beginning of this century. It was not until the 1940s, however, that protected areas began to be established in any significant number. Along with an increase in the number of protected areas and the acreage they covered, the importance of developing a comprehensive management system for protected areas was gaining recognition.

The World Parks Congress was first convened in Seattle in 1962. The conference attracted the attention of many governments and proved a catalyst for international efforts in the establishment of protected areas. For instance, prior to 1962, the entire number of sites under protection was 1,433, covering 1,324,600 square kilometres. During the 10-year period 1962–1971 alone, a total of 1,372 more sites were added under various categories of protection; and 4,422,600 km^2 was designated as protected in the two decades following the Seattle conference, thereby more than tripling the pre–1962 area. In this connection, the creation of Greenland National Park (97 million ha) in 1974 and the Great Barrier Reef Marine Park (34 million ha) in the 1980s had a marked effect on the total area that is currently protected as nature preserve (WCMC 1992).

Most of the early parks were designated in countries that today are considered developed. The establishment of parks in low-income countries did not occur until much later. The first national park in Asia, for instance, was Corbett National Park, established in India in 1935 (Dixon and Sherman 1990). By 1982, fewer than half of the developing countries had established any national parks (Blower 1984). Since the mid–1970s, however, most of the new national parks have been located in developing countries (Malik 1984).

The global increase in protected areas is shown in Figure 9.5. As of 1992 and judged by IUCN criteria, protected areas exist in 169 countries, compared to 136 countries in 1985. As of 1994 (the latest year for which data are available), there are nearly 9,800 sites covering some 960 million ha, or around 7.5% of the earth's land area (Table 9.8).

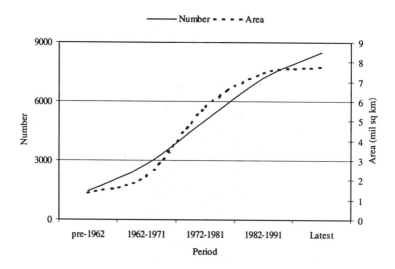

Figure 9.5 Global Increase in Numbers and Area Protected

Table 9.8: Protected Areas by Continent

Continent/	All Protected Areas			% of Land Area[a]		
Country	Number	Area ('000s ha)	Totally[b]	Partially[c]	All Categories
Africa	727	149,541	2.68	2.08	4.94
Asia	1,774	141,793	1.73	4.13	4.40
Europe	2,923	223,905	2.23	8.57	8.90
N. & C. America	2,549	230,199	7.58	4.88	10.23
Oceania	1,087	100,282	4.50	7.34	11.75
S. America	706	112,834	3.77	2.53	6.33
WORLD	**9,793**	**959,568**	**3.23**	**3.04**	**7.15**
Major Timber Producing Countries					
Canada	627	82,358	2.70	2.28	8.26
Chile	66	13,725	11.14	7.12	18.13
Finland	81	2,744	1.50	0.90	8.12
New Zealand	182	6,067	9.76	1.22	22.39
Russian Federation	209	70,536	1.07	0.02	4.13
Sweden	197	2,982	1.10	5.39	6.63
United States	1,585	130,209	4.10	6.38	13.27

Source: WCMC (1992, pp. 460–63) and UN Environmental Program (1995, p. 983).
[a] Data on totally and partially protected areas are for 1992; data for all categories are for 1994.
[b] IUCN categories I, II and III that prohibit extractive use.
[c] IUCN categories IV and V that permit local sustainable extractive use.

The largest protected area is Greenland National Park, covering 97.2 million ha. Some 1,400 sites covering more than 300 million ha have marine or coastal elements within them, and the largest marine protected area is Great Barrier Reef Marine Park (34 million ha). The median size of a protected area is only 10–30 km^2 (1,000–3,000 ha), however, and the majority of the world's protected areas are contained in a relatively few large sites.

Managed nature reserves/wildlife sanctuaries (category IV) are the most prevalent type of IUCN protected area in terms of site numbers, while national parks (category II) cover more area than any other category. Information collected by the WCMC (1992) and the UN Environmental Program (1995) indicates that, despite a global coverage of protected areas of 6.3%, there is considerable variation between countries and continents (Table 9.8). For most countries, the protected areas network covers less than 5% of the surface area. It has been an accepted approach that, for the sake of simplified comparison, categories I–V are divided into two groups, namely, totally protected areas with no extractive use (categories I, II and III), and partially protected areas with local sustainable extractive use (categories IV and V). One variation treats categories I and II as sites under strict protection in the sense that the use of these areas is much more restricted than for other categories (BC Ministry of Environment, Lands and Parks and Environment Canada 1993).

Of the world total, Europe accounts for the most number of sites, while North and Central America account for the greatest area of protection. Together with Oceania, North and Central America protect the largest proportion of their land area, and these regions are closest to the 12% target (Table 9.8). While Europe and South America protect significant proportions of their respective land areas, they still have some distance to go in achieving the target set by the Brundtland Commission, or WCED. Africa and Asia lag other regions in protecting biodiversity.

Because the IUCN categories are arranged according to the degree of human use permitted, there is a considerable variation in protected area designations among continents. For example, Asia has established a greater number of managed nature reserve/wildlife sanctuaries (category IV) than any other region. Europe has excelled in the creation of protected landscapes. North and Central America have the largest areas in national parks. South America seems to have made an even effort in developing all types of protected areas, whereas Oceania has concentrated its endeavours on national parks and managed nature reserves/wildlife sanctuaries. Africa has demonstrated a high degree of commitment to the establishment of national parks, wildlife sanctuaries and managed nature reserves. One other distinct region is the former Soviet Union. Its area of scientific reserves for strict nature protection purpose is, in absolute terms, nearly half the world's category I coverage, but, on a relative basis, it is at the bottom in terms of establishing strict nature reserves.

Ultimately it is not important how much land gets protected in total, but how much of various important biomes get protected. Protecting rock and ice may be important, but not if it comes at the expense of tropical rainforests, for example. To provide some indication of how global society is doing with respect to protecting ecosystem variety, consider Table 9.9. The data indicate that, while protection of subtropical and temperate rainforests is approaching the 12% level, protection of tropical rainforests is lagging. Protection of grassland ecosystems, particularly in temperate regions, might be a priority, but perhaps such ecosystems are not as threatened as others or have little biodiversity. It might also be the case that such areas are expensive to protect because they are privately held. This may be the case for other biomes as well, whereas others simply appear to have been neglected, perhaps because they do not conjure up the same images as those associated with tropical and temperate rainforests, or grasslands with various large wildlife herbivores and their predators.

Table 9.9: Distribution of Protected Areas by Biome Type

Biome Type	Number	Area (mil ha)	%
Tropical humid forests	506	53.8	5.1
Subtropical/temperate rainforests/woodlands	899	36.6	9.3
Temperate needle-leaf forests/woodlands	429	48.7	3.1
Tropical dry forests/woodlands	799	81.6	4.7
Temperate broad-leaf forests	1507	35.8	3.2
Evergreen sclerophyllous forests	776	17.8	4.7
Warm deserts/semi-deserts	300	98.4	4.1
Cold-winter deserts	136	36.5	3.9
Tundra communities	78	164.5	7.5
Tropical grasslands/savannahs	59	23.5	5.5
Temperate grasslands	194	10.0	0.8
Mixed mountain systems	1277	85.2	8.0
Mixed island systems	530	32.3	9.9
Lake systems	17	0.7	1.3

Source: United Nations Environmental Program (1995, p. 988)

An indication of the level of protection provided by major wood product producing and exporting countries is provided in the lower half of Table 9.8. The data indicate that, as of 1994, Chile, New Zealand and the USA had been able to attain the 12% target, protecting some 18%, 22% and 13% of their land areas, respectively. In the past several years, all of the major forest product exporters have made large strides in increasing areas officially protected. This may well be a response to lobbying by environmental groups and international efforts to certify forest products (see Chapter 11).

Of the OECD countries, Australia, Japan, Germany, the United Kingdom, Austria, New Zealand, Norway, Switzerland and the United States have now surpassed the 12% benchmark, but many countries are making efforts to do so. Thus, statistics are misleading because they are outdated or, in the case of Canada and Russia, vast forest areas are protected de facto, simply because such areas are beyond the extensive margin – they are not developed because infrastructure is inadequate, while net returns are too low. Relying on 1994 data, Russia officially protects some 4.1% of its land base, while Canada protects 8.3% and has committed to attain or exceed the 12% mark early in the next century. It is clear that most of the OECD countries have designated more sites under partially protected categories, and this feature is particularly conspicuous in Western Europe. From the early 1980s to the early 1990s, virtually all OECD countries have experienced growth in protected areas to varying degrees, with the greatest growth occurring in Denmark, Germany and Switzerland (see also Figure 9.5).

The world's 9.8 million ha of protected area is scattered among 169 countries or territories, but it is mainly concentrated in 17 countries that each have more than ten million hectares (ha) jointly account for 45% of total protected sites and 73% of area.

In terms of per capita availability of protected areas, the world average in the early 1990s was 0.15 ha per person. Oceania is well ahead of all other continents with 3.19 ha per person, while North/Central America is four times the world's average. South America and Africa are both above the world's average, while Europe and Asia are below it. Among OECD countries, Australia leads in the per capita protection of ecosystems, followed by Canada (Table 9.10).

Table 9.10: Per Capita Availability of Protected Areas, Selected OECD Countries, 1990

Country/ group	Population (millions)	Protected areas (thousand ha)	per capita (ha)
Canada	26.52	49452.3	1.86
USA	249.22	98239.9	0.39
Japan	123.46	4663.5	0.04
Australia	16.87	81309.4	4.82
EU-12	341.20	22892.1	0.07
Scandinavia	17.63	8708.9	0.49
World	**5,292.20**	**773,490.1**	**0.15**

Source: World Resources Institute (1992) and WCMC (1992)

It is not surprising that the distribution of protected areas varies with income levels in countries. For instance, the high-income countries that belong to the OECD account for 55.5% of the total number of protected sites and 34.6% of total protected areas.[12] In contrast, low-income countries, large or small, have fewer sites and a smaller total area (Table 9.11).

Table 9.11: Distribution of Protected Areas by Income Group, 1990

Income group	Number	% of total number	Area (km^2)	% of total area
low income (large)	758	8.9	421,300	5.5
low income (small)	734	8.6	1,067,300	13.8
middle income (lower)	1,051	12.4	1,338,500	17.3
middle income (upper)	1,126	13.3	1,200,400	15.5
high income (OECD)	4,713	55.5	2,677,100	34.6
high income (non-OECD)	62	0.7	990,600	12.8
income not assigned	47	0.6	39,700	0.5
TOTAL	**8,491**	**100.0**	**7,734,900**	**100.0**

Source: WCMC (1992).

---

[12] Income classes are based on World Bank classification of per capita income of a country's economy. The low-income class is subdivided according to country size, with "large" including China and India.

9.5. Conclusions

Biological diversity involves a large number of considerations ranging from measurement to implementation of conservation programs. Economists clearly have a contribution to make in thinking about biodiversity and, particularly, as it relates to public policy. Many issues remain unresolved, not the least of which is that of determining policies concerning species extinction. In this regard, biologists must be more forthright about extant rates of extinction and beliefs about future extinctions and their supposed causes. In so doing, policy issues and misconceptions about the roles of economic development and population growth, as well as that of policy formulation, can better be addressed.

Economic evidence suggests that, at the margin, random loss of species is not terribly important. Further, while the value of the earth's ecosystem services and natural capital is large (Costanza et al. 1997), costs of *in situ* preservation of species in representative ecosystems may well exceed benefits at the margin. One challenge, therefore, is to make a stronger case for sacrificing economic development benefits for increased protection of biodiversity. Another challenge is to focus to a greater extent on the potential of scientific principles of ecosystem management as a means for obtaining economic development benefits while maintaining or even enhancing biodiversity. After all, "hands off" is itself a form of management, but one that might be less efficient in providing the sorts of ecosystem benefits (including biodiversity) that society desires.

Economic evidence suggests that, at the margin, random loss of species is not terribly important. Further, while the value of the earth's ecosystem services and natural capital is large (Costanza et al. 1997), costs of *in situ* preservation of species in representative ecosystems may well exceed benefits at the margin. One challenge, therefore, is to make a stronger case for sacrificing economic development benefits for increased protection of biodiversity. Another challenge is to focus to a greater extent on the potential of scientific principles of ecosystem management as a means for obtaining economic development benefits while maintaining or even enhancing biodiversity. After all, "hands off" is itself a form of management, but one that might be less efficient in providing the sorts of ecosystem benefits (including biodiversity) that society desires.

10 Threatened and Endangered Species

In Chapter 7, we discussed the economics of extinction, the notion of endangered species as "assets", and the concept of a minimum viable population (MVP). In this chapter, we extend the treatment of endangered species by considering the conservation of elephants, rhinos and African herbivores in more detail. The methodologies and some conclusions apply to other species.

In the next section, we consider international conventions on biodiversity and "trade" in biodiversity more generally. Then, in section 10.2, we focus on a particular trade convention, the ban on international trade in ivory, because there is conflicting evidence about its effectiveness. More generally, however, we set out to explore some of the issues involved in conservation of an endangered species. More specifically, we analyse whether a ban on the trade in ivory is beneficial for elephants and economic well being.[1] For this purpose we employ increasingly complex and realistic models to evaluate the pros and cons of banning trade. Both those favouring the trade ban and those wishing to eliminate it have valid arguments to support their positions, and the main economic arguments in favour of and against the ivory trade ban are presented. We also explore the (possibly adverse) consequences of international compensation for nonuse values.

We also explore the potential of game cropping as a method to encourage landowners to preserve threatened or endangered species. In some countries, landowners graze domestic livestock (cattle, sheep and goats), ignoring wild herbivores altogether or actively seeking their demise as the wildlife compete with domestic animals for scarce forage resources. We employ the dynamic optimisation models developed in Chapter 7 to examine the case where certain rights to large wildlife herbivores are transferred from the state to landowners. The questions that we wish to consider are as follows: will a transfer of such rights increase numbers of wildlife (i.e., result in conservation)? To what extent do rights have to be transferred, and what happens when transfer of rights is incomplete? These issues are addressed in section 10.3.

---

[1] It is increasingly recognised that some species, such as elephants, play an important role in ecosystem dynamics, although they may not be "keystone species". Elephants do have the capacity to alter the landscape and, thereby, the ecosystem. There are obvious disadvantages to ecological studies of a single species (see Budiansky 1995), although it has been argued that safeguarding elephants ensures ecosystem and other species survival (Leakey and Lewin 1995).

In section 10.4, we examine a particular controversy related to international cooperation in the area of whale preservation. We apply the theory of Chapter 7, along with nonmarket values, to determine optimal stocks of minke whales. The results also indicate the extent to which whales can be harvested in sustainable fashion.

10.1 Protecting Biological Diversity by Treaties

Concern over loss of biodiversity has sparked a number of international conventions designed to protect various aspects related to biodiversity. A list of global conventions is provided in Table 10.1, but various regional agreements have also been struck (World Conservation Monitoring Centre 1992, pp. 488–9; also see Sandler 1997, p. 16). Nations act when it is in their interest, as international treaties cannot typically be enforced by third parties. The design of self-enforcing treaties is, therefore, a key issue. Depending on the circumstances, only outcomes that are not much different from non-cooperative ones may be negotiated, although sometimes compliance can be promoted by side payments. Compliance might also be promoted by coupling separate issues, such as nature conservation and trade concessions, something known as "issue linking". Barrett (1998) notes that testing theories "in this field is often difficult because we can only observe the outcome in which countries possibly sustain some cooperation, ... [and can] only try to infer what counterfactual outcomes might look like" (p. 317). For example, had there been credible mechanisms for deterring free riding, different environmental treaties may have been negotiated in the past. In any event, international treaties tend to contain escape clauses or lack an effective enforcement mechanism. Barrett (1998) describes the process and outcomes of environmental treaty making in some detail, and discusses some of the pitfalls in arriving at cooperative solutions.

Table 10.1: Some Global Conventions/Multilateral Treaties Related to Biodiversity

Year	Place	Treaty/Convention Name
1951	Rome	International Plant Protection Convention
1958	Geneva	Convention on Fishing and Conservation of the Living Resources of the High Seas
1958	Geneva	Convention on the High Seas
1971	Ramsar, Iran	Convention on Wetlands of International Importance Especially as Waterfowl Habitat
1972	Paris	Convention concerning the Protection of the World Cultural and Natural Heritage
1973	Washington	Convention on International Trade in Endangered Species of Wild Fauna and Flora
1979	Bonn	Convention on the Conservation of Migratory Species of Wild Animals
1982	Montego Bay	United Nations' Convention on the Law of the Sea (establishing 200 nautical mile, or 360 km, Exclusive Economic Zones)
1983	Geneva	International Tropical Timber Agreement
1992	Rio de Janeiro	United Nations' Framework Convention on Climate Change United Nations' Convention on Biological Diversity

Source: WCMC (1992, p. 488)

Consider some real-world examples of treaty making from the fishery. Munro et al. (1998) examine the inability of Canada and the United States to renegotiate the Pacific Salmon Treaty (see also Harris 1998). Canada and the USA have attempted jointly to manage the Pacific salmon since about 1900. A formal treaty, whereby the two countries equally shared the direct costs of salmon enhancement on the Fraser River as well as salmon harvests, was ratified in 1937. It was a highly successful treaty that lasted until the early 1960s when Canada realised that it incurred substantial indirect costs that it alone bore (e.g., inability to develop the Fraser River for hydro power). In order to bring the USA to the bargaining table, Canadians increased fishing effort and intercepted salmon bound for Washington and Oregon. The two-player (Canada-US) game of the 1930s had, by the 1980s, become a four-player game (Alaska, Washington & Oregon, Washington & Oregon natives, and Canada). This made it difficult to achieve agreement because Alaska had the most to lose from any agreement, with benefits going to the other parties. Further, Alaska's stocks of salmon were not being depleted and fish were abundant (partly as a result of the El Nino in the mid–1990s).

In 1985, there was a truce in the "fish war" because Washington and Oregon, and WA & OR natives, made a side-payment to Alaska, but this soon collapsed and the "war" resumed. Between the late 1980s and mid–1990s, the price of salmon declined by some 50%, mainly as a result of increased supply from aquaculture. To maintain incomes of fishers, Alaska had the incentive to increase its harvests. Whereas in 1985 "there was an expectation that the United States and Canada would present an example to the world of cooperative resource management and the mutual benefits which can flow therefrom" (Munro et al. 1998, pp. 1–2), quite the opposite remains the case. As of 1999, there is an ongoing fish war between Canada and the USA.[2] If two developed countries that are considered good neighbours cannot reach agreement to manage a common property resource, this does not bode well for agreements to manage the global commons.

As a second example, consider an agreement to limit whaling, where there has been more success partly because the resource's value is much smaller. Barrett (1998) points out that

1. the Soviet Union, through the offices of the KGB, falsified the data it submitted to the International Whaling Commission (IWC);
2. Iceland withdrew from the IWC after the majority of the parties to this agreement sought to ban whaling for animal welfare reasons;
3. restrictions on whaling resulted in pirate whaling, which was partly noncompliance by another name as, for example, Japanese whalers could get around restrictions by re-registring their vessels under the flag of non-party states; and
4. Norway and the Netherlands withdrew from the IWC in a dispute over quota setting in the 1950s, only to rejoin in the early 1960s when quotas were raised.

---

[2] In 1999 some stocks of US salmon were listed as endangered under ESA. This changes the "game", perhaps proving to be the catalyst for achieving an agreement.

Sandler (1997) argues that cooperation is facilitated when

1. the problem at hand concerns both present and future generations (as opposed to only future generations),
2. uncertainty is small,
3. fewer nations are needed to address the exigency, and
4. there are considerable local benefits.

For all these reasons, addressing global warming is expected to be much harder than, for example, ozone shield depletion. This is consistent with actual experience; the latter problem has been successfully tackled by the 1987 Montreal protocol, whereas the former issue continues primarily to be a subject of debate. For example, the December 1997 Kyoto agreement for reducing emissions of CO_2 failed to include mandatory trade sanctions on non-complying nations, while developing countries were excluded. (Further discussion of the Kyoto Protocol and the role of carbon uptake in forest ecosystems in provided in Chapter 11.)

Efforts to conserve biodiversity in general, and certain prominent species in particular, may yield substantial local benefits, both to current and future generations. One reason for protecting larger wildlife species is that they provide economic benefits to the countries where they are found. For example, the elephant and white rhinoceros are often considered "flagship" species because tourists are drawn to countries for the primary purpose of viewing such species. Each elephant's tourist-related worth is estimated at US$14,375 per year in Kenya (Khanna and Harford 1996).

Wildlife have other uses that contribute to the economic well being of residents. A summary of different uses and their value for Zimbabwe is found in Table 10.2. The value of wildlife is lowest when animals are used for meat (consumed by local populations – last three columns in Table 10.2).

Table 10.2: Uses and Economic Value of Wildlife Promoted in Zimbabwe, 1992

Type of Management	Gross Return (US$/ha)	Net Return (US$/ha)	Net return as % of gross return (%)
Mass tourism	100	50	100
Exclusive tourism	50	25	100
International safari hunting	7.5	5	200
Sale of live animals	5	2.5	100
Meat, hides and products	2.5	1	66
Subsistence hunting	1	0.5	100
Cattle ranching	15	3	20

Source: Edwards (1995, p. 226)

Where conservation of a particular endangered species is desired, the number of host countries involved is often relatively modest (viz. the orang-utan that is only found on Sumatra and Borneo). This implies that the prospects for international cooperation are likely favourable. However, on the side of the non-host countries, there may be considerable uncertainty about future use, as well as the nonuse values of biodiversity, that prevent them from agreeing to help (compensate) host countries for preserving species. As for the host country, the opportunity cost of conservation (foregone agricultural expansion or mining opportunities) may be significant, probably outweighing the (local) benefits of nature conservation. To the extent that conservation of nature and biodiversity yields transboundary nonuse benefits, failure to devise compensation schemes (actual, in-kind or other) could bode ill for the species to be conserved.

International cooperation can take many forms, with Swanson (1992) identifying four.

1. Direct funding constitutes a flow of money for the compensation of nonuse assets. Examples include the Global Environmental Facility, which was established to facilitate and fund environmental protection programs in low-income countries (see Chapter 1), and the World Heritage Convention, which was adopted by the UN in 1972 and provides funds to countries for preserving eligible world heritage sites. As we discuss later in this chapter, a drawback of funding programs might be collusion on the part of recipients. Swanson (1992, p. 73) identifies uncertainty and instability in funding as a problem for nature preservation and compensation of nonmarket amenities, because donor payments are largely voluntary.

2. In-kind reciprocity involves mutual commitments by participating countries. For example, Canada might be willing to designate a particular area as a Ramsar site (requiring it to expend funds to protect waterfowl habitat) in exchange for a commitment by the Netherlands to do the same. In some ways, the Pacific Salmon Treaty, or any other treaty to reduce harvests of shared resources in mutual fashion, is a form of reciprocity agreement. If the resources are unequally distributed (e.g., Canada and the Netherlands could not mutually agree to protect large wild mammals), or preferences differ (e.g., Zimbabweans may not care if Canada protects grizzly bears), then in-kind reciprocity may not be possible.

3. Property rights can be used to conserve species. Environmental NGOs and industrialised countries are able to purchase real estate in developing countries, thereby protecting ecosystems from exploitation. Debt-for-nature swaps (to protect habitats) are one vehicle that can be used to transfer property rights. Problems with this instrument are discussed in Chapter 12 in the context of tropical deforestation. Swanson (1992, pp. 84–5) argues that property rights are not only difficult to transfer between rich and poor countries, but the poor countries may have strong incentives to renege on such agreements in the future as a result of population growth, for example.

4. Finally, trade conventions can be used to regulate wildlife trade and thereby increase the revenues from sustainable harvesting and protect species. Trade conventions include export taxes, import tariffs, price and quantity controls, and certification. The effects of trade on the environment are well documented (e.g., Heerink et al. 1993; Anderson 1992; OECD 1994). Trade measures are usually a second best policy when environmental issues are involved, because trade is

often not the root cause of environmental degradation (root causes may be market and/or government failure).[3] Trade may exacerbate problems when there are market and government failures. Trade in ivory, for example, may add to excessive depletion of elephant stocks when poaching takes place (i.e., property rights are ill-defined or poorly enforced), or when nonuse values of *in situ* stocks are ignored. Burgess (1994) writes that over-exploitation of wildlife species for international trade generally plays a minor role in extinction, but that trade interventions may be warranted for certain key species (such as elephants). Recent international agreements to restrict trade in endangered species (or their products) are not often aimed at promoting economic efficiency, but rather at protecting endangered species.

Although the majority of agreements to regulate trade in species may have failed to achieve their objectives to some extent, perhaps the most important outcome has been greater monitoring or information gathering, and funding for research. This has enabled the scientific community to take stock of the current state of the environment – estimate the extent of and immediacy of the problem – while considering policies to achieve the desired ends. One of the more widely accepted and "successful" of the international treaties is the Convention on International Trade in Endangered Species of Wild Fauna and Flora (CITES). The number of parties to CITES has increased from just over 60 in 1973 to 113 in 1992. In comparison, 154 nations signed the Framework Convention on Climate Change (FCCC), although number of signatories is itself not a good indicator of whether a Convention will be successful or not (Sandler 1997).

Countries are eligible to become a party to CITES when they are members of the UN. Taiwan, which is a major actor in wildlife trade, is not a UN member so CITES rules do not apply. To its credit, Taiwan has unilaterally taken steps to regulate the trade in endangered species that are modeled on the guidelines set forth in CITES (Meecham 1997). Signing may be a formality, with actual commitment questionable. For example, Canada has ratified neither the Law of the Sea Convention or the UN agreement on straddling fish stocks, something that it pressured the international community to implement (Harris 1998, p. 313).

CITES aims to regulate commercial trade in endangered species. It employs a ranking scheme for species: Appendix I contains species banned from international commercial trade; Appendix II lists species that may be traded but for which export permits need to be issued (at the discretion of the exporting state); and Appendix III includes species that are threatened and could become endangered in the future. Consuming or importing countries agree not to trade in species (or parts of or products from species) listed in Appendix I, and ensure that proper export permits

---

[3] Often trade measures serve the interests of certain groups in society. Sometimes it is argued that trade measures should be applied to get other countries to harmonise environmental standards, typically set at high levels by industrial countries. However, different countries have different preferences for environmental quality, and willingness to accept a degraded environment may give some countries a comparative advantage. Global welfare is served by acknowledging such differences and allowing them in international trade.

accompany imports of species listed under Appendix II. States can apply sanctions on species listed under Appendix III at their discretion. All parties to CITES are obliged to submit annual reports of all trade in species included on the two lists to the Convention Secretariat. Although only some 70–80% of parties to the Convention submit reports in each year, the information is useful for the development of data bases that can be used to track trade. "Of the large number of international environmental conventions, CITES probably has the most detailed control structure. It was the first international wildlife treaty to provide for explicit obligations and international monitoring" (WCMC 1992, p. 500).

Since 1973, several important modifications have been required in an attempt to find middle ground between Appendices I and II. Since habitat is not protected under CITES, there was concern that species listed under Appendix I could be lost through destruction of habitat, with trade restrictions themselves providing an adverse incentive to habitat protection. Conserving (terrestrial) biodiversity often implies considerable opportunity costs as there are competing uses for the land. Banning trade then makes "nature conservation" a less attractive activity, inadvertently promoting land conversion to other uses. In 1981, therefore, provision was made in New Delhi (under Conference Resolution 3.15) to permit transfer of certain populations from Appendix I to Appendix II for the purposes of sustainable resource management. This became known as the "ranching criterion" that generally pertains to a particular state or operation. A further change in 1985 (Resolution 5.21) provided for the systematic re-listing of species from Appendix I to II in cases where countries of origin agree on a quota system, which enables maintenance of a population so that the species does not become endangered. No external control was exercised, with quota determined solely by the relevant states.

The third innovation under CITES was the creation of a Management Quota System (MQS) for the African elephant (Resolution 5.12). The MQS relied on management decisions taken by the producing countries (who would not deplete their stocks of elephants) that would be enforced by the consuming countries. Essentially, consuming countries would not permit imports of ivory (and other elephant products) without an accompanying MQS permit. There were no externally enforced incentives for sustainable use, with most states basing their quotas on expected confiscations of poached ivory. Since consumer states could obtain ivory from any ivory-producing state without question, and due to lack of border controls on illegal ivory, public confidence in the MQS failed and, in 1989, the elephant was moved to Appendix I status despite a current population of around 600,000 elephants. For a discussion of the fluidity of the ivory trade, see Chadwick (1992) and Burgess (1994).

10.2 The African Elephant

Undeniably, during the 1970s and 1980s, elephant stocks were severely depleted. According to Chadwick (1992), "statistics showed a species on a toboggan ride towards absolute zero". African elephant populations are estimated to have declined from some 1.2–1.3 million animals in the mid 1970s to slightly more than 600,000 by 1988 (Pearce and Warford 1993) and less than 600,000 today (Said et al. 1995). To protect the elephant, international trade in ivory and other elephant products has been banned since 1989. Five south African states – Zimbabwe, Namibia, Botswana, Malawi and South Africa – did not sign the CITES agreement, with the first four forming the South African Center for Ivory Marketing (SACIM) as an export agency for ivory from those countries. These countries have relatively large elephant stocks and have lobbied to down-list the species and re-open (limited) trade in ivory and other elephant products. Their main argument against the endangered species listing is that, in a number of areas, there are too many elephants and not too few, and that numbers need to be controlled to keep elephants from damaging agricultural lands and wildlife habitat. In addition, trade would create revenues that could potentially be invested in the conservation of elephants.

Their lobbying efforts had some results. In June 1997, signatories to CITES decided that the African elephant (*Loxodonta africana*), as well as the Asian elephant (*Elephas maximus*), would continue to be listed under Appendix I, implying no trade in ivory. However, three southern African countries – Botswana, Namibia and Zimbabwe – would be permitted to sell off nearly 60 tonnes (t) of stockpiled ivory over a 21-month period, but only if promised trade controls are in place (Daley 1997). This constitutes less than 60% of the ivory that these countries have accumulated as a result of confiscation from poachers, natural mortality, culling and destruction of problem animals (Milliken 1997). Decisions on whether to permit any trade in ivory directly affect south African states that account for some 46% of the 462.5 t of verifiable (and legitimately held) stocks of ivory in Africa, although a further 243 t of undeclared or illegal stocks are estimated to exist (Milliken 1997). Some recent empirical evidence related to elephant stocks is provided in Table 10.3.

Welfare economics of an ivory trade ban (no poaching)

A very simple static model is often used to evaluate whether banning trade in elephant products is economically efficient or not (Anderson 1992). Assume that perfect monitoring and enforcement of elephant exploitation are possible, such that "optimal management" of elephant stocks is attainable. Poaching is ignored at this stage, as are nonuse values, tourist revenues and the agricultural damage caused by elephants (restrictive omissions relaxed in later sections). With the aid of conventional applied welfare economics, it is then easy to show that a trade ban results in sub-optimal outcomes. In Figure 10.1, S and D represent the respective supply and demand curves for ivory. African countries produce and supply ivory while Asian countries are the main demanders, accounting for some 90% of consumption. Neither group of countries is assumed to care (much) about the non-consumptive (viewing and preservation) values of the elephant stock. Thus, the market equilibrium in Figure 10.1 corresponds with a supply of Q tonnes of ivory that is sold at the price P. This is the solution that maximises economic well being in the two-group static model, and is therefore considered to be economically efficient. Free trade in ivory generates a producer surplus given by area *ceP* (Figure 10.1) for African nations, and a consumer surplus of *caP* for Asian countries.

Table 10.3: Effectiveness of the Ivory Trade Ban, General Data
Selected West African Countries

Item/Country	Zimbabwe	Cameroon	Gabon	Ivory Coast	Nigeria
Elephant population					
- pre-ban (1989)	52,000	22,000	74,000	3,600	1,300
- post-ban (1994)	61,515	17,000	NK	1-2,000	1,000
- post-ban (1996)[a] (def.)	56,297	1,100	0	551	0
- probable + possible	25,558	15,513	82,012	1,060	1,065
Illegal off-take					
- pre-ban	48	77	NK	NK	NK
- 1990–91	167	100	NK	NK	NK
- 1992–93	175	42	NK	NK	NK
Enforcement budget					
- pre-ban (US$/km^2)	24.00	1.58	30%	NK	NK
- post-ban (US$/km^2)	2.63	1.23	decline[b]	NK	NK
Enforcement staff					
- pre-ban (km^2/person)	118	1,130	NK	≈50%	NK
- post-ban (km^2/person)	105	654	NK	decline[b]	NK
Ivory stockpile (mt)	> 31	NR	0.6	NR	NK
- annual increase (mt)	6.2	NR	–0.2	NR	NK

Selected East African Countries

Item/Country	Kenya	Tanzania	Malawi	Zambia
Elephant population				
- pre-ban (1989)	16,000	61,000	2,800	32,000
- post-ban (1994)	23,797	54,157	2,000	22,785
- post-ban (1996)[a] (def.)	13,834	73,459	1,111	19,701
- probable + possible	11,720	24,750	976	13,303
Illegal off-take				
- pre-ban	45	55	89	≈2,100
- 1990–91	111	8	123	≈700
- 1992–93	208	12	77	≈100
Enforcement budget				
- pre-ban (US$/km^2)	6.60	12.60	14.80	65.00
- post-ban (US$/km^2)	4.00	0.38	11.40	41.00
Enforcement staff				
- pre-ban (km^2/person)	270	87	65	69
- post-ban (km^2/person)	137	146	65	51
Ivory stockpile (mt)	5.3[c]	52.3	4.9	2.7
- annual increase (mt)	> 1	5.9	0.8	0.1

NR = not reliable; NK = not known
[a] The first row provides the "definite" number, the second provides the sum of the "probable" and "possible" categories of elephant estimates. A third category, speculative, is not included but accounts for 6.2% of the total of 579,532 elephants in Africa.
[b] Level data are unavailable, but data on change are available. Percentage change reported here.
[c] Kenya destroyed 11 tonnes of ivory in 1989 and another 6 t in 1991.
Source: Bulte and van Kooten (1999c).

The efficient solution no longer holds once we introduce a third group of nations into the model, namely, developed countries that do not want to purchase ivory (or other elephant products) but are interested in the non-consumptive use (viewing) and preservation benefits of elephants. Denote this group as the European countries (although it likely also includes the countries of North America, Australia and New Zealand). Killing elephants reduces the well-being of this group, implying that the marginal cost curve S (i.e., the supply curve) rotates upwards to S'. The original free-trade equilibrium (Q, P) is no longer efficient when the Europeans are included in the analysis. Global welfare is lower than is the case if only the well being of nations trading in ivory were maximised. A global planner (such as the CITES group) should take into account the gains and losses of all the agents, and not only of those engaged in ivory trade (Burgess 1994, p. 138).

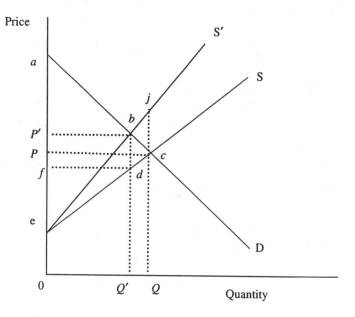

Figure 10.1 Welfare Measures in Static Model of Ivory Trade

If all agents with an interest in elephants are considered, this reduces the total supply of ivory to Q', which causes prices to rise to P'. This can be achieved, for example, by introducing an (import or export) tariff. Comparing the new equilibrium with the free-trade solution, the economic welfare of Asians and Africans is lower by *bcPP'* and *cdfP*, respectively. Tariff revenues are equal to *bdfP'*, and accrue to African (Asian) governments in case of an export (import) tariff. The same result can be achieved using export or import quotas, although the design of the scheme will determine the distribution of welfare changes, and the remaining incentives to cheat. In addition, the Europeans gain *cdbj*, such that the total net gain of reducing supply from Q to Q' equals *cbj*.

A complete trade ban (such that $Q = 0$ in Figure 10.1) is inefficient because, at the margin, an elephant harvested for its ivory is worth more than one that is allowed to live. Anderson (1992) argues that conservationists have been prepared to insist on trade bans because they have not been required to compensate the losers (Europeans compensating Africans and Asians). Take the efficient point (Q', P') as a reference. The total loss to the countries engaged in ivory trade from a complete ban on trade is given by *abde*, while the welfare gain of the Europeans (who are not engaged in ivory trade, but benefit from the preservation of elephants) is unambiguously smaller, namely, area *ebc*.[4] This static analysis thus yields the well-known economic result that a trade ban is socially undesirable. When exploitation can be controlled, restricted trade is preferred to a total ban on trade.

The ivory trade ban and elephant numbers

Bulte and van Kooten (1996) demonstrate that a trade ban may also not be in the interests of nature conservation. For this purpose, they develop a simple dynamic model that captures some of the relevant intertemporal tradeoffs that elephant producing countries encounter, but ignores poaching and enforcement. A government is assumed to maximise social well-being (perhaps narrowly defined) from elephant management. Well-being includes benefits from the sale of ivory and from eco-tourism (but nonuse values are ignored), and, as a financial cost, the damage elephants cause to agricultural crops and possibly habitat of other wildlife (see Brown and Henry 1989; Chadwick 1992; Pearce and Warford 1993). The objective function for the government can therefore be written as (suppressing the time variable):

$$(10.1) \quad \text{Maximise}_{\{y\}} \int_0^{\infty} \left(H(y) + R(x) - D(x) \right) e^{-rt} \, dt,$$

where $x(t)$ is the stock of elephants at time t; $y(t)$ is the number of elephants harvested at t; $H(y)$ are net revenues from harvesting elephants (i.e., selling ivory), or the area under the demand curve for ivory ($R'(x) \geq 0$); and $D(x)$ is damage inflicted on agricultural lands and other wildlife habitat ($D'(x) \geq 0$). The dynamics describing the stock of elephants are given as:

$$(10.2) \quad \dot{x} = G(x) - y,$$

where $G(x)$ is the growth function for elephants. From the maximum principle and assuming an interior solution, first-order conditions are:

$$(10.3) \quad H'(y) = \lambda$$

$$(10.4) \quad \dot{\lambda} = (r - G'(x))\lambda - R'(x) + D'(x) .$$

From (10.3) and (10.4):

---

[4] Anderson (1992) measures gains and losses relative to the free-trade equilibrium, with losses and gains equal to *cea* and *cej*, respectively. It is not possible to state unambiguously whether losses exceed gains in this case. But it is not particularly useful to know the magnitude of total gains and losses, because it is marginal values that are important; with a trade ban, the marginal benefits of permitting trade clearly exceed the margin al costs (*a > e* in Figure 10.1).

(10.5) $\dfrac{\dot{\lambda}}{\lambda} = r - G' + \dfrac{D'(x) - R'(x)}{H'(y)}$.

Equation (10.3) states that the marginal revenue generated by harvesting another elephant now and selling its ivory is equal to the shadow value of retaining the elephant and perhaps harvesting it at a later date. Equation (10.4) is a generalised version of Hotelling's rule, which, rewritten as in (10.5), states that the elephant population should be maintained at the level where the growth rate of the shadow value of an elephant (or, its ivory) equals the dynamic opportunity cost of not culling elephants (i.e., reducing the stock). The latter equals the discount rate minus the growth rate of the stock, plus a term that measures the change in future agricultural damages avoided plus lost future tourism benefits from culling another animal today.

Differentiating (10.3) and equating it to (10.4) gives:

(10.6) $\dot{y} = \dfrac{\left(r - G'(x)\right)H'(y) - R'(x) + D'(x)}{H''(y)}$.

Once the optimum equilibrium stock x^*, or steady-state, is reached, harvest levels will be constant; hence, $\dot{y} = 0$. The implicit optimal stock size is then determined by solving

(10.7) $r = G'(x^*) + \dfrac{R'(x^*) - D'(x^*)}{H'(y^*)}$.

If the discount rate equals the growth rate plus a stock term (see Chapter 7), the optimal stock size has been reached. Then, from (10.2), harvest (y^*) should equal the regenerated fraction of the stock ($G(x^*)$).

The effect of a trade ban can be determined by removing the term H(y) from (10.1) and solving the dynamic optimisation problem anew (assuming that a costless cull is used to manage the herd). In that case, enforcement of the trade ban reduces expression (10.7) to

(10.8) $R'(x^*) = D'(x^*)$.

The optimal population level now occurs where marginal benefits generated from tourism equal marginal agricultural damage.

Is the level of the elephant stock determined from (10.8) larger or smaller than that determined from (10.7)? Alternatively, does the trade ban increase or decrease optimal population size? An answer can only be found by specifying the underlying functions. With respect to $D(x)$, it seems reasonable to assume that agricultural damage and damage inflicted on nature reserves are directly proportional to the size of the stock.[5] Hence, assume $D(x) = \alpha x$, where $\alpha > 0$ is a parameter (see below). On the other hand, the marginal utility of watching elephants is a positive but diminishing function of stock size, as anyone who ever spent a week in a Zimbabwean game park would agree. For simplicity, assume that the convex relation between $R(x)$ and stock size is adequately represented by $R(x) = \beta \ln(x)$, with $\beta > 0$. Also assume that the growth of an elephant population can be described by a logistic growth function, $G(x) = gx(1 - x/K)$, where g is the intrinsic growth rate and K is the region's carrying capacity as described in Chapter 7. More realistically, elephants (and other large mammals) probably have a "skewed" growth function, with maximum growth occurring to the right of 0.5K. According to Millner-Gulland and Leader-Williams (1992a), hereafter MG&LW, the following function is more appropriate: $G(x) = gx(1 - (x/K)^7)$, where maximum growth occurs for $x = 0.75K$, but we do not use it here.

Estimates of Optimal Elephant Stocks

We consider two cases – an individual country that is a price taker (Kenya) and the African continent as a whole. For Kenya, the demand for elephants is given by $H'(y) = P$, where P is the (fixed) price of an elephant derived from the price of ivory. Using the functional forms described above and solving equation (10.7) for the steady-state optimal stock of elephants with trade in ivory gives:

$$(10.9) \quad x_T{}^* = \frac{(g-r)KP - \alpha K + \sqrt{8\beta gKP + (\alpha K - (g-r)KP)^2}}{4gP}.$$

What do we know about any of the parameters in the foregoing equations? Very little empirical data is available, but we can use a bit of detective work to "guess" at what the parameters might be. Parameter α is determined as the value of lost forage, and not the damage that might be caused by elephants trampling crops, since such damages can be avoided by appropriate management practices. As herbivores daily consume about 2.5% of their body weight in forage, one elephant annually consumes as much forage as required to bring 4.7 cows to full maturity, with one cow consuming some 36,500 kg of dry matter valued at about US$35. Hence, the forage displaced is valued at $164.50, which is the value of α.

The intrinsic growth rate of elephants is estimated to be 7% ($g = 0.07$), although that is an optimistic estimate that can only be obtained with appropriate management (Lindsay 1986; Forse 1987). We take the carrying capacity of Africa to be approximately double the highest population estimate of recent times (i.e., $K = 3$ million). Before the ban, Kenya had some 16,000 elephants (for 1996 estimates, see Table 10.3), which is about one-half of the numbers of several decades earlier. We

---

[5] This is a simplification since the presence of small groups of elephants may even have beneficial effects, since their feeding habits result in more sunlight on the ground, which favours growth of grasses, the preferred food of grazers. Thus, over some range, a convex curve would describe $D(x)$, while $D(x)$ might be concave over some other range (Western 1989).

assume double the latter amount as an approximation of carrying capacity for Kenya ($K = 60,000$).

In the small-country case of Kenya, β is calculated as follows. Brown and Henry (1989) estimate that the annual value from viewing elephants in Kenya is $20⁻25 million. Given that there were an estimated 16,000 elephants in Kenya for that period, then β = $25 million ÷ ln(16,000) = 2,582,553. For all of Africa, there are approximately 600,000 elephants, but there is no information about their tourism or recreational value. Taking the average estimate of Brown and Henry (1989) and assuming it applies to all of Africa (an unrealistic assumption) gives an upper estimate of viewing/recreational value of some $900 million. Then β = 67.6 million. This is considered an upper bound for the entire continent.

Using these parameter values, equation (10.9) is solved for two recent prices and different values of the discount rate, with the results provided in Figure 10.2. Under the trade ban, the optimum population is simply β/α, or 15,700 elephants (with associated annual harvest of 880 animals) irrespective of the discount rate.

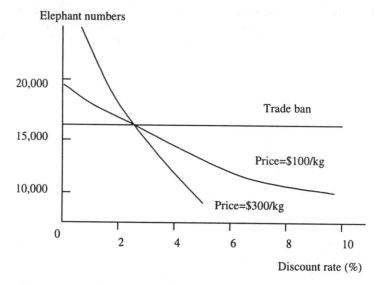

Figure 10.2 Optimal Elephant Stocks for Kenya for Given Prices and Discount Rates

From Figure 10.2, it is clear that when the discount rate is more than about 3.5%, the optimal stock of elephants under a trade ban exceeds that with trade; at lower discount rates optimal elephant stocks are greatest when trade in ivory is permitted. In the absence of recreation benefits, and damage and stock-dependent harvesting costs, the optimum stock size approaches $0.5K$ (= 30,000 animals) as r approaches zero. At the optimum population, marginal damage exceeds marginal benefits, which explains why x^* is (far) below 30,000 animals. Relatively high prices for ivory induce the government to "tolerate" more damage, giving the unusual result that the curves cross at a positive rate of discount ($r = G'(x)$). A real discount rate of 3.5% might be a good approximation of the social discount rate for developed countries, but for developing countries r probably exceeds 3.5% by a substantial amount. This would imply that elephant populations should have increased after implementation of the trade ban. This is consistent with some actual observations in recent years (Chadwick 1992), although other sources report a modest overall decline in African elephant populations for the period 1990–1995 (see Table 10.3).

If the discount rate applied by the Kenyan government equals 10% and price is $300 per kg of raw ivory (so an elephant is worth US$3,060 as derived from average tusk weight), the optimum population size should almost double after implementation of the trade ban. However, if a real social discount rate of 2% more accurately describes the rate of time preference of the Kenyan government, the optimum population size under the trade ban is almost 3,000 elephants smaller than the equilibrium stock with trade. The effect of the trade ban, or its removal, on population size is sensitive to the discount rate.

Ivory prices also play a role. When ivory prices are $300/kg (as in 1989), optimal elephant stocks are higher for low discount rates but lower for higher discount rates compared to an ivory price of $100/kg (as in 1985–86) (Harland 1988; Barbier and Swanson 1990). Increasing α reduces optimal stock levels, while increasing β enhances them. The values of the critical discount rate are found by substituting into (10.7) the appropriate functional forms and solving for r to get:

$$(10.10) \quad r^* = g(1 - \frac{2x^*}{K}) + \frac{1}{P}(\frac{\beta}{x^*} - \alpha).$$

The results of a sensitivity analysis with respect to the recreation (β) and damage (α) parameters are provided in Table 10.4. The negative values in the table indicate that, whenever we substantially underestimate α and overestimate β, there is a chance that the trade ban is always optimal. On the other hand, high values of α (accompanied by low values of β) lead to critical discount rates that are higher than 5%, meaning that a government with a lower rate of time preference than this critical value will favour elephant conservation to a greater extent when trade is permitted. The analysis illustrates the importance to the international community of obtaining good estimates of α and β before making decisions about the benefits of a trade ban in ivory products.

Table 10.4: Critical Switching Points of the Discount Rate for Various Values of α and β for Ivory Prices of $100/kg and $300/kg

	½ α	α	2 α
½ β	3.3	5.2	6.1
β	negative	3.3	5.2
2 β	negative	negative	3.3

Now consider the case of the African continent as a whole. Assume that the inverse demand function for ivory is linear and downward sloping, i.e., $H'(y) = \Omega - \gamma y$. In this case, equation (10.9) cannot be solved in straightforward manner because it is necessary to solve for the optimal harvest level y^* and optimal stock x^* simultaneously. The approach in the case of ivory trade is to find the steady-state solution by setting $\dot{x}$ and $\dot{y}$ in equations (10.2) and (10.6) to zero and solving both for y:

(10.11) $\dot{y} = 0$:
$$y = \frac{\Omega}{\gamma} - \frac{\alpha x - \beta}{gx(1 - \frac{2x}{K})\gamma - rx\gamma}$$

(10.12) $\dot{x} = 0$:
$$y = gx(1 - \frac{x}{K}).$$

It is not straightforward to solve (10.11) and (10.12) for y^* and x^* so this must be done graphically and numerically.

Unlike for a small country, a decision maker who might wish to determine the optimal stock of elephants for the entire African continent would need to take into account the effect of harvest on price. A linear demand function can be constructed from the fact that, in 1986, some 118,600 elephants were harvested and the price of ivory was about $100 per kg, while, in 1989, 75,000 animals were harvested and ivory price was $300 per kg. Average tusk sizes were reported to be 5.6 kg in 1986 and 5.1 kg in 1989. Using these values, raw ivory prices are converted into elephant values of $1,120 and $3,060 for ivory prices of $100/kg and $300/kg, respectively; then, the parameter values can be calculated as $\Omega = 6397.16$ and $\gamma = 0.044$ (with the phase-plane diagram of the saddle-point equilibrium given in Figure 7.2). A graph of the numerical results is similar to that depicted in Figure 10.2. Again, the optimal stock under a trade ban is given by β/α, although the values of these parameters are different in the case of Africa than Kenya alone. In the case of Africa, the optimal stock of elephants under a trade ban is 411,200 compared to a stock of approximately 600,000 at the time the ban was implemented (Table 10.3).

The critical discount rate in the small country case is about 3.5% compared to about 5% when harvest of ivory affects price. The critical discount rate (or internal rate of return) for the large-country case is higher because the large country has the ability to set prices and realise a higher rate of return. (For example, the price of ivory for the large country case amounts to $533 per kg, with an associated harvest of approximately 22,000 elephants). The conclusion is that a trade ban may lead to greater elephant conservation in the small-country case of Kenya (where the critical discount rate is low) than in the large-country case with a higher critical discount rate.

The potentially restrictive assumption in the large-country model is that the relation between (potential) recreation benefits and elephant population size in Africa is proportional to that for Kenya. Thus, recreation benefits for Africa equal benefits for Kenya multiplied by the ratio of the total African elephant stock to the number of elephants in Kenya. This results in recreation benefits for all of Africa equal to about $900 million. Clearly, benefits from elephant watching are lower in many African countries where potential for this activity is less well developed. For that reason, the estimate of $900 million (and the value of β derived from it) serves as an upper bound for our calculations. A sensitivity analysis over benefit values can be used to discover critical discount rates. First, solving equations (10.11) and (10.12) simultaneously for r gives:

$$(10.13) \quad r^* = g(1 - \frac{2x^*}{K}) + \frac{\alpha x^* - \beta}{[gx^*(1 - \frac{x^*}{K})\gamma - \Omega]x^*}$$

For different recreational values, it is possible to derive β from the relation $R(x)$ = β ln(x), where x = 600,000 and the remaining parameters are provided above. Critical r ranges from 5.1% for $900 million in assumed recreational benefits, to 5.9% for $500 million in assumed benefits, and to 6.8% for $100 million in assumed benefits. The result is rather stable with respect to parameter values and the earlier conclusion does not change.

Did countries with high discount rates reduce their stocks of elephants, while countries with low discount rates increase their elephant populations in response to the 1990 trade ban? Empirical tests of this hypothesis are difficult because the social discount rate, or the rate of interest as applied by the government in inter-temporal cost-benefit analyses, is not revealed on markets. Even market-determined real rates of interest are difficult to determine for many African countries due to poorly functioning financial markets. Governments of many developing countries have typically tried to "fix" nominal interest rates in the past, mainly for political purposes. Real interest rates (nominal rates minus inflation) have been negative in the seventies and eighties for many countries (International Monetary Fund 1995). These artificial interest rates provide insufficient information about the rate of time preference of governments, so applying such a rate in an empirical analysis would serve little purpose.

One interesting observation is that the rate of time preference of African governments will not be constant over time, but will change (more specifically, decline) as the economy and per capita income grow. This in turn implies that, to conserve elephants, it is necessary frequently to re-assess instruments implemented in the past. The same instrument (e.g., a trade ban) that worked well yesterday could be detrimental to elephant conservation in the future. Whether a trade ban is effective in achieving its goal of species preservation or enhancement depends crucially on the discount rate, which is an object of a country's macro-economic policies, as much as it is on intervention by the international community to protect wildlife species.

Finally, it is obvious that discount rates are only one explanation of why elephant producing countries may or may not favour a trade ban. Another has to do with the relative importance that producing countries place on market values (sale of ivory), opportunity costs of conservation and nonmarket values (viewing, preservation value). Thus, countries that place a greater value at the margin on the role of elephants in attracting tourists, or value their existence more highly, are more likely to favour a trade ban than countries that place relatively greater value on elephant products. The latter countries may already have sufficient stocks to meet nonmarket values. Not only will these two types of countries have a different stance regarding the trade ban, they will also place different emphasis on enforcement. We examine enforcement in these different situations in the next subsections.

Range States with Different Nonuse Benefits

In the foregoing analyses, we compared optimal elephant populations for a single country in situations with and without trade in ivory. It turns out that the optimum steady-state with trade is a function of the discount rate. Here we consider the difficulty of attaining an intertemporal optimum when multiple countries are involved.

Now consider a single (Asian) ivory consuming country J and two African producing countries K and Z, where, at the margin, country K places great nonmarket (use and nonuse) value on elephant stocks and Z is more interested in sales of elephant products (ivory). For now, ignore other developed countries that place nonmarket value on elephant conservation. Country K supports the trade ban on ivory, whereas country Z chooses to take a reservation. Poaching is likely in country K as ivory can be sold through Z, since ivory from different sources is hard to distinguish. The model is consistent with that of Khanna and Harford (1996), except that it is dynamic. The ivory producing countries K and Z are relatively poor compared to the consuming country J and will, therefore, probably apply a different (higher) discount rate (Barbier et al. 1990).

Let N_h denote the effort that country h (h = K,Z,J) devotes to enforcement (measured in dollars or staff) and I_Z denote the amount of ivory traded by the African country Z that takes a reservation from the ban. N_h and I_Z are thus choice variables for the optimisation problem. Define ψ_h as the net benefits accruing to country h from sale/consumption of ivory and/or the nonmarket values of elephant stocks (corrected for enforcement costs). Assuming a global planner (say CITES) that maximises the present value of net benefits for the three countries, the objective function for the optimal enforcement problem can be written as:

(10.14) $\text{Maximise} \int_0^\infty [(\psi_K + \psi_Z)\, e^{-\rho t} + \psi_J]\, e^{-rt}\, dt,$

where $\rho > 0$ is the discount rate differential due to differences in wealth between the poor African countries (K and Z) and the consuming country J, and r is the (relatively low) discount rate of the consumer country. The equations of motion for the elephant stocks are simply:

(10.15) $\dot{x}_K = G(x_K) - P_K,$

and

(10.16) $\dot{x}_Z = G(x_Z) - I_Z - P_Z,$

where P_i (i = K, Z) refers to the amount of ivory poached in African country i. In the Khanna and Harford (1996) model, poaching in country K depends on enforcement effort in countries K and J and legal ivory flows from Z to J. This observation implies that there are externalities associated with enforcement effort, suggesting that cooperation or coordination may be necessary to achieve a globally optimal solution, an extension considered below.

Applying the maximum principle and setting time derivatives equal to zero yields the following expression for the "steady-state" stocks of elephants (where i = K,Z):

$$(10.17) \quad r = G(x_i) + \frac{\dfrac{\partial \psi_K}{\partial x_i}e^{-\rho t} + \dfrac{\partial \psi_Z}{\partial x_i}e^{-\rho t} + \dfrac{\partial \psi_J}{\partial x_i}}{\lambda_i},$$

where λ_i is the co-state variable for the stock of elephants in country i (= K,Z). Since the stock term on the RHS of (10.17) is a function of time t, technically it is wrong to refer to the outcome as a steady-state. It is easy to see that the steady-state (or "compromise") elephant stocks x_K and x_Z are not constant over time because the first two terms in the numerator of the second, or complex stock, term on the RHS of (10.17) are a function of time t. Hence, to track this solution over time ($dx_i/dt \neq 0$), growth should not be equal to exploitation – $G(x_K) \neq P_K$ and $G(x_Z) \neq P_Z + I_Z$. This is at odds with the concept of a steady-state as defined in Chapter 7.

Although the optimal scheme developed above is intertemporally consistent from the perspective of the global planner (say, CITES), attaining and sticking to such a scheme may be difficult in practice, as it may provoke strategic behaviour. In early periods, relatively greater weights are given to the preferences of countries K and Z, while in the more distant future the preferences of rich country J will dominate. As $t \to \infty$ the steady-state solution is determined solely by preferences of country J because $e^{-\rho t} \to 0$. The reason of course is that the African countries place less value on benefits in the distant future than does the consumer country. As time passes, the African countries have a strong incentive to cheat and improve their welfare at the expense of the consumer country. In this respect, it is important to note that the ivory trade has proven to be fluid, or impossible to stop completely.

A potentially cumbersome coordination issue arises. Without binding agreements that contain credible threats by the consumer country to retaliate whenever the African countries deviate from the initially agreed upon plan (or sufficient side payments to abide with the plan), achieving an optimal solution may not be possible (Munro 1990; Sandler 1997). Further, the discrepancy between optimal stock sizes in the short and long run could be even greater if the (relatively rich, low-discount rate) European-type countries that derive utility from conserving elephants were included in the model.

The above analysis implies that the opportunity costs of retaining the trade ban – i.e., potential benefits from lifting the ban and allowing some trade – may be lower than anticipated. That is, because optimally managed stocks are dynamically inconsistent, the outcomes of the trade ban should not be compared to optimal, but rather to sub-optimal management schemes involving monitoring and enforcement costs. This in turn suggests that the case for retaining the ban becomes stronger.

Open-access, the trade ban and poaching

In the above models, poaching and anti-poaching enforcement have been ignored. Poaching is difficult to eliminate in range states because the products from threatened and endangered species have such great value compared to average incomes, as illustrated in the previous chapter for tiger bones. Inclusion of poaching in ivory trade models is important because, during the 1980s, approximately 80% of the ivory supplied on international markets was illegal. Indeed, it has been argued that actual management of elephants has strong characteristics of open-access exploitation, where poachers from different countries enter the killing business as long as there is a profit to be made (Burton 1998). Future benefits are discounted at an infinite rate because any poacher can never be sure that she is the one to benefit from investing in the stock (by refraining from harvesting today). Hence, elephants are regarded as an important source of income, but are not treated as a valuable asset (Barbier and Swanson 1990; Burgess 1994).

Poachers will consider *in situ* elephant stocks as an open-access resource, irrespective of whether legal trade is allowed or not. The incentives facing poachers are affected by whether or not some countries can legally trade in ivory, since illegal ivory can be laundered through those countries (as note above). Meecham (1997) provides a similar argument concerning tiger bones, while Burton (1998) reports that ivory prices were typically higher in the pre-ban period than with the ban. Thus, one might expect greater poaching effort when there are (restricted) legal sales.

An important caveat applies here. It has been noted on several occasions that legal trade in ivory may provide locals with a stake in conservation efforts. If, say, property rights are granted to local communities, which are then able to generate a sustainable flow of income from conservation, members of such communities will be less inclined to engage in poaching when trade is legalised (Hertzler and Gomera 1998). This appealing argument may be false, however. MG&LW (1992b), for example, describe elephant and rhino poaching in Luangwa Valley, Zambia. Locals are typically responsible for small-scale poaching for meat and hides on the fringes of parks, where occasional tusks and horns are considered a nice bonus. In contrast, organised poaching gangs often operate at the heart of nature reserves, and are primarily after valuable resources such as ivory and horns. The organised gangs are often composed of foreigners (e.g., Somalis in Kenya, Zambians in Zimbabwe), and it is not at all obvious why they should care about the property rights of locals. However, by providing locals with property rights, they will have an incentive to protect elephants from outside poachers, such that effective "poaching costs" increase.

To evaluate the impact of lifting the trade ban, the consequences for open-access exploitation should be considered. While some data are available to analyse steady-states and approach dynamics for the restricted trade case (i.e., data from the pre-ban period), no such data are available for the period since 1990. Hence, it is not possible to compare open-access exploitation patterns for the "restricted trade" and "no legal trade" cases. It can be inferred, however, that the incentive to poach will be greater with legal trade. The obvious question ("how much greater?") will be addressed by considering the development of estimates of elephant populations over time.

First, assume that poaching has aspects that are similar to open-access, in the sense that poaching effort will dissipate all rents (see MG & LW 1992b; Burton 1998; Bulte and van Kooten 1999c). Poachers face two types of costs: the cost of poaching effort and the (expected) fine when caught. Indeed, since the fine constitutes a form of fee equal to the expected probability of getting caught times the size of the fine, this is not really a case of open-access because poachers pay a fee equal to the expected probability of getting caught times the penalty. Here we consider the open-access steady-states and approach dynamics for the restricted trade case, using Zambian data for the pre-ban period. Suppose that effort is attracted to poaching of elephants as long as revenues exceed the opportunity costs of the production factors (i.e., as long as the rent from elephant exploitation is positive). Assume the conventional Schaefer production function $y = qxE$, where q is the catchability coefficient, x is the elephant stock (as before) and E is effort. The rents from elephant exploitation are given by:

(10.18) $\pi = pqxE - cE - \theta EF$,

where c is the per unit cost of effort, θ is the probability of detection per poaching expedition (such that θE represents total probability of detection) and F is the (expected) penalty. When new entrants are attracted to the sector with a time lag v, and the response of effort leaving the industry is subject to a similar lag, then the change in effort over time can be described by:

(10.19) $\dot{E} = v(pqxE - cE - \theta EF)$.

The parameter v will be a function of, for example, the malleability of capital in the industry, which, for the case of elephant exploitation, is probably high. The change in the elephant population over time is given by:

(10.20) $\dot{x} = G(x) - qxE$,

where $G(x) = \gamma x (1 - x/K)$. In a steady-state equilibrium, $\dot{x} = 0$ and $\dot{E} = 0$. From (10.19) this implies that $x = (c + \theta F)/pq$. Substituting the growth function into (10.20) gives:

(10.21) $E = \dfrac{\gamma}{q}(1 - \dfrac{x}{K})$.

Information on γ, c, q, p, θ and F is available from MG&LW (1992b). When $\gamma = 0.067$, $K = 1.2$ million, $c = \$180$ (per poaching expedition), $q = 0.00026$ and $p = \$450$ per elephant (approximately \$50/kg of raw ivory), $\theta = 0.05$ and $F = \$180$, the steady-state elephant stock for the entire continent is 1,615 elephants (assuming $K =$

1.2 million elephants or double the current stock for all Africa). This is obviously a very low number compared to past and current stocks, and is likely below the minimum viable population level, which is a feature not included in the current growth function (see Chapter 7; Soulé 1987).

The phase-plane diagram is depicted in Figure 10.3, but it is not drawn to scale, as the $\dot{E} = 0$ isocline (located at $x = 1,615$) would then be indistinguishable from the vertical axis. The $\dot{x} = 0$ isocline crosses the horizontal axis at the carrying capacity K. Since the isoclines intersect in the interior of the phase-plane, $x > 0$ and $E > 0$ in the steady-state.

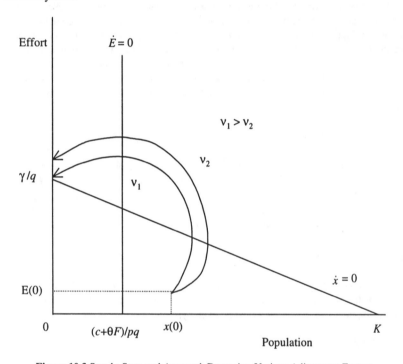

Figure 10.3 Steady-State and Approach Dynamics, Various Adjustment Factors

The existence of a positive steady-state, albeit at a low level, does not imply that survival of the elephant is guaranteed, however. It is possible that extinction occurs during the approach path due to excessive entry and delayed exit of poachers. In order to analyse entry and exit, we need information about the adjustment parameter v in order to compute changing effort and stock with equations (10.19) and (10.20) for given starting values, $E(0)$ and $x(0)$. We vary v over the range 0.00001 to 0.1.

Representative results are depicted in Figure 10.3, and these indicate that extinction during the approach dynamics is the general result.[6]

There are no data to support a similar analysis for the case where poached ivory cannot be laundered and sold as legal ivory, so direct comparison of the pre- and post-ban situation is not possible. Some tentative conclusions can be drawn, however, by examining elephant population data over time. Recent data indicate that poaching has indeed declined as a result of the trade ban, supporting the notion of a link between legal and illegal trade discussed above. The population of elephants was cut in half between 1979 and 1989 (Khanna and Harford 1996). Hence, the number of elephants in Africa was estimated at no higher than 607,000 before the ivory trade ban took effect. Based on estimates presented in Table 10.3, it appears that elephant numbers have declined by 4.5% since the ban was implemented, or some 0.6% per year. This implies that the rate of decline of the population is much lower than in the pre-ban period.

These findings suggest that the ban has contributed towards survival of the species, and conversely that lifting the ban could endanger long-run survival of the elephant. Yet, there remains a major problem related to the quality of the data. Not only is information about elephant populations not very reliable, but neither are data on raw ivory prices, legal and illegal trade (shipments of ivory), costs of poaching, costs of anti-poaching enforcement and so on. The major reason is the fact that range states are poor countries. Lack of data or poor quality data limit what the economist and resource manager can do in investigating (making) appropriate policy.

Enforcement to protect elephants

The previous model ignored enforcement by government to conserve elephant stocks, and this severely limits the usefulness of the model and the reliability of its outcomes.[7] Two schools of thought can be discerned on the matter of enforcement effort and the ivory trade ban (see, e.g., Chadwick 1992; Khanna and Harford 1996; *The Economist* 1997a; Coetzee 1989; Simmons and Krueter 1989). First, it is believed that by legitimising trade (reducing transaction costs), ivory prices will increase, providing greater incentives for legal and illegal harvests, probably resulting in declining stocks. Incentives for poaching are enhanced because legal ivory provides a cover for illegal ivory, as discussed earlier. The alternative view is that revenues from legally produced ivory could be used for enforcement, so that poaching could actually decline. Since enforcement is expensive, it is sometimes argued that such revenues may be necessary to pay for adequate protection of elephants. In addition, by allowing trade in ivory, the incentives for governments to manage sustainably the stock and enforce harvest restrictions are affected. With trade, for example, the characteristics of elephant stocks as a valuable asset are obviously

---

[6] The analysis ignores the potential effect of changing supply on prices, although some justification for assuming a flat inverse demand function is provided by Millner-Gulland (1993).

[7] Discussion in this section is based on Bulte and van Kooten (1999c).

different because living elephants represent a growing and valuable source of marketable ivory.

We extend the forgoing model to allow for poaching and enforcement. For obvious reasons, poachers do not have formal property rights, and do not consider *in situ* stocks as assets. Therefore, they are assumed to maximise a short-run (one-period) profit function, which implies that the effect of current harvests on future stocks and harvests is discounted at an infinite rate. The commercial poacher's choose poaching effort E (measured as the number of poaching expeditions in a given time period) for a given level of government enforcement B. Optimal effort translates into a reduced-form, poaching production function h. The government's problem is then solved, for both the cases where ivory trade is allowed and where it is not allowed, with the authority choosing the level of enforcement B and (possibly) legal off-take y.

The Poachers' Problem

The rents accruing to poaching are assumed to be determined as follows:

(10.22) $pf(E, x) - c(B)E - \theta(E) F(E, x),$

where p is the price of an elephant derived from the ivory it carries; E is total poaching effort (measured as the number of poaching expeditions in a given time period); x is the stock of elephants; $f(E, x)$ is the poaching production function (specified as qEx, as before); c is cost per unit of poaching effort, which is assumed to be an increasing function of enforcement effort B undertaken by the government ($\partial c/\partial B > 0$), because poachers have to take precautions to avoid getting caught, including moving to more distant, relatively unprotected lands;[8] and θ is the probability of detection (actually, it is the probability of detection, capture and subsequent sentencing), which is assumed to be an increasing function of poaching effort E. Because of data limitations, we assume that the probability of detection can be modeled adequately as θE, where θ is now a parameter (Leader-Williams et al. 1990). The probability of detection should be a function of B as well as E. There are no data relating detection to enforcement, but there is some information relating detection probability to poaching effort. Finally, F is the fine for poaching. It is assumed that the fine F, which also includes the confiscation of one trophy, is proportional to output: $F = z f(E,x) + p$, where z is the proportionality constant.[9]

As long as there remains rent, poaching continues. This implies that the open-access steady-state for a given level of enforcement effort B is determined by the level of stocks where rents are fully dissipated:

---

[8] For Zambia, Leader-Willams et al. (1990) indicate that enforcement (patrol effort) has resulted in relatively safe areas where there were less elephants initially, but to which elephants have migrated from less safe areas.

[9] In Zimbabwe, if "guards and game rangers come across anybody who might be a poacher [of black rhinos], they now have the right to shoot first and ask questions later" (*The Economist* 1997b).

(10.23) $pqEx - cE - \theta E(zqEx + p) = 0$.

Then the optimal level of open-access effort is:

(10.24) $E_\infty = \dfrac{pqx - c - \theta p}{\theta zqx}$.

The reduced form poaching function is obtained by substituting optimal effort in the poaching production function $f(E,x)$, and is given as $h(x,B;p,F)$ (Skonhoft and Solstad 1998). Poaching h is thus given by $qE_\infty x = (pqx - c - \theta p)/\theta z$. This obviously implies $\partial h/\partial c < 0$ and $\partial h/\partial z < 0$.[10] The steady-state population in the open-access case is found by utilising the fact that, in the steady-state, growth of the population equals exploitation.

The Government's Problem without Trade in Ivory

Obviously, enforcement effort B is the result of government decision making. Because B varies over time, changing because policies change or because *in situ* stocks deteriorate or grow, the steady-state computed above will not occur. That implies that x_∞ does not provide a relevant benchmark to evaluate whether the trade ban should be lifted. Instead, government preferences and responses to changing circumstances need to be modeled explicitly.

Without trade in ivory, elephants are (just) a source of potential tourism revenues $R(x)$. Elephants may also damage agricultural crops, denoted by $D(x)$, and governments have to invest in enforcement to protect them from poachers. Enforcement costs are $w(B)$, where w is the total cost of mounting anti-poaching patrol units (APUs). Assume $w'(B) > 0$, $w''(B) > 0$ and $w(0) = 0$. For the no-trade case, we assume the government chooses B to solve:

(10.25) Maximise $\displaystyle\int_0^\infty [R(x) - D(x) - w(B)]e^{-rt}\, dt$

(10.26) subject to: $\dot{x} = G(x) - h(x, B; p, F)$.

Here, we implicitly assume that the government can choose B freely. Even though government funds are scarce, and expenditures on wildlife conservation have to compete with government expenditures elsewhere in the economy, we assume that there is no binding constraint on funds for enforcement. It also implies that potential proceeds from trade in ivory after lifting the ban do not relax a binding constraint.

---

[10] According to this formula, $\partial h/\partial p < 0$ for $qx < \theta$. This results from our assumption that, after detection, a trophy is confiscated. According to MG&LW (1992a), on average one trophy was confiscated after detection. However, in the real world no confiscation takes place unless an elephant has been poached, so $\partial h/\partial p > 0$.

(There is no reason to link ivory revenues directly to enforcement; governments should spend revenues where they contribute most to social welfare at the margin). This may be more or less correct for different African nations, but, for most nations, proceeds from ivory are relatively modest compared to total revenue.

The current value Hamiltonian associated with the above problems is $H = R(x) - D(x) - w(B) + \lambda[G(x) - h(x,B;p,F)]$, where λ is the co-state multiplier measuring the shadow price of the stock at the margin. Assuming an interior solution, the maximum principle yields the following necessary conditions for an optimum:

$$(10.27) \quad \frac{\partial H}{\partial B} = 0 \rightarrow \lambda \frac{\partial h}{\partial B} = -w'(B)$$

$$(10.28) \quad \dot{\lambda} = r\lambda - \frac{\partial H}{\partial x} = (r - G'(x) + \frac{\partial h}{\partial x})\lambda - R'(x) + D'(x)$$

From (10.27), the marginal cost of enforcement should equal its marginal benefit, which equals the contribution of an additional dollar to poaching enforcement ($\partial h/\partial B < 0$) multiplied by the shadow price of the elephant stock. Equation (10.28) is a standard inter-temporal non-arbitrage condition (see Chapter 7).

Assuming a steady-state, so that the state and co-state variables are constant over time, gives:

$$(10.29) \quad r = G'(x^*) - \frac{\partial h}{\partial x^*} - \frac{(R'(x^*) - D'(x^*))\partial h / \partial B^*}{w'(B^*)}$$

$$(10.30) \quad G(x^*) = h^*$$

where * indicates an optimum solution for the no-trade scenario. For numerical analysis, it is necessary to specify functional forms for the functions in (10.29) and (10.30). We use the specifications of the previous section to describe $h(x,B;p,F)$. Assuming that $c(B) = \gamma + \phi B$ is an adequate representation of the relation between enforcement and poaching cost, and specifying $w(B) = e^{\sigma B}$, (10.29) and (10.30) reduce to:

$$(10.31) \quad r = G'(x^*) - \frac{pq}{2\theta z} + \frac{[R'(x^*) - D'(x^*)]\phi}{2\theta z \sigma e^{\sigma B^*}}$$

$$(10.32) \quad G'(x^*) = \frac{pqx^* - (\gamma + \phi B^*) - \theta p}{2\theta z}$$

Using the earlier functional forms for $G(x)$, $R(x)$ and $D(x)$, the model can be solved for optimal enforcement and elephant stock levels. Optimal stocks and enforcement in this situation can then be compared to the case where trade is allowed.

The Government Problem with Trade in Ivory

When trade in ivory is allowed, the government recognises the potential to harvest sustainably a marketable product from living elephant populations. This implies that the problem given by (10.25) and (10.26) should be slightly modified as:

(10.33) Maximise $\displaystyle\int_0^\infty [p'(y + \theta h) + R(x) - D(x) - w(B)]e^{-rt}\, dt$

(10.34) subject to $\dot{x} = G(x) - y - h(x, B; p', F)$.

In this model, y is legal off-take, θh represents confiscated tusks, and p' is the new (possibly higher) price of ivory. Poachers may face different prices after the trade ban is lifted, because poached ivory passes for legal ivory and is marketed through different channels, or because demand increases (demand function shifts out) as a result of the signal (trade is resumed) that the elephant is no longer a threatened species. The sequence of control variables in this case is as follows:

1. The government chooses an optimal level of enforcement B^* – the number of days APUs spend on patrol.
2. The poachers respond by choosing the number of elephants they will harvest h^* given B^*.
3. The government chooses the number of elephants it will cull y^*, where $y^* = G(x^*) - h^*$ (Skonhoft and Solstad 1998).

The current value Hamiltonian is $H = p'(y + \theta h) + R(x) - D(x) - w(B) + \lambda[G(x) - y - h]$, where λ is the co-state multiplier. Assuming a steady-state exists and given the above specifications, the following system of equations describes the steady-state:

$$(10.35) \quad r = G'(x^{**}) - \frac{p'q}{2\theta z} + \frac{R'(x^{**}) - D'(x^{**}) + p'\theta \dfrac{p'q}{2\theta z}}{p'}$$

$$(10.36) \quad G(x^{**}) = y^{**} + \frac{p'qx^{**} - (\gamma + \phi B^{**}) - \theta p'}{2\theta z},$$

where ** indicates optima for the trade scenario. Equations (10.35), (10.36) and $ph_B = -w$ should be solved simultaneously for x^{**}, y^{**} and B^{**}. It is clear from (10.35) that B does not enter directly into the equation describing stock size, because, for an optimum solution, the co-state variable λ should equal the price of ivory per elephant. This implies that p' (which is independent of B) can be substituted in the denominator of the stock term.

A priori, it is not clear whether x^{**} is greater or smaller than x^*, or whether the trade ban results in more or fewer elephants. This depends on the magnitude of the price change (p' versus p) and the outcomes of the complicated stock terms on the right-hand-sides of (10.32) and (10.36). (Due to the concavity of the growth function $G(x)$, increases in the stock term translate into more elephants.) We now solve the trade and no-trade models to determine whether elephant populations are likely to be greater under trade than with a trade ban.

Empirical Application to Zambia

The parameter data and functional forms employed in the model are similar to the ones applied in previous sections. The specification of the $c(B)$ function, however, requires additional explanation as this function is not described elsewhere. Define enforcement effort B as the number of days that APUs are actually in the field. According to Leader-Williams *et al.* (1990), the total number of APU days for the period 1979–1985 is about 672. This value is applied to the scenarios below. Using data on the opportunity costs of labour, MG&LW (1992b) estimate poaching costs per expedition c to be approximately $180. But one would expect higher levels of enforcement to translate into higher costs for poachers, because they have to travel greater distances to areas that are less well guarded or take other precautions to avoid APUs. Assume that $c = \gamma + \phi B$ is an adequate representation of the cost function, although the analysis can easily be repeated for other specifications. Optimal elephant stocks are computed for $c = 180$ and $B = 672$ and different combinations of γ and ϕ, (see Table 10.5).

Finally, according to Leader-Williams *et al.* (1990), the total enforcement budget for the period 1979–1985 amounted to approximately US$1 million. As mentioned above, the total number of expedition days in this period was about 672. Thus, APU expedition-days per year amounted to approximately 134, with an annual budget of $0.2 million. Fitting the curve, $w(B) = e^{\sigma B}$, through this single observation yields $\sigma \approx 0.1$. Table 10.5 gives optimal stocks for different discount rates and specifications of the poaching cost function $c(B)$, although varying the cost function does not affect the trade outcome.

Table 10.5: Optimal Elephant Stocks, No-Trade and Trade Scenarios

Discount rate	No Trade: $\gamma = 160$ $\phi = 0.03$	No Trade: $\gamma = 100$ $\phi = 0.12$	No Trade: $\gamma = 60$ $\phi = 0.18$	Trade
0%	15,890	15,790	15,780	18,100
4%	15,780	15,760	15,760	16,100
6%	15,720	15,750	15,760	15,300
8%	15,660	15,730	15,740	14,500
12%	15,550	15,700	15,720	13,200
16%	15,440	15,680	15,700	12,100

Perhaps the most important observation that follows from the results in Table 10.5 is that the optimal elephant stock for *both* the trade and the no-trade scenarios are consistently lower than current stock estimates. According to the African Elephant Database (Said *et al.* 1995), the current Zambian stock comprises some 33,000 elephants. Further, as noted earlier, culling elephants makes sense because of conflicts between elephants and agricultural activities. In this analysis, damage done by elephants, $D(x)$, is measured as the opportunity cost of foregone forage, although it is likely higher.

Not surprisingly, optimal stocks fall with an increase in the discount rate. Optimal elephant stocks for the no-trade scenario are higher than in the case where trade is permitted if the discount rate is higher than about 5%. As the real discount rate rises, the no-trade steady-state population exceeds the trade population by a significant amount in Table 10.5. Given that real discount rates in developing countries tend to be high (partly as a result of uncertainty), it is in the interests of nature conservation that an ivory trade ban remain in place.

The numerical results also indicate that the stocks are relatively robust for different specifications of the cost function $c(B)$. High values for γ reduce poaching (poachers consider average rather than marginal returns to poaching effort), while high values for ϕ stimulate enforcement (which is evaluated at the margin by the government) and thereby reduces poaching as well. On balance, the effect of the specification of $c(B)$ matters little. Robustness of the results with respect to the parameter σ has also been investigated (but not presented here); we conclude that changes in this parameter have relatively minor effects on the optimal population.

As already noted, there is considerable uncertainty about future demand and prices when the trade ban is lifted. Hence, both lower and higher price scenarios are investigated, with the results reported in Table 10.6. Burton (1998) presents average prices for ivory from hunter to middleman for the pre-ban and post-ban period. The average price has fallen some 40%, although the evidence is not conclusive for all countries. For example, prices in Zambia in the pre-ban period ranged from $18–$24 per kg, and in the post-ban period from $14–$26 per kg.

Table 10.6: Optimal Elephant Stocks, Trade Scenario and Various Prices

Discount rate	$p' = 0.8p$	$p' = 1.2p$	$p' = 1.4p$	$p' = 1.6p$
0%	17,700	18,400	18,700	19,000
4%	16,100	16,000	15,900	15,800
6%	15,400	15,000	14,800	14,500
8%	14,800	14,200	13,800	13,500
12%	13,700	12,700	12,200	11,800
16%	12,700	11,500	10,900	10,400

Higher ivory prices depress elephant numbers, except when discounting is not taken into account. In the trade scenario, harvesting by both the government and poachers is more attractive when prices go up. The government will respond by increasing its enforcement effort, but on balance the steady-state stock falls. The numerical results (not reported here) indicate that the optimal stock with trade approaches the no-trade outcome when the ivory price approaches zero.

Now, return to the issue of whether ivory trade should be banned, and consider two schools of thought regarding enforcement. As argued by some advocates of restricted trade, what happens to ivory revenues may also be important for elephant numbers. *The Economist* (1997a), for example, suggests that proceeds from the sale of harvested ivory could go "into a special pot to help finance conservation, anti-poaching and, at least in theory, rural development for local people, most of whom regard elephants as a destructive nuisance". Poor people who encounter elephants are often killed (Coetzee 1989; Simmons and Krueter 1989). What is done with revenues may be relatively unimportant because economic theory dictates that government proceeds should be invested in the economy to obtain the greatest marginal gain in social welfare, which might not necessarily be to protect elephants. However, it becomes important if those living in rural areas who are affected by elephants are provided a stake in elephant harvests. If they are given a property right to the elephants, their incentive to protect them is greater, but only if expected revenues exceed nuisance values.

Bulte and van Kooten (1999b) analyse whether investing all the ivory proceeds in elephant conservation makes a significant difference, or not. They estimated that, for a price of US$450 per elephant, optimal management of elephants results in sustainable ivory income of approximately $300,000 per year (depending on the discount rate, which determines optimal stocks and, hence, flows). This implies that about 830 hectares can be safeguarded from poaching if $500 per ha per year is needed to prevent poaching, and slightly more than 1,430 hectares if only $200 ha^{-1} per year is required. Since game management areas and parks in Zambia amount to 130,000 square km and elephants are found in an area about two times that large (Said et al. 1995), the effect of investing any ivory rents in conservation will probably be relatively modest.

Finally, in this analysis we ignored passive-use values, which may well be considerable. The optimal stock estimates in the above tables are therefore only "optimal" from the perspective of a host country that is not compensated for the external nonuse values that it generates. From a global perspective (i.e., with proper compensation for the positive externalities associated with conservation), optimal stock levels are underestimated. We now consider this issue.

Declining marginal nonuse benefits and strategic culling

What happens when, based on nonuse values of *in situ* elephants, rich countires compensate range states to maintain their elephant populations? In considering this case, we assume that countries can legally trade in ivory, and we ignore poaching. Transboundary nonuse values for which the "host country" is not fully compensated may give rise to sub-optimal low levels of supply of the amenity, sub-optimally low from an international perspective. Compensating for positive externalities should be in the interests of nature conservation, and can be pursued through international conventions and agreements.

The alleged positive effects of international transfers may never materialise, however. Conventional wisdom relies on the critical but maybe unrealistic assumption that an international governing body exists to ensure a cooperative solution or that national governments can somehow be tempted to agree to the global optimum (Folmer et al. 1993; Sandler 1997). We are not concerned with how cooperative solutions arise, but focus on the consequences of applying the naive assumption that internalising positive externalities contributes to conservation of natural resources. What happens is that a selfish national government can sometimes improve its welfare by choosing an excessive depletion strategy when confronted with international transfers. The selfish government assumption may be more relevant for policy makers than the assumption of altruistic global cooperation for the common good (Sandler 1997).

The No-compensation Solution of the Simple Elephant Model

Assume that the international community derives utility $U(x)$ from elephant conservation, but chooses not to compensate the host country for this externality. Using the same notation as before, the management problem for African countries can be represented by the following problem:

(10.37) Maximise $\displaystyle\int_0^\infty [R(x) + py - D(x)]e^{-rt}\,dt$

(10.38) subject to $\dot{x} = G(x) - y$.

Nonuse values are assumed to exist, but accrue to people in different countries who choose to free ride. Since no compensation is provided for nonuse values, they are ignored by range states. The current value Hamiltonian for problem (10.37)–(10.38) is $H = R(x) + py - D(x) + \lambda[G(x) - y]$, where λ is the co-state multiplier measuring the shadow price of the stock at the margin. Assuming an interior solution and that a steady-state exists, the maximum principle yields the following steady-state equations:

(10.39) $\quad r = G'(x^*) + \dfrac{R'(x^*) - D'(x^*)}{p}$

(10.40) $\quad G(x^*) = y^*$

where * indicates an optimum solution in the case of no compensation for the non-use benefits that accrue to foreigners. From (10.39), the optimal population of elephants results when the social discount rate equals the growth rate plus the marginal rate of substitution between leaving an elephant *in situ* and harvesting it today. Given the standard assumption that $G''(x) < 0$, it is seen from (10.39) that increasing marginal recreation benefits, $R'(x)$, raises the optimal stock x^* unambiguously, with an increase in $D(x)$ having the opposite effect. From (10.40) it follows that, at the steady-state, harvest should equal net growth.

Compensating for Nonuse Values

Now assume that the international community ceases to free ride, so that range states no longer bear the burden of protecting elephants alone. Assume that marginal preservation value is declining in stock size (i.e., there is a downward sloping demand curve for the number of elephants preserved $U'(x) > 0$, $U''(x) < 0$), and that donor countries are willing to pay compensation based on the marginal value of *in situ* elephants. It is easy to show that a cooperative solution with compensation and no strategic behaviour by the range states unambiguously increases optimal stock size. The exercise would result in an extra term $U'(x)$ in the numerator of the stock term in equation (10.39), which, due to the concavity of the growth function, implies that optimal stocks should go up (as $U'(x) > 0$).

It is likely that African countries recognise that they can manipulate the transfer payments they receive as compensation for transboundary nonuse values. Assume that African countries collude and act as a "monopolist", or, alternatively, as that the main range states (e.g. Botswana, Zimbabwe, South Africa, Gabon, Zaire) act as oligopolists, which means that they face downward sloping demand functions (Bulte and van Kooten 1999e). With marginal preservation value declining in stock size, the compensation received per elephant is subject to the discretionary culling choices of the range states. African countries can raise the price (compensation per *in situ* elephant) by restricting the stock of elephants (by culling more). The objective function for the African community can thus be written as:

$$(10.41) \quad \text{Maximise} \int_0^\infty [R(x) + py + T(x)x - D(x)]e^{-rt}\, dt$$

with T represents the transfer received per elephant, with $T(x) = U'(x)$. Consistent with economic intuition we assume $U''(x) = T'(x) < 0$. The current value Hamiltonian associated with problem (10.41) with constraint (10.38) is $H = R(x) + py + T(x)x - D(x) + \lambda[G(x) - y]$. Again, assuming a steady-state, this problem is readily solved for the following equations:

$$(10.42) \quad r = G'(x^{**}) + \frac{R'(x^{**}) + T'(x^{**})x^{**} + T(x^{**}) - D'(x^{**})}{p}$$

and

$$(10.43) \quad G(x^{**}) = y^{**},$$

where ** indicates an optimum solution for the non-cooperative solution.

Since $G(x)$ is concave, the optimal stock increases (decreases) when the stock term on the RHS of (10.42) goes up (down). Obviously, $T(x^{**}) > 0$, and thus this term contributes to conservation. This is the *conservation motive* of international transfers. On the other hand, $T'(x^{**}) < 0$ (and $T'(x^{**})x^{**} < 0$) by assumption. This is the *depletion motive*. Hence, the stock term of (10.42) is greater than the stock term of equation (10.39) when $T(x^{**}) > T'(x^{**})x^{**}$, and smaller when the reverse holds. In the latter case, international compensation for a positive externality reduces African elephant stocks. In order to gain some insights for policy purposes, we solve both models for various assumptions about preservation value at the margin.

Empirical-Numerical Results

Functional forms of $R(x)$, $G(x)$ and $D(x)$ are provided above. There is no information about the nonuse values of elephants, but some have estimated willingness-to-pay to preserve large mammals (see Chapter 9). Due to the lack of data for elephants, we heroically employ WTP for protecting gray whales as a poxy for WTP for elephants (or total WTP of approximately US$20). This assumption biases our numerical results, but in an unknown direction. We assume a linear, downward sloping marginal WTP curve, $U'(x) = \alpha - \beta x$. The area under the marginal WTP curve is total WTP, which is found by multiplying household WTP ($20) by the number of households in high-income countries (available in IBRD 1997). We analyse the impact of various assumptions about marginal WTP by varying the vertical intercept, or WTP for the first elephant. Total WTP (or the area under the curve) is kept constant when the intercept on the vertical axis increases but marginal WTP is steeper – in this case, the slope of $T(x)$. First the base case of no cooperation is determined, followed by the solution for the compensation case with no strategic behaviour by the range states (or cooperative solution). The base case results do not depend on the specification of $T(x)$ and are reported in the first column of Table 10.7. The other columns are for the cooperative solution, for various assumptions with respect to $T(x)$.

It is obvious that, relative to the base case, the cooperative solution results in a higher (or at least the same size) optimal stock. This is the standard result. Without compensation, the optimal stock is much smaller than current populations of around 600,000 elephants. However, assuming that total WTP to conserve elephants is roughly equal to WTP to conserve whales, the current stock may be sub-optimal from a global perspective.

Table 10.7: Optimum Elephant Populations in Africa for Various Discount Rates and Marginal Values of the First Elephant (α in '000s US$): Base Case and Cooperative Compensation[a]

Discount Rate	Base Case	Compensation $\alpha = 6$	Compensation $\alpha = 16$	Compensation $\alpha = 26$	Compensation $\alpha = 36$
0%	432,600	1,172,900	449,800	432,600	432,600
3%	401,800	1,170,300	449,400	401,800	401,800
6%	374,700	1,167,600	449,100	374,700	374,700
9%	350,800	1,165,000	448,700	350,800	350,800
12%	329,500	1,162,400	448,300	329,500	329,500
15%	310,500	1,159,700	447,900	310,500	310,500

[a] For the second column, the value of α is such that marginal WTP is approximately constant. For the other columns, α is arbitrarily increased.

Now consider the case where the range states behave strategically, lowering elephant populations so that they extract monopoly-type rents from the rich countries. Solving the steady-state described by (10.42) and (10.43) gives the results in Table 10.8. Strategic responses by rnage states to international compensation schemes for nonuse values may result in depletion of *in situ* elephant stocks. This is seen by comparing the last three columns in the table with the base-case column. When the marginal WTP curve (or international demand curve for nonuse values) is steeply downward sloping (i.e., when α is relatively large, in this case greater than or equal to

16,000), the depletion motive outweighs the conservation motive and stocks are lower with international compensation than without.

Table 10.8: Optimum Elephant Populations for Various Discount Rates and Marginal Values of the First Elephant (α in '000s US$): Base Case and with Strategic Culling[a]

Discount Rate	Base Case	Compensation α = 6	Compensation α = 16	Compensation α = 26	Compensation α = 36
0%	432,600	594,900	227,100	140,300	101,500
3%	401,800	593,600	226,900	140,200	101,400
6%	374,700	592,300	226,800	140,100	101,400
9%	350,800	591,000	226,600	140,100	104,400
12%	329,500	589,700	226,400	140,000	101,300
15%	310,500	588,300	226,200	139,900	101.300

[a] For the second column, the value of α is such that marginal WTP is approximately constant. For the other columns, α is arbitrarily increased.

Conclusions concerning the ivory trade ban

We summarise the main finding about trade bans that are designed to conserve an endangered or threatened species. Although the African elephant was considered in the above analysis, the conclusions apply to other species as well. We can use our models to determine the costs to the range states of protecting elephants using a trade ban, although the costs of enforcing such a trade ban are ignored and might be substantial. The results are presented in Table 10.9. These indicate that, for real discount rates of 8% or more, the costs of protecting elephants are $300 per elephant or less. Indeed, the level of compensation required is so small that a one-time payment of $1 by households in rich countries (assume there are 100 million such households) would be sufficient to compensate the range states for "putting up with" the trade ban. It would seem, therefore, that a trade ban is not only effective in preserving elephants, but that is should be a simple matter to complensate range states for the costs they incur. This conclusion is misleading, however, for a number of reasons. As shown in the forgoing analyses, a complete trade ban is unlikely to be efficient at the margin, even when the preservation benefits that accrue to some wealthy nations are taken into account. Also, banning trade may be detrimental to elephant conservation when discount rates applied by host countries are sufficiently low (as indicated in the first two rows of Table 10.9).

Table 10.9: Annual Costs to Range States of Protecting Elephants via a Ban on Ivory Trade Ban

Discount rate	Ivory Trade Ban		Trade		Trade minus No Trade		
	Benefits ($)	Optimal stock	Benefits ($)	Optimal stock	Difference $	Δ in elephant numbers	$ per elephant protected
0%	59,212	16,240	387,645	18,080	328,443	1840	Negative
4%	57,871	15,960	348,653	16,220	290,782	260	Negative
6%	57,199	15,820	331,881	15,430	274,682	-390	704
8%	56,574	15,690	316,700	14,720	260,126	-970	268
12%	55,322	15,430	290,158	13,490	234,836	-1940	121
16%	54,164	15,190	267,697	12,460	213,532	-2730	78

In the absence of nonuse values, the case against the ban is substantially weakened when poaching occurs. The first-best, restricted trade optimum may perhaps not be attainable as range states have an incentive to deviate from the optimal plan as time proceeds. Further, support for the ban becomes stronger when poaching is considered. The economic tradeoffs for governments (e.g., deciding how much effort to devote to enforcement) are affected by the trade ban, and numerical results using data for Zambia indicate that elephant stocks decline when trade is allowed. Restricted trade also gives an impetus to illegal poaching (as poached ivory can not be distinguished from what is legal) that is unmatched by increasing government enforcement.

When nonuse values are incorporated, the optimal stock of elephants increases. However, since marginal preservation values of elephants are probably declining in stock size, compensating range states to protect elephants may provoke a strategic response; range states may decide to decimate their herds to manipulate elephant conservation values at the margin, thereby increasing their payments from the rich countries. This is similar to a monopolist reducing output in order to increase revenues. Depending on the specification of the "demand for nature curve", the result may well be declining stocks and a reduction in global welfare, although range states increase their well being via the redistribution of income that their strategic behaviour entails.

It is sometimes argued that, as a result of the trade ban and absence of legal ivory on the market, prices on the illegal market will soar (see, e.g., Barbier and Swanson 1990). This provides an extra incentive for poachers to increase poaching effort. This expectation has never materialised, however, probably because of shifting demand. The trade ban itself may well have been instrumental in shifting demand, by creating a moral barrier to ivory purchases.

Finally, some authors argue that prevention of extinction may not be the only (or even the most relevant) goal of endangered species conservation. Meecham (1997), for example, investigated endangered tigers and concluded that this species is technically in no danger of extinction. Tigers breed readily in captivity and will continue to be available in circuses, zoos and animal parks. The real challenge concerning tiger conservation is maintaining wild tigers (however defined) in their natural habitat. Then the issue centres on preserving wildness, rather than species *per se*. Preservation of wilderness as a public good was discussed in Chapter 9. An alternative is to permit game ranching where wildlife exist in the wild, but on private land. Landowners are able to crop the animals for their products and/or bring tourists or hunters onto the land. We investigate this in the context of game ranching in Kenya (in the next section). First, however, we briefly consider the case of rhino conservation to illustrate a general point that was also raised in Chapter 7: multiple species may matter in wildlife management. We argue that efforts to conserve the rhino should not be taken in isolation from elephant management, because in real life poachers typically harvest both species. Thus, the foregoing analyses can only be considered an approximation of reality. So far, we have focused on elephants, disregarding rhino poaching. Since jointness is important, the types of models considered above can readily be extended to include joint harvesting of multiple (endangered) species.

Joint harvesting of endangered species: Rhinoceros and elephants

Brown and Layton (1998) consider the case of (black) rhino conservation. This section is mainly based on their work and data. Legal trade in rhino horn has been banned since 1977, but this has not stopped the dramatic decline in animal numbers. In 1960, an estimated 100,000 black rhinos roamed Africa, but, by 1980, this number had fallen precipitously to about 15,000 rhinos. Recent (1994) estimates indicate fewer than 2,200 animals, with the species locally extinct in many countries. The major reason for the decline is poaching, with prices for rhino horn as high as $3,000 per kg in recent years. Demand for horn is inelastic (it is used as traditional medicine in China, Korea and Taiwan), and prices have risen by sixfold since the ban was implemented. Enforcement effort has not kept track with increased poaching.

Brown and Layton do not believe that more enforcement effort is the key to successful rhino conservation. They advocate quite a different approach: trade should be legalised and rhino horn should be supplied at a price below the opportunity cost of poaching. Demand for rhino horn is unlikely to shift inward (as happened with demand for ivory since horn is used for medicinal purposes) and it is difficult to raise poaching costs by increasing enforcement (as is apparently the case in many poor African nations). Hence, the proposed solution is to flood the market with rhino horn, thereby driving prices down. Prices should be depressed to such a low level that profits from poaching rhino are zero, and poaching is eliminated. The threshold price is a limit or entry price.

To be more specific, the authors propose the following process. African range states should first sell their considerable quantities of stockpiled horns (from dead rhinos, confiscated horns, *etc.*) to speculators. Speculators will treat their (old and newly acquired) stocks as a non-renewable resource, and sell them as predicted by the Hotelling depletion model. African range states and speculators will play a Cournot-Nash game, with the range states supplying horn as a renewable resource by sustainable cropping of living (albeit sedated!) rhinos. Both black and white rhinos can be cropped, since horns from the two species are perfect substitutes. The range states must commit to a no poaching policy as a prerequisite to resuming legal trade. Thus African countries commit to keeping horn prices below the threshold price that makes poaching profitable. Cropping sufficient rhinos every year provides the "backstop price" for the stockpiled horns. It turns out that there are currently more than enough living rhinos to ensure that prices of rhino horn can be sustainably depressed below entry prices. According to Brown and Layton (1998), this approach will allow for full recovery of rhino populations in Africa.

This is obviously an interesting approach to wildlife conservation, and one that is consistent with textbook economics. We note one potential drawback. Brown and Layton use threshold prices of $300 and $800. While this is probably a realistic estimate when poachers are exclusively after rhinos, it may be an overestimate of the entry price in the case of "joint harvesting".

Initially assume exclusive rhino poaching (no elephants are taken as bycatch), and define poaching profits as $\pi = p_r q_r - cE$, where p_r is the price of a rhino horn, q_r is poached quantity, c is the per unit cost of poaching effort, and E is poaching effort (e.g., defined in terms of expedition days). Let output be $q_r = \phi x_r E$, where, as before,

ϕ is a catchability coefficient and x_r is the stock of rhinos. In Chapter 7 we demonstrated that the open-access stock is $x_r' = c/\phi p_r$. Optimal poaching effort is found by equating harvest $\phi x_r E$ with net growth $G(x_r')$ in the steady-state x_r'. It is now possible to compute the limit price p_r such that E falls to a value below 1.0 (i.e., less than one expedition day per year is undertaken). As mentioned, Brown and Layton assume that the threshold price is \$300–\$800.

Zambian poachers go after both rhinos *and* elephants on their poaching expeditions (MG&LW 1992b). This implies that profit should be rewritten as: $\pi = p_r q_r + p_e q_e - cE$, where p_e is now the price per unit of ivory and q_e is poached ivory. Optimal poaching effort E is now a function of both the profitability of catching rhinos and elephants. It can be argued that the marginal costs of poaching rhinos is nearly zero (the cost of one bullet plus the costs of retrieving and transporting the horn). When rhino horn prices fall, poachers may concentrate on elephants, but any rhinos encountered along the way will be a bonus as long as the marginal benefits exceed the "price of a bullet". Only when rhino horn prices fall to zero (a possibility not consistent with the Brown and Layton model) will shooting cease. In fact, when legalising rhino horn is accompanied with legalised ivory trade (something not recommended by Brown and Layton), on balance, poaching effort E (and hence illegal rhino killing) may *increase* rather than decrease. The reason is that legalised ivory and rhino trade provides an impetus for the illegal trade (see above). This observation suggests that care should be taken in formulating policies to protect endangered species.

10.3 Game Ranching to Conserve Wildlife in Kenya

Wildlife are an important resource in Kenya, generating income for the government, employment for local people and preservation benefits to those living in Kenya and elsewhere. Hence, policies to protect wildlife are important, but one must continually ask whether the policies in place are effective or whether other ones might be more efficient in conserving wildlife. We examined policies related to elephants (and, to a lesser extent, rhinos) in the previous sections. We now turn our attention to wildlife herbivores, particularly game animals. Consistent with the elephant story above, opinions are divided on the central issue of how to promote conservation of herbivores: should legal harvesting be allowed, and is legal harvesting in the interests of nature conservationists?

Rangelands are the focus of wildlife policy in Kenya, with rangelands categorised into

1. National Parks and National Reserves,
2. "dispersal areas and corridors", and
3. "non-adjacent areas" (Kenya Wildlife Service 1990).

National parks and reserves constitute some 8% of Kenya's total land area, and are protected solely for use by wildlife. The government owns National Parks and county councils own National Reserves, but management and conservation of wildlife are the responsibility of the Kenya Wildlife Service (KWS). Dispersal areas and corridors are "unprotected" lands adjacent to national parks and reserves, with wild animals "spilling over" into these areas that are privately owned. Finally, non-adjacent areas are "unprotected" lands that harbour more than half of Kenya's game animals but, in contrast to the dispersal areas and corridors, are not directly connected to the national parks and reserves. They are an important component in wildlife conservation and are privately owned.

Commercial ranches are a key land use in "adjacent areas and corridors" and "non-adjacent areas", and thus play an integral part in wildlife protection and preservation (KWS 1990). Accordingly, management of these ranches must be tailored to meet the objectives of the private landowners and the KWS; these are to secure the greatest continuous profit and to conserve wildlife, respectively.

Before the 1890s, wild animals in Kenya, and East Africa more generally, were plentiful in numbers and diverse in species because the pastoral tribes, notably *Masai*, lived in harmony with nature (KWS 1990). They accommodated wildlife by grazing their herds and flocks alongside wild animals. Without a wildlife policy, the period 1890 to 1898 witnessed substantial rifle-hunting of game animals, which was a catalyst for the development of wildlife conservation policies. The earliest wildlife conservation policy began in 1898 when legislation established game reserves and introduced controls on game hunting. But a spirit of wildlife preservation was still lacking, and heavy hunting of wild animals marked the period 1899 to the early 1930s (Murray 1993). In 1907, the Department of Game was established and empowered to manage wildlife and game hunting. As a result of a hunting "safari" in East Africa in 1909, US President Theodore Roosevelt brought with him the spirit of wildlife conservation, and, by 1938, photography began to replace rifle-shooting. In 1945, a Board of Trustees was established and mandated to administer National Parks, with Nairobi and Tsavo East National Parks established in 1946 and 1948, respectively.

In 1977, a presidential decree banned all hunting of wild animals in a bid to control poaching, and all trophy and curio dealer licenses were revoked. In 1989, the Wildlife Conservation and Management Act created the KWS as a government corporation attached to the Ministry of Tourism and Wildlife and mandated it with responsibility for conserving wildlife in Kenya. The goals of the Act are to conserve the natural environments of Kenya, and its fauna and flora, for the nation's economic development and for the people living in wildlife areas and to protect people and property from injury or damage by wildlife. By 1990, game photo-viewing had completely replaced the rifle-hunting safaris.

Prior to 1989, ranchers had no choice but to accommodate wildlife on their lands. They could not legally kill wildlife ungulates. This state of affairs was unsustainable as a preservation policy because private landowners could not continue to subsidise national and international conservation efforts. Any forage consumed by wildlife and damage to ranch investments were borne by the private landowners. Therefore, after 1989, the KWS instituted alternative policies. Ranchers could be compensated for damage caused by wildlife, but, more importantly, although wildlife continued to be owned by the state, ranchers were given conditional user rights to wildlife found on their land. Restrictions on what ranchers could do with game consisted of limits on harvest and even on the use of carcasses (e.g., until recently hides could not be sold), and a prohibition against sale of hunting safaris, with trophy sales limited to *ad hoc* licences (Sommerlatte and Hopcraft 1994).

Currently, game ranches can crop wildlife, with game meat and its by-products sold locally, but subject to harvest quota based on game populations. Game harvest quotas for ranches located south-east of Nairobi on the Athi-Kapiti Plains along the Nairobi-Mombasa road in Machakos District are provided in Table 10.10.

Table 10.10: KWS Wildlife Cropping Quotas for Machakos District, 1996.

Animal Species	Allowable Quota (% of population)	Animal Species	Allowable Quota (% of population)
Thomson's gazelle	5	Impala	7.5
Grants gazelle	7.5	Zebra	7.5
Kongoni	10	Oryx	6
Wildebeest	10	Giraffe	7.2[a]

Source: Kinyua (1998)
[a]Realised quota for the David Hopcraft Ranch. Quotas for other ranches are apportioned by KWS based on the need to crop giraffe.

There are nine private ranches in this area and they cover some 65,870 ha of range. The most progressive ranch is the David Hopcraft Ranch (8,100 ha), although it is not the largest. The David Hopcraft Ranch was allowed to practice game harvests as early as 1982, but the other ranches could do so only since 1989. This ranch is also fenced and has its own slaughterhouse (Sommerlatte and Hopcraft 1994). The game ranching policy gives ranchers an incentive to allocate scarce forage (and other ranch) resources to wildlife ungulates, but obstacles remain.

Annual rainfall in the study region (Machakos District) averages 550 mm, but the distribution of rainfall is bi-model. This gives rise to two distinct growing and grazing seasons.

It is not clear whether this conservation policy (permitting game cropping) will actually achieve the desired results of widlife conservation for several reasons. First, the value of wildlife harvest (primarily meat) is low (recall Table 10.2) and ranchers are more likely to make forage available for domestic cattle, sheep and goats than for wildlife herbivores. Second, some wildlife are transitory while other wildlife are resident, although fences can be built to keep wildlife on one's property. For transient wildlife, there is an incentive to take animals before one's neighbours harvest the animals – the open-access problem – although here we only consider the case where animals are enclosed in some fashion (either via fencing or because of a tendency to remain in place). Third, the availability of forage and wildlife populations fluctuate wildly depending on weather (forage production) and the predator-prey (herbivores and their predators) relationship. Finally, government regulations continue to be an obstacle to game management. For example, when game cropping was first permitted in Kenya, ranchers could sell game meat but not hides. This reduced the value of wildlife herbivores relative to domestic livestock. To investigate potential problems with current (and past) policies and to analyse alternative wildlife policies, we present a dynamic optimising mathematical programming model, calibrated using biophysical and economic data collected from ranchers in Machakos District near Nairobi. Data and other details are provided in Kinyua (1998) (see also van Kooten, Bulte and Kinyua 1997).

Bioeconomic model of game ranching

The rancher makes decisions on stocking levels of both domestic and wildlife herbivore (and thus species mix) through livestock sales and purchases, and through the effort devoted to the harvest of game animals. The harvest of wildlife herbivores is a function of effort. A bioeconomic model that captures the dynamics of domestic and wild herbivores, within the broader context of the dynamics of a commercial ranch grazing system, is employed to examine KWS and other wildlife conservation policies. The model is discrete since decisions are made at discrete points in time and because, rather than an analytic solution, the solution has to be found numerically. The objective of the ranch owner is to maximise discounted net returns to the ranch enterprise, with returns accruing from the sale of domestic livestock and game cropping of wildlife herbivores:

$$(10.44) \quad \text{Maximise} \sum_{t=1}^{T} \left(\rho^t \sum_{i=1}^{n} (p_i y_{it} - w E_{it}) + p_{Ca} y_{Cat} - w_{Ca} X_t \right).$$

In (10.44), $\rho = 1/(1 + r)$; $n \ (= 8)$ is the number of species of wildlife ungulates; p_i is real gross price per animal unit adjusted for all variable costs, except effort cost in the case of game and livestock purchase cost; E_{it} is effort devoted to game cropping of species i (in hours); w is the real cost of effort per hour; y_{it} is off-take of game animals measured in animal units rather than animal numbers;[11] and X_t is purchases of long yearlings (immature cattle) in period t. A decay function (Conrad and Clark 1987) describes game animal off-take as a function of the wild herbivore population (H) and effort:

$$(10.45) \quad y_{it} = H_{it} (1 - e^{-\alpha_i E_{it}}),$$

where α_i is a harvest parameter for species i and H_{it} refers to numbers at time t. We model the species in Table 10.10.

In the current game cropping specification, we assume that ranchers decide how much effort to devote towards cropping of different species. It is also possible to consider the case where ranchers choose one optimal effort level E, since a game cropping crew out to harvest a kongoni may well stumble upon a herd of impalas. Then, by substituting E for E_i in (10.45), we know how much of each species is harvested. The most satisfactory way to model game cropping, however, is probably a hybrid of these approaches. In contrast to the relatively simple case of the multi-species fishery, the game cropping crew is better able to select individuals of each of the various species to harvest.

---

[11] Range stocking rates are measured in animal units (AUs), with one AU being the amount of (dry-matter) forage consumed by a 450 kilogram cow. Wildlife AUs are determined by $(W/450)^{3/4}$, where W is the weight of the wildlife animal.

Changes in the populations of wildlife herbivores from one period to the next are given by logistic growth functions minus harvests:

$$(10.46) \quad H_{it+1} - H_{it} = \beta_i H_{it} \left(1 - \frac{H_{it} + \lambda_{iC} C_t + \sum_{j=1}^{n-1} \lambda_{ij} H_{jt}}{\delta_i R_t} \right) - y_{it}, \ \forall \ i = 1, \ldots, n, \ i \neq j.$$

Since carrying capacity depends on rainfall, R_t, it is modeled via the term $\delta_i R_t$, with δ_i representing the effect of rainfall on the carrying capacity of herbivore species i. Carrying capacity also depends on the presence of other herbivores and the size of the domestic cattle herd in period t (C_t), and this is captured by the summation term in the logistic model, with λ_{ij} describing the effect that the presence of herbivore j has on H_i, and λ_{iC} the effect of cattle on wildlife herbivore H_i. In some cases, presence of one herbivore enhances the availability of forage for another herbivore (e.g., giraffes reduce browse that competes with grass eaten by gazelle); at other times, the species are competitive (so $\lambda_{ij} > 0$). There is a separate carrying capacity for each species because each species has its own unique habitat (forage and shelter) requirements.

Ranch cattle numbers are modeled as:

$$(10.47) \quad C_{t+1} - C_t = \beta_C C_t + X_t - y_{Ct},$$

where $\beta_C C_t$ is the increase in population due to reproduction (births less deaths), X_t is purchases of long yearlings (which can be sold in the next or following periods) and y_{Ct} is cattle sales in period t.

Because the distribution of rainfall is bimodal, a time step of six months is chosen, corresponding with two growing seasons and two grazing seasons per year. We employ a discrete dynamic optimisation model that is solved using nonlinear programming. While a discrete, current value Hamiltonian can be written (Kinyua 1998), this step is unnecessary as an analytical (and steady-state) solution cannot be found when there are this many state and control variables.

Institutional constraints hamper the ability of ranchers to implement game cropping. Before the late 1980s, landowners were prevented from harvesting any wildlife (preservation policy), with the exception of the David Hopcraft Ranch; in objective (10.44), the first two terms are removed to model this. Since then, game cropping has been permitted (conservation policy), but the government has continued to place constraints on ranchers. One such constraint has already been mentioned: for a time, ranchers could sell meat, but not hides. Ranchers are not permitted to sell viewing or hunting expeditions (trophies) to tourists. Game meat is primarily destined for restaurants that cater to foreign tourists. One reason for the prohibition on sale of hides, horns and other parts is the fear that, by doing so, poaching is encouraged in other areas. As pointed out in the case of elephants, by creating legal markets for these products, illegal products can be sold more easily.

Another constraint prevents ranchers from harvesting more than a fixed number or proportion of the stock of wildlife herbivores. Indeed, the major complaint from ranchers has been the lack of a consistent game cropping policy and an inability to maximise the potential of game conservation on private lands.

In the bioeconomic model, we investigate several aspects of government policy that is designed to conserve wildlife herbivores on private lands. In particular, we use the model to investigate the effects of several institutional constraints on wildlife sustainability. The objective of the analysis is to find policies that will enable ranchers to realise high levels of income while, at the same time, maximising the numbers of wildlife found on game ranches. That is, we wish to determine whether game-cropping policies can effectively be used to conserve *in situ* stocks of wildlife.

A number of public objectives are investigated by making these constraints in the model. These include:

1. no harvesting whatsoever (preservation);
2. constraining wildlife populations at some future time to be equal to or greater than what they were when game cropping was first introduced, namely,

(10.48) $[H_{1,T}, H_{2,T}, ..., H_{m,T}] \geq [H_{1,0}, H_{2,0}, ..., H_{m,0}]$,

where T is the final period in the planning horizon and (m = 8) game animal species;
3. restricting game harvesting to be equal to or less than some fixed level or proportion of the stock of the species (the current KWS policy);
4. ensuring a certain level of biodiversity in each period, where biodiversity is measured using the Shannon index (equation 9.3), say; and
5. unconstrained harvesting.

In some sense, these scenarios represent a progression from preservation to conservation to exploitation. In what follows, the results of these "conservation scenarios" are compared to the case of "preservation" that existed until 1989.

Empirical model of game cropping in Kenya

Equations (10.45) and (10.46) are estimated using ranch-level data from Machakos District, Kenya, for the period mid–1982 through mid–1996. The data consist of monthly harvest levels, cattle sales and purchases, six-month population counts, and precipitation data. Because there are two definite growing/breeding seasons, the data are aggregated to a six-month basis; hence, there are a total of 28 observations (Kinyua 1998). Parameter estimates for the wildlife harvest functions (10.45) are presented in Table 10.11, while the parameter estimates of the logistic growth functions (10.46) are found in Table 10.12. Finally, prices and other economic variables are provided in Table 10.13.

The bioeconomic model, which consists of the objective function (10.44), with harvest levels determined by (10.45), and the population dynamics (10.46) and (10.47) as constraints (= 9), is numerically solved using GAMS (Brooke et al. 1996). There are eight wildlife herbivores and one domestic herbivore species (cattle). The rancher decides how much effort to employ in harvesting each of the eight wildlife species, plus how many long yearlings to purchase and how many cattle to sell; thus, there are ten decision variables. Additional constraints are introduced to examine various policy options. An example of such a constraint is equation (10.48).

Table 10.11: Regression Results for Harvest Production Functions

Equation	Coefficient	t-statistic	R^2	n
G. gazelle	0.0103	12.17	0.90	17
T. gazelle	0.0110	10.03	0.85	19
Giraffe	0.0148	5.65	0.78	10
Oryx	0.0148	7.20	0.86	9
Zebra	0.0158	4.44	0.66	11
Wildebeest	0.0040	6.59	0.71	19
Kongoni	0.0053	5.99	0.65	20
Impala	0.0270	10.55	0.88	15

Source: Kinyua (1998)

Table 10.12: Parameter Estimates for Logistic Population Functions (n = 28)[a]

Species	Gr	Th	Gi	Or	Zb	Wb	Ko	Im
G. gazelle	0.286		−0.677	0.198		−3.588	−2.022	
(Gr)	(4.4)**		(−3.8)	(1.1)		(−8.6)	(−2.2)	
T. gazelle		0.349						
(Th)		(3.6)						
Giraffe	−0.168		0.294	0.297				
(Gi)	(−0.7)		(4.4)	(3.9)				
Oryx (Or)				0.430	−0.651	−2.142		
				(3.4)	(−3.7)	(−2.5)		
Zebra (Zb)		3.209			0.477			
		(2.7)			(5.1)			
W/beest				−0.137		0.323		
(Wb)				(−5.1)		(6.0)		
Kongoni				−0.094			0.332	
(Ko)				(−1.8)			(4.6)	
Impala			−1.641	−0.174		−4.629	4.019	0.074
(Im)			(−3.4)	(−0.5)		(−2.6)	(1.7)	(1.8)
Cattle (C)		−0.045				0.072		
		(−1.5)				(3.6)		
Rainfall	0.231	0.580	0.134	0.059	0.153	0.478	0.685	71578
	(2.2)	(2.80)	(3.6)	(6.1)	(7.0)	(2.8)	(1.6)	(0.0)
R^2	0.44	0.40	0.52	0.7447	0.56	0.71	0.24	0.03

Source: Kinyua (1998)

[a] Explanatory variables in left-hand column. Asymptotic t-statistics in parenthesis.

Table 10.13: Economic Data for Cropping of Game Animals, Purchase of Immature Cattle and Sale of Mature Cattle ('000s 1990 Kenya shillings)

Item	Gr	Th	Gi	Or	Zb	Wb	Ko	Im	C
Gross price AU^{-1}	11.35	7.75	11.05	11.15	12.35	7.0	5.59	9.78	8.88
Net return AU^{-1}	9.78	5.71	6.97	9.27	9.88	5.30	3.92	7.92	7.70
Adjusted NR[a]	10.45	6.10	7.45	9.91	10.56	5.67	4.20	8.47	7.70
Effort cost per hour	0.18	0.18	0.18	0.18	0.18	0.18	0.18	0.18	-
Purchase cost AU^{-1}	-	-	-	-	-	-	-	-	4.17

Source: Kinyua (1998)

[a] Net return per animal unit (AU) excluding effort

The constrained, dynamic optimisation model is solved in GAMS for 30 periods (15 years). Without the constraints that model various policy options, the numerical model consists of a nonlinear objective function and 270 nonlinear constraints (Kinyua 1998). Due to difficulties in solving highly nonlinear constrained optimisation problems, it was not possible to obtain solutions for more than 15 years.

In the case where benefits accrue and costs are incurred for a period of 15 years only, any remaining wildlife at the end of the time horizon still has value to the rancher and/or society. The end-period wildlife can be valued using shadow values for the end period, but shadow values are highly interdependent. In any period, a species' shadow value depends on the price meat fetches in Nairobi and on the population of that species, which determines harvest as a function of effort (and thus cost of harvesting animals). In addition, a species' value depends on the numbers of other species, because other species affect the one under consideration via competition for forage. Attempts to determine consistent end-point shadow values failed, and no attempt is made to value animals available at the end of the time horizon. We assume ranchers have no interest in animals beyond 15 years. In other words, it is assumed that ranchers maximise their profits from game ranching and stocking of cattle over 15 years, with the wildlife that remain at the end of the time horizon simply reverting back to KWS ownership. Given the vagaries of Kenyan wildlife policies, this is not unrealistic assumption. The KWS is then assumed to rely on regulations to ensure that sufficient wildlife remain in the future to satisfy societal concerns. Different forms of these regulations are investigated in the bioeconomic model to determine which one(s) might be most successful in maximising rancher well-being while attaining conservation goals.

Economics of game cropping: Policy insights

The model is used to simulate various policies. The results of the simulation model are summarised in Table 10.14, and provide some interesting policy insights. First of all, for a time horizon of 15 years, and assuming no constraints on the model (scenario 5) and that wildlife have no value after year 15, all of the wildlife populations on the ranch are driven to extinction or to very low levels. This is not surprising given that the transversality conditions (see Chapter 7) require either that the shadow price of game in the last period be zero, or the population be driven to zero. With the exception of low value species, such as impala, the populations are harvested to near zero in the final two periods of the model.

The most interesting result is that the pre–1989 preservation policy (scenario 1) does not result in the preservation of all populations of wildlife herbivores on the ranch. Rather, it leads to the extinction of some species (oryx) and the near extinction of others (e.g., Thompson's gazelle). The reason is that the other animals, as well as cattle raising, drive out those populations that are least able to compete for forage – the marginal species. This is evident from the high stocking rates of cattle in this scenario (Table 10.14). Hence, the conservation policy that was implemented in 1989 (but previously experimented with on one ranch near Nairobi) appears to have been a positive step.

Table 10.14: Effects of Various Kenyan Government Game Ranching Policies on Ranch Returns, Population of Wildlife Herbivores and Carrying Capacity, Model Simulation Results, 15 years

Policy simulation	Net discounted return (mil. KS)	Mean AU[a]	Carrying capacity (ha AU^{-1})[a]	Effect on Wildlife Herbivore Populations
1. Preservation	100.15	2334	3.47[b]	Some wildlife herbivore populations driven to extinction due to competition from other animals, including cattle.
2. End-period population constraint	131.04	1935	4.19	Sustainable
3. KWS harvest rate	111.54	2201	3.68[b]	Sustainability threatened
4. Maintain biodiversity measure, S = 0.615	134.31	1925	4.21	Not sustainable; numbers similar to the end-period population constraint policy, except rapid harvest in final year
5. Unconstrained harvesting	136.10	1959	4.13	Game populations driven to extinction or near extinction in the final two periods

[a] Include wildlife as well as cattle animal units.
[b] Stocking rate for range exceeds recommended level of 4 ha per AU (animal unit).

Another supposedly sustainable policy is the current KWS policy that controls the rates at which ranchers cull wildlife populations (scenario 3). It is not possible for ranchers to harvest more than 10% of the population of Thompson's gazelle in any year, 12% of oryx, 15% of Grant's gazelle, impala, zebra and giraffe, and 20% of kongoni and wildebeest (recall Table 10.10). Surprisingly, sustainability is threatened as this situation is similar to the preservation scenario where some animals are better able to compete than others for forage. Since this is a game ranch with fences to keep game in and predators out, natural predators are less likely to keep populations in balance, while ranchers have a greater incentive to graze cattle – the stocking rate for cattle is also high in this scenario. Despite its low rate of harvest relative to population, Thompson's gazelle, in particular, is projected to go to extinction, at least on the ranch. This is clearly an unintended consequence of what might otherwise be considered a policy to guarantee sustainability.

Two other methods for "imposing" sustainability of wildlife populations are considered: final period populations must be equal to, or greater than, starting populations (scenario 2); and the Shannon biodiversity index (see Chapter 9) must exceed 0.615 in every period (scenario 4). The Shannon number 0.615 is the value of the biodiversity index in the initial year. In scenario 2, game ranching is clearly a sustainable enterprise. The major share of game harvests comes from wildebeest, kongoni, giraffe, oryx and Thmpson's gazelle, while few Grant's gazelle and impala are harvested. With a biodiversity constraint (scenario 4), animal populations are adjusted in the last two periods of the model in a fashion similar to the unconstrained case – all excess animals (i.e., those not needed to satisfy the biodiversity constraint) are harvested in the last period. Since the biodiversity constraint is based on the proportion of animals found on the ranch, as opposed to animal richness (i.e., total numbers), the ranchers harvest the animals to their lowest common denominator. That is, Shannon's biodiversity index as a judge of sustainability leads to erroneous conclusions about the sustainability of the system. Clearly, an end-period constraint that requires population levels to be at or above their original levels is preferred. In practice, such a constraint might require that wildlife populations are compared to the original levels every five or ten years, say.

The costs of each of the institutional constraints can be inferred from Table 10.14 by comparing the net present values of the policies. As expected, the unconstrained case yields the highest returns to the ranchers, but might also lead to the extinction of certain wildlife populations on the ranch. The biodiversity constraint results in the next highest returns, followed by the policy that constrains final period populations to be no less than initial period populations. Since this policy is also judged to be the most sustainable, we compare the remaining policies relative to it. In this regard, the Kenya Wildlife Service's policy reduces discounted net income over the 15 years by some 19.5 million Kenyan shillings, but does nothing to enhance sustainability. A policy that constrains wildlife populations at the end of the 15-year period appears to be the best in terms of profitability and sustainability. It provides ranchers with flexibility but requires them to achieve certain social objectives. The difference in net returns to ranchers between this case (scenario 2) and the unconstrained case (scenario 5) is only about 5 million shillings.

Finally, we note that, according to the model presented here, abandoning the previous preservation policy was a good decision. Not only was it not sustainable, it lowered a rancher's income by some 30.9 million KS over the 15-year time horizon.

10.4 Should Whales be Harvested?

Outcomes of models that assess optimal harvesting and stock size are highly dependent on assumptions with respect to preservation benefits. In this section, we illustrate this using the case of minke whales (Bulte and van Kooten 1999d). With a model that excludes nonuse values, Conrad and Bjorndal (1993) find that a (permanent) moratorium on minke whaling is inefficient in most circumstances. But whales have both commercial value and preservation value. By including nonuse values, Bulte et al. (1998) argue that the current stock of minkes in the Northeast Atlantic is sub-optimal, and that the current moratorium on the harvesting of minke whales is economically justified (see also Horan and Shortle 1999). Their conclusion assumes that the value of the first whale protected is just as high as that of the last whale. However, policy recommendations with respect to whaling are highly sensitive to assumptions about marginal preservation values (as shown in the case of elephants), and the conclusions of Bulte et al. (1998) may not hold when their highly restrictive assumption of constant marginal preservation values is relaxed.

The assumed objective of the International Whaling Commission (IWC), which regulates whaling primarily through the device of moral suasion, is to maximise the sum of (net) use (flow) and nonuse benefits (of the stock) of whales. Mathematically, it is to

$$(10.49) \quad \text{Maximise} \int_{0}^{\infty} [H(y) + U(x) - C(y) - P(x)] \, e^{-rt} \, dt,$$

where $H(y)$ is the benefit of consuming y whales – the area under the demand curve for whales, with $H'(y)$ being the inverse demand function; $C(y)$ is the cost of harvesting whales; $H(y) - C(y)$ is thus the sum of the producer and consumer surpluses of whaling; $U(x)$ are nonuse benefits from preserving whales, which are assumed to be an increasing function of the *in situ* stock x; and $P(x)$ is the economic cost of a biological interaction, namely, the predation that arises because minke whales and humans compete for the same prey species (e.g., herring, capelin, cod). The latter cost, according to Flaaten and Stollery (1996), amounts to approximately US$2,000 per minke whale per year, and we assume that this is the *marginal* predation cost.

The constraints to problem (10.49) consist of the population dynamics:

(10.50) $\quad \dot{x} = G(x) - y,$

where $G(x)$ is the net growth or regeneration of the population in the absence of harvest y.

Invoking the maximum principle gives the following necessary conditions for an optimum:

(10.51) $\quad H'(y) - C'(y) - \lambda + \phi = 0$

(10.52) $\quad \dot{\lambda} = (r - G'(x))\,\lambda - U'(x) + P'(x) - \gamma$

In equation (10.51), λ is the (shadow) rent to the resource, or the market price minus marginal harvesting costs. Equation (10.52) is an arbitrage condition for inter-temporal management, with a similar interpretation as the Hotelling rule for exhaustible resources.

Assuming an interior solution, the optimal steady-state stock is obtained by setting the derivatives with respect to time equal to zero, and then substituting (10.51) into (10.52):

(10.53) $\quad r = G'(x^*) + \dfrac{U'(x^*) - P'(x^*)}{H'(y^*) - C'(y^*)},$

and $y^* = G(x^*)$, where variables denoted with a * indicate optimal levels and $H'(y)$ is the inverse demand function for whales. The optimal population of minke whales results when the social discount rate equals the growth rate plus the marginal rate of substitution between leaving a whale *in situ* and harvesting it today. Given the standard assumption that $G''(x) < 0$, it is easily seen from (10.53) that increasing marginal preservation values, $U'(x)$, raises the optimal stock x^*, and that increasing *marginal* consumption benefits and/or predation costs reduces the optimal population for a given discount rate r. Equation (10.53) is solved for various assumptions with respect to $U'(x)$.

Before answering whether or not minke whales should be harvested, we briefly explain the empirical basis of the functions that appear in (10.53). The growth function most often applied in papers on the economics of whaling (such as Amundsen et al. (1995) and Conrad and Bjorndal 1993) suffers from two shortcomings:

1. the natural population (i.e., the population where natural mortality is exactly offset by recruitment) is *lower* than recent estimates of the current stock size (see below), which is clearly inconsistent; and
2. the function does not allow for a minimum viable population, although this concept is likely relevant for large mammals such as whales (see Soulé 1987, who estimates the MVP for large mammals to be "in the low thousands").

We apply a growth function that deals with the latter problem:

$$(10.54) \quad G(x) = 0.08x(\frac{x}{5,000} - 1)(1 - \frac{x}{100,000}).$$

In this specification, 5,000 approximates the MVP, consistent with Soulé's (1987) interpretation, and we assume that 100,000 is the carrying capacity of minke whales in the Northeast Atlantic. The current population estimated at some 57,000 (Amundsen et al. 1995) to 86,000 animals (Flaaten and Stollery 1996). We also assume that 0.08 is a reasonable approximation of the intrinsic growth rate, which is slightly lower than the growth rate applied by others but consistent with the fact that natural mortality is not included explicitly in the model. Finally, our model should allow for a time lag between birth and maturity, as it takes about seven years until a minke whale is recruited to the adult stock, but, for simplicity, we ignore this. Thus, optimal stocks are somewhat overestimated, but the qualitative results are not affected.

As to the inverse demand function, Bulte et al. (1998) estimated the following model:

$$(10.55) \quad H'(y) = (p^{0.6} - 1)/0.6 = 1,508.4 - 0.3 \, y$$

where p is price in 1994 Norwegian Kroners (NKr) per whale and y is the number of whales harvested. For a harvest of 300 whales ($y = 300$), price is about NKr136,000 (or $p \approx$ US\$19,500). Finally, marginal harvesting costs, $C'(y)$, are simply assumed to be constant and equal to NKr 1,000.

Suppose that total willingness-to-pay for protection of minke whales in the Northeast Atlantic equals about \$30 per household, which is not unreasonable given estimates provided in Table 9.5 for conservation of gray whales. Bulte et al. (1998) simply assumed that MVP was constant, implying thereby that the preservation value per whale amounts to multiplying WTP by the number of households N, and then dividing by the number of whales, namely, $U'(x) = (N \times \text{WTP})/x$. If we assume that total WTP equals \$30, x is 86,000 and N is 90 million (the number of households in the European Union), then the marginal value of preserving a whale is about \$30,000. The WTP for preservation of minke whales can be summed over households because preservation values are assumed to be a public good. Clearly, if the market value of a whale is $20,000 and its preservation value is $30,000, regardless of the stock of whales, it is economically efficient not to harvest any whales.

If the assumption of constant marginal value is relaxed, the impact on the economically efficient population level is dramatic as is the consequence for harvest policy. Assume a linear, downward sloping marginal preservation value curve: $U'(x) = \alpha - \beta x$. Then marginal utility (WTP) equals zero at $x = \alpha/\beta$. Given that the area under such a curve is total WTP (for minke whale preservation in Europe), we can analyse the impact of various assumptions about marginal preservation value by varying α, or the preservation value of the first whale. (The only way to keep the area under the curve constant while increasing α is to shift the MVP function inwards; hence, when α is chosen, the slope is unambiguously determined because total WTP is known.) α is the maximum sum that all Europeans together are willing to pay to protect the first minke whale.

The economics literature provides several hints at α (see Table 9.5), but there is little information that enables one to construct a marginal WTP (MWTP) function for whales or any other endangered species for that matter. Therefore, we assume a linear functional form for MWTP and use sensitivity analysis over the marginal WTP function to determine optimal stocks of minke whales in relation to valuation at the margin. This is the same method employed in the case of elephants. The optimal populations of minke whales for various combinations of α and the discount rate are provided in Table 10.15, where column 1 corresponds with the case of (approximately) constant marginal preservation value.

Table 10.15: Optimum Minke Whale Populations in the Northeast Atlantic for Various Combinations of Discount Rate and Marginal Value of the First Whale (NKr '000s)[a]

Discount rate	$\alpha = 250$	$\alpha = 1,250$	$\alpha = 2,250$	$\alpha = 3,250$	$\alpha = 4,250$	$\alpha = 5,250$
Total preservation value kept constant.						
0%	90,000	29,900	16,700	11,600	8,900	7,200
12%	90,000	29,800	16,700	11,600	8,900	7,200
½ of total WTP to ensure survival of species, ½ to protect additional whales						
0%	75,070	20,030	14,710	14,710	14,710	14,700
12%	74,570	20,010	13,380	10,800	9,440	8,590

Source: Bulte and van Kooten (1999d)

[a] For the first column, α is determined by multiplying the number of European households (90 million) by WTP per household (=US$30 or NKr 210), divided by the current whale population. K is arbitrarily increased for the other columns.

It is clear from Table 10.15 that the optimum population declines as α is increased. This is because a high value of α corresponds with a steep slope (to keep area under the curve, total WTP, constant), which implies that the marginal value of preservation falls rapidly. Lower marginal preservation values correspond with declining optimal stock levels (see equation 10.53).

The results in Table 10.15 (last column) indicate that, for high values of α, optimal stocks of whales approach the minimum viable population. Although MVP is not reached, a policy that takes minke whales to such a low level might lead to extinction of the whales in the event of some unforseen event that shocks the whale population and causes it to decline further. That is, with uncertainty, populations close to but above the MVP level can be shocked into extinction. Further, if the growth function does not explicitly include MVP, the population could be driven to extinction. This implies that both strict conservation (column 1 of Table 10.15) and eventual extinction may be optimal for the same estimate of total preservation value, depending on the true value of MVP.

The results in Table 10.15 also indicate that, for the WTP values used here, marginal preservation values are of greater importance for the optimal social management of minke whales than the choice of discount rate. Discount rate has little effect on the decision to protect whales. When household WTP is reduced to an annual amount of $10 or $5, the sensitivity of optimal stock size to choice of discount rate is greater, however.

As argued by Boman and Bostedt (1994), the concept of MVP may affect WTP to preserve a species at the margin, where preserving a species requires maintaining a minimum viable population. For example, marginal WTP for stocks below MVP is likely zero – the "all-or-nothing" choice is not amenable to marginal analysis of benefits – but MWTP is a declining function of stocks greater than MVP. That is, individuals place a particular value on the species' survival, *and* place positive but declining value on additional animals beyond the population that guarantees survival. Total WTP to preserve a species (obtained from a CV study) captures two different concepts:

1. True existence values, or values associated with survival of the species (the "all-or-nothing" value that determines whether stock preservation makes sense at all).
2. Nonuse values unrelated to the extinction decision. Due to lack of data, it is not possible to separate these contributions.

For illustrative purposes, however, we assume that total WTP is divided into two components: one half is attributable to existence value (to guarantee survival of the species) with the remainder constituting the nonuse value of preserving whales above their minimum viable population. Employing the same method as before (but with only half of the total WTP under the MWTP curve), the optimal minke whale populations for this case are provided in the lower part of Table 10.15. Notice that it is now worthwhile maintaining a population of whales greater than or equal to MVP. Comparing the optimal populations in the upper and lower parts of the table indicates that optimal steady-states can both be greater and smaller than before. What is especially relevant, however, is that in general they are different. Differences in the left-hand column amount to some 15,000 whales! However, compared to the previous case, optimal populations do not approach as close to MVP, providing a greater buffer or safety zone. For policy makers, therefore, it is important to know what is being measured when people are asked about their WTP.

Finally, the optimal population values are all less than the maximum sustainable yield population ($x^* < x_{MSY}$) even for a discount rate of 0%. The reason is that we have included predation costs in our analysis.

10.5 Conclusions

In this chapter, we employed dynamic optimisation models to examine policy implications related to the preservation of endangered and threatened mega-fauna. The examples that we provided varied in some important ways. For elephants and wildlife herbivores in Africa, a major opportunity cost is related to land. The opportunity cost of land can be substantial. This was not true of whales, as their conservation does not entail the usual opportunity cost associated with land use (as in the case of terrestrial mammals), but it does entail an opportunity cost associated with the species upon which whales feed (e.g., herring). In order to protect elephants and whales, bans on trade (elephants) and harvest (whales) have been imposed. For wildlife herbivores in Africa, a mix of strategies have been used, including game cropping. In each case, the dynamic optimisation models provide insights into how best to manage these wildlife resources.

In the case of the elephant, for example, the dynamic optimisation models suggest that an ivory trade ban on its own could fail; anti-poaching enforcement is also needed if elephants are to be protected. However, an ivory trade ban still appears to be the preferred strategy for nature conservation. This may not be the case for other species because, in the case of elephants, tourist benefits are an important driving factor leading to our conclusion in favour of the trade ban. Other species are not as charismatic, or, as in the case of rhinos, the species is difficult to view (hence, low tourism benefits). If conservation results in high opportunity costs (rhinos require large amounts of land) that are not offset by benefits, then habitat is likely to be converted.

A similar conclusion was reached in the second case study. If ranchers are not permitted to put game animals to their best use, they may decide to increase cattle stocking rates, thereby driving wildlife species out. The models clearly demonstrate that what are considered sustainable management options may simply be smokescreens, with the species to be preserved possibly driven to extinction nonetheless.

Our results for elephants and whales indicate that nonuse values may be important, but that it is necessary to determine importance at the margin. Simply knowing the total values of a biological asset in its various uses can be meaningless for management. Rather, it is important that one knows the marginal values of the asset in its various uses. This is true for wilderness protection (see Chapters 6 and 11) and preservation of wildlife species. For example, optimum stocks of elephants and minke whales are highly sensitive to assumptions about the marginal preservation utility function. For whales and a given total WTP, extinction and strict conservation can both be sensible policies depending on what is assumed about marginal WTP. This finding highlights the importance of correct formulation of contingent valuation studies: more emphasis should be placed on valuation at the margin, as estimates of total WTP for environmental and natural assets are of limited importance as a policy guide. Marginal valuation includes such things as specifying the current population and what it costs to maintain it (if anything) and the meaning of increments and decrements to this population under various assumptions, including associated probabilities of survival at different population levels.

Although economic analysis offers insights into resource conservation problems, those who want to adopt it willy-nilly must also accept that the consequences of its proper use. Economic analysis cannot be employed only if it suits one's viewpoint and doing so can be dangerous because it can lead to easily refutable policy recommendations. This is true when tourism benefits are relied upon to justify reductions in logging, or when willingness-to-pay is used as an argument to preserve all species or ecosystems. The arguments and data can sometimes be turned around to demonstrate the opposite of what is desired.

11 Forest Management

Forests cover 4.3 billion hectares or one-third of the world's land area, although 40% of the earth's land is capable of growing trees. Forests are an important source of income and employment because of the wood products they provide. Forests also contribute a natural bounty whose value is difficult to measure; they are an important carbon sink, perform a weather regulation function, absorb pollutants, provide recreational and scenic amenities, contribute wildlife habitat, and protect watersheds. Therefore, management of forestlands for both commercial timber production and other amenities is vital to the overall well-being of society.

Of the globe's forested area, 2,900 million hectares or 68% is considered productive forestland, defined as land capable of growing merchantable stands of timber within a reasonable period of time (see Table 11.1). It is estimated that the standing volume of timber on productive forestlands is some 310 billion cubic meters(m^3). Canada's forests account for about 10% of the world's forested land and 8% of its productive forestland; the United States accounts for about 7% of total forested land and the same proportion of productive forestland. As a country, only Russia has greater forest resources (Table 11.1).

Table 11.1: World Forest Resources

Country/Region	Total Forestland (10^6 ha)	Productive Forestland (10^6 ha)	Timber Volume (10^9 m^3)
Canada	418	245	25.0
United States	296	210	29.0
South and Central America	988	739	97.0
Africa	744	236	25.0
Europe (excl. former USSR)	195	141	15.2
Former USSR	957	770	86.7
Asia & Oceania	767	585	44.0
WORLD	4,364	2,926	321.8

Source: Canadian Forest Service (1997)

The USA is the largest producer of softwood lumber and wood products in the world, followed by Canada and Russia (Tables 11.2 and 11.3). Some 70% of total roundwood (Table 11.2) and 90% of all the pulp produced globally come from forests in northern latitudes (Table 11.3). The majority of wood products are produced from coniferous forests in the Northern Hemisphere.

Production of pulp from hardwood species has become increasingly important as a result of technical advances in pulp making and the existence of substantial indigenous (boreal) stands of mixed hard and softwood species, and the use of hardwood species in plantation forests. Principal producers of pulp and softwood lumber are the United States, Canada, Sweden, Finland, Russia and Japan, with Chile, New Zealand and Australia expected to become important in export markets.

Table 11.2: Global Industrial Production of Roundwood and Sawn Wood by Region, 1994[a]

Region	Industrial Roundwood ($\times 10^6$ m³)		Sawn Wood ($\times 10^6$ m³)	
	Production	Exports	Production	Exports
Developed	**1,127**	**82**	**303**	**95**
	(73%)	**(72%)**	**(73%)**	**(89%)**
North America	581	22	156	53
	(38%)	(19%)	(38%)	(49%)
- Canada	*181*	*2*	*62*	*46*
	(12%)	*(2%)*	*(15%)*	*(43%)*
- United States	*400*	*20*	*94*	*7*
	(26%)	*(17%)*	*(23%)*	*(6%)*
Western Europe	256	21	70	28
	(17%)	(18%)	(17%)	(26%)
- Sweden	*62*	*1*	*14*	*11*
	(4%)	*(1%)*	*(3%)*	*(10%)*
- Finland	*44*	*2*	*10*	*7*
	(3%)	*(2%)*	*(2%)*	*(6%)*
Oceania	35	13	6	1
	(2%)	(11%)	(2%)	(1%)
- New Zealand	*17*	*6*	*3*	*1*
	(1%)	*(5%)*	*(1%)*	*(1%)*
Eastern Europe	53	4	12	4
	(3%)	(4%)	(3%)	(4%)
Former USSR	153	20	31	8
	(10%)	(17%)	(8%)	(8%)
- Russia	*135*	*15*	*30*	*6*
	(9%)	*(13%)*	*(7%)*	*(6%)*
Other developed	49	2	27	0
	(3%)	(2%)	(7%)	(0%)
Developing	**422**	**32**	**110**	**12**
	(27%)	**(28%)**	**(27%)**	**(11%)**
Africa	48	5	6	1
	(3%)	(4%)	(2%)	(1%)
Latin America	131	9	31	4
	(8%)	(8%)	(7%)	(3%)
- Chile	*23*	*7*	*3*	*1*
	(1%)	*(6%)*	*(1%)*	*(1%)*
Northeastern Asia	16	0	5	0
	(1%)	(0%)	(1%)	(0%)
Far East	223	14	68	7
	(14%)	(12%)	(17%)	(7%)
Oceania	3	4	0	0
	(0%)	(4%)	(0%)	(0%)
Total	**1,549**	**113**	**413**	**108**

Source: FAO (1997)

[a] Proportion of global total in parentheses

It is clear from Table 11.2 that tropical forests do not contribute large amounts to global industrial wood output. Among tropical countries, only Brazil produces globally significant amounts of pulp, although the amount is relatively small, accounting for less than 5% of world production (Table 11.3). Even for countries such as Brazil that are significant in pulp production, fibre comes from plantation forests. Less than one-third of the world's industrial wood harvest originates with old-growth forests, or forests that have not previously been commercially exploited (Table 11.4).

Table 11.3: Global Production of Wood Pulp, and Paper and Board, by Region, 1994[a]

Region	Wood Pulp ($\times10^6$ tons)		Paper and Board ($\times10^6$ tons)	
	Production	Exports	Production	Exports
Developed	**139**	**27**	**213**	**65**
	(90%)	**(86%)**	**(79%)**	**(95%)**
North America	85	17	99	21
	(54%)	(52%)	(37%)	(29%)
- *Canada*	*24*	*10*	*18*	*14*
	(15%)	*(31%)*	*(7%)*	*(19%)*
- *United States*	*60*	*6*	*81*	*8*
	(39%)	*(19%)*	*(30%)*	*(11%)*
Western Europe	34	8	72	40
	(22%)	(26%)	(27%)	(55%)
- *Sweden*	*10*	*3*	*9*	*8*
	(6%)	*(9%)*	*(3%)*	*(11%)*
- *Finland*	*10*	*2*	*11*	*10*
	(6%)	*(5%)*	*(4%)*	*(13%)*
Oceania	2	1	3	1
	(2%)	(2%)	(1%)	(1%)
- *New Zealand*	*1*	*1*	*1*	*neg*
	(1%)	*(0%)*	*(neg)*	*(0%)*
Eastern Europe	2	neg	4	1
	(1%)	(1%)	(1%)	(2%)
Former USSR	4	1	4	1
	(3%)	(3%)	(1%)	(2%)
- *Russia*	*4*	*1*	*3*	*1*
	(3%)	*(3%)*	*(1%)*	*(1%)*
Other developed	12	neg	30	1
	(8%)	(1%)	(11%)	(2%)
Developing	**16**	**5**	**57**	**7**
	(10%)	**(14%)**	**(21%)**	**(10%)**
Africa	1	neg	1	0
	(0%)	(1%)	(0%)	(0%)
Latin America	9	4	12	2
	(6%)	(12%)	(4%)	(2%)
- *Chile*	*2*	*2*	*1*	*neg*
	(1%)	*(5%)*	*(0%)*	*(0%)*
Northeastern Asia	0	neg	1	0
	(0%)	(0%)	(0%)	(0%)
Far East	6	neg	43	5
	(4%)	(1%)	(16%)	(7%)
Oceania	0	0	0	0
	(0%)	(0%)	(0%)	(0%)
Total	**155**	**32**	**269**	**73**

Source: FAO (1997)
[a] Proportion of global total in parentheses; neg implies negligible

Commercial timber production from old growth occurs principally in Canada, Russia, Indonesia and Malaysia (Sedjo 1997). Industrial plantations account for more than one-third of industrial wood harvest, with the remainder accounted for by second-growth forests. The continuing trend towards intensively managed plantation forests occurs for both financial reasons and concerns related to security of supply, with increasing investment in the technology of growing trees stimulated by declining global reliance on old growth – the dwindling of the "old growth overhang" (Sedjo 1997). Increasingly trees are considered an agricultural crop, with rapidly growing trees competitive with annual crops as a land use (as is the case with loblolly pine plantations in the US South and hybrid cottonwood plantations on irrigated agricultural lands in the US Pacific Northwest).

Table 11.4: Global Timber Harvests by Management Type

Management Type	Proportion of Industrial Wood Production
Old growth	30%
Second growth, minimal management	14%
Indigenous second growth, managed	22%
Industrial plantation, indigenous species	24%
Industrial plantation, exotic species	10%

Source: Sedjo (1997)

Canada is the world's foremost exporter of wood products followed by the United States and the Scandinavian countries (Tables 11.2 and 11.3). Although not included in Tables 11.2 and 11.3, Germany and France rank ahead of the ex-Soviet Union in terms of wood product exports. Compared to other timber producing regions in the world, Canada and Russia are likely at a disadvantage in timber production because of climate (particularly in the interior regions of these countries); to a lesser degree, the same might be true of the Scandinavian countries.

Timber shortfalls have been forecast for the US Pacific Northwest and South and Canada, particularly British Columbia. In BC, a "fall down" in timber production is predicted because of the time lag between the availability of virgin forests and second growth. This is caused by past delays in plantings and silvicultural investments and the mere fact that old-growth forests contain greater timber volume and are increasingly being set aside. Globally these shortfalls will likely be covered by production of radiata pine from Chile and New Zealand. Unless adequate investments are made in planting and silviculture, countries such as Canada will decline in importance in terms of world timber production. Unfortunately, reforestation and silvicultural investments on many sites are often uneconomic and it may well be that forests in these regions provide non-timber benefits to society that exceed their commercial timber value.

In the remainder of this chapter, we investigate the management of forests from an economics perspective. We begin in the next section by providing a background to some ongoing issues pertaining to forest management and policy, namely, forestland ownership, silvicultural investment and certification of forest practises. In section 11.2, we consider optimal rotation ages, both from a financial and nonmarket perspective. Then, in section 11.3, we examine the impact of silvicultural investments by considering the allowable cut effect. Climate change and forestry is the focus of section 11.4. There we address the role of forest ecosystems in storing carbon and discuss how terrestrial ecosystems are to be treated under international climate agreements, as carbon sequestration serves to reduce atmospheric concentrations of carbon dioxide. The focus is on economic aspects, particularly those related to the costs of carbon uptake in forest ecosystems. The results of case studies involving

Canada and the Netherlands are presented in order to provide some indication of the potential for this option. Examples are provided to illustrate the economic efficiency tools developed in earlier chapters. Some conclusions follow in section 11.5.

11.1 Forest Competitiveness and Certification

Forest policy has a profound effect on the performance of a forest jurisdiction in providing environmental amenities related to the non-timber and nonuse values of forests. This is done directly through regulations and indirectly through policies that affect forest management and the performance of the commercial forestry sector. In this section, we examine government policies related to public versus private ownership of forestland, silvicultural investment and forest certification and eco-labelling.

Public ownership of forestlands

Ownership of forestlands influences the management of a country's timber and non-timber resources. The extent of public ownership for selected countries (and some regions) is provided in Table 11.5.

Table 11.5: Forest Area, Public Ownership, Mean Annual Increment and Annual Harvests, Selected Jurisdictions, Data for Early- to Mid- 1990s

Country/ Region	Working Forest (mil. Ha)	% Public	Average Annual Growth (million m³)	Annual Harvest (m³)	MAI (m³ per ha)
Finland	20	29	77	63.6	4.1
Sweden	23	13	98	68.0	4.2
New Zealand	2	4	22[a]	17.0	23.0
Chile	2	neg	22[b]	20.0	19.0
Russia	446	90	617	300+[c]	2.0
United States	198	45	612	469.0	3.4
- Pacific Northwest	16	56	82	73.0	5.0
- US South	37	11	128	117.0	5.7
Canada	227	94	233	183.0	2.0
- British Columbia	23	96	72	71.0	2.5
- Alberta	25	96	22	20.3	< 1.0

Source: Wilson et al. (1998, p. 13)
[a] New Zealand's annual growth is expected to rise to some 25 million m³ by 2005.
[b] Chile's MAI is expected to reach 47 million m³ in 2018.
[c] Russian harvests have fallen to some 232 million m³, but have exceeded 300 million m³ previously.

Regions in Canada have the highest degree of public ownership of any country or region in the world. Forestland ownership patterns are important for three reasons:

1. They determine the degree of control that government has on forestry.
2. They determine, in part, the distribution of political power.

3. They affect forest productivity and thus the perceived need to intervene or change policies.

A system with numerous small, privately owned forest stands (as in Scandinavia) reduces the ability of government to control forest management, since the transaction costs will be enormous. Coercive instruments are likely to be ineffective without prohibitively expensive enforcement. At the other extreme, a system of complete public ownership with few private rights to timber provides the government with a broad range of possible instruments for directing logging and other forestry activities. Where forestland ownership is broadly distributed, forest policy may also be an important electoral issue. In Sweden and Finland, forest-owner organisations have a significant political voice. The forest sector is probably more commercialised in regions where concentrated industrial ownership results in the mobilisation of industry associations and unions to defend their interests. Public ownership, on the other hand, broadens the forest policy debate and legitimises the role of interest groups seeking to protect the non-commercial values of forests. Ownership patterns also influence incentives to invest in forestry through silviculture and in industrial productivity in the long term.

While forest ownership should not influence the performance of the forest industry, this is only the case if tenures on public forestland give companies rights similar to those they would have under private land ownership. For example, industry should have the same incentives to invest in silviculture under public as under private ownership (i.e., receive the same benefits from such investments), and public ownership should not result in higher uncertainty for the forest companies. While such a state of affairs is potentially attainable through appropriate tenure arrangements, governments have a proclivity to establish tenures that lack appropriate incentives (see, for example, Garner 1991; Shleifer and Vishny 1998). The public owner is prone to interfere as needed to appease this or that group (labour, timber companies, resource-dependent communities, or environmental lobbyists) and enhance its prospects of gaining support for its current agenda, or at election time. This then creates uncertainty for forest companies.

Silvicultural investment and competitiveness

Also indicated in Table 11.5 are the annual growth, annual harvests and mean annual increments (MAIs) for selected jurisdictions, ones that account for the greatest proportion of global timber production and exports. Canada and Russia currently rely on harvests of virgin timber or timber that has regenerated on its own, while the Scandinavians are banking on past and continued plantings of fast-growing species (Wilson et al. 1998). Mean annual growth per hectare in Scandinavia averages about double that of Canada and Russia, for example. Rotation ages in the USA are generally much shorter than those in Canada and total annual growth greatly exceeds that in Canada, particularly in the US South where plantation forests dominate. It appears that Canada and Russia are, at best, marginal producers of timber. Compared to the Scandinavians, investment in silviculture is low or non-existent in Canada. For the most part, silvicultural investments cannot be justified on economic grounds in much of Canada, even when nonmarket benefits are taken into account (see section 11.4). This is also true in much of Scandinavia, although investments in silviculture are often viable at very low discount rates (2% or less).

Sedjo (1997) estimates that the BC Coast is now the most expensive source of fibre, followed by the US Pacific Northwest and the BC Interior. The high cost of fibre in BC is the result of high stumpage rates and environmental regulations that have added to costs. As noted in Chapter 6, the onerous environmental regulations cannot be justified on economic efficiency grounds. To improve competitiveness, in June 1998, the BC government lowered stumpage rates (by C\$8.10 per m^3 for the Coast and \$3.50 m^{-3} for the Interior) and announced it would relax environmental regulations. This has been risky for two reasons. First, according to the US Coalition for Fair Lumber Imports, the reduction in stumpage rates violates the 1996 Softwood Lumber Agreement between Canada and the USA. The Agreement runs for a five-year period, from April 1 1996 to March 31 2001, and limits exports to the USA from the four largest exporting provinces – BC, Alberta, Ontario and Quebec. The Agreement establishes an import quota of 14,700 million board feet (mmbf) from the four covered provinces (1,500 mmbf below the 1995 level). For exports exceeding this amount, a fee of US\$50 per thousand board feet (mbf) is levied for the next 650 mmbf with anything in excess of 15,350 mmbf subject to a fee of \$100 per mbf. Despite the threat of US retaliation, however, the BC government reduced stumpage rates because it recognised that it was collecting not only resource rents but quasi-rents, thereby driving firms out of business.

Second, BC relies almost exclusively on harvests of native (old-growth) timber, and environmental groups lobby BC's customers to convince them not to purchase wood products derived from old-growth forests.[1] Forest product companies in BC are now seeking certification from the Forest Stewardship Council and other agencies for harvest practises in old-growth forests (see below). For the most part, Scandinavia, New Zealand and other jurisdictions are immune from this problem, because they rely on harvests from plantation forests, or forests regenerated artificially or naturally for the specific purpose of producing commercial timber. By relaxing environmental regulations to reduce the onerous logging costs, the possibility of a backlash by environmental groups remains a threat.

The main concern of governments is generally not economic efficiency, but, rather, employment and the appeasement of various lobby groups. Silvicultural activities are often subsidised by government (even on private land via tax breaks, input subsidies, etc.) on the basis of job creation. In Sweden, for example, silvicultural investment was justified because it guaranteed a supply of fibre to the wood-processing sector, thereby creating value added and employment (Wilson et al. 1998). Likewise, BC's 1994 "Jobs and Timber Accord" was designed to encourage value-added activity, and thereby employment. Some indication of the success that policies in various timber producing regions have had in creating value-added jobs is

---

[1] The definition of what constitutes old growth is unclear. As a rule of thumb, old growth refers to trees older than 120 years in temperate rain forests, but in excess of only 80 years in boreal and interior ecosystems. Other definitions include undisturbed by humans, but that is probably an unrealistic thing to expect (Budiansky 1995).

provided in Table 11.6. Employment per 1,000 m³ of timber harvest is the standard for judging success in creating value added – in secondary manufacturing or processing of the raw fibre. While Alberta and New Zealand are clearly providers of raw material, Finland, Ontario and the Pacific Northwest appear to have higher levels of job creation, while BC and Sweden fall somewhere in the middle. However, it is important to keep in mind that job creation (or success in secondary manufacturing) is not the same as maximisation of economic well-being. Thus, policies in Alberta and New Zealand may simply be ones that enhance the welfare of their citizens.

Table 11.6: Standardised Harvest, Employment and Wage Rates for Selected Jurisdictions, 1993

	BC	Ontario	Alberta	Oregon	Wash.	Sweden	Finland	New Zealand
Fibre Consumption ('000 m³)								
Base harvest	78004	25432	14183	25252	20181	56500	42071	16028
Imports	710	1460	53	4151	3074	6019	6761	65
Recycled fibre	494	2987	149	5449	3734	5352	3469	225
Total harvest equivalent	*79208*	*29879*	*14385*	*34852*	*26989*	*67871*	*52301*	*16318*
Employment								
Base employment	82916	63000	13500	62700	53000	90534	87004	29672
Other forest employment[a]	4595	2800	267	200	200	1200	incl.	incl.
Total Full-Time Equivalent	*87511*	*65800*	*13767*	*62900*	*53200*	*91734*	*87004*	*29672*
Hourly Wage Rate (C$)								
Pulp and paper	$32.66	$25.84	$28.37	$21.61	$21.61	$26.37	$27.15	$15.64
Wood products	$23.99	$17.68	$19.68	$15.60	$16.03	$21.79	$19.53	$8.41
Weighted wage rate	$29.81	$20.88	$25.42	$20.57	$19.48	$23.98	$22.52	$12.84
Exchange rate (Per C$1993)	1.00	1.00	1.00	0.78	0.78	6.04	4.44	1.43
Employment per 1,000 m³								
Base	1.10	2.20	0.96	1.80	1.97	1.35	1.66	1.82
Wage adjusted	1.10	1.54	0.82	1.25	1.29	1.09	1.26	0.78

[a] Government employees
Source: Delcourt and Wilson (1998)

In addition to lobbyists representing the forest industry and forest workers, the environmental lobby has also become a major force in countries' forest policies (Wilson et al. 1998). Related to this, consumers of wood products are willing to pay a premium of some 5 to 10% over current market prices for the assurance that forests are harvested in a sustainable fashion, and that processes of production are environmentally sound (Haener and Luckert 1998). Thus, there appears a perception among consumers that current forest practices and production processes do not provide sufficient attention to externalities.

Market failure occurs because forest management is thought to focus too much on commercial timber at the expense of environmental amenities related to recreation, watershed protection, wildlife habitat and so on – the nonmarket values of forests. Production processes for wood products, particularly of pulp and paper, are perceived to ignore external environmental costs (e.g., damage to waterways from pulp mill wastes). In addition, consumers lack information to make appropriate judgements concerning the environmental friendliness of wood products. Information resides with the forest companies, and this information asymmetry constitutes a second form of market failure. While costs to the individual of obtaining information are prohibitive, economies of scale in gathering information led to the formation of certifying organisations. We briefly consider the issue of forest certification and eco-labelling.

Forest certification and eco-labelling

The UN Conference on Environment and Development at Rio de Janeiro dealt with forestry via a non-binding statement of principles for the management, conservation and sustainable development of all types of forests, and through Chapter 11 of Agenda 21, which deals with deforestation. UNCED also established the Intergovernmental Panel on Forests, which gave way in 1998 to the Intergovernmental Forum on Forests, but neither dealt with definitions of sustainable forest management. Governments have been reluctant to pursue common, binding standards of forest management, because each country faces unique circumstances regarding forestry that extend down to the local level. Further, certification of forest management practices and products is market driven, so that the role of government is primarily to encourage transparency, the full participation of all stakeholders, non-discrimination and open-access to any voluntary schemes.

Nonetheless, individual timber producing countries have pursued certification of forest management standards independently or in concert with several other nations. Canada, the United Kingdom, Sweden, Finland and Indonesia are in the process of developing or have already implemented national sustainable forest management (SFM) standards. SFM certification deals with how forests are managed, using environmental, economic, social and cultural criteria that vary from region to region. In this sense, SFM certification is broader in scope than environmental labelling, because the latter focuses largely on environmental impacts. While development of international SFM standards for certification should be straightforward, because it should be possible to agree on what factors to measure, getting agreement on performance levels for each indicator is more difficult. The other problem with SFM certification is that it deals only with how a particular forest is managed (it is forest specific), not with the forest company logging the stand or the "chain-of-custody" of forest products. That is, it ignores what happens to the logs, thereby providing no link between the forest practice and the customer. Determining chain-of-custody is much easier for lumber and similar products than for pulpwood. Wood chips used to produce pulp derive from various sources (pulp logs, sawmill residues) and are mixed together in the production phase, making it difficult to track pulp back to its source logs. However, chain-of-custody and labelling of products are not needed to meet sustainable forestry management objectives.

Canada has pursued SFM certification through the Canadian Standards Association (CSA), using criteria and indicators for sustainability developed by the Canadian Council of Forest Ministers. The Canadian experience indicates that the road to national SFM certification is not an easy one. Development of corporate policy statements, combined with public input into the setting of values for criteria and indicators, meant that significant management and other resources needed to be devoted to the effort. As a result, while 15 major forest companies had started to implement CSA SFM standards (covering nearly 200,000 km^2), no certification had occurred by the end of 1998. Costs to companies of obtaining certification appear to be one obstacle, although such costs will be reduced with learning.

Governments also act through the International Standards Organisation (ISO), particularly ISO 14001 and its related series of management system standards. Although designed for all sectors, ISO 14001 is relevant to the forestry sector as it deals with both resource management and the production phase. ISO 14001 seeks to establish environmental management system (EMS) standards that are site-and organisation-specific. A corporate environmental policy must apply to all forest sites, but for each site relevant data must be documented. A forest company may implement ISO 14001 in its pulp mills and sawmills. Hence, the ISO 14001 process is both complementary with and a substitute for national SFM certification. It is complementary with respect to production, but a substitute with respect to resource management.

The Forest Stewardship Council (FSC) was established in 1993 by environmental non-governmental organisations (ENGOs), particularly WWF, for the purpose of wood product certification. It has more than 200 members from 37 countries. FSC uses chain-of-custody to label products as originating from forests that are managed according to the following broad areas:

1. Compliance with local regulations and FSC principles
2. Tenure and use rights and responsibilities
3. Indigenous' peoples rights
4. Community relations and workers' rights
5. Benefits from the forest
6. Environmental impact
7. Management plan
8. Monitoring and assessment
9. Maintenance of natural forests
10. Plantations

Thus, FSC takes a performance standards as opposed to management systems approach to forestry. Because economic, environmental and social considerations are to be treated equally, FSC recognises the need for regional standards, rather than ones that apply globally. Until regional criteria are developed, however, FSC-endorsed certifiers (of which there were five at the end of 1998 – two from each of the USA and UK and one from the Netherlands) assess and certify forest operations on the basis of their interpretation of the FSC's Principles and Criteria. Until regional guidelines are available, the potential for conflict of interest between the consulting and certification roles exists. That is, the interpretation that a certifier applies could well be used as the basis for a region's future standards.

Finally, the Canadian Pulp and Paper Association (CPPA) has developed the Environmental Profile Data Sheet (EPDS) in response to customer concerns regarding the production and life-cycle environmental attributes of pulp and paper. The EPDS is meant to provide detailed information to bulk purchasers of pulp and paper about resource management and production practices (e.g., recycled fibre content, mechanical vs. chemical pulping process). Buyers can purchase pulp and paper with those attributes that are most desirable, even mixing purchases from various firms to achieve an optimal mix of attributes. Producers are encouraged to improve their environmental performance over time, which makes it a more dynamic approach than simple eco-labelling (see below). The key to this approach is third-party verification (certification).

There are three forms of environmental labelling.

1. Type I is eco-labelling, which involves attaching a symbol, mark or stamp to a product to indicate that it comes from a sustainably managed forest and/or that it meets certain production process standards. The "stamp of approval" is usually provided by an ENGO, although governments have been involved in the initial set up of such programs (e.g., Canada's Environmental Choice program founded in 1988 and privatised in 1995). Selectivity criteria are such that eco-labels are awarded to only 20⁻30% of products. Since eco-labelling is aimed at the retail customer, it is not possible to provide the type of detail found with an EPDS.

2. The second form of environmental label, Type II, consists of self-declared environmental claims, with no third-party verification. Such claims are made by a manufacturer, importer, distributor and/or retailer, but buyers must determine the truth or accuracy of such claims on their own.

3. Finally, Type III environmental labelling refers to quantified environmental life-cycle product information provided by a supplier, based on critical reviews by a third party. The product information is presented as a set of categories or parameters, with detail too great to enable its provision on the product at the retail level. The Environmental Profile Data Sheet is an example of a Type III environmental label.

Third-party verification (certification) is a key to any certification or eco-labelling scheme. In the end, success depends upon the credibility of the auditing scheme that leads to certification or the granting of a label.

A number of problems remain. Small, private woodlot owners, principally in Scandinavia, have generally opposed efforts to certify forest management practices. There it has been an obstacle in joint private, government and ENGO efforts to certify management practices, mainly because the process of certification costs money and increases management costs. Without compensation many private forest owners are unwilling to spend money in order to become certified.

Also, forestland owners are excluded from participation in the FSC process in countries where government ownership dominates (e.g., Canada, Russia), because governments cannot be members.

Further, certification that involves chain-of-custody clearly gives an advantage to vertically integrated forest companies, and large companies are also better able to fund the costs associated with the certification process. Hence, certification could lead to mergers and acquisitions and increasing concentration in global wood products markets (Haener and Luckert 1998).

Perhaps the greatest problems associated with forest certification are related to its effect upon trade. Under the rules of the World Trade Organisation (WTO), certification cannot explicitly be used as a barrier to trade. Thus, a country cannot require that imported wood be certified without also requiring that all domestically produced wood be likewise certified. Clearly, a country creates a technical barrier to trade (TBT) by imposing certification standards that domestic producers can attain, but which competitors cannot attain. A particular TBT of this nature involves the FSC's general principle 9 above, namely that natural forests are to be maintained. Canada and some other timber-producing countries (notably in the tropics) cannot possibly meet (a strict interpretation of) this requirement, because most of the timber that these countries harvest is from natural forests. Even second-growth forests have, for the most part, regenerated naturally. Trade problems can be reduced only if approaches to certification take into account local management conditions in producing countries and if such regional certification standards are developed in an open and transparent manner. Government can play a role in ensuring the latter.

11.2 Optimal Forest Rotation Age

Harvesting of timber by clear cutting a stand has an obvious and immediate impact upon land use. Selective harvesting also has an impact on land use, but it is not nearly as dramatic as clear felling, nor does it have the same visual impact. In both cases, a decision must be made about when trees should be harvested (or whether they should be left standing). Depending on the decision maker's objectives, there are a number of different criteria that are used to determine the age of harvest. We focus on economic criteria, and use a hypothetical illustration to demonstrate the effect of different harvesting strategies.

Maximising sustainable yield

Maximum sustainable yield (MSY) is used by biologists to determine optimal harvest ages for timber. As implied by its name, the objective is to find the forest rotation age that leads to the maximum possible annual output that can be maintained in perpetuity. The allowable annual cut is based on the MSY concept. The annual allowable cut is the amount of timber that can be harvested each and every year without diminishing the amount that can be harvested in the future. It is simply the net increase in timber volume in a region or district that results from tree growth – the *mean annual increment* (MAI).

Denote the growth of a stand of timber over time by $v(t)$. In the parlance of production economics, this is the total product function, where time or age, t, replaces the usual inputs labour or capital. Then average product is simply MAI, which is given by $v(t)/t$. Current annual increment is analogous to marginal product, and is given by $v'(t)$. It is well known that the marginal product curve intersects the average product function (from above) at the point where average product attains its maximum. Thus, the MSY rotation age, t_M, is simply the culmination of mean annual increment, and is found by setting the current annual increment equal to MAI:

(11.1) $\quad \dfrac{v(t)}{t} = v'(t).$

Rearranging (11.1) gives the usual relation for finding the MSY rotation age:

(11.2) $\quad \dfrac{v'(t_M)}{v(t_M)} = \dfrac{1}{t_M},$

where the LHS of this expression is the rate of growth of the timber stand.

As an illustration, suppose the following function describes the growth in the yield of commercial timber for a stand of spruce trees:

(11.3) $\quad v(t) = k\, t^a\, e^{-bt},$

where v is timber volume measured in m³. This function is easy to estimate, differentiable and $v'(t)/v(t) = (a - bt)/t$. For $k = 0.25$, $a = 2$ and $b = 0.02$, commercial timber yields and values at different ages are provided in Table 11.7, while a plot of the growth rate, $v'(t)/v(t)$, is provided in Figure 11.1. Also included in Figure 11.1 is a plot of 1/age or $1/t$. The MSY rotation age is determined by the intersection of the two functions; this occurs at point M in the figure or for rotation age t_M. The rotation ages can also be determined directly from Table 11.7. The MSY rotation age (point *M* in the figure) is found where $1/t$ equals the rate of growth, or 50 years.

For plantation forests and under a MSY rotation, the allowable annual cut (AAC) is set equal to the MSY. For uneven-age forests consisting of mature, over-mature, and young stands of trees, the AAC and MSY are subject to vagaries of harvesting and planting. If one's desire is to maximise society's well-being, the MSY rotation may not be appropriate, however.

Maximising net benefits from a single cut: Fisher rotation age

Suppose the objective of forest operations is to maximise the net benefit from a one-time harvest of the forest so future harvests are not considered. The objective is then to

(11.4) $\quad$ Maximise$_t$ $(p - c)\, v(t)\, e^{-rt},$

where p is the price of logs at the mill and c is the associated cost of felling, bucking, yarding, loading and hauling the logs to the mill. For simplicity, it is assumed that the cost of harvest is a constant marginal cost that can be subtracted from price to obtain a net price or stumpage value.

Table 11.7: Data for Determining Optimal Rotation Ages, Hypothetical Stand of Trees, per ha, r=4%

Age	Timber Volume[a] (m³)	Value of Timber[b] ($)	Rate of Growth[c]	RHS Faust-mann $R/(1-e^{-rt})$	MSY Age $1/t$	Amenity Value[d] ($)	Rate of Change in Amenity Value[e]	RHS Hartman $re^{-rt}/(1-e^{-rt})$
4	3.69	184.62	0.480	0.271	0.250	1.90	0.487	0.231
8	13.63	681.72	0.230	0.146	0.125	7.20	0.237	0.106
12	28.32	1,415.93	0.147	0.105	0.083	15.36	0.153	0.065
16	46.47	2,323.68	0.105	0.085	0.063	25.91	0.112	0.045
20	67.03	3,351.60	0.080	0.073	0.050	38.40	0.087	0.033
24	89.10	4,455.24	0.063	0.065	0.042	52.45	0.070	0.025
28	111.96	5,597.85	0.051	0.059	0.036	67.72	0.058	0.019
32	134.99	6,749.34	0.043	0.055	0.031	83.90	0.049	0.015
36	157.71	7,885.39	0.036	0.052	0.028	100.73	0.042	0.012
40	179.73	8,986.58	0.030	0.050	0.025	117.96	0.037	0.010
44	200.75	10,037.75	0.025	0.048	0.023	135.39	0.032	0.008
48	220.55	11,027.32	0.022	0.047	0.021	152.84	0.028	0.007
52	238.94	11,946.77	0.018	0.046	0.019	170.14	0.025	0.006
56	255.80	12,790.17	0.016	0.045	0.018	187.18	0.022	0.005
60	271.07	13,553.74	0.013	0.044	0.017	203.82	0.020	0.004

[a] Equation (11.3) [b] Assumes net price of $50/m³. [c] $v'(t)/v(t)$, Equation (11.2) [d] Equation (11.19) [e] $\gamma'(t)/\gamma(t)$

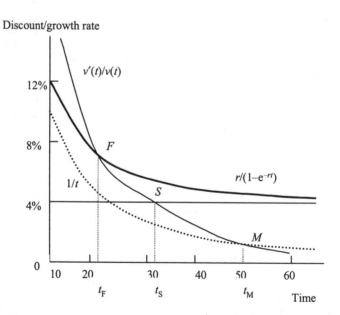

Figure 11.1 Comparison of MSY, Single-Period and Faustmann Rotation Ages (r = 4%)

The first-order conditions for a maximum give:

$$(11.5) \quad \frac{v'(t_S)}{v(t_S)} = r,$$

where r is the (instantaneous) rate of discount. The rotation age found from (11.5) is known as the Fisher rotation age, t_S (where S denotes single harvest). This condition states that trees should be left standing as long as their value (rate of growth) increases at a rate greater than the rate of return on alternative investments, as represented by the discount rate r. When the rate of tree growth is falling, the trees should be harvested the moment the rate of growth in value equals the discount rate. The forest (wood lot) owner simply keeps her investment tied up in trees until more can be earned by liquidating the investment (cutting the timber) and investing the funds from their sale at the alternative rate of return, or discount rate. Assuming a discount rate of 4%, the single rotation age can also be found in Table 11.7 by setting rate of growth to 0.04 (the discount rate); this occurs at an age of about 33 years. This is shown in Figure 11.1 by point S.

In the above analysis, the decision to harvest is independent of price as can be seen by multiplying both the numerator and denominator in conditions (11.2) and (11.5) by net price. (Alternatively, and without loss of generality, we can scale the output units so net revenue per unit is 1.0.) However, price is important in the decision for one reason: if price is too low, so that the net revenue from harvesting a stand of trees is negative, then the trees will not be harvested regardless of their rate of growth. If the cost of harvesting (c) cannot be expressed on a per unit basis, then the cost of harvesting trees can be incorporated in the decision by modifying equation (11.5) as follows:

$$(11.6) \quad \frac{pv'(t)}{pv(t)-c} = r.$$

Faustmann or financial rotation age

Assume that forestland is to be used only for the purpose of growing and harvesting trees, that it has no potential for non-timber sources of revenue, and that speculative factors are ignored. (The impact of each of these upon land value will be discussed below.) Then, the value of land depends on whether the land is managed, whether trees are currently growing on the site and whether the land is part of a larger management unit.

Begin with a situation where there are no trees growing on the site (bare land). Let V denote the discounted value of returns from all future harvests, or the value of bare land, which is also referred to as the *soil expectation*. The soil expectation is given by:

(11.7) $\quad V = \lim_{n\to\infty} \sum_{k=1}^{n} (p-c) \, v(t) \, e^{-rkt} = \dfrac{(p-c)v(t)\,e^{-rt}}{1-e^{-rt}},$

where $v(t)$ is the volume of timber growing on the site at time t, p and c are as above, and r may include a risk premium. Maximising (11.7) by setting the first derivative with respect to t equal to zero gives:

(11.8) $\quad \dfrac{v'(t_F)}{v(t_F)} = \dfrac{r}{1-e^{-rt_F}}$

where the t_F denotes the optimal Faustmann rotation age. Compared to the cutting rule in equation (11.5), the fact that the denominator on the RHS of (11.8) is less than one but greater than zero has the same effect as that of increasing the discount rate in (11.5). An increase in the discount rate would cause one to harvest sooner.

What is not taken into account in the Fisher (single-harvest) case is the possibility that, once timber is harvested, a new stand of trees can be generated on the land. The second growth can be harvested at a later date. By taking into account the potential of the land to grow another stand of trees, the harvest period is actually shortened. The reason is that, by cutting trees sooner, it also makes available a second and third harvest sooner than would otherwise be the case.

Regeneration can be hastened through reforestation and silviculture. In the one-period case, initial planting costs do not affect the optimum unless net returns are less than zero, in which case there is no solution (Samuelson 1976, p. 472). The same is true in the multiple-period case. Rotation ages for other situations, such as when the forest is of uneven age (the manager does not begin with bare land), are discussed by Montgomery and Adams (1995).

The Faustmann or financial rotation age is denoted t_F in Figure 11.1. It is given by the intersection of the timber growth curve and the "modified" discount formula, or point F in the figure. The Faustmann rotation age can also be determined directly from Table 11.7; it is the age where the rate of growth equals "RHS Faustmann", or just over 20 years of age. Where institutions permit (e.g., public ownership), biological considerations have led governments to legislate harvest ages that exceed the Faustmann age.

Assessing Bare Land Value in British Columbia

According to the BC Assessment Authority (1988, 1994), managed forestlands are those where the owner must undertake the following commitments: have an approved forest management plan, keep land fully stocked with commercial trees, tend young trees until they are free growing, and plan the harvest of trees. The main requirement for the purposes of valuing land is that of keeping land fully stocked with commercial trees, which implies owners must plant trees following denudation of land, whether that occurs as a result of harvesting or naturally.

We find that the net present value of the currently denuded forest stand is:

(11.9) $V = \dfrac{[(p-c)v(t)-C]\,e^{-rt}}{1-e^{-rt}},$

where t is the (financial) rotation age and V is the soil expectation (as before). What is different from (11.7) is that C denotes the cost of planting trees on the site immediately after harvest, which in most jurisdictions is a regulatory cost.

The existence of trees on the site does not unduly complicate the analysis. The soil expectation given by (11.9) still holds, but needs to be modified. If the trees are already mature, the net return from harvesting the site today must be added on the RHS of (11.9). If the trees are not ready to be harvested, then again the net returns from harvest must be added on the RHS of (11.9), but discounted by e^{-rk}, where k is the number of years until the trees currently growing on the site are harvested. Supposing that it pays to manage land, the formula for determining the value of land when trees are growing on the site is:

(11.10) $V = \dfrac{[(p-c)v(t)-C]\,e^{-rk}}{1-e^{-rt}}.$

If the site is part of a larger management unit, then the contribution of the site to the larger unit is required to determine its bare land value. If the rotation age t is 80 years, for example, the management unit can be viewed as divided into 80 sites, with one site harvested every year. In this case, removal of a single site from the management unit means that each of the remaining sites must be made smaller so that a new site can be made from the remaining 79. What, then, is the value of keeping the site in the management unit? It is the lost benefits that would result by taking a small amount from each of the remaining 79 units; that is, each year the loss would be equal to the amount of timber taken from one of the remaining 79 multiplied by its stumpage price $(p-c)$. As shown below, the value of the timber lost each year is equal to $mai \times (p-c)$, where mai is the timber that cannot be cut each year.

Each year the sustainable amount that can be harvested from the entire management unit equals the timber growth that accrues on the unit. The average of the annual growths (averaged over time and over sites within the unit) is referred to as the mean annual increment for the management unit, or MAI. The MAI is also the amount that can be harvested each year without jeopardising future harvests and is used to determine the allowable annual cut. The AAC is usually set equal to the MAI. Because of the allowable cut effect (discussed in section 11.3), the value that a recently harvested site (i.e., bare land) has to the management unit as a whole is the growth that the new trees (whether planted or naturally regenerated) contribute to the unit's total annual increment. If the recently harvested site is excluded from the management unit, then the contribution of the young trees growing on the site cannot be included in the calculation of the entire unit's AAC. When the management unit consists of a plantation forest, AAC = MAI; if it consists of mature stands then the *Hanzlik formula* is used to calculate AAC. This formula states that AAC = MAI + Q/t, where Q is the volume of timber in the management unit that exceeds rotation age *t* (Pearse 1990, pp. 153–69). For plantation forests, no sites exceed age *t*, so that the second term is zero.

The value of bare land when it is included in a larger management unit is given by the site's mean annual increment (*mai*) multiplied by (*p* − c) divided by the discount rate:

(11.11)   Value of bare land in management unit = $\dfrac{mai \times (p-c)}{r}$,

where *mai* = MAI × ξ, with ξ (0 < ξ < 1) being the proportion of the management unit's MAI attributable to the specific site (that is, the area proportion adjusted for productivity characteristics of the site), and (*p* − c) is the stumpage price. This is the same formula used by the BC Assessment Authority (1994, section 2.21), although the Authority adjusts (*p* − c) using several adjustment factors. In particular, stumpage is adjusted by factors that take into account differences in harvest costs due to more or less difficult terrain, nearer or further access, and the size of the parcel under consideration. Size is chosen to be one hectare as the BC Assessment Authority (1988, 1994) does not consider the value of a hectare to vary by the size of the parcel. Topography factors vary from 1.0 to 1.3 for "favourable" sites to 0.4 to 0.75 for "difficult" sites, with "average" sites assigned a factor of 0.7 or 1.0. The access factor is assigned a value between 1.2 and 1.4 for "close" sites, 1.0 for "normal" sites, and 0.75 or 0.8 for "remote" sites. (The factors themselves vary by their location in the Province.)

How does (11.11) compare with (11.9) – the value of bare land when it is not part of a larger management unit? First of all, it is important to recognise that (11.11) is simply the well-known bond formula (see Chapter 6) applied to forestland. It requires a return to be realised every year, rather than when trees reach harvest age. In actuality, a return is realised only when the stand is harvested, with the return at that time given by (*p* − c) × *v*(*t*), where *v*(*t*) = *mai* × *t*. It is easy to demonstrate that the BC Assessment Authority's valuation formula (11.11) leads to a higher bare land value than does the Faustmann formula by showing that:

(11.12) $\dfrac{mai \times (p-c)}{r} - \dfrac{[mai \times t \times (p-c)]e^{-rt}}{1-e^{-rt}} \geq 0$.

Rearranging (11.12) gives:

(11.13) $rt \geq \ln(1 + rt)$,

which holds for all $r \geq 0$ (i.e., for all positive discount rates) and $t \geq 0$ (all rotation ages). Therefore, the BC Assessment Authority formula for determining the value of bare land assumes the land is part of a larger management unit.

As an example of the magnitude of the difference, consider an *mai* of 10 m^3 per ha, a rotation length of 60 years, a stumpage price of $25 per m^3, and a discount rate of 10%, recommended by the BC Assessment Authority (1994). The Authority's equation (11.11) yields a bare land value of $2,500 ha^{-1}, while the correct formula (11.9) yields a bare land value of $49.43 ha^{-1}. Clearly, inclusion of reforestation costs results in a negative soil expectation in this example as such costs are measured in the hundreds of dollars.

Capitalisation Rate versus Interest Rate

Now consider the discrete-time version of equation (11.9), but ignore regeneration costs:

$$(11.14) \quad V = \frac{\text{MAI} \times (p - c) \times t}{(1 + r)^t - 1},$$

Equation (11.14) can be re-written as:

$$(11.15) \quad V = \frac{\text{MAI} \times (p - c)}{\delta},$$

where δ is the capitalisation rate such that

$$(11.16) \quad \delta = \frac{(1 + r)^t - 1}{t}.$$

Determining the appropriate capitalisation rate is the crux of the problem, because the BC Assessment Authority uses δ rather than r – it determines δ from observations on land sales (land which may not even be forestland), or observations of V. It is clear from (11.16) that δ is not independent of either the discount rate r or the rotation age t.

Consider the capitalisation formula (11.16). The BC Assessment Authority uses capitalisation rates between 2% and 14%. Table 11.8 gives discount (interest) rates (r) associated with various given capitalisation rates (δ) that lie in this range; this is done by specifying values for δ and t and solving (11.16) for r. Then, Table 11.9 presents capitalisation rates that are associated with various realistic interest rates; this is done by specifying values for r and t and solving (11.16) for δ.

The Assessment Authority used a capitalisation rate of 8% until 1991, when it was raised to 10% to reflect increasing risk. The rates are adjusted to account for higher land prices in observed transactions. A subsequent re-evaluation of the rate occurred again in 1993, but the bounds indicated above have remained. Based on the 8% capitalisation rate, and assuming rotation ages of 80 to 120 years, the implicit interest rate is somewhere between 2% and 2.5%. Such interest rates are low and do not reflect risk and/or inflation.

BC's Treasury Board has used a discount rate for evaluating projects of 10%, which, from Table 11.9, implies one would have to use a capitalisation rate exceeding 2,000% if the rotation age is 80 years or greater. Even using low market rates of interest, such as 4–6%, requires that the Assessment Authority use capitalisation rates that exceed 15% (see Table 11.9). The point is that one cannot separate the capitalisation rate and interest rate.

Table 11.8: Calculated Interest (Discount) Rates Associated with Various Capitalisation Rates

Capitalisation Rate (δ)	Forest Rotation Age (t)			
	60 years	80 years	100 years	120 years
2%	1.323%	1.202%	1.105%	1.025%
4%	2.061%	1.810%	1.623%	1.476%
6%	2.576%	2.222%	1.965%	1.769%
8%	2.973%	2.533%	2.222%	1.987%
10%	3.296%	2.785%	2.427%	2.161%
12%	3.569%	2.995%	2.598%	2.305%
14%	3.805%	3.176%	2.745%	2.428%

Table 11.9: Calculated Capitalisation Rates Associated with Selected Interest Rates

Interest Rate (r)	Forest Rotation Age (t)		
	60 years	80 years	100 years
4%	15.866%	27.562%	49.505%
6%	53.313%	130.995%	338.302%
8%	167.095%	588.694%	2,198.761%
10%	505.803%	2,559.250%	13,779.961%

Consider again the earlier example – an MAI of 10 m^3 ha^{-1}, a rotation length of 60 years, a stumpage price of $25 per m^3, and an interest rate of 10%. From (11.14), the land has a value of $49.43 ha^{-1}. The Assessment Authority's formula (11.10) yields $2,500 ha^{-1} for a capitalisation rate of 10%. From Table 11.8, it is clear that the Assessment Authority is assuming an interest rate of 3.3%, much lower than the 10% assumed here. Using an interest rate of 3.3% in formula (11.14) gives a value of $2,500/ha. Clearly, the Assessment Authority's interest rate for discounting future costs and returns is too low and unrealistic in comparison to market rates of interest and to interest rates used by the BC government. It is also out of line with the interest rates at which the government itself can borrow.

An interesting question is the following: In the case of land that does not have trees growing on it, why is such a low interest rate needed to render assessed values that are closer to true market values? Either buyers are irrational and would be willing to invest funds at rates much lower than those they can obtain in (riskless) money markets, or the land has some value that the assessment misses. This value must be related to the fact that the land is incorporated into a larger forest management unit (and has value because of the tenure system and BC's forestry regulations) or has commercial value outside of timber production (e.g., recreational property, speculative value).

Effect of Taxes on the Financial Rotation Age

Montgomery and Adams (1995, p. 383) consider three types of timber taxes.

1.　An *ad valorem* tax constitutes a fixed percentage levy against the market value of the timber stand (land plus timber) each year. The effect of such a tax is similar to that of increasing the rate of interest that the forest manager faces, thereby reducing the optimal rotation length. In the case of uneven-aged stands, the effect of an *ad valorem* tax is to reduce the optimal holdings of timber stocks (p. 392).

2. Yield taxes have been implemented to counter the adverse effect of *ad valorem* taxes, namely, that the timber is harvested sooner. A yield tax is based on the value of the timber when it is harvested. The effect of such a tax is a percentage reduction in the effective output price, thus extending the rotation age. In the case of uneven-aged stands, the effect of a yield tax is neutral (p. 392).

3. Finally, the effect of a an annual site or land tax that is based only on the value of the land and not the timber on it, is neutral. This is true both for even and uneven-aged stands (pp. 383, 392).

Hartman rotation age: Non-timber benefits

Where growing forests provide non-timber benefits, an economic argument can be made for extending rotations beyond the financial age. Standing trees have value to society in addition to commercial timber value; these values are derived from scenic amenities, watershed functions, waste receptor services, non-timber products such as mushrooms, wildlife habitat functions, and so on. If nonmarket values are related to timber volume, then, if society is to maximise its welfare from managing the forest, the Faustmann rotation age needs to be modified to take into account these values. External benefits need to be correlated with timber (forest) growth before it is possible to determine directly the optimal harvest age that would take external values into account. The difference between commercial timber and non-timber benefits in determining optimal rotation age is that commercial timber benefits accrue only at the end of the rotation, when the trees are harvested. Non-timber benefits, on the other hand, accrue continuously (or annually in the discrete case).

The Hartman (1976) rotation age is based on the maximisation of external or amenity values. Suppose that amenity values, denoted $\gamma(t)$, are an increasing function of the age of a forest stand, with $\gamma'(t) > 0$ and $\gamma''(t) < 0$. The amenity benefits over a rotation are then given by $A(t) = \int_0^t \gamma(s)e^{-rs}ds$. The objective is to choose the rotation age that maximises the discounted stream of such benefits, recognising that benefits fall to zero each time the stand is cut. Substituting $A(t)$ for $(p - c)\,v(t)$ in expression (11.7) gives the following problem:

$$(11.17) \quad \underset{t}{\text{Max}}\left[\frac{A(t)e^{-rt}}{1-e^{-rt}}\right] = \underset{t}{\text{Max}}\left[\frac{\left(\int_0^t \gamma(s)e^{-rs}ds\right)e^{-rt}}{1-e^{-rt}}\right].$$

Maximising expression (11.17) yields

$$(11.18) \quad \frac{\gamma'(t_H)}{\gamma(t_H)} = \frac{r\,e^{-rt_H}}{1-e^{-rt_H}}.$$

If one solves (11.18) for the Hartman rotation age, t_H, one finds that it is longer than the Faustmann age, but only if amenity values increase with stand age; if they decline with age, the Hartman rotation is shorter. This is explored further below.

For now, suppose amenity values for a stand of spruce increase with age according to the following function:

$$(11.19) \quad \gamma(t) = 0.125\, t^2\, e^{-0.0132t},$$

where $\gamma(t)$ is measured in dollars per hectare. Selected amenity or external values and their rate of change are provided in Table 11.7. In the example of Table 11.7 and Figure 11.1, the Hartman rotation age lies quite a bit to the right of $t_M = 50$ years and is not shown in the figure. It is found in Table 11.7 by finding where the "rate of change in amenity values" equals the "RHS Hartman". It is clear that this occurs when the age of the trees is significantly greater than 60 years (and, hence, is also not shown in Table 11.7).

Hartman-Faustmann rotation age

Consider the case where the manager seeks to maximise the combined commercial timber and non-timber amenities over an infinite planning horizon. In the usual formulation, the manager begins with bare land, plants trees and maximises the present value of total forest benefits (Swallow et al. 1990; Swallow and Wear 1993):

$$(11.20) \quad \underset{t}{\text{Max}} \left[\frac{((p-c)v(t)+A(t)-C)e^{-rt}}{1-e^{-rt}} \right],$$

where $(p-c)v(t)$ is the commercial timber benefit, $A(t)$ amenity benefits over rotation t, and C regeneration costs. The necessary conditions for an optimum give:

$$(11.21) \quad [(p-c)v'(t_{HF}) + \gamma(t_{HF})]\left(\frac{1-e^{-rt_{HF}}}{r} \right) = (p-c)v(t_{HF}) + e^{-rt_{HF}} A(t_{HF}) - C.$$

The Hartman-Faustmann rotation age (denoted t_{HF}) should be chosen so that the marginal present value of delaying harvest, or marginal benefit of delay (MBD), equals the marginal opportunity cost of delay (MOC). The latter is given on the RHS of (11.21) as the immediate timber benefits minus regeneration costs if the stand is harvested today, plus the amenity benefits received over the next growing period.

The forest manager who is interested in commercial timber production only would need to be subsidised to take into account non-timber amenity values. The policy would provide a subsidy of γ(t) to those who hold timber of age t, or pay $[r/(1 - e^{-rt})] e^{-rt} A(t)$ to managers who harvest at age t.

The problem is that there are many non-timber values (e.g., wilderness preservation, provision of forage for wild ungulates, wildlife habitat) that vary in different ways with forest age (see, e.g., Calish et al. 1978; Bowes and Krutilla 1989). Indeed, some amenities are unrelated to forest age. Examples of the relationship between a forest stand's age and non-timber amenities are provided in Figure 11.2. For example, amenity flows might represent the value of wildlife species (e.g., herbivores) adapted to young forests with plentiful forage (I), wildlife values that are independent of forest age (II), and the value of species reliant on more mature forests, such as trout and spotted owls. Benefit stream IV could be the sum of several amenity flows (Swallow et al. 1990). When such non-timber values are combined with commercial timber benefits to form the objective function in (11.20), the second-order conditions associated with a solution for the optimal cutting (Hartman-Faustmann rotation) age are likely to be violated, which implies existence of a *nonconvexity*.[2]

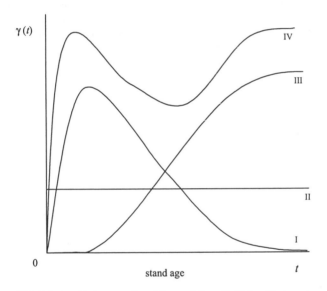

Figure 11.2 Relationship between Stand Age and Amenity Value, Various Amenities

---

[2] When a single objective function is to be maximised, it is convexity that leads to the violation of the second-order conditions. More generally, in constrained maximisation, the objective function should be concave and the constraints convex; otherwise the second-order conditions for a maximum may not hold. Other conditions hold for minimisation. But the term nonconvex has come to represent any violation of the second-order conditions.

A relevant nonconvexity prevents a tax/subsidy policy from achieving the socially desirable rotation age. The reason can be illustrated with the aid of Figure 11.3. From (11.21), the first-order conditions for a socially optimal solution occur where the marginal opportunity cost of delaying harvest equals the discounted marginal benefit of delay, or MBD = MOC.

Suppose that the Faustmann rotation age is given by rotation age t_F. Points x and y, with accompanying rotation ages t_x and t_y, represent cases where (11.21) is satisfied. The second-order conditions are violated at x but not at y. Providing the forest manager with a myopic subsidy equal to the value of the non-timber benefits will result in a rotation age, t_x, that is shorter than the financial rotation age t_F, but this is not the socially optimal solution. However, a policy that rewards the forest owner or manager with a subsidy of $\gamma(t)$, with $t_x < t \le t_F$, will achieve the desired solution at y.

Although the discussion in this subsection used bare land as a starting point, for some existing forests the external or amenity benefits (which would include preservation value) might be so great that it would not be economically feasible to harvest the forest. In this case, it may be preferable to delay harvest or never harvest. In the context of Figure 11.3, this would be the case if equilibrium points existed at ages beyond those indicated in the diagram (e.g., MOC and MBD may intersection again, with MOC upward and MBD downward sloping). If this is the case and society inherits "ancient" forests, it may be worthwhile delaying harvests, perhaps indefinitely. The case of ancient forests is considered again in section 11.4 in the context of climate change, with carbon uptake and preservation benefits used to determine how much old-growth forest to retain on Canada's West Coast.

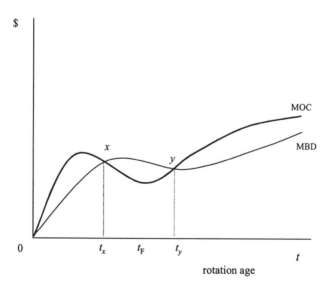

Figure 11.3 Nonconvexities and Optimal Hartman-Faustmann Rotation Age

Finally, Swallow and Wear (1993) and Swallow et al. (1997) extend the notion of convexities and external benefits to multiple use across forest stands. First consider two sites, one publicly owned and the other private. Suppose that harvest of the private forest stand affects the flow of amenity benefits from the public stand, thus shifting both the MOC and MBD functions at the public site. While it may be optimal to harvest the public stand, the public manager may wish to delay harvest in anticipation of felling of the private site, thus extending the public rotation age beyond that which would be socially optimal in the single-stand case (Swallow and Wear 1990). When both sites are managed together for their joint commercial timber and amenity values, Swallow et al. (1997) demonstrate that the sequence of harvest schedules can take rather odd forms. For example, even though two forest stands may be nearly similar in all respects, it might be socially optimal to permit one site to mature to beyond 100 years before harvesting it, while the other site is harvested several times during this period. Vincent and Binkley (1993) reach a similar conclusion about specialisation, recommending zoning rather than subsidies as a public policy for increasing social well-being.

Summary

A summary of the MSY, financial and combined financial-Hartman criteria for determining rotation ages is provided in Table 11.10. The variables are defined as above. In Table 11.11, the first-order conditions for these three criteria are given for the general growth function (11.3).

Table 11.10: Alternative Criteria for Determining Rotation Age

Item	Mathematical Statement Maximise:	First-Order Conditions
Average Annual Output (MSY)	$\dfrac{v(t)}{t}$	$\dfrac{v'(t)}{v(t)} = \dfrac{1}{t}$
Net present value of timber (Faustmann)	$\dfrac{[(p-c)v(t) - C]\, e^{-rt}}{1 - e^{-rt}}$	$\dfrac{(p-c)v'(t)}{(p-c)v(t) - C} = \dfrac{r}{1 - e^{-rt}}$
Present value of timber plus non-timber benefits[a] (Hartman-Faustmann)	$\dfrac{[(p-c)v(t) - C]\, e^{-rt} + A(t)}{1 - e^{-rt}}$	$(p-c)v'(t) + \gamma(t) = r(p-c)v(t) +$ $r\left(\dfrac{[(p-c)v(t) - C]\, e^{-rt} + A(t)}{1 - e^{-rt}} \right)$

[a] $\gamma(t)$ refers to non-timber benefits as a function of growth, with $A(t) = \displaystyle\int_{0}^{t} \gamma(s) e^{-rs} ds$.

Table 11.11: Alternative Criteria for Determining Rotation Age for $v(t) = k\,t^a\,e^{-bt}$

Average Annual Output (MSY)	$t = \dfrac{a-1}{b}$
Net present value of timber (Faustmann)	$\dfrac{(p-c)\left(\dfrac{a}{t} - b\right)v(t)}{(p-c)v(t) - C} = \dfrac{r}{1 - e^{-rt}}$
Present value of timber plus non-timber benefits[a] (Hartman-Faustmann)	$(p-c)\left(\dfrac{a}{t} - b\right) + q = \dfrac{r\left((p-c) - \dfrac{C}{v(t)}\right)e^{-rt}}{1 - e^{-rt}}$ $+ \dfrac{\dfrac{rq}{v(t)}\displaystyle\int_0^t v(s)\,e^{-rs}\,ds}{1 - e^{-rt}} + r(p-c)$

[a] Assumes $\gamma(t) = q\,v(t)$, where q is the proportionality constant

11.3 The Allowable Cut Effect and Even Flow Constraints

Governments are interested in sustainable resource use. In forestry, this is pursued through the allowable annual cut, with the AAC set equal to the mean annual increment (or, in the case of mature stands, an adjustment is added according to the Hanzlik formula). For example, BC's Chief Forester sets the AAC, but allows tenure holders to deviate from AAC by as much as 50% in a given year (to take into account market conditions). Companies are not permitted to deviate from total AAC by more than 10% over a 5-year period, however. Under this regulatory regime, the AAC will increase if slowing-growing, mature trees are harvested and replaced by faster-growing young trees. This is an example of the *allowable cut effect* (ACE). If there is much mature or over-mature timber, harvesting such timber and reforesting the site will increase growth (the MAI), and subsequently the AAC. Similarly, investments in silviculture that lead to an increase in tree growth can result in an ACE. In essence, the ACE is the "immediate increase in today's allowable cut which is attributable to expected future increases in (timber) yields". (Schweitzer et al. 1972.)

The ACE can easily be illustrated using a linear production function, as in Figure 11.4 (Binkley 1980, 1984). The production function indicates the trade-off between current and future harvests. In the figure, the maximum harvest available in period t is S, but, if no timber is harvested in t, then $(1 + g)S$ is available for harvest in period $t + 1$, where g is the growth of timber between periods t and $t + 1$. Thus, the production function gives the maximum amount that can be harvested in period t (h_t) and period $t + 1$ (h_{t+1}). Suppose that a silvicultural investment that costs c leads to an increase in growth from g to g'. (This investment might simply be the harvest and reforestation of a stand of mature timber.) Under the even-flow constraint (shown as a

$45°$ line in Figure 11.4), there is a permissible increase in timber harvest given by h_t'' $- h_t'$, which equals the ACE.[3]

Again let r denote the (social) discount rate. Then, the objective of maximising net present value from timber harvests is represented by the parallel lines denoted PV. In terms of these, the ACE effect leads to a benefit of $PV' - PV^0$. If $PV' - PV^0 > c$, then the silvicultural investment is worth undertaking. It is readily apparent that, even though investments in fertilizing and reforestation yield high rates of return via the ACE, these returns are illusory and hold only because of the even-flow constraint (Price 1990). In terms of Figure 11.4 and in the absence of the constraint, agents would harvest all of the trees in the first period, thereby gaining a discounted net benefit given by PV*, which is greater than any other possible net discounted gain. For reasons presented in the previous section, it is only if $g' > r$, and the gain in present value exceeds the cost of the investment, that the investment is worth undertaking in the absence of a constraint.

An economic decision about replanting or fertilizing ignores the regulatory constraint. The costs of replanting need to be recouped by the timber removed at the end of the rotation. Likewise, the costs of fertilizing need to be recouped when the trees are cut. Legal constraints may require companies to charge the costs of replanting to the current rotation, but this is not an economic solution. Legal constraints such as sustained yield or even flow are an effort to implement sustainable development.

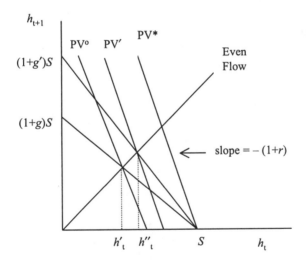

Figure 11.4 Allowable Cut Effect

---

[3] Rather than linear production, a nonlinear production frontier, $g(h_t, c)$, where c represents the level of investment in timber production. ACE is represented by a shift in this frontier, but the analysis of Figure 11.4 remains essentially unchanged (Binkley 1980, 1984).

As Price (1990) points out, sustainable development permits depletion of an old-growth stand of trees "only if an environmentally compensating project is instituted to replace it – in this case by accelerating the growth of another stand". (p. 574) The environmentally adverse effect of harvesting old growth is to be balanced by positive environmental effects (replanting, fertilizing) in each time period. This is a strong sustainability requirement. This obligation makes it is possible to escape "the bogey of rotation-long compound interest" (p. 577) that works against the viability of silvicultural investments. Nonetheless, the escape relies on the existence of a constraint or some arbitrary necessity that an environmentally compensating project be instituted. It does not address the question of whether replanting or fertilizing is the environmental project that is most efficient in achieving strong sustainability, or whether strong sustainability is even the objective of society.

Many silvicultural investments are not economically viable, particularly in temperate and boreal forests (Benson 1988; Thompson et al. 1992; Wilson et al. 1998). While long rotations and the bogey of compound interest are the main culprit, nature itself works against economic efficiency. Many sites that have been denuded for whatever reason (say clear felling) will regenerate on their own within five or at most ten years. Thus, the benefits of artificial regeneration are not given by the discounted benefits at harvest time, but by a much smaller amount determined by:

$$(11.22) \quad \frac{B}{(1+r)^T} - \frac{B}{(1+r)^{T+\Delta T}},$$

where B represents the net benefits from harvesting logs at the time of maturity, T is the rotation age, and ΔT is the time it takes to regenerate a stand naturally. Suppose that the cost of replanting is \$2,000 per ha, but that B is \$50,000 per ha after trees grow for $T = 60$ years. Assume a low discount rate of 2% ($r = 0.02$). Then the present value of B is \$15,239. If trees would not regenerate on their own, then replanting yields a net discounted benefit of \$13,239 (benefit-cost ratio of 7.6). If trees regenerate naturally, but it takes five years, then the true benefit from replanting is only \$1,436. The investment is no longer viable and the benefit-cost ratio (= 0.7) is less than one.

11.4 Climate Change and Forestry

Climate change and related global warming are caused by so-called greenhouse gases (GHGs) that permit the sun's rays to pass through the earth's atmosphere, but prevent heat from radiating back into space by trapping it. While GHGs include methane (CH_4), nitrous oxides (N_2O) and a group of artificial gases known as halocarbons (or CFCs), the most dominant GHG (outside of water vapour) is carbon dioxide (CO_2), in terms of anthropogenic emissions and potential to affect climate. It is feared that human activities, primarily fossil fuel burning and tropical deforestation (see Chapter 12), are responsible for increasing atmospheric concentrations of CO_2. This is shown in Table 11.12, which suggests an average 1.3×10^9 tonnes (i.e., 1.3 gigatons or Gt) of carbon (C) are added to the atmosphere each year as a result of human activities. Compared to the size of global sinks such as oceans and the soil, which are also indicated in Table 11.12, the contribution of humans is rather small, however.

Table 11.12: Annual Anthropogenic Flux and Size of the Globe's Carbon Sinks (Gt C)

Item	Average annual flux	Approximate sink size
CO_2 sources		
Emissions from fossil fuels and cement production	5.5 ± 0.5	
Net emissions from changes in tropical land uses	1.6 ± 1.0	
TOTAL ANTHROPENIC EMISSIONS	7.1 ± 1.1	
Partitioning amongst reserves		
Atmosphere	3.3 ± 0.2	800
Oceans	2.0 ± 0.8	40,000
Northern Hemisphere forest regrowth	0.5 ± 0.5	–
Soils	n.a.	1,500
Above ground biomass	n.a.	600‑700
Inferred Sink (Difference)	1.3 ± 1.5	≈43,000

Source: Houghton et al. (1996); n.a. means not available

Over the past two centuries, atmospheric concentrations of CO_2 have increased by about 25%, from approximately 285 parts per million by volume (ppmv) to 356 ppmv, with most of this increase occurring in the past 100 years. If other GHGs are included, equivalent CO_2 levels were approximately 290 ppmv at the beginning of the industrial revolution, 310 ppmv in 1900 and some 440 ppmv by 1995. Mean global surface temperatures have increased some 0.3° to 0.6°C since the mid–1800s, and by some 0.2°–0.3°C in the last 40 years. Between 1861 and 1910, mean global temperatures remained relatively flat, but were some 0.1°C below the 1861 level in 1910. Between 1910 and about 1940, temperatures rose by some 0.5°C, remained flat between 1940 and 1975, and then rose a further 0.2°C in the two decades since 1975 (Houghton et al. 1996, p. 26). One might have expected a greater increase in mean global surface temperatures after World War II rather than before it, because of the greater increase in fossil fuel use. Hence, controversies over climate change remain, including whether global warming currently is or will in the future even occur (e.g., Balling 1995; Emsley 1996). Currently, average global temperatures are projected to increase by 1.0–4.5°C under a double CO_2 atmosphere (Kattenberg et al. 1996).

Climate change is considered by some to be the world's most important environmental policy issue (Clinton and Gore 1993). Concern about anthropogenic emissions of GHGs led the World Meteorological Organisation and the United Nations Environment Program jointly to establish the Intergovernmental Panel on Climate Change (IPCC) in 1988.[4] The first IPCC report was published in 1990; it led to the signing of the United Nations' Framework Convention on Climate Change (FCCC) in Rio de Janeiro in June 1992. The Convention committed signatories to stabilise atmospheric CO_2, with developed countries to reduce emissions to the 1990 level by 2000 (article 4). The IPCC's second assessment report was published in

---

[4] WMO and UNEP had already convened the First World Climate Conference and established the World Climate Program in 1979.

1996 (Houghton et al. 1996) and endorsed by the Second Conference of the Parties (COP) to the FCCC. Following this, at the Third COP in December 1997 at Kyoto, Japan, developed countries agreed to curtail their CO_2 emissions relative to what they were in 1990.[5] Developed countries agreed to varying levels of emissions reduction, with the actual target date for measurement purposes being 2008–12, known as the commitment period. The USA committed to reduce emissions by 7% from 1990 levels by the commitment period, while EU countries agreed to reduce emission by 8% of 1990 levels, as did countries hoping to gain membership to the EU sometime in the future. Canada and Japan agreed to a 6% reduction, while Australia agreed to limit its increase in CO_2 emissions to no more than 8% by 2008 and Iceland to an increase of no more than 10%. Other developed countries agreed to limits that fell between the EU's 8% decrease and Australia's 8% increase. Within the EU, some countries will be required to reduce emissions by less than other countries. Thus, the Netherlands will need to reduce emissions by only 6%, while Germany will reduce them by some 20% or more (because inefficient industries in the Eastern part will be closed or rebuilt). The Kyoto Protocol does not commit developing (poorer) countries to CO_2 emission reduction targets, even though their emissions will soon account for more than one-half of total global emissions.

The Kyoto Protocol does not call for sanctions against countries failing to meet their targets – the Protocol is voluntary. Moral suasion will be brought to bear on those countries failing to live up to their agreement, but only if there is general compliance. With the exceptions of Germany and the UK, most countries signing the FCCC have been unable to meet the Rio target (e.g., Canada's emissions in 1996 exceeded 1990 emissions of CO_2 by more than 12%), and most are unlikely to meet the Kyoto target. Nonetheless, countries are committed to reducing anthropogenic GHG emissions in the long run. As an interim measure, policies to remove CO_2 from the atmosphere and store it as carbon in terrestrial ecosystems have taken on some importance. As early as 1989, 68 countries that signed the Noordwijk Declaration proposed increasing global forest cover as a means of slowing climate change.

The Kyoto Protocol allows countries to claim as a credit any C sequestered as a result of afforestation (planting trees on agricultural land) and reforestation (planting trees on denuded forestland) since 1990, while C lost as a result of deforestation is a debit (article 3.3). The Protocol has several interesting aspects, however, each of which is under review as countries seek clarification on the Protocol's interpretation of terrestrial C sinks, especially forest sinks. First, deforestation is defined as a change in land use, so when a site is harvested but subsequently regenerated there is no change in use and only the C credits associated with reforestation are counted, not the costs of C release (with not all countries accepting this interpretation). For example, if a mature forest stand is harvested sometime after 1990 and subsequently replanted before 2008, only growth of the newly established stand is counted as a credit; the debit from harvest is not counted. The amount of C to be credited as a reduction is determined by measuring the inventory on the site in 2012 minus the inventory in 2008, divided by the number of intervening years to give the annual

---

[5] The First COP in 1995 issued the "Berlin Mandate" that led to the Kyoto Protocol.

value. Although only verifiable growth during the commitment period is to be counted, inventory measurement will be difficult and costly, so data from growth models and/or MAI may be used as a fall back for determining C uptake. Only deforestation during the period 2008–12 is counted as a debit.

Forests store carbon by photosynthesis. For every tonne (t) of carbon sequestered in forest biomass, 3.667 (= 44/12) t of CO_2 is removed from the atmosphere. C is stored not only in above-ground biomass, but also in decaying material on the forest floor and, importantly, in the soil (Binkley et al. 1997). Soil carbon should be taken into account, along with other components of the ecosystem, but Kyoto only counts the commercial (and measurable) component of the trees, although the Protocol leaves open the opportunity to include additional terrestrial activities (article 3.4).

Most countries are unlikely to adopt large-scale afforestation programs before the new millennium. For most forests, such as those found in Scandinavia, Russia, Canada and the USA, the major producing regions, the increase in biomass over the first two decades after planting is generally small, and, in many instances, growth tables do not even begin until the third or fourth decade. Thus, any measure of C uptake by forests during the Protocol's accounting period 2008–2012 will be negligible, or biased upwards if MAI over the entire rotation is used as a proxy for actual growth. It would appear, therefore, that forest policies are important in the intermediate term and not the short term of the Kyoto Protocol. An exception might occur if high-yielding varieties of hardwood species are used in place of more natural and commercially valuable species, although this could result in adverse environmental consequences associated with mono-cultures.

Planting trees involves more than simply carbon uptake in forest biomass, because what happens to the C balance of the soil and to products from harvested timber is also important. Wood can substitute for fossil fuels and wood products continue to serve as a C sink for many years after the trees are harvested. Policies can be oriented towards greater substitution of wood for non-wood products (e.g., wood studs rather than aluminium ones) and simply greater use of wood products. Wood products' research is one means of encouraging greater substitution and use of wood, but so are subsidies or other policies that reduce the price of wood products. Planting trees and increasing the supply of wood is one way to reduce prices. In general, it appears that plantation forests may be a cost-effective means of sequestering C (Sedjo et al. 1995), although this is investigated further below.

The main purpose of cost-of-mitigation studies is to provide benchmarks for comparing alternative strategies, so that the least cost strategies can be implemented. Benefits are measured in physical units of carbon uptake, with some arguing that physical quantities cannot be discounted. As indicated in Chapter 1, the Global Environment Facility can allocate funds to desirable C-uptake projects in developing countries. In determining project feasibility, GEF recommends against discounting of physical C sequestered and stored in terrestrial ecosystems in the future, although future costs are to be discounted. Economists disagree with this approach, with Richards (1997) demonstrating that the time value of carbon will depend on the path of marginal damages – that is, on the concentration of atmospheric CO_2. If marginal damages are constant over time, then physical C can be discounted at the social rate;

the more rapidly marginal damages increase over time, the less future C fluxes should be discounted. Given uncertainty over the relationship between atmospheric CO_2 concentrations and global climate change, and between climate change and economic damages, we have no *a priori* reason not to discount future C fluxes (see also Richards and Stokes 1994). The problem of discounting is discussed further below in the context of afforestation.

In this section, we examine economic aspects of C uptake in forest ecosystems. The discussion needs to be separated into economic issues related to the management of existing forests (and forest plantations) and to afforestation, as planting trees on agricultural land is one means for taking CO_2 out of the atmosphere. The empirical examples used here are drawn primarily from western Canada, although some European estimates are also provided.

Managing forests for carbon fluxes

If existing forests are managed for their carbon uptake benefits, the optimal rotation age will be affected as will the area of ancient rainforest that is economically optimal to set aside as wilderness. In this section, we first investigate the effect on optimal rotation ages of subsidies for C uptake and taxes for C release. Then we consider the effect of carbon sink benefits in conjunction with preservation (and other non-timber) benefits on the protection of ancient rainforest. Illustrative examples are provided using data on boreal forests and coastal rainforests in western Canada.

Effect of Carbon Subsidy/Tax on Forest Management

When carbon uptake benefits are taken into account, it is not the age of trees or standing timber volume that is important (as with the Hartman rotation), but, rather, the rate of tree growth. As trees grow, they sequester C, but once the forest ecosystem achieves equilibrium, with decay occurring at the same rate as new growth, no further C is sequestered, and no further benefits are forthcoming. Following van Kooten, Binkley and Delcourt (1995), let carbon uptake at any time be given by $\alpha\, v'(t)$, where α is a parameter that translates m^3 of biomass into tonnes of C and v is timber volume in m^3. The proportion of C in biomass varies with tree species, although it is generally in the range of 200 kg/m^3 (van Kooten, Thompson and Vertinsky 1993). The present value of the C flux over a rotation of length t is given by the sum of the discounted C uptake benefits over the rotation minus that released at harvest:

$$(11.23) \quad PV_C = p_C \int_0^t \alpha\dot{v}(s)\, e^{-rs}\, ds \; - \; p_C\, \alpha(1-\beta)v(t)e^{-rt},$$

where p_c is the shadow price or implicit social value of carbon that is removed from the atmosphere, β is the fraction of timber that goes into long-term storage in structures and landfills – the "pickling" factor – and r is defined as before. The dot above v signifies a time derivative. Integrating the first term in (11.23) by parts results in the following revised expression for (11.23):

$$(11.24) \quad PV_C = p_C \alpha \left(\beta v(t) e^{-rt} + r \int_0^t v(s) e^{-rs} ds \right).$$

In order that forest companies correctly take into account the external benefits and costs of their decisions, they should receive a yearly subsidy of $p_C \alpha$ for each m^3 of timber added to the growing stock – an annual subsidy equal to the total value of the carbon sequestered that year. Likewise, they should face a tax levied at harvest time that equals the external cost of the C released to the atmosphere. The tax would be given by $p_C \alpha(1 - \beta)$ per m^3 of timber harvested.

The value of carbon, p_C, is the same at the margin, whether C is released (a cost to society) or sequestered (a benefit). Because C does not remain in the atmosphere indefinitely, p_C is the present value, for all time, of removing one unit of C from the atmosphere today. It is determined as the discounted value of the annual contribution to damage caused by one unit of carbon summed over the expected number of years that the unit of C is present in the atmosphere. It is simply assumed that p_C is constant over the rotation length. Issues related to the discounting of physical C are discussed further below.

The present value of the timber and C sequestration benefits over all future rotations then becomes, upon substituting equation (11.24) and the expression for commercial timber value (see equations 11.7 and 11.20),

$$(11.25) \quad PV = \frac{PV_C + pv(t)e^{-rt}}{1 - e^{-rt}} = \frac{p_C \alpha \left(\beta v(t) e^{-rt} + r \int_0^t v(s) e^{-rs} ds \right) + pv(t)e^{-rt}}{1 - e^{-rt}},$$

where p is the net price of commercial timber.

The optimal rotation age that takes into account both commercial timber values and carbon uptake values, and that includes a penalty for releasing carbon into the atmosphere at harvest, is found by differentiating equation (11.25) with respect to t and setting the result equal to zero. Upon rearranging, this gives:

$$(11.26) \quad \frac{\dfrac{v'(t)}{v(t)} + \dfrac{r}{\beta}}{1 + \dfrac{r}{\beta} \dfrac{\int_0^t v(s) e^{-rs} ds}{v(t)}} = \frac{r}{1 - e^{-rt}}.$$

Setting $p_C = 0$ gives the Faustmann result, while setting $p = 0$ gives the formula for calculating the Hartman rotation age (assuming $\beta \ne 0$):

(11.27) $$\dfrac{v(t)}{\displaystyle\int_{0}^{t} v(s)\,e^{-rs}\,ds} = \dfrac{r}{1-e^{-rt}}.$$

As a particular case, if the pickling rate also equals zero (i.e., $\beta = 0$), then we obtain the Hartman rotation age.

Van Kooten, Binkley and Delcourt (1995) employ numerical illustrations for two regions in western Canada using growth function (11.3). Background data are found in Table 11.13. Producers are subsidised and taxed for C uptake and release according to the shadow damages of carbon, p_c. Rotation ages for various assumptions about the net price of commercial timber (p), the shadow value of carbon (p_c) and the pickling rate (β) provided for such a tax/subsidy scheme in Table 11.14. The IPCC (Houghton et al. 1996) does not endorse any particular range of values for the marginal damages of CO_2 emissions, but cites published estimates of discounted future damage of US$5–$150 per tonne of C emitted. The estimates depend on, among other things, the discount rate applied to weight future costs.

Table 11.13: Forest Growth Data for Western Canada

Item	Alberta Boreal Forest	British Columbia Coastal Rainforest
Parameter values for $v(t) = kt^a e^{-bt}$		
k	0.0008	0.0006
a	2.766	3.782
b	-0.0092	-0.0310
MSY age (years)	192	90
Maximum volume (m^3 ha^{-1})	340	1,020
Age of maximum volume (years)	300	122
Value of α (kg m^{-3})	203	182

Suppose that trees have no commercial value, but stands are managed for carbon uptake only. If, in addition, timber releases its stored C at the time of harvest ($\beta = 0$), then it is optimal never to harvest trees. The same is true if only half of the stored C is subsequently pickled in landfills and structures. However, if all stored carbon can be pickled at harvest time, the optimal rotation age is 108–119 years for the coastal forest, and 269–293 years for the boreal forest (Table 11.14). Thus, even in the absence of commercial value, it is socially beneficial to harvest trees because CO_2 is removed from the atmosphere and permanently stored in structures and/or landfills, thereby mitigating the effects of climatic change. These rotation ages are greater than t_{MSY}, and relatively close to the age that maximises timber volume. When timber has commercial value, and as the price of timber increases, the optimal rotation age falls toward the Faustmann age.

As the shadow price of C increases, the optimal length of time until trees are harvested increases, *ceteris paribus*. Indeed, for low timber prices, $\beta < 1$ and high C value, it may not be optimal to harvest trees at all. An increase in timber prices and the discount rate shortens the optimal rotation age, with the discount rate having the greatest effect in reducing rotation age. On the other hand, an increase in the pickling rate reduces the time between harvests because the tax penalty from releasing carbon at harvest is lower; indeed, it is zero when $\beta = 1$.

Table 11.14: Optimal Rotation Ages when C Taxes and Subsidies are taken into Account (Years)

Item	Discount Rate (%) / Price of Carbon ($ per tonne)								
	5%			10%			15%		
	$20	$50	$200	$20	$50	$200	$20	$50	$200
Coastal									
Faustmann	43			27			20		
$\beta = 0$, $p = \$ 0/m^3$	*	*	*	*	*	*	*	*	*
15	51	68	*	34	52	*	25	41	*
25	47	56	*	31	38	*	23	29	*
50	45	49	77	29	32	63	22	23	52
$\beta = 1/2$, $p = \$ 0/m^3$	*	*	*	*	*	*	*	*	*
15	50	60	*	32	43	*	25	33	210
25	47	53	88	31	36	78	23	27	68
50	45	48	64	29	32	47	21	23	35
$\beta = 1$, $p = \$ 0/m^3$	108	108	108	116	116	116	119	119	119
15	49	56	76	32	39	61	24	29	50
25	47	51	68	30	34	51	22	26	40
50	45	48	58	29	31	41	21	23	31
Boreal									
Faustmann	42			23			16		
$\beta = 0$, $p = \$ 0/m^3$	*	*	*	*	*	*	*	*	*
15	54	100	*	31	63	*	22	46	*
25	49	64	*	27	37	*	19	26	*
50	45	50	136	25	28	95	17	20	72
$\beta = 1/2$, $p = \$ 0/m^3$	*	*	*	*	*	*	*	*	*
15	53	74	*	30	44	*	21	31	*
25	48	59	176	27	34	136	19	24	109
50	45	50	83	25	28	50	17	19	36
$\beta = 1$, $p = \$ 0/m^3$	269	269	269	287	287	287	293	293	293
15	51	64	111	30	37	73	20	26	53
25	47	56	89	26	32	55	18	22	40
50	45	49	68	25	27	40	17	19	28

Source: van Kooten, Binkley and Delcourt. (1995)
* Indicates that rotation age is infinite.

The foregoing results are not strictly applicable to over-mature timber stands. For example, Harmon et al. (1990) conclude that it is inappropriate to harvest old-growth forests in the Pacific Northwest because harvesting contributes to an overall increase in atmospheric CO_2. To achieve economic efficiency, the decision to harvest depends upon a number of factors. The economic efficiency criterion indicates that, at the current time, a stand of over-age timber should be harvested when

$$(11.28) \quad pv - p_C \alpha (1 - \beta)v + V > p_C \alpha \int_0^\infty v'(t)dt,$$

where V is the soil expectation of the land. This condition requires that the marginal benefits of cutting the trees must exceed the marginal costs. The marginal benefits (LHS of 11.28) are equal to the timber value at harvest minus the tax from releasing C to the atmosphere, plus the soil expectation of the stand. The marginal cost of harvesting the stand (or RHS of 11.28) is the discounted value of the foregone carbon subsidies from timber growth on the over-age stand.

Suppose the current harvest value of a stand of old-growth rainforest is $15,000 per ha. Such a stand stores about 150–200 tonnes of C per ha. Assume that the soil expectation is approximately equal to $1,000, p_C = $100 per tonne (a high value), and no C is stored once trees are harvested (β = 0). Then the stand should be left unharvested since the marginal benefits of harvest ($16,000) are less than the marginal costs ($20,000). If $\beta > 0$ and/or $p_C < $100 per t, the opposite conclusion can easily hold. We now consider the case of old-growth (over-mature) forests in more detail.

Carbon Sinks and Preservation of Ancient Temperate Rainforests

What role do ancient temperate rainforests play as a carbon sink? More specifically, can an economic argument be made to preserve ancient forests because of their role as a C sink? There are some 3.0 million ha of old-growth temperate rainforest on BC's West Coast. From an economic efficiency standpoint, how much of this old growth should be retained, assuming that such a decision includes all commercial timber and non-timber benefits (including carbon flux)? Van Kooten and Bulte (2000) find that, if C sink benefits are ignored, the total *average* non-timber value of mature forests amounts to no more than $5,250 per ha. If carbon is included, the benefits of retaining old growth change significantly, increasing to at most $11,330 ha^{-1} (if C is valued at $200 per t), but more realistically to some $6,250 ha^{-1} (if p_C = $20 per t). The *average* benefit from commercial forestry, on the other hand, is some $15,000 per ha, and can be as high as $40,000 on better sites. Clearly, it would be socially optimal to harvest all the ancient forest on the BC Coast, if average values are used as the basis of comparison. As demonstrated in the previous chapter, this result changes dramatically if marginal analysis is employed.

For the purpose of marginal analysis, we employ a dynamic optimisation model to provide some notion about society's optimal holdings of ancient forests. The objective is to

$$(11.29) \quad \text{maximise W} = \int_0^\infty \pi(t)\, e^{-rt}\, dt\,,$$

where

$$(11.30) \quad \pi = B[G(t)] + \int_0^{G_0-G} [F(z) + p_C\, C(z)]\, dz + [\tau(G) - p_c\, \gamma(G)]\, D(t).$$

Here $\pi(t)$ is economic benefits; $B(G)$ are non-timber benefits (i.e., the sum of benefits from exploitation of non-timber forest products, recreational benefits and the nonuse values associated with the conservation of old growth) as a function of the stock of ancient forest remaining at time t, $G(t)$; G_0 represents the initial stock of old-growth forest (or 3.0 million ha), so that $G_0 - G$ is land devoted to secondary forest production; p_C is the shadow price of carbon (as before); $\tau(G) - p_c\gamma(G)$ represents the marginal benefit or cost (price) of logging old growth as a function of the old growth remaining at t; and r is the social rate of discount, assumed to be 4%. The term $\int_0^{G_0-G} [F(z) + p_C C(z)]dz$ describes the total benefits for the $G_0 - G$ hectares of old growth converted to plantation forests, and consists of commercial timber benefits (first term) and the shadow value of C uptake benefits of plantation forests (second term). The function $\tau(G)$ represents declining commercial timber benefits from harvesting old growth as a function of remaining old growth, while $p_C\gamma(G)$ is the accompanying shadow cost of C released to the atmosphere. The required functions are discussed below.

The dynamic (subject to) constraint is

$$(11.31) \quad \dot{G}(t) = -D(t),$$

where $D(t)$ is the area of old growth harvested at time t.

The current value Hamiltonian (suppressing time notation) is defined as: $H = \pi - \lambda D$, where λ is the co-state variable. The derivation of the steady-state solution (where $D = 0$) is similar to that presented in previous chapters. The equation that describes the optimal forest stock in the steady-state is:

$$(11.32) \quad \tau(G^*) - p_C\,\gamma(G^*) + \frac{F(G_0 - G^*) + p_c C(G_0 - G^*)}{r} = \frac{B'(G^*)}{r}.$$

Equation (11.32) requires that, in equilibrium, the marginal present value of benefits of retaining ancient forest (RHS) must be equal to the sum of immediate benefits of ancient forest conversion and the present value of subsequent forest plantation production at the margin. Included in benefits are the shadow costs and benefits of C uptake and release. The difficulty in solving (11.32) lies with determining the five functions $\tau(G)$, $\gamma(G)$, $B(G)$, $F(G_0 - G)$ and $C(G_0 - G)$. The required functions for the model are described in the following paragraphs (van Kooten and Bulte 2000). (All of the equations are specified in millions of hectares, not in hectares.)

The marginal benefit from logging old growth at time t is a function of how many ancient forest sites (G) that remain:

$$(11.33) \quad \tau(G) = 7{,}451.495\, e^{0.586\,G},$$

which has been estimated using actual data for BC (van Kooten and Bulte 2000).

To calculate the lost C sink services when old growth is harvested, we begin by assuming that a proportion β $(0 \leq \beta \leq 1)$ of the C gets stored in products that decay (release C) at a rate δ (say 2%) per year. Then, the amount of C released at time of harvest is (see also below):

(11.34) $\left(\dfrac{(1-\beta)(1+r) + 2\delta\beta}{1+r-\delta} \right) \alpha v,$

where the discount rate could be zero and αv is the amount of carbon stored in the trees on the site that is harvested ($\alpha = 0.182$ t m^{-3}). Multiplying by the shadow price of C gives the contribution to climate-related damage caused by harvesting ancient forests and changing land use (i.e., deforestation). An indication of the climate-related damages from deforestation (harvesting old growth and converting the land to another use) is provided in Table 11.15 for various values of the parameters in (11.34) and shadow prices of C. The results are not very sensitive to discount rates between 4% and 10%, and are also not highly sensitive to decay rates between 0.02 and 0.10. Only if carbon is stored in wood products ($\beta > 0$) do climate-related damages vary with the discount rate.

Table 11.15: Climate-related Damages from Harvesting Ancient Forest on BC's Coast, per ha[a]

Shadow price of C ($/t)	$\beta = 0$	$\beta = 0.60$ $\delta = 0.02$ $r = 0$	$\beta = 0.60$ $\delta = 0.02$ $r = 0.04$	$\beta = 0.60$ $\delta = 0.10$ $r = 0$	$\beta = 0.60$ $\delta = 0.10$ $r = 0.04$
Deforestation (permanent land use change)					
$20	$1,830	$ 760	$ 750	$ 850	$ 840
$50	4,580	1,910	1,880	2,130	2,120
$100	9,080	3,830	3,750	4,250	4,230
Deforestation followed by replanting					
$20	$1,230	$160	$150	$ 250	$ 240
$50	3,080	410	380	630	620
$100	6,080	830	750	1,250	1,230

[a] Assuming 500 m^3 per ha and 0.182 t of C per m^3

The marginal climate-related cost of releasing carbon is given by:

(11.35) $\gamma(G) = \alpha R \times 138.437 \, e^{0.644\,G}$,

where $R = [\delta\beta/(1 + r - \delta) + (1 - \beta)]$ takes into account storage (and subsequent decay) of C in wood products.

Finally, it is necessary to determine the marginal non-timber benefits associated with retaining land in old growth. These benefits are over and above the benefits associated with the old growth already protected as parks, ecological reserves, wilderness areas, and so on. Van Kooten and Bulte (2000) estimate that the area of remaining ancient forest (3 million ha) has an annual value of $620.8 million, which is the total benefit of non-timber products and environmental amenities. Without additional information, it is simply assumed that the marginal function is linear, as in the cases of minke whales and elephants, namely,

(11.36) $B'(G) = a - \dfrac{a}{b} G$

where $B'(G)$ represents marginal benefit as a function of remaining old growth, a is the intercept on the vertical axis and b the intercept on the horizontal axis. The total non-timber benefits are given by the area under the marginal benefit function, $B'(G)$. Neither a nor b is known; only the area under the curve is known and fixed (equal to $620.8 million). Denote this area by A. Once a is known, b is also known because $b = 2A/a$, where A is the area under the curve. Parameter a is the amount households are willing to pay to protect the next ha of old growth, over and above that already set aside. The amount individuals are WTP for each additional ha of ancient forest declines as more and more ancient forest is protected from harvest. Sensitivity analysis about the intercept is used to determine the optimal area of ancient forest to preserve. Of course, the higher the value of a, the steeper the slope of the marginal (non-timber) benefit function.

Old growth area is converted to plantation or second-growth forest, with the annualised marginal benefits from logging second growth given by:

(11.37) $F(G_0 - G) = \left(\dfrac{(1+r)^t}{(1+r)^t - 1} \right) \times r \times 765.92 \; e^{-0.690 \, (G_0 - G)},$

where $(G_0 - G)$ is the amount of land taken out of old growth and allowed to regenerate naturally into the next forest to be harvested. The first term on the RHS of (11.37) takes into account the benefits of future harvests (and differs slightly from the normal formula because the estimated benefit function is already in present value terms), while multiplication by r annualises returns. The final term is an estimated relationship using actual data for BC (van Kooten and Bulte 2000). It is assumed that rotation age, t, is 80 years and r is 4%. The annual (marginal) C-uptake associated with second growth is given by:

(11.38) $C(G_0 - G) = \dfrac{\alpha}{t} \times 691.695 \; e^{-0.720 \, (G_0 - G)}.$

Using the optimality (steady-state) condition (11.32) along with results (11.33)–(11.38), it is now possible to calculate the optimal amount of old growth to preserve for various assumptions about the marginal benefit function, $B'(G)$. The results are presented in Table 11.16. Consider first the well-being of BC residents only, but include C release (from harvest of old growth) and uptake (by second growth forests). Keeping total non-timber and non-carbon benefits fixed at $620.8 million annually, the amount of the 3 million ha of ancient forest to retain is sensitive to assumptions about the ordinate intercept (steepness) of the marginal benefit function. For high values of the intercept a, the marginal benefit function is very steep and little of the remaining ancient forest would be protected (some 4% or less). If a is small, the marginal benefit function for retaining old growth is flat and lies almost everywhere below the marginal opportunity cost function; again very little old growth would be protected. For values of *a* between 300 and 5,000, and ignoring C release and uptake (p_C = 0), the optimal amount of old growth society would retain is nearly 700,000 ha, or 23% of what remains.

If carbon release and uptake are taken into account, society would want to increase its protection of old growth by between 7,000 and 33,000 ha, depending on the shadow price of C. Taking into account the role of C increases old growth protection by some 1 to 5%. If the Kyoto Protocol for counting carbon is implemented (in essence, release of C during harvest does not count if land is reforested), then less ancient forest should be preserved. Compared to the case where release of C is counted as a debit, the Kyoto rule suggests that 12,100 ha of additional old-growth forest should be converted to second growth if p_C = $20 per tonne, 30,200 ha for p_C = $50, and 60,300 ha for p_C = $100. The Kyoto rule suggests reducing the amount of ancient forest to be retained by some 2 to 9%. The results are not very sensitive to values of β and δ.

Table 11.16: Optimal Preservation of Ancient Temperate Forest in BC, Various Scenarios and Shadow Prices for Carbon ('000s ha)

Price of carbon	Vertical Axis Intercept for Non-Timber Benefit Function (Value of "a")								
	300	500	1,000	2,000	3,000	4,000	5,000	10,000	50,000
Maximum benefits for BC residents (including C uptake and release)									
$0	0	486.5	681.8	495.4	362.3	282.7	231.1	120.1	24.7
$20	10.4	500.8	688.3	497.2	363.1	283.1	231.4	120.2	24.7
$50	39.2	522.6	698.2	499.9	364.2	283.8	231.8	120.3	24.7
$100	88.5	559.8	714.8	504.4	366.2	284.8	232.5	120.4	24.7
Maximum benefits for BC residents under Kyoto rules for C uptake									
$0	0	486.5	681.8	495.4	362.3	282.7	231.1	120.1	24.7
$20	0	474.8	676.2	493.9	361.4	282.4	230.9	120.1	24.7
$50	0	457.5	668.0	491.6	360.7	281.9	230.6	120.0	24.7
$100	0	429.4	654.5	487.9	359.2	281.0	230.1	119.9	24.7
Maximum benefits for BC residents plus non-residents									
$0	0	734.1	1475.0	1604.6	1356.8	1119.4	938.4	502.9	104.2
$20	13.4	756.6	1493.0	1614.4	1361.0	1122.0	940.0	503.2	104.2
$50	50.4	791.1	1520.5	1629.1	1369.0	1126.0	942.4	503.7	104.2
$100	114.2	850.2	1567.7	1654.2	1381.4	1132.7	946.4	504.5	104.2

Consider the case where non-BC residents are interested in preservation of temperate rain forests in western Canada. Assume that households in the USA, Europe, the rest of Canada and elsewhere would be willing to pay $10 annually to protect old growth in BC. If there are some 200 million households in these regions, this increases the total non-use value of the ancient forests by $2 billion annually. Then it is optimal to increase protection of old growth to 53.5% of the 3 million ha that remain. By taking into account climate-related benefits, an additional 50,000 ha should be protected, increasing overall protection to 55.1% of the remaining ancient forest. However, it is unlikely that BC would ever be compensated for the positive externalities associated with preservation of ancient temperate rain forests. It would seem that there is a greater chance that households in rich countries would pay for protection of tropical rainforests.

Finally, it is important to recognise that the C sink benefits of ancient forests are probably less important than the nonuse values they provide. It is the nonuse values that ultimately determine how much old growth should be retained.

Planting trees on marginal agricultural land for carbon uptake

Planting trees on lands that are currently cultivated or used for grazing is considered an attractive option for removing CO_2 from the atmosphere. Indeed, some countries intend to rely on afforestation for upwards of 25% of their international commitments to reduce CO_2 emissions, while some companies have either purchased or are seriously looking into afforestation as a means of offsetting some of their greenhouse gas emissions. In this section, we explore issues related to afforestation, providing estimates of the costs of afforestation for two regions – the Netherlands and western Canada. We begin by providing a theoretical background to the economics of afforestation.

Economics of Afforestation

Calculating the carbon flux is essentially an economic exercise. Carbon flux needs to be calculated for six different accounts. The most important account is the bole or merchantable component of the tree. It is found by multiplying tree growth (i.e., merchantable component), as given by equation (11.3) for example, by the amount of carbon per m^3 (α). Carbon builds up in the bole until harvest time (t), when it is assumed to enter into another account (e.g., wood products) or the atmosphere (by burning). A new stand of trees replaces the old, with the process assumed to continue indefinitely.

Next is above-ground biomass other than the bole; this consists mainly of branches and leaves, and is usually determined as a proportion of merchantable volume. When trees are cut, all of the non-merchantable biomass is left on the site as slash. At that time, it enters the litter account (treated below). When a new stand of trees is planted, there is re-growth of the non-bole biomass. In this sense, the non-merchantable biomass is treated much like the merchantable component.

Let η be an expansion factor that translates bole biomass into total above-ground biomass and α the factor that converts growth into carbon. The total discounted C per ha for the merchantable (M) plus related above-ground biomass (B) account is given by:

$$(11.39) \quad C_{M\&B} = \frac{\eta\alpha\left(\int_0^t \dot{v}(s)e^{-rs}ds - v(t)e^{-rt}\right)}{1-e^{-rt}},$$

where t is the rotation age and the dot above v denotes a time derivative – that carbon is being sequestered at every point in time as trees grow. The first term in parentheses counts the (discounted) carbon that accumulates during the growing stage, while the second term measures the C released to another account at harvest time. Upon dividing by $1 - e^{-rt}$, we obtain the sum of the infinite series of "returns" that accrue every t years, beginning in the current period.

Third, carbon in the root pool is calculated from an estimated relationship between root biomass (R) and above-ground biomass (G = M + B). An example of such a relationship might be:

$$(11.40) \quad R(G) = a\, G^b,$$

where R and G are both measured in m^3 per ha. An assumption needs to be made about what happens to the roots when trees are cut and new ones planted. For example, one might assume that, once the first set of roots has grown, root decay causes C to enter the soil pool at a rate exactly offset by the rate at which new growth adds to the root pool. Total discounted C per ha for the root account is then:

$$(11.41) \quad C_R = \alpha \int_0^t \dot{R}(G)\, e^{-rs}\, ds.$$

Fourth, there is a change in soil C when agricultural land is converted to plantation forests. Data on soil C are difficult to obtain. For the Netherlands, Wolf and Jensen (1991) report that grassland contains 75 tonnes of C per ha in equilibrium, arable land 34 t C ha^{-1}, and forestland 52 t C ha^{-1}. Field trials in the northern Great Plains of the USA indicate that sites with hybrid poplar have an average of 191 t C ha^{-1} in the top 1 metre of soil, row crops an average of 179 t of soil C, and grass that is regularly cut 157 t C ha^{-1} (Hansen 1993, p. 435). Guy and Benowicz (1998) note that forest soils in the boreal region of western Canada store some 108 t C ha^{-1} compared to cropland that stores some 60 t. Soil C rebuilds only slowly when cultivation stops. Suppose it takes k years for soil C to achieve a new equilibrium if cultivated land is afforested. Then total discounted C per ha in the soil (S) account is

$$(11.42) \quad C_S = c_S\left(\frac{1 - e^{-kr}}{r}\right),$$

where c_s is annual addition of C to the soil sink and the term in parentheses discounts an annual flow for a k-year period to the present.

Fifth, the litter pool consists of dead or dying biomass on the forest floor that releases C to the atmosphere through fire and decay and to the soil pool. It is a relatively small pool of C that changes rapidly. For simplicity, it is often assumed that the litter account grows by a constant amount each year for k years, after which it is in equilibrium. At that point it is assumed that the litter pool is some proportion (ϕ) of the non-bole biomass. In addition, there is a spike in the pool's biomass at harvest time. It is assumed that the slash component of the litter releases a constant amount of C into the atmosphere over the next t years (linear decay) so that it is depleted by the time of next harvest. This carbon spike and subsequent decay is important because physical C is discounted – it matters when C is removed from the atmosphere. The total discounted carbon per ha accruing to the litter account (C_L) is given as:

$$(11.43) \quad C_L = (\eta - 1)\, \alpha \left[c_l \left(\frac{1 - e^{-kr}}{r} \right) + \frac{\int_0^t \dot{v}(s)e^{-rs}\,ds - v(t)e^{-rt}}{1 - e^{-rt}} \right],$$

where $c_l = v(t)/\phi$ is the constant annual addition to the litter pool. The first term constitutes the current "value" of the k-year litter pool, while the second term is the discounted sum of the infinite deposit and subsequent decay of litter beginning with the current period and continuing every t years (the spike component).

Finally, it is important to consider what happens to the commercial component of the tree (or bole). Two alternatives are considered for harvested timber: burning wood in place on an energy-equivalent amount of coal, say (thus saving CO_2 emissions from coal) or storing C in wood products. As an energy substitute, one tonne of coal emits on average about 0.707 t of C. The amount of wood needed to generate the same energy as one tonne of coal is determined by dividing 0.707 t C per tonne of coal by α t C per m^3 of wood.

To obtain carbon fluxes for wood products, assume that proportion β ($0 \le \beta \le 1$) of bole goes into wood products, that decay (release C) at a rate δ ($0 \le \delta \le 1$) per year. Assume that $(1 - \beta)$ of the bole (the waste) is burned, thereby replacing an energy-equivalent amount of coal. Then, the total discounted C per ha stored in wood products at time of harvest plus the discounted emission savings resulting from the substitution of wood for coal in energy production at time of harvest is given as:

$$(11.44) \quad C_W = \alpha\, v(t) \left[\beta \left(\frac{r}{r + \delta} \right) + (1 - \beta) \right] \left(\frac{e^{-rt}}{1 - e^{-rt}} \right),$$

where C_W refers to the discounted C uptake resulting from use of commercial timber. Each time wood is harvested, a proportion β of the C in the bole is stored immediately in wood products, but every year thereafter a proportion δ is released. The first term in the square brackets in (11.44) gives the infinite sum of the total discounted C stored in wood products at each harvest; the second term in brackets represents C saved by burning wood in place of coal. The final term in (11.44) is a factor that sums the "values" that accrue every t years over the infinite time horizon.

Skog and Nicholson (1998) argue that paper products have a half-life of one to six years, while lumber in housing has a half-life of 80 to 100 years. Winjum et al. (1998), on the other hand, point out that oxidation rates are 0.02 per year for industrial roundwood products and 0.005 for paper products that end up in landfills.

In the discussion about existing forests, not all of the accounts had to be considered. When existing forests are managed to take carbon into account, the results are unlikely to be affected by the assumption that the soil, root and litter accounts as these are essentially in equilibrium. Then the issue of whether to discount physical carbon or not is not very troublesome. However, in the case of afforestation, where changes in these accounts do matter, the issue of discounting becomes troublesome.

Suppose one does not discount physical C. Then the one-time build-ups of C in the litter, root and soil accounts are counted, but not C going into wood products since such C is inevitably released to the atmosphere (even if that occurs far in the future). In that case, afforestation results in high costs of C uptake. If wood is burned in place of coal, even if it is only a very small amount, there will be an infinite C saving if one tries to calculate everything in terms of the current year. In these situations, the response is to calculate costs and C savings in annualised terms. Unfortunately, this creates problems for the soil and other accounts that eventually attain equilibrium, where the net C flux becomes zero. For these important but limited-time fluxes, discounting is required if the flux is to be annualised; if not, C uptake will be vastly overestimated. The only way one can avoid these problems is to adopt a planning horizon and assume that the land goes back to its original land use after at the end of the planning horizon. This is done in the study of afforestation in the Netherlands, while the infinite horizon approach is adopted in the study of afforestation in western Canada.

Afforestation in the Netherlands

For the Netherlands, two species are considered for planting on agricultural land for the purpose of C uptake: poplar (*Populus spp.*, especially *Populus euramericana*) and Norway spruce (*Picea abies*). For poplar, we use a rotation age of 15 years and two growth rates – poor growth of 142 m^3 over the rotation and good growth of 217 m^3 over the rotation. For Norway spruce, the rotation is fixed at 40 years with growth of 460 m^3 over this period. Slangen et al. (1997) calculate the following changes in above-ground carbon: for poplar (poor growth), 1.49 t C ha^{-1} yr^{-1}; for poplar (good growth), 2.28 t C ha^{-1} yr^{-1}; and for Norway spruce, 1.81 t C ha^{-1} yr^{-1}. These amounts likely underestimate true uptake by about 20% because of the low value of α employed (0.158 t C m^{-3} rather than some 0.190 t C m^{-3}). Changes in below-ground biomass from changes in land use lead to an annual gain of 0.36 t C per ha when land changes from cultivation to forest, but a loss of 0.46 t C ha^{-1} yr^{-1} for a change from grassland to forest. The size of the below-ground C sink at any time since the change in land use can then be calculated as: $C_0 + \Delta C_j \times$ time. Here C_0 is the below-ground carbon associated with the original land use (arable land or grassland) and ΔC_j is the effective annual flow (addition or removal) from changing from land use j to forestry.[6]

Three options are examined. For each, the below-ground change in C stored per hectare is derived from the equilibrium levels of soil C for the three land use types – grassland (75 t C ha^{-1}), arable land (34 t C ha^{-1}) and forestland (52 t C ha^{-1}). Assume

---

[6] The data used in this section are taken from Slangen et al. (1997), but the results reported there are recalculated in what follows.

soil C takes 50 years to reach a new equilibrium after land conversion and that the annual change in soil C is constant until equilibrium is attained. Then, in converting land from cultivation to forestry, the discounted net change in below-ground carbon is 18.00 t C ha^{-1} for a discount rate of 0%, 11.31 t C ha^{-1} for 2% and 7.73 t C ha^{-1} for 4%. Comparable measures for a conversion from grassland to forestland are −23.00 t C ha^{-1}, −14.46 t C ha^{-1} and −9.88 t C ha^{-1} for discount rates of 0%, 2% and 4%, respectively.

Consider as a first option a one-time conversion of grassland or arable cropland to forests, with no subsequent harvest of timber – the *storage option*. Total above-ground C uptake is given by $\sum_{s=1}^{t} \Delta C (1 + r)^{-s}$, where ΔC is the annual C uptake and t is rotation length (15 years for poplar, 40 years for spruce). The amounts of above-ground C that would be stored per ha for the two species (and for different discount rates) are provided in Table 11.17. Below-ground changes need to be added to these amounts.

A second option is to harvest the wood and burn it in place of an energy-equivalent amount of fossil fuel, with the net gain equal to the CO_2 that would otherwise have been released by fossil-fuel burning. To achieve this gain it is necessary to continue to plant trees and harvest them for the purpose of generating energy. Thus, one achieves a balance between C emissions and uptake, with harvested biomass used only as an energy source. Two processes are important, namely, C uptake during tree growth and fossil fuel substitution. Earlier we discussed substituting wood for coal, but in the Netherlands we substitute wood for natural gas as the Netherlands is a major gas producer. On an energy-equivalent basis, 2.042 m^3 of wood are needed for every m^3 of natural gas, so it is necessary to divide the amount of C sequestered in trees and subsequently released through burning by 2.042 to obtain the true saving in CO_2 emissions. Further, based on natural gas prices and adjusting for energy equivalence, wood as fuel is less valuable than wood used for products. Only the above-ground carbon fixed in wood biomass is available for generating energy, while changes in soil C are as before. The total C saving by burning wood in place of natural gas over a period of T years – the *energy option* – is $\sum_{s=1}^{t} \Delta C (1 + r)^{-s}$. We assume a project of 120 years (= T). Results are provided in Table 11.17.

The final option is to harvest the trees and store carbon in wood products. Wood can be used as raw material for the production of capital goods or as consumption goods in place of synthetic materials, concrete, aluminium and steel. Then the wood products become an important sink, with the life of the sink equivalent to the duration or life of the capital or consumption good, or beyond if the wood is subsequently disposed of in a land fill. For simplicity, we assume that wood products made from poplar release their carbon back to the atmosphere after 30 years, while products made from spruce release their stored C after 40 years. A wood product sink has a smaller drop off in total carbon uptake compared to the fuel substitution option. Total above-ground carbon uptake is

$$(11.45) \quad C_{\text{product substitution}} = \sum_{s=1}^{T} \frac{\Delta C}{(1+r)^s} - \sum_{j=1}^{h} \frac{\sum_{s=1}^{t} \frac{\Delta C}{(1+r)^s}}{(1+r)^{(j+i)t}},$$

where $T = 120$ and ΔC is the annual carbon uptake by forest growth. For poplar, $j = 3$, $h = 8$, $i = 2$ and $t = 15$; for spruce, $j = 2$, $h = 3$ $i = 1$ and $t = 40$. A summary of per hectare carbon uptake for this *product substitution option* is also provided in Table 11.17.

Table 11.17: Discounted Above-Ground Carbon Saving over 120 Years, Various Scenarios (t ha^{-1})

Option/ Discount rate	Poplar (poor growth)	Poplar (good growth)	Norway Spruce
Storage			
0%	22.365	34.178	72.452
2%	13.393	20.467	49.549
4%	12.093	18.481	35.851
Energy			
0%	87.620	133.898	106.443
2%	33.117	50.608	40.231
4%	18.089	27.643	21.975
Product substitution			
0%	44.730	68.355	72.452
2%	37.933	57.968	60.562
4%	28.581	43.677	41.075

Consider planting 150,000 ha of agricultural land to forest. Afforestation of 150,000 ha, or 7.5% of total Dutch agricultural land, reduces annual Dutch CO_2 emissions by 0.15–0.35% depending on the species that is planted, rate of planting and the discount rate employed. Further, assume that planting takes place over 10 years for both poplar and Norway spruce, implying that 15,000 ha yr^{-1} are planted either entirely to poplar or to Norway spruce.

When trees are harvested at the end of a rotation, replanting occurs immediately. Planting occurs at an initial rate of 15,000 ha per year for 10 years. When trees are harvested at the end of a rotation, replanting occurs immediately. Land reverts back to its original agricultural use at the end of 120 years (releasing or storing below-ground C over a 50-year period). After 120 years standing trees release all CO_2 back to the atmosphere under the storage option, are harvested and burned under the energy option, and are harvested and used entirely for wood products (spruce) or some combination of wood products (15%) and release of CO_2 to the atmosphere (85%) (poplar). Total discounted physical carbon benefits over the 120 years under each of the options and species are provided in Table 11.18.

Some interesting observations follow from these results. Whether cropland or grassland is converted to forest, the option that reduces atmospheric CO_2 the most is the energy option (burning wood in place of natural gas) if physical C is not discounted. If a good growth rate can be assured, then poplar should be planted. Further, the storage option should be avoided because the C stored in biomass when the forest is initially established is all lost when the land reverts back to agriculture after 120 years (thus explaining the equality of results for the options under the no discount scenario of Table 11.18). If carbon is discounted, however, the preferred strategy is to plant Norway spruce and use the harvested timber for wood products. With a 2% discount rate and a conversion of grassland to forest in the case of poor-growth poplar, the storage option actually leads to an increase in atmospheric CO_2 because the early increase in C stored in wood biomass cannot overcome the gradual loss of below-ground C. The preferred option cannot be determined from physical considerations alone, but will depend on both the amounts of C removed and the associated costs.

Table 11.18: Total C Removed on 150,000 ha over 120-Year Cycle, Various Scenarios (10^6 tonnes)

Species	Option	0%	2%	4%
Arable cropland to forest				
Poplar (poor)	Storage	0	3.051	2.482
	Energy	13.143	5.949	3.257
	Product substitution	4.697	6.423	4.566
Poplar (good)	Storage	0	3.925	3.281
	Energy	20.085	8.352	4.466
	Product substitution	7.177	9.078	6.465
Norway spruce	Storage	0	7.516	5.456
	Energy	15.966	6.926	3.749
	Product substitution	10.868	9.720	6.165
Grassland to forest				
Poplar (poor)	Storage	0	−0.270	0.277
	Energy	13.143	2.766	1.052
	Product substitution	4.697	3.241	2.361
Poplar (good)	Storage	0	0.742	1.076
	Energy	20.085	5.170	2.261
	Product substitution	7.177	5.896	4.260
Norway spruce	Storage	0	4.334	3.251
	Energy	15.966	3.744	1.544
	Product substitution	10.868	6.538	3.960

(Discount rate column group: 0%, 2%, 4%)

Social cost-benefit analysis is used to compare investments in tree plantations for C uptake purposes. The analysis focuses only on land currently used for crop production or dairy farming and eligible for conversion to forestry; of eligible land, 37% is arable and 63% is grassland. The weighted shadow value for agricultural land is 1,059.50 gld ha^{-1} yr^{-1} (Slangen et al. 1997). Given that the economy has been robust in recent years, the labour and capital that are released when agricultural land is converted to forests are assumed to have an opportunity cost that is approximately equal to what they earned in agriculture. If released labour and capital are less productive outside of agriculture, however, then the results underestimate the true costs of C sequestration.

The costs and benefits of the tree-planting project are provided in Table 11.19. Planting costs are distributed over two years, and two price scenarios are assumed.

Wood biomass used in the production of energy is valued at only 30 gld per m^3, while timber used in wood products (lumber and pulp) is valued at 50 gld per m^3. Under an alternative (high price) scenario, they are valued at 40 gld/m^3 and 60 gld/m^3, respectively. The net social benefits (discounted benefits minus discounted costs) from planting trees over a 120-year period under the three options, with two discount rates, are provided in Table 11.20.

Table 11.19: Assumptions for Afforestation in the Netherlands

Item	Poplar (Poor)	Poplar (Good)	Norway Spruce
Rotation period (in years)	15	15	40
Timber produced (m^3/ha)	142	217	460
Mean annual increment (m^3/ha)	9.5	14.5	11.5
Planting cost year 1 (gld/ha)	1,144	1,144	1,275
- Planting material	1,120	1,120	1,075
- Plant protection	24	24	200
Planting cost year 2 (gld/ha)	136	136	308
- Planting material	112	112	108
- Plant protection	24	24	200
Annual management cost (gld/ha)	130	130	130
Timber return after harvest cost (gld/ha)			
- net stumpage price of 30 gld/m^3	4,260	6,510	13,800
- net stumpage price of 50 gld/m^3	7,100	10,850	23,000
Planting subsidy (gld/ha)[a]			
- from EU	1,475	1,475	1,475
- from Dutch government	1,475	1,475	1,475
Annual subsidy (gld/ha)[a]			
- from EU	600	600	600
- from Dutch government	900	900	900

Source: Slangen et al. (1997)
[a] The EU pays a half of the subsidy, but, for the purposes of this study, it is assumed that the annual subsidy paid by the Dutch government is higher although this may not be permitted under EU rules.

It is possible to develop a number of measures of the cost per tonne of carbon uptake (CO_2 removed from the atmosphere) using the values in Tables 11.18 and 11.20. (Since the data in Table 11.20 are based on converting 37% of land from arable cropland and 63% from grasslands, it is first necessary to obtained weighted C uptake values from Table 11.18.) Cost-benefit estimates are provided in Table 11.21. If physical C is not discounted, the preferred option is the energy option. If a good growth rate can be assured, then poplar should be planted.

The last two columns of Table 11.21 are estimates of the costs of C uptake when both physical C and financial costs and returns are discounted at the same rates. These results indicate that the preferred strategy is product substitution – to use harvested timber for wood products. Again, poplar should be planted if good growth can be assured. The storage option should generally be avoided because the costs of C storage under this option are large, ranging from nearly 1,000 gld per tonne to infinite cost when physical C is not discounted.

Table 11.20: Discounted Cost of Afforesting 150,000 ha of Agricultural Land for C Uptake

Option	Low Price[a]		High Price[a]	
	2%	4%	2%	4%
Poplar (poor)	(10^6 guilders)			
Storage	7,585.7	3,915.1	7,565.9	3,913.2
Energy	6,572.7	3,548.2	6,065.1	3,326.2
Product substitution	5,617.0	3,110.0	5,121.4	2,889.1
Poplar (good)				
Storage	7,533.4	3,910.0	7,503.2	3,907.1
Energy	5,768.5	3,196.4	4,992.8	2,857.2
Product substitution	4,308.0	2,526.7	3,550.5	2,189.2
Norway spruce				
Storage	7,405.3	3,931.0	7,341.2	3,924.8
Energy	6,416.6	3,647.7	5,943.7	3,495.7
Product substitution	5,470.8	3,343.7	4,998.0	3,191.7

Source: Authors' calculations.
[a] Low price scenario has price for wood used for energy set to 30gld/m³ and for products set to 50 gld/m³; wood for energy and products is set to 40gld/m³ and 60gld/m³, respectively, under the high price scenario.

Table 11.21: Cost of C Uptake in the Netherlands, Various Scenarios (gld per tonne)[a]

Item	Discount rate for physical carbon			
	0%	0%	2%	4%
Social discount rate	2%	4%	2%	4%
Poplar (poor)				
- Storage	∞	∞	7,911.86	3,582.45
- Energy	500.09	269.97	1,666.62	1,899.64
- Product substitution	1,195.88	662.12	1,271.30	978.95
Poplar (good)				
- Storage	∞	∞	3,924.24	2,066.76
- Energy	287.20	159.15	908.80	1,038.87
- Product substitution	600.25	352.06	609.05	497.79
Norway spruce				
- Storage	∞	∞	1,343.65	966.60
- Energy	401.89	228.47	1,303.83	1,545.74
- Product substitution	503.39	307.66	709.09	700.12

[a] Using prices of 30 gld per m³ for energy option and 50gld per m³ for product substitution

If discounting of C is accepted, the costs of terrestrial C sequestration in the Netherlands range from 497.79–609.05 gld per tonne C if good-growth poplar can be planted to 700.12–709.09 gld per tonne C if Norway spruce is planted. This amounts to US$260–375 per tonne of C uptake. (The cost would be 159.15–500.09 gld per t C, or about $85–$265 t C, if physical carbon is not discounted and the socially efficient strategy is chosen.) Given that a low value of α was employed, the costs in Table 11.21 likely overstate actually costs by as much as 20%. Even so, this would costs only to the US$200–$300 range, still unacceptably high. Finally, the results indicate that correct choice of species and disposal option is important to achieving these costs. Choosing strategically and proper forest management can save substantial economic costs.

The costs of C uptake on agricultural land in the Netherlands are high, and there is likely little room for this option in the Dutch government's policy arsenal. There certainly must exist methods for reducing CO_2 emissions that are better in terms of having lower net social costs. In particular, there are possibilities for planting trees outside of the Netherlands, where agricultural land values are not as high as in the Netherlands but rates of growth are at least as great. Subsidising or operating land conversion schemes in other countries is one means by which the Dutch can lower their contributions to atmospheric CO_2. For comparison, we present similar calculations for western Canada. Although the methodology is somewhat different between the studies, the results can be considered roughly comparable nonetheless.

Afforestation in Western Canada

Unlike the Netherlands, Canada has large areas of marginal agricultural lands that could be afforested in order to sequester carbon for mitigating future climate change. In 1990, Canadian emissions of CO_2 amounted to 596 million metric tonnes (Mt) of CO_2-equivalent GHG emissions, or 162.5 Mt of C; in 1996 (the latest year for which data are available), emissions amounted to 669 Mt of CO_2, or 182.4 Mt of C. Business as usual scenarios project annual emissions to remain stable to 2000, and then rise to 203.2 Mt of C in 2010 and 225–230 Mt in 2020. To meet the Kyoto target, Canadian emissions must be 152.7 Mt C (560 Mt CO_2), some 25% (or 50.5 Mt C) below the level expected in the commitment period. Canada expects a large part of its international commitment to reduce atmospheric CO_2 to come from forestry, with perhaps 10% to nearly 25% of its Kyoto commitment coming via tree planting.

To investigate the potential for and costs of terrestrial C sequestration in western Canada, we focus on the Province of Alberta (immediately east and adjacent to BC) and the Peace River region of Northeast BC. We do not consider the southern most region of Alberta because it is too dry for growing trees, except under irrigation. Marginal agricultural land area and annual net returns to various activities on marginal land in the BC Peace River region and six Agricultural Reporting Areas (ARA) in Alberta are provided in Table 11.22 (van Kooten et al. 1999). ARAs 1 and 2 are located in southern Alberta and are not considered here. There are some 7.033 million ha of available marginal agricultural land, not including unimproved pasture in the BC Peace region that is considered to have too much canopy cover to include in the analysis.

Table 11.22: Marginal Farmland Area and Annual Net Returns, Classified by Land Use

Region	Area Available in Activity ('000s ha)			Annual Net Returns ($ per ha)		
	Forage	Improved pasture	Unimproved Pasture	Forage	Improved pasture	Unimproved pasture
BC Peace	119.6	97.0	282.5	184.98	34.45	n.a.
Alberta Agricultural Reporting Area (ARA)						
3 (Southwest)	216.4	194.1	1,039.6	310.20	35.82	17.33
4a (East central S)	115.9	180.6	498.0	101.47	24.84	12.42
4b (East central N)	128.4	186.4	338.9	116.80	28.35	14.02
5 (Mid central)	435.7	360.8	557.4	260.56	46.93	20.26
6 (Northeast)	446.7	351.1	685.6	168.63	58.01	21.04
7 (Northwest)	334.1	245.0	501.4	178.75	34.45	15.15

Estimates of the costs per tonne of carbon sequestered for each of these land types requires data on the net returns associated with the current agricultural activity (the opportunity cost of afforestation), the direct costs of afforestation, and the C uptake associated with the trees to be planted. Net returns to forage crops were calculated using data on hay production and prices for the different regions of Alberta and British Columbia (van Kooten et al. 1999). Pasture is treated somewhat differently. A good market exists in both BC and Alberta for private pasture rental. Rents are based on a standardised animal unit month (AUM), which is the forage consumed per month by a 450-kg cow. Using data for each ARA on stocking rates in AUMs per ha and the private market value of an AUM of pasture use, the opportunity costs of lost pasture is estimated (van Kooten et al. 1999). The opportunity costs of foregone agricultural activities are also provided in Table 11.22.

Tree planting costs depend on the species chosen for planting. For various regions of the Canadian Prairies, there are different species that could be considered for planting on agricultural land, but only fast growing hybrid poplar is chosen for C uptake because of its rapid rates of growth. Since the main purpose of this study is to provide estimates of the costs of C sequestration, other issues, such as the reduced potential for biodiversity gains from planting only one species, are not taken into account. Plantation establishment costs range between C$1,270 and $4,000 per ha (van Kooten 1999b; van Kooten et al. 1999).

Calculation of the stream of C uptake requires estimates of tree growth. For this purpose, the Chapman-Richards function is employed:

$$(11.46) \quad v(t) = \gamma (1 - e^{-kt})^m,$$

where γ is maximum stem wood volume and k and m are parameters (Guy and Benowicz 1998). Many clones of hybrid poplar exist and "... quoted growth rates of hybrid poplar vary tremendously across Canada and the northern USA making it difficult to estimate average values for each region" (Guy and Benowicz 1998, p. 8). Available data on growth rates have been obtained under various management regimes, including fertilization and irrigation. Parameter values for the study region are provided in Table 11.23.

Table 11.23: Parameters for the Chapman-Richards Growth Function for Hybrid Poplar, by Region and Potential Land Productivity

REGION	Forage	Improved Pasture	Unimproved Pasture
BC Peace	$\gamma = 330, k = 0.16$	$\gamma = 330, k = 0.14$	n.a.
Alberta, ARA			
3 (Southwest)	$\gamma = 300, k = 0.16$	$\gamma = 330, k = 0.14$	$\gamma = 270, k = 0.15$
4a (East central S)	$\gamma = 300, k = 0.16$	$\gamma = 300, k = 0.14$	$\gamma = 270, k = 0.15$
4b (East central N)	$\gamma = 300, k = 0.16$	$\gamma = 300, k = 0.14$	$\gamma = 270, k = 0.15$
5 (Mid central)	$\gamma = 300, k = 0.16$	$\gamma = 300, k = 0.16$	$\gamma = 270, k = 0.15$
6 (Northeast)	$\gamma = 330, k = 0.15$	$\gamma = 300, k = 0.16$	$\gamma = 270, k = 0.14$
7 (Northwest)	$\gamma = 330, k = 0.16$	$\gamma = 330, k = 0.14$	$\gamma = 270, k = 0.14$

Total C uptake is calculated from the growth function (11.23), which gives the merchantable component of the trees, plus the following parameter values: $\alpha = 0.187$ t per m^3, $\eta = 1.57$ in equation (11.39), and $a = 1.4139$ and $b = 0.639$ in equation

(11.40). Van Kooten et al. (1999) examine both wood burning for energy (substituting for coal in the generation of electricity) and timber used in wood products. The results of these calculations are summarised in Figures 11.5 and 11.6.

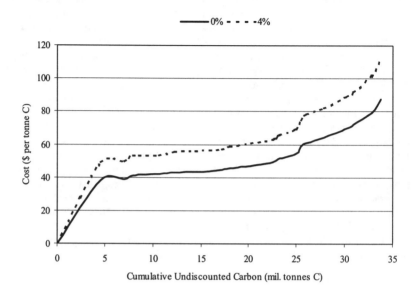

Figure 11.5 Marginal Costs of C Uptake by Afforestation, Western Canada, Wood Burning Option

The results suggest that marginal costs of carbon uptake rise dramatically as increasingly better marginal agricultural land is converted to hybrid poplar plantations, but that C uptake costs are significantly higher for the wood burning option than for the wood products option.

For a cost of C uptake of less than $20 per tonne of carbon, the wood burning option is not likely to be viable, and one would expect very little (marginal) agricultural land to be planted to trees for this purpose. How realistic is a cost of $20 per t C? In late 1999, Ontario Power Generation Inc. pruchased C rights from Zahren Alternative Power Corp. in the USA for about $C50 per tonne of carbon.[7] Even at that cost, from Figure 11.5 the wood burning option does not seem to be very feasible.

---

[7] This is as reported in the *Globe and Mail* newspaper, October 26, 1999. Such newspaper accounts leave out many details, however, such as the timing of the carbon benefits and the time frame over which payments are to be made. Hence, costs may well be much lower than those based on the information reported.

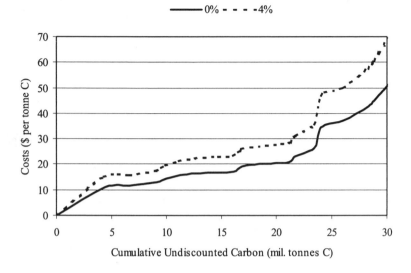

Figure 11.6 Marginal Costs of C Uptake by Afforestation, Western Canada, Wood Product Option

If, on the other hand, wood is harvested and wood products subsequently store C for a long time, then afforestation of marginal agricultural land could be a useful component in Canada's policy arsenal. For C uptake costs of $20 per tonne C or less, it may be worthwhile to plant hybrid poplar on 2.3 million ha of a potential 7 million ha of marginal agricultural land. Note that this is less than one-third of the agricultural land that a non-economist might identify as suitable for afforestation. On the 2.3 million ha, some 9.9 Mt of C would be sequestered annually, or some 19.6% of Canada's Kyoto commitment. If these results hold for other regions of Canada, then as much as 60% of Canada's requirements could be met via afforestation!

We might ask whether this is the optimal amount of agricultural land to convert to tree plantations. In order to investigate this question, it is necessary to employ a dynamic optimisation model. Following van Kooten (1999b), the objective is to maximise the discounted flow of present and all future net benefits, including benefits of carbon uptake:

$$(11.47) \quad \text{maximise} \int_0^\infty \pi(t)\, e^{-rt}\, dt,$$

where

$$(11.48) \quad \pi = \int_0^A B'(s)\, ds + \int_0^{A_0-A} [sF(z) + p_c C(z)]\, dz - \tau(R)\, R(t).$$

Here $\pi(t)$ is economic benefits; A_0 represents the initial stock of (marginal) agricultural land available for afforestation (7.033 million ha for the study area) and $A(t)$ the land in agriculture at any time, so that $A_0 - A$ is land converted from agriculture to plantation forest for the purpose of sequestering C; $R(t)$ is the agricultural area afforested at time t; $B'(A)$ are the marginal benefits of agricultural production, which decline as more of the available agricultural land is retained in agriculture rather than converted to forest, $B''(A) < 0$, indicating that the poorest agricultural land is afforested first; s is the stumpage value of timber; p_c is the shadow price of carbon; $F(z) + p_cC(z)$ are the marginal benefits of afforestation; and r is the social rate of discount. The term $\int_0^{A_0-A} [sF(z) + p_cC(z)]dz$ describes the total benefits for the $A_0 - A$ hectares of farmland that is afforested. Marginal benefits of tree planting equal the sum of the marginal commercial timber benefits, $sF(z)$, and the shadow value of the marginal C uptake benefits, $p_cC(z)$. Recognising that $z = A_0 - A$, $F'(z) < 0$ and $C'(z) < 0$. The function $\tau(R)$ represents the cost of planting a hectare of farmland to trees, which increases as one attempts to plant more area in a given year.

The dynamic (subject to) constraint is

(11.49) $\dot{A}(t) = -R(t)$,

where the dot over the variable A indicates a time derivative. The focus is on conversion of agricultural land into plantation forest, because cost of converting land from forest to agriculture is ignored.

Maximisation takes place subject to the equation of motion (11.49). The current value Hamiltonian (suppressing time notation) is defined as: $H = \pi - \lambda R$, where λ is the co-state variable. Assuming an interior solution, the necessary conditions for an optimum solution are:

(11.50) $\dfrac{\partial H}{\partial R} = 0 \Rightarrow \lambda = -\tau'(R)R - \tau(R)$

(11.51) $\dot{\lambda} = r\lambda - \dfrac{\partial H}{\partial A} \Rightarrow \dot{\lambda} = r\lambda - [B'(A) - sF(A_0 - A) - p_c C(A_0 - A)]$.

The interpretation of (11.50) is that the rate of conversion of agricultural land to forest should be chosen so that the discounted marginal net benefit from current conversion, λ, equals the marginal benefit (marginal costs avoided) of delaying conversion. The discounted marginal benefits of current conversion take into account the opportunity cost of lost agricultural production, while τ could be constant. Equation (11.51) provides a standard intertemporal arbitrage condition.

The steady-state occurs when the co-state multiplier and the area retained in agricultural production are constant ($\dot{\lambda} = \dot{A} = 0$) so no further afforestation takes place ($R = 0$). The equation that describes the optimal amount of land to keep in agriculture in the steady-state is:

$$(11.52) \quad -\tau(0) + \frac{sF(A_0 - A^*) + p_c C(A_0 - A^*)}{r} = \frac{B'(A^*)}{r}.$$

Equation (11.52) says that, in equilibrium, the marginal present value of the benefits of afforestation minus planting costs must equal the discounted stream of benefits of keeping land in agricultural production at the margin. Included in benefits are the shadow costs and benefits of C uptake and release.

Notice that the current problem and its solution are nearly identical to the above problem concerning the optimal area of ancient forest to retain. Only the context differs, and that there are no nonuse benefits to consider in the current analysis. However, due to its similarity with the earlier problem, we only consider the final results. Van Kooten (1999b) provides functional forms for each of $F(A_0 - A)$, $C(A_0 - A)$, $\tau(R)$, and $B'(A)$, thereby enabling one to solve (11.52).

The steady-steady, optimal solutions are provided in Table 11.24. These indicate that, for a shadow price of C not exceeding $20 per tonne, no more than about 50% of available marginal agricultural land should be planted to trees to meet Canada's Kyoto target. At shadow prices for C of $50 per t or more, about three-quarters of marginal agricultural land can be afforested. Compared to the static cost-benefit analysis, the dynamic optimisation model finds that a great proportion of the available marginal agricultural land should be afforested.

Table 11.24: Optimal Proportion of Total Available Land for Afforestation (7.033 mil ha) to Plant to Trees for Carbon Uptake, Sensitivity Analysis

P_C ($ per tonne)	Discount Rate (Base Parameter Values)			Steeper slope of marginal agricultural benefits function	Higher intercept of marginal agricultural benefits function	Lower Stumpage value	Higher tree planting costs
	2%	4%	6%				
10	0.41	0.29	0.09	0.15	0	0.21	0.21
20	0.53	0.50	0.46	0.39	0.34	0.42	0.47
50	0.73	0.76	0.79	0.71	0.71	0.64	0.75
100	0.90	0.95	1.00	0.94	0.92	0.86	0.95

To determine the sensitivity of the results to various assumptions, the marginal benefits of land in agricultural activities were increased, the returns to forestry were reduced and the costs of tree planting were increased (see Table 11.24). When the marginal benefit function for land in agricultural activities has a lower slope or larger intercept (so land in agriculture is slightly more valuable at the margin), the optimal amount of agricultural land to convert to forests declines by 0.5–1.5 million ha (for lower shadow prices of C). At a shadow price of C of $20 per t, a decline in timber revenue of 1% results in a 0.27% decline in the optimal area to be afforested. Finally, the results are most sensitive to the marginal value of tree planting costs. If costs of planting hybrid poplar are significantly higher ($2000 per ha) than originally assumed ($1270 per ha), it is possible that no more than one-third of available marginal agricultural land should be planted to trees for C uptake purposes. If planting costs are $3000 per ha or higher, regardless of the type of agricultural land, no agricultural areas should be afforested.

We investigate the role of planting costs in greater detail by examining the dynamic approach path. Taking the time derivative of (11.50) gives:

$$(11.53) \quad \dot{\lambda} = - \dot{R} \ [\tau''(R) R + 2 \ \tau'(R)].$$

Substituting (11.50) and (11.53) into (11.51) and solving for $\dot{R}$ gives:

$$(11.54) \quad \dot{R} = \frac{r[\tau'(R)R + \tau(R)] + B'(A) - sF(A_0 - A) - p_C C(A_0 - A)}{\tau''(R)R + 2\tau'(R)}.$$

Assuming a 4% discount rate for both monetary values and physical carbon, and with $p_c = \$20$ per t C, equations (11.53) and (11.54) can be used to construct the phase-plane diagram shown in Figure 11.7.

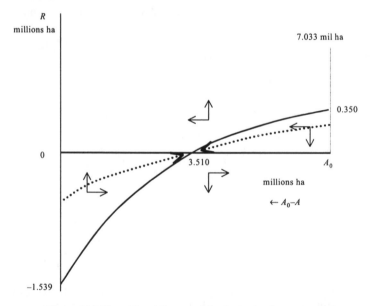

Figure 11.7 Phase-Plane Diagram of the Optimal Afforestation Path

The optimal approach path cannot be determined numerically for this autonomous, infinite horizon problem (Conrad and Clark 1987). Nonetheless, the phase-plane diagram can be used to shed some light on this problem. The optimal solution is necessarily a saddle point equilibrium (Leonard and Van Long 1992, pp. 289–99). The $\dot{R} = 0$ isocline intersects the vertical line A_0 at 350,000 ha, which corresponds to the maximum area that can be planted in one year without social benefits becoming negative. Along the optimal approach path, shown by the dotted line (separatrix), annual plantings cannot exceed some 200,000 ha. Even if 200,000 ha are planted annually, it will take some 18 years to achieve the optimal level of afforestation (3.5 million ha). However, plantings along the optimal path decline each year, so it is more likely an average of less than 100,000 ha per year would be planted along the optimal path, in which case it could take more than 35 years to achieve the optimal level of afforestation. Further, any other approach path will result in higher, probably unacceptable, carbon uptake costs.

Foresters are generally optimistic about Canada's ability to meet its carbon uptake commitments by planting hybrid poplar on marginal agricultural land. This is partially confirmed by the results presented here, which show that, for a shadow price of C of $20 per t, it may be optimal to afforest as much as 50% of identifiable marginal agricultural land. In that case, some 12.3 Mt of carbon will be sequestered per year in the study area, or nearly one-quarter of Canada's Kyoto commitment. If this result can be extended to marginal agricultural land in the rest of Canada, then some 70% of Canada's Kyoto commitment could be attained through forestry policies. Of course, this is a most optimistic scenario. Under different assumptions, the optimal, steady-state level of afforestation would be lower. Even if it were half as much, afforestation remains an important, if not the most important, policy instrument available to Canada. However, the results also suggest that the time required to plant trees is important, and this will certainly prevent Canada from using afforestation in its policy arsenal to meet Kyoto obligations.

There are two issues that remain. First, the costs considered here are related only to the opportunity costs of marginal agricultural land, tree planting costs, and costs related to the logging and hauling of logs to a place where they are burned or processed. Transaction costs are ignored, although these could be significant when millions of hectares of (marginal) land are to be teased out of agricultural production. While design of economic incentives and institutions will be important, account also needs to be taken of on-farm economies of scale (reducing land in forages and pasture might result in reduced cattle herds and associated higher per unit production costs) and farmers' attitudes (farmers may oppose mono-culture forests because of their potential to harbour pests and reduce scenic landscapes). This means that the costs of land in agriculture are higher than indicated in the above analysis.

Sohngen and Sedjo (1999) point to an even more disturbing problem. If large forest plantations are established in many countries in an effort to reduce C emissions, there will be an increase in wood fibre at a future date (as soon as a decade). This increased availability of wood fibre (whether for pulp or solid wood products) will reduce prices. If sufficient area is afforested globally (say some 50 million ha), current wood lot owners will reduce their forest holdings in anticipation of reduced stumpage prices in the future. That is, the carbon benefits of afforestation on a large scale will be offset to some extent by the liquidation of existing forest plantations. This is an important leakage that is usually neglected in studies of the C benefits of afforestation.

11.5 Conclusions

Forests are and have historically been important natural resources. They have long provided wood for burning and even today fuel wood accounts for about one-half of all wood use. Industrial wood accounts for the remainder, with roundwood logs, saw timber (lumber) and fibreboard important for construction and decoration, and pulp for paper and paper products. Because forests are a renewable resource, their future commercial use is assured; from an environmental standpoint, an attractive option is to rely more on wood products, through their substitution for non-wood products in construction (replacing concrete and aluminium studs) or burning (replacing fossil fuels). As demonstrated in this Chapter, forests play an important role in sequestering carbon and will continue in this role in the future. However, as the non-commercial timber value of forests increases with greater environmental awareness and need to reduce atmospheric concentrations of CO_2, the pressure on forestland owners to take into account such values in their land-use decisions will increase.

Given the commercial timber and non-timber demands on forestlands, it is important that they are managed efficiently. For example, global demand for wood fibre is growing by some 70 million m^3 per year, approximately equal to the entire annual growth of British Columbia. If non-timber demands of forests are to be satisfied in the future, it will be necessary to produce more fibre on less land area. This requires investment in research and development on genetics to improve stand growth and improve wood utilisation. It will also require greater investments in forest farms, where trees are grown much like an agricultural crop, with a short rotation age. Without these developments, there will continue to be great pressure on existing forest. As more forestland is reserved in the industrialised countries, and without greater investment in fibre production, logging in tropical forests will continue to be profitable, even should such forests be more valuable as a store of biodiversity. This issue is pursued further in Chapter 12.

12 Tropical Deforestation

Denudation of forests occurs by natural means (fires, disease, windfall) or as a result of human activities (harvest of timber, clearing of land). Human activities to cut trees for commercial wood products, or to clear land for agriculture, are of great concern to environmentalists and the general public. Deforestation refers to the removal of trees from a forested site and the conversion of the land to another use, most often agriculture. Deforestation is primarily confined to developing countries, and mainly in the tropics. Some see tropical deforestation as a failure of the market system (or capitalism more generally) to account for non-commercial timber values of the forest, a failure often linked to inadequate property rights over biological assets other than timber.

As noted in Chapter 1, the binding Helsinki intergovernmental ministerial agreements and the non-binding Montreal agreement represent key developments in the management of forests. They outline for the first time a common understanding of measures to monitor at the national level biological and social conditions associated with most of the world's temperate forests. Since they are directed specifically at temperate and boreal forests, the Helsinki and Montreal Processes have influenced moves to protect old-growth, temperate rain forests in the US Pacific Northwest and British Columbia. Concern has also been expressed about depletion of old-growth forest in Russia, some of which has been harvested for mills in Finland.

Timber harvests from federal lands in the US Pacific Northwest have nearly been halted, while BC has reduced harvest levels and implemented stringent environmental controls, as have Finland and Sweden (Wilson et al. 1998; Sedjo 1997). With the globalisation of wood product markets, timber harvests from forests in northern latitudes have important impacts on forestland use in southern and tropical countries (Sedjo 1996). A reduction in northern harvests increases fibre prices in the short term, increasing the attractiveness of timber mining in tropical regions. Higher prices also increase the value of forestlands, thereby reducing incentives to convert them to agriculture, and raise the profitability of plantation forests whose outputs reduce pressure on pristine forests. In most industrial forested nations (e.g., Finland, Sweden and Canada), forest laws require reforestation of sites after harvest, and evidence indicates that forests in temperate and boreal areas have actually expanded (Korotov and Peck 1993; Chapter 11).

Deforestation in developing countries is another matter, and it is mainly in these countries where tropical forests are found. The UN's Food and Agricultural Organisation (FAO) defines tropical forests as ecosystems with a minimum of 10% crown canopy of trees and/or bamboo; they are generally associated with wild flora, fauna and natural soil conditions and not subject to agricultural practices (FAO 1997). Tropical forests cover a large portion of the globe's land surface between the

Tropics of Cancer and Capricorn, 23° north and south of the Equator. The largest expanse of tropical forest is found in the South American equatorial region, predominantly in the Amazon Basin, but extending up into Central America and down into northern Argentina. Large tropical forests are also found in the equatorial regions of Africa and West Africa and in Southeast Asia, running from India to Malaysia, north into China, and continuing to the islands of the East Indian Archipelago and extending into north-eastern Australia. While the climate of the tropics is uniform in terms of a steady year-round temperature, differences in tropical ecosystems are the result of different soil and slope conditions, and variation in the amount and timing of annual rainfall. For example, annual rainfall may vary from less than 10 millimetres (mm) along the Peruvian coast to more than 10 meters (m) along the Colombian coast only a few hundred km to the north (Terborgh 1992).

Tropical forests range from open savannahs where precipitation is limited, to dense tropical rainforests, where rainfall is most abundant. Large areas of dry tropical forests exist in almost all of the above regions, covering large areas in South and Central America as well as Africa and, to a lesser extent, Southeast Asia. Obviously, the type of tropical forest that occurs in an area depends critically upon the availability of precipitation and moisture. The annual cycle of seasonal change is also an important feature of tropical climates, but the seasons are characterised by variation in rainfall rather than temperature. Evergreen forests occur where there is little or no dry season.

One feature of tropical forests is that they contain much, if not most, of the world's biodiversity in the trees and plants that comprise the vegetative system and in the animals, especially anthropoids, which exist in the forest soils, floor and canopy. Tropical forests, especially wet tropical forests, typically contain far more species of trees, plants, birds, butterflies, and so forth than their temperate counterpart. Another feature is that, despite soils that are poor in nutrients and minerals, net primary productivity (NPP) of tropical ecosystems is higher than that of temperate and boreal ecosystems. For example, NPP amounts to 224 grams (g) per m^2 per year in boreal forests, 360 to 590 g m^{-2} yr^{-1} in temperate forests (depending on type – conifer, deciduous or broadleaf evergreen), but nearly 900 g m^{-2} yr^{-1} in tropical forests (FAO 1992).[1]

In this chapter, we examine the economics of tropical deforestation. The subject is complex and there are many misconceptions. One purpose is to identify some of these misconceptions. The other purpose is to examine the extent of deforestation, its causes and policies that can protect those attributes (e.g., biodiversity and carbon storage) that are really the objective of efforts to reduce or halt deforestation. We also consider the values of various forest products other than commercial timber products

---

[1] However, ecologists argue that biotic complexity of ecosystems is inversely related to net primary productivity. "The inverse relation between ecosystem complexity and net primary productivity explains why monocultures are necessary when the management objective is to maximise net yield and profit. In fact, most agricultural and silvicultural prescriptions for maximising yield involve the simplification of ecosystems ... including weeding or poisoning of any species that may compete with those most favored for their high yield and low respiration"(Lugo et al. 1993, p.106).

(e.g., pharmaceutical values, non-timber products), ecosystem functions and preservation values as these are a major component of economic arguments to prevent deforestation. We begin in the next section by examining global rates of deforestation. Economic values of tropical forests are reviewed in section 12.2. The role of tropical forests as a carbon sink is emphasised, because this is thought to be the most important non-timber value of tropical ecosystems. Causes of tropical deforestation are analysed in section 12.3. Then, in section 12.4, we ask whether rates of deforestation are excessive from an economic standpoint, and briefly discuss options for the international community to intervene should it wish to do so. Some conclusions follow.

12.1 Tropical Deforestation: Global Patterns and Rates

As noted in Chapter 11, tropical forests do not contribute large amounts to global industrial wood output. Even for countries such as Brazil that are significant in terms of pulp production, fibre comes from plantation forests. Although unimportant on a global scale, the forests in the Philippines, Malaysia and Indonesia, and more recently Papua New Guinea, the Solomon Islands, Laos, Vietnam, Burma and Cambodia, have been an important source of tropical logs for Japan (Dauvergne 1997, especially pp. 186–7). While preserving their own forests, the Japanese have relied upon tropical log imports and imports of softwood logs, lumber and wood pulp from the developed countries, mainly the USA and Canada. Tropical deforestation in other regions, notably Africa, India, and Central and South America, has been driven by conversion of land to agriculture.

Global patterns of deforestation are indicated in Table 12.1. Deforestation generally refers to forestland conversion to non-forest uses, principally agriculture. Forest degradation, on the other hand, involves significant degrading of the forest ecosystem without eliminating all of the forest cover outright (Downton 1995, p. 23). Degradation is an arbitrary concept, although the term is used interchangeably with deforestation. As noted above, the UN's FAO defines tropical deforestation as occurring when canopy cover is reduced to 10% or less, but, for developed countries, deforestation results when canopy cover is reduced to 20% or less. Therefore, given the different thresholds, direct comparisons between developed and developing countries need to be made with caution. Also provided in Table 12.1 are population densities, the proportion of the population that is rural and the extent to which the forest cover is natural and not secondary forest.

Approximately 40% of forest cover is secondary growth (having been reforested naturally or replanted), with some 55% of the secondary forest consisting of residual forest cutover in the past sixty to eighty years (and never completely felled) and the remainder (termed "fallow" forest) having invaded after periodic cultivation (Sedjo 1992). Residual secondary forests maintain many of the ecosystem characteristics (physiognomy, systemic processes, tree species and other organisms) of natural forests. Fallow forests, on the other hand, consist of a large number of species that declines rapidly as tree sizes increase; while many of the ecosystem characteristics of natural forests have disappeared, these return as the forest matures.

Table 12.1: Forest Area and Rates of Deforestation, 1981–90 and 1990–95

Region/Country	1995 Population		1995 Forest Cover[a]		Annual Δ in Forest Cover, 1981–90[b]		Annual Δ in Forest Cover, 1990–95[a]	
	Density (#/km²)	% Rural	10⁶ ha	% Natural	Area ('000s ha)	Rate (%)	Area ('000s ha)	Rate (%)
Africa	24.8	56.7	520.2	99.1	–4,100	–0.7	–3,748	–0.7
Tropical	24.6	58.8	504.9	99.6	c	–0.7	–3,695	–0.7
Non-tropical	25.2	49.9	15.3	82.9	c	–0.8	–53	–0.3
Asia	126.5	65.7	474.2	c	c	c	–3,328	–0.7
Tropical	203.4	71.4	279.8	91.4	–3,791	–1.2	–3,055	–1.1
- South Asia	300.5	73.5	77.1	80.2	–551	–0.8	–141	–0.2
- SE Asia	111.2	66.4	202.6	95.7	–3,240	–1.4	–2,914	–1.3
Europe	107.0	26.5	146.0	c	c	c	+389	+0.3
Northern	16.5	24.6	52.5	c	c	c	+8	+0.0
Western	148.9	22.5	59.5	c	c	c	+358	+0.6
Eastern	106.1	38.8	34.0	c	c	c	+23	+0.1
Former USSR	13.3	32.1	816.2	c	c	c	+557	+0.1
Canada	3.2	23.3	244.6	c	c	c	+175	+0.1
United States	28.7	23.8	212.5	c	c	c	+589	+0.3
Central Am. & Mexico	52.3	32.0	75.0	99.7	–1,112	–1.5	–959	–1.2
Caribbean	156.7	37.5	4.4	93.4	–122	–0.3	–78	–1.7
South America	18.3	22.0	870.6	99.2	c	c	–4,774	–0.5
Tropical	19.3	23.8	827.9	99.3	–6,173	–0.7	–4,655	–0.6
- Brazil	19.1	21.8	551.1	99.1	–3,671	–0.6	–2,554	–0.5
Temperate	14.2	12.9	42.6	96.0	c	c	–119	–0.3
Oceania	3.3	20.9	90.7	c	c	c	–91	–0.1
Tropical	12.2	39.7	41.9	99.6	–113	–0.3	–151	–0.4
Temperate	2.7	15.1	48.8	c	c	c	+60	+0.1
Global Total	c	c	**3,454.4**	c	c	c	**–11,269**	**–0.3**

[a] Source: FAO (1997)
[b] Source: FAO (1993)
[c] Not available or not applicable

Throughout North America, Europe (Western and Eastern), the former USSR and Oceania, forested area increased between 1990 and 1995. These regions also account for the bulk of global wood production (Table 11.2). Increasingly, forest practices in the rich countries take into account ecological concerns, but, given globalisation of the forest products industry, reducing fibre output in (some) developed countries provides incentives for poor countries to develop their forest resources. This is a reason cited for Venezuela's decision in 1997 to open to logging the country's largest forest reserve – the 37,000 km² Sierra Imataca rainforest reserve near the Guyanese border (*The Economist* 1997b).

In contrast to northern latitudes, forest cover in poor countries is declining (Table 12.1). Tropical forests in particular are felt to be disappearing at a rapid rate, alarmingly so because they are thought to account for most of the globe's biodiversity, perhaps some two-thirds of the earth's approximately 14 million species (see Chapter 9). FAO data on tropical deforestation are provided in Table 12.2.

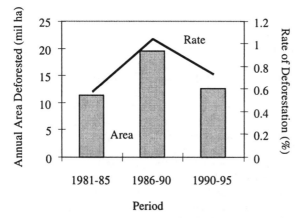

Figure 12.1 Annual Area and Rate of Deforestation, 1980–95

Table 12.2: Estimates of Forest Cover Area and Rate of Deforestation by Main Forest

Forest Formations	Land Area	Population Density 1990	Annual Population Growth (1981–90)	Forest Area 1990		Deforestation (1981–1990)	
	10^6 ha	persons/km^2	%	10^6 ha	%	10^6 ha yr^{-1}	%
FOREST ZONE	4,186.4	57	2.6	1,748.2	42	15.3	0.8
Lowland formations	3,485.6	57	2.5	1,543.9	44	12.8	0.8
- Tropical rainforest	947.2	41	2.5	718.3	76	4.6	0.6
- Moist deciduous forests	1,289.2	55	2.7	587.3	46	6.1	0.9
- Dry deciduous forests	706.2	106	2.4	178.6	25	1.8	0.9
- Very dry zone	543.0	24	3.2	59.7	11	0.3	0.5
Upland formations	700.9	56	2.9	204.3	29	2.5	1.1
- Moist forests	528.0	52	2.7	178.1	34	2.2	1.1
- Dry forests	172.8	70	3.2	26.2	15	0.3	1.1
NON-FOREST ZONE[a]	591.9	15	3.5	8.1	1	0.1	0.9
TOTAL TROPICS[b]	**4,778.3**	**52**	**2.7**	**1,756.3**	**37**	**15.4**	**0.8**

[a] Hot and cold deserts
[b] Totals may not tally due to rounding.
Source: FAO (1993).

It now appears that annual rates of tropical deforestation were greater on average in the latter half of the 1980s than in the first, but that there was a subsequent decline in the 1990s (Figure 12.1). For example, consensus estimates of the rate of deforestation for the Legal Amazon Region of Brazil are as follows (Downton 1995):

1978–1988	2.20 million ha per year
1988–1989	1.90 million ha per year
1989–1990	1.38 million ha per year
1990–1991	1.11 million ha per year

These figures indicate a significant decline in forestland conversion.

In 1995, tropical forests were estimated to cover an area of about 1,733.9 million ha (Table 12.2) or about 13.4% of the globe's land area, excluding Antarctica and Greenland. This is down from an estimated 1,756.3 million ha in 1990 and 1,910.4 million ha in 1981. The annual deforestation rate for the period 1981 to 1995 averaged 11.8 million ha, although the rate within this period varied considerably (Figure 12.1). Further, rates of deforestation have varied substantially throughout the tropics. Somewhat surprisingly, the tropical rainforest experienced the slowest relative rate of overall deforestation at 0.6% annually (Table 12.2). The highest rates of deforestation were experienced in the upland forests. Both moist and dry upland forests experienced a 1.1% annual rate of deforestation.

By major region, the Caribbean experienced the highest rate of deforestation at 1.7% per annum for the period 1990–1995, followed by Southeast Asia at 1.3% and Central America, including Mexico, at 1.2%; by contrast, South Asia had the lowest rate at 0.2% annually (Table 12.1). Interestingly, the Caribbean had the lowest rate – 0.3% per annum – during the period 1981–90. Similarly, the rate for Southeast Asia had increased from 1.5% in the 1981–90 period to 1.7% in the latest period. Rates of deforestation for Africa are about average.

Some authors, such as Myers (1991, 1994), report different figures for deforestation. According to the FAO, if forest cover declines from 15 to 8%, the area has been deforested; however, if forest cover declines from 90 to 15% no deforestation has taken place. Myers argues that the 10% threshold criterion for determining when deforestation has taken place is too strict; instead, he defines deforestation as having occurred when the remnant ecosystem no longer resembles a natural forest in appearance or in terms of the services that it is able to provide. Myers' is concerned with forest degradation and, in his view, a planted forest would not be treated as a forest in his statistics. In Myers' words, a forest can be reduced to a "travesty of a natural forest as properly understood" without reducing the tree crown cover to less than 10%. Not surprisingly, Myers' estimates of deforestation exceed those of the FAO by a considerable margin; compared to an FAO estimate of a 10.7 million ha per year decline in tropical moist forest area, Myers (1991) provides an estimate of 14.2 million ha per year (van Soest 1998, p. 32).

The advantage of the FAO estimates is that they are likely the most consistent and reliable for international comparisons, but there remain problems with FAO data on deforestation. For example, in the 1990 FAO Assessment, deforestation data for only 23% of the countries are based on two or more national forest inventories. For the remaining countries, deforestation for the period 1980–90 is based on only one inventory, with some as old as 1965. "Forest cover and deforestation were extrapolated from that single data point using a deforestation model where population density and ecological classes are the only explanatory variables, ... [so] the data reflect more population growth than actual deforestation" (Kaimowitz and Angelsen 1997, p. 54). It is expected that data limitations will be mitigated in the near future as remote sensing permits more accurate assessment of global forest stocks (FAO 1997).

It is estimated that 90% of (modern) tropical deforestation occurred between 1970 and 1990 (Skole et al. 1994). If this estimate is correct, the tropical forest of the world at its apex would have covered about 22 million km^2 (2.2×10^9 ha), or about 16.8% of the earth's land surface. Although reduced in size, the world's tropical forests still constitute an area equal to that of the whole of South America. Even at the current rate of tropical deforestation, the world's tropical forests would continue to exist through the entire twenty-first century and well into the twenty-second century. Of course, the current rate of tropical deforestation will almost surely change over time.

In many respects, tropical deforestation today is not dramatically different from temperate deforestation that occurred one and two centuries earlier. During that period pressures for land use change, primarily the demand for new lands for agriculture, resulted in large-scale deforestation of areas of Europe and North America. In the USA much of the forestlands of the eastern seaboard, the south and the Lake States were converted to cropland and pasture. This same phenomenon had begun earlier in Europe, and continued in places well into the early part of the twentieth century. The denuding of the forest landscape was often the result of spontaneous actions, but also reflected government policies. In the USA, for example, the Homestead Act required land clearing as a prerequisite for obtaining land title. For North America and Europe much of the early land clearing has been offset by the renewal of the forest, largely through natural processes. Today, the European forest has reclaimed large areas once deforested (Kuusela 1994; Table 12.1). Similarly, in America the forest has reclaimed much of the area deforested in New England (Barrett 1988), the Lake States and the south, as abandoned agricultural lands regenerated naturally into forest and, more recently, planted forests cover many former tobacco, cotton and other crop lands.

It has sometimes been claimed that it is difficult to renew tropical forests, but evidence suggests otherwise, given a long enough time span. For example, it is believed that large areas of the American tropics had been in terraces, irrigated agriculture and agro-foresty in the pre-European settlement (or pre-Columbian) period, but reverted to forests as local populations were decimated by disruptions and disease. These areas then returned to tropical forest. Turner and Butzer (1992) argue, that "the scale of deforestation, or forest modification, in the American tropics has only recently begun to rival that undertaken prior to the Columbian encounter". Similarly, the great temples of Angkor Watt in Cambodia, Borobodor in Java and other similar large structures in Southeast Asia, once located in the midst of a high level of human activity, were lost for centuries due to the incursion of tropical forest when human activity declined (Budiansky 1995, pp. 113–19).

12.2 Economic Value of Tropical Forests

Tropical forests, indeed all forests, provide many products and amenities that humans value. Human benefits often involve the collection of various forest items for food and fibre, such as various timber and non-timber forest outputs, but they also include nonuse values associated with the knowledge that tropical forests exist now (existence value) and in the future (option and bequest value). In addition, tropical forests provide local and regional ecological services in the form of watershed protection, mitigation of soil erosion and reduction of downstream flooding. Tropical ecosystems also provide habitat for much of the world's biodiversity and, together with the rest of the world's forests, provide a sink for carbon. How do these various values compare? Do forestland owners take them into account in their decision calculus?

Market failure occurs because social benefits from natural tropical forests, such as their value in contributing genetic material that may lead to new pharmaceutical drugs and their existence values, spill over to other countries – citizens in other countries benefit from the preservation of forests. As long as forest owners are not compensated to take into account these benefits, they will choose to ignore them in making decisions about the use of natural forests. This increases the probability that an agricultural alternative to preservation or sustainable tropical forest management is preferred.

Conservation of tropical forest ecosystems is often more difficult than conservation of marine biological assets because the opportunity costs of holding on to natural forests are higher. The reason is that land has more alternative uses capable of producing economic surpluses. Absent government, if forest ecosystems are to be protected, the returns from sustained forestry should be competitive with those of alternative land uses, such as agriculture and mining (Barbier and Burgess 1997). Government intervention is justified only if it can be shown that the total economic value (market plus nonmarket benefits) of the next hectare left as natural forest is greater than the market returns from a competitive use, with the difference being greater than the (marginal) cost of the government intervention. Since nonmarket values do not accrue to forest owners, governments can intervene to reflect such benefits, either by regulating conversion or by providing payments to landowners to prevent land conversion. Unfortunately, the records of most governments, rich and poor, in representing this constituency are spotty.

One way to compare the social returns to different land uses is to estimate the value of the various functions in monetary terms, where possible, so that straightforward comparisons can be made. For this purpose, we distinguish between production functions (production of timber and non-timber forest products), regulatory functions (e.g., carbon sink, watershed protection) and wildlife habitat/biodiversity functions, where the latter include nonuse values associated with preservation.

Production functions of tropical forests

Tropical rainforests produce tangible products such as timber, fuelwood and non-timber forest products (e.g., rattan, oils, fruits, nuts, ornamental flowers, bush meat), plus less tangible assets such as opportunities for eco-tourism. As we note in section 12.3, clear felling is not a common practice in the tropics. If clear felling does occur, say to make room for other activities such as agriculture or growing pulpwood for paper, net discounted returns can be high. Tropical stands contain some 200 m^3 to 400 m^3 of timber per ha (Thiele and Wiebelt 1993; Pearce and Warford 1993, p. 130), but much of this consists of noncommercial species and unusable wood. If 30–40% of the harvest is usable and assuming total rents of US$30 per m^3, clear felling yields a rent (or social surplus) of $1,800–$4,800 per ha, not including returns from subsequent land uses. Subsequent use of the land in forestry yields a positive but small return (less than $1 ha^{-1} yr^{-1} for artificially regenerated stands), while managed plantations frequently yield negative returns and proceed only with government subsidies (Sedjo 1992).

Estimates of the value of sustainable selective logging per hectare vary considerably, with differences due to (among other things) discount rates, stumpage prices, management costs, site conditions and productivity; see, for example, Vincent (1990) and Pearce and Warford(1993). Evidence from Costa Rica suggests that sustainable timber extraction from primary forest range from 0.5 to 2.0 m^3 ha^{-1} yr^{-1} (Carranza et al. 1996; Quiros and Finigan 1994). For Indonesia, Pearce and Warford (1993) estimate that selective logging yields a discounted net return of $2,409 per ha (assuming a 6% discount rate). Presumably selective logging is synonymous with *sustainable* logging, which is the ability to extract the same physical volume (or value) of commercial timber from a site indefinitely, absent discounting. Other estimates of the value of *sustainable* selective logging per hectare vary considerably. Vincent (1990) provides estimates of present value ranging from a positive $850 down to a loss of $130 ha^{-1}, with the outcome of the most realistic scenario in the vicinity of +$250 ha^{-1}.

Small scale gathering of non-timber forest products (NTFP) such as rattan, oils, fruits, nuts and bush meat is competitive with commercial logging only in some regions. The value of these products can be large on occasion (de Beer and McDermott 1989; Peters et al. 1989) and, in some cases, large numbers of forest dwellers depend critically on them for survival. Many authors have cautioned against extrapolating these high figures to large stretches of tropical rainforests due to, for example, downward sloping demand for NTFP, uncertainty concerning sustainable supply, and increasing costs of production and transportation. For the case of Latin America, most researchers produce relatively low estimates of about $10 ha yr^{-1} (Bulte et al. 1997). Hence, reliance on such activities alone may perpetuate poverty (Homma 1994).

Likewise, eco-tourism is only locally important. Although tropical (moist) forests are generally not very attractive to tourists because of the humid climate and their limited scenic value (compared to East African game parks, say), recreation and tourism have the potential to become important sources of foreign exchange. Based on observations for South and Central America (especially Ecuador), de Groot (1992) estimates that eco-tourism may contribute as much as $26 per hectare per year (measured in 1988 US dollars) to the national economy of a country with tropical forests. Ruitenbeek (1989) estimates the present value of tourism in Korup National Park (Cameroon) to be approximately $13 ha^{-1}. However, the role of eco-tourism in promotion of forest conservation will likely remain small, and its value will fall on a per hectare basis as more areas are made available for tropical forest recreation. Further, these values do not take into account the costs of providing eco-tourist services, and hence cannot be viewed as a true economic surplus (van Kooten 1995c).

Regulatory functions of tropical forests

Tropical ecosystem services consist of watershed protection, prevention of soil loss, carbon storage, and other regulatory functions. Although Costanza et al. (1997) have estimated the earth's entire ecosystems' services to be worth some US$33×10^{12}, the method they used to obtain their estimate is suspect because it is based on GDP-type components, and global GDP only amounts to $25×10^{12} (see Chapter 9). The globe's ecosystems provide services that have a large value by any standard, and must be considered infinite as life ultimately depends on (some minimal amount of) them, but knowing this is not very helpful for policy making. Economic decisions are made at the margin; decisions need to be made about whether to harvest the next elephant, whale or bear, or whether to cut the next hectare of forest. It is necessary, therefore, to determine the value of ecosystem services at the margin, or on a small region basis.

Postel and Heisse (1988) estimate that deforestation in Costa Rica resulted in revenue losses of $133–$274 million from sedimentation behind one dam. Ruitenbeek (1989) computes the benefits of forest conservation by examining fishery protection and agricultural productivity gains from forests in Korup National Park; these amount to some $3 ha^{-1} yr^{-1}, or a present value of about US$60 per ha using a 5% discount rate

Apart from protection against soil erosion and sedimentation, tropical forests are believed to provide protection against floods and a more balanced supply of water when there are seasonal differences in precipitation because the soil acts as a sponge. Ruitenbeek (1989) estimates the present value of the watershed function to be $23 per ha of forest protected in Korup National Park. However, it is important to recognise that tropical forests are not the only ecosystem capable of producing these effects. In fact, there is evidence that it is not deforestation *per se* that is important, but rather the nature of the succeeding land use. Clearcutting followed by agricultural practices that leave soils exposed during the wet season creates erosion problems and nutrient losses, and will be more damaging than land uses that provide crop cover all year long, such as coffee plantations or pasture.

Finally, release of carbon may be the most important nonmarket cost associated with tropical deforestation. Changing land use is a contributing factor to the recent build-up of CO_2 in the atmosphere. Tropical forests typically sequester larger amounts of carbon per hectare than other forests, as reflected by their high NPP (noted above). They release some 50 to 140 tonnes of C per hectare upon conversion to another land use (pasture, permanent or swiddon agriculture), although the actual amount of C stored in tropical forest ecosystems is higher. Release of C is offset by land uses that in turn sequester C (e.g., pasture or plantation forest).

In recent decades probably all of the net carbon releases from forests have come from tropical deforestation, since temperate and boreal forests are in approximate C balance (see Table 12.1).[2] Houghton (1993) estimates that tropical deforestation was the cause of between 22 and 26% of all greenhouse gas emissions in the 1980s. This is roughly consistent with findings of Brown et al. (1993), who report that total annual anthropogenic emissions are nearly 6.0 gigatons (Gt or 10^9 tonnes) of C, with tropical deforestation contributing some 0.6 to 1.7 Gt per year. Since the benefits of C

---

[2] Some analysts believe that the failure to account fully for the sources of all of the build-up of carbon in the atmosphere, the so-called "missing carbon sink", is explained by the expanding forests of the Northern Hemisphere.

uptake are the discounted sum of avoided future damages (see Chapter 11), uncertainty about the extent and costs of global warming (due to changes in the frequency of extreme events such as droughts and hurricanes, rising sea level and changes in agricultural productivity) has direct implications for the value of this regulatory function. Without knowledge of the shadow damage caused by carbon released to the atmosphere, it is impossible to unambiguously determine the value of tropical forests as a carbon sink, or the damages brought about by tropical deforestation.

Habitat, biodiversity and nonuse values

While the problem of valuing regulatory functions is intrinsically related to the diversity of effects and consequences, and the uncertainties that surround them, a major problem in valuing habitat functions of tropical forests is rooted in ethics. Tropical forests are home not only to millions of people for whom forests may be an integrated part of economic, social and religious life, but also to millions of animal and plant species, most of which are endemic to the local forest ecosystem. The various species have both use and nonuse (preservation) value. The direct use values of biodiversity have attracted the attention of economists and ecologists alike, not in the least spurred on by the belief that demonstration of high values provides a convincing argument against human intervention in "vulnerable" ecosystems. Thus Leakey and Lewin (1995), for example, describe how lucrative and important the drugs Vincristine and Vinblastine, alkaloids from the rosy periwinkle from Madagascar, have been in curing acute lymphocytic leukemia and Hodgkin's disease. The rainforest may be a valuable source of new medicines, and searching for these uses is referred to as "biodiversity prospecting", which was discussed in Chapter 9. There it was found that, at the margin, tropical forestland was worth no more than about $25 per hectare in biodiversity prospecting. Thus, this could not be used as a strong argument to prevent deforestation.

Obviously, limited direct use value does not imply that the economic value of biodiversity is modest. For example, ecosystem stability may be positively linked to diversity.

In addition to direct and indirect use values, nonuse values are also important. As a rough indication of the magnitude of these existence values, Pearce and Warford (1993, pp. 131–2) guess that the annual existence value of tropical forests amounts to some US$8 per adult in Australia, Western Europe and North America. This implies that total existence value is no less than 3.2×10^9 a year. This is much higher than estimates of household willingness-to-pay obtained by Kramer and Mercer (1997) for the USA. They estimated that preservation of global tropical forests had a one-time value of US$1.9–$2.8 \times 10^9$ ($21–$31 per household), or annual value of only $95–$140 million (using a 5% discount rate). Conservatively multiplying by four to take into account Canada, Australia, New Zealand and Western Europe yields an estimate of annual existence value of $0.38–$0.56 \times 10^9$, much less than the figure used by Pearce and Warford. Upon dividing the larger (Pearce and Warford) estimate by total tropical forest area (about 1,750 million ha in 1990), existence value is approximately

$1.80 per ha. Dividing instead by the total area of tropical rainforest (about 720 million ha), existence value per hectare rises to $4.50 per year. Using a discount rate of 5%, this gives present values of $36 and $90 per ha, respectively. These values are small compared to those from logging and other land uses (such as agriculture), and their value is based on dubious assumptions. Further, since nonuse values likely decline at the margin as the forest stock increases, the marginal preservation value is lower than the average preservation value.

Summary

A summary of the values of tropical forests is provided in Table 12.3. For comparison, estimates of the economic values of tropical forests as calculated by Costanza et al. (1997) are also provided in Table 12.3. The estimates in the table represent very general numbers, with values for particular areas or regions likely to vary considerably. As discussed in Chapter 9, Costanza et al. estimate average and not marginal values. It is easy to demonstrate that, even for very large average non-timber values, high rates of deforestation may be economically optimal, depending on what is assumed about changes in nonmarket values at the margin (van Kooten 1995b; Bulte et al. 1997; Chapter 11).

Table 12.3: Summary of the Economic Values of Tropical Forests (US$ ha^{-1} yr^{-1})

Item	Marginal[a]	Average[c]
Commercial logging		
- clear felling	72–192	Not calculated
- natural forest management	≈ 1	315 (all raw materials)
Agriculture[b]	120–140	not calculated
Sustainable land use		
- Selective logging	10–145	Not calculated
- Non-timber forest products	≈ 10	32
- Tourism	≈ 1	112 (all outdoor recreation, incl. tourism)
Preservation		
- Watershed protection[b]	≈ 2	8
- Prevention of soil loss	≈ 3	245
- Flood preventation	≈ 1	6
- Other	not calculated	1,024
- Global climate change	2–140	223
- Biodiversity prospecting	1–2	41
- Nonuse value	1–4	2

[a] Unless otherwise indicated, these data are based on discussion in the text. Values are annualised using a 4% discount rate.
[b] Source: van Soest (1998, p. 25)
[c] Source: Costanza et al. (1997). Not all categories correspond to those in the marginal column.

While it is true that tropical forests provide a wide range of ecosystem services and other non-timber amenities, their marginal value is small compared to that of logging and land use conversion (with the exception perhaps of carbon uptake). Nonetheless, as more of the tropical forest is converted to other land uses, it is likely that the costs of further conversion (the value of foregone ecosystem and other non-timber amenities) will increase as well. At some point, the marginal costs of additional land conversion, including the costs of associated risks, will equal or exceed marginal benefits and no further deforestation of tropical forests should occur. Halting further deforestation should be induced by establishing well-defined and enforced property rights, and by internalising external effects. Based on the various values presented above, compensating developing countries for the C-uptake benefits of forests could prove important in this respect. However, it does not appear that the discounted net economic benefits of sustainable forest management are higher than those of alternative land uses; in some cases they will, but in others not, depending on the profitability of alternative land use options (and location) (Sedjo 1992). It would appear, therefore, that it may not yet be globally optimal to stop all tropical deforestation and land use conversion. The issue of optimal forest stocks is examined further in section 12.4 below.

12.3 Causes of Tropical Deforestation

The causes of tropical deforestation are complex and not well understood. It is complicated by:

1. poor and inadequate data,
2. a failure to define properly terms such as "deforestation" and "shifting cultivation",
3. neglect in distinguishing between "logged" areas converted to another use in the long term and residual forest cutovers and "fallow" forest that retain their natural characteristics or revert back to natural forest over time, and
4. confusion regarding final and proximate causes of deforestation.

Proximate causes refer to the mechanical circumstances of deforestation, while final causes require establishment of a connection between events (deforestation) and the purpose or intent behind the event (Bromley 1999, p. 275). While building roads into remote forest may trigger deforestation by peasants, this is a proximate cause as roads do not cause deforestation. Rather, we must look at the reason (purpose) for road building as this constitutes the ultimate or final cause of deforestation. Finally, we note that conversion of tropical forest to other uses is the most important fact of deforestation.

Different proximate and final causes of deforestation can be identified depending on the viewpoint of the investigator, the level of analysis (local or small region, country-level or cross-country comparisons), the region considered (Southeast Asia versus Latin America, say) and the type of model (normative, positive, statistical, structural, *etc.*) employed. Because of these differences, there is often no consensus about the actual causes of deforestation. Nonetheless, we investigate some of the main factors that have been raised – commercial logging, conversion to agriculture, population pressure, poverty and the role of government. We also discuss the difference between final and proximate causes, highlighting the relevance of the asset-portfolio approach to nature, as discussed in previous chapters.

Commercial logging

A common but simplistic view, now largely rejected by most analysts familiar with tropical forests, is that tropical deforestation is due to commercial timber logging. Commercial logging in the tropics rarely results in significant direct land conversion, although, as discussed below, it does make indirect contributions to the process of deforestation. Unlike much of the commercial logging in the temperate forest, commercial logging in the tropics almost never involves clear cutting. Rather, the usual approach is to select and log only trees that are suitable for commercial uses, leaving large numbers of live trees in the forest. In the past, relatively few trees were removed, and those that were felled were done by hand and commonly transported out of the forest by animals. The forest would be periodically re-logged as trees reached desired sizes. With the arrival of modern logging – involving chainsaws, roads and equipment – larger areas have been logged, reflecting expanded demand.

Selective cutting continues to be almost universally practised with only the larger trees of desired species harvested. This reflects the fact that, due to the high diversity of tree species, only a relatively few of the total trees in a tropical forest are commercially suitable (Panayotou and Sungsuwan 1994). Studies of Western Africa, for example, indicate that few trees are harvested per hectare, frequently less than 10 out of a total of more than 350 trees (see Grainger 1993; Panayotou and Ashton 1992). For Cameroon, Thiele and Wiebelt (1993) estimate that, from a hectare of primary forest endowed with on average 250 m^3 of timber, only about 8 to 33 m^3 are extracted per round of harvesting. Within the tropical belt there are strong regional differences in logging intensity, with highly selective logging in Africa and Latin America and more intensive timber harvesting in Asia (where sometimes 40% of the trees is extracted, and sometimes clearfelling takes place). There are two main factors that determine logging intensity:

1. The share of marketable trees per hectare (which is typically much lower than in temperate zones) depending on species composition and output demand.
2. Transport costs that depend on the proximity of markets and the mode of transport (river or road) (van Soest 1998).

Selective logging is generally conducive to forest regeneration and re-growth. Although selective logging can be damaging in practice (e.g., because of careless logging induced by perverse incentives, or simply because it is too costly to untangle trees that are linked by lianas and vines), in most cases the forest is able to regenerate (Grainger 1993). During the period immediately following logging, sunlight reaches the forest floor, stimulating growth of seeds and seedlings, especially of the so-called pioneer species, which include many of the more important timber species such as teak, mahogany and many of the dipterocarp (i.e., commercially valuable) species. Typically the stock of seed and seedlings is adequate, but this can be supplemented by human activities if required. The idealised tropical forest management regime following logging varies with forest type. In the timber rich forests of Southeast Asia it is common to allow a period of 30–70 years after logging for the forest to recover and grow new trees of the desired size. Additionally, existing saplings and medium size trees will continue and in some cases accelerate their growth now that the dominant trees are gone. When such an approach is followed, a viable and sustainable forest system can be achieved. The most damaging aspect of the harvesting process (both directly and indirectly) may be the construction of roads, resulting in significant felling of trees, soil compaction and erosion (Myers 1980; Grainger 1993; Panayotou and Ashton 1992). However, the latter effect is most likely to occur for roads that are used frequently, and is in general not important for skidding tracks and feeder roads that usually revert back to forest after they are abandoned (van Soest 1998).

Estimates of the contribution of commercial logging to deforestation are therefore modest, typically varying from 2% to 10% (Amelung and Diehl 1992). According to Myers (1991), the share of commercial logging in deforestation is no less than 20%. Nonetheless, even with this higher estimate, it is clear that the bulk of tropical deforestation should be attributed to other causes, although it likely remains a catalyst for those other causes.

Conversion to agriculture

Deforestation is primarily caused by a desire to convert forests to agriculture, which is particularly true in Latin America but perhaps less so in Asia. About 80% of the world supply of tropical timber comes from the Asia-Pacific region because tropical forests in the Amazon basin, for example, are characterised by a higher degree of heterogeneity, with a relatively lower proportion of trees having commercial value (Sedjo 1992). Nonetheless, there is an indirect relation between logging and agricultural conversion (see, e.g., Barbier et al. 1994; Bulte and van Soest 1996; Sunderlin and Resosudarmo 1997). To transport the logged wood from isolated rainforest areas to ports or markets, commercial foresters have to construct a road network. The roads facilitate access for cultivation and increase the profitability of producing cash crops by reducing transportation costs. Further, the actual conversion process is easier in selectively logged forests than in pristine rainforests because the biggest trees have been removed and because the micro-climate is more favourable for burning (Panayotou and Sungsuwan 1994). Hence, agricultural conversion proceeds at a much higher pace in secondary or over-logged forests as compared to pristine, undisturbed primary forests (Amelung and Diehl 1992). This evidence suggests that commercial logging is a catalyst for the deforestation process by providing the necessary infrastructure. This is the indirect damage of selective harvesting.

The general consensus then is that agricultural conversion (shifting cultivation and conversion for "permanent" agriculture) is the most prominent cause of tropical deforestation, although commercial logging may be the catalyst. However, a fundamental distinction needs to be made between "shifting cultivators" and "forest pioneers", with a continuum between these two extremes (Sunderlin and Resosudarmo 1997; also Myers 1994). The former clear the forest, crop the land for one to three years and then leave the land fallow for a period of 20 or more years, during which time it reverts back to natural forest. Traditional shifting cultivation is capable of sustainable resource management, with products consisting of crops (low yield rice) plus a wide range of timber and non-timber products. The "forest pioneers" clear the forest with the intention of establishing permanent or semi-permanent agricultural production. Slash-and-burn is used in both cases, but the implications for sustainable resource management differ substantially along the continuum. Myers (1991) attributes a relatively higher share of tropical deforestation to shifting cultivation (about 60%), at the cost of the share of permanent agriculture in the FAO statistics; the sum of permanent agriculture, mining, etc., amounts to no more than 18% in his statistics. From the point of view of sustainability, this may be a good thing. Forest clearing followed by a short cropping period and subsequent reversion back to natural forest is not the same as a permanent change in land use.

Forests are converted to both permanent and shifting agriculture as a result of factors such as high agricultural prices, conversion subsidies, access roads, population pressure, lack of tenure security, and so on, although the significance of these factors varies (as discussed below). Once established, permanent agriculture is clearly, in most cases, less of a factor in deforestation than shifting agriculture, *ceteris paribus* (Kaimowitz and Angelsen 1997). By its very nature, shifting agriculture continues to be a contributing factor to deforestation, and anything that causes farmers to change from sedentary or permanent to shifting cultivation will increase rates of deforestation. However, shifting cultivation may be well suited for agricultural production in areas with low and medium levels of population density, but it is ill-suited to situations where in-migration (or high population densities) put pressure on land use. Thus, increasing integration in the (inter)national economy and increasing population pressure (especially brought about by regional migration of landless or otherwise displaced peasants) results in the abandonment of traditional cultivation patterns and their replacement by less sustainable production techniques.

Economic models of deforestation: Farm-level, regional and global

The complex nature of tropical deforestation implies that, in many instances, economic explanations have to account for the behaviour of firms and governments, on the one hand, and that of peasants and small-scale farmers on the other (Brown and Pearce 1994; Kaimowitz and Angelsen 1997). The former stakeholders are guided by timber prices, security of concession rights, budgetary concerns and the macro economy, but factors such as poverty, population pressure, regional migration and attitudes towards risk affect the behaviour of peasants. Identifying the role of the micro-level factors has been difficult, however. One reason has to do with the scale of models, with scale varying from the farm to the region to the global levels. Another has to do with the types of economic models employed at each scale.

At the farm level, one has a choice between subsistence models and open economy models, or hybrid (in-between) models that have some forms of quantity or other restrictions (known as Chayanovian models). In subsistence models, small-scale farmers are not responsive to market prices (households only seek to achieve a consumption target) and labour markets are assumed not to exist. Compared to open-economy models, or at least models that permit sale of labour off the farm, subsistence models yield different conclusions regarding the factors that are important in explaining deforestation. For example, open economy models predict an increase in deforestation as a result of increases in agricultural output prices and agricultural productivity, and lower transportation costs; wage increases reduce deforestation rates, while population growth has no effect. Hicks-neutral technological change in agriculture raises the value of the marginal product of land in agricultural production, thereby triggering an expansion of cultivated land. In subsistence models, however, increases in agricultural output prices and agricultural productivity reduce rates of deforestation, as does lower transportation costs; the effect of wage increases is not available from subsistence models, while population growth increases deforestation rates in these models. Now technological change reduces deforestation as less land is required to produce the desired agricultural output. A summary of the conclusions from farm-level models is presented in Table 12.4.

Table 12.4: Summary of Factors Affecting Deforestation from Farm-level Models[a]

Factor	Effect on Deforestation
Increase in transportation cost of agricultural outputs	Reduce
Increase in wage rates in agriculture	reduce or no effect
More off-farm employment	reduce
More agricultural credit availability	increase or reduce
Higher agricultural output prices	increase or reduce
Increase in agricultural productivity	increase or reduce
Increase in price of fertilizers	increase or no effect
Increase in other agricultural input prices	reduce
Population growth	increase
Soil quality	increase
Increase in household size	increase or reduce
Length of forest concession	no clear effect

[a] Results from both empirical and simulation models, which implies that some conclusions are not based on empirical evidence but follow from the model itself.
Source: Developed from information in Kaimowitz and Angelsen (1997)

Regional models focus primarily on a single country and use spatial (cross-section) or regional (time series) regressions. General conclusions from spatial regression models are that more access roads, proximity of forest edges to urban areas, nearness to markets, and better and drier soils all contribute to increasing rates of deforestation. Regional regression models rely on data for more than one period to study the effects of various potential contributing factors to deforestation. Most models employ county-level and/or provincial data for a single country, using deforestation, forest cover, cropped area, forest reserve area, or crop and pasture area as dependent variables. General conclusions from these studies indicate that any variables that raise agricultural profitability (higher prices, more credit, better access to markets, more roads, higher productivity) also increase rates of deforestation. Conclusions with regard to the role of higher population and per capita income as factors in increasing deforestation are mixed. Rather than population growth causing deforestation, it is the underlying sources of population in-migration into regions with a low-population density (due to road access, available high quality agricultural lands, and growing demand for agricultural outputs) that results in deforestation. With regard to income, in some studies per capita income has a negative effect on the remaining forest cover (Chakraborty 1994), but in others it has a positive effect (Panayotou and Sungsuwan 1994). Finally, designating forests with protected status reduced deforestation marginally in regional models, while increased security of land tenure lowered levels of deforestation.

Macroeconomic variables as causes of deforestation are best addressed using analytical or computable general equilibrium models, but only because there is no real alternative means for considering interactions among sectors. Only two or three sectors can be modeled at one time in the case of analytical models, while onerous data requirements are an obstacle to meaningful computable general equilibrium models (CGEs). Nonetheless, such models are "useful tools for understanding feedback mechanisms which can invalidate otherwise intuitive results based on partial equilibrium models" (Kaimowitz and Angelsen 1997, p. 46). Even so, models disagree on the impacts that currency devaluations, trade liberalisation, changes in tax/subsidy regimes, and other macroeconomic variables might have on deforestation. The reasons for such disagreements are rooted in the model assumptions (in the case of analytic models) or the country of application (in the case of CGEs). Currency devaluation leads to an increase in deforestation in most models, but the cause differs between Brazil and the Philippines, for example. In Brazil, the higher agricultural prices that devaluation brings about will cause an expansion of cultivation into forest areas as agricultural land is now more valuable relative to forestland. In the Philippines, on the other hand, devaluation raises timber prices causing more timber to be harvested. For African countries, reduced government spending decreases deforestation as demand for agricultural commodities declines, but, in Southeast Asia, it leads to increased deforestation due to the higher export elasticity of demand for agricultural products and timber in those countries. Reduced fertilizer subsidies and elimination of agricultural output price supports affects agricultural productivity, thus reducing deforestation, but it also increases rural unemployment which increases forest encroachment; the net effect is indeterminate and varies among countries. In general, trade liberalisation and other macroeconomic policies that raise agricultural output prices (e.g., reductions in agricultural export taxes) will increase rates of deforestation in the same way as currency devaluation.

Finally, regarding technological change in agriculture, when production is for the domestic market (i.e., prices are endogenous) and demand for agricultural products is inelastic (so there is no trade), small increases in output cause substantial declines in agricultural prices. This tends to reduce deforestation.

Global regression models use either cross-section or panel data for various countries to explain possible factors leading to deforestation, but such models may suffer from serious data problems. Dependent variables include forest cover, decline in forest cover between two (arbitrary) dates, area logged, roundwood production and agricultural land. The data are usually obtained from FAO, and suffer from the shortcomings mentioned earlier. Numerous explanatory variables are used, including GDP, growth in GDP, population, population density, proportion of the population that is rural, agricultural output (total or exports), exchange rates, indebtedness, etc. The independent variables can be divided into direct sources of deforestation, immediate causes and underlying causes (Kaimowitz and Angelsen 1997, p. 50), but, by failing to model and thus distinguish between sources of deforestation and its causes (mixing independent variables with varying degrees of direct and indirect causality), conclusions are limited.[3] Nonetheless, the results from such models tend to reinforce those found in other types of models. A summary of conclusions is provided in Table 12.5. Both logging and agricultural activities contribute to deforestation. Results concerning population and growth of population are mixed, with Cropper and Griffiths (1994) finding that these had no positive effect on rates of deforestation. Rather, they find the existence of a Kuznets' curve – deforestation is positively correlated with income at low levels, but negatively correlated at high levels. Likewise, the impacts of external debt, political stability and whether a country is democratic are unclear, partly because different researchers employed different measures for these variables and different models to analyse their impacts.

Table 12.5: Some Factors Influencing Deforestation as Determined from Global Regression Models

Factor	Correlation with Deforestation Variable
Importance of agriculture in the economy	positive
Timber production	positive
Population density	no clear effect
Population growth	no clear effect
Per capita income	positive, no effect or Kuznets
Growth in per capita income	no clear effect
External indebtedness	no clear effect
Higher export prices for forest products	positive
Currency devaluation	positive
Road construction	positive
Drier climate	positive
Unequal land tenure	positive
Political stability	no clear effect
Democracy	no clear effect

Source: Developed from information in Kaimowitz and Angelsen (1997)

A major conclusion to draw from the various studies is that some explanatory variables are highly significant in some studies and insignificant in others. Apart from fundamental differences in the deforestation processes in various countries, lack of good explanatory variables in empirical work can be explained by the fact that, first, the underlying models of deforestation are often not fully identified and, second, the dependent variable in some analyses is ill-chosen. The former centres on the argument that some variables explain more than one cause of deforestation. For example, an increase in per capita income may increase demand for forest products and thus contribute to deforestation, but it may also trigger expansion of alternative employment (in services and manufacturing in urban areas), and thereby reduce the need to seek employment in the primary sectors (van Soest 1998). With regard to the second explanation, Kummar and Sham (1994) point out that, in many cross sectional

---

[3] A two-stage regression model should be used. In the first stage, a correlation is established between direct causes (forest and agricultural product prices, exports, changes in land uses) and deforestation. Then, in the second stage, a link is made between the first (direct) and second (indirect) factors explaining deforestation. In some cases, there remains the problem of determining which variables are first as opposed to second level causes. Therefore, it is important to provide an appropriate econometric framework *a priori*.

studies, (%) forest cover serves as a proxy for deforestation as time series data on deforestation for specific countries are often lacking. If anything, forest cover represents cumulative deforestation rather than recent or current deforestation. This implies that parameter coefficients in econometric models will not measure adequately the impact of the explanatory variables on deforestation when either the initial forest stock or the period during which past deforestation has occurred differs among countries in the (cross-sectional) sample. These insights imply that care must be taken when interpreting the results of econometric work.

A strong case can be made that explanations of tropical deforestation are situation dependent. The forces that bring about deforestation differ by region and country, and over time. Factors relevant in one time period may not be important in another. Factors influencing one country at some point in time are not relevant at that time for another country, although they may become important at a later date (Dauvergne 1997). Three of the more contentious factors are considered in greater detail below – a country's per capita income, population growth and the role of government.

Income and deforestation

The relation between income and deforestation is complex and ambiguous, with direct and indirect effects (Palo 1994). The Kuznets' "inverted-U" hypothesis suggests that deforestation is positively correlated for low levels of income, but negatively correlated with high levels of income (see also Chapter 8). One explanation for this relationship is that, as income rises, people demand more wood products as well as more of the amenities associated with natural forests. As a country's citizens become better off, there comes a point where the demand for natural forest amenities exceeds a desire to permit further deforestation. Further, associated with increases in per capita income are higher education levels (and potentially less corruption in resource management), improved land tenure arrangements, fewer individuals engaged in primary production (agriculture and forestry) as a proportion of the population, and general improvements in the economy as a result of technical changes. In reference to tropical deforestation, Cropper and Griffiths (1994) argue that economic development and associated higher incomes will:

1. reduce the conversion of forests into arable land by stimulating the use of modern agricultural practices (lowering land requirements) and inducing a shift of labour to non-agricultural sectors;
2. initially stimulate commercial logging as the ability to process logs improves and demand for agricultural products increases (raising their price), but, at a later stage of development, reduce reliance on logging as industrialisation provides opportunities for alternative employment; and
3. increase the demand for energy, including fuelwood, with more efficient and cleaner-burning energy sources substituting for fuelwood at higher income levels.

As a result, an environmental Kuznets' curve, or inverted-U relationship between rates of deforestation and income, is expected.

While the environmental Kuznets' result has been demonstrated for a number of environmental pollutants (Chapter 8; Panatoyou 1995), empirical evidence in the case of tropical deforestation is mixed, and turning points vary among studies from annual incomes of US$500 to $3,500 to $5,000 (Kaimowitz and Angelsen 1997). We provide further support for the hypothesis in the case of deforestation with a model similar to that of Cropper and Griffiths (1994), but using more recent FAO (1997) data for 131 countries. This data set relies on some remote sensing information, but generally suffers from the same problems as those mentioned above.

The relationship is specified as follows:

$$(12.1) \quad FC_{jt} = a_0 + a_1 RPD_{jt} + a_2 POP\%_{jt} + a_3\,GDP_{jt} + a_4\,GDP\%_{jt} + a_5 GDP_{jt}^2 + \mu_{jt},$$

where FC_{jt} is the percentage change in forest area in country j at time t, measured as $(F_{j,t+1} - F_{jt})/F_{ijt}$; RPD_j is rural population density; $POP\%_j$ is the percentage change in population; GDP_j is the per capita gross domestic product of country j; $GDP\%_j$ is the percentage change in per capita GDP; a_k ($k = 1,...,5$) are parameters to be estimated; and μ_{jt} is an error term. We deviate from Cropper and Griffiths (1994) by leaving out the timber price variable for two reasons. First, a large proportion of timber consumption in the developing world is in the form of fuelwood for which an international market price does not exist. Second, the demand for timber is derived from the demand for wood products such as lumber, pulp and various paper products. Given the heterogeneity of forest-based products traded in the world market, it is difficult to decide which particular price or price index to use. The regression results are provided in Table 12.6.

Table 12.6: Factors Affecting Tropical Deforestation: Global OLS Regression Results (Dependent Variable is Rate of Change in Area Covered by Forest)

Variable	Coefficient	t-value
Rural population density	0.0106	1.75
Growth rate of population	- 0.1993	- 2.35
Per capita GDP	0.0002	3.34
Per capita GDP squared	- 0.0001	- 2.72
Growth in GDP	- 0.0765	- 2.48
Constant	- 1.1307	- 2.78
N = 131		
Adjusted R² = 0.1833		

With the exception of rural population density, all of the explanatory variables in Table 12.6 are significant at the 0.05 level or better. Even rural population is a statistically significant variable at the 0.10 level. The results indicate that deforestation is positively correlated with rural population density, while it is inversely correlated with population growth. The results also provide support for the Kuznets' hypothesis: Deforestation initially increases as per capita GDP rises, but eventually it falls.

If deforestation is narrowly defined to exclude the re-establishment of natural forests, it will be considered irreversible, meaning that the rate of deforestation will decrease in any event as forests disappear. Hence, the relevance of the inverted-U relation in the case of deforestation may also be limited. The only conclusion from studies of deforestation is the unsatisfying one that the relation between income and deforestation is poorly understood and probably indeterminate; and see also Kaimowitz and Angelsen (1997) Brown and Pearce (1994). Therefore, it would be inappropriate to conclude that economic growth *per se* is a panacea for reducing or preventing deforestation.

Population and deforestation

The effect of population growth and population density on rates of deforestation is also ill-understood. This is partly because there are two views about the role of population. The neo-Malthusian view is that current trends in population growth will inevitably result in large-scale deforestation with its associated massive species extinctions and loss of agricultural potential; people and trees compete for space, as more people imply greater demand for fuel and food. Those subscribing to this view generally find evidence of a positive relation between population and deforestation (Saxena et al. 1997; Palo 1994; Repetto and Gillis 1988). The (technological) optimists, on the other hand, argue that more people results in more labour, more skills, changing relative scarcity, potential for greater innovation and so on (Beisner 1997; Simon 1996). Studies of population change that take this view have found evidence that increased population density leads to less erosion and more forests (Tiffen and Mortimore 1994) and that accompanying wood scarcity leads to increased tree planting (Hyde and Seve 1991). The role of population in development and environmental degradation is discussed in more detail in Chapter 8.

Historical evidence indicates that there have been cases where population and forest have increased together, but most is for temperate countries. For example, the forest resources of France have been expanding since the late eighteenth century. An estimate of the forested area in 1890 was almost 50% higher than the area estimated in 1790, while the area of forest estimated for 1994 is again some 50% higher than that of 100 years earlier (Ministry of Agriculture and Fisheries 1995). Similarly, as noted earlier, the forest area of New England has been expanding since the 1860s despite increasing population (Barrett 1988). However, studies that look only at the tropics have population increasing and forest decreasing in almost all examples (see Table 12.6).

Nonetheless, the overall picture for tropical forests remains unclear, primarily because the direction of causality has not been identified (see Sunderlin and Resosudarmo 1997; Brown and Pearce 1994). The matter is much as Kummar and Sham (1994) note:

> we feel it is impossible to draw any firm conclusions regarding the effect of population on deforestation. For example, population per square kilometer in 1990 for five selected countries was as follows: Brazil (18), Indonesia (100), Malaysia (54), Thailand (108), Philippines (220). Absolute rates of deforestation are higher in Indonesia, Malaysia and Thailand than in the Philippines. ... Brazil, which has the most extensive ongoing deforestation in the world, has a population density which is only 8% of that of the Philippines. (p. 156)

The lack of a clear relation between population density and tropical deforestation is also evident from Table 12.2. Here it is worthwhile to point again to the limitations of the FAO data. If deforestation data are obtained from a single observation of forest stock and models of deforestation that link it to population growth, it is only tautological that one would find a positive link between the deforestation data and population growth.

Kaimowitz and Angelsen (1997) summarise the potential links between population and deforestation. Population growth affects deforestation directly through demand for fuel, other wood products and agricultural outputs, although trade and barriers to trade (e.g., tariffs) need to be taken into account. It affects deforestation indirectly through labour markets (lower wages make forest conversion more profitable), induced technological change and institutions. The latter is discussed in the context of the role of government.

Role of government in tropical deforestation

Policy or government failure may be as important or a more important underlying cause of tropical deforestation than market failure. Repetto and Gillis (1988), Panayotou (1993b), and Mendelsohn (1994), among others, demonstrate that government policies, whether deliberate or inadvertent, can result in deforestation at the cost of reducing welfare for society at large. According to (Sunderlin and Resosudarmo (1997), Repetto (1997), Repetto and Gillis (1988), and Binswanger (1989), there are many major forms of public intervention:

1. Direct subsidies to cut down forests
2. Indirect subsidies to forest companies through forest concessions that fail to capture all of the available rents and encourage excessive harvesting and wasteful rent seeking
3. Creation and protection of an inefficient ("log demanding") domestic forest industry (e.g., in Indonesia)
4. Direct subsidies to cattle ranchers (e.g., in Brazil) to generate foreign exchange;
5. Generous investment tax credits
6. Exemption of agricultural income from taxation;
7. Subsidised credit for agriculture
8. Rules on public land allocation that favour large land holders or require "development" of land to demonstrate ownership
9. Development of public infrastructure (roads for access, hospitals, *etc.*)
10. Overpopulation and migration policies (sometimes rooted in ethnic politics)

In essence, government action distorts incentives, consequently wasting valuable assets and tilting the balance against conservation (Brown and Pearce 1994).

Clearly, governments often deliberately seek to exploit forest resources knowing full well that this leads to deforestation. Here are some of the reasons why governments may choose to promote deforestation:

1. Governments overstate the value of forests for timber and understate the value of non-timber products, and their regulatory and habitat functions.
2. The value of forest soils for agriculture is often overstated, with soils quickly depleted by cropping.
3. Forest regions sometimes serve as an outlet for crowded populations, with peasants encouraged to move into forested regions rather than the cities, thereby avoiding social unrest (Reed 1992).
4. Resource prices are kept artificially low to encourage industrial and agricultural activity, and economic growth.
5. Investment in the forestry sector may be promoted to secure doubtful employment and other benefits (Osgood 1994).
6. The value of minor forest products is systematically ignored because the majority of economic benefits accrues to powerless social groups (de Beer and McDermott 1989).
7. Forests are not considered essential for economic development, more or less consistent with experience in the Western world. Forests may even be viewed as an asset to be liquidated in order to diversify the economy.

We briefly consider public policies concerning land tenures in forestry and agriculture, and restrictions on log exports, as sources of inefficiency and deforestation in tropical countries.

Forest Management and Land Tenure

Tenure plays an important role in deforestation. Markets cannot function properly without some degree of tenure security, be it formal or not. Forest companies are often "awarded" logging concessions of 20 years or (much) less, and are charged low stumpage fees, implying low rent capture (Jepma 1995; Amelung and Diehl 1992). The incentive to take care, sustainably and carefully, of logging operations and to "protect" the forest from agricultural expansion will depend on the subjective probability that the concession will be renewed. Further, concessionaires are often allocated too much land, partly because royalties are volume-based rather than area-based and partly for political reasons. Again, this provides companies little incentive (or ability) to prevent encroachment by agricultural interests (peasants or other).

The result of the short tenures and low rent capture (see Chapter 4) is rent seeking behaviour that encourages concessionaires to exploit the forest resource as quickly as possible in case fees are raised at a future date. It also encourages "premature re-entry", where companies re-enter sites prior to expiry of their concessions, thereby damaging immature timber. Thus, lack of (secure) tenure rights and low rent capture – forms of government failure – promote rapid exploitation and destructive harvesting. The result is poor forest management. In order to improve management practises, therefore, four recommendations are made:

1. Royalty fees be raised and the degree of rent capture be improved,
2. Concession cycles be lengthened and tenure security be enhanced,
3. Market competition in the allocation of concessions be introduced, and

4. The amount of area-based fees be raised relative to volume-based fees (Sunderlin and Resosudarmo 1997).

By increasing area-based fees, companies will hold less area while managing more intensely those areas that are held.

Using subsidies, governments often encourage conversion of natural forests to tree plantations for development purposes. Plantation forests provide more jobs than sustainable logging in natural forests. However, with the exception of some high quality sites, the discounted net returns of plantation forestry are below those associated with sustainable logging of natural forests. The reason is that establishment costs are high, while returns (harvests) accrue too far in the future (Sedjo 1992).

Finally, the timber in natural forests often has significant value over and above the costs of harvesting trees and bringing them to market. These resource rents may be captured by national or local governments, timber firms, local "strongmen", and/or others involved in the wood products chain, or they can be squandered through directly unproductive rent-seeking activities that involve any of the players in the chain. The existence of rents results in patronage and patron-client relations in the exploitation of tropical forest resources. According to Dauvergne (1997), Japan has been a catalyst for tropical deforestation in Southeast Asia as a result of its policies that deliberately keep domestic log prices low (Japanese firms do not maximise short-term profits), thereby encouraging wasteful consumption. The Japanese have encouraged patron-client links that "distort state timber management guidelines, weaken state supervision, channel profits to a small elite, encourage logging companies to hide profits overseas, and undermine implementation of logging rules" (p. 4). Illegal logging is supported by patrons at the state (region) level. Illegal logs are smuggled overseas or enter "legal" markets via inefficient local mills (that survive partly as a result of the illegal logs). Regional governments receive a low share of the royalties, if any, and this gives them little incentive to implement policies that protect forests.

While Dauvergne (1997) has focused on Southeast Asia and the role of the Japanese, others have examined similar political factors as an explanatory factor in deforestation. Deacon (1994) found deforestation to be positively linked to political instability and lack of accountability, and associated tenure insecurity. Reed (1992) mentions that in Côte d'Ivoire extraction of rents from the forestry sector is a principal tool of patronage and a method for preserving social privileges for the ruling elite.

Agricultural Land Tenure

As mentioned earlier, forestland (hinterland) serves to relieve population pressure on urban areas. Some governments actively encourage peasant farmers to locate in forested regions, while others simply do not enforce rules over land use. In Ecuador, for example, nearly all of the tree-covered land is designated as national parks. In the past, the government allowed peasants to make claims on forestland, but they had to clear the land in order to acquire formal property rights (Southgate et al. 1991). Indeed, for small landowners, land clearing for agriculture is often a prerequisite to gaining title, as it was with the Homestead Act in the USA. This encourages deforestation and conversion to production of tree crops (rubber, coconut and palm oil), even where it is more profitable to keep land in natural forests.

Using an optimal control model of land use in tropical forests, Mendelsohn (1994) demonstrates that insecure property rights lead a society wastefully to destroy its forests. This is true even if land ownership is not directly tied to forest clearing. Suppose that sustainable forestry yields higher net returns than agriculture, but that returns to forest activities are more evenly spread out over time, while those in agriculture are high initially but decline quickly as land is degraded (a common situation in tropical rainforests). Then, even a low probability that a peasant farmer will be evicted from the land will lead to the choice of the more destructive land use. The conclusion is that full property rights must be secured in an efficient and prompt manner.

Log Export Trade Restrictions

Governments restrict log exports for industry development, employment and well-being reasons. It is argued that, by preventing log exports, processing is encouraged, thereby leading to greater employment and economic development. However, such a forest industrialisation strategy often leads to lower overall social well-being and lower forest sector revenues (Margolick and Uhler 1986; Barbier et al. 1995). Many tropical countries have in place restrictions on log exports. Indonesia implemented a log export ban in 1985 that was replaced by export taxes in 1992 that effectively perpetuated the ban. Malaysia has banned log exports from the peninsula since 1971, while royalty rates for exported logs are ten times higher from Sabah and a 15% *ad valorem* tax exists on hardwood log exports from Sarawak. Papua New Guinea imposes a 10% tax on the value of logs that are exported, while the Philippines has restricted log exports to 25% of the annual allowable cut since 1979 (Barbier et al. 1995, p. 419).

Restrictions on trade in logs reduce domestic prices of fibre, leading processing firms to substitute greater use of fibre for improvements in technology that reduce wood waste. For example, Indonesia's trade restrictions have resulted in the use of 15% more wood to produce the same plywood as elsewhere in Asia. With respect to deforestation, two forces operate against each other – lower fibre prices reduce demand for fibre (but wood wastage has offset this effect to some extent), reducing incentives to cut trees, while the lower opportunity cost of converting land to agriculture increases the incentive to cut trees. Overall, restrictions on exports of logs dissipate available resource rents.

Proximate and Final Causes

The discussion of the role of government highlights the importance of distinguishing between proximate and final (ultimate) causes of deforestation. "Deforestation occurs because governments wish for it to happen, ... [and] most governments know precisely what they are doing and why they are doing it" (Bromley 1999, pp. 283, 279). Deforestation is intentional because it serves the purpose of government or of those who know how to manipulate government (Dauvergne 1997). While econometric work may point to road building, population growth, indebtedness or other factors as causes of tropical deforestation, this is only part of the story – the part related to the mechanics of removing trees, or the proximate causes of deforestation. To understand tropical deforestation and formulate policies to address it, deforestation should not be considered the end of a causal chain, but an intermediate step to some other goal. It is only when we consider the purpose that deforestation serves that we can understand its final causes.

Bromley (1999) distinguishes two plausible final causes – to earn revenue from timber rents and to clear land for other (possibly more valuable) uses. In other words, the government considers the opportunity cost of forest conservation as being too high, and the forest as an impediment to economic development. In that sense, even the government policies discussed above represent proximate causes of deforestation as the ultimate cause is government wishing to remove forest from their asset portfolios. Many governments in tropical regions simply regard forest as an inferior investment.

It may well be that tropical forest represents an inferior investment and that social welfare is enhanced by converting some part of it to other uses, as discussed in the next section. However, government intentions need not be benevolent. For example, governments may permit or encourage forest conversion by peasants to avoid dealing with land reform, thereby maintaining the status quo in which most of the privileges accrue to the ruling elite. Thus, while population growth is a proximate cause of deforestation, the ultimate or final cause is the government's unwillingness to deal with the institutional changes required to alleviate poverty and bring about a more equitable distribution of income. Therefore, studying proximate causes of deforestation provides little insight into policy reform.

> As long as a particular nation state is driven by a desire to earn rents from harvesting tress, and as long as land hunger (itself often the result of other policy failures) drives governments to open up remote areas, then very little is to be gained by suggesting that nations stop building roads, or that property rights be made more secure, or that population growth be implemented, or that government corruption be rectified, or that the powerful logging interests be reined in. The only way to fonfront deforestation is to focus on its final cause. (Bromley 1999, p. 278)

12.4 Is Tropical Deforestation Excessive?

As a result of market and government failures, it is often assumed that current rates of deforestation must be excessive (Barbier and Burgess 1997). But conservation of tropical forests involves considerable opportunity costs (the foregone benefits of log sales and subsequent returns to agriculture). What then is the optimal stock of tropical rainforest that the world community (a country) should protect in order to maximise the present value of global (national) welfare? Empirical work to determine optimal forest stocks is surprisingly scarce.

In one of the few studies, Ehui and Hertel (1989) compute an optimal tropical forest stock for Côte d'Ivoire, which had the highest rate of deforestation of any nation during the 1980s but also achieved the fastest agricultural growth in sub-Saharan Africa. Their empirical analysis does not include all forest services, but focuses only on the relation between forest preservation and agricultural productivity (Ehui and Hertel 1992). The authors assume that society maximises the discounted utility of net revenues from forest and agricultural output over an infinite time horizon. Net revenue is defined by:

(12.2) $\pi(D, x, F) = p_F F + (L - F)(p_A Q(D, F, x) - p_x x)$,

where L is the total land in forestry and available for agriculture, $F(t)$ is the stock of forestland at time t (in hectares), $D(t)$ is the current rate of deforestation, $x(t)$ is purchases of inputs for production of agricultural commodities (e.g., fertilizer), p_F represents the per hectare net return to forestry, p_A is the price of agricultural output (per kilogram), p_x is the per unit price of purchased agricultural inputs, and Q represents the aggregate agricultural production function. The cumulative amount of deforested land is given by $F(0) - F(t)$, where $F(0)$ ($= L$) refers to the beginning stock of forested land. Crucial assumptions, supported by empirical evidence, are that average yield increases in purchased inputs and current deforestation, and declines with increases in cumulative deforestation. It was found that $\partial Q / \partial D = Q_D > 0$, because of the nutrient content of the ash left after burning the forest, while $\partial Q / \partial (F(0) - F(t)) = Q_{F(0)-F(t)} < 0$ because of productivity losses from increased erosion that results from deforestation.

The formal optimal control model can then be expressed as:

(12.3)   Maximise $W = \int_0^\infty \pi(D, x, F)\, e^{-rt}\, dt$

(12.4)   subject to $\dot{F} = -D(t)$, with $F(t), D(t), x(t) \geq 0$,

where the decision maker chooses the rate of deforestation and purchases of agricultural inputs. Solving the dynamic optimisation problem (13.2)–(12.4) for its first-order conditions leads to the following conclusions:

1.   Purchased inputs should be applied until marginal costs equal marginal benefits (i.e., $p_x = p_A Q_x$) in each time period.
2.   The rate of deforestation should be chosen so that the marginal utility of deforestation (U_D) is equal to the opportunity cost of harvesting – the value of having access to the stock in the future.
3.   Along an optimal path the marginal utility of forest capital – the sum of the direct contribution of forestry and the indirect marginal contribution through its effect on agricultural productivity (Ehui and Hertel 1989) – should equal the social cost of this capital (which includes both an interest charge and a capital gains term).

In the steady-state, $\dot{F} = 0$, so no further deforestation takes place ($D = \dot{D} = 0$). The equation describing the optimal forest stock in the steady-state is:

$$(12.5) \quad \frac{\pi_F(D^*, F^*, x^*)}{r} = \pi_D(D^*, F^*, x^*).$$

This says that, in equilibrium, the present value of marginal net revenue from sustainable forest management must equal the marginal net revenue from deforestation.

Ehui and Hertel (1989) estimate a quadratic functional form for the aggregate agricultural output function (Q) using data for Côte d'Ivoire. This function is then substituted into (12.5), and optimal steady-state forest stocks are computed for various combinations of the remaining parameter values. For the baseline scenario, using 1984 returns to agriculture and forestry, the optimal forest stock ranged from 5.4 million ha (for a discount rate of 3%) to 1.9 million ha (for a discount rate of 11%). The authors' estimates of the optimal steady-state forest stock exceed the actual (1990) forest stock of approximately 3.2 million ha for discount rates lower than 8%. This implied that further deforestation was only optimal when social discount rates are higher than 9%. Whether this is the case is an open question. In the short term, real rates of discount exceeding 20% are not uncommon in developing countries.[4] Ehui and Hertel conclude that their estimates of optimal forest stock size are underestimates of the true optimal stock, since positive externalities like preservation of biodiversity and climate benefits are not taken into account. Also excluded are the values of non-timber forest products, possibilities for eco-tourism and existence values, although some of these values may not be entirely incompatible with some forms of logging, although one would suspect that their inclusion would lead to higher optimal forest stocks.

It is straightforward to expand Ehui and Hertel's analysis to include preservation benefits from forests. Formally, this requires rewriting π in equation (12.2) as: $(B + p_F)F + (L - F)(p_A Q - p_x x)$, where B denotes additional annual (global or national) benefits per ha of forest. The effect of adding B to the analysis will depend on its magnitude relative to p_F and p_A. To obtain some notion of its importance, some crude calculations are provided. Assume that the marginal pharmaceutical value per hectare of rainforest is constant for Côte d'Ivoire, and equal to $10, which is almost certainly an overestimation, if the results reported in Table 12.3 are representative. Further, assume non-timber products contribute $10 ha^{-1} year^{-1}, eco-tourism generates an annual return of $2 ha^{-1}, local regulatory functions contribute $5 ha^{-1} year^{-1}, and that annual existence values are $4.50 per ha. Given a shadow price of C storage of $13 per tonne C, and assuming a C sink of 100 t ha^{-1} of tropical forest, the C storage benefits amount to $1,300 per ha, or annual benefits of $52 per ha assuming a discount rate of 4%. The overall estimate of B then turns out to be about $75 ha^{-1}

---

[4] Most economists would agree that discount rates over very long time periods should be lower than the 9-12% used for [public] medium-term investments in developing countries, but how much lower is a subject of debate, even among economists. (Serageldin 1993)

year^{-1} under these assumptions. Assuming that average annual timber production equals 0.70 m^3 ha^{-1} year^{-1}, and that the log price is \$300 per m^3, p_F amounts to approximately \$210 per ha.[5]

It appears that the environmental functions that are overlooked in conventional analysis are a highly significant, but certainly not a dominant feature in land use allocation problems for tropical rainforests. Rather, they would add approximately 35% to the value of a hectare of sustainably managed forest. As a sensitivity analysis, Ehui and Hertel report the effect of doubling p_F; for a discount rate of 3%, the optimal, steady-state forest area increases from 5.4 to 5.7 million ha. For a discount rate of 11%, the optimal steady-state forest area should be almost 2.5 million ha, as opposed to 1.9 million ha when these additional benefits are not taken into account. Since B equals approximately 1/3 p_F, an indication of what might happen when B is included can be obtained by looking at 35% of the increase that results from doubling p_F.[6] Including B leads to modest increases in the steady-state forest stock of 0.15 million ha for $r = 3\%$, and 0.3 million ha for $r = 11\%$. Comparing these optimum stocks (5.6 million ha for $r = 3\%$ and 2.2 million ha for $r = 11\%$) with the current stock of 3.2 million ha shows that, for fairly high values of the social discount rate (say $r > 10\%$), further deforestation may be socially optimal even when (global) nonmarket values are taken into account. As noted earlier, it is not clear what is the real discount rate in developing countries.

Empirical research by Bulte et al. (1997) for the Atlantic Zone of Costa Rica is slightly more pessimistic about tropical forest conservation as a competitive investment, mainly because the opportunity cost of forest conservation (or the agricultural benefits foregone) are much higher in Costa Rica. Using a dynamic optimisation model that takes into account agricultural and commercial forestry returns, as well as the carbon sink benefits of tropical forests and non-timber forest products, the authors conclude that the optimal forest stock is below the current stock. That is, "since the bulk of Costa Rican forests are located in protected areas, we conclude that the government of Costa Rica has set aside too much (as opposed to not enough, as claimed by some critics) of its forests". This conclusion holds even when the per-ha value of non-timber forest products is increased to a value that is five times the authors' optimistic estimate of its true value.

International forest conservation measures

International compensation for forest preservation in poor countries raises issues concerning property rights. If the rights to the forest assets are global in nature, then the country depleting its forests at a globally excessive rate should compensate

---

[5] This value is much larger than that used by Vincent (1990). The difference is due to costs: Vincent focuses on financial profits, while the computations of Ehui and Hertel are based on returns in which the costs of infrastructure, etc., are ignored.

[6] Due to non-linearities in the model solution, this is clearly not a correct approach, but it serves an illustrative purpose, because the difference in the model between p_F and $2p_F$ is relatively small.

foreigners for such deforestation, based on the polluter pays principle. It is unlikely that such a system of property rights could ever be enforced, however, nor would it be agreed upon by sovereign nations. The reason is that what applies for externalities related to forest preservation could, in principal, apply to other situations; for example, foreigners could then oppose any domestic policy on the grounds that it creates a negative spill over, whether real or imagined. We adopt the principle that tropical forests (and their assets) are owned by sovereign nations; any other guiding principle could constitute grounds for international intervention in domestic affairs. Two possible forms of international intervention are evident: trade measures and transfers or aid. Since the advantages of these measures in a first-best world are well known, we briefly point out some of the pitfalls.

Barbier and Rauscher (1994) analyse trade measures and transfers as alternative mechanisms to reduce deforestation, but they do not model deforestation as an irreversible process, where $\dot{F} = -D$ (as in the previous model). Instead, they model the forest as a standard renewable resource, with the capacity to regenerate. The forest stock is thus easier understood in terms of units of biomass, and not in terms of hectares. Another difference is that Barbier and Rauscher do not specify the link between standing timber and agricultural productivity. Instead, they postulate a general utility function that includes the standing stock as an argument.

In their model, the objective function is specified as:

(12.6) $U(q - e, c, F)$,

where U is social welfare, q represents harvest of tropical timber; e is timber exports (so $q - e$ equals domestic consumption of timber); c is consumption of imported goods; and F is the forest stock (expressed in biomass or m^3). The partial derivatives of the utility function with respect to each of these arguments are positive. The discounted value of the infinite stream of social welfare is maximised subject to the following constraints:

(12.7) $P e + s = c$

and

(12.8) $\dot{F} = g(F) - a\,q$,

where P represents the terms of trade (p_e/p_c); s represents international transfers provided to the host country; $g(F)$ is a standard regeneration function; and a is defined as the deforestation rate.

Solving the dynamic optimal control problem in the usual way, and assuming an interior solution, gives the following conditions:

(12.9) $U_{q-e} - \lambda\,a = 0$,

(12.10) $U_{q-e} - P\,U_c = 0$,

and

(12.11) $\dot{\lambda} = (r - g')\lambda - U_F.$

Along an optimal path, the marginal utility of extraction should equal the opportunity cost of harvesting (12.9). Further, the relative marginal utility of domestic timber consumption to consumption of imported goods should be equal to the terms of trade (12.10). Finally, the rate of change in the shadow price of forest holding should equal the difference between the opportunity cost of holding a unit of the forest resource, $(r - g')\lambda$, and the marginal social value of that unit, U_F (Barbier and Rauscher 1994, p. 79).

In the steady-state ($\dot{F} = \dot{q} = \dot{e} = 0$),

(12.12) $U_{q-e} = P\, U_c$

(12.13) $g(F^*) = a\, q^*$

(12.14) $(r - g')\, U_{q-e} = a\, U_F$

The difference between (12.14) and the corresponding steady-state condition in Ehui and Hertel's model, equation (12.5) above, is due to the fact that Barbier and Rauscher allow for growth of the resource, which rewards keeping the resource *in situ*, over and above U_F. Obviously, growth of the resource in equilibrium also explains (12.13) as opposed to Ehui and Hertel's equilibrium condition $\dot{D} = D = 0$. With the aid of Barbier and Rauscher's model, some features of international policies aimed at promoting forest conservation can be analysed.

Trade measures

Roughly speaking, two types of trade measures are possible – those that reduce the level of logging (demand reducing measures such as trade bans and import levies) and those that affect the way exploitation takes place (e.g., forest management certification). These measures are motivated by the belief that currently a very small percentage of tropical wood production takes place sustainably (Poore et al. 1989). In any event, the effects of trade measures on deforestation are probably modest.

Assume that there are no international transfers, so that $s = 0$. A ban or an import tax on tropical timber will reduce the terms of trade, p_e/p_c. The effect on the steady-state forest stock of lowering P can be analysed using comparative statics. Invoking Cramer's rule, Barbier and Rauscher (1994) demonstrate that the sign of dF/dP is ambiguous:

(12.15) $\dfrac{dF^*}{dP} = \dfrac{(1+\eta)U_c - a(r - g')U_{q-e,q-e}}{H},$

where η is the elasticity of marginal utility with respect to imported consumption goods, and $H < 0$ is the determinant of the Hessian matrix of the system (12.9), (12.10) and (12.11). Worsening of the terms of trade has both an income and a substitution effect, and, depending upon which dominates, the optimal forest stock F^* can go up or down.

Several additional comments are relevant. Reducing the terms of trade may negatively affect the steady-state of the forest stock when alternative forms of land use are explicitly modeled. Earlier we considered the case where agriculture competes with sustainable forestry. When the returns of sustainable forestry decline (when p_F falls in Ehui and Hertel's model), the relative attractiveness of alternative land use options increases, and forest cover F should fall in the long run (Barbier and Burgess 1997; Ehui et al. 1990). Further, as argued by Barbier and Rauscher (1994), timber exports may be considered an important source of foreign exchange for some countries. When the terms of trade fall, this implies that the marginal utility of consuming imported goods increases (depending on demand elasticity), and the marginal utility of forest conservation should also increase. According to conventional economic reasoning, this is done by reducing the forest stock. Finally, the effects of trade measures on deforestation are probably modest. Barbier et al. (1994, p. 8) argue that the share of trade in total tropical roundwood production is small: only 17% of the tropical wood is used for industrial purposes, with the majority of the remainder consumed as fuelwood. Of the industrial amount, no more than 31% is subsequently exported, so exports account for only about 5¼% of total tropical roundwood production.

Trade measures aimed at affecting harvesting practises, specifically to promote sustainable harvesting by preferential treatment, may also impact land allocation decisions of governments. To the extent that these measures will affect the profitability of forest management (it is likely that both costs and benefits of adopting a new management regime will be altered), such a measure may increase or reduce the competitiveness of forestry as a land use option. When the costs of meeting sustainability requirements are more than compensated for by increased revenues, the profitability of applying sustainable production techniques increases. According to results from Barbier et al. (1994) and Rice et al. (1997), the scope for a "green premium" for sustainably produced timber is limited, but it is an open question whether this will have a big impact on land allocation decisions. When selective trade measures reduce profitability of non-sustainable forest management, it is possible that conversion of forests for alternative land use options is accelerated, giving rise to a tradeoff between short-run and long-run conservation objectives.

International transfers

Consider next the case of international transfers to compensate for the transboundary externality effects. According to Pearce and Warford (1993) such transfers take the form of

1. lump sum payments to prevent development of a resource,

2.   compensation (and technical assistance and/or loans) for environmentally benign projects, or
3.   debt relief in return for sustainable resource management.

Barbier and Rauscher (1994) address a fourth possibility. In their model, transfers are provided to developing countries without further restrictions on the use of natural resources. Consider the case where transfers are provided: $s > 0$. The comparative statics are as follows:

$$(12.16) \quad \frac{dF^*}{ds} = \frac{P U_{cc}[-a(r-g')U_{q-e,q-e}]}{H} > 0.$$

In other words, a direct international transfer will unambiguously increase the long-run equilibrium forest stock. The reason is that imports must be paid for with foreign exchange, earned by selling tropical timber. Transfers will ease the stringency of the foreign exchange constraint, which implies that more imports can be purchased. As a result, the marginal value of these imports (U_c) falls. In equilibrium, the marginal value of owning forests (U_F) should also fall, and thus the steady-state forest cover should increase (because $U_{FF} < 0$).

Debt relief, on the other hand, may not be a very good mechanism for attaining the desired aims of the international community. The reason is that money markets are trading the debt of developing countries at a discount that accounts for an inability to repay. Bolivia's debt was discounted at $0.06 to the $1 when Bolivia paid $34 million to buy back $308 million in bonds in 1988. The price of remaining bonds rose from $0.06 to $0.11 as a result, with the real value of outstanding debt declining from $40.2 million ($670 million at six cents on the dollar) to $39.8 million ($362 million at 11 cents) (Pearce et al. 1995). In effect, Bolivia paid $34 million to reduce its debt by only $400,000. The problem of debt-for-nature swaps is that, while they protect vulnerable ecosystems in some cases, the large nominal reductions in debt barely touch nations' real burdens, and may even increase expected repayments. The same might also be true for other types of transfers, such as lump sum payments and other forms of compensation.

12.5 Conclusions

This chapter raises a number of issues concerning tropical deforestation. First, although rates of tropical deforestation might be considered to be excessive by some, it may well be that global stocks of tropical forests are too large from an economic efficiency standpoint. The local discounted benefits of further conversion of tropical forests into agriculture or other uses may exceed the global discounted costs (e.g., foregone potential benefits due to loss of species, lost existence values). Not preventing or even promoting further deforestation may be an optimal policy choice for some countries, and the ultimate cause of ongoing tropical deforestation. While the most important value of tropical forest preservation might be as a carbon sink, evidence suggests that other values, such as those related to biological prospecting and nonuse value, are small, particularly at the margin. The problem with carbon sink benefits is that they are difficult to determine as too much uncertainty surrounds issues of climate change and benefits of preventing global warming.

There is no consensus on the main proximate causes of tropical deforestation, although change in land use is its identifying characteristic. Reasons probably vary with each particular situation that a region or country finds itself in. Clearly, logging is not a main factor, but is certainly a catalyst as it opens up natural forests to peasants seeking land for growing agricultural crops. Countries with tropical forests might well be reducing their stocks of forests because they are going through development stages similar to that experienced in Europe and North America. If this is the case, we should expect stocks of natural forests to increase at some future date.

It is unlikely that market failure is a primary or even major factor in tropical deforestation. Forestland owners are likely to convert land to other uses even if they are properly compensated for the external benefits of preserving forests. Global transfers to tropical nations to encourage them to preserve forests are unlikely to get off the ground (no agreements to transfer large sums of money will be agreed to), and, if they do, are likely to fail. When all is said, however, market failure may be less of a factor in deforestation than policy failure. Government policies in many countries encourage deforestation for development and revenue purposes, thereby providing some support for the idea that tropical forest stocks may be excessive – that tropical forests are an inferior asset in a nation's asset portfolio.

13 Concluding Remarks

In Chapter 7, we discussed the portfolio approach to the management of biological assets and sketched the conditions under which conventional economic arguments can be used to advocate conservation of nature. In other chapters, we applied economic theory to determine whether biological assets represented competitive investments, worthy of inclusion in the human portfolio. We considered conservation of elephants and whales, tropical and temperate forests, and biological diversity more generally. In all of the case studies, we aimed to measure value at the margin. Conclusions from the case studies were remarkably consistent, generally painting a rather bleak picture for the role of biological assets in the human portfolio. When valued at the margin and including both market and nonmarket benefits, the (social) rate of return on many biological assets is modest, and probably not sufficient to warrant substantial public investment in retaining them. Policy makers who adhere to principals of economic efficiency should probably disinvest in many biological assets. Thus, for many realistic assumptions, we conclude that many biological assets are *not now competitive* in the human portfolio.

Before abandoning the economic efficiency paradigm in favour of some alternative, consider what still remains to be done. First, as biological assets become scarcer, we would expect their marginal value to rise, making them a more attractive asset to include in society's portfolio of assets. Economists have little information about the rate of change in society's valuation of nature. Perhaps, the marginal willingness-to-pay function for many biological assets, or large ecosystems, is quite flat (at some low value) over a large range, but rises dramatically as biological assets fall below some threshold level (somewhere above minimum viable population in the cases of specific species, say). At that point, such biological assets become highly attractive and competitive assets.

Second, as was noted in Chapter 9, the science of nature conservation, as opposed to its management, remains unclear. There is controversy about what constitutes a species, and about how many species can be lost before biodiversity is seriously impacted. Some people simply feel that scientists are crying wolf, while others take seriously loss of even a single species. There is controversy about whether it is ecosystem function that is important, or whether it is the composition of the ecosystem that matters. If it is the former, then ecosystems can be managed, and an ecosystem with exotic species is not different than one with native, indigenous species. If composition matters, then the homogenisation of the globe's ecosystems and loss of endemic species constitutes a potentially large loss in nonuse value. However, neither economists nor biologists have shown that composition is sufficiently important to justify the public investments required to preserve composition of ecosystems over and above preservation of their function.

Third, we have for the most part ignored uncertainty and irreversibility, although, in Chapter 6, we did discuss the safe minimum standard as an approach to managing for it. No examples of how to apply it in practice were provided (but see Berrens et al. 1998). In the numerical analyses, we assumed that current and future market and nonmarket benefits and costs of conservation, and biological growth, are known with certainty. Although we examined stochastic economic models and the concept of quasi-option value as a component of the total economic value of conservation (see Chapter 9), we did not explicitly include such values. It is likely that quasi-option value is not all that large, however. Nonetheless, uncertainty could possibly render biological assets more competitive than indicated by the deterministic models.

Fourth, efficient portfolio management prescribes that the risk that matters is how an asset influences the portfolio's overall risk. For completeness, the covariance of the risk of various assets, biological and reproducible, should be considered. Doing so goes beyond the scope of this book, but the consequences of ignoring this aspect could be important. Two issues may be relevant here. Fluctuations in the "earnings" of biological assets can be positively (or negatively) correlated with fluctuations in the earnings of other assets. As decision makers care about the expected returns and risks of the entire portfolio, rather than those of its separate components, risk correlation may provide an incentive to increase (or reduce) the stock of biological assets. To our knowledge, empirical work in this field is lacking, and perhaps nonexistent. Further, as explained in Chapter 9, conservation of species and biodiversity may contribute to ecosystem stability and resilience, and thus affect the riskiness of holding some reproducible assets. Including this insight in a numerical model is also far from straightforward as there is considerable uncertainty about the (potential) contribution of biodiversity in general and certain species in particular (e.g., Baskin 1994). Ignoring system-wide consequences in the management of certain biological assets probably implies that their rates of return are underestimated.

Fifth, conventional assumptions with respect to temporal preferences (and associated discount rates) may be overly simplistic. While theory predicts that people are more averse to risks that occur early on, experimental evidence suggests that people hate delaying consequences (Knetsch 2000). Indeed, Lowenstein and Prelec (1991) found that people like to put off desired events (presumably to enjoy the prospect of such events occurring), but want to get undesired events over with as quickly as possible. This suggests that outcomes are discounted at different rates. This requires that the dynamic models and the steady-state solutions used in our case studies be modified to take into account different discount rates. Determining the appropriate rates for different outcomes may be troublesome, however.

Finally, as noted in Chapter 5, measurement of nonmarket values, particularly those related to preservation, remains problematic. Again, a major reason has to do with uncertainty (Loomis and Ekstrand 1998). Even in the absence of risk and uncertainty, people generally value gains and losses differently, although theory typically assumes that, apart from a minor income effect, valuations of gains and losses are equivalent. Thus, it is often assumed that the WTP to retain a certain level of some biological asset is the same as the compensation demanded (or WTA) to permit its loss, but this is probably not true. As explained in Chapter 2, WTP and

WTA compensation are not the same when there are few substitutes for the good or amenity in question. (Indeed, indifference curves may be kinked at the endowment level.) Knetsch (1993) notes that "people usually evaluate gains and losses not in terms of end states, but in terms of changes from some reference position". (p. 254) People appear more sensitive to losses than to gains, so valuations based on WTP for stock increments likely underestimate the true welfare loss when stocks are depleted. One implication is that specification of property rights is important for propoer management of resources and the environment, as we have argued throughout. In fact, as WTA compensation for losses is unbounded by income, the costs of drawing down stocks of biological assets may well be considerable if the property rights for such stocks belong to the public. These issues are still hotly debated, and we expect that future work in experimental economics will shed more light on the issue.

Clearly, economic efficiency is a worthy objective, but it need not take pre-eminent status in decision making as many issues concerning biological assets involve ethical considerations. Indeed, it is by no means obvious that efficiency considerations should dominate decision making with respect to nature (Johansson-Stenman 1998). Policy makers need to balance efficiency considerations, which are at the core of conventional economics, with other, perhaps more important, objectives. Concern for equality and fairness is one appealing consideration. Should species be included in deliberations of equality and fairness? For example, if notions of fairness extend to other species, it is hard to conceive how harvesting of "non-competitive" (slow growing) species to extinction can ever be considered truly optimal. However, few people would argue that species hold a moral trump card over humans; rather, as discussed in Chapter 9, the rights of humans trump those of other species. Further, one simply has to be realistic about what is and is not possible in the real world. As pointed out in Chapter 8, people are unwilling to make significant sacrifices to their lifestyles. In the real world, tradeoffs are inevitable. As Shogren (1998) argues, "resources spent on species protection are resources not spent on kids' health" (p. 567). In the real world, concern about children's health will override issues pertaining to loss of species when that loss has no immediate and readily identifiable consequences for society.

Nonetheless, in addition to economic efficiency, ethical or moral imperatives often serve as a guiding principle in the management of biological assets. For example, as noted in Chapter 8, the safe minimum standard of conservation (SMS) is based on ethical considerations. But "it is not just a matter of balancing interests with interests, it is a matter of balancing interests with morality and balancing one morality with another morality" (Sagoff 1988a, p. 98). In other words, while economic reasoning is important in developing instruments to achieve certain objectives (such that these objectives are reached cost effectively), the same reasoning should probably not be allowed to determine the goals themselves (Common 1995). Conversely, if public investment in certain biological assets is perceived unfair or to the detriment of the poor in particular, and it is difficult to compensate them, such investment may be undesirable, even if the investment is deemed economically efficient.

In practice, careful balancing of potentially conflicting objectives is required, and economic efficiency is but one of those objectives. Although economists have not been on the forefront in the development or application of multiple objective decision-making (MODM) models, such models do offer a framework for analysing trade-offs in a systematic and consistent fashion. While the SMS approach, for example, prescribes *temporarily* defaulting to safety and buttressing economic efficiency, MODM requires constant balancing of sustainability and efficiency considerations, so neither objective achieves priority status.[1] In the real world of politics, however, efforts to identify explicitly the tradeoffs among objectives, or analyse them in quantitative fashion, are rarely made, and especially not in a dynamic decision-making framework, such as that employed in this book.

We conclude that economic efficiency considerations provide powerful insights into the conservation of biological assets, and that much of the current mismanagement of nature could be avoided if managers would apply the insights of the kinds of models that we have presented in this book. Throughout this book and despite what might be considered negative conclusions regarding investment in biological assets, we have endeavoured to demonstrate that an economic efficiency model, properly specified, may lead to policies favouring preservation of species and biodiversity. Yes, we argue that, using marginal analysis, the stock of African elephants should probably be reduced, but we also favour continuing the trade ban on ivory. In the case of minke whales, where we include nonmarket values in a dynamic optimisation model, we do favour some harvesting of whales, but not to extinction. We argue that economic efficiency in the case of game ranching (get rid of arbitrary government rules) will do much to protect the stocks of wildlife herbivores. For the case of old growth, we show that, at the margin, society should protect some 40–50% of remaining virgin forest, although an analysis based only on average values (including preservation and all other non-timber values) gives the result that all of the old growth should be liquidated. We show that inclusion of carbon uptake benefits will extend the rotation age of forests, and we discuss how economic efficiency arguments can be tempered with the SMS, actually arguing in favour of the SMS against the precautionary principle that says you must preserve species *regardless of cost*. We also point out how dynamic models might change with time as a result of changing conditions, although we do not address this explicitly (see Chapter 8). The conclusion is that the management of nature and the conservation of biological assets are enhanced, and possibilities for extinction and wasteful use of natural resources reduced, when economic efficiency is take into account in policy making.

Unfortunately, economists often find that economic efficiency is missing when decisions are made about the conservation and exploitation of biological assets. There is a litany of examples where this is the case. Harris (1998) provides a recent sample in the case of the fishery; see also Roberts (1997) and Ludwig et al.(1993). Despite many indications during the 1980s that stocks of northern cod off Canada's East Coast were disappearing, the federal government, which is responsible for fishery policy, allowed very high annual total allowable catches through the latter part of the

---

[1] A general criticism of MODM has been that objectives had to be ranked or somehow weighted in order to make them commensurable within the mathematical programming framework. Fuzzy MODM has mitigated this requirement (Pickens and Hof 1991; Zimmermann 1996; Ells et al. 1997).

decade and into the 1990s. Why? There was some uncertainty about the science, whether it was overfishing or weather changes and seals that were causing the decline in stocks, and decision makers exploited this uncertainty to permit large harvests so that fishermen would be employed. Canada subsidises employment in the fishery to the tune of billions of dollars, and it is not alone. Globally, some US$124 billion is spent every year to produce about $70 billion of product. This is not economically efficient.

Similar conditions hold in other resource industries. Currently (late 1990s), in Canada, companies harvest old-growth, temperate rainforests even though they are losing some $5–$10 per cubic meter by logging trees because government regulations require that they harvest trees; otherwise they lose the right to harvest trees in the future. The reason for such a policy is job creation (retention) and to provide the government with revenues.

Canada is a signatory to Convention on international trade in endangered and threatened species and has its own legislation protecting wild animals and plants – the Wild Animal and Plant Protection and Regulation of International and Interprovincial Trade Act of 1996. Despite its best intentions and the fact that Canada is a developed country, enforcement of trade in endangered and threatened species is lax. During mid–1998, for example, federal game officers in Vancouver and Victoria, Canada, seized 2,897 pharmaceutical products contained substances from endangered and threatened species (Pynn 1998). Investigations of 110 Chinese herbal medicine shops found that 46 shops carried products that contained substances from endangered species listed under Appendix I of CITES (including tiger bone and rhino horn) and 80% contained substances from animals listed under Appendix II. Further, 49 shops carried illegal bear products, mainly gall bladders from grizzly bears. These shops were in contravention not only of international agreements, but also of domestic laws. Although the shops could have been fined a total of C$28,175, warning were issued instead.

Canada has not yet ratified the Law of the Sea Convention and other international agreements that it has signed. While this does not imply lack of compliance, it also suggests that enthusiasm for international treaties that protect the earth's ecosystems is lacking. The same holds true for other countries, whether they ratify international agreements or not. Politics gets in the way, with many nations agreeing to do one thing in the international arena but behaving in a contrary fashion when implementing a host of domestic policies that directly or indirectly affect the agreements signed. It is our contention that, by paying greater attention to economic efficiency as opposed to politics in the management of nature, there is greater hope for protecting the ecosystems that society feels are threatened.

References

Abdalla, C. W., B. A. Roach and D. J. Epp, 1992. Valuing Environmental Quality Changes Using Averting Expenditures: An Application Groundwater Contamination, *Land Economics* 68:163–9.

Adamowicz, W. L., P. Boxall, M. Williams and J. Louviere, 1998. Stated Preference Approaches to Measuring Passive Use Values: Choice Experiments versus Contingent Valuation, *American Journal of Agricultural Economics* 80(February): 64–75.

Adamowicz, W. L., 1995. Alternative Valuation Techniques: A Comparison and Movement to a Synthesis. Chapter 9 in *Environmental Valuation. New Perspectives* by K. G. Willis and J. T. Corkindale (eds.). Wallingford UK: CAB International.

Adamowicz, W. L., J. J. Fletcher and T. Graham-Tomasi, 1989. Functional Form and the Statistical Properties of Welfare Measures, *American Journal of Agricultural Economics* 71: 414–20.

Ahrens, W. and V. Sharma, 1997. Trends in Natural Resource Commodity Prices: Deterministic or Stochastic? *Journal of Environmental Economics and Management* 33: 59–74.

Albers, H. J., A. C. Fisher and W. M. Hanemann, 1996. Valuation and Management of Tropical Forests: Implications of Uncertainty and Irreversibility, *Environmental and Resource Economics* 8: 39–61.

Alchian, A. A. 1987. Rent. In *The New Palgrave: A Dictionary of Economics* edited by J. Eatwell, M. Milgate and P. Newman. Volume 4. London: Macmillan. pp. 141–3.

Amelung T. and M. Diehl, 1992. Deforestation of Tropical Rain Forests: Economic Causes and Impact on Development. Tubingen: J. C. B. Mohr.

Amundsen, E. S., T. Bjorndal and J. B. Conrad, 1995. Optimal Harvesting of the Northeast Atlantic Minke Whale, *Environmental and Resource Economics* 6: 167–85.

Anderson K., 1992. The standard Welfare Economics of Policies Affecting Trade and the Environment. Chapter 2 in *The Greening of World Trade Issues* edited by Anderson K. and R. Blackhurst. Hertfordshire: Harvester Wheatsheaf.

Anderson, L. G., 1977. *Economic Impacts of Extended Fisheries Jurisdiction*. Ann Arbor, MI: Ann Arbor Science.

Anderson, L. G., 1989. Conceptual Constructs for Practical ITQ Management Policies. In *Rights Based Fishing* edited by P. Neher, R. Arnason and N. Mollet. NATO ASI Series E: Applied Sciences 169. Dordrecht: Kluwer

Anderson, L. G., 1995. Privatizing Open-access Fisheries: Individual Transferable Quotas. Chap. 20 in *The Handbook of Environmental Economics* (pp. 453-74) edited by D. W. Bromley. Cambridge MA: Basil Blackwell.

Andersson, J. and Z. Hgazi, 1991. Marine Resource Use and the Establishment of a Marine Park: Mafia Island, Tanzania, *Ambio* 20(1): 2–8.

Arrow, K. J., 1951. *Social Choice and Individual Values*. New Haven: Yale University Press.

Arrow, K. J. and A. C. Fisher, 1974. Environmental Preservation, Uncertainty, and Irreversibility, *Quarterly Journal of Economics* 88: 312–9.

Arrow, K. J., B. Bolin, R. Constanza, P. Dasgupta, C. Folke, C. S. Holling, B. O. Jansson, S. Levin, K. G. Maler, C. Perrings, D. Pimental, 1995. Economic Growth, Carrying Capacity and the Environment, *Science* 268: 520–21.

Arrow, K., R. Solow, E. Leamer, P. Portney, R. Randner and H. Schuman, 1993. Appendix I – Report of the NOAA Panel on Contingent Valuation, *Federal Register* Vol. 58, No. 10 (January 15), pp. 4602–14.

Asheim, G. B., 1986. Hartwick's Rule of Open Economies, *Canadian Journal of Economics* 19: 395–402.

Aylward, B., 1992. Appropriating the Value of Wildlife and Wildlands. Chapter 3 in *Economics for the Wilds* edited by T. M. Swanson and E. B. Barbier. London: Earthscan.

Ayres, R. U., 1998. Comment: The Price-Value Paradox, *Ecological Economics* 25: 17–9.

Baland, J. and J. P. Platteau, 1996. *Halting Degradation of Natural Resources*. Oxford, UK: Clarendon Press.

Balling, Jr., R. C., 1995. Global warming: Messy models, decent data and pointless policy. Chapter 3 in *The True State of the Planet* edited by R. Bailey. New York: The Free Press.

Bandemer, H. and S. Gottwald, 1996. *Fuzzy Sets, Fuzzy Logic, Fuzzy Methods with Applications*. Chichester, UK: John Wiley & Sons.

Barbier, E. B. and B. A. Aylward, 1996. Capturing the Pharmaceutical Value of Biodiversity in a Developing Country, *Environmental and Resource Economics* 8: 157–81.

Barbier E. B. and J. Burgess, 1997. The Economics of Tropical Forest Land Use Options, *Land Economics* 73: 174–95.

Barbier E. B. and A. Markandya, 1990. The Conditions for Achieving Envrionmentally Sustainable Development, *European Economic Review* 34: 659–69.

Barbier E. B. and M. Rauscher, 1994. Trade, Tropical Deforestation and Policy Interventions, *Environmental and Resource Economics* 4: 75–90

Barbier, E. and T. Swanson, 1990. Ivory: The Case Against the Ban, *New Scientist*, November 17, pp. 52–4.

Barbier, E. B., N. Bockstael, J. C. Burgess and I. Strand, 1995. The Linkages between the Timber Trade and Tropical Deforestation – Indonesia, *World Economy* 18(3): 411–42.

Barbier, E. B., J. C. Burgess and C. Folke, 1994. *Paradise Lost? The Ecological Economics of Biodiversity*. London: Earthscan.

Barbier, E., J. C. Burgess, J. T. Bishop and B. A. Aylward, 1994. *The Economics of the Tropical Timber Trade*. London: Earthscan.

Barbier, E, J. Burgess, T. Swanson and D. Pearce, 1990. *Elephants, Economics and Ivory*. London: Earthscan Publications.

Barnett, H. J. and C. Morse, 1963. *Scarcity and Growth*. Baltimore: The Johns Hopkins Univ. Press.

Barrett, J. W., 1988. The Northeast Region. In *Regional Silviculture of the United States* (pp. 25–66) edited by J. W. Barrett. New York: John Wiley & Sons.

Barrett, S., 1991. Optimal Soil Conservation and the Reform of Agricultural Pricing Policies, *Journal of Development Economics* 36: 167–87

Barrett, S., 1998. On the Theory and Diplomacy of Environmental Treaty Making, *Environmental and Resource Economics* 11(3–4): 317–33.

Barten, A. P., 1964. Consumer Demand Functions Under Conditions of Almost Additive Preferences, *Econometrica* 32(January–April): 1–38.

Barten, A. P., 1968. Estimating Demand Equations, *Econometrica* 36(April): 213–51.

Baskin, Y., 1994. Ecologists Dare to Ask: How Much Does Diversity Matter? *Science* 264: 202–3.

BC Assessment Authority, 1988. *1988 Commissioners Rates. Land and Cut Timber*. Report prepared by the Appraisal Services Division, Timber Appraisal Section, Victoria.

BC Assessment Authority, 1994. *1994 Commissioners Rates. Land and Cut Timber.* Report prepared by the Farm and Forest Section, Technical Services Division, Victoria.

BC Ministry of Environment, Lands and Parks and Environment Canada, 1993. *State of the Environment Report for British Columbia.* Victoria: Queen's Printer.

BC Ministry of Environment, Lands and Parks, 1996. *British Columbia Land Statistics.* Victoria, BC: Government of British Columbia.

BC Ministry of Forests, 1991. *Outdoor Recreation Survey 1989/90. How British Columbians Use and Value their Public Forest Lands for Recreation.* Recreation Branch Technical Report 1991-1. Victoria: Queen's Printer for British Columbia.

BC Ministry of Forests, 1992a. *An Old Growth Strategy for British Columbia.* Victoria: Queen's Printer for British Columbia.

BC Ministry of Forests, 1992b. *An Inventory of Undeveloped Watersheds in British Columbia.* Recreation Branch Technical Report 1992:2. Victoria: Queen's Printer for British Columbia.

BC Ministry of Forests, 1996. *Forest Practices Code: Timber Supply Analysis.* Victoria: Queen's Printer for British Columbia. 33pp.

Becker, G. S., 1965. A Theory of the Allocation of Time, *Economic Journal* 75: 493–517.

Beckerman, W., 1992. Economic Growth and the Environment. Whose Growth? Whose Environment? *World Development* 20: 481–96.

Begon, M., M. Mortimer and D. J. Thomson, 1996. *Population Ecology.* 3rd Edition. Oxford: Blackwell Science.

Beisner, E. C., 1990. *Prospects for Growth.* Westchester, Illinois: Crossway Books.

Beisner, E. C., 1997. *Where Garden Meets Wilderness.* Grand Rapids, MI: William B. Eerdmans Publishing.

Benson, C. A., 1988. A Need for Extensive Forest Management, *The Forestry Chronicle* 64: 421–30.

Bentkover, J. D., 1986. The Role of Benefits Assessment in Public Policy Development, Chapter 1 in *Benefits Assessment: The State of the Art* edited by J. D. Bentkover, V. T. Covello and J. Mumpower. Dordrecht: D. Reidel Publishing Co.

Berck, P., 1995. Empirical Consequences of the Hotelling Principle. Chapter 10 in *The Handbook of Environmental Economics* edited by D. W. Bromley. Cambridge MA: Basil Blackwell.

Berck, P. and M. Roberts, 1996. Natural Resource Prices: Will They Ever Turn Up? *Journal of Environmental Economics and Management* 31: 65–78.

Berrens, R. P., D. S. Brookshire, M. McKee and C. Schmidt, 1998. Implementing the Safe Minimum Standard Approach, *Land Economics* 74(May): 147–61.

Binkley, C. S., 1980. Economic Analysis of the Allowable Cute Effect, *Forest Science* 26(4): 633–42.

Binkley, C. S., 1984. Allowable Cute Effects with Even Flow Constraints, *Canadian Journal of Forest Research* 14(3): 317–20.

Binkley, C. S., 1991. Imperfections in Timber Markets: Theory and Practice. Vancouver: University of British Columbia, Faculty of Forestry, mimeograph.

Binkley, C. S., M. J. Apps, R. K. Dixon, P. E. Kauppi and L. -O. Nilsson, 1997. Sequestering Carbon in Natural Forests, *Critical Reviews in Environmental Science and Technology* 27(Special): S23–S45.

Binswanger, H. P., 1989. *Brazilian Policies that Encourage Deforestation in the Amazon.* Environment Dept. Working Paper No. 16. Washington: The World Bank.

Bishop, R. C., 1978. Endangered Species and Uncertainty: The Economics of a Safe Minimum Standard, *American Journal of Agricultural Economics* 60(Feb): 10–18.

Bishop, R. C. and T. A. Heberlein, 1979. Measuring Values of Extra-Market Goods: Are Indirect Measures Biased? *American Journal of Agricultural Economics* 61: 926–30.

Bishop, R. C. and T. A. Heberlein, 1990. The Contingent Valuation Method. Chapter 6 in *Economic Valuation of Natural Resources: Issues, Theory and Application* edited by R. L. Johnson and G. V. Johnson. Boulder: Westview Press.

Bishop, R. C. and M. P. Welsh, 1993. Existence Values in Benefit-Cost Analysis and Damage Assessment. Chapter 8 in *Forestry and the Environment: Economic Perspectives* edited by W. L Adamowicz, W. White and W. E. Phillips. Wallingford UK: CAB International.

Bishop, R. C., P. A. Champ and D. J. Mullarky, 1995. Contingent Valuation. Chapter 28 in *The Handbook of Environmental Economics* edited by D. W. Bromley. Oxford UK: Basil Blackwell Ltd.

Bjorndal T. and J. Conrad, 1987. The Dynamics of an Open-access Fishery, *Canadian Journal of Economics* 20: 74–85

Bjorndal, T., 1988. The Optimal Management of North Sea Herring, *Journal of Environmental Economics and Management* 15: 9–29

Blamey, R. K., M. S. Common and J. Quiggin, 1995. Respondents to Contingent Valuation Studies: Consumers or Citizens? *Australian Journal of Agricultural Economics* 39: 263–88.

Blower, J., 1984. National Parks for Developing Countries, In J. A. McNeely and K. R. Miller (eds.), *National Parks, Conservation and Development*. Washington, D. C., Smithsonian Institution Press.

Boadway, R. W. and N. Bruce, 1984. *Welfare Economics*. New York: Basil Blackwell.

Boadway, R. W., 1974. The Welfare Foundations of Cost-Benefit Analysis, *Economic Journal* 84: 426–39.

Bockstael, N. E. and K. E. McConnell, 1993. Public Goods as Characteristics of Nonmarket Commodities, *Economic Journal* 103(9); 1244–57.

Bockstael, N. E., 1995. Travel Cost Models. Chap. 29 in *The Handbook of Environmental Economics* (pp.655-71) edited by D. W. Bromley. Oxford UK: Basil Blackwell.

Boman, M. and G. Bostedt, 1994. A Bioeconomic Approach to Wolf Population Management, *Scandinavian Forest Economics* 35: 250–63.

Boserup, E., 1965. The Conditions of Agricultural Growth: The Economics of Agrarian Change under Population Pressure. Chicago: Aldine.

Bowes, M. D. and J. V. Krutilla, 1989. *Multiple-Use Management: The Economics of Public Forestlands*. Washington: Resources for the Future.

Boyce, J. K., 1994. Inequality as a Cause of Environmental Degradation, *Ecological Economics* 11: 169–78.

Boyce, J. R., 1995. Optimal Capital Accumulation in a Fishery: A Nonlinear Irreversible Investment Model, *Journal of Environmental Economics and Management* 28: 324–39.

Boyle, K. J., F. R. Johnson, D. W. McCollum, W. H. Desvousges, R. W. Dunford and S. P. Hudson, 1996. Valuing Public Goods: Discrete versus Continuous Contingent-Valuation Responses, *Land Economics* 72(August): 381–96.

Boyle, K. J., G. L. Poe and J. C. Bergstrom, 1994. What Do We Know About Groundwater Values? Preliminary Implications from a Meta Analysis of Contingent-Valuation Studies, *American Journal of Agricultural Economics* 76(December): 1055–61.

Bradford, D. F., 1975. Constraints on Government Investment Opportunities and the Choice of Discount Rate, *American Economic Review* 65: 887–99.

Brannlund, R., P. O. Johansson, and K. G. Lofgren, 1985. An Econometric Analysis of Aggregate Sawtimber and Pulpwood Supply in Sweden, *Forest Science* 31: 595–606.

Bratton, S. P., 1992. *Six Billion & More: Human Population Regulation and Christian Ethics*. Louisville, KY: Westminster/John Knox Press, 1992.

Bromley, D. W., 1999. Sustaining Development. Environmental Resources in Developing Countries. Cheltenham, UK: Edward Elgar.

Brooke, A., D. Kendrick and A. Meeraus, 1996. GAMS Release 2. 25. A User's Guide. Washington, DC: GAMS Development Corporation.

Brown, G. M., Jr. and W. Henry, 1989. *The Economic Value of Elephants.* LEEC Paper 89–12. London: IIED/London Environmental Economics Centre.

Brown, G. M. and D. Layton, 1998. Saving Rhinos. Paper presented at the First World Conference of Environmental and Resource Economists, Venice, June 25–27.

Brown, G. M. and J. Roughgarden, 1997. A Metapopulation Model with Private Property and a Common Pool, *Ecological Economics* 22: 65–71.

Brown, G. M. Jr. and J. F. Shogren, 1998. Economics of the Endangered Species Act, *Journal of Economic Perspectives* 12(3): 3–20.

Brown, G. M., D. Layton and J. Lazo, 1994. *Valuing Habitat and Endangered Species.* Institute for Economic Research Discussion Paper #94–1, Univ. of Washington, Seattle. Jan. 26pp.

Brown, K. and D. W. Pearce (Eds.), 1994. *The Causes of Tropical Deforestation.* London: UCL-Press.

Brown, S., C. Hall, W. Knabe, J. Raich, M. Trexler and P. Woomer, 1993. Tropical Forests: Their Past, Present, and Potential Future Role in the Terrestrial Carbon Budget, in Terrestrial Biospheric Carbon Fluxes. In *Quantification of Sinks and Sources of CO_2* (pp. 71–94) edited by J. Wisniewski and R. N. Sampson. Dordrecht: Kluwer Academic Publishers.

Budiansky, S., 1995. *Nature's Keepers.* New York: The Free Press.

Bulte, E. H. and G. C. van Kooten, 1996. A Note on Ivory Trade and Elephant Conservation, *Environment and Development Economics* 1: 433–43

Bulte, E. H. and G. C. van Kooten, 1999a. Metapopulation Dynamics and Stochastic Bioeconomic Modeling, *Ecological Economics* In press.

Bulte, E. H. and G. C. van Kooten, 1999b. Economic Efficiency, Resource Conservation and the Ivory Trade Ban, *Ecological Economics* 28(February): 171–83.

Bulte, E. H. and G. C. van Kooten, 1999c. Economics of Anti-Poaching Enforcement and the Ivory Trade Ban, *American Journal of Agricultural Economics* 81(May):453–66.

Bulte, E. H. and G. C. van Kooten, 1999d. Environmental Valuation and Declining Marginal Utility of Preservation: The Case of Minke Whales in the Northeast Atlantic, *Environmental and Resource Economics*, In press.

Bulte, E. H. and G. C. van Kooten, 1999e. Downward Sloping Demand for Environmental Amenities and International Compensation: Elephant Conservation and Strategic Culling. Working paper. Tilburg University, Netherlands.

Bulte, E. H. and D. P. van Soest, 1996. Tropical Deforestation, Timber Concessions and Slash-and-Burn Agriculture: Why Encroachment may Promote Conservation of Primary Forests, *Journal of Forest Economics* 2: 55–65.

Bulte, E. H. and D. P. van Soest, 1999. A Note on Soil Depth, Failing Markets and Agricultural Pricing Policies, *Journal of Development Economics* 58: 245–54.

Bulte, E. H, H. Folmer and W. J. M. Heijman, 1998. Dynamic and Static Approaches to Mixed Good Management: The Case of Minke Whales in the Northeast Atlantic, *European Review of Agricultural Economics* 25: 73–91.

Bulte, E., M. Joenje and H. Jansen, 1997. Socially Optimal Forest Stocks in Developing Countries: Theory and Application to the Atlantic Zone of Costa Rica. Department of Development Economics Working Paper, Wageningen Agricultural University, Wageningen, Netherlands. Mimeo. 18pp.

Bunnell, F. L., D. K. Daust, W. Klenner, L. L. Kremsater and R. K. McCann, 1991. *Managing for Biodiversity in Forested Ecosystems.* Victoria: Report to the Forest Sector of the Old-Growth Strategy, mimeograph, July 25. 56pp. plus Appendices.

Burgess J., 1994. The Environmental Effects of Trade in Endangered Species. In *The Environmental Effects of Trade.* Paris: OECD.

Burt, O. R. and R. D. Johnson, 1967. Strategies for Wheat Production in the Great Plains, *Journal of Farm Economics* 49(November): 881–99.

Burton, M., 1998. An Assessment of Alternative Methods of Estimating the Effect of the Ivory Trade Ban on Poaching Effort, *Ecological Economics* In press.

Calish, S., R. D. Fight and D. E. Teeguarden, 1978. How Do Nontimber Values Affect Douglas-fir Rotations? *Journal of Forestry* 76(April): 217–21.

Campbell, H. F., 1991. Estimating the Elasticity of Substitution Between Restricted and Unrestricted Inputs in a Regulated Fishery: A Probit Approach, *Journal of Environmental Economics and Management* 20: 262–74.

Canadian Forest Service, 1997. *Selected Forestry Statistics Canada 1996*. Ottawa: Minister of Supply and Services Canada.

Carranza, C. F., Aylward, B. A., Echeverria, J., Tosi, J. A. and R. Mejias, 1996. *Valoracion de los servicios ambientales de los bosques de Costa Rica*. Document prepared for ODA-MINAE. San Jose, Costa Rica: Centro Cientifico Tropical. 78 pp.

Carson, R. T., N. E. Flores and N. F. Meade, 1996. Contingent Valuation: Controversies and Evidence. Discussion paper #96–36, Department of Economics, University of California, San Diego.

Carson, R. T., W. H. Hanemann, R. J. Kopp, J. A. Krosnick, R. C. Mitchell, S. Presser, P. A. Ruud, V. K. Smith, M. Conaway and K. Martin, 1997. Temporal Reliability of Estimates from Contingent Valuation, Land Economics 73(2): 151–63.

Castle, E. N., 1993. A Pluralistic, Pragmatic and Evolutionary Approach to natural Resource Management, *Forest Ecology and Management* 56: 279–95.

Castle, E. N., R. P. Berrens and R. M. Adams, 1994. Natural Resource Damage Assessment: Speculations About a Missing Perspective, *Land Economics* 70(August): 378–85.

Chadwick D. H., 1992. *The Fate of the Elephant*. London: Penguin Books.

Chakraborty, M., 1994. An Analysis of the Causes of Deforestation in India. Chapter 16 in *The Causes of Tropical Deforestation: The Economic and Statistical Analysis of Factors giving Rise to the Loss of Tropical Forests* edited by K. Brown and D. W. Pearce. London: UCL Press.

Chant, J. F., D. G. McFetridge and D. A. Smith, 1990. The Economics of the Conserver Society. Chapter 1 in *Economics and the Environment* edited by W. Block. Vancouver, BC: The Fraser Institute.

Chiang, A. C., 1992. *Elements of Dynamic Optimization*. New York: McGraw-Hill.

Chipman, J. S. and J. C. Moore, 1976. The Scope of Consumer's Surplus Arguments. In *Evolution, Welfare, and Time in Economics: Essays in Honor of Nicholas Georgescu-Roegen* (pp. 69–123) by A. M. Tang (ed.). Lexington MA: Heath-Lexington Books.

Chipman, J. S. and J. C. Moore, 1978. The New Welfare Economics 1939–1974, *International Economic Review* 19(October): 547–84.

Chipman, J. S. and J. C. Moore, 1980. Compensating Variation, Consumer's Surplus, and Welfare, *American Economic Review* 70(December): 933–49.

Christensen, L. R., D. W. Jorgenson and L. J. Lau, 1975. Transcendental Logarithmic Utility Functions, *American Economic Review* 65 (June): 367–83.

Ciriacy-Wantrup, S. V., 1968. *Resource Conservation. Economics and Policies*. 3rd ed. Berkeley: Univ. of California, Agricultural Experiment Sta. (Original 1952).

Clark, C. W., 1973a. Profit Maximization and the Extinction of Species, *Journal of Political Economy* 81: 950–61.

Clark, C. W., 1973b. The Economics of Overexploitation, *Science* 181: 630– 3.

Clark, C. W., 1985. Bioeconomic Modelling and Fisheries Management. New York: Wiley.

Clark, C. W., 1990. *Mathematical Bioeconomics*. 2nd edition. New York: Wiley.

Clark, C. W., F. H. Clarke and G. R. Munro, 1979. The Optimal Exploitation of Renewable Resource Stocks: Problems of Irreversible Investment, *Econometrica* 47: 25–47.

Clawson, M., 1959. *Measuring the Demand for and Value of Outdoor Recreation*. RFF Reprint #10. Washington: Resources for the Future.

Clinton, W. J. and A. Gore, Jr., 1993. *The Climate Change Action Plan*. Washington, DC: Office of the President. 50pp.

Coase, R., 1960. The Problem of Social Cost, *Journal of Law and Economics* 3(Oct): 1–44.

Cobb, J. B. Jr., 1988. A Christian View of Biodiversity. Chapter 55 in *Biodiversity* edited by E. O. Wilson with F. M. Peter. Washington: National Academy Press.

Coetzee G., 1989. Conspiracy of Silence? *South African Panorama*, October: 10–14

COFI, 1994. Review of Government Estimates of the Costs and Benefits of the Proposed Forest Practices Code. Vancouver: Council of Forest Industries of British Columbia. March.

Colborn, T., D. Dumanoski and J. P. Myers, 1996. *Our Stolen Future*. New York: Penguin Group.

Common, M., 1995. *Sustainability and Policy: Limits to Economics*. Sydney: Cambridge University Press.

Common, M. and C. Perrings, 1992. Towards an Ecological Economics of Sustainability, *Ecological Economics* 6: 7–34.

Common, M. S., I. Reid and R. K. Blamey, 1997. Do Existence Values for Cost Benefit Analysis Exist? *Environmental and Resource Economics* 9: 225–38.

Conrad, J. M., 1995. Bioeconomic Models of the Fishery. Chapter 18 in *The Handbook of Environmental Economics* edited by D. W. Bromley. Cambridge, MA: Basil Blackwell. .

Conrad, J. M. and T. Bjorndal, 1993. On the Resumption of Commercial Whaling: The Case of the Minke Whale in the Northeast Atlantic, *Arctic* 164–71.

Conrad, J. M. and C. W. Clark, 1987. *Natural Resource Economics: Notes and Problems*. Cambridge: Cambridge University Press.

Conrad, R. F. and M. Gillis, 1985. Progress and Poverty in Developing Countries: Rents and Resource Taxation. In *Henry George and Contemporary Economic Development* (pp. 25–47) edited by S. R. Lewis.

Conservation Foundation, 1987. *State of the Environment: A View toward the Nineties*. Washington, DC: Conservation Foundation and the Charles Stewart Mott Foundation,

Cooter, R. and P. Rappoport, 1984. Were the Ordinalists Wrong About Welfare Economics? *Journal of Economic Literature* 22(June): 507–30.

Copes, P., 1986. A Critical Review of the Individual Quota as a Device in Fisheries Management, *Land Economics* 62(3): 278–91.

Copithorne, L., 1979. *Natural Resources and Regional Disparities*, Report prepared for the Economic Council of Canada. Ottawa: Ministry of Supply and Services.

Costanza, R., R. d'Arge, R. de Groot, S. Farber, M. Grasso, B. Hannon, K. Limburg, S. Naeem, R. V. O'Neill, J. Paruelo, R. G. Raskin, P. Sutton and M. van den Belt, 1997. The Value of the World's Ecosystem Services and Natural Capital, *Nature* 387 (15–May): 253–61.

Cox, E., 1994. *The Fuzzy Systems Handbook*. Cambridge, MA: Academic Press.

Cropper, M. L., 1988. A Note on the Extinction of Renewable Resources, *Journal of Environmental Economics and Management* 15: 64–70.

Cropper, M. L. and C. Griffiths, 1994. The Interaction of Population Growth and Environmental Quality, *American Economic Review* 84: 250–54.

Crowards, T., 1997. Nonuse Values and the Environment: Economic and Ethical Motivations, *Environmental Values* 6: 143–67.

Csuti, B., Polasky, S., Williams, P. H., Pressey, R. L., Camm, J. D., Kershaw, M., Kiester, A. R., Downs, B., Hamilton, R., Huso, M. & Sahr, K., 1997. A Comparison of Reserve Selection Algorithms using Data on Terrestrial Vertebrates in Oregon. *Biological Conservation* 80: 83–97.

Cummings, R. G., D. S. Brookshire and W. D. Schulze (editors), 1986. *Valuing Environmental Goods: An Assessment of the Contingent Valuation Method*. Totowa, NJ: Rowman & Allanheld.

Currie, J. M., J. A. Murphy and A. Schmitz, 1971. The Concept of Economic Surplus and its Use in Economic Analysis, *Economic Journal* 81(Dec): 741–91.

Daley, S., 1997. Ban on Sale of Ivory is Eased to Help 3 African Nations, *The New York Times*, June 20, p. A3.

Daly, H. E., 1998. The Return of Lauderdale's Paradox, *Ecological Economics* 25: 21–3.

Daly, H. E. and J. B. Cobb Jr., 1994. *For the Common Good.* 2nd edition. Boston: Beacon Press.

Darwin, C., 1979 (1859). *The Origin of Species.* New York, NY: Gramercy Books.

Dasgupta, P. S., 1993. Natural Resources in an Age of Substitutability. Chapter 23 in *Handbook of Natural Resource and Energy Economics, Vol. 3* edited by Kneese A. V. and J. L. Sweeney. Amsterdam: Elsevier.

Dasgupta, P. S., 1995. The Population Problem: Theory and Evidence, *Journal of Economic Literature* 33: 1879–1902.

Dasgupta, P. S. and G. Heal, 1979. *Economic Theory and Exhaustible Resources.* Welwyn, UK: Cambridge University Press

Dasgupta, P. S., S. Marglin and A. K. Sen, 1972. *Guidelines for Project Evaluation.* New York: United Nations International Development Organization.

Dauvergne, P., 1997. Shadows in the Forest. Japan and the Politics of Timber in Southeast Asia. Cambridge, MA: The MIT Press.

Davidse, W. P., 1995. Fishery regulations and the Creation of Property Rights: The Dutch Case. Paper presented at EAFE Conference, Portsmouth, UK April.

de Beer J, and M. J. McDermott, 1989. The Economic Value of Non-Timber Forest Products in Southeast Asia. Amsterdam: IUCN.

de Groot, R., 1992. *Functions of Nature.* Dordrecht: Wolters-Noordhoff.

Deacon, R., 1994. Deforestation and the Rule of Law in a Cross-Section of Countries, *Land Economics* 70: 414–30

Deaton, A. and J. Muellbauer, 1980. *Economics and Consumer Behavior.* Cambridge: Cambridge University Press.

Delcourt, G. and B. Wilson, 1998. Forest Industry Employment: A Jurisdictional Comparison, *Canadian Public Policy* 24(May): S11–S25.

Diamond, P. A. and J. A. Hausman, 1994. Is Some Number Better than No Number? *Journal of Economic Perspectives* 8(Fall): 45–64.

Dixit, A. K. and R. S. Pindyck, 1994. *Investment under Uncertainty.* Princeton NJ: Princeton University Press.

Dixon, J. A. and P. B. Sherman, 1990. *Economics of Protected Areas.* Washington DC: Island Press.

Downton, M. W., 1995. Measuring Tropical Deforestation: Development of Methods, *Environmental Conservation* 22(Autumn): 229–40.

Drake, L., 1992. The Non-Market Value of the Swedish Agricultural Landscape, *European Review of Agricultural Economics* 19: 351–64.

Dreze, J. and N. Stern, 1987. The Theory of Cost-Benefit Analysis. Chapter 14 in *Handbook of Public Economics* edited by A. J. Auerbach and M. Feldstein. Amsterdam: North-Holland.

Duarte, C. C., 1994. Renewable Resource Market Obeying Difference Equations: Stable Points, Stable Cycles, and Chaos, *Environmental and Resource Economics* 4: 353–81.

Dublin, H. T., T. Milliken and R. F. W. Barnes, 1995. *Four Years After the CITES Ban: Illegal Killing of Elephants, Ivory Trade and Stockpiles.* Report of the IUCN/SSC African Elephant Specialist Group. January. 110pp.

Dupont, D. P., 1990. Rent Dissipation in Restricted Access Fisheries, *Journal of Environmental Economics and Management* 19: 26–44.

Dupont, D. P., 1991. Testing for Input Substitution in a Regulated Fishery, *American Journal of Agricultural Economics* 73: 155–64.

Eberstadt, N., 1995. Population, Food and Income: Global Trends in the Twentieth Century. Chapter 1 in *The True State of the Planet* edited by R. Bailey. New York: The Free Press.

Eckstein, O., 1958. Water Resource Development: The Economics of Project Evaluation. Cambridge: Harvard University Press.

Edwards, J. A., K. C. Gibbs, L. J. Guedry and H. H. Stoevener, 1976. *The Demand for Non_unique Outdoor Recreational Services: Methodological Issues.* Corvallis, OR: Oregon Agricultural Experiment Station. May.

Edwards, S. R., 1995. Conserving Biodiversity. Resource for Our Future. In *The True State of the Planet* (pp. 212–65) edited by R. Bailey. New York, NY: The Free Press.

Eggert, M., 1998. Bioeconomic Analysis and Management, *Environmental and Resource Economics* 11(3–4): 399–411.

Ehrenfeld, D., 1988. Why Put a Value on Biodiversity. Chap. 24 in *Biodiversity* edited by E. O. Wilson with F. M. Peter. Washington: National Academy Press.

Ehrlich, P. R. and A. H. Ehrlich, 1972. *Population. Resources. Environment. Issues in Human Ecology.* 2nd Edition. San Francisco, CA: W. H. Freeman.

Ehrlich, P.R. and A.H. Ehrlich, 1990. *The Population Explosion.* New York: Random House.

Ehrlich, P.R. and A.H. Ehrlich, 1991. *Healing the Planet.* New York: Addison Wesley.

Ehrlich, P. R. and E. O. Wilson, 1991. Biodiversity Studies: Science and Policy, *Science* 253(August 16): 758–62.

Ehui, S. K. and T. W. Hertel, 1989. Deforestation and Agricultural Productivity in the Côte d'Ivoire, *American Journal of Agricultural Economics* 71(August): 703–11.

Ehui, S. K. and T. W. Hertel, 1992. Testing the Impact of Deforestation on Aggregate Agricultural Productivity, *Agriculture, Ecosystems and Environment* 38: 205–18.

Ehui, S. K., T. W. Hertel and P. V. Preckel, 1990. Forest Resource Depletion, Soil Dynamics and Agricultural Dynamics in the Tropics, *Journal of Environmental Economics and Management* 18: 136–54.

Eisgruber, L. M., 1993. Sustainable Develoment, Ethics, and the Endangered Species Act, *Choices* (3rd Q): 4–8.

El Serafy, S., 1989. The Proper Calculation of Income from Depletable Natural Resources. In *Environmental Accounting for Sustainable Development* edited by Y. J. Ahmad, S. El Serafy and E. Lutz. Washington: The World Bank. 100pp.

Ells, A., E. Bulte and G. C. van Kooten, 1997. Uncertainty and Forest Land Use Allocation in British Columbia: Fuzzy Decisions and Imprecise Coefficients, *Forest Science* 43(4): 509–20.

Emsley, J. (editor), 1996. *The Global Warming Debate.* Report of the European Science and Environment Forum. Dorset, UK: Bourne Press Limited. 288pp.

Englin, J. E. and M. S. Klan, 1990. Optimal Taxation: Timber and Externalities, *Journal of Environmental Economics and Management* 18: 263–75.

Epstein, R. A., 1985. *Takings. Private Property and the Power of Eminent Domain.* Cambridge, MA: Harvard University Press.

Erwin, T. L., 1991. An Evolutionary Basis for Conservation Strategies, *Science* 253: 750–52.

FAO, 1987. *Tropical Forestry Action Plan.* Prepared by FAO, the World Bank, World Resource Institute and the UNDP. Rome: Food and Agricultural Organization of the United Nations.

FAO, 1992. *FAO Yearbook: Forest Products, 1981–1992.* FAO Forestry Series No. 27. Rome: Food and Agricultural Organization of the United Nations.

FAO, 1993. *Forest Resources Assessment 1990.* Paper 112. Rome: Food and Agricultural Organization of the United Nations.

FAO, 1997. *State of the World's Forests 1997.* Rome: Food and Agricultural Organization of the United Nations.

Farmer, M. C. and A. Randall, 1998. The Rationality of a Safe Minimum Standard, *Land Economics* 74(August): 287–302.

Farrow, S., 1995. Extinction and Market Forces: Two Case Studies, *Ecological Economics* 13: 115–23

Farzin, Y. H., 1984. The Effect of the Discount Rate on Depletion of Exhaustible Resources, *Journal of Political Economy* 93: 841–51.

Farzin, H., 1992. The Time Path of Scarcity rent in the Theory of Exhaustible Resources, *Economic Journal* 102: 813–30.

Farzin, H., 1995. Technological Change and the Dynamics of Resource Scarcity Measures, *Journal of Environmental Economics and Management* 29: 105–20.

Fedrizzi, M., 1987. Introduction to Fuzzy Sets and Possibility Theory. In *Optimization Models Using Fuzzy Sets and Possibility Theory* edited by J. Kacprzyk and S. A. Orlovski. Dordecht, Netherlands: D. Reidel Publishing Co.

Feeney, D., S. Hanna and A. F. McEvoy, 1996. Questioning the Assumptions of the 'Tragedy of the Commons' Model of Fisheries, *Land Economics* 72: 187–205.

Fisher, A. C., 1981. *Resource and Environmental Economics*. Cambridge, UK: Cambridge University Press.

Fisher, A. C., 1988. Key Aspects of Species Extinction: Habitat Loss and Overexploitation. In *Environmental Resources and Applied Welfare Economics* (pp. 59–69) edited by V. K. Smith. Washington: Resources for the Future.

Fisher, A. C., 1996. The Conceptual Underpinnings of the Contingent Valuation Method, in D. J. Bjornstad and J. R. Kahn, eds., pp. 19–37, *The Contingent Valuation of Environmental Resources*, Cheltenham: Edward Elgar.

Fisher, A. C. and W. M. Hanemann, 1986. Environmental Damages and Option Values, *Natural Resource Modeling* 1: 111–24.

Fisher, A. C. and W. M. Hanemann, 1990. Option Value: Theory and Measurement, *European Review of Agricultural Economics* 17: 167–80.

Fisher, A. C. and J. V. Krutilla, 1985. Economics of Nature Preservation. Ch. 4 in *Handbook of Natural Resource and Energy Economics*, Vol. I edited by A. V. Kneese and J. L. Sweeney. Amsterdam: North Holland.

Flaaten, O. and E. Kolsvik, 1996. On the Optimal Harvesting of a Wild Population when the Opportunity Cost of Feed is Considered. University of Tromso, Discussion Paper.

Flaaten, O. and K. Stollery, 1996. The Economic Cost of Biological Predation: Theory and Application to the Case of the Northeast Atlantic Minke Whale's, *Balaenoptera acutorostrata*) Consumption of Fish, *Environmental and Resource Economics* 8: 75–95.

Flowerdew, A. D. J., 1972. Choosing a Site for the Third London Airport: The Roskill Commission's Approach. Chapter 17 in *Cost-Benefit Analysis* edited by R. Layard. Harmondsworth, UK: Penguin Books.

Folmer, H., P. van Mouche and S. Ragland, 1993. Interconnected Games and International Environmental Problems, *Environmental and Resource Economics* 3: 313–35.

Forse, B., 1987. Elephant Decline Blamed on Ivory Poachers, *New Scientist*, June 18, p. 33.

Freeman, A. M. III, 1979a. *The Benefits of Environmental Improvement. Theory and Practice.* Baltimore: The Johns Hopkins Univ. Press.

Freeman, A. M. III, 1979b. Approaches to Measuring Public Goods Demands, *American Journal of Agricultural Economics* 61(December): 915–20.

Freeman, A. M. III, 1993. The Measurement of Environmental and Resource Values: Theory and Methods. Washington, DC: Resources for the Future.

Freeman, A. M. III, 1995. Hedonic Pricing Methods. Chapter 30 in *The Handbook of Environmental Economics* edited by D. W. Bromley. Oxford UK: Basil Blackwell Ltd.

Furubotn, Erik G. and Rudof Richter, 1997. *Institutions and Economic Theory. The Contribution of the New Institutional Economics.* Ann Arbor, MI: University of Michigan Press.

Gaffney, M.M., 1965. Soil Depletion and Land Rent, *Natural Resources Journal* 4(January): 537–57.

Gallant, R. A., 1981. On the Bias in Flexible Functional Forms and an Essentially Unbiased Form: The Fourier Flexible Form, *Journal of Econometrics* 15: 211–45.

Garner, J., 1991. Never Under the Table. A Story of British Columbia's Forests and Government Mismanagement. Nanaimo BC: Cinnabar Press.

George, H., 1879 (1929). Progress and Poverty: An Inquiry into the Cause of Industrial Depression and of Increase of Want with Increase in Wealth. New York: Modern Library.

Georgescu-Roegen, N., 1966. *Analytical Economics. Issues and Problems*. Cambridge MA: Harvard University Press.

Georgescu-Roegen, N., 1968. Utility. In *International Encyclopedia of the Social Sciences* edited by David L. Sills. Vol. 16. New York: Macmillan and The Free Press. pp. 236–67.

Gillis, M., 1988. Indonesia: Public Policies, Resource Management, and the Tropical Forest. In *Public Policies and the Misuse of Forest Resources* (pp. 43–113) edited by R. Repetto and M. Gillis. Cambridge: Cambridge University Press.

Gittinger, J. P., 1982. *Economic Analysis of Agricultural Projects*. 2nd Edition. Baltimore: The Johns Hopkins University Press.

Gleick, J., 1987. *Chaos. Making a New Science*. New York: Viking (Penguin Group).

Gordon, H. S., 1954. The Economic Theory of a Common Property Resource: The Fishery, *Journal of Political Economy* 62: 124–42.

Gould, S. J., 1995. *Dinosaur in a Haystack*. New York: Harmony Books.

Government of Canada, 1990. *Canada's Green Plan*, Ottawa: Minister of Supply and Services Canada.

Government of Canada, 1991. *The State of Canada's Environment*. Ottawa: Minister of Supply and Services Canada.

Gowdy, J. M., 1997. The Value of Biodiversity: Markets, Society and Ecosystems, *Land Economics* 73: 25–41.

Grafton, R. Q. and J. Silva-Echenique, 1997. How to Manage Nature? Strategies, Predator-Prey Models, and Chaos, *Marine Resource Economics* 12: 127–43.

Grafton, R. Q., R. W. Lynch and H. W. Nelson, 1998. British Columbia's Stumpage System: Economic and Trade Policy Implications, *Canadian Public Policy* 24(May): S41–50.

Graham-Tomasi, T., 1995. Quasi-Option Value. Chap. 26 in *The Handbook of Environmental Economics* edited by D. W. Bromley. Cambridge MA: Basil Blackwell Publishers.

Grainger, A., 1993. *Controlling Tropical Deforestation*. London: Earthscan Publications

Graves, P. E., R. L. Sexton, D. R. Lee, and S. Jackstadt, 1994. Alternative Fishery Management Policies: Monitoring Costs versus Catch Limits, *Environmental and Resource Economics* 4: 595–8.

Gregory, R., S. Lichtenstein and P. Slovic, 1993. Valuing Environmental Resources: A Constructive Approach, *Journal of Risk and Uncertainty* 7(Oct): 177–97.

Gribbin, J., 1985. In Search of the Double Helix. Darwin, DNA and Beyond. Aldershot: Wildwood House.

Grizzle, R. E. and C. B Barrett, 1998. The One Body of Christian Environmentalism, *Zygon* 33(June): 233–53.

Grossman, G. M., 1995. Pollution and Growth: What do we Know? In *The Economics of Sustainable Development* (pp. 977–87) edited by I. Goldin and L. Winters. OECD Publication. Cambridge, UK: Cambridge University Press.

Grossman, G. M. and A. B. Krueger, 1995. Economic Growth and the Environment, *Quarterly Journal of Economics* 112: 353–78.

Guy, R. D. and A. Benowicz, 1998. Can Afforestation Contribute to a Reduction in Canada's Net CO_2 Emissions? Report prepared for the CPPA. Department of Forest Sciences, UBC. Mimeograph. March 25. 21pp.

Haener, M. K. and M. K. Luckert, 1998. Forest Certification: Economic Issues and Welfare Implications, *Canadian Public Policy* 24(May): S83–94.

Hagen, D. A., J. W. Vincent and P. G. Welle, 1992. Benefits of Preserving Old-Growth Forests and the Spotted Owl, *Contemporary Policy Issues* 10(April): 13–26.

Hall, J. A., 1985. Powers and Liberties. The Causes and Consequences of the Rise of the West. London: Penguin Books.

Hall, D. and J. Hall, 1984. Concepts and Measures of Natural Resource Scarcity, *Journal of Environmental Economics and Management* 11: 363–79.

Halstead J. M., B. E. Lindsay and G. . M. Brown, 1991. Use of the Tobit Model in Contingent Valuation: Experimental Evidence from the Pemigewasset Wilderness Area, *Journal of Environmental Management* 33: 79–89.

Halvorsen, R. and T. Smith, 1991. A Test of the Theory of Exhaustible Resources, *Quarterly Journal of Economics* 56: 123–46.

Hamilton, G., 1997. Frustrated silviculture contractors get less work, *Vancouver Sun*, Friday, February 7. pp. D1, D19.

Hamilton, J. R., N. K. Whittlesey, M. H. Robison and J. Ellis, 1991. Economic Impacts, Value Added, and Benefits in Regional Project Analysis, *American Journal of Agricultural Economics* 73(May): 334–44.

Hanemann, W. M., 1984. Welfare Evaluations in Contingent Valuation Experiments with Discrete Responses, *American Journal of Agricultural Economics* 66: 332–41.

Hanemann, W. M., 1991. Willingness to Pay and Willingness to Accept: How Much can they Differ? *American Economic Review* 81(June): 635–47.

Hanemann, W. M., 1994. Valuing the Environment through Contingent Valuation, *Journal of Economic Perspectives* 8(Fall): 19–44.

Hanemann, W. M. and B. Kriström, 1995. Preference Uncertainty, Optimal Designs and Spikes. Chapter 4 in *Current Issues in Environmental Economics* edited by P. -O. Johansson, B. Kriström and K. -G. Maler. Manchester UK: Manchester University Press.

Hanley, N., J. F. Shogren and B. White, 1997. *Environmental Economics in Theory and Practice*. New York: Oxford University Press.

Hanley, N., R. E. Wright and V. Adamowicz, 1998. Using Choice Experiments to Value the Environment, *Environmental and Resource Economics* 11(Special): 413–28.

Hansen, E. A., 1993. Soil Carbon Sequestration beneath Hybrid Poplar Plantation in the North Central United States, *Biomass and Bioenergy* 5(6): 431–6.

Hanski I. and M. Gilpin, 1991. Metapopulation Dynamics: Brief History and Conceptual Domain, *Biological Journal of the Linnaen Society* 42: 3–16.

Harberger, A. C., 1971. Three Basic Postulates for Applied Welfare Economics, *Journal of Economic Literature* 9(September): 785–97.

Harberger, A. C., 1972. *Project Evaluation. Collected Papers*. Chicago: University of Chicago Press.

Hardaker, J. B., R. B. M. Huirne and J. R. Anderson, 1997. *Coping with Risk in Agriculture*. Wallingford, UK: CAB International.

Harland, D., 1988. The Ivory Chase Moves On, *New Scientist*, January 7, pp. 30–31.

Harmon, M. E., W. K. Ferrell and J. F. Franklin, 1990. Effects on Carbon Storage of Conversion of Old-Growth Forests to Young Forests. *Science* 247: 699–702.

Harris, M., 1998. *Lament for an Ocean*. Toronto: McClelland & Stewart.

Harrison, G. W., 1989. Theory and Misbehaviour of First-Price Auctions, *American Economic Review* 79(September): 749–62.

Harrison, G. W. and B. Kriström, 1995. On the Interpretation of Responses in Contingent Valuation Surveys. Chapter 3 in *Current Issues in Environmental Economics* edited by P. -O. Johansson, B. Kriström and K. -G. Maler. Manchester UK: Manchester University Press.

Hart, Oliver, Andrei Shleifer and Robert W. Wishny, 1997. The Proper Scope of Government: Theory and an Application to Prisons, *Quarterly Journal of Economics* CXII(November): 1127–61.

Hartman, R., 1976. The Harvesting Decision when a Standing Forest has Value. *Economic Inquiry* 16: 52–8.

Hartwick, J. M., 1977. Intergenerational Equity and the Investing of Rents from Exhaustible Resources, *American Economic Review* 66: 972–4.

Hartwick, J. M. and N. Olewiler, 1998. *The Economics of Natural Resource Use*. Second Edition. New York: Harper and Row.

Hastings, N. A. J., 1973. Dynamic Programming with Management Applications. London: Butterworths.

Hauser, A., G. C. van Kooten and L. Cain, 1994. Water Quality and the Abbotsford Aquifer: Overview and Cost-Benefit Analysis of Livestock Waste Disposal Alternatives using Contingent Valuation Methods. Agricultural Economics Working Paper #94–2. Vancouver: UBC. 41pp.

Hausman, J. A. (editor), 1993. *Contingent Valuation: A Critical Assessment*. Amsterdam: North Holland.

Heerink N. B. M, J. F. M. Helming, O. J. Kuik, A. Kuyvenhoven and H. Verbruggen, 1993. International Trade and the Environment. Wageningen Economic Studies 30. Wageningen Agricultural University, Netherlands.

Henry, C., 1974. Investment Decisions under Uncertainty: The Irreversibility Effect, *American Economic Review* 64: 1006–12.

Herriges, J. A. and C. L. Kling, 1997. The Performance of Nested Logit Models when Welfare Estimation is the Goal, *American Journal of Agricultural Economics* 79(August): 792–802.

Hertzler, G. and M. Gomera, 1998. Has the Convention on International Trade in Endangered Species Saved the African Elephant? Paper presented at the First World Conference of Environmental and Resource Economists, Venice, June 25–7.

Heywood, V. H. and S. N. Stuart, 1992. Species Extinctions in Tropical Forests. In *Tropical Deforestation and Species Extinction* (pp. 91–117) edited by T. C. Whitmore and J. A. Sayer. London: Chapman & Hall.

Heywood V. H., G. M. Mace, R. M. May and S. N. Stuart, 1994. Uncertainties in Extinction Rates, *Nature* 368: 105.

Hicks, J. R., 1939. The Foundations of Welfare Economics, *Economic Journal* 49(December): 696–712.

Hilborn, R., C. J. Walters and D. Ludwig, 1995. Sustainable Exploitation of Renewable Resources, *Annual Review of Ecological Systems* 26: 45–67.

Holling, C. S., 1973. Resilience and Stability of Ecological Systems, *Annual Review of Ecological Systems* 4:1–24.

Holling, C. S., D. W. Schindler, B. W. Walker, and J. Roughgarden, 1995. Biodiversity in the Functioning of Ecosystems: An Ecological Synthesis. In *Biodiversity Loss* (pp. 44–83) edited by C. Perrings, K. -G. Maler, C. Folke, C. S. Holling and B. -O. Jansson. New York, NY: Cambridge University Press.

Homma, A. K. O., 1994. Plant Extractavism in the Amazon: Limitations and Possibilities. In *Extractavism in the Brazilian Amazon: Perspectives on Regional Development* (pp. 34–57) edited by M. Clüsener-Godt and I. Sachs. Paris: MAB Digest 18, UNESCO.

Horan, R. D. and J. S. Shortle, 1999. Optimal Management of Multiple Resource Stocks: An Application to Minke Whales, *Environmental and Resource Economics* 13(June): 435–58. .

Horan R., J. S. Shortle and E. H. Bulte, 1999. Renewable Resource Policy when Distributional Impacts Matter, *Environmental and Resource Economics* In Press.

Hotelling H., 1931. The Economics of Exhaustible Resources, *Journal of Political Economy* 39: 137–75.

Houghton, J. T., L. G. Meira Filho, B. A. Callander, N. Harris, A. Kattenberg and K. Maskell (editors), 1996. *Climate Change 1995. The Science of Climate Change*. Cambridge, UK: Cambridge University Press.

Houghton, R. A., 1993. The Role of the World's Forests in Global Warming. In *The Worlds Forests for the Future: Their Use and Conservation* edited by K. Ramakrishna and G. M. Woodwell. New Haven: Yale University Press.

Howarth, R. B. and R. B. Norgaard, 1993. Intergenerational Changes and the Social Discount Rate, *Environmental and Resource Economics* 3(4): 337–58.

Howarth, R. B. and R. B. Norgaard, 1995. Intergenerational Choices under Global Environmental Change. Chapter 6 in *Handbook of Environmental Economics* edited by D. W. Bromley. Oxford: Basil Blackwell.

Howe, C. W., 1979. *Natural Resource Economics*. Toronto: John Wiley & Sons.

Hueting, R., 1989. Correcting National Income for Environmental Losses: Towards a Practical Solution. In *Environmental Accounting for Sustainable Development* edited by Y. Ahmed, S. El Serafy and E. Lutz. Washington, DC: The World Bank.

Hueting, R., 1992. The Economic Functions of the Environment. In *Rela-Life Economics* edited by P. Ekins and M. Max-Neef. London, UK: Routledge and Kegan Paul.

Hughes, J. B., G. C. Daily and P. R. Ehrlich, 1997. Population Diversity: Its Extent and Extinction, *Science* 278: 689–92.

Hyde, W. F. and R. A. Sedjo, 1992. Managing Tropical Forests: Reflections on the Rent Distribution Discussion, *Land Economics* 68(3): 343–50.

Hyde, W. F. and J. E. Seve. 1991. Malawi: A Rapid Economic Appraisal of Smallholder Response to Severe Deforestation. In *Pre-proceedings of Working Groups S6. 03–03 and S6. 10–00; Meetings at the 10th World Congress* edited by R. Haynes, P. Harou and J. Mirowski. Paris, France: International Union of Forest Research Organizations.

IBRD, 1992. World Development Report 1992: Development and the Environment. New York: Oxford University Press.

IBRD, 1997. World Bank Development Report 1997: The State in a Changing World. Washington: Oxford University Press.

Innes, R., S. Polasky and J. Tschirhart, 1998. Takings, Compensation and Endangered Species Protection on Private Lands, *Journal of Economic Perspectives* 12(3): 35–52.

International Monetary Fund, 1995. *International Financial Statistics Yearbook*. Washington DC: IMF.

Irwin, J. R., P. Slovic, S. Lichtenstein, and G. H. McClelland, 1993. Preference Reversals and the Measurement of Environmental Values, *Journal of Risk and Uncertainty* 6(Jan): 5–18.

Jepma, C. J., 1995. Tropical Deforestation. A Socio-economic Approach. London: Earthscan.

Johansson, P. -O., 1987. *The Economic Theory and Measurement of Economic Benefits*, Cambridge: Cambridge University Press.

Johansson, P. -O., 1993. *Cost-Benefit Analysis and Environmental Change*. Cambridge: Cambridge University Press.

Johansson-Stenman, O., 1998. The Importance of Ethics in Environmental Economics, *Environmental and Resource Economics* 11: 429–42.

Just, R. E., D. L. Hueth and A. Schmitz, 1982. *Applied Welfare Economics and Public Policy*. Englewood Cliffs, N. J. : Prentice-Hall.

Kahneman, D. and J. L. Knetsch, 1992a. Valuing Public Goods: The Purchase of Moral Satisfaction, *Journal of Environmental Economics and Management* 22:57–70.

Kahneman, D. and J. L. Knetsch, 1992b. Contingent Valuation and the Value of Public Goods: Reply, *Journal of Environmental Economics and Management* 22: 90–94.

Kahneman, D. and I Ritov, 1994. Determinants of Stated Willingness to Pay for Public Goods: A Study in the Headline Method, *Journal of Risk and Uncertainty* 9: 5–38.

Kahneman, D. and A. Tversky, 1979. Prospect Theory: An Analysis of Decisions under Risk, *Econometrica* 47: 263–91.

Kahneman, D., J. L. Knetsch and R. H. Thaler, 1990. Experimental Tests of the Endowment Effect and the Coase Theorem, *Journal of Political Economy* 98(December): 1325–48.

Kaimowitz, D. and A. Angelsen, 1997. *A Guide to Economic Models of Deforestation*. Jakarta, Indonesia: Centre of International Forestry Research, Mimeograph. 96pp.

Kaldor, N., 1939. Welfare Propositions of Economics and Interpersonal Comparisons of Utility, *Economic Journal* 49(September): 549–52.

Kamien, M. I. and N. L. Schwartz, 1994. Dynamic Optimization: The Calculus of Variations and Optimal Control Theory in Economics and Management. Amsterdam: North-Holland.

Kanninen, B. J., 1993. Optimal Experimental Design for Double-Bounded Dichotomous Choice Contingent Valuation, *Land Economics* 69: 138–46.

Kattenberg, A., G. Giogi, H. Grassl, G. A. Meehl, J. F. B. Mitchell, R. J. Stouffer, T. Tokioka, A. J. Weaver and T. M. L. Wigley 1996) Climate Models – Projections of Future Climate. Chapter 6 in *Climate Change 1995. The Science of Climate Change* edited by J. T. Houghton, L. G. Meira Filho, B. A. Callander, N. Harris, A. Kattenberg and K. Maskell. Cambridge, UK: Cambridge University Press.

Kealy, H. J. and R. W. Turner, 1993. Test of the Equality of Close-Ended and Open-ended Contingent Valuations, *American Jouirnal of Agricultural Economics* 75: 321–31.

Kellert, S. R., 1995. Concepts of Nature East and West. In *Reinventing Nature: Responses to Post-Modern Deconstruction* (pp. 103–21) edited by M. E. Soulé and G. Lease. Washington DC: Island Press.

Kelly, A. C., 1988, Economic Consequences of population Change in the Third World, *Journal of Economic Literature* 26: 1685–728.

Kennedy, J. O. S., 1986. *Dynamic Programming. Applications to Agriculture and Natural Resources*. London and New York: Elsevier Applied Science Publishers.

Kenya Wildlife Service, 1990. *A Policy Framework and Development Program, 1991–96.* Nairobi: Government of Kenya. 220pp.

Khanna J. and J. Harford, 1996. The Ivory Trade Ban: Is it Effective? *Ecological Economics* 19: 147–55.

Kinyua, P. I. D., 1998. Game Cropping in Kenya: Dynamic Optimization Analysis of Policy Options. Unpublished Ph. D. Dissertation. Vancouver, BC: UBC.

Klir, G. and T. Folger, 1988. *Fuzzy Sets, Uncertainty, and Information*. Englewood Cliffs, New Jersey: Prentice Hall.

Knetsch, J., 1989. The Endowment Effect and Evidence of Nonreversible Indifference Curves, *American Economic Review* 79(December): 1277–84.

Knetsch, J. L., 1993. Resource Economics: Persistent Conventions and Contrary Evidence. Chapter 13 in *Forestry and the Environment: Economic Perspectives* edited by W. L Adamowicz, W. White and W. E. Phillips. Wallingford UK: CAB International.

Knetsch, J. L., 1995. Asymmetric Valuation of Gains and Losses and Preference Order Assumptions, *Economic Inquiry* 33: 134–41.

Knetsch, J. L., 2000. Behavioural Economics and Current Environmental Valuations: Findings, Lessons and an Alternative. In *International Yearbook of Environmental and Resource Economics 2000/2001* edited by H. Folmer and T. Tietenberg. Aldershot, UK: Edward Elgar. In press. 36pp.

Knetsch, J. L., F-F. Tang and R. H. Thaler, 1998. The Endowment Effect and Repeated Market Trials: Is the Vickery Auction Demand Revealing? Working Paper, University of Chicago.

Knight, F. H., 1944. Realism and Relevance in the Theory of Demand, *Journal of Political Economy* 52(December): 289–318.

Korotov, A. V. and T. J. Peck, 1993. Forest Resources of the Industrialized Countries: An ECE/FAO Assessment, *Unisylva* 434:

Kosko, B., 1992. *Neural Networks and Fuzzy Systems*. Englewood Cliffs, NJ: Prentice Hall.

Kramer, R. A. and D. E. Mercer, 1997. Valuing a Global Environmental Good: U. S. Residents' Willingness to Pay to Protect Tropical Rain Forests. *Land Economics* 73(May): 196–210.

Krcmar-Nozic, B. Stennes, G. C. van Kooten and I. Vertinsky, 1999. Uncertainty and Climate Change: An Application of Fuzzy Multiple Objective Decision Making FEPA Working Paper. Vancouver: UBC.

Kriström, B., 1997. Spike Models in Contingent Valuation, *American Journal of Agricultural Economics* 79(August): 1013–23.

Krutilla, J. V., 1967. Conservation Re-Considered, *American Economic Review* 57: 777–86.

Kummar, D. and C. S. Sham, 1994. The Causes of Tropical Deforestation: A Quantitative Analysis and Case Study from the Philippines. Chapter 10 in *The Causes of Tropical Deforestation* edited by D. W. Pearce and K. Brown. London: UCL Press.

Kuusela, K., 1994. *Forest Resources in Europe*. European Forest Institute Report. Cambridge, UK: Cambridge University Press.

Kuznets, S., 1955. Economic Growth and Income Inequality, *American Economic Review* 49: 1–28.

Lande, R., S. Engen and B. Saether, 1994. Optimal Harvesting, Economic Discounting and Extinction Risk in Fluctuating Populations, *Nature* 372: 88–90.

Larmour, P., 1979. The Concept of Rent in 19th Century Economic Thought. Ricardo, Mill, Marx, Walras, and Marshall. Resources Paper No. 36. Vancouver: Department of Economics, Univ. of British Columbia. May. P. 45.

Larson, D. M., 1993. On Measuring Existence Value, *Land Economics* 69(November): 377–88.

Layard, R., 1972. Introduction. In *Cost-Benefit Analysis* (pp. 9–70) edited by R. Layard. Harmondsworth, UK: Penguin Books.

Leader-Williams, N., S. D. Albon and P. S. M. Berry, 1990. Illegal Exploitation of Black Rhinoceros and Elephant Populations; Patterns of Decline, Law Enforcement and Patrol Effort in Luangwa Valley, Zambia, *Journal of Applied Ecology* 27: 1055–87.

Leakey, R. and R. Lewin, 1995. *The Sixth Extinction*. London: Weidenfeld and Nicolson.

Leonard, D. and N. Van Long, 1992. *Optimal Control Theory and Static Optimization in Economics*, Cambridge: Cambridge University Press.

Lesser, J. A., D. E. Dodds and Z. O. Zerbe, Jr., 1997. *Environmental Economics and Policy*. Reading, MA: Addison-Wesley.

Levins, R., 1969. Some Demographic and Genetic Consequences of Environmental Heterogeneity for Biological Control, *Bulletin of the Entomological Society of America* 15: 237–40

Levins, R., 1970. Extinction. In: *Some Mathematical Problems in Biology* (pp. 77–107) edited by M. Gerstenhaber. Providence, RI: American Mathematical Society.

Li, C-Z., 1996. Semiparametric Estimation of the Binary Choice Model for Contingent Valuation, *Land Economics* 72(November): 462–73.

Li, C-Z. and L. Mattsson, 1995. Discrete Choice under Preference Uncertainty: an Improved Structural Model for Contingent Valuation, *Journal of Environmental Economics and Management* 28: 256–69.

Li, S., 1989. Measuring the Fuzzines of Human Thoughts: An Application of Fuzzy Sets to Sociological Research, *Journal of Mathematical Sociology* 14(1): 67–84.

Lind, R., 1990. Federal Discount Rate Policy, The Shadow Price of Capital and Challenges for Reforms, *Journal of Environmental Economics and Management* 18: 29–50.

Lindsay, K., 1986. Trading Elephants for Ivory, *New Scientist*, November 6, pp. 48–52.

Lipsey, R. G., 1996. *Economic Growth, Technological Change, and Canadian Economic Policy*. Benefactors Lecture, November 6, Vancouver. Toronto: C. D. Howe Institute. 87pp.

Little, I. M. D., 1957. *A Critique of Welfare Economics*. New York: Oxford University Press.

Little, I. M. D. and J. A. Mirrlees, 1974. *Project Appraisal and Planning for Developing Countries*. New York: Basic Books.

Loewenstein, G. and D. Prelec, 1991. Negative Time Preferences, *American Economic Review* 81: 347–52.

Loomis, J. and E. Ekstrand, 1998. Alternative Approaches for Incorporating Respondent Uncertainty when Estimating Willingness to Pay: The Case of the Mexican Spotted Owl, *Ecological Economics* 27: 29–41.

Loomis, J. B. and K. Giraud, 1997. Economic Benefits of Threatened and Endangered Fish and Wildlife Species: Literature Review and Case Study of Values for Preventing Extinction of Fish Species. Fort Collins, CO: Department of Agricultural and Resource Economics, Colorado State University. Mimeograph. 45pp.

Loomis, J. B. and D. M. Larson, 1994. Total Economic Values of Increasing Gray Whale Populations: Results from a Contingent Valuation Survey of Visitors and Households, *Marine Resource Economics* 9: 275–86.

Loomis, J. B. and D. S. White, 1996. Economic Benefits of Rare and Endangered Species: Summary and Meta-analysis, *Ecological Economics* 18: 197–206.

Lopez, R., 1998. Common Property Resources and the Farm Household, *Environmental and Resource Economics* 11: 443–58.

Lotka, A. J., 1925. *Elements of Physical Biology*. Baltimore: Williams and Wilkins.

Luckert, M. K. and J. T. Bernard, 1993. What is the Value of Standing Timber?: Difficulties in Merging Theory with Reality, *The Forestry Chronicle* 69: 680–5.

Luckert, M. K. and D. Haley, 1993. Canadian Forest Tenures and the Silvicultural Investment Behavior of Rational Firms, *Canadian Journal of Forest Research* 23: 1060–4.

Ludwig, D., R. Hilborn and C. Walters, 1993. Uncertainty, Resource Exploitation and Conservation: Lessons from History, *Science* 260: 17–36

Lugo, A., J. Parrotta and S. Brown, 1993. Loss of Species Caused by Tropical Deforestation and Their Recovery through Management, *Ambio* 22(2–3): 106–9.

MacArthur, R. and E. O. Wilson, 1967. *The Theory of Island Biogeography*. Princeton NJ: Princeton University Press.

Maddala, G. S., 1983. *Limited-Dependent and Qualitative Variables in Econometrics*. Cambridge: Cambridge University Press.

Malik, A., 1984. Protected Areas and Political Reality, In *National Parks, Conservation and Development* edited by J. A. McNeely and K. R. Miller. Washington, DC: Smithsonian Institution Press.

Malthus, T. R., 1815. An Inquiry into the Nature and Progress of Rent and the Principles by Which it is Regulated. London: John Murray.

Mann, C., 1991. Extinction: Are Ecologists Crying Wolf? *Science* 253 (Aug. 16): 736-8.

Mann, C. and M. L. Plummer, 1992. The Butterfly Problem, *Atlantic Monthly* 269(1): 47–70.

Mann, C. and M. L. Plummer, 1995. *Noah's Choice*. New York: Alfred A. Knopf.

Manne, A. S., 1979. ETA Macro. In *Advances in the Economics of Energy and Resources. Volume 2* edited by R. S. Pindyck. Greenwich, NJ: JAI Press.

Marchak, M. P., 1995. *Logging the Globe*. Montreal and Kingston: McGill-Queen's University Press.

Marglin, S. A., 1963. The Social Rate of Discount and the Optimal Rate of Investment, *Quarterly Journal of Economics* 77: 95–111.

Margolick, M. and R. S. Uhler, 1986. The Economic Impact of Remvoing Log Export Restrictions in British Columbia. FEPA Report 86–2. Vancouver: Forest Economics and Policy Analysis Research Unit.

Mattey, J. P., 1990. The Timber Bubble That Burst: Government Policy and the Bailout of 1984. New York: Oxford University Press.

Maurice, C. and C. W. Smithson, 1984. *The Doomsday Myth*. Stanford, CA: Hoover Institution Press.

May, R. M., 1994, The Economics of Extinction, *Nature* 372: 42–3

May, R. M. and J. Seger, 1986. Ideas in Ecology, *American Scientist* 74: 256–67

Mayr, E., 1982. The Growth of Biological Thought: Diversity, Evolution, and Inheritance. Cambridge MA: Belknap Press.

McConnell, K. E., 1997. Does Altruism Undermine Existence Value? *Journal of Environmental Economics and Management* 32: 22–37.

McIntosh, R. A., M. L. Alexander, D. C. Bebb, C. Ridley-Thomas, D. Perrin and T. A. Simons, 1997. *The Financial State of the Forest Industry and Delivered Wood Cost Drivers*. Report prepared for the BC Ministry of Forests. Vancouver: KPMG. 51pp. plus App.

McKean, R. N., 1958. *Efficiency in Government Through Systems Analysis*. New York: John Wiley and Sons.

McKenzie, G. W., 1983. *Measuring Economic Welfare: New Methods*. Cambridge: Cambridge University Press.

McKenzie, G. W. and S. Thomas, 1984. The Econometric Modelling of Aggregate Consumer Behaviour, *European Economic Review* 25 (August): 355–72.

McNeely, J. A., M. Gadgil, C. Leveque, C. Padoch, K. Redford and 64 others. 1995. Human Influences on Biodiversity. Chapter 11 in *Global Biodiversity Assessment* edited by V. H. Heywood and R. T. Watson. UN Environmental Program. Cambridge, UK: Cambridge University Press.

McNeill, D. and P. Freiberger, 1993. *Fuzzy Logic*. New York: Touchstone.

Mead, W. J. 1967. *Competition and Oligopsony in the Douglas Fir Lumber Industry*. Los Angeles, CA: University of California Press.

Meadows, D. H., D. L. Meadows, J. Randers and W. W. Behrens III, 1972. *The Limits to Growth*. New York: Universe Books.

Meecham C. J., 1997. How the Tiger Lost its Stripes: An Exploration into the Endangerment of a Species, Orlando: Harcourt Brace.

Mendelsohn, R., 1994. Property Rights and Tropical Deforestation, *Oxford Economic Papers* 46: 750–56.

Mendelsohn, R. and M. J. Balick, 1995. The Value Of Undiscovered Pharmaceuticals In Tropical Forests, *Economic Botany* 49: 223–28.

Metrick, A. and M. L. Weitzman, 1996. Patterns of Behavior in Endangered Species Preservation, *Land Economics* 72(1): 1–16.

Metrick, A. and M. L. Weitzman, 1998. Conflicts and Choices in Biodiversity Preser-vation, *Journal of Economic Perspectives* 12(3): 21–34.

Mill, J. S., 1961 (1848). Principles of Political Economy with some of their Applications to Social Philosophy edited by Sir W. J. Ashley. New York: Kelley.

Miller, R. E., 1979. Dynamic Optimization and Economic Applications. New York: McGraw-Hill.

Milliken, T., 1997. The Status of Ivory Stocks in Africa 1990–1996, *Traffic Bulletin* 16(3): 93–106.

Milner-Gulland E. J., 1993. An Econometric Analysis of Consumer Demand for Ivory and Rhino Horn, *Environmental and Resource Economics* 3: 73–95.

Milner-Gulland, E. J. and N. Leader-Williams, 1992a. Illegal Exploitation of Wildlife. Chapter 9 in *Economics for the Wilds* edited by T. M. Swanson and E. B. Barbier. London: Earthscan.

Millner-Gulland, E. J. and N. Leader-Williams, 1992b. A Model of Incentives for the Illegal Exploitation of Black Rhinos and Elephants: Poaching Pays in Luangwa Valley, Zambia, *Journal of Applied Ecology* 29: 388–401.

Ministry of Agriculture and Fisheries (France), 1995. *Forestry Policy in France*. Paris: Countryside and Forest Department.

Mishan, E. J., 1959. Rent as a Measure of Welfare Change, *American Economic Review* 49: 386–95.

Mishan, E. J., 1971. *Cost-Benefit Analysis*. London: George Allen and Unwin Ltd.

Mishan, E. J., 1972 (1970). What is Wrong with Roskill? Chapter 18 in *Cost-Benefit Analysis* edited by R. Layard. Middlesex, UK: Penguin Books.

Mishan, E. J., 1981. *Introduction to Normative Economics*. New York: Oxford University Press.

Mitchell, R. C. and R. T. Carson, 1989. *Using Surveys to Value Public Goods: The Contingent Valuation Method*. Washington, DC: Resources for the Future.

Mitchell, R. C. and R. T. Carson, 1995. Current Issues in the Design, Administration, and Analysis of Contingent Valuation Surveys. Chapter 3 in *Current Issues in Environmental Economics* edited by P. -O. Johansson, B. Kriström and K. -G. Maler. Manchester UK: Manchester University Press.

Montgomery, C. A. and D. M. Adams, 1995. Optimal Timber Management Policies. Chapter 17 in *The Handbook of Environmental Economics* edited by D. W. Bromley. Oxford, UK: Basil Blackwell.

Montgomery, C., G. M. Brown, and D. M. Adams, 1994. The Marginal Cost of Species Preservation: The Northern Spotted Owl, *Journal of Environmental Economics and Management* 26: 111–28.

Moore, P., 1995. Energy and Power Sources, *The Wall Street Journal Europe*, Oct. 20–21, p. 10.

Moran, D. and Pearce, D., 1997. The Economics of Biodiversity. Chapter 4 in *The International Yearbook of Environmental and Resource Economics 1997/1998* edited by H. Folmer and T. Tietenberg. Aldershot, UK: Edward Elgar.

More, T. A., J. R. Averill and T. H. Stevens, 1996. Values and Economics in Environmental Management: A Perspective and Critique, *Journal of Environmental Management* 48: 397–409.

Munro, A., 1997. Economics and Biological Evolution, *Environmental and Resource Economics* 9: 429–49.

Munro, G. R., 1990. The Optimal Management of Transboundary Fisheries: Game Theoretic Considerations, *Natural Resource Modeling*, 4: 403–26.

Munro, G. R and A. D. Scott, 1985. The Economics of Fisheries Management. Chapter 14 in *Handbook of Natural Resources and Energy Economics* (Vol. 2) edited by A. V. Kneese and J. L. Sweeney. Amsterdam: Elsevier.

Munro, G., T. McDorman and R. McKelvey, 1998. Transboundary Fishery Resources and the Canada-United States Pacific Salmon Treaty, *Canadian-American Public Policy*, Number 33, February, 48pp.

Murray, J. A. (ed.), 1993. *Wild Africa: Three Centuries of Nature Writing from Africa,* New York: Oxford University Press.

Murty, M. N., 1994. Management of Common Property Resources: Limits to Voluntary Action, *Environmental and Resource Economics* 4: 581–94.

Musgrave, R. A., 1969. Cost-Benefit Analysis and the Theory of Public Finance, *Journal of Economic Literature* 7: 759–806.

Myers, N., 1979. *The Sinking Ark*. Oxford UK: Pergamon Press. 127pp.

Myers, N., 1980. *Conversion of Tropical Moist Forests*. Washington: National Academy of Sciences.

Myers, N., 1991. Tropical Forests: Present Status and Future Outlook, *Climatic Change* 19: 3–32.

Myers, N., 1994. Tropical Deforestation: Rates and Patterns. In *The Causes of Tropical Deforestation* edited by D. W. Pearce and K. Brown. London: UCL Press.

Nath, S. K., 1969. *A Reappraisal of Welfare Economics*. London: Routledge & Kegan Paul.

Nautiyal, J. C. and D. L. Love, 1971. Some Economic Implications of Methods of Charging Stumpage, *Forestry Chronicle* 47: 25–8.

Nautiyal, J. C. and J. L. Rezenck, 1985. Forestry and Cost Benefit Analysis, *Journal of World Forest Management* 1: 184–98.

Nee, S. and R. M. May, 1997. Extinction and the Loss of Evolutionary History, *Science* 278: 692–4.

Neher, P. A., 1990. *Natural Resource Economics: Conservation and Exploitation*. Cambridge UK: Cambridge University Press.

Nelson, R. H., 1997. Does Existence Value Exist? Environmental Economic Encroaches on Religion, *The Independent Review*, I, 499–521.

Niewijk, R. K., 1992. Ask a Silly Question. . . : Contingent Valuation of Natural Resource Damages, *Harvard Law Review* 105(June): 1981–2000.

Niewijk, R. K., 1994. Misleading Quantification. The Contingent Valuation of Environmental Quality, *Regulation* 1: 60–71.

Norgaard, R. B., 1984. Coevolutionary Development Potential, *Land Economics* 60(May): 160–73.

Norgaard, R. B., 1985. Environmental Economics: An Evolutionary Critique and a Plea for Pluralism, *Journal of Environmental Economics and Management* 12: 382–94.

Norgaard, R. B., 1990. Economic Indicators of Resource Scarcity: A Critical Essay, *Journal of Environmental Economics and Management* 19: 19–25.

Norton, B. G. and M. A. Toman, 1997. Sustainability: Ecological and Economic Perspectives, *Land Economics* 73(November): 553–68.

Nozick, R., 1974. *Anarchy, State, and Utopia*. New York: Basic Books.

Olsen, R. J and J. S. Shortle, 1996. The Optimal Control of Emissions and Renewable Resource Harvesting under Uncertainty, *Environmental and Resource Economics* 7(2): 97–115. .

Olson, M., Jr., 1996. Big Bills Left on the Sidewalk: Why Some Nations are Rich, and Others Poor, Journal of Economic Perspectives 10: 3–24

Organization for Economic Cooperation and Development, 1991. *OECD Environmental Data Compendium*. Paris: OECD.

Organization for Economic Cooperation and Development, 1994. *The Environmental Effects of Trade*. Paris: OECD.

Osgood, D., 1994. Government Failure and Deforestation in Indonesia. In *The Causes of Tropical Deforestation* edited by D. W. Pearce and K. Brown. London: UCL Press.

Ostrom, E., 1998. A Behavioral Approach to the Rational-Choice Theory of Collective Action, *American Political Science Review*. 92 (March 1998): 1–22.

Pahl-Wostl, C., 1995. The Dynamic Nature of Ecosystems: Order and Chaos Intertwined. Chichester, UK: John Wiley & Sons.

Palo, M., 1994. Population and Deforestation. In *The Causes of Tropical Deforestation* (pp. 42–56) edited by D. W. Pearce and K. Brown. London: UCL Press.

Panayotou, T., 1993a. *Green Markets*. San Francisco: ICS Press.

Panayotou, T., 1993b. Empirical Tests and Policy Analysis of Environmental Degradation at Different Stages of Economic Development. Working Paper WP238, Technology and Employment Program. Geneva: International Labour Office.

Panayotou T., 1995. Environmental Degradation at Different Stages of Economic Development. In *Beyond Rio: The Environmental Crisis and Sustainable Livelihoods in the Third World* (pp. 13–36) edited by I. Ahmed and J. A. Doeleman. Houndmills and London: Macmillan.

Panayotou, T. and P. Ashton, 1992. Not by Timber Alone: Economics and Ecology for Sustaining Tropical Forests. Washington D. C. : Island Press.

Panayotou, T. and S. Sungsuwan, 1994. An Econometric Analysis of the Causes of Tropical Deforestation. In *The Causes of Tropical Deforestation* edited by D. W. Pearce and K. Brown. London: UCL Press.

Pearce, D. W. and G. Atkinson, 1995. Measuring Sustainable Development. Chapter 8 in *The Handbook of Environmental Economics* edited by D. W. Bromley. Oxford, UK: Blackwell.

Pearce, D. W. and R. K. Turner, 1990. *Economics of Natural Resources and the Environment.* Baltimore: Johns Hopkins University Press.

Pearce, D. W. and J. J. Warford, 1993. *World without End.* New York: Oxford University Press.

Pearce, D. W., N. Adger, D. Maddison and D. Moran, 1995. Debt and the Environment, *Scientific American* June, pp. 52–6.

Pearce, D. W., G. Atkinson and K. Hamilton, 1998. The Measurement of Sustainable Development. Chapter 9 in *Theory and Implementation of Economic Models for Sustainable Development* edited by J. C. J. M. van den Bergh and M. W. Hofkes. Dordrecht, NL: Kluwer Academic Publishers.

Pearse, P. H. (Commissioner), 1976. *Timber Rights and Forest Policy.* Report of the Royal Commission on Forest Resources (2 Volumes). Victoria: Queen's Printer.

Pearse, P. H. 1990. *Introduction to Forestry Economics*, Vancouver: UBC Press.

Pearse, P. H., 1980. Property Rights and Regulation of Commercial Fisheries, *Journal of Business Administration* 11: 185–209.

Pearse, P. H., 1985. Obstacles to Silviculture in Canada, *The Forestry Chronicle* 61(April): 91–6.

Pearse, P. H., 1993a. It's time to break the log jam, *The Globe and Mail*, June 17.

Pearse, P. H., 1993b. Forest Tenure, Management Incentives and the Search for Sustainable Development Policies. Chapter 5 in *Forestry and the Environment: Economic Perspectives* edited by W. L Adamowicz, W. White and W. E. Phillips. Wallingford, UK: CAB International.

Percy, M. B., 1986. *Forest Management and Economic Growth in British Columbia.* Report prepared for the Economic Council of Canada. Ottawa: Ministry of Supply and Services.

Perez-Garcia, J., and B. Lippke, 1991. The Future Supply of Timber from Public Lands: Recent Sales Will Not Support Competitive Processing. Cintrafor Working Paper 32, University of Washington, Seattle.

Perman, R., Y. Ma and J. McGilvray, 1996. *Natural Resources and Environmental Economics.* New York: Longman Publishing.

Perrings, C., 1998. Resilience in the Dynamics of Economy-Environment Systems, *Environmental and Resource Economics* 11: 503–20.

Perrings, C., K. -G. Maler, C. Folke, C. S. Holling, and B. -O. Jansson (editors), 1995. *Biological Diversity: Economic and Ecological Issues.* Cambridge: Cambridge University Press.

Pesaran, M. H., 1990. An Econometric Analysis of Exploration and Extraction of oil in the U. K. Continental Shelf, *The Economic Journal* 100: 367–90.

Peters, C., A. Gentry and R. Mendelsohn, 1989. Valuation of an Amazonian Rainforest, *Nature* 339: 655–6.

Pezzey, J., 1989. Economic Analysis of Sustainable Growth and Sustainable Development, Environment Department Working Paper No. 15. Washington: The World Bank, March.

Pezzey, J. C. V., 1997. Sustainability Constraints versus "Optimality" versus Intertemporal Concern, and Axioms versus Data, *Land Economics* 73(November): 448–66.

PFRA and Saskatchewan Water Corporation, 1985. *Saskatchewan Irrigation Project Appraisal Study*. Regina, SK: Prairie Farm Rehabilitation Administration. October.

Phillips, W. E., W. L. Adamowicz, J. Asafu-Adjaye and P. C. Boxall, 1989. An Economic Assessment of the Value of Wildlife Resources to Alberta. Dept. of Rural Economy Project Report No. 89–04. Edmonton: Univ. of Alberta.

Pickens, J. and J. Hof, 1991. Fuzzy Goal Programming in Forestry: An Application with Special Solution Problems, *Fuzzy Sets and Systems* 39: 239–46.

Pielou, E. C., 1977. *Mathematical Ecology*. New York, NY: John Wiley and Sons.

Pimm, S. L., 1984. The Complexity and Stability of Ecosystems, *Nature* 307: 321–26.

Pimm, S. L., G. J. Russell, J. L. Gittleman and T. M. Brooks, 1995. The Future of Biodiversity, *Science* 269: 347–50.

Pindyck, R. S., 1980. Uncertainty and Exhaustible Resource Markets, *Journal of Political Economy* 86: 841–61.

Pindyck, R. S., 1984. Uncertainty in the Theory of Renewable Resource Markets, *Review of Economic Studies* 51: 289–303.

Polasky, S. and A. Solow, 1995. On the Value of a Collection of Species, *Journal of Environmental Economics and Management* 29: 298–303.

Poore, D., P. Burgess, J. Palmer, S. Rietbergen and T. Synott, 1989. *No Timber Without Trees*. London: Earthscan Publications

Portney, P. R., 1994. The Contingent Valuation Debate: Why Economists Should Care, *Journal of Economic Perspectives* 8(Fall): 3–17.

Postel, S. and L. Heisse, 1988. Reforesting the Earth. Worldwatch Paper No. 83.

Prendergast, J. R., R. M. Quinn, J. H. Lawton, B. C. Eversham and D. W. Gibbons, 1993. Rare Species, the Coincidence of Diversity Hotspots and Conservation Srategies, *Nature* 365: 335–7.

Pressey, R. L., Humphries, C. J., Margules, C., Vane-Wright, R. I. & Williams, P. H., 1993. Beyond Opportunism: Key Principles for Systematic Reserve Selection. *TREE* 8: 124–8.

Prest, A. R. and R. Turvey, 1974. Cost-Benefit Analysis: A Survey. In *Readings in Natural Resource Economics* (pp. 145–71) by J. E. Reynolds, J. M. Redfern and R. N. Shulstad (eds.). New York: MSS Information Corporation.

Price, C., 1990. The Allowable Burn Effect: Does Carbon-fixing Offer a New Escape from the Bogey of Compound Interest? *The Forestry Chronicle* 66: 572–8.

Pynn, L., 1998. Shop Raids Net Animal Parts, *Vancouver Sun*, October 16, pp. A1–A2.

Quammen, D. 1996. The Song of the Dodo: Island Biography in an Age of Extinctions. London: Pimlico.

Quiros, D. and B. Finnegan, 1994. Menejo Sustenable de un Bosque Natural Tropical en Costa Rica. Proyecto Silvicultura de Bosques Naturales. Informe Técnico, No. 225. Colección Silvicultura y Manejo de Bosques Naturales. No. 9. Turrialba, Costa Rica: CATIE.

Randall, A., 1988. What Mainstream Economists have to Say About the Value of Biodiversity. Chapter 25 in *Biodiversity* edited by E. O. Wilson. Washington: National Academy Press.

Randall, A., 1991. Thinking About the Value of Biodiversity. Columbus, Ohio: Department of Agricultural Economics and Rural Sociology, Ohio State Univ. mimeograph.

Randall, A., 1994. A Difficulty with the Travel Cost Method, *Land Economics* 70(February): 88–96.

Randall, A. and M. C. Farmer, 1995. Benefits, Costs, and the Safe Minimum Standard of Conservation. Chapter 2 in *The Handbook of Environmental Economics* edited by D. W. Bromley. Cambridge MA: Basil Blackwell.

Randall, A. and J. R. Stoll, 1980. Consumer's Surplus in Commodity Space, *American Economic Review* 71(June): 449–57.

Rawls, J., 1971. *A Theory of Justice*. Cambridge: Harvard University Press.

Ready, R. C., 1995. Environmental Evaluation under Uncertainty. Chap. 25 in *The Handbook of Environmental Economics* edited by D. W. Bromley. Cambridge MA: Basil Blackwell Publishers.

Ready, R. C., J. C. Buzby and D. Hu, 1996. Difference between Continuous and Discrete Contingent Value Estimates, *Land Economics* 72(August): 397–411.

Reed D., 1992, *Structural Adjustment and the Environment*. London: Earthscan Publications.

Reisner, M., 1986. *Cadillac Desert*. New York: Penguin.

Rennings, K. and H. Wiggering, 1997. Steps Towards Indicators of Sustainable Development: Linking Economic and Ecological Concepts, *Ecological Economics* 20: 25–36.

Repetto, R. and M. Gillis, 1988. *Public Policies And The Misuse Of Forest Resources*. Cambridge: World Resources Institute/Cambridge University Press.

Repetto, R., 1997. Macroeconomic Policies and Deforestation. In *The Environment and Emerging Development Issues Volume 2* edited by P. Dasupta and K. G Maler. Oxford: Clarendon Press.

Rettig, R. B., 1995. Management Regimes in Open Ocean Fisheries. Chap. 19 in *The Handbook of Environmental Economics* (pp. 433–52) edited by D. W. Bromley. Cambridge, MA: Basil Blackwell.

Ricardo, D., 1977 (1817). *Principles of Political Economy and Taxation*. London: J. M. Dent and Sons Ltd.

Rice, R. E., R. E. Gullison and J. W. Reid, 1997. Can Sustainable Management save tropical Forests? *Scientific American* 276: 34–9.

Richards, K. R., 1997. The Time Value of Carbon in Bottom-Up Strategies. *Critical Reviews in Environmental Science and Technology* 27 (Special): 279–307.

Richards, K. R. and C. Stokes, 1994. *Regional Studies of Carbon Sequestration: A Review and Critique*. Report prepared for the U. S. Department of Energy. Washington, D. C. : Pacific Northwest Laboratory. 43pp.

Roberts, C. M., 1997. Ecological Advice for the Global Fisheries Crisis, *TREE* 12(January): 35–8.

Rollins, K. and A. Lyke, 1997. The Case for Diminishing Marginal Existence Values. Paper presented at the American Agric. Econ. Assoc. Annual Meeting, July 27–30, in Toronto. pp. 24.

Romer, P. M., 1994. The Origins of Endogenous Growth, *Journal of Economic Perspectives* 8: 3–22.

Rowthorn, B. and G. Brown, 1995. Biodiversity, Economic Growth and the Discount Rate. Chapter 3 in *The Economics and Ecology of Biodiversity Decline* edited by T. M. Swanson. Cambridge, UK: Cambridge University Press.

Ruitenbeek, H. J., 1989. Social Cost-Benefit Analysis of the Korup Project. Report prepared for the Worldwide Fund for Nature and the Republic of Cameroon. London: WWF.

Ruzicka, I., 1979. Rent Appropriation in Indonesian Logging: East Kalimantan 1972/3 – 1976/7, *Bulletin of Indonesian Economic Studies* 15(July): 45–74.

Sagoff, M., 1988a. *The Economy of the Earth*. Cambridge: Cambridge University Press.

Sagoff, M., 1988b. Some Problems with Environmental Economics, *Environmental Ethics* 10(Spring): 55–74.

Sagoff, M., 1994. Should Preferences Count? *Land Economics* 70(May): 127–44.

Said, M. Y., R. N. Chunge, G. C. Craig, C. R. Thouless, R. F. W. Barnes and H. T. Dublin, 1995. *African Elephant Database 1995*. Occasional Paper of the IUCN Species Survival Commission No. 11. Gland, Switzerland: IUCN. 225pp.

Salvanes, K. G. and D. Squires, 1995. Transferable Quotas, Enforcement Costs and Typical Firms: An Empirical Application to the Norwegian Trawler Fleet, *Environmental and Resource Economics* 6: 1–21.

Salz, P., 1991. De Europese Atlantische Visserij: Structuur, Economische Situatie en Beleid. Onderzoekverslag 85. Den Haag: LEI-DLO.

Samuelson, P. A., 1976. Economics of Forestry in an Evolving Society, *Economic Inquiry* 14(December): 466–92.

Sandler T., 1997. Global Challenges: An Approach to Environmental, Political and Economic Problems. Cambridge: Cambridge University Press.

Sassone, P. G. and W. A. Schaffer, 1978. *Cost-Benefit Analysis: A Handbook*. New York: Academic Press.

Saunders, H., 1993. The Cost of Implementing *A Proposed Forest Practices Code for British Columbia*. Report prepared for the Ministry of Forests. Vancouver: H&W Saunders Associates Ltd. Mimeograph. September. 58pp. Appendices.

Saxena, A. K., J. C. Nautiyal and D. K. Foote, 1997. Analyzing Deforestation and Exploring Policies for its Amelioration: A Case Study of India, *Journal of Forest Economics* 3(3): 253–89.

Schaefer, M. F., 1957. Some Considerations of Population Dynamics in Relation to the Management of Commercial Marine Fisheries, *Journal of the Fisheries Board of Canada* 14: 669–81.

Schaeffer, F. A., 1972. *Genesis in Space and Time*. Downers Grove, Ill., Intervarsity Press.

Schmidt, C. C., 1993. The Net Effects of Over-Fishing, *The OECD Observer* 184: 9–12

Schweitzer, D. L. R., R. W. Sassaman and C. H. Schallou, 1972. Allowable Cut Effect: Some Physical and Economic Implications, *Journal of Forestry* 70: 415–18.

Schwindt, R., 1992. Report of the Commission of Inquiry into Compensation for the Taking of Resource Interests. Victoria: Government of BC Printing Office.

Schwindt, R. and S. Globerman, 1996. Takings of Private Rights to Public Natural Resources: A Policy Analysis, *Canadian Public Policy* 22(September): 205–24.

Scitovsky, T., 1941. A Note on Welfare Propositions in Economics, *Review of Economic Studies* 9(November): 77–88.

Scott, A., 1973. *Natural Resources. The Economics of Conservation*. 2nd. Edition. Toronto: McClelland and Stewart.

Scott, A. and P. H. Pearse, 1992. Natural Resources in a High-Tech Economy: Scarcity versus Resourcefulness, *Resources Policy* 18(3): 154–66.

Scruggs, L., 1998. Political and Economic Inequality and the Environment, *Ecological Economics* 26: 259–75.

Sedjo, R. A., 1992. Can Tropical Forest Management Systems be Economic? In *Emerging Issues in Forest Policy* (pp. 505–17) edited by P. N. Nemetz. Vancouver: UBC Press.

Sedjo, R. A., 1996. Environmental Impacts of Forest Protection: Some Complications. Paper presented at the International Seminar on Forest Industries toward the Third Millennium: Economic and Environmental Challenges, European Forestry Institute and University of Joensuu, Joensuu, Finland, March 18.

Sedjo, R. A., 1997. *The Forest Sector: Important Innovations*. Discussion Paper 97–42. Washington, DC: Resources for the Future. 50pp.

Sedjo, R. A., J. Wisniewski, A. V. Sample and J. D. Kinsman, 1995. The Economics of Managing Carbon via Forestry: Assessment of Existing Studies, *Environmental and Resource Economics* 6: 139–65.

Selden T. M. and D. Song, 1994. Environmental Quality and Development: Is There a Kuznets Curve for Air Pollution? *Journal of Environmental Economics and Management* 27: 147–62.

Self, P., 1972. *Econocrats and the Policy Process*. London: MacMillan.

Sellar, C., J. Chavas and J. R. Stoll, 1986. Specification of the Logit Model: The Case of Valuation of Nonmarket Goods, *Journal of Environmental Economics and Management* 13: 382–90.

Sen, A. K., 1977. Rational Fools: A Critique of the Behavioural Foundations of Economic Theory, *Philosophy and Public Affairs* 6(4): 317–44.

Serageldin, 1993. Making Development Sustainable, *Finance and Development* pp. 6–10.

Sethi, R. and E. Somanathan, 1996. The Evolution of Social Norms in Common Property Resource Use, *American Economic Review* 86(September): 766–88.

Shafik, N. and S. Bandyopadhyay, 1992. Economic Growth and Environmental Quality: Time Series and Cross-Country Evidence. Background Paper for the World Development Report 1992. Washington, DC: The World Bank.

Shleifer, Andrei, 1998. State versus Private Ownership. Department of Economics, Harvard University, Cambridge MA. Mimeograph. 32pp.

Shleifer, A. and R. W. Vishny, 1998. *The Grabbing Hand: Government Pathologies and their Cures*. Cambridge MA: Harvard University Press.

Shogren, J. F., 1998. A Political Economy in an Ecological Web, *Environmental and Resource Economics* 11: 557–70.

Shogren, J. F., S. Y. Shin, D. J. Hayes and J. B. Kliebenstein, 1994. Resolving Differences in Willingness to Pay and Willingness to Accept, *American Economic Review* 84(March): 255–70.

Silberberg, E., 1978. The Structure of Economics. A Mathematical Analysis. New York: McGraw-Hill.

Simmons, P. and W. Weiserbs, 1979. Translog Flexible Functional Forms and Associated Demand Systems, *American Economic Review* 69(December): 892–901.

Simmons T. R. and U. P. Krueter, 1989. Herd Mentality: Banning Ivory Sales is no Way to Save the Elephant, *Policy Review* Fall: 46–9.

Simon, C. P. and L. Blume, 1994. *Mathematics for Economists*. New York: W. W. Norton.

Simon, J. L., 1996. *The Ultimate Resource 2*. Princeton, NJ: Princeton University Press.

Simon, J. L. and A. Wildavsky, 1984. On Species Loss, The Absence Of Data, And Risks To Humanity. In *The Resourceful Earth: A Response to Global 2000* (pp. 171–83) edited by J. L. Simon and H. Kahn. New York: Basil Blackwell.

Simon, J. L. and A. Wildavsky, 1995. Species Loss Revisited. In *The State of Humanity* (pp. 346–61) edited by J. L. Simon. Oxford UK: Blackwell.

Simpson, R. D. and R. A. Sedjo, 1996a. Investments in Biodiversity Prospecting and Incentives for Conservation. Discussion Paper 96–14. Washington DC: Resources for the Future.

Simpson, R. D. and R. A. Sedjo, 1996b. Valuation of Biodiversity for Use in New Product Research in a Model of Sequential Search. Discussion Paper 96–27. Washington DC: Resources for the Future.

Simpson, R. D., R. A. Sedjo and J. W. Reid, 1996. Valuing Biodiversity for Use in Pharmaceutical Research, *Journal of Political Economy* 104: 163–85.

Sinclair, A. R. E., 1999. Is Conservation Achieving its Ends? Working Paper. Centre for Biodiversity, University of British Columbia, Vancouver. 12pp.

Skog, K. E. and G. H. Nicholson, 1998. Carbon Cycling through Wood Products: The Role of Wood and Paper Products in Carbon Sequestration, *Forest Products Journal* 48: 75–83.

Skole, D. L., W. H. Chomentowski, W. A. Salas and A. D. Nobre, 1994. Physical and Human Dimensions of Deforestation in Amazonia, *BioScience* 44 (5): 314–22.

Skonhoft A. and J. T. Solstad, 1998. The Political Economy of Wildlife Exploitation, *Land Economics* 74(February): 16–31.

Slade, M. E., 1982. Cycles in Natural Resource Prices: An Analysis of the Time Domain, *Journal of Environmental Economics and Management* 9: 122–37.

Slade, M., 1991. Market Structure, Marketing Method and Price Instability, *Quarterly Journal of Economics* 106: 1309–40.

Slangen, L. H. G., G. C. van Kooten and J. -P. P. F. van Rie, 1997. Economics of Timber Plantations on CO_2 Emissions in the Netherlands, *Tijdschrift voor Sociaal Wetenschappelijk Onderzoek van de Landbouw* 12(4): 318–33.

Smith, A., 1976 (1776). *An Inquiry into the Nature and Causes of theWealth of Nations.* Books I–IV edited by E. Cannan. Chicago: University of Chicago Press.

Smith, F. D. M., G. C. Daily and P. R. Ehrlich, 1995. Human Population Dynamics and Biodiversity Loss. Chapter 11 in *The Economics and Ecology of Biodiversity Decline* edited by T. M. Swanson. Cambridge, UK: Cambridge University Press.

Smith, V. K., 1986. A Conceptual Overview of the Foundations of Benefit-Cost Analysis. Chapter 2 in *Benefits Assessment: The State of the Art* edited by J. D. Bentkover, V. T. Covello and J. Mumpower. Dordrecht: D. Reidel Publishing Co.

Smith, V. K., 1992. Arbitrary Values, Good Causes, and Premature Verdicts, *Journal of Environmental Economics and Management* 22: 71–89.

Smith, V. K., 1997. Pricing What is Priceless: A Status Report on Non-Market Valuation of Environmental Resources. Chapter 6 in *The International Yearbook of Environmental and Resource Economics 1997/1998* edited by H. Folmer and T. Tietenberg. Cheltenham, UK: Edward Elgar.

Smith, V. K., and L. L. Osborne, 1996. Do Contingent Valuation Estimates Pass a "Scope" Test? A Meta-analysis, *Journal of Environmental Economics and Management* 31: 287–301.

Sohngen, B. and R. Sedjo, 1999. Estimating Potential Leakage from Regional Forest Carbon Sequestration Programs. RFF Working Paper. Washington, DC. August. 26 pp.

Solow, A., S. Polasky and J. Broadus, 1993. On the Measurement of Biological Diversity, *Journal of Environmental Economics and Management* 24: 60–8.

Solow, R. M., 1974. Intergenerational Equity and Exhaustible Resources, *Review of Economic Studies* 41(Symposium): 29–45.

Solow, R. M., 1986. On the Intertemporal Allocation of Natural Resources, *Scandinavian Journal of Economics* 88: 141–9.

Solow, R. M., 1993. An Almost Practical Step Toward Sustainability, *Resources Policy* 19(September): 162–72.

Sommerlatte, M. and D. Hopcraft. 1994. The Economics of Game Cropping on a Kenyan Ranch 1981–1990, *Palea* 13: 71–9.

Soulé, M. E., 1987. *Viable Populations for Conservation.* Cambridge: Cambridge University Press.

Soulé, M. E., 1991. Conservation: Tactics for a Constant Crisis, *Science* 253: 744–50.

Southgate, D., R. Sierra and L. Brown, 1991. The Causes of Deforestation in Ecuador: A Statistical Analysis, *World Development* 19: 1145–51.

Spence, A. M., 1973. Blue Whales and Applied Control Theory. Technical Report 108, Institute for Mathematical Studies in the Social Sciences, Stanford University, Stanford, CA.

Squire, L. and H. G. van der Tak, 1975. *Economic Analysis of Projects.* Baltimore: Johns Hopkins University Press (A World Bank Research Publication).

Squires, D., 1987. Fishing Effort: Its Testing, Specification and Internal Structure in Fisheries Economics and Management, *Journal of Environmental Economics and Management* 14: 268–82.

Stabler, J. C., G. C. van Kooten and N. Meyer, 1988. Methodological Issues in Appraisal of Regional Resource Development Projects, *The Annals of Regional Science* 22(July): 13–25.

Stern, D. I., M. S. Common and E. B. Barbier, 1996. Economic Growth and Environmental Degradation: The Environmental Kuznets Curve and Sustainable Development, *World Development* 24: 1151–60.

Sterner, T., and J. C. M. J. van den Bergh, 1998. Frontiers of Environmental and Resource Economics, *Environmental and Resource Economics* 11: 243–60.

Stevens, T., J. Echeverria, R. J. Glass, T. Hager, and T. More, 1991. Measuring the Existence Value of Wildlife: What do CVM Estimates Really Show? *Land Economics* 67(4): 390–400.

Stollery, K., 1983. Mineral Depletion with Cost as the extraction Limit: A Model Applied to the Behavior of Prices in the Nickel Industry, *Journal of Environmental Economics and Management* 10: 151–65.

Stroup, R. L., 1997. The Economics of Compensating Property Owners, *Contemporary Economic Policy* 15(October): 55–65.

Sunderlin,W. D. and I. A. P. Resosudarmo, 1997. Rate and Causes of Deforestation in Indonesia: Towards a Resolution of Ambiguities. Occasional Paper No. 9. Jakarta: CIFOR.

Sutinen, J. and P. Anderson, 1985. The Economics of Fisheries Law Enforcement, *Land Economics* 61: 387–97.

Swallow, S. K. and D. N. Wear, 1993. Spatial Interactions in Multiple-Use Forestry and Substitution and Wealth Effects for the Single Stand, *Journal of Environmental Economics and Management* 25: 103–20.

Swallow, S. K., P. J. Parks and D. N. Wear, 1990. Policy-Relevant Nonconvexities in the Production of Multiple Forest Benefits, *Journal of Environmental Economics and Management* 19: 264–80.

Swallow, S. K., P. Talukdar and D. N. Wear, 1997. Spatial and Temporal Specialization in Forest Ecosystem Management under Sole Ownership, *American Journal of Agricultural Economics* 79(May): 311–26.

Swanson, T. M., 1992. The Role of Wildlife Utilization and Other Policies for Diversity Conservation. Chapter 4 in *Economics for the Wilds* edited by T. M. Swanson and E. B. Barbier. London: Earthscan.

Swanson, T. M., 1994a. *The International Regulation of Extinction*. New York: Macmillan.

Swanson, T. M., 1994b. The Economics of Extinction Revisited and Revised: A Generalised Framework for the Analysis of Endangered Species and Biodiversity Losses, *Oxford Economic Papers* 46: 800–21.

Swanson, T. M., 1995. Why does Biodivesrity Decline? The Analysis of Forces for Global Change. Chapter 2 in *The Economics and Ecology of Biodiversity Decline* edited by T. M. Swanson. Cambridge, UK: Cambridge University Press.

Sweeney, J. L., 1993. Economic Theory of Depletable Resources: An Introduction. In *Handbook of Natural Resource and Energy Economics* (Volume 3), edited by A. V. Kneese and J. L. Sweeney (eds.). Amsterdam: Elsevier Science Publishers.

Tahvonen, O. and J. Kuuluvainen, 1995. The Economics of Natural Resource Utilization. In *Principles of Environmental and Resource Economics: A Guide for Students and Decision Makers* edited by H. Folmer, H. L. Gabel and H. Opschoor. Aldershot: Edward Elgar.

Tanguay, M., W. Adamowicz, P. Boxall, W. Phillips and W. White, 1993. A Socio-Economic Evaluation of Woodland Caribou in Northwestern Saskatchewan. Department of Rural Economy Project Report 93–04, University of Alberta, Edmonton.

Taylor, C. R. (editor), 1993. Applications of Dynamic Programming to Agricultural Decision Problems. Boulder, CO: Westview Press.

Terborgh, J., 1992. *Diversity and the Tropical Rain Forest*. New York: Scientific American Library.

Teter, D., 1997. Briefing Paper on Forestry Revenue. Memorandum 256/96/377 to W. Nitisastro in Jakarta, Indonesia, August 15. 12pp.

The Economist, 1997a. Tusks and Horns and Conservationists, *The Economist*, May 31, p. 42.

The Economist, 1997b. The Rhino's Return. Shooting the Shooters, *The Economist*, September 20, p. 96.

The Economist, 1997c. Venezuela. Forest Gold, *The Economist*, July 12, p. 30.

Thiele R. and M. Wiebelt, 1993. National and International Policies for Tropical Rain Forest Conservation: A Quantitative Analysis for Cameroon, *Environmental and Resource Economics* 3: 501–33.

Thomas, G. B. Jr., 1968. *Calculus and Analytical Geometry*. 4th Edition. Reading, Mass. : Addison-Wesley Publishing Co.

Thompson, W. A., P. H. Pearse, G. C. van Kooten and I. Vertinsky, 1992. Rehabilitating the Backlog of Unstocked Forest Lands in British Columbia: A Preliminary Simulation Analysis of Alternative Strategies. Chapter 4 in *Emerging Issues in Forest Policy* edited by P. N. Nemetz. Vancouver: UBC Press.

Thrice, A. H. and S. E. Wood, 1958. Measurement of Recreation Benefits, *Land Economics* 34(August):

Tietenberg, T., 1996. *Environmental and Natural Resource Economics*. 4th Edition. New York: Harper Collins College Publishers.

Tiffen M. and M. Mortimore, 1994. Malthus Converted: The Role of Capital and Technology and Environmental Recovery in Kenya, *World Development* 22: 997–1010.

Tinbergen, J. and R. Hueting, 1991. GNP and Market Prices: Wrong Signals for Sustainable Economic Success that Mask Environmental Destruction. In *Environmentally Sustainable Economic Development: Building on Brundtland* edited by R. Goodland, H. Daly, S. El Serafy and B. von Droste. Paris: UN Educational, Scientific and Cultural Organisation.

Toman, M., 1998. Why Not Calculate the Value of the World's Ecosystem Services and Natural Capital, *Ecological Economics* 25: 57–60.

Toman, M. A. and M. Walls, 1995. Nonrenewable Resource Supply: Theory and Practice. Chap. 9 in *The Handbook of Environmental Economics* (pp. 182-201) edited by D. W. Bromley. Cambridge, MA: Basil Blackwell.

Toman, M. A., J. Pezzy and J. Krautkraemer, 1995. Neoclassical Economic Growth Theory and "Sustainability." Chap. 7 in *The Handbook of Environmental Economics* (pp. 139–65) edited by D. W. Bromley. Cambridge, MA: Basil Blackwell.

Torras, M. and J. K. Boyce, 1998. Income, Inequality and Pollution: A Reassessment of the Environmental Kuznets Curve, *Ecological Economics* 25: 147–60.

Treasury Board Secretariat (Planning Branch), 1976. *Benefit-Cost Analysis Guide*. Ottawa: Canadian Government Publishing Centre.

Turner II, B. L. and K. I. Butzer, 1992. The Columbian Encounter and Land-Use Change, *Environment* 34 (8): 16–20, 37–44.

United Nations Environment Program, 1995. *Global Biodiversity Assessment*. Cambridge, UK: Press Syndicate of the University of Cambridge.

US Inter-Agency Committee on Water Resources, 1958. *Proposed Practices for Economic Analysis of River Basin Projects*. Report to the Inter-Agency Committee on Evaluation Standards, rev. ed. (The Green Book).

US Inter-Agency Committee on Water Resources, 1962. Policies, Standards and Procedures in the Formulation, Evaluation, and Review of Plans for Use and Development of Water and Related Land Resources. Senate Document No. 97, 87th Congress, Second Session.

US Inter-Agency River Basin Committee (Sub-Committee on Costs and Budgets), 1950. *Proposed Practices for Economic Analysis of River Basin Projects*. (The Green Book) Washington, D. C.

US National Research Council (Policy Division), 1996. *Linking Science and Technology to Society's Environmental Goals*. National Academy Press.

US Water Resources Council, 1973. Water and Related Land Resources: Establishment of Principles and Standards for Planning, *Federal Register* 38(174 December 10): 24778–869.

US Water Resources Council, 1979. Principles and Standards for Planning Water and Related Land Resources, *Federal Register* 44(242): 72878–976.

US Water Resources Council, 1983. Economic and Environmental Principles and Guidelines for Water and Related Land Resources Implementation Studies. Washington, D. C. : Mimeograph, March 10. pp. 137.

van den Bergh, J. C. M. J. and M. W. Hofkes, 1998. A Survey of Economic Modelling of Sustainable Development. Chapter 2 in *Theory and Implementation of Economic Models for Sustainable Development* edited by J. C. J. M. van den Bergh and M. W. Hofkes. Dordrecht: Kluwer Academic Publishers.

van den Bergh, J. C. M. J. and H. Verbruggen, 1999. Spatial Sustainability, Trade and Indicators: An Evaluation of the "Ecological Footprint", *Ecological Economics* 29(1): 63–74.

van Kooten, G. C., 1988. Economic Impacts of Supply Management: Review and Comparison of Alternative Measures of Consumer Welfare Loss, *Canadian Journal of Agricultural Economics* 36(Nov): 425–41.

van Kooten, G. C., 1995a. Modeling Public Forest Land Use Tradeoffs on Vancouver Island, *Journal of Forest Economics* 1(2): 189–215.

van Kooten, G. C., 1995b. Economics of Protecting Wilderness Areas and Old-Growth Timber in British Columbia, *The Forestry Chronicle* 71(Feb/Mar): 52–8.

van Kooten, G. C., 1995c. Can Nonmarket Values be used as Indicators of Forest Sustainability? *The Forestry Chronicle* 71(Nov/Dec): 1–10.

van Kooten, G. C., 1998. Benefits of Improving Water Quality in Southwestern British Columbia: An Application of Economic Valuation Methods. Chapter 22 in *Economics of Agro-Chemicals* edited by W. A. Wossink, G. C. van Kooten and G. H. Peters. Aldershot, UK: Ashgate.

van Kooten, G. C., 1999a. Preserving Species without an Endangered Species Act: British Columbia's Forest Practices Code. Chapter 4 in *Topics in Environmental Economics* edited by M. Boman, R. Brännlund and B. Kriström. Dordrecht: Kluwer.

van Kooten, G. C., 1999b. Economic Dynamics of Tree Planting for Carbon Uptake on Marginal Agricultural Lands. FEPA Working paper. Vancouver: FEPA Research Unit, UBC. Mimeograph. 16pp.

van Kooten, G. C. and L. M. Arthur, 1997. Economic Development with Environmental Security: Canadian-made Strategies for Co-existence, *American Journal of Agricultural Economics* 79(December): 1508–14.

van Kooten, G. C. and E. H. Bulte, 2000. How Much Primary Forest Should Society Retain? Carbon Uptake, Recreation and Other Values, *Canadian Journal of Forest Research.* In press.

van Kooten, G. C. and A. Scott, 1995. Constitutional Crisis, the Economics of Environment and Resource Development in Western Canada, *Canadian Public Policy – Analyse de Politique* 21(June): 233–49.

van Kooten, G. C., R. Athwal and L. M. Arthur, 1998. Use of Public Perceptions of Ground Water Quality Benefits in Developing Livestock Management Options, *Canadian Journal of Agricultural Economics* 46(November): 273–85.

van Kooten, G. C., C. S. Binkley and G. Delcourt, 1995. Effect of Carbon Taxes and Subsidies on Optimal Forest Rotation Age and Supply of Carbon Services, *American Journal of Agricultural Economics* 77(May): 365–774.

van Kooten, G. C., E. H. Bulte and P. I. D. Kinyua, 1997. Game Cropping and Wildlife Conservation in Kenya: A Wildlife Simulation Model with Adaptive Control, *Agricultural Systems* 54(August): 439–62.

van Kooten, G. C., R. A. Schoney and K. A. Hayward, 1986. An Alternative Approach to the Evaluation of Goal Hierarchies among Farmers, *Western Journal of Agricultural Economics* 11: 40–49.

van Kooten, G. C., B. Stennes, E. Krcmar-Nozic and R. van Gorkom, 1999. Economics of Fossil Fuel Substitution and Wood Product Sinks when Trees are Planted to Sequester Carbon on Agricultural Lands in Western Canada, *Canadian Journal of Forest Research*. In press.

van Kooten, G. C., W. A. Thompson and I. Vertinsky, 1993. Economics of Reforestation in British Columbia when Benefits of CO_2 Reduction are Taken into Account. Chapter 12 in *Forestry and Environment: Economic Considerations* edited by W. L. Adamowicz, W. White and W. A. Phillips. Wallingford, UK: CAB International.

van Kooten, G. C., W. P. Weisensel and D. Chinthammit, 1990. Valuing Tradeoffs between Net Returns and Stewardship Practices: The Case of Soil Conservation in Saskatchewan, *American Journal of Agricultural Economics* 72(February): 104–113.

van Kooten, G. C., W. P. Weisensel and E. de Jong, 1989. Estimating the Costs of Soil Erosion in Saskatchewan, *Canadian Journal of Agricultural Economics* 37(Mar): 63–75.

van Kooten, G. C., D. L. Young and J. A. Krautkraemer, 1997. A Safety-First Approach to Dynamic Cropping Decisions, *European Review of Agricultural Economics* 24(1): 47–63.

van Soest, D. 1998. *The Economics of Tropical Deforestation*. Ph.D. Thesis. Groningen: University of Groningen, Department of Economics.

Varian, H. R., 1992. *Microeconomic Analysis*. Third Edition. New York: W. W. Norton.

Vartia, Y. O., 1983. Efficient Methods of Measuring Welfare Change and Compensated Income in Terms of Ordinary Demand Functions, *Econometrica* 51:79–98.

Victor, P. A., 1991. Indicators of Sustainable Development: Some Lessons from Capital Theory, *Ecological Economics* 4: 191–213.

Vincent, J. R., 1990. Rent Capture and the Feasibility of Tropical Forest Management, *Land Economics* 66(May): 212–23

Vincent, J. R., 1993. Managing Tropical Forests: Comment, *Land Economics* 69(August): 313–18

Vincent, J. R. and C. S. Binkley, 1993. Efficient Multiple-Use Forestry May Require Land-Use Specialization, *Land Economics* 69(November): 370–76.

Vold, T., B. Dyck, M. Stone, R. Reid and T. Murray, 1994. Wilderness Issues in British Columbia: Preliminary Results of a 1993 Province-wide Survey of British Columbia Households. Victoria: BC Forest Service, BC Parks and BC Environment, mimeograph. 30pp. App.

Volterra, V., 1931. Lecons sur la Throie Mathmatique de la Lutte pour la Vie. Paris: Gauthiers-Viallars.

von Thuenen, J. H., 1966 (1840). *The Isolated State*. New York: Pergamon.

Wackernagel, M., L. Onisto, P. Bello, A. C. Linares, I. S. L. Falfan, J. M. Garcia, A. I. S. Guerrero and Ma. G. S. Guerrero. 1999. National Natural Capital Accounting With The Ecological Footprint Concept, *Ecological Economics* 29: 375–90.

Wackernagel, M. and W. Rees, 1996. *Our Ecological Footprint: Reducing Human Impact on the Earth*. Gabriola Island, BC and Philadelphia, PA: New Society Publishers.

Wackernagel, M. and W. Rees, 1997. Perceptual and Structural Barriers to Investing in Natural Capital: Economics from an Ecological Footprint Perspective, *Ecological Economics* 20: 3–24.

Walker, D. J. and D. L. Young, 1986. The Effect of Technical Progress on Erosion Damage and Economic Incentives for Soil Conservation, *Land Economics* 62(February): 83–93.

Walsh, R. G., J. B. Loomis, and R. A. Gillman, 1984. Valuing Option, Existence, and Bequest Demands for Wilderness, *Land Economics* 60(February): 14–29.

Wang, S. and G. C. van Kooten, 1999. Silvicultural Contracting in British Columbia: A Transaction Cost Economics Analysis, *Forest Science* 45(2): 272–9.

Wang, S., G. C. van Kooten and B. Wilson, 1998. Silvicultural Contracting in British Columbia, *The Forestry Chronicle* 74(6): 899–910.

Watson, R. A., 1979. Self-Consciousness and the Rights of Non-human Animals, *Environmental Ethics* 1: 99.

Watson, R. T., M. C. Zinyowera and R. H. Moss (editors), 1996. *Climate Change 1995. Impacts, Adaptation and Mitigation of Climate Change: Scientific-Technical Analysis.* IPCC Working Group II. New York: Cambridge University Press.

Weisberg, H. F., J. A. Krosnick and B. D. Bowen, 1989. *An Introduction to Survey Research and Data Analysis.* 2nd. ed Glenview, Illinois: Scott, Foresman and Company.

Weisensel, W. P. and G. C. van Kooten, 1990. Estimation of Soil Erosion Time Paths: The Value of Soil Moisture and Top Soil Depth Information, *Western Journal of Agricultural Economics* 15 (Jul): 63-72.

Weitzman, M., 1974. Free Access versus Private Ownership as Alternative Systems for Managing Common Property, *Journal of Economic Theory* 8: 225–34.

Weitzman, M. L., 1992. On Diversity, *Quarterly Journal of Economics* CVII(May): 363–405.

Weitzman, M. L., 1993. What to Preserve? An Application of Diversity Theory to Crane Conservation, *Quarterly Journal of Economics* CVIII(Feb): 157-83.

Weitzman, M. L., 1998. The Noah's Ark Problem, *Econometrica* 66: 1279–98.

Western, D, 1989. The Ecological Value of Elephants: A Keystone Role in African Ecosystems. In *The ITRG Report, the Ivory Trade and the Future of the African Elephant* prepared for the second meeting of the CITES African Elephant Working Group, Gabarone, Botswana, July.

Weymark, J. A., 1980. Duality Results in Demand Theory, *European Economic Review* 14(November): 377–95.

White, L., Jr., 1967. The Historic Roots of Our Ecologic Crisis, *Science* 155(March): 1203–7.

Whiteman, A., 1996. Economic Rent and the Appropriate Level of Forest Products Royalities in 1996. Indonesia-UK Tropical Forest Management Program Report SMAT/EC/96/1. Jakarta: UK Overseas Development Administration. 17pp.

Winjum, J. K., S. Brown, and B. Schlamadinger, 1998. Forest Harvests and Wood Products: Sources and Sinks of Atmospheric Carbon Dioxide, *Forest Science* 44(2): 272–84.

Withagen, C., 1998. Untested Hypotheses in Non-Renewable Resource Economics, *Environmental and Resource Economics* 11: 623–34.

Whitmore, T. C. and J. A. Sayer (editors), 1992. *Tropical Deforestation and Species Extinction.* London and New York: Chapman & Hall.

Wilen, J. E., 1976. Common Property Resources and Dynamics of Overexploitation: The Case of the North-Pacific Fur Seal. Resource Paper No. 3. Vancouver: UBC.

Williams, P., D. Gibbons, C. Margules, A. Rebelo, C. Humphries and R. Pressey, 1996. A Comparison of Richness Hotspots, Rarity Hotspots, and Complementary Areas for Conserving Diversity of British Birds, *Conservation Biology* 10: 155–74.

Willig, R., 1976. Consumer's Surplus Without Apology, *American Economic Review* 66(Sep): 589–97.

Wilman, E. A., 1988. Modeling Recreation Demands for Public Land Management. In *Environmental Resources and Applied Welfare Economics* (pp. 165–90) edited by V. K. Smith. Washington, D. C. : Resources for the Future.

Wilson, B., G. C. van Kooten, I. Vertinsky and L. M. Arthur, 1998. *Forest Policy: International Comparisons.* Wallingford, UK: CABI Publishing.

Wilson, E. O. (editor), 1988. *Biodiversity.* Washington, DC: National Academy Press.

Wilson J. A., 1982. The Economical Management of Mulispecies Fisheries, *Land Economics* 58: 417–34.

Wilson, J. A., J. M. Acheson, M Metcalfe and P. Kleban, 1994. Chaos, Complexity and Community Management of Fisheries, *Marine Policy* 18: 291–305.

Winrich, J. S., 1984. Self-Reference and the Incomplete Structure of Neoclassical Economics, *Journal of Economic Issues* 18(December): 987–1005.

Wolf, J. and L. H. J. M. Jansen, 1991. Effects of Changing Land Use in the Netherlands on Net Carbon Fixation, *Netherlands Journal of Agricultural Science* 39: 237–46.

World Bank, 1993. Production Forestry: Achieving Sustainability and Competitiveness. Draft of working paper. Jakarta: The World Bank. 160pp.

World Commission on Environment and Development (Brundtland Commission), 1987. *Our Common Future*. Oxford: Oxford University Press.

World Conservation Monitoring Centre, 1992. *Global Biodiversity. Status of the Earth's Living Resources*. London: Chapman & Hall.

World Resources Institute, 1992. *World Resources 1992–93*. Washington, DC: World Resources Institute.

World Resources Institute, 1995. *World Resources 1994–1995*. Oxford: Oxford University Press.

Zadeh, L. A., 1965. Fuzzy Sets, *Information and Control* 8: 338–53.

Zebrowski, Jr., E., 1997. Perils of a Restless Planet. Scientific Perspectives on Natural Disasters. Cambridge, UK: Cambridge University Press.

Zerbe Jr., R. O. and D. O. Dively, 1994. *Benefit-Cost Analysis in Theory and Practice*. New York: Harper Collins College Publishers.

Zimmermann, H.-J., 1996. *Fuzzy Set Theory – and its Applications*. Boston: Kluwer.

Index